The American Society for Public Administration (ASPA)

The American Society for Public Administration (ASPA) is a nationwide nonprofit educational and professional membership organization dedicated to excellence in public management and the promotion of public service. The Society seeks to achieve these objectives through

- The advancement of the science, art, and processes of public administration
- The development and exchange of public administration literature and information, and
- Advocacy on behalf of public service and high ethical standards in government

With more than eighteen thousand members and subscribers, ASPA represents a broad array of professional interests and disciplines from all levels of government, the nonprofit and private sectors, and the academic community, both in the United States and abroad.

ASPA has provided national leadership in the areas of public administration and management since its inception in 1939. The Society and its members have been involved and influential in virtually every significant development in the theories and practice of public administration for half a century.

Through its network of 124 local chapters, 17 national special-focus sections, individual and agency members, and organizational supporters, ASPA promotes recognition of public service achievements, develops a substantive dialogue on relevant issues, and enhances the professional development of its membership. To further its mission, ASPA

- Communicates the importance and value of public service
- Promotes high ethical standards in public administration
- Speaks out in support of public service and seeks to improve the public's perception of government and to restore confidence in public servants
- Develops positions on significant public management and public interest issues
- Publishes a prestigious journal—*Public Administration Review*—an issues-oriented newspaper—*PA Times*—and other special books and publications, and
- Recognizes excellence in public service through annual awards for special accomplishments in the literature or practice of public adminstration

For additional information or membership materials, contact

Advancing excellence in public service...

AMERICAN SOCIETY FOR PUBLIC ADMINISTRATION
1120 G STREET, N.W., SUITE 500
WASHINGTON, D.C. 20005
(202) 393-7878
FAX (202) 638-4952

Handbook of
Public Administration

James L. Perry, Editor

Handbook of
Public Administration

 Jossey-Bass Publishers

San Francisco   •   London   •   1989

HANDBOOK OF PUBLIC ADMINISTRATION
by James L. Perry, Editor

Copyright © 1989 by: Jossey-Bass Inc., Publishers
350 Sansome Street
San Francisco, California 94104
&
Jossey-Bass Limited
28 Banner Street
London EC1Y 8QE

Library of Congress Cataloging-in-Publication Data

Handbook of public administration.

(The Jossey-Bass public administration series)
Bibliography: p.
Includes indexes.
1. Public administration. I. Perry, James L. II. Series.
JF1351.H276   1989   350   88-46078
ISBN 1-55542-128-8 (alk. paper)

Manufactured in the United States of America

The paper in this book meets the guidelines for permanence and durability of the Committee on Production Guidelines for Book Longevity of the Council on Library Resources.

JACKET DESIGN BY WILLI BAUM

FIRST EDITION

Code 8901

The Jossey-Bass
Public Administration Series

Contents

Preface

Governmental activity has grown enormously since the turn of the century, when public administration first became recognized as a field for research and practice. Since that time the missions of government and, concomitantly, the knowledge and skills to accomplish them have evolved significantly in scope and complexity. These changes pose tremendous challenges to the institutions and individuals charged with administering public programs and services. There is little margin for failure. The vitality of our civic life and the legitimacy of our political institutions hinge on how well public administrators are able to respond to these challenges.

The obstacles public administrators face in rising to the challenges of modern government are substantial. Many public administrators come to their positions without formal administrative and managerial training. They achieve responsibility because of their excellence in such other professional fields as engineering, law, social work, and education. They confront dual obstacles to their effectiveness; they need both to develop new skills and to adapt to new performance expectations. Even individuals with formal training in public administration face the prospect of falling short of the demands imposed on them because of the broad range of skills necessary for effective performance and the persistence of changes in their environment.

Intended Audience

The *Handbook of Public Administration* is intended to help public administrators cope with the many challenges facing them and to update or fill gaps in their knowledge base. Written by public administration experts from all areas of the field—law, politics, public policy, finance, personnel, operations, and others—it is designed to meet the needs of the range of professionals who work in government or who interact with public agencies. The handbook is intended to help public administrators act effectively in accomplishing their delegated missions.

The *Handbook of Public Administration* is unique in the recent history of public administration. It is a detailed overview of the field, grounded in both research and theory, written for public administration professionals. Its forty-three chapters cover a broad range of problems and situations that confront public administrators at all levels of government and in all types of services. These situations and problems are carefully analyzed in light of research, theory, and administrative experience. Each chapter offers a guide to effective practice, as well as some ideas about how to improve performance. But the handbook is more than a "how to" book; it is also a "how do we know it" book. Each of the chapters places professional practice in the context of relevant research and theory. Because the chapters are grounded in theory and research, readers should find the material useful not only for handling current problems but also for grappling with new situations.

The handbook offers a unified picture of public administration. Public administration is legitimately recognized as a diverse field, encompassing many different administrative roles, occupational specialties, policy arenas, and levels of government. This fragmentation has often masked both the high degree of overlap among these subareas and the relevance of each to effective practice in public administration. The *Handbook of Public Administration* illustrates that effective public administration is built on many disciplines. It emphasizes the mutual dependence of many perspectives for healthy public service.

The handbook provides a vehicle for communicating the accumulated body of knowledge about public administration to people with varying degrees of responsibility and levels of experience. It is directed to line administrators—public sector executives, managers, and supervisors—who are accountable for the success of public programs and the productivity of public services. It is also directed to staff personnel, including policy, personnel, and financial analysts, who may be responsible for evaluating administrative performance, assessing human resource requirements, or preparing annual budgets. The handbook should be helpful to judicial and legislative staff, oversight bodies, corporate public affairs personnel, and public interest groups concerned about obtaining a better understanding of the activities and requirements of administrative effectiveness. Finally, because the handbook conveys the accumulated body of knowledge about public administration, it is a valuable resource for faculty and students involved in degree and certificate programs in public administration. In short, the audience for this handbook is anyone who works in public administration or is interested in the field.

Overview of the Contents

The contributors, selected for their expertise and professional experience, have prepared original chapters on many facets of public administration. The book is organized into eight parts, representing domains of knowledge and practice essential to effective public administration. Readers can proceed sequentially through the book for an overview of the entire field or can turn to individual parts or chapters for information on specific areas or topics. Each chapter brings fresh insights to familiar problems or situations.

Part One, "Public Administration in a New Era," looks at the changing context of public administration and the challenges it poses to today's public administrator. The changes currently affecting government have been characterized as megatrends, but, regardless of their magnitude, they bring forth new challenges and require novel adaptations. The authors examine the character of these challenges at the federal, state, and local levels. They also examine the implications of the explosion of science and technology, shifting social and demographic trends, and global interdependence.

Part Two, "Effective Administrative and Organizational Systems," focuses on broad issues of governance and effectiveness in administrative and organizational systems. Administrative accountability, responsiveness, and effectiveness are influenced by administrative arrangements, just as they are by the quality of the people who serve. The authors show how laws and institutions shape administrative behavior and thereby promote major governance goals. They also identify means for managing intergovernmental and strategic processes and for designing effective organizational systems.

Part Three, "Strengthening Relationships with Legislatures, Elected and Appointed Officials, and Citizens," focuses on the administrator's ties with key actors in the environment. An administrator's environment is segmented into different actors and institutions, among them legislatures, elected executives, appointees, and citizens. The administrator needs to approach these relationships strategically, securing support from and serving the needs of all segments of the environment. Therefore, the authors provide insights into and methods of managing these relationships.

Part Four, "Establishing Successful Policies and Programs," addresses the public administrator's roles as manager, formulator, and implementer of public policies and programs. Success in making policy requires public administrators to master a range of technical, substantive, and political skills. These skills contribute to an administrator's ability to understand the policy process, to assess policies before and after execution, and to intervene effectively (or defer from doing so) when necessary. The authors convey the political requirements of establishing effective policies through the administrator's role in setting agendas and formulating, implementing, and evaluating programs. They also discuss the policy analyst's role and how the contributions of the analyst can improve the results of public policy.

Part Five, "Effective Budgeting and Fiscal Administration," focuses on issues involving revenues and expenditures in government. The authors look at processes for making choices about the allocation of financial resources and about how resources can be efficiently managed and utilized. On the budgetary side, the authors discuss relationships between budget methods and budgetary objectives, strategies administrators employ to achieve budgetary goals, and systems and methods of accounting for government expenditures. With respect to fiscal affairs, they discuss criteria for assessing a jurisdiction's portfolio of revenue sources and methods for managing debt.

Part Six, "Managing Human Resources," parallels the preceding part but looks at human, in contrast to financial, resources. Many human resource problems in government are similar to those in private organizations, but the constraints, priorities, and methods often differ. Over the years, many governmental jurisdictions have adopted some form of civil service structure, which typically provides for selection by examination, political neutrality, and job security. Civil service systems do succeed in buffering public administrators from arbitrary political interference, but the cost of discretion is often flexibility. The authors provide guidelines on how to manage human resources in this context and on how to overcome such common problems as those involved in appraising and rewarding performance, managing poor performers, and achieving equal employment goals.

Part Seven, "Improving Operations and Services," focuses on operational considerations facing public administrators. Government's role in society encompasses more than strategies for effecting and securing compliance with public policies. It also involves such routine and mundane activities as collecting trash, sweeping streets, and procuring services from the private sector, services that happen to be vital for promoting confidence in government. The authors communicate some of the methods and approaches for ensuring that government operations provide high-quality results. Several of the chapters address readily recognizable operational problems of government, including the measurement of performance and the management of contracts. Other issues—public enterprises, coproduction, information systems, and cycles of growth and decline—have more recent origins but will be quickly recognized by seasoned administrators.

Part Eight, "The Professional Practice of Public Administration," concludes the handbook by reflecting on what it means to be a member of the public administration profession. The authors identify values appropriate to the social and political roles of the public administrator, rules of legal liability, and precepts for administrative conduct. The final chapter summarizes the lessons that this volume offers on being an effective public administrator.

The handbook is sponsored by the American Society for Public Administration (ASPA), an association of approximately fifteen thousand practitioners and academicians dedicated to advancing the art, science, and processes of public administration.

Acknowledgments

To my associates whose contributions appear in this handbook, I offer my sincere thanks. Their cooperation, which in some cases involved extensive reorganizing and rewriting of chapters in response to reviewers' comments and my editorial suggestions, helped to produce an integrated volume. I hope the final product measures up to their original expectations.

I also thank the editorial advisory board of distinguished scholars and public administrators. Members of the board helped at many stages of this project, commenting on the draft table of contents, offering advice about potential authors, and reviewing draft chapters.

I thank the American Society for Public Administration (ASPA) for its willingness to sponsor this volume, which commemorates the fiftieth anniversary of the society. Special thanks go to the ASPA Publications Committee and to ASPA's past and present executive directors, Keith Mulrooney and Shirley Wester.

Special thanks go to David Arnold, Charles Bingman, and Robert Denhardt for devoting many hours of their time to reviewing the manuscript in its entirety and offering helpful criticism, praise, and wisdom. I also thank the many other colleagues who reviewed parts of the manuscript, and I hope they see the fruits of their labors reflected in this volume.

The School of Public and Environmental Affairs at Indiana University provided generous secretarial, office, and telephone support. My secretaries during this project, Cindy Backherms, Rebecca Bouse, and Tammy Hancock, diligently tended to many details and helped to keep everything on track.

To my wife, Wendy, I express deep appreciation for her flexibility and tolerance of my work schedule.

Bloomington, Indiana   James L. Perry
January 1989

On September 23, 1988, Charles H. Levine, distinguished professor of government and public administration at American University, died suddenly from a heart attack at the age of forty-nine. Charlie, as he was known to so many friends, played a special role in the development of this handbook. As chair of the ASPA Publications Committee, Charlie was instrumental in developing the concept for the handbook and obtaining approval for it. He also served on the handbook's editorial advisory board. Charlie's contributions to public administration, however, went far beyond this handbook. He was an eminent scholar, valued colleague, caring teacher and mentor, and an activist for better government. Above all else, Charlie was a wonderful human being. It is to his memory that we dedicate this book.

The Editor

James L. Perry is professor of public and environmental affairs in the School of Public and Environmental Affairs at Indiana University, Bloomington. He received his B.A. degree (1970) in public affairs from the University of Chicago and his M.P.A. (1972) and Ph.D. (1974) degrees in public administration from Syracuse University.

Perry's research has focused on public management, public personnel administration, and public sector labor relations. From 1979 to 1983, he was principal investigator of a major evaluation of the Civil Service Reform Act of 1978. In 1986, he received the Yoder-Heneman Award for innovative research from the American Society for Personnel Administration. His articles have appeared in *Academy of Management Journal, Academy of Management Review, Administration and Society, Administrative Science Quarterly, American Political Science Review,* and *Public Administration Review.* Perry's books include *Technological Innovation in American Local Government* (1979, with K. L. Kraemer), *Labor-Management Relations and Public Agency Effectiveness* (1980, with H. A. Angle), and *Public Management: Public and Private Perspectives* (1983, with K. L. Kraemer).

Perry is past president of the Section on Personnel Administration and Labor Relations of the American Society for Public Administration and past chair of the Public Sector Division, Academy of Management. He was a Fulbright Scholar at the Chinese University of Hong Kong, Department of Government and Public Administration, in 1986.

Contributors

Robert Agranoff is professor of public and environmental affairs in the School of Public and Environmental Affairs at Indiana University, Bloomington, where he specializes in public administration, intergovernmental management, and human services management. He is the author of *Intergovernmental Management: Human Services Problem-Solving in Six Metropolitan Areas* (1986) and has contributed to *Public Administration Review, Publius: The Journal of Federalism, American Behavioral Scientist,* and the *New England Journal of Human Services.* He is currently studying the role of governments in managing intergovernmental networks that deal with such human crises as homelessness and hunger. He received his B.S. degree (1962) in political science from the University of Wisconsin, Riverside. His M.A. (1963) and Ph.D. (1967) degrees are from the University of Pittsburgh, also in political science.

Robert Berne is associate dean and professor of public administration at the Graduate School of Public Administration, New York University, where he also coordinates the specialization in public finance and financial management. His research in finance focuses on the assessment of governments' financial condition and the measurement of equity in school finance. He is completing a study on the relationship between accounting and financial reporting and the measurement of financial condition. He coauthored *The Financial Analysis of Governments* (1986, with R. Schramm). He received his B.S. degree (1970) in industrial engineering and operations research, his M.B.A. degree (1971), and his Ph.D. degree (1977) in business and public administration, all from Cornell University.

Jeffrey M. Berry is professor of political science at Tufts University. His works include *Lobbying for the People: The Political Behavior of Public Interest*

Groups (1977), *Feeding Hungry People: Rulemaking in the Food Stamp Program* (1984), *The Interest Group Society* (1984), and *The Challenge of Democracy* (1987, with K. Janda). He received his A.B. degree (1970) from the University of California, Berkeley, and his M.A. (1972) and Ph.D. (1974) degrees from the Johns Hopkins University.

Robert L. Bland is associate professor of public administration in the Division of Public Administration, University of North Texas. His areas of research include the municipal bond market and the financing of state and local government. He is the author of *Financing City Government* (1986), which in 1987 received the Government Finance Officers Association's award for excellence in research, and *Managing Local Government Revenues* (1988). He received his B.S. degree (1973) in biology from Pepperdine University. He has both an M.P.A. (1975) and an M.B.A. degree (1976) from the University of Tennessee. His Ph.D. degree (1981) is from the Graduate School of Public and International Affairs, University of Pittsburgh.

Barry Bozeman is director of Syracuse University's Technology and Information Policy Program. He is professor of public administration at the Maxwell School and affiliate professor of engineering at the L. C. Smith College of Engineering. His research focuses on organization theory and public management, as well as on policy in science and technology. Bozeman has authored or coauthored books on science and technology, including *Strategic Management of Industrial R&D* (1985, with M. Crow and A. Link), *Investments in Technology* (1983, with A. Link), and *Synthetic Fuel Technology Development in the United States* (1988, with M. Crow, W. Meyer, and R. Shangraw). His B.A. degree (1968) and M.A. degree (1970), both in political science, are from Florida Atlantic. He received his Ph.D. degree (1973) in political science from the Ohio State University.

Jeffrey L. Brudney is associate professor of public administration in the Department of Political Science, University of Georgia. He received his B.A. degree (1972) in political science from the University of California, Berkeley, and his M.A. (1974) and Ph.D. (1978) degrees in political science from the University of Michigan, Ann Arbor. His areas of primary interest and specialization include citizen participation and research methods.

Gerald E. Caiden is professor of public administration in the School of Public Administration, University of Southern California. He received his B.S. degree (1957) in economics and his Ph.D. degree (1959) in government from the University of London, where he attended the London School of Economics and Political Science. He has taught at universities in Canada, Australia, and Israel and has published over twenty-five books and monographs in public policy and management and comparative public administration.

Kim S. Cameron is associate professor of organizational behavior and industrial relations in the Graduate School of Business Administration and associate professor of higher education in the School of Education at the University of Michigan, Ann Arbor. He received his B.S. degree (1970) in sociology and his M.S. degree (1971) in social psychology from Brigham Young University. His M.A. degree (1976) and his Ph.D. degree (1978), both in administrative science, are from Yale University. He is the author or coauthor of five books and some thirty refereed publications on topics including organizational effectiveness, management of decline and downsizing, and management skills.

Ralph Clark Chandler is professor of political science at Western Michigan University, Kalamazoo, where he teaches courses in public administration and constitutional law and is editor-in-chief of the New Issues Press. He received his B.A. degree (1956) in social science interdisplinary studies from Stetson University, his M.A. degree (1962) in political science from Rutgers University, and his Ph.D. degree (1970) in public law and government from Columbia University. He also holds the B.D. degree (1965) from Union Theological Seminary in New York City and the Th.M. degree (1966) from Princeton Theological Seminary, both in ethics.

Eleanor Chelimsky is director of the U.S. General Accounting Office's (GAO) Program Evaluation and Methodology Division, which conducts studies of individual government programs for Congress. Before coming to the GAO, she directed the MITRE Corporation's work in program evaluation. Earlier, she was an economic analyst at NATO and a Fulbright Scholar in Paris.

Beverly A. Cigler is professor of public administration and policy at Pennsylvania State University, Harrisburg, where she is also a faculty research associate at the Institute for State and Regional Affairs and a cocoordinator of the National Small Government Research Network. She received her B.A. degree (1968) from Thiel College and her M.A. (1972) and Ph.D. (1977) degrees from Pennsylvania State University, University Park, all in political science.

James K. Conant is assistant professor of public administration in the Graduate School of Public Administration, New York University. His research and publications are focused on executive-branch organization and leadership in the states. His professional experience includes private-sector management, as well as public service in the Office of the Governor and the State Budget Office in Wisconsin. His writings have appeared in *Public Administration Review, State and Local Government Review, Public Administration Quarterly, State Government,* and *Environmental Forum.* He received his B.A. (1971), M.A. (1974), and Ph.D. (1983) degrees in political science from the University of Wisconsin, Madison.

Phillip J. Cooper is associate professor of political science, public administration, and public policy in the Rockefeller College of Public Affairs and Policy, State University of New York, Albany. His recent books include *Public Law and Public Administration* (second edition, 1988) and *Hard Judicial Choices* (1988). He received his B.A. degree (1975) in government from California State University, Sacramento, and his M.A. (1977) and Ph.D. (1978) degrees in political science from the Maxwell School, Syracuse University.

Glen Hahn Cope is associate professor of public administration at the American University School of Public affairs. She is on leave from the Lyndon B. Johnson School of Public Affairs, University of Texas, Austin, where she is associate professor of public affairs. She was previously a budget analyst and acting budget director of the Michigan Department of Social Services. Her Ph.D. (1981), in public administration, is from the Ohio State University. She received her A.B. degree (1971) in economics from the University of Michigan and her M.P.A. degree (1972) from Syracuse University. She has published research on budgeting and public management.

John Thomas Delaney is associate professor of business in the Columbia University Graduate School of Business. He received his B.S. degree (1977) from Le Moyne College and his A.M. (1980) and Ph.D. (1983) degrees from the University of Illinois, all in industrial relations. His research on public sector labor relations has appeared in various journals for scholars and practitioners.

Douglas C. Eadie is founder and president of Strategic Development Consulting, Inc., a Shaker Heights, Ohio, firm specializing in the design and implementation of strategic management processes, in policy-body development, and in senior management team building. Eadie is coauthor of *The Game Plan: Governance with Foresight* (1982) and has published articles in *Civic Review, Economic Development Commentary, Public Administration Review,* and *Public Management.* Eadie is a Phi Beta Kappa graduate (1964) of the University of Illinois, Urbana, and he received an M.S. degree (1980) in management from the Weatherhead School of Case Western Reserve University.

Loretta R. Flanders is project manager for research in the Office of Executive Personnel, U.S. Office of Personnel Management. She has held several managerial and research positions in that agency and was on its teaching faculty at the Federal Executive Institute as a National Association of Schools of Public Affairs and Administration Faculty Fellow in 1977–78. She has published articles on management development and executive qualifications in several professional journals. She holds a B.A. degree (1960) from the University of Kentucky, an M.A. degree (1966) from the University of Florida, and a Ph.D. degree (1975) from the University of Georgia, all in political science.

Jeffrey J. Fuller is a consultant with Hay Management Consultants in Chicago. He formerly served as assistant city manager in Park Ridge, Illinois. He is a past president of the Illinois City Management Association and the Illinois Association of Municipal Management Assistants. He received a B.A. degree (1972) in English from Illinois Wesleyan University and an M.A. degree (1978) in public affairs from Northern Illinois University.

James L. Garnett is associate professor of public policy and administration in the Graduate Department of Public Policy and Administration at Rutgers University, Camden. He is author of *Reorganizing State Governments: The Executive Branch* (1980) and *Communicating Strategically* (forthcoming). He received his B.A. degree (1967) in government from Carleton College and his M.P.A. (1971) and Ph.D. (1978) degrees in public administration from the Maxwell School, Syracuse University.

Charles T. Goodsell is professor and director of the Center for Public Administration and Policy at Virginia Polytechnic Institute and State University. He is the author of several books, including *Administration of a Revolution* (1965), *American Corporations and Peruvian Politics* (1974), *The Case for Bureaucracy* (revised edition, 1985), and *The Social Meaning of Civic Space* (1988). He received his B.A. degree (1954) from Kalamazoo College and his M.P.A. (1958), M.A. (1959), and Ph.D. (1961) degrees from Harvard University, concentrating in political science and public administration.

Harry P. Hatry is a principal research associate and director of the State and Local Government Research Program at the Urban Institute. He is a member of the National Academy of Public Administration and is on the editorial boards of *New Directions for Program Evaluation, Evaluation Review, National Civic Review,* and *The Bureaucrat.* He received the 1984 American Society for Public Administration (ASPA) Management Science Section award for outstanding contributions to the literature of management science and policy science. He received his B.S. degree (1952) in industrial administration from Yale University and his M.S. degree (1955) in business from the School of Business, Columbia University.

Raymond D. Horton is professor of business in the Columbia University Graduate School of Business, where he directs the program in Public and Nonprofit Management. He received his B.A. degree (1962) in history from Grinnell College, his J.D. degree (1965) from Harvard University, and his Ph.D. degree (1971) in political science from Columbia University.

Peter W. House has been director of the Division of Policy Research and Analysis at the National Science Foundation since 1983. He previously directed research and policy groups at the Department of Energy and the Environmental Protection Agency. In 1985, he received ASPA's practitioner award for outstanding contributions to public administration. His most recent book is *Rush to Policy* (1987, with R. Shull), which describes many actual cases in which large mathematical models have been misapplied to the analysis of policy. His M.A. degree (1960) in economics is from Clark University. He received his Ph.D. degree (1968) in public administration from Cornell University.

Kenneth L. Kraemer is professor in the Graduate School of Management and the Department of Information and Computer Science at the University of California, Irvine, where he is also director of the Public Policy Research Organization. He received his B.A. degree (1959) in architecture from the University of Notre Dame, his M.S.C. and R.P. (1964) degrees from the University of Southern California, and his M.P.A. (1965) and Ph.D. (1967, in public administration) degrees from the University of Southern California. His most recent books are *Datawars* (1987), *Wired Cities* (1987), and *Change and Control in Computing* (forthcoming).

Thomas P. Lauth is professor and head, Department of Political Science, the University of Georgia. His articles on budgeting and on state and city administration have appeared in numerous professional journals. He is the coauthor of *Compromised Compliance: Implementation of the 1965 Voting Rights Act* (1982, with H. Ball and D. Krane) and *The Politics of State and City Administration* (1986, with G. Abney). He received his B.A. degree (1960) in government from the University of Notre Dame and his Ph.D. degree (1976) in political science from the Maxwell School of Citizenship and Public Affairs at Syracuse University.

James Leigland is director of public enterprise studies at the Institute of Public Administration. He is the author of *WPPSS: Who is to Blame?* (1986) and of many reports and articles in public policy and finance. He holds a Ph.D. degree (1981) in political science from Columbia University.

Nicholas P. Lovrich is professor of political science and director of the Division of Governmental Studies and Services at Washington State University. He serves on the editorial boards of *Review of Public Personnel Administration, Social Science Quarterly,* and the *Western Political Quarterly.* He received his B.A. degree (1966) in political science from Stanford University and his M.A. (1967) and Ph.D. (1971) degrees, also in political science, from the University of California, Los Angeles.

Jeffrey S. Luke is director of the Bureau of Governmental Research and Service and associate professor of public affairs in the Department of Planning, Public Policy, and Management at the University of Oregon. He received his B.A. (1972), M.P.A. (1974), and Ph.D. (1982) degrees, all in public administration, from the University of Southern California. He is coauthor of *Management Training Strategies in Third World Countries* (1987, with J. Kerrigan) and of *Managing Economic Development* (1988, with C. Ventriss, B. J. Reed, and C. Reed).

Jerry L. Mc Caffery is professor of public budgeting at the U.S. Naval Postgraduate School in Monterey, California. He received his B.A. degree (1959) in history and English, his M.A. degree (1969) in political science, and his Ph.D. degree (1972) in political science, all from the University of Wisconsin. His research has focused on budgetary decision making under fiscal stress, budget innovations, and techniques for teaching budgeting. He served for seven years as a budget analyst in the Wisconsin state government.

Eugene B. McGregor, Jr., is professor of public and environmental affairs in the School of Public and Environmental Affairs at Indiana University, Bloomington. He holds an A.B. degree (1964) in government from Dartmouth College and a Ph.D. degree (1969) in political science from the Maxwell School at Syracuse University. He has taught at Indiana University since 1973.

John L. Mikesell is professor of public and environmental affairs in the School of Public and Environmental Affairs at Indiana University, Bloomington. He received his B.A. degree (1964) from Wabash College and his M.A. (1965) and Ph.D. (1969) degrees from the University of Illinois, all in economics.

Ronald J. Oakerson is senior scientist at the Workshop in Political Theory and Policy Analysis, Indiana University, Bloomington, where he does research on local and metropolitan governance. Previously, he was senior analyst at the U.S. Advisory Commission on Intergovernmental Relations (ACIR) and is author of the ACIR report *The Organization of Local Public Economies* (1987). He received his B.A. degree (1966) from Taylor University and his M.A. (1973) and Ph.D. (1978) degrees from Indiana University, all in political science.

Laurence J. O'Toole, Jr., is professor of political science at Auburn University. His primary research interests include administrative theory, intergovernmental relations, policy implementation, and the regulatory process. He received his B.S. degree (1970) in chemistry from Clarkson University and his M.P.A. degree (1972) and Ph.D. degree (1975) from the Maxwell School, Syracuse University. He currently serves on the editorial boards of *Public Administration Review, State and Local Government Review,* and the *Journal of Politics.*

Jone L. Pearce is associate professor of administration in the Graduate School of Management and director of Orange County Business and Economic Studies at the University of California, Irvine. She has published research on public sector organizational behavior in the *Journal of Applied Psychology, Academy of Management Journal,* and *Public Administration Review.* She has also written a book (forthcoming) on volunteer organizational behavior. She received her A.B. degree (1974) in psychology from the University of California, Berkeley, and her M.A. (1976) and Ph.D. (1978) degrees in administrative sciences from Yale University.

Kent E. Portney is associate professor of political science and director of the Citizen Survey Program at Tufts University. He is the author of *Approaching Public Policy Analysis* (1986) and coeditor of *The Distributional Impacts of Public Policies* (1988, with S. Danziger). Portney serves as director of survey research for the National Citizen Participation Development Project. He received his A.B. degree (1973) in political science from Rutgers University, his M.A. degree (1975) in political science/public administration from the University of Connecticut, and his Ph.D. degree (1979) in government from Florida State University.

Charles A. Pounian is a senior consultant with Hay Management Consultants in Chicago. He is a former director of personnel for the city of Chicago, past president (1986) of the International Personnel Management Association, and a former member of ASPA's National Council (1980–1983). Pounian has served as adjunct professor in the M.P.A. program at Illinois Institute of Technology. He received his B.A. degree (1949) from Lake Forest College and his M.S. (1951) and Ph.D. (1960) degrees from the Illinois Institute of Technology, all in psychology.

Robert E. Quinn is associate professor of organizational behavior and industrial relations at the University of Michigan Business School. For the past six years, he has been executive director of the Institute for Government and Policy Studies at the Rockefeller College, State University of New York, Albany. His research is on managerial and organizational change and effectiveness. He received his B.S. degree (1970) and M.S. degree (1972) in sociology from Brigham Young University. His Ph.D. degree (1975) in organizational behavior and applied behavioral science is from the University of Cincinnati. Quinn is the author of *Beyond Rational Management* (1988).

Dianne Rahm is assistant professor of public administration in the Department of Public Administration at Pennsylvania State University. She received her B.A. degree (1975) in liberal arts from Wichita State University, her M.A. degree (1976) in American history from Wichita State University, and her M.S. degree (1985) in computer science from Fitchburg State College. She received her Ph.D. degree in public administration from Syracuse University. She has written several articles on policy in science and technology.

Hal G. Rainey is professor of political science at the University of Georgia. His research concentrates on the comparison of public, private, and hybrid organizations and managers and on citizens' perceptions of government. He received his B.A. degree in English and psychology from the University of North Carolina, Chapel Hill. He holds an M.A. degree (1972) in psychology and a Ph.D. degree (1978) in public administration from the Ohio State University.

Michael V. Reagen is director of the Missouri Department of Social Services. He previously served seven years as commissioner of the Iowa Department of Human Services, an agency recognized as one of the ten best in the country. Reagen has received numerous national awards for his progressive leadership, especially in forging partnerships between the private and the public health care sectors. His awards include the 1985 National Public Service Award and the 1982 Iowa Distinguished Service Award. He is the author of two books and forty publications on human services. He received his B.S. degree (1964) in marketing and philosophy from Fordham University, his M.S. degree (1965) in advertising and marketing from the University of Illinois (where he was a James Webb Scholar), and his Ph.D. degree (1972) in communications research and social psychology from Syracuse University.

Wilbur C. Rich is associate professor of political science at Wayne State University, Detroit, where he was director of the graduate program in public administration from 1980 to 1986. He is the author of *The Politics of Urban Personnel Policy* (1982) and of numerous articles on personnel management. He received his B.S. degree (1960) in education from Tuskegee Institute and his Ph.D. degree (1972) in political science from the University of Illinois.

Irene S. Rubin is associate professor of public administration at Northern Illinois University, where she is also a research associate at the Center for Governmental Studies. She received her B.A. degree (1967) in oriental studies from Barnard College, her M.A. degree (1969) in East Asian studies from Harvard University, and her Ph.D. degree (1977) in sociology from the University of Chicago. Her singly authored books include *Running in the Red: The Political Dynamics of Urban Fiscal Stress* (1982), *Shrinking the Federal Government: The Effects of Cutbacks on Five Federal Agencies* (1985), and *Getting and Spending, Borrowing and Balancing: The Politics of Public Budgeting* (forthcoming). She is coauthor of *The Politics of Retrenchment* (1981, with C. Levine and G. Wolohojian) and coauthor of *Community Organizing and Development* (1986, with H. Rubin). She is editor of *New Directions in Budget Theory* (1988) and coeditor of *Fiscal Stress and Public Policy* (1980, with C. Levine).

Grace Hall Saltzstein is assistant professor in the Department of Political Science at the University of California, Riverside. She received her B.A. degree (1973) in political science from the University of Houston and her Ph.D. degree (1980) in political science from the University of California, Riverside.

Roger D. Shull is senior technical analyst with the National Science Foundation's (NSF) Division of Policy Research and Analysis. He managed research and policy programs in the Atomic Energy Commission, the Department of the Interior, the Environmental Protection Agency, and the Department of Energy before joining NSF. He received his B.S. (1962) and M.S. (1963) degrees in civil engineering from Michigan State University and his Ph.D. degree (1968) in environmental engineering from the University of Texas.

Roger L. Sperry is director of Academy Studies at the National Academy of Public Administration, Washington, D.C. During the 99th Congress, he was a professional staff member of the U.S. Senate Committee on Governmental Affairs and previously served (1969–1971) as a GAO consultant to the Congressional Joint Committee on Atomic Energy. Sperry spent twenty-five years with the GAO as a senior group director, special assistant to the comptroller general, and legislative adviser in the Office of Congressional Relations. His publications include *GAO 1966–1981: An Administrative History* (1981) and numerous journal articles, principally on public management. He is policy issues editor for *The Bureaucrat.* He has a B.B.A. degree (1963) from the University of New Mexico and an M.P.A. degree (1976) from Harvard University.

Frank J. Thompson is professor of public administration, policy, and political science in the Graduate School of Public Affairs at the State University of New York, Albany. He has written extensively about public personnel administration, policy implementation, and health policy. Before joining the faculty at the State University of New York, Thompson served on the faculty of the University of Georgia for fifteen years. He received his B.A. degree (1966) in political science from the University of Chicago and his M.A. (1967) and Ph.D. (1973) degrees, in the same discipline, from the University of California, Berkeley.

Ken Thomson is director of citizen participation programs at the Lincoln Filene Center, Tufts University. He received his B.S. degree (1968) in physics from Harvey Mudd College and his M.Phil. degree (1970) from Yale University. Thomson has worked in citizen participation for the past fifteen years. For the past eight years, he has been managing editor of the *Citizen Participation Newsmagazine.* His primary focus has been on developing evaluative frameworks for citizens' group and government-involvement programs.

Dave Ulrich is assistant professor of organizational behavior at the School of Business and faculty associate at the Institute for Social Research at the University of Michigan. He serves on the editorial boards of *Academy of Management Journal, Human Resource Management,* and *Human Resource Plan-*

ning. He has published over twenty-five articles and book chapters on competitive advantage, organizational capability, strategic human resources, and leadership. He received his B.A. degree (1976) in English and social science from Brigham Young University and his Ph.D. degree (1982) in management from the University of California, Los Angeles.

Annmarie Hauck Walsh is Luther Gulick Scholar in Residence and former president of the Institute of Public Administration, New York City. She is a consultant to state and local governments on management systems and author of *The Public's Business* (1978), *The Urban Challenge to Government* (1969), and numerous articles and reports. She received her M.A. and Ph.D. degrees from Columbia University.

Barton Wechsler is assistant professor of public administration at Florida State University, where he is also director of the Florida Center for Productivity. His primary research interests are strategic management of public organizations and executive transition processes in government. He received his B.A. degree (1970) in liberal arts from Antioch College, his M.S. degree (1975) in social and applied economics from Wright State University, and his Ph.D. degree (1985) in public administration from Ohio State University.

Walter Williams is professor of public affairs at the Graduate School of Public Affairs, University of Washington. His books include *Social Policy Research and Analysis* (1971), *Government by Agency* (1980), *The Implementation Perspective* (1980), *Studying Implementation* (1982, senior author), *Disaster Policy Implementation* (1986, with P. May), and *Washington, Westminster and Whitehall* (1988). He has been visiting scholar at the London School of Economics (1983) and at Bergen University (1988). His B.B.A. (1955) and M.B.A. (1956) degrees are from the University of Texas, Austin. His Ph.D. degree (1960) in economics and business is from Indiana University.

Charles R. Wise is associate professor in the School of Public and Environmental Affairs at Indiana University, Bloomington. He served as special assistant for policy analysis in the Office of Legislative Affairs, U.S. Department of Justice, from 1982 to 1983 and as director of intergovernmental affairs in 1984. He was managing editor of *Public Administration Review* from 1977 to 1983. Author and editor of a number of articles, he was the recipient of the Frederick Mosher Award for the best scholarly article published in the *Public Administration Review* in 1985. His B.A. degree (1967) is from Arizona State University and his M.A. (1970) and Ph.D. (1972) degrees are from Indiana University, all in political science.

Chilik Yu is a research associate in the Department of Political Science at the University of North Texas. His research interest is in debt administration in state and local government, and he has authored several articles on the subject. Most recently, he has examined the cost-effectiveness of different approaches used by state governments to enhance the investment appeal of school bonds. He received his B.A. degree (1981) in political science from Tunghai University and his M.P.A. degree (1987) from the University of North Texas.

Editorial Advisory Board

Handbook of
Public Administration

Part One

Public Administration in a New Era

In a few years, we enter the twenty-first century, a historic juncture that is sure to trigger volumes speculating about a new era. For most public administrators, the new era has already arrived, although its precise beginning is subject to debate. Some would associate it with the tax revolt of the late 1970s. Others might peg its beginning to the election of Ronald Reagan. Regardless of the starting date, there can be no doubt that public administrators and the institutions they steer have entered a new and exciting age. Part One examines this new age and the changing face of public administration.

The new era we have entered signals changes in all realms of public administration. Federal, state, and local governments are confronted with needs to assess both what they do and how they do it. The federal government is adapting its operational and managerial initiatives to a new strategic environment. State governments are similarly assessing the responsibilities for which they must exercise leadership. Local governments, buffeted by changes at the federal and state levels, are attempting to preserve their limited autonomy. Intragovernmental shifts at the federal, state, and local levels are necessitating intergovernmental adjustments as well.

Not only has the new era meant changes in traditional governmental institutions, it has also brought with it entirely new instruments for achieving public purposes. Third parties, private contractors, and nonprofit organizations play increasingly large roles in shaping public policies and delivering public services. In the face of the proliferation of new public organizational forms, institutional distinctions between the terms *public* and *private* have been blurred, but ideological and value distinctions remain.

Changes in public administrators' environments are driven by fundamental shifts along several dimensions. One area of accelerating change is science and technology. Computing, telecommunications, and biotechnology represent the tide of scientific and technological changes that are altering public administration. Computer and telecommunications technologies give us the capacity to process and rapidly transmit large volumes of data. At the same time, such technologies permit unprecedented intrusions into individual privacy and impose tremendous obligations on government. Biotechnology creates possibilities not only for improving life but also for changing it altogether.

Changing technologies have helped in part to stimulate a fundamental shift in another domain: relations among nations. Once insular countries have become highly interdependent. National economic, resource, and political decisions now have global ramifications.

Fundamental shifts are also occurring in the demographic makeup of American society. While the populations of many Third World countries explode, the decline of fertility rates in the United States has produced a "birth dearth." This decline, together with the end of the baby boom of the 1940s and 1950s, is dramatically altering the age profile of the American population. Such changes are precipitating a reassessment of some of the most basic assumptions underlying social policy.

These fundamental shifts complicate the challenges public administrators have traditionally faced. Effective and ethical service is certain to become more difficult in the future. Part One provides insights into both the new era we have entered and the challenges confronting public administrators.

1

James L. Perry

Challenges Confronting
Public Administrators

An early-twentieth-century novel (House, 1912), set in the 1920s, depicted the life of an idealistic West Point graduate repelled by the exploitation of the weak by the physically and mentally strong. The young idealist led an army of insurgents in a civil war against government troops and won a decisive victory at the Battle of Elma, in upstate New York. Shortly after his victory, the young general marched on Washington, accepted the formal surrender of the president, and declared himself administrator of the Republic. In the days that followed, the administrator introduced a series of reforms that changed the face of American government, making it truly responsive to the will of the people. Taxes became more progressive, election ballots were shortened, and indigents were guaranteed government employment. The title of the novel? *Philip Dru: Administrator.*

Times have changed. The saga of Philip Dru is an unlikely plot for a modern best-seller. Public administrators seldom are cast as heroes in modern novels. These days, they are more likely to be depicted as shadowy figures who exercise powers similar to those of the fictional Philip Dru but who lack legitimacy for their actions.

But some things do not change. Public administrators still reside in one of the most demanding niches in American life. Admittedly, they are not required, as Philip Dru was, to create a governmental system from scratch, but they are expected to facilitate the workings of one of the most complex governmental systems in the world. What, specifically, are the challenges that face the public administrator today? Part One of this handbook identifies specific challenges that confront public administrators because of changes at different levels of government and in science, technology,

3

society, and the international arena. This chapter identifies some of the cross-cutting features of the challenges discussed both in Part One and throughout the remainder of the handbook.

Five areas, given here in no particular order of priority, capture the challenges of the public sector: (1) maintaining constitutional order, (2) achieving technical competence, (3) coping with public expectations, (4) managing complexity, uncertainty, and change, and (5) behaving ethically. This list makes no claim to empirical validation for all public administrators for all time, but I believe it will be recognizable to many who have recently pursued public service careers.

Maintaining Constitutional Order

A hallmark of American government is its reliance on the Constitution, which serves as the ultimate arbiter for the appropriateness of public and private actions. Although constitutional rule is central to American public administration, the Constitution offers little direct guidance about the role of public administration or public administrators. In fact, as Waldo (1980, p. 66) has observed, "the Constitution does not contain the words administration or management," and it is clear that the framers "did not envisage an apparatus with even one one-hundredth the size, variety, and complexity of that today."

Despite the Constitution's lack of definitiveness, the nation's founders possessed clear views about the role of administration in American government. Rohr (1986, p. 1) notes that "the word administration and its cognates appears 124 times in *The Federalist Papers;* more frequently than Congress, President, or Supreme Court." Rohr argues persuasively that the Constitution legitimates the administrative state, not in the language of the Constitution itself but in the debates between the Federalists and the anti-Federalists that preceded its ratification.

Whether or not one agrees with Rohr, the centrality of the Constitution to American government imposes a special duty on public administrators to behave according to its charter and consistently with its promise. Near the end of the nineteenth century, Woodrow Wilson (1887, p. 201), then a professor of history and political science, had already recognized the challenge of fulfilling this mandate: "It is getting harder to run a constitution than to frame one." The practical details of administering "with enlightenment, with equity, with speed, and without friction" (pp. 198–199) were becoming more problematic than the constitutional principles being administered.

How can public administrators today, in an era of unprecedented change and complexity, hope to meet a challenge that Woodrow Wilson considered so difficult a hundred years ago? The answer lies in part with the vision of the nation's founders. They foresaw the values of the American regime maintained through the interaction of three elements: constitutional correctives, honor, and education (Richardson and Nigro, 1987). Public administrators can contribute to the maintenance of constitutional order by appreciating and actively supporting the constitutional correctives—among them the separation of powers—that protect against the self-interest of citizens. They must also seek public esteem through their service to others and prepare for it with a well-rounded education about constitutional principles, history, politics, law, government, and management (Richardson and Nigro, 1987). These prerequisites of constitutionally responsible administration are at the core of public administration's most enduring challenge.

Achieving Technical Competence

One of the foremost expectations of public administrators is that they will be technically capable of performing roles assigned to them by political and administrative superiors and by citizens. Technical competence has been central to public administration since the late nineteenth century. One of the objectives of Woodrow Wilson's (1887) landmark essay was to improve the personnel of government. In a similar vein, the city manager movement and other progressive reforms of the early twentieth century reflected the commitment of our society to politically neutral competence as a centerpiece of governmental design (Kaufman, 1969).

By itself, however, the requirement for technical competence would not confront a public administrator with a challenge distinguishable from, say, one presented to a business executive, an engineer, or an accountant. But the job domains of public administrators often involve unique challenges, because government has been allocated tasks either that markets are unable to fulfill or that are not deemed appropriate to the private sector. Thus, the public administrator's challenge is to perform, in a technically competent manner, tasks that are too difficult or too sensitive to be entrusted to other societal institutions.

There are often immense impediments to performing such tasks successfully. For example, after analyzing the history of implementation of a federal jobs program in Oakland, California, Pressman and Wildavsky (1979) concluded that it was a wonder that government could achieve any success at all, given the incredible odds against which such intergovernmental programs had to struggle. Not all government activities necessarily face low prospects for success, but it can be a very humbling experience for an administrator to be asked to preside over programs with relatively small probabilities for success, a success for which cause-effect relations are unknown or only vaguely understood.

As challenging as it is to attain the level of technical competence necessary for effective public service, achieving such competence poses yet another challenge: reconciling technical competence with popular rule. Willbern (1954) observed many years ago that professionalization of the public service has the disadvantage of simultaneously insulating public servants from both political favoritism and political control, in the public interest. Thus, maintaining a balance between professional judgment and popular control is an inevitable extension of the challenge of technical competence.

Coping with Public Expectations

Ladd (1978) has labeled Americans institutional conservatives and operational liberals for their dual propensities: to conserve basic institutional arrangements, and to extend government provision of social and economic programs. At no time was this form of American dualism more prominent than during the California tax revolt of 1978. On the heels of Proposition 13 and the reduction of over $7 billion in public revenues, Californians expressed expectations that services would not be reduced and might in fact be expanded.

One reason for the sometimes puzzling pattern of public expectations is that problems are highly subjective. Lindblom (1980) has observed that public problems are not givens but rather the subjective determinations of participants in the policy process. The public and the media are given to labeling a host of situations as problematic—housing, environment, child care—without any yardstick for measuring the direction and depth of problems (Dery, 1984).

Goodsell (1985) offers a litany of reasons for the substantial, occasionally unrealistic, expectations about American public administration. He suggests that one of the major reasons for the public's "impossible" expectations is that public administrators are often asked to pursue goals that are inconsistent and contradictory. Another problem is that most public agencies are judged not by their efforts but by the societal outcomes of their actions. Unfortunately, the scope and magnitude of many public problems—poverty, crime, drug abuse, AIDS—are so great that small progress or holding fast may represent enormous accomplishment. But citizens, motivated both by political rhetoric and promises and by their own instincts about human betterment, expect more from public agencies and are not satisfied with holding fast against even intractable problems.

The culture created by public expectations presents public administrators with a vexing paradox (Whorton and Worthley, 1981). They are simultaneously exposed to two sets of philosophical stimuli: one that represents a positive expression of high ideals, and another that represents a negative expression of distrust and limitations. These stimuli leave public administrators facing an awkward reality: "They wear the hat of agent for the social good as well as the hat of incipient wrongdoer" (Whorton and Worthley, 1981, p. 358). The consequences of this paradox of public administrative culture can take several forms: the development of defense mechanisms for resisting change, perceptions that any encroachments by outsiders or other organizational units are adversarial, and establishment of special performance norms for "government work."

In the face of the American public's deep ambivalence, public administrators are challenged to maintain perspective on their roles. They must strive to be responsive to citizens' and clients' viewpoints, even when these viewpoints conflict with one another. Simultaneously, public administrators must recognize that the public prefers them to be unobtrusive and impartial. Finally, public administrators must resist defending their ambiguous position by sacrificing the public interest.

Managing Complexity, Uncertainty, and Change

American public administration today resides in a two-century-old political system designed to enhance complexity—a characteristic that, as we enter the late twentieth century, is reinforced by rapid technological, scientific, economic, and social change. The legacy of the Federalists has endured. Government should not be entrusted to the good intentions of citizens; citizens sought to impose their selfish interests on others. A government of free people required a design that prevented control by one or even many interests, so that factions could be deterred from tyrannical rule. The design of American government ensured not only a pluralism of structural arrangements but also a pluralism of values, political orientations, and interests.

An inventory of governmental units shows how the complexity envisioned by James Madison has multiplied exponentially. In 1982, there were 82,341 governmental units in the United States, representing three levels of government and a variety of hybrids: one national government; fifty state governments; 3,041 counties; 16,734 townships; 19,076 cities and towns; 28,588 special districts, delivering services ranging from flood control and irrigation to fire protection to libraries and hospitals; and 14,581 school districts (Wright, 1988). The network of associations between and among units—that is, *intergovernmental relations*—defies simple or enduring characterizations, but it has been depicted variously by such metaphors as layer cake, marble cake, picket fence, and whiplash.

If inherent structural complexity were not challenging enough, the web of government now extends to thousands of nonprofit organizations that have been enlisted to deliver public services. In 1980, federal, state, and local support to the nonprofit sector totaled almost $50 billion (Salamon, 1987). On average, over 40 percent of all government spending for social services, employment, housing, health, and the arts went to nonprofit organizations. Although some observers have argued that the widespread use of third sector organizations reduces the performance potential of government, "administration by proxy" (Hood, 1976) appears to be preferable to what might exist in its absence—either massive government or vastly diminished services.

One further complicating factor emanates from the nature of the American political economy. Business exercises influence by virtue of many of its routine decisions—for example, price adjustments, plant openings, hirings, and layoffs. This influence extends beyond the bounds of simple economic transactions, because government relies on business performance and must facilitate that performance by its actions. Noting this privileged position of business, Lindblom (1977, p. 175) writes: "They appear as functionaries performing functions that government officials regard as indispensable."

Complexity is a double-edged sword. It can invigorate the people called on to manage it, and it helps to preserve a system of governance. But complexity can also exceed our capacity to respond and cope with it, thereby frustrating our noble aims. Mosher (1980, p. 542) has written: "Some scholars have extolled complexity in public administration and legislation; it is a challenge, it is fun. But it is at least possible that complexity may grow beyond the bounds of the most brilliant minds. I suspect that it already has." If complexity represents both a challenge and a potentially insurmountable barrier to successful public action, then public administrators must be prepared to follow different strategic paths. One path would be to put the best minds to work on complex problems, facilitating their successful resolution. Another would be to design systems for collective action that overcome the impediments of complexity and permit human beings to triumph despite their individual inadequacies. Another path would be to recognize the inefficacy of intervention and refrain from establishing unrealizable goals. These difficult choices are integral parts of the challenge posed by complexity.

Behaving Ethically

Expectations for the ethical behavior of public officials originated with the founding of the Republic. The founders considered themselves people of good breeding, capable of exercising the duties thrust on them by the demands of their time (Mosher, 1968). Public administrators today, however, find themselves in a more ambiguous ethical milieu. As moral discourse becomes less popular, moral absolutes appear to be in decline. Waldo (1980, p. 112) writes: "The twentieth century has hardly been distinguished either by its observance of agreed moral codes or by its concentration on ethical inquiry. On the contrary, it has been distinguished by a 'decay' of traditional moral codes, a widespread feeling that morality is 'relative' if not utterly meaningless, and a disposition to regard ethical inquiry as frivolous, irrelevant."

At the same time that ethical inquiry has become muddled, the consequences of administrative decisions have become far more consequential. Administrative determinations today cover the spectrum of our physical and social environments, from the cleanliness of our air to opportunities for organ transplants to the security of our neighborhoods.

At the heart of the ethical challenge for public administrators are two questions (Brown, 1986): For whom is the public administrator an agent? What are the justifications for individual conduct and institutional practices and modes of thought? To continue questioning, is the public administrator the servant of one group (that is, administrative superiors) or of several (including legislators and the sovereign public)? Should administrators act to maximize the positive consequences of public action, or are there categorical imperatives to which the administrator must attend? There are obviously no simple answers to these questions. From these quandaries, however, springs the challenge for public administrators to reflect seriously on the moral obligations of their social roles.

Summary

Unlike the corruption and favoritism confronted by the fictional administrator of the Republic, Philip Dru, there is nothing fictional about the challenges faced by today's public administrator. All public administrators must learn to deal with the five challenges discussed in this chapter, which reflect the American system of administration and the technological, social, and international changes that currently engulf it. These challenges can both frustrate and exhilarate. Public administration has risen to the challenges that have confronted it in the past. We can hope it will continue to cope with future challenges successfully, because the quality of public and private life depends on their being met. The remainder of this handbook is devoted to exploring these challenges and providing public administrators with insights and tools for dealing with them.

References

Brown, P. G. "Ethics and Education for Public Service in a Liberal State." *Journal of Policy Analysis and Management,* 1986, *6,* 56–68.

Dery, D. *Problem Definition in Policy Analysis.* Lawrence: University Press of Kansas, 1984.

Goodsell, C. T. *The Case for Bureaucracy.* (2nd ed.) Chatham, N.J.: Chatham House, 1985.

Hood, C. C. *The Limits of Administration.* New York: Wiley, 1976.

House, E. M. *Philip Dru: Administrator.* New York: B. W. Huebsch, 1912.

Kaufman, H. "Administrative Decentralization and Political Power." *Public Administration Review,* 1969, *29* (1), 3–15.

Ladd, E. C., Jr. "What the Voters Really Want." *Fortune,* Dec. 18, 1978, 40–48.

Lindblom, C. E. *Politics and Markets.* New York: Basic Books, 1977.

Lindblom, C. E. *The Policy-Making Process.* (2nd ed.) Englewood Cliffs, N.J.: Prentice-Hall, 1980.

Mosher, F. C. *Democracy and the Public Service.* New York: Oxford University Press, 1968.

Mosher, F. C. "The Changing Responsibilities and Tactics of the Federal Government." *Public Administration Review,* 1980, *40,* 541–548.

Pressman, J. L., and Wildavsky, A. *Implementation.* (2nd ed.) Berkeley: University of California Press, 1979.

Richardson, W. D., and Nigro, L. G. "Administrative Ethics and Founding Thought: Constitutional Correctives, Honor, and Education." *Public Administration Review,* 1987, *47,* 367–376.

Rohr, J. A. *To Run a Constitution: The Legitimacy of the Administrative State.* Lawrence: University Press of Kansas, 1986.

Salamon, L. "Partners in Public Service: The Scope and Theory of Government-Nonprofit Relations." In W. W. Powell (ed.), *The Nonprofit Sector:*

A Research Handbook. New Haven, Conn.: Yale University Press, 1987.

Waldo, D. *The Enterprise of Public Administration.* Novato, Calif.: Chandler and Sharp, 1980.

Whorton, J. W., and Worthley, J. A. "A Perspective on the Challenge of Public Management: Environmental Paradox and Organizational Culture." *Academy of Management Review,* 1981, *6,* 357–361.

Willbern, Y. "Professionalization in the Public Service: Too Little or Too Much?" *Public Administration Review,* 1954, *14,* 13–21.

Wilson, W. "The Study of Administration." *Political Science Quarterly,* 1887, *2,* 197–222.

Wright, D. S. *Understanding Intergovernmental Relations.* (3rd ed.) Monterey, Calif.: Brooks/Cole, 1988.

2

Eugene B. McGregor, Jr.

The Evolving Role
of the Federal Government

Federal public administration—like all national systems of administration—confronts large and complex issues of bureaucracy, politics, and national problem solving. The federal government directly employs 2.8 million civilians and 2.5 million uniformed military personnel. It spends roughly $1 trillion annually, roughly 24 percent of the U.S. gross national product. The national effort is funneled through thirteen line departments, each of which represents a complex conglomerate of bureau-level firms covering from 350 to 400 *bureau leaders,* a general term describing the powerful heads of the major federal operating units (Held, 1982, p. 41). Also included are more than sixty independent agencies, public corporations, and regulatory boards and commissions. Finally, if federally sponsored corporations are included (Seidman, 1975, pp. 106–108), another seventeen enterprises chartered since 1960 must be added to the federal list. The result is a thick and seemingly inpenetrable administrative jungle. Sheer size also makes the analytical task forbidding. Moreover, a glance at the federal budget "bible," the *Appendix* of the budget of the United States, should convince any first-time reader of the complexity of the federal enterprise.

Direct measures of administrative size merely outline the edge of the jungle, however. The real jungle derives from the leverage generated by these numbers. Furthermore, the *Appendix* numbers are incomplete. They omit a contractual work force that exceeds federal employment by a crudely estimated ratio range of from 4:1 to 6:1 (Mosher, 1980). They ignore the leveraging of whole enterprises by a dependence on patronage from the federal customer and by careful design of corporate charter (Weidenbaum, 1969). They are partially blind to a recent dramatic shift toward the use of off-budget

11

expenditures and monetary instruments (Leonard, 1986) as a means of using nonappropriated statutory entitlements, loans, loan guarantees, and government-sponsored enterprise to implement public policy. Thus, as much, or more, federal administration may lie outside the federal government as inside (Mosher, 1980; Walsh, 1978; Kettl, 1988).

A large and complex system cannot be adequately characterized without a simplifying scheme that discerns and separates the significant from the insignificant aspects of federal administration. In this argument, at least three simplifying dimensions are required, by which complex systems of public administration can be understood. The major finding is paradoxical. Decomposed into its multiple dimensions, the federal administrative jungle appears much more comprehensible and penetrable than an initial scan of federal government size and structure might suggest. The complexity arises when the dimensions must be combined and government must act. The term *public administration* is reserved to denote the generation of purposive public action whose success depends on reconciling the competing demands of administrative operations, democratic governance, and public problem solving.

The first dimension deals with the "administrative state" as government operations (Van Riper, 1987, p. 6) and with Woodrow Wilson's (1887, p. 209) notion: "The field of administration is a field of business." Thus, at one level, federal public administration consists of budgets, funding formulas, and career administrative staff remaining at their stations regardless of political change.

The second dimension deals with the administrative state as a system of politics (Seidman and Gilmour, 1986; Nathan, 1975; Held, 1982). In this perspective, federal administration can be viewed as a system of democratic governance and accountability wherein political power is exercised.

Third, federal administration can be viewed as a system that strives to deal effectively with public problems (Dery, 1984). *Public problem solving* is taken here to mean the collective impact of governmental action on a nation of more than 240 million persons that currently employs a labor force of over 110 million workers and generates a $4.5 trillion economy. Thus, public problems appear in the form of threats to national security, slow economic growth, poverty, crime, and other collective issues that affect a whole public. The list could go on, but the point is simple: The administrative state strives to be operationally efficient and organizationally effective, certainly. It exists to govern democratically, to be sure. But it continues to survive because it solves public problems (Caldwell, 1976). The extent to which federal administration produces effective solutions to public problems is termed *policy effectiveness*.

In effect, public administrators are engaged simultaneously in the pursuit of efficient operation, democratic accountability, and problem-solving effectiveness. The three goals pose conflicting objectives and complex trade-offs. For example, democratic accountability strives to achieve democratic objectives that make some business "inefficiency" inevitable (Pressman,

1975). Too-zealous pursuit of "business efficiency" (Grace, 1984) can render government useless as an effective instrument of public policy (Kelman, 1987) and may even threaten democratic accountability in the bargain (Nathan, 1975). Each of the three problem areas is treated briefly in the sections that follow.

Operations

Two general sets of facts constrain and direct federal administrative operations. One is the size and structure of federal funding. The other is the size of the federal work force. Taken separately, however, each factor presents a misleading picture of government activity. For example, at the federal level, a separate treatment of finance and personnel would overlook the obvious discontinuity between an enormous federal fiscal engine and the relatively small work force assigned to run it. Spending data suggest governmental growth. Federal employment data, on the contrary, suggest declining government, compared to the rapidly growing national work force. Neither factor accurately portrays the true size and structure of federal operations.

A perusal of standard statistical and budgetary sources reveals that total government spending (all governments) has risen steadily as a percentage of gross national product (GNP). In 1983 federal, state, and local governments collectively spent nearly 41 percent of GNP, compared with nearly 37 percent in 1975, nearly 28 percent in 1965, and 25 percent in 1955. The greatest contributor to government spending, however, is the federal government, whose spending over the past twenty years held constant at 60 to 61 percent of total government spending. During that time, the federal outlays grew from under 20 percent of GNP in 1967 to 24 percent in 1985.

Federal receipts exceeded outlays only once in the last twenty-five years. Indeed, over the past ten years, the lowest federal deficit (1979) was $40 billion, and over the period from 1982 to 1985, roughly $1 trillion had been added to the federal debt (approximately one-quarter of the current U.S. GNP). Thus, federal deficits represent structural gaps between revenue-generation constraints and the political and public problem-solving agendas that determine expenditures. Much of the current deficit represents a "scissors crisis," brought about by automatic increments built into entitlement expenditures during the late 1960s and the 1970s and by the Reagan administration's success in cutting personal income taxes without making proportional cuts in expenditures (Behn, 1985).

The scope of recent resource shifts is partly revealed by a simplistic disaggregation of federal financial outlays. Crudely put, federal budget totals are derived from decisions in six basic areas: national defense, individual cash transfers, interest on the national debt, grants-in-aid to state and local government, research and development (R&D) expenditures, and residual outlays. By definition, *residual outlays* are programmatic services provided by civil servants spending budgeted funds appropriated to the numerous executive-branch bureaus and operating agencies. Two of the categories—cash transfers and interest on the debt—are uncontrollable in the sense that public policy has removed them from the control of the annual appropriations process. For instance, cash transfers involve categorical entitlements coded in statute. Thus, social security and veterans' benefits, unemployment compensation, food stamps, Aid to Families with Dependent Children, Medicaid, and Medicare involve cash disbursement to persons through direct payments or services vouchered through third-party payment mechanisms. In the case of social security, payments are still partially indexed to inflation.

What is most striking, however, is that a few strategic decisions determine most of the federal budget. Decisions on national security, taxation, and entitlement policy are clearly key points. For example, the decision to reverse the military spending decline of the 1970s (following the Vietnam buildup) resulted in the movement of resources to the Pentagon and an *increase* in defense spending, from 23 percent of the federal budget in 1978 to 26.7 percent by 1985. Over the same period, however, individual cash transfers and entitlements approached 50 percent of the federal budget. Entitlements rose from 27.4 percent of federal outlays in 1967 to 45.0 percent in 1985 and hit a peak share of 48.9 percent in 1983 (Behn, 1985, p. 170). Thus, decisions in three areas—commitments to massive increases in defense outlays, to uncurtailed entitlements, and to lifting the national debt ceiling—resulted in a preemptive claim on 85.4 percent of the federal expenditure total. During this time, the interest on the debt more than doubled and is now the third-largest budget item.

Two major conclusions follow from the preceding discussion. The first is that there has been long-term real growth in total government expenditures. Regardless of the "cutback" rhetoric and recent attempts to shrink government, aggregate federal expenditures increased, rather than decreased, from 1981 to 1985, both in absolute terms and in terms of GNP shares. The simple fact is that the federal government continues to be an increasingly important fiscal engine of U.S. public policy.

The second conclusion is that within the federal fiscal aggregate, enormous realignments of resources have occurred. These have been exacerbated in part by recent massive failures of the federal revenue generator to cover both uncontrollable and controllable outlays. The result is that the controllable budget items—service-based programs, R&D, and nonentitlement grants-in-aid—have come under enormous pressure from the preemptive strikes of national security policy and partially indexed entitlements. Thus, when aggregate spending cutbacks occur, budget cuts are concentrated in three principal categories: non–cash-transfer financial assistance programs for state and local government, R&D, and other programs (not R&D) of federal service delivery.

The result of recent federal fiscal scarcity has been unstable and declining controllable spending. For example, nonentitlement federal grants-in-aid claimed 6.6 percent of federal outlays in 1967, peaked at 11.7 percent in 1978, and by 1985 had shrunk to 6.1 percent of the budget. Nonmilitary R&D moved from 8.2 percent at the beginning of the post-Sputnik buildup of science and technology to 12.3 percent in 1965 and declined slowly and steadily to 5.2 percent by 1985. Finally, program spending (that is, residual outlays) presented one of the most volatile pictures, bouncing from 3.6 percent of outlays in 1967 to 6.4 percent in 1980 and down to 3.3 percent in 1985. A consequence is that federal domestic service-delivery agencies in such diverse fields as air traffic control, public works, natural resource management, the census, parks management, law enforcement, public health, regulation, and science and technology have had to contemplate alternative and perhaps permanent alterations in program design to accommodate the strategic realities already described.

The trend is a secular one and antedates the presidency of Ronald Reagan. For example, intergovernmental grants-in-aid have been a declining share of the budget since 1978, and a rise of fend-for-yourself federalism has been one result (Shannon, 1988, p. 17). Long-term R&D spending has declined during the era of post-Apollo cuts in the National Aeronautics and Space Administration. Domestic service-based programs have shown no consistent funding trend over the past decade.

Public finance tells only part of the story, however, for the growing fiscal claim on the U.S. economy completely swamps the lack of growth in federal personnel. The great anomaly of federal bureaucracy is the enormous growth in financial outlays processed by a work force whose aggregate size has changed very little in over two and one-half decades; indeed, growth in the federal work force occurred at a rate of only three-fifths of the population growth rate. One of the ironies is that during the Reagan years 1981 to 1985, total executive-branch civilian employment actually rose by twenty-four thousand, representing the net of a Department of Defense increase of sixty-six thousand and a nondefense employment decline of forty-two thousand persons.

Stability of absolute work force size is only one strategic fact. The other is that over a twenty-year period, the federal employment share of all direct civilian government employment declined from 27 percent to 18 percent (compare the 1962 and 1982 census of governments). In addition, the declining federal share occurred in a declining "industry": Whereas all government civilian work forces—federal, state, and local—in 1968 accounted for 16.8 percent of all jobs in a national labor force of over 82 million workers, it claimed only 15.2 percent twelve years later, in 1980, when the labor force numbered nearly 107 million workers. By 1984, however, the governmental share had shrunk to 14.2 percent of a total labor force of 115 million persons. Notwithstanding a modest recent employment surge, the federal civilian work force is shrinking, both absolutely (since the late 1960s) and relatively, in a public labor market that is itself shrinking relative to the U.S. labor force.

No public management system can remain untouched by the policy demand that ever larger policy results be achieved by a declining work force spending fewer program dollars on direct service delivery. This demand has meant that federal administrators, for example, have had increasingly to implement national policy through the use of remote instruments of production, in which workers other than federal civil servants have been engaged in the production of final products and services. In no other way could a work force of 2.8 million civilians dispose of nearly one-quarter of the U.S. GNP. Thus, the definition and structure of federal service have undergone continuous reform in the face of changing policy demands and resource constraints.

Governance

Federal administrators also confront a governance problem. Management of the modern instruments of the administrative state involves the exercise of enormous power (Walsh, 1978; Heymann, 1987). How can the power of the administrative state be rendered obedient to democratic institutions and processes? The American answer to the ancient question is unique: No one person or institution is in charge! The result has been the development of a complex administrative state based on a complex system of political accountability that derives from a carefully crafted constitutional confusion (Sundquist, 1986). This guardianship of democratic institutions and processes through the careful fragmentation of power and authority presents federal public administrators with a governance issue that centers on the question of accountability (Smith and Hague, 1971; Rosen, 1982) and the determination, according to Seidman and Gilmour (1986, p. 28), of "who shall control . . . [political power] and to what ends?"

The issue is easy to underestimate and dismiss as profoundly nonmanagerial and unprofessional. Nevertheless, public administration has classically treated democratic governance as a final purpose of government and happily endures administrative inefficiencies in order to attain its goal of accountability (Pressman, 1975). This is implied in governmental machinery established to ensure civilian control of the military (U.S. Senate, 1985). It is implied in the Freedom of Information Act. It is contained in congressional oversight of the bureaucracy and the many constraints deliberately placed on public management practice, including procurement regulations, compliance with merit systems administration, and so forth.

Furthermore, political accountability is buttressed by a layer of politically appointed persons constitutionally empowered with the visible task of democratic governance. The governance system historically has been stressful. Descriptive research (Heclo, 1977) has revealed enormous strains between governance personnel and the permanent staff who manage operations. For example, federal political executives at the assistant secretarial level and up have been consistently characterized by a high degree of turnover (average tenure is two years), little prior experience in public service, and low levels of specialized training in the policy fields to which they were appointed (Mackenzie, 1987). Top federal career administrators, in contrast, were notable for their lack of career mobility, civil service protection from political manipulation, and specialized technical and professional training (McGregor, 1974).

The existence of dichotomized political and career federal services has implied a corollary: Much of public policy making has been de facto in the hands of career experts and not in those of political persons holding non-career policymaking and confidential positions. The latter group was widely regarded as insufficiently experienced and, if trained and experienced, too mobile to be effective in making and implementing public policy (McGregor, 1974). The result is a "government of strangers" formed by an institutional competition between administrative careerists and amateur politicians over the control of public policy programs (Heclo, 1977).

Less well understood is that the confusion over governance has its roots in the U.S. Constitution. The establishment of a governance system based on separation of powers and on checks and balances among separated powers was designed to prevent predatory and unproductive exercises of power in the absence of concurrent majorities in the courts and in the legislature. The unforeseen corollary is that in their role as operations managers, career civil servants have been thrust into the breach and, as a consequence, have come to exercise extraordinary discretion and power (Nathan, 1975; Seidman and Gilmour, 1986; Rourke, 1978). The result is that career public administrators have assumed a political significance arguably (Rohr, 1986) not foreseen in the original constitutional design of 1787.

The strains of career and political services surface periodically. Notable were the attempts of two presidents, Jimmy Carter and Ronald Reagan, to reform the civil service, cut back on the size and cost of government, and privatize the delivery of public services. Indeed, the presidency of Ronald Reagan was characterized as one in which the president made, in at least one view, "perhaps the most determined effort of any recent president to bend the permanent government to his will" (Lynn, 1984, p. 339). Thus, the traditional competition between the partisan forces of governance and those of career administrators appears to have taken a nasty turn to the disadvantage of careerists. Evidence of a "federal service malaise" consists of the following:

1. The last two administrations—Carter's and Reagan's—made vigorous use of the noncareer appointment limit to appoint the maximum number of elite, noncareer Senior Executive Service (SES) members possible, leading to the charge that the federal executive branch was being politicized (Goldenberg, 1984).
2. An aggressive attempt by the Reagan administration to deliver on a campaign pledge to cut the size and cost of government has led to vigorous attempts to privatize the delivery of public services (Savas, 1987).
3. An investigation of federal staffing, overgrading, and pay has contributed to the widespread public suspicion that federal bureaucracies are overstaffed with mediocre people holding overgraded and overpaid positions (Grace, 1984).

Not surprisingly, disillusionment has been reported in the ranks of senior career executives (Seidman and Gilmour, 1986, p. 134), 70 percent of whom, questioned in one 1983 poll (Federal Executive Institute Alumni Association, 1983), responded that they would advise bright young people not to seek employment with the federal government. More recent surveys of federal executives at the level of division chief and of the SES report only modest improvements in morale (Federal Executive Institute Alumni Association, 1988).

How are recent events to be understood? A two-dimensional answer views the problem as a clash of governance politics and administrative operations. It is only part of the story, however. The other part is that large portions of the federal business are growing, rather than shrinking, over time. The institutional antagonisms between career public administrators and politicians are coming to be mediated by new structures of governance and public administration that do not fit neatly into the paradigms of either administrative operations or governance politics. These structures constitute new, less visible instruments of the administrative state. Their advent antedates the political moves of the Reagan administration and therefore cannot have been caused by Reaganism. Indeed, Reagan policies may simply have redirected a watershed of accumulated public policy problems, which have the ironic effect of accelerating both the public need for and the power of public administrators at the same time that the visible portions of the administrative state are being trimmed and rearranged. This shift can be seen only by shifting to a third perspective, that of public problem solving.

Policy Effectiveness

How do public problems get solved? The pattern of moving public productivity out of the governmental domain and into remote production units is the only strategy that simultaneously satisfies both a large, growing public problem-solving agenda and resource limitations. The first post–World War II round of redesign activity followed a well-described and predictable pattern. A complex system of intergovernmental financial assistance moved federal missions into local government during the 1960s through the use of categorical grants. In addition, states were encouraged to join the national agenda during the 1960s (Weidenbaum, 1969) and further encouraged in the 1970s through the use of block grants (Advisory Commission on Intergovernmental Relations, 1977).

Furthermore, an elaborate system of contracting for goods and services has developed. This can only be expected when public policy, backed by an enormous and growing fiscal engine, attempts to implement ambitious programs without expanding the government work force. The instruments of the ''new political economy'' were fashioned increasingly from interorganizational networks of public agencies and private and not-for-profit firms (Savas, 1987; Smith, 1975; McGregor, 1981). In short, U.S. public policy is increasingly implemented through instruments resembling those employed by strategic corporate planners (Thorelli, 1986; Seidman and Gilmour, 1986), including the following:

- *Project and contract management,* including turnkey contracting, rather than line management of service production
- *Multiple "in-sourcing and out-sourcing"* of services and products among operating agencies and between federal agencies and private firms
- *Public-private joint ventures* whose activities are supported through private and off-budget public financing for combinations of franchises, user fees, risk guarantees, insurances, and the sheltering of capital investment from taxes
- *Franchising and chartering of new government-sponsored enterprises*—for example, mortgage associations, health maintenance organizations, and community mental health centers

These are the adaptive responses that circumvent constitutional debt limitations, spending limits, and operational ceilings placed on budgets and bureaucrats (Leonard, 1986).

Adaptive Federal Management

The great strength of federal public administration derives from the continuous adaptation of federal administrators to the challenges of operations management, governance, and public policy. Federal administrators are under constant pressure from turbulent policy environments to experiment, change, and respond to the nation's productivity demands. Paradoxically, the basis of adaptive federal management is an enduring and stable administrative structure built on a large number of independently chartered bureaus and agencies (Heymann, 1987). These operating bureaus have their own statutory and budget authorizations, personnel systems (McGregor, 1974), and methods of managing information and resources (Bragaw, 1980). Thus, the Federal Bureau of Investigation, the Bureau of Labor Statistics, the U.S. Patent Office, the U.S. Coast Guard, the Forest Service, the Federal Aviation Administration, the National Aeronautics and Space Administration, and all their associated institutes and field centers form the stable operating core of federal public administration.

Notwithstanding program failures (Trento, 1987), the structure has from most accounts served public policy well. Deliberate redundancies (Landau, 1969) of agency and program encourage substantial competition among the many federal "businesses" (Trento, 1987; Bragaw, 1980). When administrative complexity is combined with the checks and balances of the American Constitution, the result is an invisible institutional stimulus that encourages management excellence and is as powerful as the vaunted stimulus of the competitive economic marketplace (Bragaw, 1980; Webb, 1969).

Over time, however, the federal system has slowly changed its focus. A brief historical digression leavens the conclusion about the federal contribution to American public administration. During the first hundred years after the constitutional convention of 1787, questions of governance prevailed, at least through the end of the Civil War. During the second hundred years, public debate shifted to the design and operation of an administrative engine that would serve the public will. Woodrow Wilson (1887), writing at the time of the constitutional centennial, not only announced the end of the constitution-building period in American history but also correctly foresaw the rise of the administrative state.

Wilson could not have anticipated the extent to which questions of what to do about public affairs would establish a public policy agenda as powerful as the exercise of governance and the management of administrative operations (Van Riper, 1987, p. 29). The great questions of national public policy now require, in turn, substantive answers to questions of national security and economic revival (Kennedy, 1987), questions of whether and how to accelerate the postindustrial conversion of the U.S. economy (Drucker, 1969) during a period of intense global competition (Hudson Institute, 1987), and questions of how to design, build, and test new and highly sophisticated technologies (Trento, 1987). Furthermore, solutions to problems will be formulated and executed in turbulent environments under conditions of extreme financial pressure (Grace, 1984; Levine, 1986).

The ascending public policy problems appear to transcend the product lines of single operating bureaus and agencies. National security, for instance, is really the product of many agencies. The same could be said of public welfare, health, economic development, and so forth. Gone is a simpler administrative era (if, indeed, it ever existed) in which the term *public administration* could be made synonymous with the term *operations management* (Rosenthal, 1982), with the politics of governance (Heymann, 1987), or, for that matter, with public policymaking. It is simply more complete to say that federal public administration involves the simultaneous solution of problems of public policy, governance, and operations management. Whether all three competencies will be contained in the persons of an elite corps of federal executives or divided among teams of specialists remains unclear. What is clear is that the failure to engage the three dimensions has enormous potential costs. For example, whether the annexation of the private sector by public policy leads to a "government by proxy" (Kettl, 1988) is not really a function of using government's many contractual instruments; "contracting out" will convert public power to private proxy only when government fails to retain the in-house talent necessary to manage, monitor, and intervene effectively in program implementation (Trento, 1987, p. 54).

The joining of public administration's three dimensions has profound implications for designing central federal administrative functions. Questions of finance, personnel, acquisitions, and political oversight are not easily separable. For example, the purchase of sophisticated computer and communications systems for automating program management has simultaneous implications for staffing levels, financial obligations, and purchasing systems. Even more important is that contracting for complex public systems, on either effectiveness or efficiency grounds, still begs the question of what civil service staffing pattern will ensure that public money is well spent and that federal sovereignty is not compromised by contract activity.

Somehow, federal administrators will have to develop a continuing conversation among personnel, budget, and acquisitions offices, which was not required when federal administration proceeded at a less pressured pace and with a less constrained resource base. Thus, there are numerous proposals to restructure central federal administrative functions (Benda and Levine, 1986, p. 388) such that budget, personnel, and procurement agencies become less insular. It is not at all clear, however, that structural reshuffling, or even the creation of a central federal management agency, will do the job. Regardless of structure, federal administrators will have to develop a sophisticated multilevel system for resource management that cuts across administrative disciplines.

Summary

Federal administrators simultaneously pursue the goals of operating efficiency, democratic accountability, and public policy effectiveness. Engaging all three dimensions comprises the federal public management challenge. The modern challenge is particularly exciting because of the severe resource constraints likely to be imposed. One obvious conclusion, however, is that the attempt to shrink the visible portions of operations (budgets and administrators) can, under some conditions, force the hidden federal government to grow. In effect, federal public administration grows, even while attributes of the administrative state are cut back.

Ironically, if cutbacks are thoughtlessly applied in the name of operating efficiency, program effectiveness and democratic accountability can be lost. In such a case, it will be truly appropriate to speak of a government by proxy. The supreme irony, however, is that the power and prestige of the career public service may well be most augmented by precisely those actions favored by politicians who wage war against government, budgets, and bureaucrats. Absent a paring of the problem-solving agenda, ideologically motivated attempts to cut the cost and size of government theoretically accomplish three things. They hasten the pace of the public-private merger, encourage the invention of increasingly sophisticated and invisible instruments of public policy, and escalate the skill requirements of public administrators. The likely result is an enhancement of the power, prestige, and skill requirements of the true federal administrator.

References

Advisory Commission on Intergovernmental Relations. *Block Grants: A Comparative Analysis.* Washington, D.C.: Advisory Commission on Intergovernmental Relations, 1977.

Behn, R. "Cutback Budgeting." *Journal of Policy Analysis and Management,* 1985, *5* (2), 155–177.

Benda, P. M., and Levine, C. H. "OMB and the Central Management Problem: Is Another Reorganization the Answer?" *Public Administration Review,* 1986, *46* (5), 379–391.

Bragaw, L. K. *Managing a Federal Agency: The Hidden Stimulus.* Baltimore, Md.: Johns Hopkins University Press, 1980.

Caldwell, L. K. "Novus Ordo Seclorum: The Heritage of American Public Administration." *Public Administration Review,* 1976, *36* (5), 476–488.

Dery, D. *Problem Definition in Policy Analysis.* Lawrence: University Press of Kansas, 1984.

Drucker, P. F. *The Age of Discontinuity.* New York: Harper & Row, 1969.

Federal Executive Institute Alumni Association (FEIAA). *Newsletter.* McLean, Va.: Federal Executive Institute Alumni Association, Jan. 1983.

Federal Executive Institute Alumni Association (FEIAA). *FEIAA 1987 Membership Survey.* McLean, Va.: Federal Executive Institute Alumni Association, Apr. 5, 1988.

Goldenberg, E. N. "The Permanent Government in an Era of Retrenchment and Redirection." In L. M. Salamon and M. S. Lund (eds.), *The Reagan Presidency and the Governing of America.* Washington, D.C.: Urban Institute Press, 1984.

Grace, P. J. *War on Waste.* New York: Macmillan, 1984.

Heclo, H. *A Government of Strangers: Executive Politics in Washington.* Washington, D.C.: Brookings Institution, 1977.

Held, W. G. "Decision Making in the Federal Government: The Wallace S. Sayre Model." In F. S. Lane (ed.), *Current Issues in Public Administration.* (2nd ed.) New York: St. Martin's Press, 1982.

Heymann, P. B. *The Politics of Public Management.* New Haven, Conn.: Yale University Press, 1987.

Hudson Institute. *Workforce 2000.* Indianapolis, Ind.: Hudson Institute, 1987.

Kelman, S. *Making Public Policy: A Hopeful View of American Government.* New York: Basic Books, 1987.

Kennedy, P. *The Rise and Fall of the Great Powers: Economic Change and Military Conflict from 1500 to 2000.* New York: Random House, 1987.

Kettl, D. F. *Government by Proxy: (Mis)Managing Federal Programs.* Washington, D.C.: Congressional Quarterly Press, 1988.

Landau, M. "Redundancy, Rationality and the Problem of Duplication and Overlap." *Public Administration Review,* 1969, *29* (4), 346–358.

Leonard, H. B. *Checks Unbalanced: The Quiet Side of Public Spending.* New York: Basic Books, 1986.

Levine, C. H. "The Federal Government in the Year 2000: Administrative Legacies of the Reagan Years." *Public Administration Review,* 1986, *46* (3), 195–206.

Lynn, L. E., Jr. "The Reagan Administration and the Renitent Bureaucracy." In L. M. Salamon and M. S. Lund (eds.), *The Reagan Presidency and the Governing of America.* Washington, D.C.: Urban Institute Press, 1984.

McGregor, E. B., Jr. "Politics and the Career Mobility of Bureaucrats." *American Political Science Review,* 1974, *68* (1), 18–26.

McGregor, E. B., Jr. "Administration's Many Instruments: Mining, Refining and Applying Charles Lindblom's *Politics and Markets.*" *Administration and Society,* 1981, *13* (3), 347–375.

Mackenzie, G. C. (ed.). *The In-and-Outers.* Baltimore, Md.: Johns Hopkins University Press, 1987.

Mosher, F. C. "The Changing Responsibilities and Tactics of the Federal Government." *Public Administration Review,* 1980, *40,* 541–548.

Nathan, R. P. *The Plot That Failed: Nixon and the Administrative Presidency.* New York: Wiley, 1975.

Pressman, J. L. *Federal Programs and City Politics: The Dynamics of the Aid Process in Oakland.* Berkeley: University of California Press, 1975.

Rohr, J. A. *To Run a Constitution: The Legitimacy of the Administrative State.* Lawrence: University Press of Kansas, 1986.

Rosen, B. *Holding Government Bureaucracies Accountable.* New York: Praeger, 1982.

Rosenthal, S. R. *Managing Government Operations.* Glenview, Ill.: Scott, Foresman, 1982.

Rourke, F. E. (ed.). *Bureaucratic Power in National Politics.* (3rd ed.) Boston: Little, Brown, 1978.

Savas, E. S. *Privatization: The Key to Better Government.* Chatham, N.J.: Chatham House, 1987.

Seidman, H. *Politics, Position, and Power: The Dynamics of Federal Organization.* (2nd ed.) New York: Oxford University Press, 1975.

Seidman, H., and Gilmour, R. *Politics, Position, and Power: From the Positive to the Regulatory State.* (4th ed.) New York: Oxford University Press, 1986.

Shannon, J. "The Faces of Fiscal Federalism." *Intergovernmental Perspective,* 1988, *14* (1), 15–17.

Smith, B.L.R. (ed.). *The New Political Economy: The Public Use of the Private Sector.* New York: Wiley, 1975.

Smith, B.L.R., and Hague, D. C. (eds.). *The Dilemma of Accountability in Modern Government.* London: Macmillan, 1971.

Sundquist, J. L. *Constitutional Reform and Effective Government.* Washington, D.C.: Brookings Institution, 1986.

Thorelli, H. B. "Networks: Between Markets and Hierarchies." *Strategic Management Journal,* 1986, *7* (1), 37–51.

Trento, J. J. *Prescription for Disaster: From the Glory of Apollo to the Betrayal of the Shuttle.* New York: Crown, 1987.

U.S. Senate. *Defense Organization: The Need for Change.* Staff Report to the Committee on Armed Services, S. Prt. 99–86. Washington, D.C.: U.S. Senate, 1985.

Van Riper, P. P. "The American Administrative State: Wilson and the Founders." In R. C. Chandler (ed.), *A Centennial History of the American Administrative State.* New York: Free Press, 1987.

Walsh, A. H. *The Public's Business: The Politics and Practices of Government Corporations.* Cambridge, Mass.: MIT Press, 1978.

Webb, J. E. *Space Age Management.* New York: McGraw-Hill, 1969.

Weidenbaum, M. L. *The Modern Public Sector: New Ways of Doing the Government's Business.* New York: Basic Books, 1969.

Wilson, W. "The Study of Administration." *Political Science Quarterly,* 1887, *2* (2), 197–222.

3

James K. Conant

The Growing Importance
of State Government

Over the past decade or so, a number of scholars and journalists have commented on the growing importance of the states' role in the federal system. President Reagan's attempt to reduce the size and role of the national government has been the principal cause of the renewed interest in and growing visibility of the states. Indeed, it was President Reagan's "new federalism" that put the spotlight on the states in the early 1980s, and it is the ongoing preoccupation of national policymakers with deficit reduction that has heightened the intensity of that spotlight in recent years (Stenberg, 1985). Of course, other factors have also contributed to the growing visibility and importance of the states. Among the most important are the growth in state expenditures and employment, the growing fiscal and institutional capacity of the states, the nature of the states' role in the intergovernmental system, and new policy initiatives undertaken by the states.

In this chapter, the role each of these factors has played in generating the current visibility and renewed importance of the states will be discussed. In addition, some of the major challenges faced by state policymakers and administrators will be identified and analyzed. It is important to acknowledge at the outset of this chapter that there are many significant differences in the economic, political, sociocultural, and administrative systems of the fifty states. Indeed, in some areas, the differences may be more important than the similarities. By necessity, however, the principal focus of this chapter is on the shared dimensions of the states' environment and activities and the shared challenges that state policymakers and administrators have faced and are likely to face in the future.

25

New Federalism and National Deficits

A key fact of life for state policymakers and administrators is that they live and act in a federal system. Mandates established by the national government heavily influence what the states do and how they do it. In addition, the national government supplies approximately 25 percent of the money that state governments spend. Given this situation, changes in national government priorities and policies can have an important or even profound effect on the states.

For more than a quarter of a century, from the early 1950s through the late 1970s, national policy and fiscal decision making seemed to have a common direction. The number of mandates given to state and local governments was increasing, and the amount of intergovernmental revenue was expanding. Although President Carter was the first president to interrupt the upward trajectory of intergovernmental aid (Wright, 1988), Ronald Reagan's election to the presidency in 1980 was a more visible signal that changes in national policy and the federal system were forthcoming.

In his 1980 inaugural address, President Reagan said, "It is my intention to curb the size and influence of the federal establishment and to demand recognition of the distinction between the powers granted to the federal government and those reserved to the states or the people." The significance and meaning of the president's objectives were simply and eloquently summed up by Palmer and Sawhill (1982, p. 1): "After a half century of growing federal efforts to stabilize the economy, insure individuals against misfortune, redistribute income and opportunity and respond to other perceived national needs," the authors said, President Reagan intended to initiate a counterrevolution.

One element of this counterrevolution was President Reagan's commitment to establishing a more limited role for the national government in domestic affairs. A second element was his desire to restore the traditional separation of responsibility among governments. President Reagan viewed the national government as a competitor, rather than a partner, with state and local governments (Palmer and Sawhill, 1982). Furthermore, he believed that this intergovernmental competition distorted the priorities of state and local governments.

The principal methods members of the Reagan administration used to cut back the national government's size and role were tax cuts, elimination or reduction of national government programs, and tightened eligibility requirements, particularly in social welfare and health programs. The principal methods used to shape the new intergovernmental relationships were cuts in grants-in-aids to lower levels of government, the creation of block grants to increase state governments' budget flexibility, and an attempt to strengthen the national-state, rather than the national-local, government connection.

President Reagan achieved significant changes in each of these areas. In the Omnibus Budget Reconciliation Act of 1981, he secured the biggest tax cut in history, as well as cutbacks in some national government programs and activities. In addition, the president achieved some important changes in the intergovernmental aid system. More than a hundred of the existing grant authorizations for state and local governments were cut, sixty were zeroed out, and seventy-seven categorical grants were consolidated into nine block grants (Wright, 1988, p. 203, p. 212). The fiscal effects of these changes, in constant (1972) dollars, was that federal aid declined from $48 billion in 1980 to $43 billion in 1985. Total federal aid, however, continued to rise despite the cutbacks.

　　The effects of the Omnibus Reconciliation Act of 1981 were felt across a broad spectrum of state agencies and state programs. Administrators in social service and health agencies, however, were most adversely affected. Since the cutbacks in federal aid occurred during the nation's deepest recession since the Great Depression, most states did not immediately attempt to restore the lost funds (Palmer and Sawhill, 1982; Nathan and Doolittle, 1983). The result was that state administrators in many social service and health agencies faced the difficult challenge of trying to maintain programs for the poor and the working poor in the face of growing demands and resource cutbacks.

　　The Reagan administration's efforts to make additional cuts in federal aid were generally blunted or rejected by Congress between 1982 and 1985. Both nominal and real reductions in the level of intergovernmental aid occurred after 1985 (Wright, 1988), however, as Congress attempted to reduce deficits and meet the provisions of the Gramm-Rudman-Hollings Act. Among the most controversial cutbacks in the intergovernmental aid system was the elimination of general revenue sharing (GRS) for both state and local governments. The fact that state and local governments used GRS funds to offset the costs of national government mandates made the elimination of these funds particularly difficult for state and local officials to swallow.

　　While some state officials have strong negative views of the Reagan administration's attempt to decentralize through the new federalism, others have been more favorably disposed. For example, governors, legislators, and administrators who felt that the states were being "strangled" (Broder, 1980) by federal rules and regulations appreciate the flexibility they have gained through the expansion of block grants. Moreover, they have applauded the slowdown, caused by the preoccupation with deficit reduction, in Congress's attempts to establish new national goals and mandates. Even these state officials, however, are sensitive to the fact that the annual cost of federal mandates to state and local government is estimated to be in excess of $200 billion (Moore, 1986). Furthermore, many share the concern expressed by Mayor Ed Koch of New York over the "ever widening gulf separating the programmatic demands of an activist Congress from its concurrent fiscal conservatism" (Koch, 1980, p. 43). In short, cuts in federal aid have not been welcomed even by the state officials most favorably disposed to the new federal-state relationship of the 1980s.

The Growing Size of State Government

Growth in expenditures and employment is a third reason for the growing visibility and importance of the states. Between 1970 and 1985, employment in state government bureaucracies nearly doubled, growing from 2.3 million in 1970 to almost 4 million in 1985. State expenditures also grew dramatically during that period, moving from $131.3 billion in 1970 to $503.4 billion in 1984. Even with constant dollars as the basis of comparison, that is an increase of almost 40 percent in the fifteen-year period. National mandates, population growth, and economic growth have served as a spur for the growth in state employment and expenditures. Citizens' demands for new services, the desire of state officials to provide new services, and local governments' demands for additional aid have also contributed to this growth.

One way to gain perspective on the growing size and scope of state activity is to compare state governments to America's largest industrial companies. To establish its list of the top five hundred American companies, *Fortune* magazine ranks corporations on the basis of sales. In a similar fashion, state governments can be ranked on the basis of revenues. Behn and Behn's (1986) comparative rankings of the fifty states and the largest industrial companies show that ten states—California, New York, Texas, Pennsylvania, Michigan, Illinois, Ohio, New Jersey, Florida, and Massachusetts—displace ten corporations on *Fortune*'s top-fifty list. In addition, twenty-four states displace twenty-four corporations on the *Fortune* list of the top one hundred. Even Vermont, the state with the smallest amount of general revenue, is ranked 383 on the combined *Fortune* list of five hundred.

The fact that the states are now such large business enterprises means that there is a pressing need for effective management of state agencies. Indeed, making sure that every state agency can and does perform its core tasks effectively is one of the principal challenges that elected state officials and state administrators currently face and will face in the near future. An adequate level of resources is a necessary, but not sufficient, condition for creating, sustaining, and renewing this capacity. Other factors, like management strategy, organizational structure, culture, and systems, and employee skills, must be managed effectively to create this capacity (Peters and Waterman, 1982).

Fiscal Capacity

A fourth reason for the growing visibility and importance of state governments is the growth in the states' fiscal capacity. One reflection of this growing capacity is the fact that most states have had healthy surpluses since the early 1980s, while the national government has had large deficits. For example, the states' surplus for fiscal year 1985 was $4.3 billion (Stenberg, 1985), while the national deficit was approaching $200 billion. Prudent financial management has contributed to the generally healthy financial condition of the states, but growth in state revenues has also been a key factor. For example, state general revenues climbed from $77.8 billion in 1970 to $365.3 billion in 1985.

State taxes were the source of almost 60 percent of the 1985 state general revenue. Charges and miscellaneous sources accounted for 18 percent, and federal aid accounted for 23 percent. The relative share that each of these sources has contributed to state revenues has changed somewhat between 1970 and 1985, and adjustments of this type will undoubtedly continue in the future. For example, the proportion of general revenue generated from tax sources declined from 62 percent in 1970 to 60 percent in 1980 and then remained stable at 60 percent through 1985. The proportion of revenue drawn from user fees increased steadily, moving from 12 percent in 1970 to 14 percent in 1980 and to 18 percent in 1985. Federal aid expanded as a source of state general revenue between 1970 (26 percent) and 1980 (28 percent) but fell to 25 percent in 1985.

The growth in total taxes raised has been a key factor in the states' growing fiscal capacity, even though taxes have declined somewhat between 1970 and 1985 as a share of total state general revenue. Specifically, state tax collections have grown at an average rate of 10 percent a year over the past thirty years. In contrast, national government tax collections have grown at an average annual rate of only 5.8 percent, and local tax revenues have grown at an average annual rate of 8.4 percent (Wright, 1988).

Economic growth and inflation contributed to this growth in tax revenues, but decisions made by state policymakers also contributed significantly. For example, policymakers in thirty states raised taxes in 1981. In 1982, tax rates were raised in twenty-one states, and in 1983 they were raised in thirty-one states (Wright, 1988). Furthermore, new taxes—personal income taxes, corporate income taxes, or sales taxes—were established in a number of states. As a result, forty-one states have broad-based personal income taxes, forty-six have corporate income taxes, and forty-five have general sales taxes (Stenberg, 1985, p. 320).

Governors and legislators, of course, are acutely aware of the political risks involved in imposing new taxes and expanding existing income and sales taxes. The fact that this risk was taken with such frequency over the past decade seems to show that there is a good deal of political courage in the states. These decisions also serve as a barometer of the kinds of pressures faced by elected state officials in recent years. Governors and legislators have had to cope with increasing numbers of federal mandates, economic recession, cutbacks in federal aid, demands for new services, and local government requests for more support. The risks involved in raising taxes or imposing new taxes have also motivated state officials to pursue user fees aggressively as a means of avoiding tax increases or spending cuts.

This aggregate picture of the growth in the states' fiscal capacity does, however, mask some dimensions of the states' fiscal condition that are less favorable. For example, state tax and revenue growth has been uneven across the states over the past two decades. Between 1982 and 1985, for example, economic growth created a tax revenue boom in states like Massachusetts and New Jersey. In states like Iowa and Oklahoma, however, shrinking demand levels, and falling prices for farm products and oil, adversely affected tax revenues. Likewise, the tax revolt that began in 1978 with the passage of Proposition 13 in California motivated elected officials in many states to cut tax rates, limit tax rates, or cap spending at state and local levels. Drastic measures to cut taxes, like Proposition 13, were approved in only two other states over the past decade—in Iowa (1978) and Massachusetts (1980)— and they were defeated in five states (Oregon, Michigan, Nevada, South Dakota, and Utah) (Mikesell, 1986, p. 7). Referenda to limit and contain spending, appropriations, and revenues were approved, however, by voters in fourteen of the nineteen states where such issues were on the ballot (Mikesell, 1986, p. 8).

Institutional Capacity

Growth in the institutional capacity of state legislatures and executive branches is the fifth factor that has contributed to the states' growing importance and visibility. In many legislatures, for example, the changes that took place between the mid 1960s and the mid 1970s amounted to a transformation. The composition of the state legislatures changed, legislative facilities were expanded, legislative structure and procedures were modified or overhauled, and the number of bills introduced and enacted rose substantially.

One way to gain an appreciation of the transformation that has taken place in state legislatures is to consider the kinds of complaints legislative leaders voiced about their institutions in the 1960s. For example, the "former speaker of the Massachusetts house recalled that, on his assumption of the speakership in 1967, the average legislator did not have a desk or secretarial assistance or simple office amenities. . . . The minority leader of the New York assembly recalled that when he arrived in Albany in 1961 'we had one secretary for every nine assemblymen, and only leaders had an office'" (Rosenthal, 1981, p. 205). By 1980, there were over sixteen thousand full-time professional, administrative, and clerical staff working in state legislatures. An additional nine thousand people were employed during each legislative session (Rosenthal, 1981, p. 206).

Changes in the composition of state legislatures were driven by the Supreme Court's decision in *Baker* v. *Carr,* which mandated reapportionment of state legislatures on the basis of population. As a result of that decision, urban areas gained greater representation during the 1960s and the 1970s. In more recent years, as legislatures in many states have become full-time bodies, a new breed of legislator has begun to emerge. Contemporary legislators are younger and better educated than their predecessors, they are more likely to hold office as full-time professionals rather than part-timers, and they are more likely to be female. In addition, contemporary legislators are more likely to serve for extended periods of time. The turnover rate in legislatures declined from about 40 percent in 1967 to 23 percent for lower houses and 20 percent for state senates in 1981 (Bowman and Kearney, 1986).

Improved working conditions have contributed to the growing longevity and continuity of legislative service. For example, legislators in California, Florida, Massachusetts, Michigan, Nebraska, New Jersey, Ohio, Pennsylvania, Texas, and Wisconsin currently have personal staff support, professional staff support, or both (Rosenthal, 1981). In addition, legislative facilities have improved. Most legislators now have their own offices or at least share an office, and chambers and hearing rooms in many states have been remodeled. Legislative pay and daily expense allowances have also been increased in many states. In several states, however, pay remains very low, and staff support and facilities remain minimal.

In addition to the changes described above, modifications in the organization and procedures of state legislatures have also been made. These changes were designed to improve the processing of bills. Indeed, fragmented committee structures and antiquated procedures became increasingly problematic during the 1960s and the 1970s, as the number of bills introduced each session rose steadily. In some states, committee structures and procedures for processing bills were overhauled through reorganization; in other states, they were modified and improved gradually. As a result of these changes, the number of standing committees has been reduced in many states, and the number of committee assignments for individual legislators has fallen. Consequently, the prospects for specialization by legislators have improved. In addition, tighter and more effective scheduling systems have been established for committee and house action on bills (Bowman and Kearney, 1986).

These changes have helped state legislators and state legislatures cope with an ever growing number of demands. While committee structures, procedures, and staff support remain weak in many states, compared to the U.S. Congress, significant improvements have been made over the past thirty years. State legislatures now have the capacity to do more, and they are doing more. The number of bills introduced into the legislative hopper each year now exceeds one hundred thousand. Furthermore, the average legislature is likely to pass almost five hundred new pieces of legislation each year (Council of State Governments, 1987). In short, the combination of greater demands and greater institutional capacity has led to a higher level of output by state legislatures over the past several decades.

The growth in the volume of new legislation has made quality control an increasingly important issue in recent years. Furthermore, it will undoubtedly continue to be a key challenge for legislative leaders in the future. There are indications, however, that most state legislatures are coping responsibly and effectively with this challenge. A poll conducted in 1979 by Lou Harris showed that state legislatures were viewed more favorably than Congress on a number of dimensions, including the use of taxpayers' money, management of the day-to-day business of government, response to specific policy problems, and trust or confidence (Advisory Commission on Intergovernmental Relations, 1985). Similar findings were reported from a 1984 public opinion poll (Advisory Commission on Intergovernmental Relations, 1984).

As in state legislatures, the institutional capacity of the executive branch in most states has grown significantly over the past several decades. Gubernatorial power has been strengthened, the structure of the executive branch has been modified or overhauled, and administrative procedures have been modernized. The arrival of a new breed of governors who were younger, better educated, and more "managerially minded" than their predecessors was a key stimulus for these changes (Sabato, 1983). The expanding activities of the state legislatures and Congress, growing national and state economies, and citizens' demands for more and better services were also important stimuli.

The growth and development of executive-branch capacity in the states has taken place in three ways since the early 1960s: comprehensive reorganization, limited reform initiatives, and evolutionary (incremental) change. Comprehensive executive-branch reorganization initiatives took place in twenty-one states between 1965 and 1978 (Michigan, Wisconsin, California, Colorado, Delaware, Florida, Massachusetts, Maryland, Montana, Arkansas, North Carolina, Virginia, Georgia, Maine, South Dakota, Kentucky, Missouri, Idaho, Louisiana, New Mexico, and Connecticut). Since 1978, there has been only one comprehensive executive-branch reorganization, in Iowa during 1985–86.

Diffusion of executive (gubernatorial) authority, fragmentation of program responsibility, and unplanned growth were the problems that these comprehensive reorganization initiatives were designed to solve (Conant, 1988). For example, elected constitutional officers, boards, and commissions controlled as many as two-thirds of the agencies in some states, while gubernatorial appointees headed less than one-third. In addition, the number of executive-branch agencies in the twenty-two states that had reorganized ranged from sixty to three hundred (Conant, 1988), and many of these agencies had program responsibilities that overlapped or were duplicated. Furthermore, staff support and agency support for the chief executive were limited, and administrative systems and procedures were either antiquated or non-existent.

As a result of the comprehensive reorganization initiatives in these twenty-two states, gubernatorial appointment power was expanded, executive-branch agencies were consolidated into large departments, staff and central agency support for chief executives was expanded, and administrative systems and procedures were installed and modernized. Among the most widely publicized of these reorganization initiatives was the one that took place in Georgia while Jimmy Carter was governor. As part of that reorganization, sixty-five executive-branch agencies, boards, and commissions were consolidated into twenty-two large departments, and the governor gained the authority to appoint sixteen of the twenty-two department heads.

During the 1980s, efforts to improve the capacity and performance of the executive-branch agencies shifted away from comprehensive reform efforts to limited or focused initiatives. One reason for this shift was that so many states had recently completed comprehensive reorganizations. A second reason is that comprehensive reorganization initiatives consume large amounts of gubernatorial and executive-branch time. A third reason is that legislatures tend to react negatively to reorganization proposals. More than two-thirds of the comprehensive executive-branch reorganization initiatives in the states have been ignored, rejected, or significantly watered down by legislatures over the past seventy years (Garnett, 1980; Conant, 1986b). Legislative determination to block the expansion of gubernatorial power has been the principal cause of this negative response (Conant, 1986b, 1988). The result is that governorships in states like South Carolina, Indiana, Alabama, and Nevada remain very weak (Beyle, 1982).

Almost every state had an organized initiative to improve executive-branch capacity and performance during the 1980s (Chi, 1986). The Governor's Management Improvement Program (GMIP) in New Jersey (1982–1984) had the broadest scope and impact of these state initiatives (Conant, 1986a). As part of the GMIP initiative, the structures and procedures of two-thirds of the state's eighteen cabinet departments were modified or overhauled, and central staff agencies were created or expanded. In contrast to the reorganization initiatives of the 1960s and the 1970s, however, the focus of the New Jersey initiative was intradepartmental rather than interdepartmental (Conant, 1986b). No attempt was made to reduce the number of executive-branch departments or to shift programs from one department to another. Instead, the GMIP process was designed to reduce the number of management layers within each department and to group similar functions.

The fact that many state executive-branch departments are now large entities means that management effectiveness and continuity are increasingly important factors in determining the performance of these institutions. Indeed, the two factors are sometimes closely related. Many political appointees know little about the departments they are appointed to head, and so they need time to learn their jobs. Consequently, the increasing rate of turnover at the top of these state organizations is not a positive sign. Over the two-year period from 1981 to 1983, only 50 percent of state agency heads remained in office. The comparable figure for the period from 1959 to 1961 was 70 percent (Haas and Wright, 1987, p. 6).

Agency age and policy type are two factors that have been linked to the growing turnover rate. The 1981–1983 turnover rate in newer state agencies (such as environmental protection, consumer protection, occupational health and safety, mass transit, and mental retardation) was 60 percent. In contrast, the turnover rate for older agencies (such as agriculture, labor, higher education, motor vehicle, and taxation) was 45 percent (Haas and Wright, 1987, p. 9). Retention rates for redistributive agencies were also found to be lower than retention rates for regulatory or distributive agencies (Haas and Wright, 1987). Other factors that have been linked to the increasing turnover rate are the growing demands and pressures of these top-level jobs (Conant, forthcoming) and the relatively low rate of pay, as compared to that of chief executives in private sector organizations.

The Nature of the States' Role

The sixth factor that has contributed to the growing visibility and importance of the states is the nature of the states' role in the intergovernmental system. Sometimes referred to as "intergovernmental middlemen," the states have three basic roles: to implement national policy, to make and implement their own policies, and to provide financial and technical support for local governments. The first two roles put the states in the position of being direct service providers or regulators; the third involves raising and distributing revenues.

The states' role as implementers of national policy expanded rapidly during the 1960s and the 1970s. During that time, Congress established a host of new national programs and expanded many existing programs. "As a general rule," says Derthick (1987, p. 67), "when Congress essays new domestic responsibilities it relies on cooperation of the states, with the result that the two levels of government in our federal system are today massively and pervasively intertwined." In this massive intertwining, the states are generally given the opportunity to be the prime implementing sources of these national programs. One result is that state employment is substantially greater now than it was twenty years ago or even ten years ago, while growth in employment at the national level has been very small over the past decade. Another result is that the states play a pivotal role in determining whether national policy is actually implemented and whether it succeeds or fails.

Some scholars, journalists, and practitioners, however, see this expanded administrative role as evidence that the states' role in the federal system is declining, rather than growing. They view congressional intrusion into domains once considered the territory of the states as something like a zero-sum game: The feds win and the states lose. Nevertheless, even in areas where the tendency toward national preemption of state policymaking authority has been highest (such as in income maintenance and environmental protection), responsibility for implementation of national goals and policies gives the states a good deal of freedom and discretion.

Indeed, numerous studies of the implementation process show that it is characterized by negotiation and bargaining, rather than by command and obedience. Furthermore, as Derthick (1987) and others have pointed out, it is the states' strengths and the national government's weaknesses that have ensured this type of relationship. The states' strengths include their administrative institutions and capacity, intergovernmental lobbies, and ability to bring suit when they believe that constitutional or statutory boundaries have been violated. The national government's weaknesses include the limited response repertoires available to national agencies that are unable to gain states' compliance with national rules and regulations. The two principal options for a national agency are to take over administration of the program and to withhold funds. Attempting to replace state administrative personnel and efforts can be time-consuming and expensive, and taking away a state's funds may result in less, rather than more, compliance. Furthermore, such a move is likely to draw sharp criticism from members of the state's congressional delegation.

The states' role as independent policymaker has also grown significantly over the past decade. Equally important, however, is the fact that implementation of these new state policies, like implementation of existing national and state policies, generally involves direct service delivery to citizens and direct regulation of business organizations. The result is that state agency employees have daily contact with hundreds or even thousands of citizens and private sector employees. This contact provides these citizens and business employees with important data about the performance of government organizations.

When citizens or private sector employees have to wait in long lines to conduct their business, when the forms they are required to fill out and submit are not processed in a timely manner, when their letters are not answered, when their phone calls are handled in a brusque manner, or when they find that mistakes are made in their transactions with state agencies, they are not likely to have a positive impression of government. Indeed, transactions of this type are likely to contribute to the current frustration with government performance that some authors (Sundquist, 1980; Lynn, 1982; Savas, 1982) have described as a crisis of competence in government. In short, state policymakers and administrators have a unique opportunity to shape citizens' impressions of government. Whether that opportunity is used effectively depends heavily on resource commitments made by state policymakers and on the skills and commitment of state administrators and employees.

Finally, the states' role as resource supplier for local governments has also contributed to their growing visibility and importance. Like the other two roles, this one has also been expanding over time. Many states currently provide half the revenue that local governments have available; a few supply two-thirds or more. Three factors, however, have made state aid to local government even more important in the 1980s than it was in the past: economic dislocation, cutbacks in federal aid to local governments, and the growing complexity of modern society. Indeed, the cutbacks in federal aid, and particularly in general revenue sharing, have hit most big cities very hard. Consequently, local officials, like other interest groups and their lobbyists, are increasingly looking to state governments for help (Hagstrom, 1985; Moore, 1987a, 1987b).

Local governments' needs and demands pose a tough challenge to state officials. State policymakers may be sympathetic to local governments' requests, but the resources needed to meet those requests can easily exceed the annual increment of growth available in state budgets. Therefore, new taxes, higher tax rates, or cuts in state operations may be required before the amount of intergovernmental aid distributed to local governments can expand significantly. Furthermore, even in a state where there is a healthy surplus in a given year or two, new commitments to expanded local support can quickly turn the surplus into a deficit (Conant, 1983).

New Policy Initiatives

The seventh factor that has contributed to the growing visibility and importance of state government is the new policy initiatives undertaken in many states over the past decade. Indeed, Naisbitt (1982, p. 105) argues that the states have regained their "traditional function as the laboratories of democracy." State officials have taken new initiatives across a wide range of policy areas, including education, drug abuse, economic development and international trade, consumer protection, mergers and acquisitions, infrastructure redevelopment, hazardous waste management, land-use planning, local transportation, housing and urban renewal, income maintenance and employment, social services, health care, and worker safety.

Of these initiatives, efforts to improve the quality of education in primary and secondary schools have been the most heavily publicized over the past five years. Indeed, the level of action and experimentation in the states has been impressive. Since 1983, every state has taken some action to improve education (Beck, Namuth, Miller and Wright, 1988), and twenty-four states have passed broad educational packages (Reinhold, 1987). Among the components of those packages are minimum salaries for teachers, across-the-board increases in teachers' salaries, master teacher programs to give top performers extra pay, a longer school year, expanded testing of students, and curriculum reform. To support these changes, the states increased aid to public schools by 26 percent above the rate of inflation between 1980 and 1986 (Rheinhold, 1987). Tennessee, South Carolina, and Texas have been leaders in education reform.

A number of states have also experimented with welfare reform in the past five years or so. For example, Massachusetts and California have attempted to link welfare, education, training, and employment programs. A number of states have also experimented with new housing and urban development policies and programs. Fifteen states are currently active in this area, with Massachusetts and New York among the leaders (Steinbach and Neal, 1987). Land-use planning is another area where some states have taken some new policy initiatives. New York and Florida are among these states, but New Jersey is where the largest experiment has taken place. In that state, commercial and housing development in the Pinelands, an area that covers more than 20 percent of the state's total acreage, has been prohibited or highly restricted (Collins and Russell, 1988).

Some of the state experiments in the policy areas already mentioned have been bold new approaches, some have been incremental changes in existing approaches, and still others have been combinations of big changes and small steps. As one might expect, the results of these initiatives have been mixed. In a few cases, such as in housing development, significant results have been achieved in relatively short time periods (Steinbach and Neal, 1987). In other cases, the experiments have had mixed results. Some education reform initiatives, for example, have generated a good deal of resistance from teachers and administrators, while others have created new paperwork requirements that have reduced the hours that teachers can spend on classroom instruction.

Mixed results and the passage of time will remove some of the glow from the current round of state experimentation. The need to oversee and make ongoing adjustments to these experiments, the costs of the experiments, changing financial conditions, the conflict that major new initiatives create— all these factors are likely to make state policymakers and administrators more cautious. Consequently, the commitment to keep the "laboratory" going will be an important challenge to state policymakers and administrators in the future.

Summary

The states' role in the federal system is more visible and important now than it was during the 1960s and the 1970s. A number of factors have contributed to the states' expanding role. Among the most important are President Reagan's "new federalism," large national budget deficits, the expanding size of state governments, the growing fiscal capacity of the states, the growing institutional capacity of the states, the nature of the states' role in the intergovernmental system, and new policy initiatives. Three of these seven factors—President Reagan's "new federalism," the large national budget deficits, and the new policy initiatives—are essentially products of the 1980s. The other four are largely products of longer-term trends or constitutional design.

Environmental changes, particularly recent shifts in political and economic conditions, have driven growth in the size, role, and capacity of state governments. Choices made by state policymakers and administrators have also been key factors in the states' revitalized and expanded role. In turn, these changes in state governments have improved the states' ability to respond to citizens' demands and local governments' needs. Much old business still needs to be addressed, and new problems will undoubtedly emerge as the nation moves into the 1990s. Through their track record over the past three decades, however, state policymakers and administrators have provided good reasons for us to believe that they will be ready to respond to these challenges.

References

Advisory Commission on Intergovernmental Relations. *Changing Public Attitudes on Government Taxes.* Washington, D.C.: Advisory Commission on Intergovernmental Relations, 1984.

Advisory Commission on Intergovernmental Relations. *The Question of State Government Capability.* Washington, D.C.: Advisory Commission on Intergovernmental Relations, 1985.

Beck, M., Namuth, T., Miller, M., and Wright, L. "A Nation Still at Risk." *Newsweek,* May 2, 1988, pp. 54–55.

Behn, R., and Behn, J. *The Governor as CEO.* Washington, D.C.: Center for Policy Research, National Governors' Association, 1986.

Beyle, T. L. "The Governors' Power of Organization." *State Government,* 1982, *55* (3), 79–87.

Bowman, A. O'M., and Kearney, R. C. *Resurgence of the States.* Englewood Cliffs, N.J.: Prentice-Hall, 1986.

Broder, D. "The Governors, Feeling Burned." *Washington Post,* Aug. 24, 1980, p. C7.

Chi, K. S. *Alternative Service Delivery and Management Improvement in State Government: A Bibliography.* Lexington, Ky.: Council of State Governments, 1986.

Collins, B. R., and Russell, E.W.B. *Protecting the New Jersey Pinelands: New Directions in Land Use Planning.* New Brunswick, N.J.: Rutgers University Press, 1988.

Conant, J. K. "Executive Decision Making in the State." Unpublished doctoral dissertation, Department of Political Science, University of Wisconsin Madison, 1983.

Conant, J. K. "Reorganization and the Bottom Line." *Public Administration Review,* 1986a, *46* (1), 48–56.

Conant, J. K. "State Reorganization: A New Model?" *State Government,* 1986b, *58* (6), 130–138.

Conant, J. K. "In the Shadow of Wilson and Brownlow: Executive Branch Reorganization in the States, 1965–87." *Public Administration Review,* 1988, *48* (5), 59–69.

Conant, J. K. "Stability, Change and Leadership in State Administration." *State and Local Government Review,* forthcoming.

Council of State Governments. *Book of the States, 1986–87.* Lexington, Ky.: Council of State Governments, 1987.

Derthick, M. "American Federalism: Madison's Middle Ground in the 1980s." *Public Administration Review,* 1987, *47* (1), 66–74.

Garnett, J. L. *Reorganizing State Government: The Executive Branch.* Boulder, Colo.: Westview Press, 1980.

Haas, P. J., and Wright, D. "Administrative Change in State Government." Unpublished manuscript, 1987.

Hagstrom, J. "Liberal and Minority Coalitions Pleading Their Cases in State Capitols." *National Journal,* 1985, *17* (8), 426–428.

Koch, E. "The Mandate Millstone." *The Public Interest,* Fall 1980, pp. 42–57.

Lynn, L. E., Jr. *Managing the Public's Business: The Job of the Government Executive.* New York: Basic Books, 1982.

Mikesell, J. L. "The Path of the Tax Revolt: Statewide Expenditure and Tax Control Referenda Since Proposition 13." *State and Local Government Review,* 1986, *18* (1), 5–12.

Moore, J. W. "Mandates Without Money." *National Journal,* 1986, *18* (40), 2366–2370.

Moore, J. W. "Cut Off at Town Hall." *National Journal,* 1987a, *19* (15), 862–866.

Moore, J. W. "Have Smarts, Will Travel." *National Journal,* 1987b, *19* (48), 3020–3025.

Naisbitt, J. *Megatrends.* New York: Warner Books, 1982.

Nathan, R. P., and Doolittle, F. C. *The Consequences of Cuts.* Princeton, N.J.: Princeton Urban and Regional Research Center, 1983.

Palmer, J. L., and Sawhill, I. V. *The Reagan Experiment.* Washington, D.C.: Urban Institute Press, 1982.

Peters, T. J., and Waterman, R. H., Jr. *In Search of Excellence: Lessons from America's Best-Run Companies.* New York: Harper & Row, 1982.

Reinhold, R. "School Reform: 4 Years of Tumult, Mixed Results." *New York Times,* Aug. 10, 1987, pp. A1, A14.

Rosenthal, A. *Legislative Life.* New York: Harper & Row, 1981.

Sabato, L. *Goodbye to Good-Time Charlie.* (2nd ed.) Washington, D.C.: Congressional Quarterly Press, 1983.

Savas, E. S. *Privatizing the Public Sector: How to Shrink Government.* Chatham, N.J.: Chatham House, 1982.

Steinbach, C. F., and Neal, R. P. "Picking Up Hammers." *National Journal,* 1987, *19* (23), 1464–1468.

Stenberg, C. W. "States Under the Spotlight: An Intergovernmental View." *Public Administration Review,* 1985, *47* (2), 319–326.

Sundquist, J. L. "The Crisis of Competence in Government." In J. A. Pechman (ed.), *Setting National Priorities: Agenda for the 1980s.* Washington, D.C.: Brookings Institution, 1980.

Wright, D. S. *Understanding Intergovernmental Relations.* (3rd ed.) Monterey, Calif.: Brooks/Cole, 1988.

4   *Beverly A. Cigler*

Trends Affecting
Local Administrators

Local administrators have always faced tough challenges, since local governments are the key service providers of citizens' daily needs. Protecting the public's health, safety, and welfare is complicated and expensive and, unlike administrators at other levels, local leaders must maintain face-to-face citizen interaction, including dealing with controversial life-style issues, such as housing, education, and zoning. As the 1990s approach, administrators face redefined challenges requiring greater sophistication and skill because of dramatic economic, demographic, technological, ideological, and political changes in their environment.

This chapter examines the trends affecting local administrators' environment, suggests the types of skills necessary in this redefined environment, and discusses several key challenges facing local administrators, to demonstrate how skills and knowledge can be brought to bear on handling problems.

The Administrators' Changing Environment

The reduction of governmental activism at all levels, a long-term Reagan administration goal, has not occurred. Governmental spending at all levels continues to rise, although at a slower rate than in the 1966–1977 period. Reaganism, in addition, has not brought a major federal withdrawal from the intergovernmental grant and regulatory arenas. When Supreme Court actions and federal preemptions are considered along with the actions of the congressional and executive branches, some argue that the basic trend has been increased centralization. Nevertheless, the devolutions of programs and regulations that did occur in the 1980s had a dramatic effect on local governments, whose officials no longer view Uncle Sam as Santa Claus (Walker, 1986).

The long-term intergovernmental centralizing trend that began in the 1930s was at least redirected in the 1980s, especially in terms of local fiscal impacts. Whether there is now a bias toward decentralization will continue to be debated, but in the minds of local officials there has been a shift (Gage, 1987). The respective responsibilities of national, state, and local governments and of the private sector are in the midst of a sorting-out process. Leadership, imagination, and resourcefulness at all levels of government are needed to deal with the crosscurrents of centralization, decrementalism, decentralization, deregulation, and devolution that are likely to continue in the 1990s (Stenberg, 1986).

A fiscal environment that forces local officials to become more self-reliant stands out as the key feature in what Shannon (1987) calls ''fend-for-yourself federalism.'' Local governments have sustained dwindling federal financial assistance, which has declined 67 percent since 1979, despite an overall federal spending increase of 102 percent and a federal debt increase of 261 percent. The federal government now spends more for foreign aid than it does for total direct assistance to all local governments.

Less federal aid, and especially the elimination of general revenue sharing, means that fewer communities have direct financial ties to the federal government, a deterioration of the previous dominant ''vertical federalism.'' Recognition of the reality of federal aid reductions, coupled with an understanding that much of what is called state and local aid is actually a categorical pass-through to individual citizens, results in a situation in which most local governments receive no federal revenue. Approximately 80 percent of U.S. counties, for example, no longer receive any direct federal financial assistance (J. P. Thomas, 1987). Pressures abound for more cooperation with the private sector, and tight finances and policy spillovers create the need for more ''horizontal'' federalism in metropolitan areas and regions.

Emerging changes in the form (not the scope) of governmental activity have led to a different local political environment, known as third-party government, government by proxy, or, more narrowly, privatization (Salamon, 1986; Seidman and Gilmour, 1986; Kettl, 1988). What is new is that proxies—intermediaries responsible for actually producing goods or services—have replaced, in many cases, the direct administration of programs by government. Local governments carry out federal and state policies, and local units themselves contract with the private sector or not-for-profit organizations. The administrator's environment is a fluctuating one, which crosses over from the public to the private to the nonprofit sector. Learning how to provide services without actually producing them is the administrative challenge associated with this trend, which includes increased concern for accountability, since power is no longer centralized in a community's elected officials (who exercise control over administrators) but is shared with more parties.

Examples of the third, or nonprofit, sector in the local administrator's environment include public-private partnerships for economic development, community planning organizations whose board members include government officials, and charitable organizations (including social agencies, health care organizations, and museums) that supplement government service provision and sometimes provide public services under government contract or with tax revenues (Kramer, 1986). Human services agencies receive more than 40 percent of their support from government and derive 28 percent of their revenues from service-related fees. Over 30 percent of public funds in some cities is spent through nonprofit organizations (Salamon, 1987).

As localities receive fewer federal resources, federal and state mandates—legal requirements that communities undertake specific activities or provide services meeting minimum standards—are increasing, with a burdensome cumulative financial effect. Current mandates relate to civil rights, environmental policy, personnel, public and employee health and safety, taxes, and service levels. Water pollution control, stormwater sewers, employee benefits and rights, and landfill site mandates are increasing and once again highlight the growing need for more "horizontal" cooperation. Recent federal tax reforms redefined public purpose bonds, further limiting local governments' ability to raise revenues.

Federal changes involve more than money and mandates. Two 1987 Supreme Court decisions (*First English Evangelical Lutheran Church of Glendale* v. *County of Los Angeles* and *Nollan* v. *California Coastal Commission*) took a close look at the severity of the impact of local land-use regulations on landowners. The decisions deter harsh land-use regulations and warn officials that private property restrictions must be based on sound research. Increased litigation triggered by these decisions gives local government a financial incentive to develop careful regulatory strategies and promotes increased cooperation between regulators and the regulated.

Much federal aid for local activities is channeled to communities through the states, with state-local relations also expanding both through cooperation (comprehensive economic development programs) and through conflict (state mandates). Giving local governments more discretion in raising revenues, reviewing state mandates, and assuming the costs of compliance; evaluating state-local responsibilities for various activities of service delivery and financing; and responding to new federal mandates (for example, that states develop revolving loan funds for local water and sewer financing) are key state concerns (Gold, 1987).

Increased citizen and special-interest activism, especially among the well educated, has resulted in greater citizen power and new organizational arrangements. Earlier, the grass-roots tax-limitation movement questioned local governments' right to tax and led to demands for decentralized service delivery and to pressures for increased governmental accountability and productivity. Currently, the "not in my backyard" issue symbolizes continuing public distrust of government, as efforts are resisted to place even environmentally sound disposal sites for hazardous waste in communities. Local officials are liable to be sued, whether they fail to provide safe disposal sites or whether they site facilities in communities. These are just two examples of a much broader liability crisis at the local level.

Citizens also expect local governments to provide new and better services. Demographic, economic, technological, and political changes help explain the rising expectations. The populations of many communities are changing in size and composition and redefining the need for infrastructure and services. Average household size is getting smaller, and more households are nonfamily in composition, which increases the demand for housing, water, sewers, and highways. More elderly residents and fewer youth in a community have implications for public investment in schools, housing, and medical, recreational, and other kinds of facilities. Increased urbanization requires more infrastructure than would a more rural, low-density population distribution. Changing social needs and priorities continually redefine local roles. Minority population increases have led to racial minorities' being the majority populations in some cities, a situation that changes the political climate.

Technological and economic changes render the economic foundations of some communities obsolete and create boom-town economies in others. Retrenchment, revitalization, and the growth phase characteristic of suburban areas with expanding tax bases all require different political and management strategies. Computers facilitate cooperation and collaboration with other organizations, and the result is a leveling effect among governments with different resources. Telecommunications, the information explosion, and advances in transportation technology are all transformational factors. Global economic interdependence (Drucker, 1986) demands that even rural and small-town areas be aware of their diminishing control over local destiny and of the difficulties of local self-sufficiency.

Changes in the external environment bring changes to the administrators' workplace. Citizens' activism and increased service demands stir greater policy activism among elected officials. The search for improved public productivity and accountability leads to new types of relationships within and among governments and other sectors. Aid reductions force local officials to scrutinize programs and measure effectiveness. More systematic and accurate data are needed to convince decision makers to support programs. Such problems as the necessity for an adequate water supply or a landfill increase the need for intergovernmental cooperation, since watersheds do not fall within single municipal boundaries and land is scarce and expensive. Aid reductions and public distrust of government decrease employees' morale. Employees' personal problems (for example, abuse of drugs and alcohol) affect the workplace.

Skills Necessary for Local Administration

Honadle (1981) defines *government capacity* as government's ability to anticipate and influence change, make informed intelligent decisions about policy, develop programs to implement policy, attract and absorb resources, manage resources, and evaluate current activities to guide future action. For administrators, a sound foundation in the basic internal management skills—including the control functions of budgeting and personnel systems and knowledge about specific kinds of service delivery—is mandatory.

A narrow focus on control functions, however, is unlikely to produce effective managers (Kerrigan and Hinton, 1980; Becker, Banovetz, and Zar, 1986). Technical expertise must be coupled with an understanding of the political context in which the administrator functions, and effective political skills must be nurtured. Support for administrative actions must be developed, as well as practical and politically feasible implementation strategies. Understanding differences in goals between the local unit and its proxies is essential, so that administrators can provide leadership in offering feedback to elected officials.

Greater attention must be paid to accountability and performance in an environment where traditional management techniques that emphasize internal control (budgeting, personnel) are inadequate for dealing with the complex network of private and nonprofit actors and institutions over which public actors have only limited control. Not only must local administrators promote innovation in this complex environment, they must also control it through creative interaction among and between sectors. Finally, they must convince others that they have succeeded.

The new skills for local management include the abilities to think, plan, and manage strategically; create self-evaluating organizations; create conditions for employee and organizational excellence, as well as for the image of excellence; negotiate and mediate conflict among diverse groups in and out of government; and act as a social entrepreneur.

The development of these skills is constrained by the uneven resource base among local governments. Professionalization is associated with larger units of government, but more than 90 percent of the municipal and town-township governments in the United States serve communities of fewer than ten thousand residents. More than 80 percent of U.S. municipalities serve under five thousand people each, and about thirty thousand local governments (40 percent of the nation's total) are zero-employee governments (Schenker, 1986). More than three-fourths of county governments serve populations of fewer than fifty thousand people. Approximately one-third of the population of the United States lives in rural areas, and approximately two-thirds of all governmental units exist there. Although most people live in urban areas, most local governments, inside and outside of metropolitan areas, serve small populations and have limited management capacity.

The diversity of local government types increases the fragmentation of the local system. In recent years, the 3,138 U.S. counties have become key delivery units for health, welfare, transportation, and education services. Special districts, excluding those for education, continue to proliferate (numbering nearly twenty-nine thousand) because of their territorial flexibility and political popularity. The diversity of local governments, as well as their adaptation to change, is exemplified by regional councils that have become increasingly entrepreneurial. Regional councils provide direct services to member local governments, such as data services, grantwriting, and technical assistance. They serve as brokers for discussions of such regional policies as promotion of state policy for regional water problems. Regional councils also develop and promote regional policy approaches—concerning growth management, for example (McDowell, 1987).

Local officials deal with a complex variety of ''horizontal'' and ''vertical'' intergovernmental relationships. State authority patterns, in particular, offer local governments differing abilities to control their own futures, with local taxation and borrowing limited by constitutional and statutory fiscal restrictions (Zimmerman, 1983).

In the next section of this chapter, several key and overlapping challenges that face local administrators are used to assess necessary knowledge and skills. These challenges are the search for increased revenues, economic development strategies, program implementation, and alternatives for service delivery.

Bringing Knowledge to Bear

The Search for Increased Revenues. Cutback management—that is, adaptation to fiscal stress—is routine for most local governments and forces a consideration of which services and activities to reduce, maintain, and expand. In the past, two basic ways of enhancing public revenue have been considered: taxation (new or increased) and fees for service. Local administrators have only recently begun to consider strategies for expenditure reduction and increased productivity or reorganization as revenue enhancers, rather than as separate concerns (Levine, 1980; Clark and Ferguson, 1983; Cigler, 1986). By increasing overall local finances through a variety of ways (including revenue diversification, expenditure reduction, and program innovation), local governments move beyond retrenchment and toward self-renewal or revitalization.

Research to uncover a sequential set of responses to stress (Levine, Rubin, and Wolohojian, 1981) and to understand the process itself (Morgan and Pammer, 1985) has had only qualified success. It may be that local officials' coping mechanisms are nonrational when they are dealing with unfamiliar problems, limited knowledge, and unpredictable outcomes (Starling, 1986), or perhaps officials adapt to the uniqueness of their communities, rather than following particular sets of prescribed actions. In any case, substantial savings can result when officials think strategically about the services they deliver and create links across such responsibilities as revenue enhancement, expenditure reduction, and program innovation.

For example, personnel costs, the largest item in local operating budgets, are a focus of local productivity improvements. Only rarely are attempts to reduce energy costs (usually the second-highest item in an operating budget) linked to personnel policies or viewed as cost-savings strategies, yet when police and sanitation employees are taught more efficient driving techniques, both energy and money are saved. Washnis (1980) fails to link energy management to cost-savings strategies, but a wealth of other literature documents the innovations of local governments that have had the vision to develop energy management programs (Cigler, 1986). The lesson is that strategic thinking in an organization would find managers from different units talking with each other about such ''generic'' problems as cost savings.

Economic Development Strategies. Local financial stability and self-reliance can also result from comprehensive economic development strategies, which lessen the need for stark retrenchment options and create movement toward revitalization. In the 1970s, the national government played a key role in the leveraging of local investments. Today, local officials are more entrepreneurial and promote economic change by developing packages of inducements, subsidies, and other incentives to influence private investment and locational choices, largely on their own (Judd and Ready, 1986). Administrators, working with elected officials, must develop new skills in the marketing of their communities, in the formation of partnerships with the private sector, and in the use of local public funds to leverage private investment.

Despite local enthusiasm for local economic development, there are many pitfalls. Targeting strategies to distressed areas or social groups is difficult. Public leveraging of funds can result in local governments' being held captive by businesses that threaten to leave if even more public support is not offered. Moreover, growing competition for economic investment among local governments leads to diminishing returns for any one unit. Thus, a sharp contrast exists between those who praise the benefits of economic development programs and those who note the failure to regenerate depressed urban economies through quick-fix, ideologically acceptable solutions whose pursuit, it is argued, has redefined *urban governance* to mean *civic marketing* (Barnekov and Rich, 1988).

Wildavsky's (1979) notion of the self-evaluating organization suggests skills that seem necessary for a successful economic development program and, indeed, for any other kind of policy implementation. Wildavsky argues that public organizations should be held accountable on two dimensions: the content of policy decisions (with goals and purposes considered in the attempt to determine whether those purposes should continue to direct the organization's activities) and the implementation of programs designed to achieve those goals and purposes. An effective local administrator would consider evidence for and against each alternative, select the most promising one, and implement it. Formal evaluation is the means to effectiveness (although Wildavsky recognizes the obstacles that make evaluation difficult in practice).

The virtual revolution in government information management, fueled by increased availability and versatility of affordable computers and software programs, lends hope that local governments can develop the self-evaluative skills to choose economic development options, measure targeting attempts, assess privatization options, determine cost-effective rates for user fees, monitor progress, and measure service costs and quality. It is helpful to use the print, electronic, and face-to-face information services developed by municipal and professional organizations and universities, which provide data banks, innovative program exchanges, "how to" publications, training workshops, and other valuable tools (International City Management Association, 1984). Conscious development of one's own professional network and the conduct of self-audits are always important.

Program Implementation. Writings on strategic management processes (Olsen and Eadie, 1982; Sorkin, Ferris, and Hudak, 1984), as well as the literature developed by researchers on organizational process and on program and policy implementation (Beyer, Stevens, and Trice, 1983; Mazmanian and Sabatier, 1983), help administrators develop self-evaluating, accountable organizations that successfully implement programs. Successful implementation requires the following elements:

- Commitment of the top elected local leadership
- Careful consideration of mission (the role local government will and can play)
- An action plan tied to a commitment of resources and an explicit description of expected results
- An understanding of the external and internal environments in which the government operates, including the threats and opportunities faced and the strengths and weaknesses of the community and the local government
- Payoff guarantees that show direct, measurable public return on investments in exchange for public resources
- Clearly targeted, implementable goals that build on the community's set of unique strengths
- An early focus on program implementation
- A clear locus of responsibility for action within the governmental organization, which usually means the designation of a key person or agency with authority and support
- Visible results on initial projects, to create the image that fosters future success

These preconditions of program success highlight the necessity of building strong relationships among administrators and other actors in any project—elected officials, staff, citizens, and private groups. Again, the example of economic development illustrates this point. Administrators can educate elected leaders about the need for more economic self-reliance and can provide information on payoffs for public investments. Staff members can be encouraged and shown how to work with the private sector. Citizens can be assured that government has bargained with the private sector to guarantee new jobs for local residents. Marketing skills can be used to negotiate with the private sector. Creativity and innovation can help restore public confidence in government. Government administrators can learn entrepreneurial skills from their counterparts in the private sector.

Alternatives for Service Delivery. The search for new revenues, along with efforts to lessen and redefine government's role in service delivery, also highlights the necessity of building new types of relationships. The basic concerns of service delivery remain the same—high quality, equity, and efficiency—but administrators must become more entrepreneurial, more familiar with more options, and more innovative in a "government by proxy." This means improving internal procedures to make government more competitive with the private sector, overcoming bureaucratic inefficiencies, and developing ways to assess and monitor alternatives.

There are many facets of the privatization alternative for service delivery (Savas, 1987). For routine commercial activities that are not unique to government (building, vehicle, and grounds maintenance, data and word processing, billing, claims), government can hire the private sector. Contracts with private companies for the delivery of traditional services (such as garbage pickup) are also an option, although human service activities are also provided through contracts. Municipalities and counties hire attorneys and engineers from the private sector. Full-service privatization of large capital works projects (private financing, building, or operating of wastewater treatment plants or waste-to-energy plants) may also sometimes be a viable alternative.

Privatization poses a number of challenges to local government. Criticisms include several arguments. Privatization may make local communities captives of the private sector, in terms of costs and information. Contractors may increase fees and charges excessively after an initial period of cost containment. Public accountability may be reduced. The costs of governmental monitoring may seldom be measured. Poorly prepared service agreements intended to limit the liability and financial exposure of contractors may make it difficult to receive reasonable responses to unforeseen circumstances. Finally, quality may suffer from the need to make a profit: Contractors may skimp on the quality of materials, work, equipment, and staff and may defer maintenance expenditures.

Again, the need to create an organization that can evaluate itself and its needs is obvious. Whether the criticisms of privatization are accurate or not is unclear. Nevertheless, without proper planning and sound legal, financial, and technical advice, communities can be victims rather than beneficiaries of privatization. Administrators must develop sound service agreements with contractors. This action can ensure efficient and well-maintained operations and high-quality staff, eliminate excessive and escalating costs, and protect localities against poor performance.

Protection of a community against the pitfalls of privatization is possible, but it requires sophisticated analytical skills that assess the extent to which citizens are getting value for their dollars, even when government is the service provider. Data on service improvements caused by governmental activities are rarely collected, and most governments do not survey citizens to ascertain their perceptions of the services they have received. Efficiency is rarely measured systematically or regularly. Complaints are heard and answered, but few citizens use available channels for voicing their complaints.

Small governments with tight resources have less flexibility than larger units to respond to fiscal constraints. They are unable to cut back on programs already confined to the delivery of basic public services—police and fire departments, street maintenance, water, sewers—and even these basic services are hard to maintain in the face of revenue losses. It is tempting for small governments to turn to privatization, but they have only limited managerial expertise to evaluate options and monitor third-party service deliverers. Especially attractive alternatives—use of volunteers and paraprofessionals, citizen coproduction of services, self-help, neighborhood organization of service delivery—also raise unique problems for local personnel management. Increased involvement of citizens could mean real or perceived antagonism, interference with professional judgments, increased costs due to program revisions necessary to satisfy activists, and costly delays in decision making and implementation (J. C. Thomas, 1987).

Participative decision-making can mitigate these possibilities and perhaps improve the quality of public decisions by providing better information and thereby increasing the likelihood of citizens' acceptance of decisions that are made, as well as increasing trust in government's efficiency (J. C. Thomas, 1987). Building these new relationships and developing information is costly, however. Learning about citizen groups is time-consuming, as is developing decision approaches that involve large numbers of participants and opinions. Ways must be found to structure citizens' involvement according to the public interest, and not geographical or functional interests. Citizens must be afforded more than token power; staff, time, and other resources must be devoted to interaction.

Intergovernmental arrangements for service delivery—that is, arrangements for services to be delivered by another unit of government, to be shared among governments, or to involve such shared functions as data processing and planning—also involve new relationships and data needs. Regional councils especially have become active in this arena, taking an entrepreneurial approach to problems that require the willingness of governments and the private sector to negotiate differences and share power, whether through special arrangements or in partnership.

Local administrators no longer ask what the states are doing to replace federal programs, but rather what the states and local governments can plan to do together to establish effective programs. Matters of organization and respective responsibility are paramount in debates over legal powers, mandates, and fiscal control. As states embark on more capacity building, more technical assistance, and more local programs, more cooperative mechanisms for involving local officials are also emerging (Advisory Commission on Intergovernmental Relations, 1985). Local administrators now work with state officials to assess governmental functions and responsibilities within the states and, sometimes, to transfer tasks to other levels (the county or the state, for example). This practice requires cooperation among local officials and the ability to convince state legislators to support new ideas.

Implications for Improved Practice

In a world of interconnections, the local administrator's job is more difficult, since no one person or organization is in charge. Local officials need information to define what they can control, to maximize resources in response to changed circumstances, and to develop coherent strategies for action. The kinds of issues confronting local governments (events beyond their control; changes that affect basic choices of management, financing, technology, and personnel; new opportunities for improving service quality and quantity in more efficient ways) point to the need for strategic planning, thinking, and management (Bryson, Van de Ven, and Roering, 1987).

The elements of successful program implementation, as well as the strategic process itself, are too often the missing ingredients when local administrators attempt to work with others to build the capacity to respond to change. Even if administrators think and act strategically, it takes strong leadership to organize human and organizational commitment and then to take action.

The local pursuit of excellence, requiring the transformation of both organizations and people, is one means of transforming and revitalizing local governments and their employees. Administrators can be "change masters," adept at the arts of anticipating and leading productive change (Kanter, 1983). This call for excellence, however, comes at a difficult time. The national government is programmatically less involved than it was earlier, and its regulatory agenda is broader. Managing resources, influencing others, and implementing change must be accomplished effectively, efficiently, and equitably, but with limited resources. Employees' morale and motivation, in an environment that challenges the worth of the public sector and the effectiveness and responsiveness of its employees, are difficult to nurture, since the necessary relationships—participatory, team-oriented, and cooperative—demand substantial time, commitment, and resources.

Summary

A clear theme emerges from this chapter: There will be less government (in the traditional sense) in the future, but local government administration will become more complex. The skills needed by today's local administrators go far beyond traditional control functions. Public service spans the arenas of government, not-for-profit organizations, and private institutions. In the new organizational environment, it is necessary to think, plan, and manage strategically; exercise analytical skills to create self-evaluating organizations; create conditions for employees' and organizations' excellence; build relationships among diverse groups in and out of government; and become more entrepreneurial. The building of the new relationships, and the development of the information required for local governance, require relationship- and task-motivated individuals, who will have to work more closely together than in the past. Administrators geared to technical decision making alone may be uncomfortable with the necessity for group-negotiated decisions with citizens, private and nonprofit organizations, and other governments. Nevertheless, the complexity of local government, the rapid rate of change, and the information explosion all demand that administrators have sharp analytical skills attuned to making their organizations self-evaluating. The difficulties of local governance in the 1990s are clearly matched by the excitement of the challenges.

References

Advisory Commission on Intergovernmental Relations. *The Question of State Government Capability.* Washington, D.C.: Advisory Commission on Intergovernmental Relations, 1985.

Barnekov, T., and Rich, D. "Privatism and the Logic of Local Economic Development." Paper presented at the 18th annual meeting of the Urban Affairs Association, St. Louis, Missouri, March 10, 1988.

Becker, F. W., Banovetz, J. M., and Zar, C. "The Need for Entrepreneurship and Analytical Ability in City Management." *Management Science and Policy Analysis,* 1986, *3* (4), 21–31.

Beyer, J. M., Stevens, J. M., and Trice, H. M. "The Implementing Organization: Exploring the Black Box in Research on Public Policy." In R. H. Hall and R. E. Quinn (eds.), *Organizational Theory and Public Policy.* Newbury Park, Calif.: Sage, 1983.

Bryson, J. M., Van de Ven, A. H., and Roering, W. D. "Strategic Planning and the Revitalization of the Public Service." In R. B. Denhardt and E. T. Jennings, Jr. (eds.), *The Revitalization of the Public Service.* Columbia: University of Missouri, 1987.

Cigler, B. A. "Capacity-Building Policy for Local Energy Management." In B. W. Honadle and A. M. Howitt (eds.), *Perspectives on Management*

Capacity-Building: Challenge for the Eighties. Albany: State University of New York Press, 1986.

Clark, T. N., and Ferguson, L. C. *City Money: Political Processes, Fiscal Strain, and Retrenchment.* New York: Columbia University Press, 1983.

Drucker, P. F. "The Changed World Economy." *Foreign Affairs,* 1986, *64,* (4), 768–791.

First English Evangelical Lutheran Church of Glendale v. *County of Los Angeles,* 107 S. Ct. 2378 (1987).

Gage, R. W. "A Reality Check: How Much Intergovernmental Change Is Really Out There?" *SIAM Intergovernmental News,* 1987, *10* (3), 1, 4.

Gold, S. D. "NCSL State-Local Task Force: The First Year." *Intergovernmental Perspective,* 1987, *13* (1), 11–13.

Honadle, B. W. "A Capacity-Building Framework: A Search for Concept and Purpose." *Public Administration Review,* 1981, *41* (5), 575–580.

International City Management Association. *Excellence in Local Government Management.* Washington, D.C.: International City Management Association, 1984.

Judd, D. R., and Ready, R. L. "Entrepreneurial Cities and the New Politics of Economic Development in the United States." In G. E. Peterson and C. W. Lewis (eds.), *Reagan and the Cities.* Washington, D.C.: Urban Institute Press, 1986.

Kanter, R. M. *The Change Masters: Innovation for Productivity in the American Corporation.* New York: Simon & Schuster, 1983.

Kerrigan, J. E., and Hinton, D. W. "Knowledge and Skill Needs for Tomorrow's Public Administrators." *Public Administration Review,* 1980, *40* (5), 468–472.

Kettl, D. F. *Government by Proxy: (Mis?)Managing Federal Programs.* Washington, D.C.: Congressional Quarterly Press, 1988.

Kramer, R. M. *The Future of Voluntary Organizations in Social Welfare.* Independent Sector 1986 Spring Research Forum Working Papers. Washington, D.C.: Independent Sector, 1986.

Levine, C. H. (ed.). *Managing Fiscal Stress: The Crisis in the Public Sector.* Chatham, N.J.: Chatham House, 1980.

Levine, C. H., Rubin, I., and Wolohojian, G. *The Politics of Retrenchment.* Newbury Park, Calif.: Sage, 1981.

McDowell, B. "Regional Council Roles in the 1980s." *SIAM Intergovernmental News,* 1987, *10* (4), 6.

Mazmanian, D. A., and Sabatier, P. A. *Implementation and Public Policy.* Glenview, Ill.: Scott, Foresman, 1983.

Morgan, D. R., and Pammer, W. J. "Municipal Fiscal Austerity: Examining the Use of Retrenchment Strategies." *Management Science and Policy Analysis,* 1985, *3* (2), 1–9.

Nollan v. *California Coastal Commission,* 107 S. Ct. 3141 (1987).

Olsen, J. B., and Eadie, D. C. *The Game Plan: Governance with Foresight.* Washington, D.C.: Council of State Planning and Policy Agencies, 1982.

Salamon, L. M. "The Rise of Third-Party Government: Implications for Public Management." Speech delivered to the National Academy of Public Administration spring meeting, Washington, D.C., June 5, 1986.

Salamon, L. M. "Partners in Public Service: The Scope and Theory of Government-Nonprofit Relations." In W. W. Powell (ed.), *The Nonprofit Sector: A Research Handbook.* New Haven, Conn.: Yale University Press, 1987.

Savas, E. S. *Privatization: The Key to Better Government.* Chatham, N.J.: Chatham House, 1987.

Schenker, A. "Zero Employment Governments: Survival in the Tiniest Towns." *Small Town,* 1986, *16* (2), 4–11.

Seidman, H., and Gilmour, R. *Politics, Position, and Power: From the Positive to the Regulatory State.* (4th ed.) New York: Oxford University Press, 1986.

Shannon, J. "The Return to Fend-for-Yourself Federalism: The Reagan Mark." *Intergovernmental Perspective,* 1987, *13* (3/4), 34–37.

Sorkin, D. L., Ferris, N. B., and Hudak, J. *Strategies for Cities and Counties: A Strategic Planning Guide.* Washington, D.C.: Public Technology, 1984.

Starling, J.D. *Municipal Coping Strategies.* Newbury Park, Calif.: Sage, 1986.

Stenberg, C. W. "New Federalism and the States: Crosscurrents, Challenges and Crossroads." *SIAM Intergovernmental News,* 1986, *10* (2), 1, 7.

Thomas, J. C. "Citizen Involvement in Public Management: Lessons from Municipal Administration." In R. B. Denhardt and E. T. Jennings, Jr. (eds.), *The Revitalization of the Public Service.* Columbia: University of Missouri, 1987.

Thomas, J. P. "Perspective on County Government Services and Financing." *State and Local Government Review,* 1987, *19* (3), 119–121.

Walker, D. B. "New Federalism, 1981–1986." *SIAM Intergovernmental News,* 1986, *9* (2), 1, 4.

Washnis, G. J. *Productivity Improvement Handbook for State and Local Government.* New York: Wiley, 1980.

Wildavsky, A. *Speaking Truth to Power: The Art and Craft of Policy Analysis.* Boston: Little, Brown, 1979.

Zimmerman, J. F. *State-Local Relations: A Partnership Approach.* New York: Praeger, 1983.

Barry Bozeman
Dianne Rahm

5

The Explosion of Technology

The purpose of this chapter is to comment on the current and future prospects for scientific and technical change affecting public administration. The focus is not on any particular policy domain or type of public administrator but on public administration in general. Some technologies—computers, telecommunications, and photocopying come quickly to mind—have the potential to affect large segments of public administration. Our concern here is with those broad changes in science and technology that alter the way most public administrators think about their work.

After discussing some of the categories of scientific and technical advance viewed as most significant for current and future public administrators, we identify certain problems that administrators inevitably confront in the wake of new technology, as well as some general strategies for dealing with these problems.

Scientific and Technical Change and Public Administrators

A welfare worker, drawn to the profession by its opportunities for human contact and direct problem solving, labors to enter case data into a spreadsheet format. A city manager struggles to understand the pollution impact of alternative garbage-burning steam plant technologies. A firefighter considers the chemistry of ''slippery water.'' Science and technology have their place, and their place is everywhere. Public administrators are drawn to their occupations by diverse factors, including, in some instances, a desire for nontechnical work. But technophobes and technophiles alike share a need to cope with technical change.

In the United States, particularly since World War II, applications of science and technology have rapidly altered the political, social, and economic environment of the entire nation. Technical sophistication has replaced simplicity. With the new complexity has come a higher standard of living but also an ever present need for detailed planning, functionally compartmentalized organizations, specialization, and new management techniques (Galbraith, 1967).

Administrators, in both the public and the private sectors, have had to deal with changes in science and technology as an ongoing phenomenon. Public administrators, however, are particularly affected by issues of science and technology because they are the guardians of the public interest. It is the task of the public administrator to carefully analyze the social impacts of new science and technologies so as to anticipate potential problems, minimize risks, and maximize benefits.

Science and technology often affect administrators (and not just techno-science administrators) in ways difficult to anticipate. Consider a few recent examples.

Public education offers several illustrations. For one, there is the debate over the use of calculators, computers, and computer-assisted instruction by children enrolled in the public schools. Should children be permitted to make use of calculators to simplify computations, or should they be required to learn the mathematical tables? If use of a calculator is permitted, at what grade level should its employment be initiated? Should calculators be authorized for use in standardized exams, such as state and national examinations? How many computers should a school system purchase, running what software, and from what vendors?

Overcrowding of prisons is a major issue, and so electronic imprisonment in one's own house, made possible by a device that monitors the location of the wearer of a nonremovable "bracelet," has been considered as an alternative. In one recent twist—one with heavy irony—a Los Angeles slumlord was sentenced not to prison but to confinement in his own rat-infested apartment building. He was monitored by just such an electronic "bracelet."

One of the major technological problems of the 1980s is the deterioration of infrastructures. The collapse of a bridge on a New York State freeway in June 1987 may have been just a portent of problems to come. Among other issues, this event brings the issue of technological standards to the fore. To ensure public safety (Florman, 1981), should managers of civil engineering projects trust the guidelines set forth by private organizations? (The American National Standards Institute, Underwriters Laboratories, the National Fire Protection Association, and the American Society for Testing and Materials are just a few of the approximately four hundred voluntary-standards organizations in operation today.) This concern over standards also applies clearly to administrators in areas of consumer protection.

The ever increasing use of computers and information-processing equipment in most areas of government administration also creates concern among administrators with respect to sabotage, theft of services, property crimes, financial crimes, individual privacy, security of data, and accuracy of data banks (Mandell, 1984).

These few examples clearly show that a great many fields of public administration—diverse fields, at that—are affected by scientific and technical change. As new sciences and technologies are developed, they affect public administrators by offering them new choices, as well as new dilemmas.

Before we continue this discussion of challenges that public managers can expect from technical change, it will be worth our time to consider briefly the most likely sources of such change. Where are today's and tomorrow's big breakthroughs, big advances, and big problems?

Science and Technology Today

Four categories of emerging science and technology seem to offer the greatest potential for vigorous transformation of the technoscience status quo: information technologies, artificial intelligence, biotechnology, and materials science. Advances in these areas are producing some startling innovations, and public administrators would be wise to be familiar with them. A basic understanding of the capabilities of these technologies will enable administrators to anticipate potential applications, as well as problems that could arise from their use, and to plan accordingly. A capsule description, rather than a detailed analysis, of each of these technologies follows.

Information Technologies. Pioneering areas of information technologies include microelectronics, computers, telecommunications, and networking. The term *microelectronics* refers to the basic electronic circuitry of computers and communications devices. Improvements in microelectronics usher in new and improved computers and associated peripheral devices. Likewise, improvements in computers enable better telecommunications and networking.

Since its development in the mid 1960s, the basic building block of all information technologies has been the integrated circuit, or chip. Improvements in chips over the past few years, coupled with software advances, keep computers and communications devices high on the list of technologies to watch. Very Large Scale Integration, a mechanism for increasing the speed of electronic and computing devices by minimizing the distance electricity has to travel, continues to augment computer capacity.

Few better demonstrations of the vastly improved capacity of microelectronics exist than those to be seen in the recent improvements in computers. For example, in comparison to computers on the market today, early microcomputers were quite slow and had only small memories. It was normal to see microcomputers with main memory capacities limited to from 4,000 to 16,000 bytes, or characters. Now, roughly a decade later, standard microcomputers contain between 256,000 and 640,000 bytes. From personal computers to supercomputers, hardware continues to improve and, as the hardware is enhanced, better software is created to take advantage of increased capacities.

Microcomputer software, in particular, has made significant advances in the past few years. Apart from integrated software packages (software systems that permit multiple applications to interface with spreadsheets, graphics, and word processors), new software releases now allow users to interact with systems and applications in powerful ways. New software capabilities include user-generated customized software (available without the writing of a program) and sophisticated information-organization capabilities that let users combine texts, graphics, sound, and computer-generated animation (Rogers, 1987).

Just as advances in micro, mini, and mainframe computers are improving office productivity, so also are those in supercomputers changing the reality of scientific research and engineering. Supercomputers are powerful, for several reasons. They can handle arrays or vectors of numbers all at one time, rather than dealing with each number separately, and they can pipeline, or process, several instructions from a program concurrently. Supercomputers are enabling scientists and engineers to solve problems that previously were thought intractable because of the massive number of necessary computations. This development has had an energizing effect on many fields of science and technology, including astrophysics, aeronautics, meteorology, physics, computer design, and chemical engineering (National Science Board, 1985).

Still, many scientific and engineering problems will require even greater computer capacities before the solutions will be deemed workable. Research is proceeding on a new computer architecture, described as *parallel,* which aims at boosting computer speeds to twenty thousand million instructions per second. A handful of parallel computers are now operating, but they are still largely experimental. The time seems to be rapidly approaching, however, when these powerful devices will be readily available as tools for scientists and engineers (National Science Board, 1985).

Telecommunications—that is, communication at a distance—and computer networking—that is, the linking of computers to telecommunications lines—continue to revolutionize information sharing and acquisition. Telecommunications itself involves various technologies, including cable television and communications satellites.

Cable television, which began in the 1940s as a way to improve reception for households on the fringes of broadcasting centers, has grown enormously since 1975, when RCA launched its commercial communications satellite, SATCOM I. In large part, the growth was due to satellite-interconnected programming businesses. Two-way cable systems that can transmit both from and to the individual households are another growing feature of general cable services. Common household applications include burglar, fire, and medical-alert security systems. There are also interactive cable systems, which allow the viewer to enter responses to public opinion polls. Teletext and Videotext are two communications services that bridge the gap between communications and computer networks. Teletext is one-way communication that permits television reception of text and graphics. Videotext is a two-way connection between a television set and a computer that offers information and allows the user to shop and perform banking transactions (Singleton, 1983).

Data banks are also available via commercial computer network systems, enabling any computer equipped with a modem (and any user prepared to pay a fee) to access a variety of information. The Source, Dow Jones/Retrieval Service, and CompuServe, Inc., are just three examples (Mandell, 1986). Many more systems exist, offering the user access to information as varied as Scholastic Aptitude Test scores, national newspaper indexes, and tax advice.

The cost effectiveness of networks has been a large factor in promoting their success. Computers are cheaper than communications facilities, and so it makes good sense to adopt networking strategies. Before 1970, when computers were still more expensive than communications devices, it would not have made any sense for regional offices of, say, the Environmental Protection Agency to analyze data at each collection site. Instead, detailed data were transmitted to one central location (and one computer) for processing. Now the reverse is true. Microcomputers and minicomputers are relatively inexpensive, compared to data-transmission costs. To network the computers together, do detailed analysis on site, and transmit periodic summary reports across geographically separate locations is more cost-effective than to process data centrally (Tanenbaum, 1981).

Artificial Intelligence. The recent advances in computer design, with the advent of extremely powerful supercomputers, have facilitated the development of artificial intelligence (AI). AI is the long-sought-after goal of making a computer interact with humans (through its program) as if the computer were intelligent. AI activity has focused on several areas: visual perception, natural language recognition, automatic programming, game playing, and expert systems (Yazdani and Narayanan, 1984).

But there is considerable reason to believe that what is today referred to as the separate field of AI will soon no longer exist as a distinct subdivision of computer science. This concept was presented by W. Joe Watson, an employee of Texas Instruments and vice-president of the American Association for Artificial Intelligence (Waldrop, 1987). Watson argues that this will occur, not because AI will disappear, but rather because the techniques pioneered by AI will become standard for all mainstream programming. Programming now is based on detailed algorithm specification, around which programs are written. Simple changes in specifications can and regularly do cause expensive modifications or wholesale recoding. AI programming style is different in that it does not concentrate codes around precise and rigid specifications. Instead, AI programming instructs the computer about what must be known to solve a problem, and the computer uses that knowledge to determine what to do as specifications change.

Expert systems—commercially profitable today, and marketed by many vendors—were the first spinoffs of AI programming techniques. In this kind of system, experts' knowledge is encoded in programs that use one of a variety of techniques, called *rules, semantic networks, frames,* and *logical expressions.* These techniques are used to arrange and relate facts. There are a host of expert systems currently available, as well as commercial expert-system tools that enable users to design and build their own customized systems.

Some of the most famous expert systems were designed before 1980. MYCIN aids physicians in diagnosing and treating meningitis and bacteremia infections. DENDRAL functions as a chemistry expert in predicting molecular structures from unknown molecules. MYCSYMA helps mathematicians and engineers solve complex mathematical problems. INTERNIST diagnoses diseases. PROSPECTOR is used in exploratory geology. Recent systems have been designed for commercial purposes and provide a guide to the types of systems one might expect to see in the next few years. XCON, for instance, is used by Digital Equipment Corporation to configure its VAX line of computers. GENESIS is a collection of smaller expert systems, sold by IntelliCorp, which assist in genetic engineering. CATS-1, a computer-aided troubleshooting system, was developed by General Electric to help railroad maintenance personnel maintain locomotives. DRILLING ADVISOR, marketed by Teknowledge, helps oil rig managers resolve problems that otherwise could cause costly shutdowns of drills (Harmon and King, 1985). There are also a host of fourth-generation tools available on the market that enable users to design and implement their own expert systems, many of which can be written and run on standard microcomputers.

Another area of AI research is natural language recognition. Several programs are able to handle questions expressed in simple English. These programs include Larry Harris's INTELLECT and Gary Hendrix's LIFER (Winston, 1984). Natural language systems that accept inputs, answer questions about knowledge bases, make inferences, and generate natural language responses are complex and are not yet fully developed. More complete grammars are being developed, though, and it should not be long before natural language processing becomes completely viable (Harris, 1985).

Biotechnology. Genetic engineering, gene splicing, recombinant DNA, and *biotechnology* are names used to describe a relatively new branch of science that manipulates living organisms (microorganisms, plants, and animals) to develop new organisms that have applications useful to a wide variety of fields, including agriculture, pharmaceuticals, and energy. This area has been making sustained and noticeable progress for the past few years (Turney, 1984).

When biotechnology was first emerging, scientists themselves slowed its development until they could be satisfied that the risk of releasing newly created (and possibly harmful) organisms into the environment was not large (Wade, 1974). As the commercial potential of this technique became more obvious, and as knowledge about the potential risks was gathered, the scientific community became less hesitant. The National Academy of Sciences has recently argued that the release of biologically engineered organisms outside of laboratories is safe. The academy's position is that governmental evaluation of the environmental safety of these organisms should be based on their specific properties, rather than on how they are made (Sun, 1987).

In fact, the scientific community is seeking substantial federal funds to proceed with a project that reputedly will push biotechnology far ahead. The plan—to map and sequence the human genome—has the Department of Energy and Congress interested, even with its projected $1 billion price tag (Roberts, 1987).

The human genome is made up of approximately one hundred thousand genes. Each gene serves a function in determining an individual's characteristics, from color of eyes to susceptibility to certain diseases. Mapping the genome will give scientists the location of each gene, and sequencing the genome will reveal the chemical bases of each gene. The reliability of the technology to map and sequence has been proved; some twelve million chemical bases have already been sequenced, although even this total is less than 1 percent of all bases. This proposed "genome initiative" will speed up the process of knowing the bases. It will take over one thousand years to complete at the current rate of unveiling (Begley, Katz, and Drew, 1987).

Whether the government actually funds the project is of some concern to private industry, which has also shown considerable interest. If the project goes to the private sector, however, chances are that corporations will try to either patent or copyright the results. If a private company sequences the genome, will other researchers have to pay for what may become proprietary knowledge (Roberts, 1987)?

Materials Science. Materials science grew out of the field of metallurgy in the 1940s, as scientists expanded their efforts to explain the behavior of metals (in terms of the basic laws of physics and chemistry) to nonmetallic substances as well. Materials science now seeks to explain the complex behaviors of ceramics, plastics, organic solids, and glass.

The most exciting area of materials science today centers on the search for a room-temperature superconductor. Since the turn of the century, it has been known that certain materials, when sufficiently cooled, lose their resistance to electricity. A substance that can carry a useful current of electricity with no resistance is called a superconductor. One major advantage of superconductors is their ability to create very intense magnetic fields without the loss of power associated with the heat and resistance of standard electromagnets. Superconducting magnets are currently in use today (particularly in particle accelerators), but they need to be cooled with liquid helium. As a consequence, the utility of present superconductors is restricted (National Science Board, 1985). Recently, though, great advances have been made in the search for a room-temperature superconductor. Experiments at Lawrence Berkeley Laboratory and at the University of California at Berkeley have caused ceramics to briefly superconduct at sixty-six degrees Fahrenheit (Thomsen, 1987). Other labs have had equally astounding progress. The problem is that researchers still do not know why the new ceramics work they way they do, and therefore scientists have no theoretical guide for improving them (Robinson, 1987).

Nevertheless, the Reagan administration has shown considerable interest in rapid commercialization of the new technology, so that the United States can maintain its lead in the field over foreign competitors, who are not far behind. Accordingly, the Federal Conference on Commercial Applications of Superconductivity was held, and 1,500 government, university, and industry researchers were invited. The plan was to increase interaction among researchers and federal labs (Crawford, 1987; Hartley, 1987). Nevertheless, a decision, made by presidential science adviser William Graham, to exclude noncitizens from the conference upset many foreign diplomats, especially the Japanese (Marshall and Sun, 1987). Such willingness to offend other nations indicates the intensity with which the Reagan administration hopes today's sciences and technologies will restore American competitiveness.

Enduring Problems of Technical Change

The preceding discussion contains intimations of some of the problems ushered in by technical change. Among the many categories of problems, three seem particularly important to public administrators: public participation, the sorting out of experts' advice, and anticipation of technological change. Each of these categories will be discussed, but first it will be useful to note some other dimensions of scientific and technological impact and some additional roles of public administrators.

Our chief concern here has been with the kinds of technical change that have such sweeping impact that virtually all public administrators are caught up in them. Nevertheless, many of the impacts of science and technology are more distributed, in terms of their nature and the intensity of their impact on public administrators. The role we have emphasized here is that of the public administrator as a receiver of science and technology, of its blessings as well as its curses. There are many other roles, however, so many that space will not permit us to do more than mention them, although mentioning them does at least draw attention to the special focus of this chapter.

The role of the public administrator as a developer of science and technology is often overlooked. Obviously, scientists and engineers working in government laboratories produce technical and intellectual goods and services and purvey them, via technology transfers and spinoffs, to other segments of society. Still, many more public administrators are involved in the development of social and managerial technologies that have important impacts on the ways in which the core tasks of public administration are performed.

Science and technology are often important to the public administrator in terms of their economic implications. Thus, the role of the public administrator as a commercial agent for science and technology is often prominent. Particularly at the state level, science and technology are increasingly viewed as centerpieces of economic development programs, and the challenge for public administrators is to find ways to contain the economic benefits of science and technology locally.

Until recently, the role of the public administrator as a governor of science has been approached with much trepidation and reluctance. It has been assumed that science is best kept outside the public administrator's purview and that scientific inquiry should proceed in a free market of ideas directed by the curiosity of individual investigators. With the recent emphasis on public policy in approaches to competitiveness, however, public administrators and policymakers are somewhat less hesitant to intrude on the autonomy of scientists and, usually through the more passive means of manipulated incentives, try to shape the direction of science. (There has never been great reluctance, of course, to help govern the course of technology.)

A familiar role of the public administrator is that of regulator of science and technology. In any of a variety of fields—public health, occupational health and safety, conservation—public administrators have long been charged with overseeing science and technology as a means of guarding public welfare, a mission that includes ensuring the integrity of the physical environment. Advances in science have made this role even more complex, as public managers, among others, seek to develop approaches to such complex issues as inhibiting the spread of AIDS, ensuring environmental safety with respect to genetic research, and determining the origin of acid rain.

An increasingly important role of the public administrator is that of educator of the general public about science and technical issues. This is a difficult and demanding role. Given issues as diverse as the siting of a resource-recovery garbage-burning steam plant, the routing of transported nuclear waste, and the dynamics of contagion, the first and most important step is to inform the public. Often, the level of technical detail required is not that of a practicing scientist or engineer but is of the sort that can be mastered (perhaps not easily) by a layperson. In such cases, the ability of the public administrator to educate and communicate is sometimes one of the most important ingredients of a productive public dialogue.

The issues described in the following sections do not touch on all the roles that public administrators play with respect to science and technology. Instead, the focus is on the types of problems likely to confront any public administrator, not just those working directly and routinely with science and technology.

Public Participation. While concern for public participation in science and technology is not unique to the public sector, public administrators must be particularly mindful of the public's right to participate. At the same time, there is an inevitable need for the expertise of specialists, often scientists and engineers. In many cases, this need seems to oppose the public's rights and the experts' superior knowledge. This conflict is played out in a wide variety of public policy disputes, including those that involve nuclear power (Nelkin, 1977), airport siting (Nelkin, 1979), pollution, and public health (Levine, 1982; Mazur, 1981).

It is tempting to offer simple nostrums for such disputes, but the complexity of the problems is not amenable to universal prescriptions. For example, it is easy to suggest that the public is best suited to establishing values, setting levels of technical risk, and choosing among broad alternatives. After these parameters have been established, experts' (and public administrators') mission is to choose scientific and technological alternatives consistent with those values. This simple prescription overlooks a number of factors, however. In the first place, "the public" is not a homogeneous, single-minded entity. The public varies with respect to knowledge of issues, interest in issues, and ability to articulate concerns. Even highly rational and extremely knowledgeable people often disagree, because of different stakes in a decision. It is difficult to aggregate public opinion about a garbage-burning steam plant when one person lives a block from the proposed site and another lives a mile away. Likewise, a rational actor who has a store or a business near the path of a proposed high-speed superconducting magnetic train may have a quite different view than a rational actor who lives near the same spot. Nor can we, with some Bentham-like calculus (such as cost-benefit analysis), make disparate values commensurate. Parties to technical disputes have different resources. Some have access to and skills with mass media, and others do not. Some have greater political clout, and some have greater economic clout. Some have organized interest groups working on their behalf. Public participation is never subject to convenient formulas.

What, then, can public administrators do to elicit and use public opinion? In the first place, they can strive to be public educators. This is not so demanding a task as it might seem, because in many instances the level of knowledge one needs to express an informed opinion is really rather low. Public administrators cannot themselves, nor can they help citizens, become scientists overnight, but public administrators can often provide information about the rudimentary functions of technology or pollutants in terms that anyone can understand. This task, of course, is often viewed as a function of the mass media, but in many cases, especially in city government, technological issues are reported in the media only after many early decisions have hardened.

Public administrators can act as go-betweens and technological brokers. By knowing the parties to a dispute, knowing their views, and even knowing about what scientific and technical evidence exists (or knowing where to find it), public administrators can often bring groups together to express their values and, under the best of conditions, pool their knowledge. Even if such activity does not always lead to happy syntheses, it is usually superior to having groups with disparate views work in separate "armed camps."

Sorting Out of Experts' Advice. Even if effective forums for public participation are constructed, it is the rare technological dispute that elicits agreement among experts. A common and invariably mistaken practice is to equate the exactness of the sciences with exactness in science and technology policymaking (Bozeman and Bozeman, 1981). The sciences are well suited to giving theoretical explanations at a high level of generalization, but they are not so well suited to predicting the composition and flow of the particulate emissions from garbage-burning steam plants in unique environmental settings.

Faced with such dilemmas, what can public administrators do? A first step is to realize that in the vast majority of disputes that involve science and technology there are no true experts but only degrees of expertise and, most important, different types of knowledge. The public administrator's responsibility is to structure dialogue in such a fashion that an argument is considered on its face (rather than from its source) and to ensure that the scientist speaks from his or her own perspective and not "for science." Likewise, it is the citizen's (or citizen group's) responsibility to represent its perspective adequately, and it is the public administrator's responsibility to seek other perspectives. If this statement seems to suggest that a technical dispute is less a search for rationality than a dialectic mixing the political with the scientific in an indecipherable blend, then the public administrator can at least take comfort in the thought that that is the best that can be done. The public administrator is a guarantor of process, rather than an arbiter of ultimate truth.

Anticipation of Technological Change. Broadly speaking, the impacts of science and technology on public administration can be classified as societal or local in origin. An example of a local-origin technological change would be the installation of a local-area network in one's office. An example of a societal-level change would be the development of microcomputer technology powerful enough to drive a local-area network. It is almost always important for public administrators to be able to anticipate scientific and technological change at one or both levels, and it is usually exceedingly difficult to do so. Even among technically trained public administrators, the prospects for effectively monitoring scientific and technical change are bleak. Scientific and technical information is accumulating at a remarkable rate. In most scientific fields, the reaction to the pace of change has been specialization. Most public administrators, however, need greater breadth of scientific and technical knowledge, and less depth.

Public administrators can keep attuned to scientific and technical change that is local in origin in many of the same ways they keep abreast of local policy and political developments: interactions with colleagues (particularly the more specialized) within an agency, and communication with the agency's clients and vendors. Staying abreast of societal technological change is usually much more difficult, but it is often quite rewarding. Given the pace of societal change in some fields (information technology is the prime example), the time required for moving innovative technology from the laboratory to the market to a government agency is remarkably brief. Often, a public administrator who last year was unfamiliar with the terms *laser printer* and *electronic mail* is this year a key decision maker in their installation. By staying just a bit ahead of the diffusion curve, public administrators can often save money, enable more effective programs, and avoid disasters in the local implementation of technology.

Despite the obvious need for many public administrators to be able to monitor and anticipate scientific and technical change, the nature of the work is such that little time is devoted to activities that might support this need (Lau and Pavett, 1980). What can be done? A number of specific strategies for public administrators' acquisition of externally based scientific and technical information have been suggested elsewhere (Bozeman, Roering, and Slusher, 1978; Bozeman and Cole, 1982; Bozeman, 1981), but it now seems time for a more radical proposal: that the very nature of public administration work be reexamined.

Traditionally, public administrators have been evaluated, both externally and by themselves, in terms of a "can do" ethos that emphasizes action and high energy over detachment and reflection. This claim is documented by the fact that administrators, both public and private (Mintzberg, 1972), spend less than an hour per week reading anything other than correspondence. At some point, however, it will become necessary to stop equating the expenditure of energy with effectiveness. Increasingly, the information public administrators require to be able to anticipate and deal effectively with scientific and technical change will come from sources external to agencies, perhaps even external to government. A myopic view, concentrating almost exclusively on the local impacts of rapidly unfolding events, will not permit the acquisition of external technical knowledge. We argue that the current concern about crisis-driven management and the renewed interest in strategic management can be interpreted as, in part, an embryonic recognition of the need to move from high-energy, parochial public administration to steady-energy, reflective public administration. Technical change and complexity will reward the deliberate and punish the desperate.

References

Begley, S., Katz, S., and Drew, L. "The Genome Initiative." *Newsweek,* Aug. 31, 1987, pp. 58–60.

Bozeman, B. "Public Managers and Scientific and Technical Information." *R&D Management,* 1981, *11* (1), 33–35.

Bozeman, B., and Bozeman, J. "Technical Information and Policy Choice: The Case of the Resource Recovery 'Nondecision.'" *Journal of Public Policy,* 1981, *1* (2), 51–63.

Bozeman, B., and Cole, E. "Scientific Information Acquisition in Public

Agencies: The Role of Channel Preference and 'Gatekeeping.'" *Administration and Society,* 1982, *14* (3), 479–493.

Bozeman, B., Roering, K., and Slusher, E. "Social Structures and the Flow of Scientific Information in Public Agencies: An Ideal Design." *Research Policy,* 1978, *7* (4), 384–405.

Crawford, M. "White House Spotlights New Superconductors." *Science,* 1987, *237* (8415), 593–394.

Florman, S. C. *Blaming Technology: The Irrational Search for Scapegoats.* New York: St. Martin's Press, 1981.

Galbraith, J. K. *The New Industrial State.* Boston: Houghton Mifflin, 1967.

Harmon, P., and King, D. *Expert Systems: Artificial Intelligence in Business.* New York: Wiley, 1985.

Harris, M. D. *Introduction to Natural Language Processing.* Reston, Va.: Reston Publishing, 1985.

Hartley, K. "No Resistance to Superconductivity." *Science News,* 1987, *132,* 85.

Lau, A., and Pavett, C. "The Nature of Managerial Work: A Comparison of Public-Private-Sector Managers." *Group and Organization Studies,* 1980, *5* (4), 453–466.

Levine, A. G. *Love Canal: Science, Politics, and People.* Lexington, Mass.: Lexington Books, 1982.

Mandell, S. L. *Computers, Data Processing, and the Law: Text and Cases.* New York: West, 1984.

Mandell, S. L. *Computers and Data Processing Today.* (2nd ed.) New York: West, 1986.

Marshall, E., and Sun, M. "Stumbling on Superconductors." *Science,* 1987, *237* (8414), 477.

Mazur, A. *The Dynamics of Technical Controversy.* Washington, D.C.: Communications Press, 1981.

Mintzberg, H. *The Nature of Managerial Work.* New York: Harper & Row, 1972.

National Science Board. *Science Indicators: The 1985 Report.* Washington, D.C.: U.S. Government Printing Office, 1985.

Nelkin, D. *Technological Decisions and Democracy: European Experiments in Public Participation.* Newbury Park, Calif.: Sage, 1977.

Nelkin, D. (ed.). *Controversy: Politics of Technical Decisions.* Newbury Park, Calif.: Sage, 1979.

Roberts, L. "Who Owns the Human Genome?" *Science,* 1987, *237* (4813), 358–361.

Robinson, A. "Chains May Not Be Needed for 90K Superconductivity." *Science,* 1987, *237* (4812), 249–250.

Rogers, M. "Hyper-Excitement at Apple." *Newsweek,* Aug. 31, 1987, p. 45.

Singleton, L. A. *Telecommunications in the Information Age.* Cambridge, Mass.: Ballinger, 1983.

Sun, M. "Recombinant Organisms Pose No Special Hazard." *Science,* 1987, *237* (4817), 840.

Tanenbaum, A. S. *Computer Networks.* Englewood Cliffs, N.J.: Prentice-Hall, 1981.

Thomsen, D. "Superconductivity Glimpsed Near 300K." *Science News,* 1987, *132* (1), 4.

Turney, J. (ed.). *Sci-Tech Report.* New York: Pantheon, 1984.

Wade, N. "Genetic Manipulation: Temporary Embargo Proposed on Research." *Science,* 1974, *185* (4148), 332–334.

Waldrop, M. M. "Artificial Intelligence Moves into Mainstream." *Science,* 1987, *237* (4814), 484–485.

Winston, P. H. *Artificial Intelligence.* (2nd ed.) Reading, Mass.: Addison-Wesley, 1984.

Yazdani, M., and Narayanan, A. (eds.). *Artificial Intellience: Human Effects.* New York: Wiley, 1984.

6   *Michael V. Reagen*

Shifting Demographic and Social Realities

Public administration is a dynamic and ever changing process. We live in an era of uncertainty, rapid transition, and complex interrelationships. We can learn from history, but it is myopic to think our future will replicate the past. Today, public administrators face a multiplicity of dilemmas, each loaded with critical and often unintended consequences. Each dilemma encountered must be approached as an interdependent part of a complex whole, where administration of public policy, programs, and services is affected by demographic variables and external economic and political authorities. Some contend that public administration is in an era of resource reallocation and molecular politics, where economic and political resources are finite. Interest groups with shared characteristics are emerging and competing for increasingly slender slices of a diminishing resource pie.

The groups barter and dicker among themselves. They cajole and communicate with political authorities, usually in a narrowly defined environment. Thus, the political nature of their demands is fragmented and particularistic. Compounding these two epochal phenomena are markedly changing and inexplicably interdependent economic and demographic trends, scientific and technological advances, and value and life-style changes that affect the administrator's decision-making world.

Serious disturbances in our economic and social life, along with the rapid technological development of the last few years, suggest that fundamental structural alterations are taking place (Kennedy, 1987). Moreover, some say these changes show a pattern consistent with macroeconomic cycles or

Note: The author wishes to thank Donna Checkett, Mary Honse, Stephen King, Richard Koon, Edwin Walker, and Sheryl Wright for their patience and help.

68

"waves" of forty-five to sixty years, which coincide with recent ebbs and flows of economic growth and decline. The changes, however, escape historically classic, conventional explanations, and they seem to be driven by the start, growth, and later overexpansion of an interrelated set of complex technological and industrial processes that eventually reach diminishing returns (Erickson, 1985).

Kennedy (1987) claims that the current erosion of America's economic foundation and the consequent social and political challenge to public administrators began gradually and are fueled by several factors: U.S. agricultural export policies, a decline in industrial production relative to overall world production, and the great turbulence in America's finances and governmental budgetary policies. According to Peters (1987), America's economic decline is being accelerated by the "chaos" in foreign trade.

Clearly, then, we are in an era of resource reallocation and molecular politics. We must learn how to shift finite resources among increasingly valued priorities to resolve problems, instead of assuming that we can continually allocate infinite resources to solve them. In addition, public administrators must become accustomed to a more narrowly defined view of politics. Molecular politics suggest that we need to know how to balance the demands of increasing groups of people, who are emerging with legitimate and reasonable needs to challenge our politicians, who want to satisfy all constituents' wishes while maintaining blanket popularity.

In this chapter, I shall summarize some of these economic, social, and demographic changes by discussing the impact of shifting patterns of age, fertility, and migration on our society. Finally, I shall summarize future issues and challenges that public administrators must face, and I shall discuss the implications of these changes for the administrative and political environment.

Shifting Patterns

Global Population. There are approximately 4.5 billion people on the earth today. Because of advances in food distribution, sanitation, and immunology, the world's population has tripled since 1900, and experts say it will reach 10.4 billion in the year 2105 (Vu, 1985, p. 2). Nine out of every ten infants are born in Third World countries, and the result is a major world population shift. In 1950, the developed countries had 22 percent of the world population. Today, they have 15 percent. By the year 2030, they will have 9 percent (Wattenberg, 1987b, p. 58).

Not only is growth shifting to less developed nations; the more developed countries are also aging disproportionately. Western Europe, for example, full of old churches, old history, and old people, is shrinking in population, power, and economic muscle, and Japan is currently burdened with more old people than its workers can support.

In fact, the industrial world is beginning to experience a "birth dearth." According to Wattenberg, a birth dearth "deals with a total fertility rate

(TFR) below the replacement rate of 2.1 children per woman'' (Wattenberg, 1987a, p. 14n). For over a century, fertility has fallen in the western world. For fifteen years, the industrial nations have not borne enough children to reproduce themselves over an extended period of time. Many demographers thought the fertility rate drop would stop when it reached about 2.1 births per woman over her childbearing years, the level required to keep a population stable over an extended period of time. Instead, the fertility rate has reduced even more.

In contrast to the projected shrinkage in the modern democracies, the Communist Bloc nations are growing moderately. Today, as a whole, they have a TFR of 2.3 births per woman, well above the replacement rate of 2.1 TFR and 28 percent higher than the 1.8 TFR rate of the Western democracies.

In Third World countries, there has been a decline from 6.1 TFR in 1970 to 4.1 TFR in 1985. But there are 1.1 billion women of childbearing age in the less developed world. Even if the Third World reduces its future TFR, the increase in Third World babies will continue. The Third World population of 3.7 billion will rise to 8 billion by the middle of the next century. The earth's soil, fuel, water, and forests will be dramatically exploited unless public policies are changed to accommodate these dramatic population increases.

America's Birth Dearth. The United States is also affected by these demographic shifts. In 1984, America's median income was approximately $26,433, the highest in the world. In 1985, public school enrollments rose for the first time since 1969 and are expected to increase by about 15 percent by the early 1990s. By 1995, the number of Americans between the ages of thirty-five and fifty-five will have risen by a third; the nation's median age, thirty in 1980, will then be thirty-five. By 1995, the number of Americans between the ages of twenty and thirty-four will have dropped by nearly 6 million (Wattenberg, 1987b, p. 59).

Our middle-aged culture is stable, serious, and careful. It is even beginning to affect the nation's mood and concerns. Baby boomers are changing society, prompting higher school spending: Because of anxiety over competitiveness, baby boomers form a constituency for better schools for their children. We also have less leisure: Baby boomers are more time-sensitive because of the conflicting demands of work, children, and personal pleasure. Moreover, we are seeing the death of the youth culture: Baby boomers place middle age in a positive light, preferring, for example, such television programs as ''The Cosby Show,'' ''Family Ties,'' and ''thirtysomething'' to those that focus on singles and work.

Nevertheless, although we exhibit a blend of traditional values—home, family, work—our attitudes and experiences often differ profoundly from those of our parents. Divorce is now acceptable, and two-earner couples are the norm. Conflicting values abound. We are relabeling, if not reinventing, middle age. We are aging rapidly, and our minority population is growing disproportionately. We experience substantial immigration, especially from Hispanics, and we are very mobile.

In 1890, the U.S. population was 65 million. The 1990 U.S. census is expected to record 230 million. Our past growth has always meant a demand for more of everything. Now, however, because of the birth dearth, we have shrinking domestic markets and an older population, and we need fewer people to produce fewer of the items in demand.

From 1990 to 2000, the number of Americans between the ages of twenty-five and thirty-four will shrink by 18 percent because of the low fertility rates of the late 1960s and the 1970s (Wattenberg, 1987b, p. 58). During 1986, for example, only sixty-five babies were born per one thousand U.S. women of childbearing age, the lowest rate in American history. More elderly people will also die, leaving vacant residences and further shrinking the need for new housing. Without a stable home market, the export market will suffer.

Traditional wisdom suggests that only populous nations that optimize large labor forces and economies of scale can become big powers. Brute economic production is crucial to national strength and security. Nations with large populations can do many things. They can more easily build the infrastructure to support national defense. They can attain technological leadership through larger pools of scientists. They can support broader-based industrial and scientific innovation. They can also tax their people to finance major military research and development, build and sustain modern weapons systems, and provide workers for armed services in an economically interdependent world. The sheer sizes of domestic markets and labor forces are critical and competitive variables in determining the economic clout and the social and political stability of a country. America's wealthy continental market of 230 million people gives it a geopolitical leverage that nations with smaller populations cannot enjoy (Wattenberg, 1987b, p. 60).

Population growth in U.S. nonmetropolitan areas now outpaces growth in metropolitan areas. In fact, in such major metropolitan areas as Chicago and New York, more than one-third of all households contain only one person. The number of young adults living alone increased by 1.2 million during the 1970s and decreased by 402,000 between 1980 and 1985, but it is again on the rise. Women constitute 62 percent of people who live alone, with a median age of 65.5 (Schmich, 1987, p. 1H). It is apparent that the shifting of populations to nonmetropolitan areas forces public administrators to reevaluate strategies for directing available resources to shrinking urban populations. More administrative time and attention will need to be devoted to the nonurban sector.

In most U.S. cities, the overall growth rate is now less than the national growth rate (Kemp, 1987, p. 2). Only Los Angeles and San Francisco have grown significantly since 1970. Increases in the nonmetropolitan population, however, are taking place almost entirely in nonfarm areas, a trend that is associated with outer suburban development, less expensive housing, relocation of retired persons, and new employment opportunities that have been created as industry has spread to these more cost-effective areas.

Of total U.S. population growth during the 1970s, 90 percent was in the southern and western states. Today, over half the U.S. population lives there. The countryside that once served a shrinking population of farmers is now filling back up with nonfarmers who work at home, commute long distances to work, or find jobs in the new small industries attracted to rural areas. More traditional social and political behavior will be displayed in these areas than in the metropolitan areas from which these "new rurals" came.

Today, 80 percent of the total U.S. population is of white, ex-European stock. At current fertility and immigration rates, demographers project that the white, ex-European share of the U.S. population will shrink to 60 percent by the year 2080. Influxes of undocumented foreign workers, as well as growing ill will among various ethnic groups, often help to incite social turbulence.

The "Graying" Dilemma. The declining fertility and mortality rates and the inevitable aging of the baby boomers are combining to change the nation's age structure dramatically. A decade ago, 10 percent of the total population was elderly, a percentage expected to double in the next fifty years. The "old old"—those over eighty who have special needs—will grow to about 7 percent of the population, nearly triple their current share (Urban Institute, 1986). Obviously, an aging population requires greater attention to social security policy, among other things.

In 1985, there were 145 million U.S. workers available to pay social security taxes for 29 million elderly (a ratio of 5:1). In 2035, as baby boomers retire and younger people make up the labor force, the ratio will be 2.5:1.

Educational achievement, improved pension coverage, and medical technology have created an unprecedented U.S. retired population. Today, the over-fifty market is growing, changing, and spending. Consider these few facts: People over fifty-five years old did 30 percent of all estimated U.S. travel in 1984. They control an estimated $7 trillion of U.S. wealth, nearly 70 percent of the net worth of U.S. households. They account for 33 percent of all memberships in health spas. And those between sixty-five and seventy-five years old have more average income per person than those under forty-five (Futures Group, Inc., 1987).

Unless real reforms are enacted soon, some literature suggests, the social security system is precariously close to defaulting (Ferra, 1985; Meyer, 1987). If Medicare liabilities are shifted to current younger groups, this process will quicken. The slender legions of the birth dearth may be unwilling to shoulder additional taxes and sacrifice quality of life. Assuming a continuance of current domestic, defense, and foreign-program financing, there will be fewer taxpayers to fund the new life- and health-extending medical technology for the elderly.

Poverty and the Underclass. Cohen (1987) argued that there are more poor in the United States than the statistics indicate, because poverty guidelines are outdated and based on decade-old census data, which necessarily exclude year-to-year changes in such groups as the aged, children, and one-parent families.

Samuel Halperin of the W. T. Grant Foundation's Commission on Work, Family, and Citizenship cites three statistics to show that poverty is a growing reality in single-parent families (U.S. Department of Commerce, Bureau of the Census, 1987):

- The number of persons below the poverty line who were living in families headed by a woman, with no husband present, jumped 27.1 percent between 1979 and 1986, from 9.4 million to 11.9 million.
- A single parent working at the federal minimum wage of $3.35 per hour would have to support herself and two children at 20 percent below the current official poverty line ($8,737 per year for a family of three).
- In March 1985, 67.8 percent of single mothers with school-age children were in the labor force at least part time or part of the year.

Halperin, noting that half of all poor families are headed by women, also writes: "While the number of in-poverty individuals increased 27.1 percent among single-parent families, among other households, composed almost entirely of married couples, poverty soared 21.3 percent between 1979 and 1986, from 10.5 million to 12.8 million individuals" (U.S. Department of Commerce, Bureau of the Census, 1987, p. 38). Poverty must be reckoned with at all three levels of government before the number of poverty-stricken people reaches a point of no return.

According to Magnet (1987), many reports neglect data that indicate that 50 percent of inner-city high school students drop out before graduation and that, because of civil rights and expanded housing and job opportunities for blacks, millions of middle-class, working inner-city minorities have fled to suburbs, leaving behind an underclass with clusters of deficits. Once economically diverse, urban communities have turned into homogeneous enclaves of poverty.

Inner-city occupants, mostly black males, form a one-dimensional and often demoralized culture, with few traditional role models to demonstrate the mainstream educational and work ethics. Some researchers suggest that few contingents remain in some American inner cities to counter the underclass or to alert youngsters to job openings (Reischauer, 1987).

Other researchers have long argued that community institutions—schools, churches, stores, recreation centers—have lost the support of the family structure. Social stability in many American inner-city areas is in an almost downward spiral. Vandalism hastens business flight, reduces employment opportunities, and leaves little but the culture of failure, unemployment, hustling, drugs, and welfare (Auletta, 1982).

The results have been overwhelmingly crushing to minorities, especially blacks (Wilson, 1987). Today, because of scarce jobs and the lack of necessary skills, only 44 percent of black men between sixteen and twenty-four are employed, down from 59 percent a quarter-century ago. This decline is associated with marked increases in violent crime among blacks. Robbery and rape rates quadrupled between 1963 and 1980. Burglary and assault rates tripled, and the murder rate doubled between 1963 and 1980. In 1987, a twelve-year-old black American boy had an 89 percent chance of being a victim of violent crime in his lifetime, and an urban household has a 93 percent chance of being burgled sometime during the next twenty years. Nevertheless, poor blacks get robbed four times more than middle-class whites, and the leading cause of death among young black men is murder (Magnet, 1987).

Many elderly people have not escaped poverty. The poverty rate for the elderly in the United States fell from roughly 25 percent in 1970 to 13 percent in 1986. Despite these significant reductions, there are still major pockets of poverty among the elderly. In 1985, the poverty rate for elderly female-headed families was 23 percent, and the rate for black elderly families was 31 percent. Poverty rates for elderly adults with disabilities are very high: In 1983, more than 30 percent of elderly disabled persons were poor.

The Cost of Illness. Increasing health care costs pose yet another obstacle to the overall betterment of society. The cost of illness in the United States is rising to epic proportions, and the end is not in sight. Americans spent $458 billion on health care in 1986. Spending was up 18 percent over the 1984 level of $387 billion. As a percentage of gross national product (GNP), health care spending increased from 10.6 percent to 10.9 percent over that two-year period. On the basis of trends from the past two decades, we can predict that spending will be $1.5 trillion in the year 2000. Spending per capita will be $5,500, and health care will take 15 percent of GNP. Expenditures for hospitals' and physicians' services will be about three and a half times higher. The main factor in these increases will be inflation in the health care sector that will far exceed the general inflation rate.

In 1984, all national and local taxes (including social security contributions) constituted 29 percent of U.S. GNP. The only industrialized country with a lower rate was Japan (27.4 percent). Canada had 33.7 percent, and France and the Netherlands exceeded 45 percent. Scandinavian countries were even higher. These other nations give health care to their poor and aged through universal national health insurance systems. Each country has tight controls over health care costs. For example, while U.S. national health expenditures exceed 11 percent of GNP, these other nations limited their costs to about 9 percent of GNP.

Although U.S. health care costs continue to grow dramatically each year, relatively poorer nations—specifically Canada and West Germany— provide greater access to high-quality care for the elderly and the poor by taxing themselves more than Americans do. Thirty-seven million Americans in 1986 had no health insurance and, in 1984, America's aged self-financed about one-third of their health expenditures. Out-of-pocket insurance expenses took an average of 22 percent of the resources of the elderly poor with annual per capita income of less than $5,000. The payments amounted to only 3 percent for those with per capita income of over $20,000. Hundreds of thousands of elderly Americans still bear more than $2,000 in annual out-of-pocket expenses.

Cost-containment pressures, together with the presence of more physicians, are causing highly competitive modes of health care delivery. The current major issues are equity, coverage, and cost policies of Medicare and Medicaid programs; access to care for the uninsured and the underinsured; the growing elderly population's need for more long-term care; and the impact of medical malpractice insurance on physicians, hospitals, and health care costs. The public administrator's role is to attempt to redirect and monitor scarce resources and accommodate interest groups' demands while still trying to satisfy the public interest.

Implications for Change

Each of the patterns of change discussed here creates a defined area of concern for the public administrator. Typically, the administrator will outline the specific problem, establish priorities, allocate additional resources, and focus additional personnel on solving the problem. For example, consider poverty and welfare programs. Howe (1988, p. 2) writes: "American society's response to poverty is rooted in two major assumptions. The first: that a capitalistic, free-enterprise system brings more benefits to more people than any other general economic policy. . . . The second . . . is that Americans have a collective responsibility to help individuals who do not succeed in the economic system."

Since poverty was viewed in the past as a consequence of the national economy, as a socially rooted problem, or even as a result of poor national planning, politicians directed public administrators to limit their focus to crafting entitlement programs that would ease the impacts or effects of poverty. Administrators reacted by engaging in episodic, short-sighted actions that were narrowly defined and focused and that did not allow for evaluation or reexamination of unintended consequences. Today, however, administrators, public officials, businesspeople, and others recognize that entitlements have become entrapments for many, perpetuating dependency and deepening poverty. Leaders increasingly recognize that multifaceted problems cannot be solved in one-dimensional ways.

There is a growing desire for greater activism and strategic thinking to provide continuity of services and put an end to program fragmentation (Amidei, 1987). The complex social, economic, and political realities of the 1980s have forced government to seek new and innovative ways to provide essential government services to citizens while simultaneously coping with diminished financial resources. Chase (1984, p. 6) argues that these new realities are having a corresponding impact on corporate executives as well: "A growing number of chief executive officers have perceived that exclusive preoccupation with profit now creates public policy problems. . . . The management of public policy is increasingly perceived . . . to be part of sound management of profit, now and in the future." Strategic thinking, public-private partnerships, and service integration are methods that public administrators must use to counter the negative effects of these recurring changes.

Strategic thinking is an organizational function that involves a planned response to change, rather than a simple reaction to it. Strategic thinking focuses on choices that are related to overall organizational purposes, oriented toward the future, and tied to uncontrollable environmental forces. It is a philosophy, an attitude, and a mode of approach that is more of a thought process—an intellectual exercise—than a prescribed set of procedures, structures, and techniques. It links strategic plans, medium-range programs, and short-range budgets and operating programs. The primary purpose of strategic thinking is to devise comprehensive solutions that incorporate alternatives calculated to provide integrative service mechanisms.

One area where strategic thinking is proving successful is welfare reform. There is consensus that our current public welfare system does not work well and needs fixing. The issue under debate is how to fix it. Instead of debating the enhancement of entitlements, however, elected officials, public administrators, and business executives are recognizing that for many—perhaps as many as half the adults receiving Aid to Families with Dependent Children (AFDC) payments, for example—the current system fails to open the door to progress and only reinforces barriers to eventual entry into the labor market.

It is important to engage in strategic thinking to reconfigure the components of specific current programs into holistic, interactive, targeted approaches if these barriers are to be lowered for the truly disadvantaged. Public administrators need to integrate the components of public education, job training, early childhood development, and public health programs with low-cost health insurance, economic development, and child care incentives for low-income families and single mothers. This approach may, among other things, positively influence the multidimensional problems of welfare so that recipients can be empowered to break the web of dependency and become independent.

One example of an innovative approach to attacking welfare dependency is the Women's Employment Network (WEN). WEN is a program in Kansas City, Missouri, jointly funded by state, local, corporate, and foundation sources. It is designed to provide job-readiness training to low-income women who are interested in improving their marketability. Essentially a "resocialization" program, WEN enhances existing skills and emphasizes the traditional work ethic. The program is an example of an effective public-private partnership, with state and local public service agencies joining the corporate, business, and labor sectors. The Department of Social Services provides child care and Medicaid coverage and performs case finding and assessments to refer AFDC recipients who lack high school diplomas to the program. Employment Security staff assist with job search and placement. The corporate and foundation funding provides leverage to the state dollars and has the effect of doubling the efforts of the program.

At this writing, Congress is debating welfare reform, and twenty-four states, with the encouragement of the federal executive branch, are experimenting with models along these very lines.

The debate over welfare reform currently focuses on the conflicting strategies necessary to address the objectives of reducing poverty and reducing welfare dependency. *Poverty,* as a concept, emphasizes the level of one's income; *dependency* focuses on the source of that income. Care must be taken because, in the short term, strategies aimed at reducing dependency may not reduce poverty rates, and strategies targeted at reducing poverty may increase dependency. A strategic and comprehensive effort is needed to ensure progress.

Redefinition of Roles

Before society can reap the benefits of strategic planning and innovative thinking, it is imperative to redefine the roles of each governmental level and the business and labor market sectors as well. The current roles of each of these entities are anathema to the implementation of strategic planning and innovative thinking.

The national government has too many rules and regulations that result in a hodgepodge of strategies and programs. Program objectives are vague, with shifting definitions. Program objectives are directed at problems on which programs have limited impact. Objectives cannot be adequately assessed, and responsibility for the management of programs is diffuse. Conversely, the federal role should deal less with the direct provision of services and more with the development of institutions to provide services, including nonprofits and the corporate sector. This should include a new national focus on the problem and new mechanisms for addressing it.

State governments affect local governments' management of human resources through administration of state human service programs and state policies and regulations governing implementation of federal programs. Instead of engaging in just the administration of programs, state governors, for example, should be empowered to grant greater flexibility to local governments and agencies by in turn empowering them to act. Indeed, there needs to be an increased emphasis on regional and local efforts in combatting human service problems. We must move from entitlement to empowerment. For example, regional planning bodies (such as the Area Agency on Aging and the Council of Governments) or an interagency cooperation (such as Youth 2000, in Missouri) are prerequisites for instituting strategic plans in the attempt to solve human service problems.

Today, as in the past, local entities, for the most part, are the receivers of national and state funds and are essentially restricted to administration of services. Local governments should convene community roundtables to establish a common language and an awareness of interrelated goals and priorities. Local business and government leaders need to create coordinating councils and community profiles that will determine communities' needs and available resources.

Finally, it is necessary to rethink the role of the private sector. In the past, the only stipulation the public sector placed on the private sector was to contribute dollars to a project or program. Today, the partnership needs to be rooted in strategic thinking. Local business and other community stakeholders must critically reexamine their input in a partnership agreement by asking "Whom are we doing this for? Why are we doing it?" The answers to these questions will significantly shape the future public-private partnerships.

For public-private partnerships to work effectively, there are five organizational axioms that the participants in the partnerships must understand.

First, all participants are biased. Initially, private executives, whose motives public administrators question, assume public administrators are inflexible and unmotivated. Likewise, public administrators contend that the executives are concerned only with profits and not with delivery of services or products. The biases must be dealt with collegially if the public-private alliances are to work.

Second, for the most part, partnerships in the past have meant only the acquisition of dollars. It is essential for private executives to realize that the formation of partnerships requires reciprocity, so that both parties contribute ideas, inventions, and innovative thinking, rather than just financial resources.

Third, the process must be formalized. Otherwise, without an institutional framework, the partnership will lose sight of its predetermined goals, and leadership will falter. Once leadership slips, direction may become unclear.

Fourth, all parties must be committed to the goals set and the actions implemented. Without agreement and commitment to the goals and actions, the results derived will not be satisfactory to all parties.

Fifth, outside experts should be used. Experts in any given field can offer new information and empower the partnership with support for the tasks. Links with the academic community, for example, are essential if substantive progress is to be made.

These five axioms provide a guideline for progress. Without them, such partnerships, instead of ameliorating or even solving problems, may actually exacerbate them.

Progress in effective service delivery, however, can take place without the private sector. Service integration is the key.

What is service integration? "Service integration focuses on the multiple needs of individuals and families through community-wide service delivery networks, bringing all community services together in a coherent whole, working toward unified approaches to policy development, administration, planning, and service delivery'' (Hageback, 1979, p. 575). It is composed of three elements: policy development and policy management cutting across independent programs and categories of human services; a delivery system designed to meet the needs of clients whose problems go beyond a single agency or program; and an organizational structure supportive of policy management or service delivery or both.

What are some examples of service integration? Generally located at the state and local levels under national government influence and guidance, these mechanisms are designed to link service providers together. The following are some common integration mechanisms:

- Joint planning, the joint determination of total system needs and priorities through a structured planning process
- Joint development of operating policies, a structured process in which the policies, procedures, regulations, and guidelines governing the administration of a project are jointly established
- Joint programming, the joint development of programmatic solutions to define problems in relation to existing resources
- Outstationing, placement of a service provider in the facility of another service agency, without the transfer of line authority or payroll
- Organizational change across agencies, whereby service agencies in the integrated system, or newly created agencies, receive staff or units from other agencies in the system, or whereby an umbrella organization is created
- Joint use of staff, whereby two different agencies deliver services by using the same staff, with both agencies retaining separate line authority over staff
- Case teams, the arrangement in which a number of staff members of a given family work together to relate a range of services of autonomous providers to a given client

Each of these mechanisms links the services delivered by state or local agencies. Although the mechanisms are not necessary for the simple delivery of services, they are essential if different agencies wish to integrate services and resources to improve service to clients.

The Families First program, in Missouri, is an excellent example of an interagency agreement for the effective provision of services. Families First is an interagency effort between the Department of Social Services and the Department of Mental Health to provide in-home crisis treatment to child welfare clients with mental disorders and school problems. Interagency service integration will continue to be an important means of delivering services.

Summary

The emerging trends discussed at length in this chapter—demographic changes, the aging of society, poverty, rising health care costs—combine to force public administrators to reevaluate how they approach decision making. It is critical that public administrators raise the level of problem identification, policy analysis, debate, and evaluation. Public administrators must act in an environment of molecular politics, where the arena of action is particularized, and of reallocation of resources, where resources are becoming more finite.

In addition, these trends can also be expected to emerge in public organizations in three ways (Wolf, Neves, Greenough, and Benton, 1987). First, there has been an overall slowing of organizational growth since the late 1970s, most dramatically reducing the number of middle-level managerial positions in the public sector. This trend is expected to continue and, indeed, to be exaggerated by a shortage of applicants for entry-level jobs in both the public and the private sectors.

Second, the upward mobility of the baby-boom generation will be severely restricted by both a decline in middle-level positions and the fact that most middle- and upper-level positions are already occupied by persons only slightly older than themselves. The present occupants of those positions will not reach retirement age for at least ten to twenty years, and this delay may mean career plateauing and underuse of skilled staff.

Third, the inability to motivate managerial staff with the promise of challenging work or promotional opportunities may well give rise to new perspectives on work, careers, and self-fulfillment. Without deliberate intervention, public administrators will increasingly derive satisfaction from their endeavors outside their organizations.

The implications of these dynamics for public administrators are legion. New principles of supervision in the public sector, emphasizing the quality of interpersonal relationships instead of extrinsic rewards, may be appropriate. Alternative strategies for promoting affirmative action may be required if traditional avenues of advancement are clogged. The public sector as a whole may need to be restructured to compensate for a dearth of applicants for entry-level jobs and a concurrent oversupply (in terms of jobs available) of persons trained for middle- and upper-level management.

Strategic thinking can help us recognize the external and internal forces acting on us and on our work. It can promote better management decisions and enhance our ability to cope with change, both within and outside organizations. Strategic thinking can prompt us to shape policies proactively and can project us beyond the status quo and into the future.

Innovation, imagination, and *boldness* are terms for the future, to be used by administrators today. The one-dimensional solutions of the past do not apply to the multifaceted problems of today. Administrators must redefine and reexamine their management capability while exhibiting leadership abilities.

References

Amidei, N. "The New Activism Picks Up Steam." *Public Welfare,* 1987, *45* (3), 21–26.

Auletta, K. *The Underclass.* New York: Random House, 1982.

Chase, W. H. *Issue Management: Origin of the Future.* Stamford, Conn.: Issue Action Publications, 1984.

Cohen, W. "There Are More Poor Than the Statistics Indicate." *Kansas City Star,* May 24, 1987, p. 6K.

Erickson, S. "The Transition Between Eras: The Long-Wave Cycle." *Futurist,* 1985, *19* (4), 40–44.

Ferra, P. J. (ed.). *Social Security: Prospects for Real Reform,* Washington, D.C.: Cata Institute, 1985.

Futures Group, Inc. *Notes: Workshop on the Future for the Senior Executive Staff, Social Security Administration, U.S. Department of Health and Human Services.* Baltimore, Md.: Futures Group, Inc., 1987.

Hageback, B. R. "Local Human Service Delivery: The Integration Imperative." *Public Administration Review,* 1979, *39* (6), 575–582.

Howe, H., III. "Poverty in American Society and Its Effects on Youth." Paper prepared for W. T. Grant Foundation's Commission on Youth, Family, Work, and the Future, New York, Mar. 7, 1988.

Kemp, A. Unpublished notes from census briefing, U.S. Department of Health and Human Services, Region VII, Kansas City, Missouri, May 1, 1987.

Kennedy, P. "The (Relative) Decline of America." *Atlantic,* Aug. 1987, pp. 29–38.

Magnet, M. "America's Underclass: What to Do?" *Fortune,* May 11, 1987, pp. 130–150.

Meyer, C. W. (ed.). *Social Security: A Critique of Radical Reform Proposals.* Lexington, Mass.: Heath, 1987.

Peters, T. J. *Thriving on Chaos.* New York: Knopf, 1987.

Reischauer, R. D. "America's Underclass." *Public Welfare,* 1987, *45* (4), 26–31.

Schmich, M. T. "Living Alone but Not Lonely." *Kansas City Times,* July 26, 1987, p. 1H.

U.S. Department of Commerce, Bureau of the Census. *Money, Income and Poverty Statistics of Families and Persons in the United States: 1985.* Washington, D.C.: U.S. Government Printing Office, 1987.

Urban Institute. *Annual Report.* Washington, D.C.: Urban Institute Press, 1986.

Vu, M. T. *World Population Projections 1985: Short- and Long-Term Estimates by Age and Sex with Related Demographic Statistics.* Baltimore, Md.: Johns Hopkins University Press, 1985.

Wattenberg, B. J. *The Birth Dearth.* New York; Pharos Books, 1987a.

Wattenberg, B. J. "The Birth Dearth: Dangers Ahead?" *U.S. News & World Report,* June 22, 1987b, pp. 56–63.

Wilson, W. J. *The Truly Disadvantaged.* Chicago: University of Chicago Press, 1987.

Wolf, J. F., Neves, C. M., Greenough, R. T., and Benton, B. "Greying at the Temples: Demographics of a Public Service Occupation." *Public Administration Review,* 1987, *47* (2), 190–198.

Jeffrey S. Luke
Gerald E. Caiden

7

Coping with Global Interdependence

In the last twenty years, public administration has been transformed by an increasingly complex globalized environment. Characteristic of this new international order are spreading networks of subtle and direct interconnection and interdependence that enmesh public officials at all levels of government, from one part of the planet to another. Such networks have always existed, although for the most part they have been weak, temporary, and insignificant. But since World War II, and particularly in recent years, global interdependence has gained strength, permanence, and significance.

Historically separate and autonomous jurisdictions are now closely linked in elaborate overlays of formal and informal arrangements. Global, regional, and local interdependence is connecting the political and economic fortunes of city, county, and state governments more closely than ever before. Modern self-governance has now become a process of managing global and local interdependence. Consequently, a major function of public executives—both elected and appointed officials—is to manage this increasing interdependence.

Increasing interdependence among formally separate and distinct jurisdictions creates both problems and opportunities. On the one hand, it adds new constraints on self-governance and administrative performance. It seriously challenges the viability of traditional political boundaries and administrative accountability and diminishes the relevance of many traditional approaches to public administration. On the other hand, global interdependence generates possibilities for new opportunities. To take advantage

Note: The authors wish to thank John Kincaid and Curt Ventriss for their comments on earlier drafts.

of these new opportunities, the public interest now demands administration that emphasizes a broader strategic vision, a capacity for integrative thinking, a catalytic style of leadership, an interest in multicultural learning, and a more fundamental change in ideology from separation to interconnectedness.

Global Interdependence

Globalization—the internationalization of trade, finance, and technology transfer—has been progressing for several decades. Compared to other Western countries, American citizens were late in recognizing global interdependence because of our emergence from World War II in a position of economic dominance (Kline, 1984). Awareness among American public administrators of expanding global interdependence began in the early 1970s as a result of a series of economic shocks stemming from the world energy crisis in 1973, followed by a world recession and by the emergence in the 1980s of recurrent and record export trade deficits. Separation and isolation are no more; they have been replaced by intricate networks of interdependence, first noted in the economic sphere and now spreading to a wide variety of other public policy areas, such as immigration, law enforcement, energy consumption, and public health. This "passing of remoteness" (Cleveland, 1985) forces public administrators to look outside their organizations more, and inward less.

Essentially, interdependence means interactions characterized by reciprocal effects among public administrators and involves "mutual dependence," where actions of one individual or agency both influence and are constrained by actions of another. Interdependence—high-cost, very important mutual dependence—can be further distinguished from interconnectedness (that is, low-cost, relatively unimportant mutual dependence) (Keohane and Nye, 1977). Although interdependence has evolved since the 1950s, fundamental changes have recently occurred in three particular areas: communications, economics, and natural resources.

Global "Infostructure." International space has shrunk; technology has dramatically lessened geographical and social distance. The world is being rendered smaller and smaller, making the interaction of international, national, and local systems more pervasive and intense (Rosenau, 1980). Recent advances in communications, transportation, and information processing have linked countries in such an interlocking system that actions in one country can have both immediate and delayed effects on American states and communities. And there can be no reversal. With satellite communications, jet transport, and personal computers, every part of the world is accessible and potentially visible to every other part. Distance has been rendered less relevant as the new "infostructure" makes it possible to reach anywhere electronically. Portable dishes now fit into small packing crates and are assembled like petals of a flower to receive pictures and data transmitted by satellites. Any organization can broadcast or receive video information from remote disaster areas and the most isolated hamlets. The result is a quantum jump in ability to identify, sort, retrieve, transmit, create, and apply information (Clarke, 1986). States, counties, and cities now easily interact with provinces and communities around the globe. Another result is expansion of the political arena, drawing in new participants and multiplying potentially influential actors in policymaking.

Global Economy. Perhaps the most important impact of the new global infostructure is that it has ushered in a truly global economy that goes well beyond mere international trade. All countries in recent years—including some, like Albania and Burma, that tried to cut themselves off—have experienced an escalation of economic and resource interdependence. The global economy is now characterized by an increasing reliance on foreign trade for the sale of domestic products, the acceleration of financial flows and capital movement across national boundaries, the growth of labor migration from one country to another, and the expansion of multinational corporations that globally link branch offices through electronic networks.

There has been a progression from local to regional markets, and from regional to national and then to international markets. There are more foreign companies competing in the United States, and more American companies are exporting or operating abroad. Currently in the United States, nearly 80 percent of new manufacturing jobs are related to exports. International trade, in terms of gross national product, has almost doubled over the past decade, despite a decline in the U.S. share of world manufacturing exports from 25 percent in 1960 to about 17 percent (Shelp, 1985). Where once national economies may have been relatively insulated from one another, there now exists one global interdependent economy, which forces openness, erodes national independence, and forces state and local government executives to think in global terms.

Natural Resources. Every government—local, regional, or national—now functions in a situation of resource scarcity. No jurisdiction is immune; none is self-sufficient and insulated from the outside world. National and local self-sufficiency is no longer possible in the production and consumption of natural resources. Furthermore, there is a growing awareness of interdependence among natural resources, particularly of the interconnectedness of natural life-support systems on the planet, and of the need to protect the ozone layer, the equatorial forests, and phytoplankton in the oceans. The concept *ecosystems* captures the essence of this interdependence among various levels of our biological and environmental systems.

Impacts on Public Policy

The global "infostructure," the international economic fabric, and the biological ecosystems create a web of overlapping interconnections and reduce separateness. Few problems can be isolated. Local unemployment, for example, cannot be resolved without reference to world trade problems and the relative strength of currencies. The substance of foreign policy is increasingly related to internal domestic issues, rather than just to international affairs. Foreign policies influence domestic policies; domestic variables shape and determine foreign policies. All national actions in foreign policy thus have state and local consequences.

The emerging links between international issues (usually considered foreign policy) and local problems (traditionally considered domestic policy) are expanding the arenas necessary for self-governance. Increasing numbers of critical policy issues facing local and state governments—such as job creation and environmental protection—are simultaneously and inseparably both domestic and international. Simple and local problems that were once isolated now tend to be replaced by interrelated problems that are more complex, are broader in scope, and require a multiplicity of corporate and public executives to share responsibility for corrective action. Critical policy problems can no longer be handled as if they were primarily domestic issues. Similarly, foreign policy directly affects the capacity for self-governance at the state and local levels. As a result, cities and states are now making their own foreign policies.

One pragmatic outcome of the new interdependence is that public administrators are forced to react not only to local, regional, and national events but also to international events and to initiate contacts with counterparts abroad. In the United States, the once-exclusive control of foreign affairs by the federal government has been broken by state and local governments (Elazar, 1984). States and cities are asserting their local interests in the global arena and are shaping their own foreign policies by pursuing three strategies. First, they and their umbrella organizations, such as the National Governors' Association and the National League of Cities, are learning how to successfully lobby federal government agencies on such issues as the trade barriers that directly affect their own jurisdictions and interests (Kincaid, 1984; Kline, 1984). Second, they are conducting their own independent transborder policies (Duchachek, 1984), crossing national borders to negotiate with their counterparts in Canada and Mexico over matters of mutual concern. The northern border states, for example, have signed over six hundred protocols with Canadian provinces on fire protection, international bridges and highways, and seaways and commerce, while the southern border states have negotiated agreements with Mexican authorities concerning industrial development, agriculture, undocumented workers, and cultural exchanges (Kincaid, 1984). Third, state and local administrators can be found in larger numbers conducting constituent diplomacy around the world—foreign diplomacy over the unique interests of their local constituents (Kincaid, 1988). They maintain permanent liaison offices in foreign countries, they organize missions to promote foreign investment, trade, and tourism, and they schedule trade and investment shows overseas.

International Economic Development. Many of these initiatives in domestic lobbying, transborder relations, and constituent diplomacy have been prompted by the need to stimulate state and local economic development. It is estimated that the United States lost as many as two and a half million jobs in the first half of the 1980s as a result of foreign competition, foreign capture of domestic markets, and the relocation of investment and employment by multinational corporations to Third World countries. The globalization of the economy, as well as the need to export, have stimulated firms and industries to look to state and local governments for assistance (Luke, Ventriss, Reed, and Reed, 1988).

In response, public administrators have encouraged local exports and sought foreign investment and tourism in order to foster economic development. Cities, counties, and states have developed a wide variety of international trade initiatives. Many programs involve nothing more than providing counseling, information, and technical assistance to business enterprises willing to try exporting. Most states now provide export information and conferences, trade missions, sales promotion, export consulting, trade shows, and international market studies and newsletters (Luke, Ventriss, Reed, and Reed, 1988). The second approach by state and local governments to stimulating international trade is the creation of export finance mechanisms. By 1988, twenty-three states were helping to finance local exports by providing loan guarantees, credit insurance, and direct subsidies (Sylvester, 1988). Promotion of exports by states, although there is considerable diversity of approaches, appears to have a positive impact on job creation (Coughlin and Cartwright, 1987).

International Public Finance. The globalization of the economy has created a second international arena for public administrators: international public finance. First, as financial markets become more interconnected and the U.S. tax-exempt bond market shrinks, state and local finance officers are turning to offshore capital markets as potential sources of funds for infrastructure and capital projects. Foreign debt is increasingly attractive because it can be a source of lower-cost financing, it is a new pool of debt financing for most municipal borrowers, and there are financing structures available in overseas capital markets that may not be available in the United States (McCarthy, 1988).

In addition to selling debt, public administrators are engaging in international investing. Overseas investments by pension plans of cities, special districts, and states have increased dramatically. In 1983, the total invested by these public agencies overseas was $144 million. This jumped 1,000 percent, to $1.4 billion in 1984, and by 1986 had reached $6 billion. States as varied as North Dakota and Massachusetts invest 10 percent of their pension funds in international markets (Emken, 1988). Moreover, the percentage of all public pension assets invested abroad is expected to increase, highlighting the increased global financial interdependence of state and local governments.

Other Emerging Policy Issues. Although fiscal issues have propelled public administrators into the global arena, the internationalization of state and local policy issues now includes a wider variety of social and environmental questions that demand attention, particularly immigration, law enforcement, environmental pollution, and education. Illegal immigration is of critical concern to border states and cities that have to provide public services for a swollen population and for a permanent underclass of economically marginal families. Environmental pollution, often bitterly contested across the borders, is a perennial problem, one that can become a strong local issue. For instance, Oregon billed the Soviet Union for costs incurred by state agencies as a result of radioactive contamination from the Chernobyl fallout. These are only a few examples of the expansion of social and political arenas that has created a truly interconnected intergovernmental and intersectoral web, which challenges the traditions of self-governance, local autonomy, and independent action.

Ideological Switch

Every generation inherits intellectual "baggage" that contains outdated or increasingly outmoded patterns of believing and behaving. Customary beliefs run counter to contemporary experience. Increasing interdependence in the realm of public business now requires a switch in the thinking of public administrators, from separation to interconnectedness. This ideological switch will not be easy to make. The idea of separation is strong in the American tradition. It predates the War of Independence and goes back to English legal theory, to the philosophies of Locke and Montesquieu, to the concept of town government in New England, to frontier individualism, and to the vision of a land with abundant room for all and an open door to all comers who wished to preserve their separate identities. It is embedded in the theory and application of the Constitution, in free competition and laissez-faire capitalism, and in political parochialism.

But the idea of separation is rooted in a past that is no more and cannot be recreated. The future belongs to interconnectedness. Effective public administration must implicitly assume the existence of global interdependence. Government jurisdictions and private bodies certainly have their own separate identities and their own unique internal governance or management systems. They are also legally separate entities; but they are no longer independent. The notion of separation is no longer even a useful fiction. Government jurisdictions are no longer autonomous self-reliant entities, separate from one another, separate from the private sector, or separate from global dynamics. The crystallization of global interdependence demands the replacement of the idea of separation with that of interconnectedness. Such an ideological shift entails changes in perceptions, values, and priorities. In addition, new policy approaches and managerial responses are required.

Policy Implications

The new interdependence arising from increasing interconnectedness is eroding conventional public administration and management. The experience and past working knowledge of public administrators are increasingly outdated and can even be detrimental. The new environment is significantly different from yesteryear's, where independence and self-sufficiency (that is, separation) guided politics and administration. The new constraints are real and compelling. Public action occurs in expanding and crowded policy arenas where power is dispersed and shared by multiple overlapping publics and policy actors. The capacity for any one jurisdiction or policy actor to act unilaterally is significantly reduced. Public administrators are increasingly vulnerable to outside influences, and they are increasingly dependent on others beyond their view. Policy choices and public actions often have unforeseen, unintended, undesirable, and indirect consequences beyond the normal externalities.

New public policies, based on the existence of global interdependence, are needed. They must now be formulated from larger frames of reference that assume an expanded set of interrelated variables to produce successful outcomes. American economic policy has failed to recognize adequately the profound changes that have taken place in the global economy (Thurow, 1980). Basic assumptions governing monetary policy, for example, are now quite misleading and certainly inaccurate (Bryant, 1980).

In an environmental context of interconnectedness, each problem becomes linked to every other problem, interweaving and causing unpredicted new problems. Each new public policy typically interacts with other policies, greatly increasing the probability of unanticipated outcomes. Thus, policies can easily create more problems that they solve, generating ripple effects that unpredictably extend far into the future (the temporal dimension), cross jurisdictional boundaries (the spatial dimension), and interfere with other governmental functions and policies (the functional dimension).

More appropriate policy strategies now require more modest programs and policy initiatives, which are based on longer-term goals or visions pursued collaboratively by intergovernmental and intersectoral stakeholders who inhabit particular policy domains. Such a collaborative strategy entails mobilizing interorganizational resources and formulating appropriate action for governmental and nongovernmental agencies. It requires a systematic response by policy actors, based on a shared interest in certain outcomes. New government policymaking strategies should be devised that can more effectively guide public action in an interconnected environment. They should be based on enlarged frameworks and models that assume interdependent relationships among increasing numbers of variables, be smaller in scope—incremental and experimental—yet sustained by some larger vision of policy goals, and be collective, collaborative efforts that mobilize a variety of interorganizational actors in the public, private, and nonprofit sectors.

Managerial Responses

Increasing global interdependence dissolves jurisdictional boundaries and weakens capacities for traditional self-governance. Public administrators concerned with organizational performance are now forced to pay increasing attention to the external dynamics of organizational environment and less attention to internal operations and productivity. In an interconnected context, public administrators are impelled to bring to their work an understanding of sectoral and governmental interdependence. More important, successful public administrators will have developed and will continue to refine skills in three specific areas: strategic thinking, catalytic leadership, and multicultural learning.

Strategic Thinking. The artful public administrator now becomes a "weaver" who sees patterns and connections in the global environment and threads them into effective networks capable of local public action. The public interest requires skills in strategic thinking: being able to think globally and act locally. At the administrative level, it involves moving incrementally and opportunistically toward strategic, longer-term goals. Strategic thinking also includes the following elements (Botkin and others, 1979; Luke, 1986; Mitroff and Kilmann, 1984):

- Stimulating the formulation of an overarching macropurpose from several different micropurposes
- Thinking about a web of local and global strategies that can be constantly updated and refined
- Considering the broadest possible set of local, national, and international stakeholders
- Detecting local-global interrelationships and assessing the importance of their linkages
- Anticipating what the future will demand of the public agency in order to shorten response time to problems
- Thinking systematically—that is, seeing multiple, rather than single, causes and effects

Catalytic Leadership. Strategic thinking alone will not suffice. It must also be joined by an ability to interact with policy actors and groups outside one's agency and to manage organizational interfaces. A leader in an interconnected environment must be skillful in stimulating action by a variety of stakeholders toward a particular goal or vision. This requires building coalitions and collaborating in situations where multiple stakeholders need to agree on goals and strategies. At the practical level, it requires more telephone calls, attendance at more meetings, and more travel outside the office.

More specifically, this interpersonal skill can be characterized as *catalytic leadership*—the ability to coalesce key public and private stakeholders around a critical global-local issue, such as acid rain, immigration, or economic diversification. A catalytic leader stimulates the development of a critical mass of diverse policy actors motivated by a goal or vision created collectively among them. Only such facilitators are able to move the interdependent web of government and corporate actors. A charismatic leader, with his or her individual vision, is seldom able to move the web of government and corporate actors in a particular policy direction.

Whereas most traditionally oriented public executives view environmental constraints created by the various webs of interdependence as a source of substantial grief, catalytic leaders understand that interconnectedness generates possibilities for new and as yet undiscovered opportunities. Emerging interdependence provides new opportunities for public action and an equally new set of available resources. The opening of international capital markets for financing local government bonds provides a good example. Interdependence and interconnectedness provide new resources and new patterns for initiating action in arenas previously thought separate and insulated. This increases the number of potential access points and creates new avenues for catalytic action to initiate particular policies.

Multicultural Learning. There is an increasing need for multicultural, international skills. First, an international perspective is required that reflects the current interdependent global economy, as well as an expanded knowledge of values, viewpoints, capital markets, and government structures in other nations. Second, increased skills in international communications and foreign languages will enable public administrators to observe, think, and act in an interdependent world.

The globalization of the economy, in particular, creates a need for heightened understanding of the cultures, markets, and languages of other countries. Public administrators must learn, for example, how to discuss exports, deal with foreign officials, and develop understanding of investment opportunities abroad that affect the vitality of a state's or a community's economy.

Summary

Public administrators are discovering that there is much that can be learned from the new interdependence. Their problems are shared by many, and possible solutions are already being implemented elsewhere. To be effective, public administrators will need a lively intellectual curiosity. They are going to have to read more, inform themselves about the international and national scenes, travel more, spend more of their time reflecting on world events and working out their real implications, mix more with foreign counterparts, negotiate more border crossings, and facilitate more combined operations and cooperative ventures.

Strategic thinking is also required. It involves an awareness of global interconnectedness and the ability to assess the international ripples that emanate from different directions at the same time and are occasionally obscured by the shock waves sent out from exceptional events. Sooner or later, external influences will affect local situations, and it is better to have anticipated such influences than to have to react hastily and improvise.

One clear implication is that any distinction that may still exist between politics and management in the conduct of public business is fast disappearing. Elected and appointed officials have to master the identical challenge of managing global interdependence. To do this, elected officials must comprehend the new realities of the much-enlarged managerial world, while appointed officials must think in broader political, economic, social, and cultural terms. Together, they may realize that while effective action may have become more difficult, the internationalization of public business and the enlargement of personal networks have made their jobs easier. No longer do they have to be so original. They can now borrow more from better practice elsewhere, with greater certainty that such practice will probably work better locally, too. Improving the performance of public organizations depends on understanding the new interconnected environment of public administration and mastering the new interdependence.

References

Botkin, J. W., and others. *No Limits to Learning: Bridging the Human Gap.* Elmsford, N.Y.: Pergamon Press, 1979.

Bryant, R. *Money and Monetary Policy in Interdependent Nations.* Washington, D.C.: Brookings Institution, 1980.

Clarke, M. *Revitalizing State Economies.* Washington, D.C.: National Governors' Association, 1986.

Cleveland, H. *The Knowledge Executive: Leadership in an Information Society.* New York: Dutton, 1985.

Coughlin, C. C., and Cartwright, P.A. "An Examination of State Foreign Exports and Manufacturing Employment." *Economic Development Quarterly,* 1987, *1* (3), 257–267.

Duchachek, I. D. "The International Dimension of Subnational Self-Government." *Publius,* 1984, *14* (4), 5–31.

Elazar, D. "Introduction: Symposium on Federated States and International Relations." *Publius,* 1984, *14* (4), 1–4.

Emken, A. R. "International Investing in State and Local Governments." *Government Finance Review,* 1988, *4* (1), 33–42 (special supplement).

Keohane, R., and Nye, J. S. *Power and Interdependence.* Boston: Little, Brown, 1977.

Kincaid, J. "The American Governors in International Affairs." *Publius,* 1984, *14* (4), 95–114.

Kincaid, J. "Implications of Constituent Diplomacy for the Nature and Future of the Nation State." In H. J. Michelmann and P. Soldators (eds.), *Federalism and International Relations: The Role of Subnational Units.* Oxford, England: Oxford University Press, 1988.

Kline, J. "The International Economic Interests of U.S. States." *Publius,* 1984, *14* (4), 81–94.

Luke, J. S. "Finishing the Decade: Local Government to the 1990s." *State and Local Government Review,* 1986, *18* (3), 132–137.

Luke, J. S., Ventriss, C., Reed, B. J., and Reed, C. *Managing Economic Development: A Guide to State and Local Strategies.* San Francisco: Jossey-Bass, 1988.

McCarthy, C. "Offshore Financing and State/Local Government Capital Financing Needs." *Government Finance Review,* 1988, *4* (1), 25–32 (special supplement).

Mitroff, I., and Kilmann, R. *Corporate Tragedies.* New York: Praeger, 1984.

Rosenau, J. *The Study of Global Interdependence: Essays on the Transnationalization of World Affairs.* New York: Nicholas, 1980.

Shelp, R. K. "A New Strategy for Economic Revitalization." *Economic Development Review,* 1985, *3* (3), 24–31.

Sylvester, K. "Exporting Made Easy." *Governing,* 1988, *1* (4), 36–42.

Thurow, L. *The Zero-Sum Society: Distribution and the Possibilities for Economic Change.* New York: Basic Books, 1980.

Part Two

Effective Administrative and Organizational Systems

Public administrators are creatures of their environments. They function within a variety of complex systems that are intended to shape their behavior and decisions. At the same time, the effectiveness of the systems within which public administrators work often depends on their choices and actions. Part Two explores these facets of the context of administrative action.

What are the primary systems that create the context of administrative action? Among them are laws, governmental institutions, the intergovernmental system, work organizations, and strategic plans. The character and permanence of each of these systems differ quite radically. At one extreme, the U.S. Constitution embodies the relatively permanent principles that are at the heart of the American social contract. At the other extreme, strategic plans epitomize temporary, ad hoc systems designed to impose order on the sometimes chaotic and often incomprehensible worlds within which public officials must function effectively.

The structure and content of these systems provide a variety of cues and messages to which public administrators must be attentive. Some of the messages—public access, due process, public control—are mandates of our governmental system that depend on administrative compliance. Without such compliance, our system of governance would soon lose its legitimacy and thereby its moral and instrumental force. Other messages—coordination with other jurisdictions, the thinking through of long-term consequences—are less binding but still important for the effective functioning of government.

The public administrator is not passive, someone who simply reacts to cues and lives with the constraints inherent in these systems. Instead, the public administrator plays a variety of active, discretionary roles within legal, governmental, and organizational systems. One of the most important roles is that of energizer of inert rules and processes. Laws and organizations become living entities via the people who implement, enforce, and manage them. Ironically, much of what public administrators do to energize these systems involves routine transactions, but, because of the fragmented nature of our governmental systems, public administrators are also often called on to patch together solutions to problems. A common venue of patchwork solutions involves problems that span multiple levels and units of government: the intergovernmental system.

Within these systems, public administrators also fill a creative role. Because the problems that gravitate to the public agenda may be novel, chronic, or highly charged, they demand innovation and ingenuity if they are to be solved. For instance, the state government administrator attempting to cope simultaneously with federal mandates, demands for local autonomy, and a fixed budget is pressed to seek flexible solutions that permit all parties to a relationship to achieve their objectives.

Public administrators also serve as designers of the environments in which they operate. Although some of the systems within which public administrators function are relatively stable, others change at the discretion of administrators. The legal system, for example, has been relatively stable over the course of American history, but the design of administrative organizations has changed radically.

Public administrators are creatures of their environments, but they respond proactively to them. Part Two addresses the problems and situations that public administrators confront, as well as appropriate responses to them.

8

Phillip J. Cooper

Legal Tools for Accomplishing Administrative Responsibilities

Americans are fond of repeating that ours is a government of laws, not men. Yet as administrators, we are frustrated and fearful about legal restrictions on managerial discretion. Nevertheless, even those who accept the proposition that administrative responsibility ought to come from within the public service, rather than be externally imposed by threat of sanction, expect the law to be a necessary guarantor of proper public behavior.

In truth, ours is a system of laws and people. Administrative law is not a rigid, rule-bound barrier to good management. Although the law of administration was intended to meet a variety of broad demands for responsibility, it was devised largely by people who understood the problems faced by administrators. Moreover, while it is necessarily true that legal requirements do constrain administrators, they also embody a variety of concepts and procedures that are useful administrative tools. Beyond their utility, though, legal mechanisms of accountability are important because they have a legitimating capacity, which contributes to the perception that public administration is acceptable within the American constitutional framework.

This chapter will stress the utility of due process requirements, rule-making guidelines, and judicial review. While attention will be given to these specific mechanisms for ensuring that the link between the constitutional framework and administration is preserved, the touchstone for the discussion is the supremacy of law.

The Rule and Supremacy of Law

Unlike the approaches discussed in other chapters of this volume, legal forms of responsibility trace their force back to the supremacy of law. Although the term seems abstract, and remote from routine administrative activities, it is very much associated with day-to-day problems. Indeed, one of the major struggles in administrative law has been to operationalize this concept in some workable fashion.

Rule Versus Supremacy. One distinction that is essential to an understanding of the supremacy of law is the difference between the *rule of law* and the *supremacy of law*. Under the tradition of the rule of law (an ancient idea), subjects were to live under law crafted by the ruler, obey its dictates, and deal with each other accordingly. The idea of the supremacy of law, which came later, was an important change because it insisted that the law binds both the rulers and the ruled.

The notion of supremacy was clearly comprehended by the framers of the Constitution: "In framing a government which is to be administered by men over men, the great difficulty lies in this: you must first enable the government to control the governed; and in the next place oblige it to control itself" (Hamilton, Madison, and Jay, 1961, p. 322). The Constitution created the basic law to govern both the rulers and the ruled, but, by the nature of constitutions, it could do so only in broad compass. The closest the Constitution comes to a specific mention of the supremacy of law is in Article VI, which states: "This Constitution, and the Laws of the United States which shall be made in Pursuance thereof . . . shall be *the supreme law of the Land;* and the Judges in every State shall be bound thereby, any Thing in the Constitution or Laws of any State to the Contrary notwithstanding" (emphasis added).

The phrase "a government of laws, not men" came to us by a circuitous route, which can be traced from Aristotle's *Politics* through Harrington's *Oceana* to the Massachusetts Constitution, before it was ultimately placed in our constitutional law through dictum in Chief Justice Marshall's opinion in *Marbury* v. *Madison* (1803). The maxim that no man is above the law came to American jurisprudence in another Supreme Court opinion. The Court warned, "No man is so high that he is above the law. No officer of the law may set that law at defiance with impunity. All the officers of government, from the highest to the lowest, are creatures of the law, and are bound to obey it" (*United States* v. *Lee*, 1882, p. 220). Unlike earlier governments, in which subjects took oaths of obedience to those who governed, officers of American government, from the president down, are sworn to uphold the Constitution and the laws made under its authority.

Contemporary Manifestation. While virtually everyone subscribes to the concept of supremacy of law, there is substantial disagreement about just what that principle entails. The need to define and implement this fundamental norm is particularly acute where unelected officials exercise substantial power. Most commentators have argued that the supremacy of law requires the use of legally established principles (rather than arbitrary decisions), equality before the law, protection of individual rights, constraint on agencies by authoritative legal rules, the application of administrative power by authorized and regular processes, impartiality, uniformity, and some degree of certainty or predictability in administrative behavior (see Dickinson, 1927; Pound, 1942).

The problem is that administrators must have discretion to apply their expertise and experience to public problems in order to achieve effective and efficient solutions. If the constraints of law are so tightly applied that everything requires excessively formal processes, administrators will be deprived of that essential flexibility. It was precisely this dilemma that prompted Frank (1942) and, later, Davis (1969, pp. 28–41) to warn about "extravagant versions of the rule of law." Davis argued that the goal of administrative law must be to find a proper accommodation between the need for protection against abuse of power and the importance of ensuring sufficient discretion. Frank made a similar claim (1942, p. 9), asserting that we must not believe that we can really have a government of laws and not men. Rather, he said, we must work toward the more realistic goal of "a government of laws, administered by the right kind of men."

Modern administrative law has evolved with this sense of the need to maintain the ideal of the supremacy of law and to temper it with recognition of administrative reality. Although it places constraints on administrative flexibility, its procedural requirements and substantive standards can be useful administrative tools, serving day-to-day needs while also supporting the fundamental values that underlie the American constitutional system.

Constitution, Statute, and Rules: The Family of Tools

The same authorities most often cited as bases for holding administrators accountable are also the foundations for administrative power and discretion. In that sense, the constitutions, statutes, and rules that govern administration are tools to accomplish administrative responsibilities. Among the most important legal devices employed are constitutional powers, statutes, executive orders, administrative orders, and rules.

Constitutional Foundations. Public administration is very much a constitutional activity, even if the United States Constitution does not specify the nature and powers of public bureaucracy (Rohr, 1986). State constitutions may establish administrative agencies (usually commissions), but they rarely provide detailed information on how those or other agencies created by state legislatures are to use the legal power they possess. Nevertheless, all legal authority flows from a constitutional foundation.

Broad interpretations of commerce powers, taxing and spending powers, and the so-called necessary and proper clause have served as foundations both for the legislative acts that established administrative agencies (known as enabling acts) and for others that, over time, have assigned them additional responsibilities. While there have been renewed challenges to the constitutional foundations of administrative authority (see *Commodity Futures Trading Commission* v. *Schor,* 1986; *Bowsher* v. *Synar,* 1986), there is no evidence that the judiciary is on the verge of substantially restricting the role or importance of administrative agencies. Neither is there any substantial movement to prevent legislatures from initiating new types of organizations or new tasks for existing agencies.

Nevertheless, there are limits on the constitutional authority that Congress or state legislatures may confer, and on the constraints that can be included in delegations of administrative authority. These constitutional restrictions generally fall within the categories of separation of powers, federalism, and Bill of Rights guarantees.

The Constitution creates three branches, and there are occasional disputes among them that require resolution, but most participants have realized that it is extremely difficult to draw those boundaries. Even if it can be done, it is not in the best political interest of any of the players to press the point too far. Thus, Fisher has argued forcefully that we function most often under a political system in which power is shared (Fisher, 1981, 1985a).

Even so, there are limits to just how far such informal working arrangements can be maintained. Hence, the Supreme Court was recently called on to resolve the clash over the Gramm-Rudman-Hollings Deficit Reduction Act and, before that, the expanded use of the legislative veto of proposed administrative rules (*Bowsher* v. *Synar,* 1986; *Immigration and Naturalization Service* v. *Chadha,* 1983). In both cases, it found violation of the doctrine of separation of powers. The lesson from recent history seems to be that questions concerning separation of powers are far more alive than many had assumed in the early 1970s but that, in general, the judiciary is unlikely in the near term to fundamentally alter the practices by which agencies have been accorded responsibility and authority in the past half-century.

The increasing American intergovernmental complexity over the past two decades has presented a variety of issues of federalism. Despite the fact that the Supreme Court and, to some extent, the lower courts have recently been staffed with judges who are more conservative than some of their predecessors, there are few indications that states and localities will be able to successfully block federal legislative or administrative initiatives. In cases challenging the degree to which federal actions could preempt participation by states or localities in a variety of policies, the courts have usually upheld the federal claims (see *Capital Cities Cable* v. *Crisp,* 1984; *Michigan Canners and Freezers Assn.* v. *Agricultural Marketing and Bargaining Board,* 1984). The only significant recent exception was the Supreme Court's ruling upholding the California nuclear moratorium that blocked new power plants until the issue of nuclear waste is resolved (*Pacific Gas & Electric* v. *California State Energy Commission,* 1983). That case is generally regarded as an exception to the trend, rather than a new direction.

For a brief period, there appeared to be a change in the judicial definition of just how close the federal government could come to the core of local government decisions, with a ruling that the Fair Labor Standards Act, as applied to local government employees, violated the principle of federalism (*National League of Cities* v. *Usery,* 1976). The apparent change was cut short when the Supreme Court overturned that case in *Garcia* v. *San Antonio Metropolitan Transit Authority* (1985). The courts have also continued their general willingness to allow the federal government to employ grant programs to regulate indirectly what it cannot get at directly, although the Supreme Court has warned that there are outer boundaries to federal demands under grants (*Pennhurst State School and Hospital* v. *Halderman,* 1981).

The final limits to administrative authority in the Constitution are those generally associated with the Bill of Rights. As it always has, the judiciary stands ready to block governmental action that violates free speech or association protections under the First Amendment, prohibitions against unreasonable searches and seizures, due process guarantees, or assurances of equal protection of the law. There has been a movement, however, to assess constitutional requirements in light of administrative realities. Hence, the Supeme Court has done the following:

- Allowed administrators greater latitude to prevent and punish allegedly insubordinate and disruptive behavior by employees (*Connick* v. *Myers,* 1983)
- Permitted agencies to limit, to some degree, the settings in which First Amendment activities are permitted by persons from outside the agency (*Perry Education Assn.* v. *Perry Local Education Assn.,* 1983; *Cornelius* v. *NAACP Legal Defense and Education Fund,* 1985)
- Sanctioned a modified standard of probable cause for purposes of search warrants sought by administrative agencies (*Donovan* v. *Dewey,* 1981; *Dow Chemical* v. *United States,* 1986)
- Created a more relaxed standard for determining whether, when, and what kind of a process is due a person with a case before an agency, a standard that takes into consideration the administrative burden and costs to the agency of additional or substitute safeguards (*Mathews* v. *Eldridge,* 1976)

If the Court has gone too far in several of these areas, that does not change the fact that these decisions allow increased administrative discretion.

Importance of Statutes. Constitutional powers and limits are not self-enforcing, of course. Indeed, on a day-to-day basis, most administrators must rely principally on statutory authority and must be alert to statutory limits.

Statutes create agencies and define the outer boundaries of their powers. They also establish the jurisdictions within which those powers can be exercised. It is one thing to have legal power, but it is another to possess jurisdiction to exercise it in a given context. Furthermore, there are several procedural statutes defining the manner in which granted powers may be used. Although the exact requirements vary, the same types of procedural statutes are often found at both the federal and the state level. They include administrative procedure acts (APAs), governmental contracting laws such as the Federal Property and Administrative Services Act (FPASA), and human resource management statutes such as the Civil Service Reform Act (CSRA). In several cases, there are packages of statutes (such as in the case of the APA, which incorporates not only the original procedure act but also the Freedom of Information Act, Right to Privacy Act, Regulatory Flexibility Act, and so on, or the CSRA, which incorporates by reference the provisions of the federal legislation prohibiting various forms of job discrimination). While these statutes place limits of one sort or another on agencies' action, they also provide tools and legal support for actions that are properly performed.

In general, courts interpret the provisions of statutes strictly, on the grounds that the legislature can remedy erroneous interpretations without great difficulty. Legislators, however, are rarely able to anticipate all the specific situations that may arise under their statutory mandates, and so they generally wish to leave agencies some discretion in enforcement. Hence, agencies play important ongoing roles in statutory interpretation. Under the doctrine of contemporaneous administrative construction, courts are obliged to grant considerable discretion to the interpretation of a statute by the agency charged with its enforcement, on the grounds that the agency has both experience and expertise in that field (*Commodity Futures Trading Commission* v. *Schor,* 1986, pp. 688–689; *Chevron U.S.A.* v. *Natural Resources Defense Council,* 1984, pp. 844–845).

Further, the Supreme Court and the U.S. Circuit Court of Appeals for the D.C. Circuit have permitted administrators to exercise substantial enforcement discretion under acts that the agencies are charged with enforcing. Two areas of activity have been particularly important. The first concerns the decision to act in a given case. The Supreme Court has said that administrative discretion is presumptively unreviewable and should be overturned only if the statute involved contains standards that require enforcement in certain situations (*Heckler* v. *Chaney,* 1985). There has also been a trend, particularly in the Supreme Court, away from permitting so-called private attorneys general to enforce statutory provisions where an agency would not or could not do so (see *Middlesex County Sewerage Authority* v. *National Sea Clammers Assn.,* 1981).

The courts have also allowed agencies substantial discretion in choosing to engage in deregulation from within, even if the legislature has not indicated a desire for administrative retrenchment (*FCC* v. *WNCN Listeners*

Guild, 1981; *Office of Communications of the United Church of Christ* v. *FCC,* 1983). That does not relieve agencies of their procedural responsibilities in, for example, rescinding rules (see *Motor Vehicle Manufacturers* v. *State Farm Mutual,* 1983), but it does demonstrate a willingness to permit considerable judgment to agencies, so long as the decision is supported by an adequate record that provides evidence and reasoning supporting the deregulatory decision.

Judges are stressing the use of legislative history to determine congressional intent in cases where the legislature's mandate is unclear. This suggests that the prudent administrator should ensure that everyone in his or her agency is as well trained as possible in the legislation that the agency is charged with implementing.

The nature of legislation has changed considerably since about 1970. Statutes have become more detailed and include a variety of boilerplate provisions. These mandate rulemaking, set time limits for implementation by rule or otherwise, prescribe adjudication requirements beyond what might be mandated by an administrative procedure act or the due process clause of the Constitution, call for legislative veto devices or some variation on them, and set sunset deadlines that call for complete examination of an agency's performance within a certain time or provide for an end to the agency's legislative authorization. The fact that federal courts have struck down the legislative veto on the grounds of separation of powers has not affected the many state legislative vetoes. For that matter, Congress has continued to include veto provisions in new legislation (Fisher, 1985b). Finally, legislatures at both the state and the federal levels have increased their use of regulatory analysis clauses, which require one or another form of impact assessment. These most often take the form of cost-benefit requirements or assessments of burden, with particular attention to the impact of administrative actions on small businesses.

The Executive Order. In the past several years, presidents and governors have moved to shape policy through the use of executive orders. As mandates having the force of law, these orders have been valuable tools. While executive orders must state the authority on which the executive purports to act, that has not proved to be a formidable barrier to the use of this particular tool, since presidents and governors alike have been willing to assert broad constitutional delegations of executive power as the basis of their pronouncements. Executive orders may not violate properly enacted statutes, and they may be overturned by the legislature (although such actions are rare).

The executive order is a particularly useful device, since it allows a chief executive to make legally binding policy throughout the executive branch. It allows for the creation of standardized procedures and permits a substantial amount of executive control in an administrative environment that tends to resist centralized dominance.

The executive order is a troublesome device, however, because it allows the chief executive to exercise powers that may indirectly prevent agencies from carrying out their legal obligations. That has been the experience, for example, under President Reagan's Executive Orders 12291 and 12498, which govern agency rulemaking. Although the orders contain language limiting their applicability to "the extent permitted by law," their practical effect has been to prevent agencies from promulgating rules required by Congress within statutorily defined time limits (*Environmental Defense Fund* v. *Thomas,* 1986). Similarly, although executive orders are justified as affecting only those within the executive branch, such mandates inevitably have an impact on those who deal with agencies, because they shape the behavior of those agencies in fundamental ways. The orders can also create situations in which other important elements of administrative law, designed to ensure effective and legitimate administration, are undermined (Cooper, 1986).

Rules as Tools. Administrative law recognizes three tools that can be used by administrative agencies in the performance of their duties. The first is a *rule,* which is characteristically a general statement intended to cover future actions, and which applies to many or all of those with whom an agency does business. Rates established by regulatory agencies are considered, for all intents and purposes, to be rules. Those who issue rules often see themselves simply as implementers of adopted policies, rather than as quasi-legislators, and yet that is the legal character of their acts. The other two types of tools are *orders* and *licenses.* Orders are statements about the rights, duties, or legal status of those over whom an agency has jurisdiction. They usually concern specific parties and events that have already taken place. A license is a special form of order. Many administrators, particularly direct service providers, do not think of themselves as issuing orders, yet that is what they do each time they grant or disallow a claim or a request for service.

Orders (or decisions, as many laypersons describe them) are taken for granted as the output that one desires from administrative agencies. Rules, by contrast, have often been regarded, particularly during the 1970s and the 1980s, as useless, wasteful, constraining edicts, issued by overzealous, excessively intrusive bureaucrats. Indeed, political candidates have committed themselves to the goal of reducing the number of pages printed each year in the *Federal Register,* the official organ for dissemination of executive-branch policy pronouncements. Notwithstanding all the political rhetoric and the traditional American resistance to anything that constrains our behavior, rules are useful and important tools. There are legal, historical, and pragmatic reasons for this seemingly odd assertion.

For many agencies in which the promulgation of rules is simply required by statute, there can be no serious question about whether rules should be issued. The fact that agencies are often required by law to adopt rules on matters that the legislators who framed a law could not themselves resolve does not alter that administrative obligation. Further, courts have sometimes held that agencies are required to issue rules, even if the statutes involved did not specify such a requirement (see *Allison* v. *Block,* 1983; *Ford Motor Co.* v. *FTC,* 1981).

A complex set of historical forces culminated in the federal Administrative Procedure Act's discussion of rules and rulemaking. After two decades of administrative experience under that act, virtually every knowledgeable student of the subject called for wider use of rules and fewer announcements of agency policies on a case-by-case basis through orders (see Friendly, 1962). Critics explained that the case-by-case approach smacked too much of making up the rules in the middle of the game. Moreover, one of the critical purposes of administrative law reform in 1946 was the development of a mechanism for agencies' policy pronouncements.

There are several practical arguments in favor of rules as tools. First, rules provide predictability for those outside as well as within the agency. Within, predictability enhances the likelihood of orderly and efficient operation. Outside, rules convey the idea that those who comply can avoid costly conflicts with agencies and will be able to obtain grants or other forms of largesse that agencies may be able to dispense.

Rules also have importance for the future. They provide policy history, against which later administrators can evaluate performance and develop new approaches. Similarly, rules assist legislators in conducting oversight, so that they can assess agencies' performance and determine whether modifications should be made in legislatively mandated programs. While it is true that rules are constraining while in force, they can also be changed.

Legal Approaches to Responsible Administration

The administrative procedure acts adopted by the federal government and the states pursue effective and responsible administration by prescribing a set of procedures. Critics of the proposed acts had argued that administrative agencies could be said to comport with the rule of law only if their policymaking was open, orderly, and participative, if adjudications were characterized by the assurance of minimum due process protections, and if some device were available to ensure that agency decisions were subject to judicial review. The essential elements of administrative law that came from these demands for reform included rulemaking, adjudication, judicial review, and requirements for fair information practices. These procedures are themselves instruments for the administrator.

Rulemaking. Procedures for rulemaking have changed since the federal Administrative Procedure Act was adopted in the 1940s. While some of the modifications were designed to make the process more effective, others were added in an effort to inhibit the promulgation of regulations. Those facts notwithstanding, rulemaking is still a useful administrative device.

Under the basic requirements of administrative law, substantive or legislative rules, which are rules intended to implement legislation and carry the force of law, should be made through a procedure that is regular, open, and participative. Other types of rules, such as procedural or interpretative rules (sometimes called *guidelines*), can be adopted without these steps. The essential elements of rulemaking are notice and an opportunity to comment (hence, the term *notice and comment rulemaking*). At its base, this procedure requires publication of a proposed rule in the *Federal Register* (or its state equivalent), time for interested parties to communicate their views in writing, and, in due course, publication of the final rule. In addition to this informal rulemaking process, there is also a formal rulemaking procedure that has more of the character of a formal adjudication. It is used in those few cases where the legislature has called for it.

The procedure generally employed today is termed *hybrid* because it has at its base a notice and comment process that is supplemented by other features intended to create an adequate rulemaking record. An adequate rulemaking record is one that demonstrates that the agency has made serious attempts to provide notice to interested parties, with sufficient time for them to respond; that serious efforts have been made to obtain comments, either in writing or through informal hearings; that the agency has considered the criticisms and comments it has received (generally, summaries of comments and brief responses are provided); that there is a body of evidence and data on which the agency has relied in reaching its final decision, and which is described in sufficient detail for legislators and others to examine the bases of the agency's action; and that there is an explanation of how the agency reasoned from that evidence to its conclusion.

Even when an agency could get away without observing its minimum requirements, rulemaking provides a number of advantages over ad hoc announcements of policy. For one thing, it encourages orderly policymaking. Second, it encourages participation, without yielding control of the process to political interests. In addition to participation, rulemaking also supports a sense that the agency is accessible and open to public involvement, which helps an agency build coalitions in support of its actions and, on some occasions, to coopt some of its opponents. It also provides for development of the kind of decision-making record that will permit future administrators to assess past performance and shape new policies. Finally, it provides a defensible position for an administrative agency whose decisions are challenged in court or in the legislature. These arguments in favor of the process remain valid, even though rulemaking has been discouraged by the addition in the past decade of complex requirements for regulatory analysis and regulatory flexibility analysis, mandated by executive order and legislation.

Adjudication. One of the major criticisms lodged against administrative law in its formative years was precisely that it violated that most basic tenet of the supremacy of law, which held that before anyone could be seriously injured by government, he or she was entitled to the commonly accepted principles of due process of law. Legally, of course, procedural due process is mandated by the Fifth Amendment when federal action is involved and by the Fourteenth Amendment when states or localities are the decision makers. Even so, there has been considerable disagreement over the years about whether, in a given situation, process is due, what kind of process is due, and when procedural protections are due.

At the heart of this discussion is a dramatic difference in perspective on the purpose of due process (Tribe, 1978, Section 10-7). During much of the 1960s and into the 1970s, administrative due process was considered intrinsically important. Its value stemmed from the idea of protecting any citizen from harm at the hands of arbitrary administrators. Thus, the Supreme Court spoke of the need to provide due process protection whenever someone was made to suffer a ''grievous loss'' at the hands of government. During the Burger Court years, however, the approach switched to an instrumental perspective. Under this approach, adjudication is viewed as a simple fact-finding process. Its value is in its ability to accurately find fact in properly limited legal circumstances. Moreover, the Court has adopted the idea that in determining the process due, courts should take a narrower view of the kinds of injuries that qualify for due process protection and consider the administrative and fiscal burdens placed on an agency (*Mathews* v. *Eldridge,* 1976, p. 335). While the judiciary had been moving for two decades to expand procedural due process, the more recent trend has been in the other direction.

Due process requirements may come from legislation or agency rules as well as from the Constitution. Those requirements may mandate more process than the Constitution requires, but they may not permit less. When state or local governments are involved, of course, they must also attend to the requirements of state constitutions.

The basic requirements of due process are generally known. The party involved must be given notice of the proposed action and the authority on which it is based. There must be some opportunity to respond, although not always in a formal hearing. There must be a fair decision maker, one with sufficient independence to allow an unbiased judgment. There is an obligation to render a decision on the record (rather than from information acquired from rumor or the like). Finally, there should be some vehicle of appeal.

Despite the apparently burdensome character of due process, adjudication, like rulemaking, is a useful administrative tool. Its utility has to do with internal management and external interaction with agency clientele. Externally, the availability of some kind of due process conveys both a sense of fundamental fairness in the way the agency behaves and a concomitant sense of equal treatment. It enhances the decision-making process, not so much because adjudicative decisions are necessarily best calculated to reach truth but because it keeps the decision maker aware of the individual character of the decision and alert to its impact on individuals. Internally, it enhances morale by conveying a sense of fair treatment. It also tends to assist in squelching rumors by eliminating the belief that decisions are reached by some mysterious conspiratorial process.

Due process would be worthwhile even if administrative law required relatively extensive procedures; but, in fact, considerable flexibility is permitted. Some administrators have found that such alternative dispute-resolution techniques as rudimentary mediation and arbitration lend themselves to particular environments. The form is not nearly so critical as the presence of the basic conceptual elements of due process and, above all, the sense of fundamental fairness.

Judicial Review. One of the last aspects of law that most public administrators would think of as useful is judicial review. Indeed, the very idea that a judge is assessing one's performance conjures up a mixed image of failure (Why else would we be in court?), determination (We're going to show those people!), and anxiety (What's going to happen to all our efforts?), yet judicial review is a normal part of the policy process, a part that has positive as well as negative significance.

Judicial review of administrative action generally poses a series of questions to administrators. These inquiries ask whether the agency violated constitutional provisions or statutory obligations, failed to adhere to procedural requirements, was arbitrary and capricious, abused discretion, or acted without substantial evidence on the record as a whole to support its decision. The task of the courts is to determine not whether the agency reached the best conclusion but rather whether its decision could have been reached by a reasonable person on the basis of the record that was before the agency at the time of the administrative action.

In addition to judicial review, challengers of agencies' actions may seek criminal prosecution, pursue claims for money damages, or request injunctive relief (an order requiring an agency to cease illegal conduct and perhaps to take actions to remedy previous violations). Criminal prosecution is rare. Damage claims are important and may be threatening, but many jurisdictions indemnify their employees (that is, pay their fines if they lose lawsuits). The trade-off has been the movement of the federal courts, in particular, to reduce the frequency, scope, and depth of their injunctions in return for providing injured citizens the opportunity to recover damages later. That may not be the best arrangement for administrators, but we cannot have things both ways. We cannot claim immunity from money damages and simultaneously insist that courts avoid using injunctions to correct violations.

Most court involvement, however, is judicial review in which the plaintiff seeks reversal of an administrative decision. Judicial review can provide a number of benefits. First, it offers feedback on statutory interpretation and tells administrators whether they are correct in their understanding of legislation. When legislators have handed difficult or ambiguous laws to administrative agencies, such feedback can be useful. Among other things, it permits an agency some defense against repeated claims by legislators that their manifold post hoc interpretations of statutes should govern agency action. Courts also provide feedback on procedural questions. Often these decisions are favorable, providing administrators with external validation of their actions. Courts also produce interpretations of potentially conflicting legal requirements, helping beleaguered administrators out of difficult situations. Judges can provide instructions that protect agencies against political interference from the executive branch as well as from the legislature.

At a more general level, judicial review provides a mechanism for integrating the decisions made by agencies into the existing body of law. Without that, administrative decisions would not operate under the same rule of law as all other elements of American life. With it, rulemaking proceedings and adjudications can be reconciled with the requirements of constitutional law, statutory interpretations, and the rest of American law. Judicial review, then, conveys a sense of administration as a legitimate part of the constitutional whole, as opposed to a system of disconnected, unaccountable, exotic decisions rendered by unelected elites.

There are even cases in which administrators have been able to use the fact that their agencies have been found in violation of the law to compel political officials to respond to basic needs. Decisions about prisons, mental hospitals, and schools have allowed politicians to provide services they knew were necessary without having to take the politically difficult position of voting expenditures for, say, prison reform outside the context of a judicial mandate.

The point is not that one should make decisions with the hope that they will be overturned, but that judicial review in itself is not necessarily without benefits. It certainly plays an absolutely essential role in supporting the legitimacy of administrative power.

Information Policy. The remaining common element of administrative procedure that acts at the federal and state levels is what can be called fair information practices laws. These usually include some variation on the *Federal Register* Act, which requires publication of executive-branch official decisions. Most such practices contain open-government statutes, such as a freedom-of-information provision and a so-called ''government in the sunshine'' act. The former makes information in the possession of agencies presumptively public and available, unless it fits specified exemptions; the latter usually requires that high-level policymaking meetings be open or, if they are closed, that some record of the meetings be kept. The next element of a fair information policy is some sort of privacy section, which protects citizens against abuses in the collection, use, and dissemination of information by government agencies. Such policies also commonly involve prevention of conflict of interest (by financial reporting requirements) or, in the case of the Federal Advisory Committee Act, provide information on who was advising officials on various types of decisions, when those advisers could have influenced decisions in favor of regulation in industry or in favor of some particular constituency.

A number of problems in these fair information policies have yet to be resolved. There are often clashes between the freedom-of-information provisions and the right-to-privacy requirements. These laws frequently require substantial reporting obligations, which can be burdensome for agencies that lack funding. Many exemptions make it difficult for people dealing with agencies to understand their rights and the agencies' obligations.

Despite these difficulties, the laws requiring both the availability of information and guidelines for its proper handling make possible some degree of order and predictability in the midst of an information explosion. On an extremely practical level, these laws ensure a degree of accountability. They provide some measure of quality control in an area where supervision can be difficult. They encourage efficiency in the management of information resources by discouraging unnecessary data collection and inappropriate information flow. They provide opportunities for error correction, since people about whom data are kept may gain access and register challenges. They also represent important aspects of legitimacy, since current laws concerning fair information practices are quite clearly reactions to post-Watergate public demands for protection against abuse of power by those with access to sensitive information about the lives of citizens.

Legal Accountability and Political Legitimacy

The administrator who wields substantial discretion in a constitutional democracy should not underestimate the issue of legitimacy. The connections between the broad conception of supremacy of law and the day-to-day application of administrative law practices are considerably more immediate than they may appear. The law can support claims by administrators to the legitimate exercise of power. Lack of attention to legal concerns jeopardizes the status of any administrative action, even if it evades judicial reversal. There are three issues worthy of consideration by administrators when they deal with those whose responsibility it is to ensure that officials honor the supremacy of law. They are an awareness of the perspective of the judge, a sensitivity to the elements needed for forging a working relationship with the courts, and an acquired ability to learn the benefits of defeat in the legal forum.

Judges are socialized in a tradition quite different from that of administrators. Judges' environment is characterized by adversary relationships, as opposed to the consensus-oriented training of administrators. They are wary of the tendency to undervalue fundamental fairness or equality, while administrators are admonished to set efficiency and effectiveness as primary criteria of success. Judges tend to focus primarily on the problems and the parties in the cases before them, while administrators must contemplate the wider clientele and constituencies who will respond to their actions.

The fact that judges and administrators begin from quite different intellectual and professional foundations does not preclude the establishment of useful working relationships. There are some steps administrators can take to help shape that interaction. The first step is to act with the assumption that courts will probably be called on to judge administrative decisions. Above all, this step requires attention to the substantive elements of administrative law. Beyond that, it requires administrators to establish records supporting their actions at the time they are taken, and not after the fact. Courts refer to justificatory memoranda prepared after the fact as *post hoc rationalizations,* which are not acceptable for upholding administrative action. Courts will refuse to fill in the blanks when administrators have not provided reasons for action.

Candor and cooperation are important. Judges are experienced in the business of determining which participants in the process are telling the whole truth. As in other administrative relationships, the person who loses credibility in one case has an extremely difficult time recovering it in another.

Judges take a dim view of administrators who assume an unbending posture of opposition when a cooperative spirit, even an effort at education, might be helpful. For example, judges in some institutional reform cases have been told that agencies cannot carry out proposed orders requiring reform, but they are often not told precisely why. The use of financial interposition is not calculated to engender a positive exchange with a judge. If an agency cannot act for financial reasons, its representatives should be prepared to make a feasibility case that suggests a willingness to work with the court in pursuit of the goals required by law while simultaneously explaining the nature of the limits that bar agency action.

Finally, conflict conversion is a bad idea. Sometimes administrators choose to make the judge the adversary. Cooperative interaction with a court does not constitute a waiver of an agency's right to appeal what it perceives to be an adverse decision. Hostility is unnecessary and usually counterproductive.

Administrators must be alert to the likelihood that, despite all their efforts, their agencies will lose cases in court. It is possible to benefit from those defeats. The tendency is to determine precisely what must be done to respond to an adverse ruling and then move on to other things, but careful study of adverse opinions can yield important information. It may provide leverage for the agency. It may suggest the need for strategic planning and policy development. It may recommend options that would be acceptable substitutes for the practice that was overturned. An adverse decision is an input into the decision process, not merely a constraint on administrative action.

Summary

The essential elements of administrative law are not merely or primarily troublesome constraints on the discretion that public administrators must exercise in their quest for effective and efficient performance of the people's business. They are tools, essential devices for the accomplishment of the responsibilities entrusted to administrators. The first responsibility of an administrator is to carry out the law. Failure to do so is not excusable on the basis of the end dictating the means, for an administrator has no authority except that delegated by law. An act in violation of the law is by definition an act by someone who has placed himself or herself above the law and is fundamentally illegitimate. Moreover, such an action is counterproductive: It undermines the compromise that permits unelected officials to render decisions having the force of law in a constitutional democracy, which claims as the source of its authority the rule and supremacy of law.

Finally, these legal devices are also administrative tools. They aid orderly decisions, enhance efficiency, reduce arbitrariness, improve morale, and provide defenses when agencies' actions are challenged. They require little more than reasoned decisions and fundamental fairness. They also provide defenses against political interference and policy errors. For all these reasons, the tools of legal responsibility for administrators are extremely valuable.

List of Cases Cited

Allison v. *Block,* 723 F.2d 631 (8th Cir. 1983).
Bowsher v. *Synar,* 92 L.Ed. 2d 583 (1986).
Capital Cities Cable v. *Crisp,* 467 U.S. 691 (1984).
Chevron U.S.A. v. *Natural Resources Defense Council,* 467 U.S. 837 (1984).
Commodity Futures Trading Commission v. *Schor,* 92 L.Ed. 2d 675 (1986).
Connick v. *Myers,* 461 U.S. 138 (1983).
Cornelius v. *NAACP Legal Defense and Education Fund,* 473 U.S. 788 (1985).
Donovan v. *Dewey,* 452 U.S. 594 (1981).
Dow Chemical v. *United States,* 90 L.Ed. 2d 226 (1986).
Environmental Defense Fund v. *Thomas,* 627 F.Supp. 566 (D.D.C. 1986).
FCC v. *WNCN Listeners Guild,* 450 U.S. 582 (1981).
Ford Motor Co. v. *FTC,* 673 F.2d 1008 (9th Cir. 1981).
Garcia v. *San Antonio Metropolitan Transit Authority,* 469 U.S. 528 (1985).
Heckler v. *Chaney,* 470 U.S. 821 (1985).
Immigration and Naturalization Service v. *Chadha,* 462 U.S. 919 (1983).
Marbury v. *Madison,* 5 U.S. (1 Cranch) 137 (1803).
Mathews v. *Eldridge,* 424 U.S. 319 (1976).
Michigan Canners and Freezers Assn. v. *Agricultural Marketing and Bargaining Board,* 467 U.S. 461 (1984).
Middlesex County Sewerage Authority v. *National Sea Clammers Assn.,* 453 U.S. 1 (1981).
Motor Vehicle Manufacturers v. *State Farm Mutual,* 463 U.S. 29 (1983).
National League of Cities v. *Usery,* 426 U.S. 833 (1976).
Office of Communications of the United Church of Christ v. *FCC,* 707 F.2d 1413 (D.C. Cir. 1983).

Pacific Gas & Electric v. *California State Energy Commission,* 461 U.S. 190 (1983).
Pennhurst State School and Hospital v. *Halderman,* 451 U.S. 1 (1981).
Perry Education Assn. v. *Perry Local Education Assn.,* 460 U.S. 37 (1983).
United States v. *Lee,* 106 U.S. 196 (1882).

References

Cooper, P. ''By Order of the President: Administration by Executive Order and Proclamation.'' *Administration & Society,* 1986, *18* (3), 233–262.

Davis, K. *Discretionary Justice: A Preliminary Inquiry.* Baton Rouge: Louisiana State University Press, 1969.

Dickinson, J. *Administrative Justice and the Supremacy of Law in the United States.* New York: Russell and Russell, 1927.

Fisher, L. *The Politics of Shared Power: Congress and the Executive.* Washington, D.C.: Congressional Quarterly Press, 1981.

Fisher, L. *Constitutional Conflicts Between Congress and the President.* Princeton, N.J.: Princeton University Press, 1985a.

Fisher, L. ''Judicial Misperceptions About the Lawmaking Process: The Legislative Veto Case.'' *Public Administration Review,* 1985b, *45* (6), 705–711.

Frank, J. *If Men Were Angels: Some Aspects of Government in a Democracy.* New York: Harper & Row, 1942.

Friendly, H. *The Federal Administrative Agencies.* Cambridge, Mass.: Harvard University Press, 1962.

Hamilton, A., Madison, J., and Jay, J. *The Federalist Papers.* New York: Mentor, 1961.

Pound, R. *Administrative Law: Its Growth, Procedure and Significance.* Pittsburgh, Pa.: University of Pittsburgh Press, 1942.

Rohr, J. A. *To Run a Constitution: The Legitimacy of the Administrative State.* Lawrence: University Press of Kansas, 1986.

Tribe, L. *American Constitutional Law.* Mineola, N.Y.: Foundation Press, 1978.

9

Ronald J. Oakerson

Governance Structures for Enhancing Accountability and Responsiveness

To be accountable means to have to answer for one's actions or inaction, and depending on the answer, to be exposed to potential sanctions, both positive and negative. Accountability can bring either blame and censure or recognition for a job well done. Patterns of accountability depend on the sanctions that can be imposed, who can impose them, and the unit that is affected. Administrative agencies—the subject of this chapter—can be held collectively accountable in ways that individual administrators cannot (Rosenbloom, 1978). The choice of basic units of accountability—the size and number of administrative agencies within a general-purpose government, and the size and number of governments in a multigovernmental arrangement—strongly influences the way that governance affects administration.

The purpose of public accountability is responsiveness, the assumption being that responsiveness is largely patterned on the requirements of accountability ("He who pays the piper calls the tune"). Accountability does, however, have costs. Something less than complete accountability, and therefore something less than perfect responsiveness, is always a preferred outcome. Moreover, some patterns of accountability are more economical than others, depending on circumstances. Accountability, like administration, is subject to a criterion of efficiency. Any pattern of accountability must include reference to objects—accountable to whom, and for what? Maintaining an economical pattern of accountability is a problem of institutional design, an effort that depends on more than vigilance.

The orthodox point of view on these issues has been a reform orientation, which seeks both to strengthen hierarchical organization on the administrative side and to simplify public organization on the governance side. Efforts to strengthen executive control of administration, consolidate administrative agencies, simplify legislative processes, shorten election ballots, and move toward metropolitan or regional governments in place of a multiplicity of local jurisdictions—all were reforms intended to streamline the structure of administration and connect it through a single strong executive to an equally streamlined structure of governance. Yet the traditional structures of American governance have been remarkably resistant to these orthodox reform prescriptions and, with few exceptions, have become more, not less, complex as the overall responsibilities of American public administration have grown. Explaining, understanding, and learning to work with complexity have assumed high priority in the study of governance and administration today.

Simplicity retains a strong intuitive appeal, however. Even in science, other things being equal, the simpler explanation is considered the better. The same criterion applies to administration and governance. Complexity is something we embrace only of necessity. The first question to consider, therefore, is whether complex governance structures are a gratuitous historical accretion or a useful complement of public administration in a large democratic society. To figure out how to approach the design of governance structures, it is necessary to examine the circumstances that have led to administrative fragmentation and overlap.

Fragmentation and Overlap in Administrative Structures

Orthodox public administration theory looked on fragmentation and overlap as bad organization, unnecessary impediments to efficiency and accountability. One difficulty with this approach was that it lumped a lot of different patterns of fragmentation and overlap together as a wholesale phenomenon to be avoided. Gulick's (1937) famous set of criteria for dividing work among administrative units—purpose, process, clientele, and place or territory—were intended as a guide to sorting the heterogeneous functions of government into homogeneous units. The criteria of purpose and place are also useful for distinguishing quite different configurations of fragmentation and overlap.

Fragmentation of Purpose. One of the orthodox principles of public administration is departmentalization, that is, division of work among the departments and agencies of a government according to such criteria as Gulick's. An effort to departmentalize by major purpose is common. Fragmentation of purpose occurs when some of the resources—money, information, authority—necessary to accomplish the purpose of one department are controlled by other departments. Overlap, with respect to purpose, occurs when two or more departments each have the same authority to act in the same circumstances. Jurisdictional fragmentation divides authority, while jurisdictional overlap generates redundant authority. Orthodox theory holds that fragmentation makes government ineffective and that overlapping jurisdictions are wasteful and inefficient.

Much of the concern expressed about fragmentation and overlap is directed to fairly broad purposes—protecting the environment, helping the poor, fighting crime. The precise focus of criticism varies with the active policy agenda. It is sometimes narrower, sometimes broader. Nevertheless, purposes can be divided into subpurposes, and departments into bureaus, agencies, offices, and other units; the same principles would apply as work is subdivided. Gulick's "principle of homogeneity" holds that no administrative unit should attempt to perform heterogeneous functions or, in terms of purpose, to serve competing purposes. A closely related principle holds that all responsibility for a single homogeneous function, or purpose, ought to be placed in a single unit. This is the principle of nonfragmentation.

Simon (1946) demonstrated that many of the orthodox principles of public administration were like proverbs: Each principle could be paired with an equally compelling counterprinciple, so that each contradicted the other. Contradictory principles cannot be followed consistently. The principle "Do not fragment responsibility" also cannot be followed consistently, because *to unify responsibility with respect to one purpose is often to fragment responsibility with respect to another.* The purposes pursued by government overlap (quite apart from government organization), often in complex ways.

A coherent attack on drug abuse, for example, cuts across other purposes associated with education, law enforcement, public assistance, and public health. If each of these purposes is organized separately by department, and if each houses a unit on drug abuse, orthodox administrative analysts will complain that the fight against drug abuse is fragmented; yet to form a separate agency to fight drug abuse would contribute to the fragmentation of a host of program efforts organized with reference to education, law enforcement, public assistance, and public health. The jurisdiction of such an agency would necessarily overlap a number of others. It would also violate orthodox prescriptions to minimize the span of control for executive officers and be open to the charge of agency "proliferation." The only other option, to create a superagency that would absorb all relevant functions, would violate the principle of homogeneity by combining the pursuit of widely disparate purposes under a single jurisdictional roof. The desire for a comprehensive policy on this or that broad social problem is frequently accompanied by a call for a comprehensive agency (Steiner, 1981). Many social problems, however, are so broad that to combine the authority and resources necessary to address any one problem in a single agency would be to roll the entire government into a single administrative unit.

Thus, fragmentation of responsibility among the administrative units of general-purpose governments is an unavoidable fact of life. To complain about fragmentation per se is meaningless, for to organize a general-purpose government is necessarily to fragment responsibilities with respect to some important purposes. Jurisdictional overlap, rather than an additional source of waste and inefficiency, can be viewed as a useful and necessary complement of jurisdictional fragmentation, increasing both the effectiveness and the comprehensivenes of public policy by providing for redundancy (Landau, 1969).

Fragmentation of Place. Returning to Gulick's (1937) criteria for administrative organization, fragmentation of purpose can be distinguished from fragmentation of place or territory. The standard critique of local-government or metropolitan fragmentation is addressed to the fragmentation of territorial responsibility. What is viewed as a single interdependent place—a metropolitan area—is fragmented among multiple local agencies organized by multiple units of government. Organization by territory is viewed as fragmentation of territory when there are common problems that affect an entire area and require a coordinated response among multiple jurisdictions. Overlapping jurisdictions occur in a territorial sense when the agencies of counties and special districts, among other units, add redundant local jurisdictions that geographically overlap municipal agencies. The orthodox view has been that a single metropolitan government is appropriate to govern a metropolitan area. This is a governance structure that is thought to eliminate both fragmentation and overlap.

Some advocates of metropolitan reform make the case for a two-tiered system that sorts basic functions between two levels of local government (Zimmerman, 1972). The difficulty with the usual pattern of overlap, from this perspective, is that territorial overlap is accompanied by both overlap and fragmentation of purpose. County and municipal agencies, for example, generally share authority for police, and each has some functional responsibility for police protection. The two-tiered approach to metropolitan reform assumes that fragmentation and overlap in the purposes served by territorially overlapping jurisdictions can be removed by a process of sorting out—assigning one set of functions, or purposes, to a layer of small local governments and another set to an overlapping unit. A similar approach is frequently proposed as a way to reform federal-state relations.

If it is impossible to sort responsibilities neatly among administrative units within governments, eliminating both fragmentation and overlap of purpose, it is even less likely that responsibilities can be neatly sorted out between governments that overlap territorially (Grodzins, 1966). If, for example, parks are assigned to a county agency, and police patrol to small municipal units, which jurisdiction is responsible for patrolling parks? Overlapping territories almost guarantee overlapping problems and shared functions among agencies in different units of government.

If administrative fragmentation within large general-purpose units of government is inherent in public organization, it also follows that metropolitan reform cannot, as widely believed, eliminate fragmentation. Metropolitan reform can only trade one pattern of fragmentation for another. Sayre and Kaufman's (1965) classic study of New York City, for example, describes extensive fragmentation accompanied by complex patterns of accountability in a large metropolitan unit of government. Just as multiple local governments fragment responsibility for major functions (from the metropolitan standpoint) among local communities, large consolidated "local" governments fragment responsibility for discrete communities—or places—among functional agencies (Mudd, 1976, p. 114). In the latter case, responsibility for a place, such as a neighborhood, is fragmented among the police, fire, education, public works, and other functional departments or agencies of government. Instead of seeking to eliminate or minimize fragmentation and overlap, the relevant problem is to choose between different patterns of fragmentation and overlap. The need for economical patterns of accountability is an important consideration in this choice.

A Theory of Complex Governance Structures

If administrative jurisdictions are necessarily fragmented, what sorts of governance structures are appropriate to obtaining accountability and responsiveness? Orthodox administrative theory argued for simple governance structures—single centers of command and control—linked to hierarchically organized, nonfragmented administrative structures (Wilson, [1885] 1956). The assumption that simpler is better no longer holds on the governance side when the administrative side is unavoidably fragmented and complex. At least as plausible is an assumption that complex administrative structures can be controlled only by equally complex governance structures.

Instead of being created whole at one point in time, complex structures tend to emerge from series of incremental decisions. The lack of overall planning, however, does not necessarily mean that each incremental step is unplanned. Because complex structures of decision making cannot be observed in their entirety in any great detail at a particular point in time, our understanding of them is necessarily somewhat abstract, based as it is on simplifying assumptions, concepts, and inferences. The first tool of governance is a theory of governance.

Ostrom (1974) has argued that traditional American governance structures are consistent with (and may even derive from) a theory of democratic administration, identified by Max Weber as an alternative to "bureaucratic administration" but elaborated much earlier by Alexis de Tocqueville ([1835–40] 1945) in *Democracy in America* (see especially vol. I, chap. 5). In a theory of democratic administration, strict hierarchical accountability on the administrative side is relaxed. Implementing agencies, not "the government," are regarded as the basic units of accountability. Vertical hierarchy is augmented by multilateral arrangements in which implementing agencies are subject to multiple constraints of different sorts, both political (sometimes electoral) and legal. The links between governance and administration are many.

American society is organized according to two quite different patterns of democratic administration. Instead of relying on the same general structure of governance to organize administration in terms of both purpose and place, we use two different types of governance structure. The first is general-purpose government, characterized by the organization of diverse departments, bureaus, and agencies, which are organized internally to serve different but overlapping *purposes*. The second is multigovernmental arrangement, characterized by numerous units of government, which are organized to serve different but overlapping *places*. The second structure reaches greatest complexity in metropolitan areas. One of the most significant features of American governance is the independence between organization by purpose in the national government and organization by place in the states, integrated by the U.S. Constitution in a common system of governance called federalism.

To this dimension of governance we can add another, making a distinction between general structures of governance and specific structures developed to govern specific purposes or places. A general structure of governance provides an institutional framework for the development of more specific governance structures organized around specific problems, programs, functions, policies, or communities.

Governance Within Large, General-Purpose Governments

The general structure of governance for American national government, or for any large, general-purpose government in America, can be viewed as a complex mechanism of administrative accountability, with many working parts. Most federal agencies are directly accountable to four committees of Congress—an appropriations committee (or subcommittee) in both the House and Senate, and a substantive policy committee in each chamber. An agency is dependent on these committees for two basic resources: money and authority. Each agency is also potentially accountable to the federal courts for the legal exercise of its authority and can be found *ultra vires* (without authority) if a court concludes that the agency has exceeded its congressional charter (or its constitutional powers). These mechanisms of accountability operate in addition to hierarchical mechanisms, often exercised in a routine manner through such executive staff agencies as the Office of Management and Budget. Agencies are also often informally accountable to clientele groups, whose source of influence lies in their access to formal decision makers, especially congressional committees. Added to this mix are the scrutiny of the General Accounting Office, which works for Congress, and the ever inquiring press.

Within this general structure, specific governance structures—often called *subgovernments*—are created to govern particular policy domains. In response to different policy problems, Congress has created a diverse array of governmental agencies (see Seidman, 1975, p. 221) distinguished by their governance structures. Some programs, for example, establish structures of collective decision making that require collegial deliberation and agreement before action can be taken. The National Science Foundation was created in this fashion, to emulate the governance structure of a university and to tie federal decisions on research closely to the system of higher education (Seidman, 1975, pp. 22–23). The Cooperative Extension Service is a highly decentralized administrative structure with a parallel governance structure that relies on collective decision making at both the state and the local levels. Independent regulatory commissions were designed to provide quasi-judicial arrangements as a governance mechanism that might protect decision making from certain types of political pressures.

Some governance structures require citizen advisory committees that become a source of both constraint and support for administrators (Derthick, 1979). Other governance structures are characterized by interagency competition (such as the rivalry between the Army Corp of Engineers and the Bureau of Reclamation), which increases their responsiveness to political and legislative sponsors (see Niskanen, 1971; Downs, 1976, p. 230; Seidman, 1975, pp. 174–177). Still others entail extensive intergovernmental relationships that create reciprocal patterns of legal and political accountability among administrative agencies in the federal and state governments. Although organized around categorical grants that establish contractual obligations on the part of recipient units, the terms of the relationships are also responsive to state and local interests (Derthick, 1970, 1975; Peterson, Rabe, and Wong, 1986).

Basic Units and Tools of Accountability. Perhaps the fundamental question in relating governance to administration is the choice of basic units of accountability, the designation of responsible agencies. Democratic administration depends first upon giving discretion to implementing agencies and then holding them accountable for the exercise of their discretion. Fragmentation, it has been argued, is a necessary feature of administrative organization, but fragmentation has another side. Division of authority among a large number of agencies tends to place the responsibility for discrete programs with the implementing agency, and not with a large overhead bureaucracy. This is the positive side of fragmentation—the use of implementing agencies as basic units of accountability, closely tying responsibility to action. It is also the reason that implementing agencies are generally created by legislatures, not by the executive: to determine the basic units of accountability.

A specific governance structure is built with rules of law that determine the allowable scope of action by each relevant agency and who is authorized or required to take action under what conditions or circumstances, using what procedures, and subject to what potential challenges or vetoes from outside. The general structure of governance provides an array of alternatives in each case, thus making available a very large and somewhat indefinite matrix of possibilities. What is usually called policymaking can also be viewed as a process of microinstitutional design, where the purpose of legislation is to craft a specific governance structure around basic units of accountability.

Three main legislative tools are used in this process:

- Legal mandates directing administrators to take certain actions in certain circumstances
- Legal proscriptions prohibiting administrators from taking certain actions in certain circumstances
- Assignment of permissive authority, allowing administrators to take a range of actions in a variety of circumstances, also possibly subject to expiration after a certain date (sunset legislation)

Most legislation is permissive. The usual assumption is that in the absence of a grant of authority from the legislature (or directly from a constitution), administrative agencies lack authority to act. Legislation is used more often to create action possibilities within a set of boundaries than to issue commands. The extent of permissive authority is frequently defined, however, in part by specific prohibitions—administrative actions that are explicitly forbidden. Less frequently, legislation directs that specific actions be taken, thus limiting administrative discretion much more sharply.

This pattern of legislation requires mechanisms of accountability that perform different functions. One mode of accountability is needed to police the boundaries of permissive authority and, in the process, define those boundaries precisely. For the most part, this is legal accountability. Other mechanisms are needed to hold administrators accountable for the way they use their discretion, the question being not one of lawfulness but of judgment, efficiency, and faithfulness to purpose. For the most part, these are mechanisms of political accountability, aided by fiscal accountability. Such reliance on diverse mechanisms necessarily fragments the responsibility of governance—among courts, legislative committees and agencies, and executive agencies—as well as creating redundant or overlapping channels of accountability.

Legal Accountability. A basic issue in the design of a governance structure is who should have authority to invoke the law—to claim permissive authority to act, to command action by others, or to veto a proposed action—in response to a particular set of circumstances. Some federal laws, for example, are invoked only by decisions of the president, although these decisions are subject to challenge in various ways. For example, the president is authorized by law to seek a court injunction halting a strike if the national interest is seriously impaired. Only the president may take such an action in court, but his petition is then subject to judicial scrutiny on the facts. In 1973, Congress endeavored to fashion a new governance structure with respect to American involvement in military hostilities, hoping to increase presidential accountability. The president, however, is assigned exclusive discretion to invoke the War Powers Resolution and set its procedures in motion. As a result, the constraints built into this structure have not been regularly used as American military personnel are deployed into hostile situations in various parts of the globe.

The Bill of Rights of the U.S. Constitution, as well as the Equal Protection Clause of the Fourteenth Amendment, in contrast, are predicated on the authority of *any person* (see Ostrom, 1987) to claim legal protection for certain individual liberties. These liberties establish constitutional boundaries around the permissive authority that may be granted to and exercised by any government official or agency.

Allowing affected individuals to challenge an administrative agency in court is also an effective means of policing the statutory boundaries of administrative discretion. Statutes frequently provide explicitly for citizens' standing, and occasionally they deny it. Even if a statute is silent on this point, however, as a requirement of due process of law under the Fifth Amendment, persons who are directly affected by an agency's action usually have standing to contest its legality. State courts often maintain a more liberal form of taxpayers' standing as the base rule, in which any taxpayer is held to be directly affected by any government action that involves spending taxpayers' money. Within constitutional limits, legislatures are permitted to expand or contract citizens' standing as a matter of policy.

Citizens are often able defenders of widely shared interests, while agency discretion may be responsive to narrower, more highly concentrated interests. For this reason, Sax (1970) recommended reliance on citizens' lawsuits to hold administrators accountable to standards of environmental law. A number of states have enacted statutes based on Sax's model. Citizens' standing is intended to allow individual citizens to make legal claims to legitimate public interests—that is, interests that have legal protection under current legislation if the law is invoked. The objects of such suits may be public agencies or private parties whose activity is subject to regulation by law.

Political Accountability. Policing the boundaries of discretion, however, is only one aspect of accountability. Equally important is accountability for how discretion is exercised. Assigning authority directly to implementing agencies enhances their responsiveness to the legislative committees that write the agencies' organic legislation, while it relaxes the hierarchy that links agencies to executive officers, including the chief executive. The strengthening of hierarchical management, once understood as an absolute good, is regarded today with greater skepticism in view of its high costs, primarily in the form of elaborate clearances and the proliferation of administrative rules that tighten and restrict the boundaries of discretion on the part of those who act (Warwick, 1975). Stronger hierarchical ties increase the size of the basic organizational unit of accountability, producing more elaborate bureaucratic processes as a defense against external monitoring.

Size and number of administrative agencies are crucial variables in creating an economical pattern of accountability. Efforts to reduce fragmentation, which is often measured simply by counting separate agencies, may lead to the consolidation of agencies or to the centralization of responsibility in upper levels of management. This consolidation or centralization produces larger units of accountability and may result in extensive patterns of administrative clearance intended to protect the larger unit from suffering from the decisions of subunits. Multiplying the number of required clearances in large administrative structures reduces discretion and increases administrative costs. The idea that a chief executive or a department head is ultimately responsible for the conduct of every administrative agency—"the buck stops here"— is not a useful principle, because it obscures the basic unit of accountability.

The president's constitutional responsibility to "take care that the laws be faithfully executed" (Art. II, Sec. 3) is consistent with a relaxed view of hierarchical accountability. A chief executive has a political role (to obtain accountability for how discretion is exercised) more than a managerial role (taking responsibility for how discretion is exercised). A president fails, not when agencies fail, but when agencies are not held accountable for their failure. Yet accountability is not intended simply to enforce the political preferences of the chief executive but to contribute to the faithfulness of public agencies to public purposes. This is a role that, almost by definition, is shared with others.

Oversight is the process by which legislatures participate in political accountability (see Schick, 1976). Unlike executive power, which is based primarily on control over personnel, legislative power is based on control of an agency's charter, or basic grant of authority, and its annual appropriation. Oversight consists of monitoring by committees charged with writing the legislation that pertains to agencies' authority and annual appropriations. Control over money and authority gives legislative oversight committees considerable leverage over the exercise of agency discretion, beyond the requirements of the law. Legislative oversight, nevertheless, cannot adequately substitute for rules of law enforceable by citizens in the courts. Oversight is best used to monitor the effects of legal rules on relevant values and interests.

The relationships among administrative agencies, congressional committees, and clientele groups, as Fisher (1981, p. 192) wrote, "are too complex and variable to warrant shorthand descriptions of 'iron triangles.'" This popular textbook imagery was based on the tendency of specific governance structures to seek closure and to limit the community of interested parties. The incentives to do so are clear: The more inclusive the community, the higher the bargaining costs, and the more difficult it is to get the ability to act. Specific governance structures may remain relatively stable until external events bring about a change. The general structure of governance in the United States, which makes it possible for excluded groups to find various points of political leverage, results in countervailing tendencies toward inclusiveness in specific governance structures. The environmental movement, for example, eventually brought environmentalists into the governance process of the U.S. Army Corps of Engineers (Mazmanian and Nienaber, 1979). Efforts to obtain closure are never quite successful. Heclo (1978) described these same relationships as open and permeable "issue networks" in which knowledge and the ability to contribute to an ongoing discussion are the major criteria of admission.

The choices made among different mechanisms of accountability are best viewed as contingent on the purposes of legislation and the circumstances of administration. Various trade-offs exist. Legislative oversight, for example, depends on the limited time and effort of committee members and staff, while citizens' lawsuits take up the time and effort of the courts. Direct legal requirements, as opposed to permissive authority, are a more certain method of obtaining compliance; but permissive authority adds discretion and flexibility when legislators cannot anticipate precisely what may or may not need to be done. Reliance on a single mechanism to the exclusion of others is, however, the choice most likely to lead to frustration and failure. If accountability is mostly political (see Lowi, 1969), then policy depends entirely on political accommodations, and individual citizens may be left without sufficient leverage in the political process. If accountability becomes mostly legal, as happens when specific policy outcomes are treated as constitutional entitlements, then policy becomes independent of political accommodation, and the political demands of individuals become law.

Metropolitan Governance

In American national government, the general governance structure composed of Congress, the president, and the Supreme Court is highly visible, while specific governance structures are less so. The opposite is true in highly fragmented metropolitan areas. Here, the specific governance structures—specific with respect to place—are conspicuous, readily apparent from maps that display cities, towns, and villages, while general governance structures are less visible.

Metropolitan governance in America does not ordinarily consist of a metropolitan government. In its place is a multigovernmental structure, associated with a set of rules formally supplied by state constitutions and state laws. Included are rules of association or incorporation that allow communities to organize governments, fiscal rules that establish the taxing powers available to different types of units, boundary adjustment rules that allow for changes in the territorial domains of governmental units, and contracting rules that pertain to relationships among units (Advisory Commission on Intergovernmental Relations, 1987, p. 39). Frequently, special legislation is used to devise unique sets of rules for particular metropolitan areas. Local delegations to state legislatures then become key groups of decision makers in metropolitan governance. Just as important, however, are associations of local government officials that serve informally as forums for raising issues, accommodating differences, and proposing state legislation (Advisory Commission on Intergovernmental Relations, 1988).

To a great extent, citizens are empowered as voters to create, by means of initiative and referendum, the specific governance structures—towns, villages, cities, and special districts—that are organized with respect to specific places. Citizens, not officials, can then be viewed as the basic legislators in a metropolitan area. The citizen-legislators of metropolitan areas in the United States, when given the opportunity to choose, have usually shown a strong preference for maintaining a variety of relatively small local governments as the basic units of accountability. The use of governments as basic units allows citizens to draw on elections as instruments of administrative accountability, a device that is generally unavailable in the specific governance structures organized by major purpose in large general-purpose governments. Citizens in small local governments generally enjoy much more favorable citizen-to-elected-official ratios than citizens in large general-purpose local governments (Advisory Commission on Intergovernmental Relations, 1988). Metropolitan organization and fragmentation (by place) are associated with a pattern of accountability much different from those of national organization and fragmentation (by purpose).

The ability to organize territorially overlapping units allows citizens even greater flexibility in the creation of specific governance structures. Accountability for small-scale interests need not be sacrificed to accountability for large-scale interests. The use of both subarea and areawide special-purpose districts to provide fire protection, water and sewers, education for handicapped persons, and community colleges—to name only a few possibilities—is a governance mechanism that allows citizens to combine small-scale, community-oriented patterns of accountability for many services with supplementary patterns of organization, as needed.

The extent of jurisdictional fragmentation on the governance side does not determine the extent of functional fragmentation on the administrative side (Oakerson, 1987). For example, St. Louis County, Missouri—one of the most fragmented metropolitan counties in the nation—has ninety-one municipalities, each with authority to provide police protection alongside county government, yet St. Louis County has only sixty-four full-time police departments. Communities without their own departments receive police services through various contracting arrangements with other departments. Moreover, each department does not produce in-house all the components of police service; only 45 percent produce their own dispatch services. Instead, a number of municipalities have organized joint dispatch centers. All of St. Louis County is served by a joint police-training academy and a major-case squad to investigate serious crimes. This complex overlay of joint service arrangements is what advocates of metropolitan reform, who are preoccupied by administration within governments, tend to ignore when describing the fragmented structures of metropolitan areas.

The general governance structures of metropolitan areas differ, however, especially from state to state, in the degree to which citizens are allowed to govern. Various rules are used for municipal incorporation and special-district formation, annexation and consolidation, and transfer of jurisdiction. Some governance structures allow citizens in an unincorporated area to incorporate as a municipality by invoking rules of petition and majority vote in a popular referendum; others require approval by an areawide or state agency that represents existing jurisdictions (Martin and Wagner, 1978). Some rules allow existing municipalities to annex unincorporated territory unilaterally, subject perhaps to a judicial proceeding. Others require approval by concurrent majorities in elections held in both the annexing municipality and the area to be annexed. Still others allow the overlapping county government to be represented in the process. The consolidation of units may occur on the petition of citizens or officials, may or may not be submitted to a vote of the electorate, and may require either concurrent majorities in the units to be consolidated or only a majority throughout the proposed consolidated unit. The variety of special districts that citizens can create through petition and referendum may consist of many different types or of only a few. Large, general-purpose municipalities do not ordinarily allow the independent formation of subunits. The greater the range of citizen choice, the greater the capacity of citizens to determine the basic units of accountability (Advisory Commission on Intergovernmental Relations, 1987).

Summary

Fragmentation occurs, not because of poor organization or antiquated governance structures, but because the problems that governments address overlap and cannot therefore be neatly sorted among government agencies or legislative committees. Administrators, legislators, and policy analysts should treat both fragmentation and overlap, in the generic sense, as givens. Any division of labor fragments at least some important responsibilities. Shared jurisdiction must be regarded as basic (Fisher, 1981, p. 200), and a streamlined system of governance and administration as infeasible. The relevant question is not whether to share, but how.

One method of dividing and sharing responsibility is found in large, general-purpose governments, such as American national government, state governments, and large municipalities. Organization by purpose or function also creates fragmentation of purpose and function, addressed in part by allowing redundant or overlapping responsibilities among both administrative agencies and mechanisms of accountability. Extensive patterns of negotiation, collaboration, competition, and litigation, in addition to hierarchical supervision, all contribute to responsiveness and help maintain accountability. Efforts to reduce fragmentation among implementing agencies, in contrast, may lead to uneconomical patterns of accountability within large, overhead bureaucracies.

Any such pattern of accountability, however, is costly. The costs of accountability consist mainly of what economists call transaction costs (Williamson, 1979): the time and effort devoted to exploring alternatives, making decisions, reaching agreements, and monitoring results. A simple proposition can be stated: The larger the population of a territorial jurisdiction, and the greater the number of functions for which that jurisdiction has responsibility, the higher tend to be the transaction costs of securing accountability. The reasoning goes like this: The larger the size and the greater the number of functions, the greater are the number and variety of interests to be taken into account. The more varied the interests to be accounted for, the more complex the pattern of accountability will tend to be. The more complex the pattern of accountability, the greater the transaction costs required to sustain a course of decisions. Moreover, the smaller and more homogeneous a community, the more likely that responsiveness can derive from shared norms and interests, as opposed to strict accountability.

Analysts have frequently expressed concern that levels of citizen participation appear to be lower in small local communities than in large general-purpose governments (see Riedel, 1972). The assumption is that if small local governments offer better opportunities to participate, citizens should tend to participate more. Citizens' preferences for small local governments, however, may rest on precisely the opposite consideration: the ability to obtain a responsive set of local services without having to incur high transaction costs. The preferences of citizens for relatively small local governments may be better explained by the economics of accountability than by an abstract desire for participation.

A substantial trade-off exists between dividing governance and administration primarily according to major purpose or primarily according to place or territory. General-purpose governments divide responsibility by major purpose, engendering one type of fragmentation and overlap. Federalism and local government are based on territorial divisions and produce a much different pattern of fragmentation and overlap. The use of state and local governments—governance by place—can be viewed as a way of economizing on the costs of accountability and, especially in the case of small local governments, relying to a greater extent on shared interests between administrators and citizens to obtain responsiveness. Stigler's (1965) prescription, to rely on the smallest feasible unit of government to address any given question of public policy, is sound advice, in terms of the economics of accountability.

The empirical question of service responsiveness, comparing relatively small local governments to large consolidated departments, has been investigated systematically and in depth with respect to police services. An extensive series of studies, using different methodologies and employing various indicators of responsiveness and effectiveness (including, but not limited to, citizens' expressions of satisfaction), found not a single large police department (over 350 officers) that was more responsive or effective in delivering services directly to citizens in similar neighborhoods than the small to medium-size departments that were studied (Ostrom and Parks, 1987; Ostrom, 1976). Interjurisdictional arrangements and overlapping jurisdictions add a complex overlay. While adding new transaction costs, relationships based on cooperation can be expected to be cost-effective for the parties concerned and thus not to increase costs overall. This argument is supported by research showing that the more complex the police service delivery system in a metropolitan area, the better it performs. A key finding is that fragmentation with overlap is preferred both to full functional consolidation and to fragmentation without overlap (see Parks, 1985).

Whether jurisdictions are organized on the basis of purpose or place, the old nemeses of fragmentation and overlap have an important place in structures of both administration and governance. Administrative fragmentation of major purposes, on the one hand, cannot be eliminated from general-purpose governments; efforts to do so, beyond some point, tend to increase the costs of accountability by obscuring the basic units of accountability. Jurisdictional fragmentation by place, on the other hand, tends to reduce the costs of accountability, provided that there are overlapping jurisdictions to take account of different communities of interest. Only complex structures of governance and administration, using both fragmentation and overlap, can produce economical patterns of accountability.

References

Advisory Commission on Intergovernmental Relations. *The Organization of Local Public Economies.* A-109. Washington, D.C.: Advisory Commission on Intergovernmental Relations, 1987.

Advisory Commission on Intergovernmental Relations. *Metropolitan Organization: The St. Louis Case.* M–157. Washington, D.C.: Advisory Commission on Intergovernmental Relations, 1988.

Derthick, M. *The Influence of Federal Grants: Public Assistance in Massachusetts.* Cambridge, Mass.: Harvard University Press, 1970.

Derthick, M. *Uncontrollable Spending for Social Service Grants.* Washington, D.C.: Brookings Institution, 1975.

Derthick, M. *Policymaking for Social Security.* Washington, D.C.: Brookings Institution, 1979.

Downs, A. *Urban Problems and Prospects.* (2nd ed.) Chicago: Rand McNally, 1976.

Fisher, L. *The Politics of Shared Power: Congress and the Executive.* Washington, D.C.: Congressional Quarterly Press, 1981.

Grodzins, M. *The American System: A New View of Government in the United States.* Chicago: Rand McNally, 1966.

Gulick, L. H. "Notes on the Theory of Organization." In L. H. Gulick and L. Urwick (eds.), *Papers on the Science of Administration.* New York: Institute of Public Administration, Columbia University, 1937.

Heclo, H. "Issue Networks and the Executive Establishment." In Anthony King (ed.), *The New American Political System.* Washington, D.C.: American Enterprise Institute, 1978.

Landau, M. "Redundancy, Rationality, and the Problem of Duplication and Overlap." *Public Administration Review,* 1969, *29* (4), 346–358.

Lowi, T. J. *The End of Liberalism.* New York: Norton, 1969.

Martin, D. T., and Wagner, R. E. "The Institutional Framework for Municipal Incorporation: An Economic Analysis of Local Agency Formation Commissions in California." *Journal of Law and Economics,* 1978, *21* (2), 409–425.

Mazmanian, D. A., and Nienaber, J. *Can Organizations Change? Environmental Protection, Citizen Participation, and the Corps of Engineers.* Washington, D.C.: Brookings Institution, 1979.

Mudd, J. "Beyond Community Control: A Neighborhood Strategy for City Government." *Publius,* 1976, *6* (4), 113–135.

Niskanen, W. A., Jr. *Bureaucracy and Representative Government.* Hawthorne, N.Y.: Aldine, 1971.

Oakerson, R. J. "Local Public Economies: Provision, Production and Governance." *Intergovernmental Perspective,* 1987, *13* (3/4), 20–25.

Ostrom, E. "Size and Performance in a Federal System." *Publius,* 1976, *6* (2), 33–73.

Ostrom, E., and Parks, R. B. "Neither Gargantua nor the Land of Lilliputs: Conjectures on Mixed Systems of Metropolitan Organization." Paper presented at the Midwest Political Science Association meetings, Chicago, Apr. 9–11, 1987.

Ostrom, V. *The Intellectual Crisis in American Public Administration.* (2nd ed.) University: University of Alabama Press, 1974.

Ostrom, V. *The Political Theory of a Compound Republic.* (2nd ed.) Lincoln: University of Nebraska Press, 1987.

Parks, R. B. "Metropolitan Structure and Systematic Performance: The Case of Police Service Delivery." In K. Hanf and T.A.J. Toonen (eds.), *Policy Implementation in Federal and Unitary States.* Dordrecht, The Netherlands: Martinus Nijhoff, 1985.

Peterson, P. E., Rabe, B. G., and Wong, K. K. *When Federalism Works.* Washington, D.C.: Brookings Institution, 1986.

Riedel, J. A. "Citizen Participation: Myths and Realities." *Public Administration Review,* 1972, *32* (3), 211–220.

Rosenbloom, D. H. "Accountability in the Administrative State." In S. Greer, R. D. Hedlund, and J. L. Gibson (eds.), *Accountability in Urban Society: Public Agencies Under Fire.* Newbury Park, Calif.: Sage, 1978.

Sayre, W. S., and Kaufman, H. *Governing New York City: Politics in the Metropolis.* New York: Norton, 1965.

Sax, J. L. *Defending the Environment: A Handbook for Citizen Action.* New York: Vintage Books, 1970.

Schick, A. "Congress and the 'Details' of Administration." *Public Administration Review,* 1976, *36* (5), 516–528.

Seidman, H. *Politics, Position, and Power: The Dynamics of Federal Organization.* (2nd ed.) New York: Oxford University Press, 1975.

Simon, H. A. "The Proverbs of Administration." *Public Administration Review,* 1946, *6* (1), 53–67.

Steiner, G. Y. *The Futility of Family Policy.* Washington, D.C.: Brookings Institution, 1981.

Stigler, G. J. "The Tenable Range of Functions of Local Government." In E. S. Phelps (ed.), *Private Wants and Public Needs.* New York: Norton, 1965.

Tocqueville, Alexis de. *Democracy in America.* New York: Vintage Books, 1945. (Originally published 1835–1840.)

Warwick, D. P. *A Theory of Public Bureaucracy: Politics, Personality, and Organization in the State Department.* Cambridge, Mass.: Harvard University Press, 1975.

Williamson, O. E. "Transaction-Cost Economics: The Governance of Contractual Relations." *Journal of Law and Economics,* 1979, *22* (2), 223–261.

Wilson, W. *Congressional Government: A Study in American Politics.* New York: Meridian Books, 1956. (Originally published 1885.)

Zimmerman, J. F. *The Federated City: Community Control in Large Cities.* New York: St. Martin's Press, 1972.

10

Robert Agranoff

Managing Intergovernmental Processes

This chapter explains how public administrators work at the margins of their jurisdictions. As governmental systems become more interdependent, new routines are emerging for operating within the federal system. This process is intergovernmental management (IGM), which is emerging as an activity distinct from but related to intergovernmental relations and federalism. Understanding and managing in this arena are emerging challenges, since the public administration tradition is geared toward single organizations.

IGM Situations

In rural Louisiana, a parish health department administrator wishes to negotiate state approval to use funds for nurse practitioners. These funds would be combined with pass-through federal Primary Care Block Grant funds. No physician currently practices in the parish, and state law prohibits nurses to practice without physicians' supervision. The state disapproves the initial request, claiming lack of authority, but two legislators representing the county call the state health officer, urging her to approve the request for funding. The local health officer travels to Baton Rouge and makes his case, demonstrating distance to physicians and distribution problems. After considerable discussion and problem exploration, it is agreed that purchase of nurse practitioners' services can proceed on an experimental basis by the use of a system of physician-supervised authorized care plans and by consultation with physicians in surrounding parishes.

131

The Indiana Department of Environmental Management's Water Quality Program discovers, through an Environmental Protection Agency (EPA) field audit, that several streams are out of compliance with the Clean Water Act. The water division head and the agency head meet with a member of the governor's staff to discuss the situation. The meeting is not only to inform the governor's office of possible problems with the federal government over penalties and litigation but also to calculate the costs of noncompliance in lost federal funds if the state takes no action. The officials jointly decide that the costs of delay will exceed any benefits, and so they prepare a draft compliance plan that will minimize the cost to the state. State officials, along with staff of the state's two U.S. senators, then proceed to negotiate with EPA regional officials in Chicago. Extended discussions and negotiations result in a compliance plan that satisfies EPA but is considerably less costly to the state than it could have been had the state waited until noncompliance had clearly been established.

In suburban Chicago, seven clustered municipalities use intergovernmental agreements to provide fire protection services. Under Illinois law, incorporated municipalities are required to supply services but are not necessarily required to supply them directly. Two of the municipalities do provide direct services. Two adjacent cities purchase services from the two municipalities that provide them. The remaining three municipalities have formed a fire district that operates as one unit within the borders of the three municipalities. Through a mutual aid compact, the seven municipalities provide backup services for one another in case of fires that require personnel and equipment that exceed the standard arrangement.

Defining IGM as Practice

As the three preceding vignettes suggest, *IGM* means routine transactions or working out of relationships between governmental units as programs unfold. *Federalism* refers to a system of governments; it focuses on roles of levels of government and delineation of functions. *Intergovernmental relations* (IGR) focuses on connecting behaviors as governments share in the performance of expanded functions (Reagan and Sanzone, 1981). Wright (1982, p. 13) suggests that IGR features the behaviors of officials, representing multiple units of governments, as they pursue goals and implement policy. IGM emphasizes the goal-achievement processes that are inherent in IGR, since management is a process by which cooperating officials direct action toward goals. Policy development and implementation processes are also operative in IGM, but the primary emphasis is on the process by which specified objectives are met.

These vignettes also demonstrate the special qualities of IGM. These include a problem-solving focus, that is, "an action-oriented process that allows administrators at all levels the wherewithal to do something constructive" (Mandell, 1979, pp. 2, 6); a means of understanding and coping with the system as it is; and an emphasis on contacts and the development of communication networks (Wright, 1983, p. 431). These qualities operate within a goal-oriented framework, as parties develop joint solutions while confronting and making accommodations among the structural and legal issues related to jurisdictional independence, partisan and jurisdictional politics, and the technical and operational questions involved. IGM is thus a complex and interdependent managerial process in which actors search for feasible courses of joint management action (Agranoff and Lindsay, 1983, p. 228).

The study of IGM began indirectly, through examination of the changing federal system and through the study of policy implementation. Studies conducted by the Advisory Commission on Intergovernmental Relations (1977, 1985) focused on trends and patterns and on the need for management. One representative study called for four management reforms: reorganization of the federal government, standardization and simplification of administrative procedures, improvement of communications between governmental levels, and the strengthening of state and local grant discretion and management.

Policy implementation studies indirectly provided valuable generalizations about routine and nonroutine workings. Pressman and Wildavsky's (1973) study of economic development identified the myriad steps involved in making a federal program work. They trace at least thirty decision points requiring dozens of clearances and documenting the "complexity of joint action." Thompson's (1981) study of health programs identified the importance of the legal basis of IGM. Among the variables he identified were statutory precision (whether a policy is regulatory or distributive) and the degree to which it allocates major implementation decisions to state and local governments. Derthick's (1975) study of social services spending demonstrated the game played by states as they switch federal reimbursement across titles to maximize their gain. Bardach's (1977) study of state mental health legislation pointed to the important role of politicians at postenactment stages in adjusting a program as it is carried out. Finally, Radin's (1977) study of desegregation policy pointed to the educational administrator's technical power in carrying out daily routines.

Rosenthal (1984, p. 471) suggests that traditional single-organization models of management do not apply to IGM. In IGM, responsibilities for producing a service or seeking compliance usually must be met through organizations that are not necessarily under the administrator's direct control. From a federal perspective, Rosenthal suggests that "indirect" management can be understood in terms of the four conditions under which it exists. First, program delivery requires that state or local (public or private) agents be partially but not fully accountable to a federal agency. Second, those who are responsible for various aspects of the program are likely to differ, in some important respects, about the objectives of the program. Third, the program is ongoing. Fourth, mechanisms or devices are specified for the exchange of resources and information across formal organizational boundaries.

Howitt (1984, p. 26) also identifies IGM as indirect. Its structure can be viewed either as top-down (from the perspective of officials trying to make a program work from its enactment) or as bottom-up (from the perspective of officials at the other end, whose problem is to make the program work for their own government's purposes while satisfying external requirements). Howitt identifies IGM transactional arrangements as grants-in-aid, eligibility requirements, application review and approval, performance controls, financial controls, technical assistance, grantsmanship, constituency building, and developing implementation capacity.

Wright (1983, pp. 428–430) identifies three central IGM activities that can be linked to growth and complexity: *calculation,* that is, the need to weigh the costs and benefits of federal grants, to play the game of who benefits by formula distribution of funds, and to assess the risk of noncompliance with requirements versus the costs of compliance; *fungibility,* or the ability to shift or exchange resources received for one purpose in order to accomplish another purpose; and *overload,* leading to excessive costs, ineffectiveness, and overregulation. These conditions, Wright explains, have highlighted the roles of appointed officials who apply their experience, expertise, and knowledge to the workings of IGM.

Within this framework, an IGM research tradition is emerging. Studies of process components have examined such topics as regulatory management (Massey and Straussman, 1985), states' planning and participation processes after block grant enactment (Agranoff, 1987), management of the state takeover of the Small Cities Block Grant program (Jennings and others, 1986), IGM techniques used as alternatives for service delivery (Agranoff and Pattakos, 1985), and political accommodation and shared values in program management (Peterson, Rabe, and Wong, 1986).

The interorganizational nature of IGM provides potential bridges from the research tradition in interorganizational relations (IOR). While too broad to cover here (Aldrich and Whetten, 1981), such concepts as resource exchange, organizational domain, partial conflict, authority patterns, and power/resource dependence all relate to the interdependence of interacting government organizations. Few IOR studies, however, confront the jurisdictional nature of IGM or deal with the differences between political and governmental organizations. Among the exceptions is Rubin's (1984) study of the role of municipalities as "meshing" entities, that is, governments that blend the individual goals of the focal government with the collective goals of other local governments. Most central to the IOR research tradition is the concept of networks as means of contact and communication.

A network includes the totality of all organizational units connected by a certain type of relationship (Aldrich and Whetten, 1981, p. 369).

Mandell (1988a, 1988b) has defined IGM networks as ''a number of diverse actors that are connected through a specific type of interaction and within a certain context.'' She emphasizes not only the legal-jurisdictional character of intergovernmental networks but also the autonomy of managers within networks and the varying degrees of permanency among such networks. Of particular importance to IGM are functional networks, those that exhibit high degrees of interaction, interdependence, trust, and areas of agreement. Such networks transcend mere linking and build cohesiveness, Mandell concludes.

A basic synergy between the IGM concept and IGM practice therefore exists. Examination of the dimensions of IGM has been suggested by practice. The greater the knowledge about IGM practice, the more realistic and useful will be academic discourse and, ultimately, action.

IGM Techniques

A variety of IGM techniques have emerged in practice. Related topics and approaches include grantsmanship, regulation, program management, capacity, policy management, bargaining, problem solving, cooperative management, and system changes. There appears to be no specific formula for choosing the techniques of one approach over those of another in particular situations. Their use is situational; all appear useful in certain situations, either alone or in combination.

Grantsmanship. Acquisition and administration of grants have been among the hallmarks of IGM as the availability of nonformula discretionary grants has increased. There are actually two managerial perspectives in grants, one for the funder and one for the recipient. Pressman (1973, pp. 107–108) identifies funders' needs to transfer money to recipients, gather information about recipients' performance, control recipients' performance, justify that projects are worthwhile, and establish stable relationships with recipients. Recipients need to attract funders' attention, achieve a steady flow of money, develop some autonomy over spending funders' money, and achieve stability in relations with funders. Funders face additional managerial constraints due to the indirect nature of IGM, which must be addressed at the design stage (Hale and Palley, 1981, pp. 81–92).

Stories of grants acquisition during times of more abundant funding are legion. One small-town mayor, for example, attracted over $16 million in project grants over a ten-year period. His success was said to be related to his regular reading of the *Catalogue of Federal Domestic Assistance,* to his working with a series of advisory committees, and to his personally filling out applications and working with many federal officials (Hale and Palley, 1981, p. 80). Many hard-pressed governments have looked for money from various available sources by similarly focusing their efforts on any opportunities. Local governments often have needed only knowledge of opportunities and time to fill out applications.

Anderson (1983, p. 199) has identified the critical activities of grants management as writing applications, negotiating and building relations with grantor agencies, administering grant programs within regulations, coping with audit exceptions, and participating in the incremental improvement of programs and regulations. Many of these activities are conducted by grant or program specialists, but administrators must also become involved in securing and administering grants. Anderson identifies seven executive tasks: determining community attitudes and making legislative proposals; calculating the costs and burdens versus the expected benefits, and communicating them; establishing procedures for monitoring funding opportunities and for circulating them through the government; ensuring that management procedures are followed; understanding grants acquisition as an aspect of the job; participating in the resolution of major controversies and impasses with grantor agencies; and making sure that grantsmanship training and resources are available to staff.

A new politics of grantsmanship has emerged because funds for programs and services are declining, because selection criteria for funds are becoming more objective and stringent, and because the level of competition has therefore increased. Administrators must become more adept at the grants game. They must increase their political contacts, improve the targeting of funds, garner greater support from external groups, pay more attention to program detail and quality, and focus on measurable outcomes (Lorenz, 1982, p. 247).

Regulation. Intergovernmental regulation is management by attempts on the part of one government to influence the actions of another government. At least three manifestations of IGM regulation exist:

- Regulatory programs that totally or partially preempt state and local actions (the Occupational Safety and Health Act, the Clean Water Act)
- Program requirements attached to grants (the proviso to provide active treatment for all mentally handicapped persons receiving Medicaid payments)
- Regulations that make a particular action a condition of receiving federal aid (highway funds tied to the lowering of the speed limit; grants for urban development tied to environmental impact reports)

Grant administrators use regulations as means of controlling programs through rules conditioning how money can be used. Unless a regulating agency chooses to totally preempt enforcement, it must ensure program results by such means as stating program goals, setting personnel requirements, making rules, and working to develop implementation capacity (Reagan, 1987, pp. 158, 198–200). Kettl has identified the 1970s as the era of federalism by regulation, where uncertainties over program results created the complicated mix of monitoring and controls in grants programs (Kettl, 1987, p. 33).

Kettl (1987, pp. 95–98) identifies several important purposes of grant regulations: identification of beneficiaries, definition of an agency's posture, setting of standards for local compliance, reestablishment of communication with field offices, provision of the battleground for intraagency conflicts, and continuation of the policymaking process.

As regulators apply rules, the regulated are increasingly involved in calculating costs and benefits. Wright (1983, pp. 428–429) identifies calculations of the regulated as estimating the dollar and compliance costs and the benefits of getting federal grants, assessing the risk of noncompliance with mandates, and selecting appropriate standards and rules (that is, arranging for partial compliance, since programs have so many requirements that all cannot be met). As an IGM strategy, calculating involves thinking before acting, forecasting or predicting the consequences of anticipated actions, and counting, figuring, or computing in a numerical sense the dollar or resource-commitment costs.

Successful implementation of regulatory programs is a political as well as a technical process. Reagan (1987, pp. 194–195) maintains that the degree of workability of the managerial approach depends on the prior success of political bargaining. He identifies three key elements of success. First, a program can work only if adequate political support can be generated and maintained. Second, along with political support, a "sound theory" of regulation must embody appropriate action. Third, harmony of values, or belief integration, must be shared by the diverse participants.

In this context, management of regulations involves the routines of enforcement authorized by law in relation to the regulated parties' adherence to standards. The approach is difficult and sometimes successful. One chronicled success is the federal government's enforcement of southern school desegregation through regulatory actions related to compensatory education (Peterson, Rabe, and Wong, 1986, p. 190). The federal government also used program regulations to get the state of Massachusetts to change its welfare program from a locally administered to a state-administered program (Derthick, 1970). Some provisions are harder to enforce. Massey and Straussman (1985, pp. 292–300) found that regulatory enforcement of fair housing provisions was variable, with performance and compliance spotty. They concluded that the impact of federal aid mandates is overstated.

Program Management. Effective program management involves the actions taken by managers to ensure that a program is developed and administered within the needs of a jurisdiction's perspective. In a grant program, for example, funders must be concerned with such issues as statutory provisions, funding rules, eligibility and service restrictions, and program standards. Ordinarily, these concerns are translated into administrative regulations, written guidelines, and verbal interpretations.

Recipients have their own concerns, starting with developing acceptable responses to funders' requirements. Beyond this, recipients need to plan, organize, and operate programs within their own administrative processes. Making a program responsive involves responding to local political agendas, shaping programs with a jurisdictional or agency emphasis, selecting key program elements, and using policy space. The latter term refers to the residual program authority left when funders' requirements are met. Policy implementation studies reveal these tactics as part of the program management game (Bardach, 1977; Pressman and Wildavsky, 1973; Radin, 1977). In all, the interstices and moves in program management involve incredible complexity, time, costs, and detail that are hidden from public view but are very real to donors and recipients.

Capacity. This is an elusive concept that has been the subject of much discussion. Honadle (1981) has defined *capacity* as the ability of a governmental jurisdiction to anticipate and influence change; make informed and intelligent policy decisions; develop programs and implement policy; attract, absorb, and manage resources; and evaluate current activities in order to guide future action. Capacity is an important IGM tool because governments that have such abilities are better able to manage intergovernmental programs, accomplish funders' program purposes, and make programs suitable to jurisdictional needs.

Considerable debate has occurred in the past few years over the status of state governmental capacity. A number of studies have generally concluded that states have increased their capacities through structural-constitutional modernization, reapportionment, overhaul of their revenue systems, court restructuring, and such managerial reforms as improved budgeting and professional staffing. As a result, states have expanded services in some important areas, provided tax relief to targeted groups, and become more sympathetic to the plight of urban areas. One recent capacity study concluded that states "are more representative, more responsive, more activist and more professional in their operations than ever before." Moreover, as a group, they have been "transformed" and are more equipped to assume their expanded roles as "middlemen" in the federal system (Advisory Commission on Intergovernmental Relations, 1985, p. 15).

Local government capacity is also a crucial factor in the success of intergovernmental programs. Pressman's (1973) study of federal programs in Oakland pointed to political managerial capability as more essential than goal commitments. A survey of city and county officials' responses to federal grants revealed that they believe grant requirements have improved local administrative capacity in such areas as personnel standards, organization, and service quality. Thus, despite the difficulties grantees often find with requirements, they find them to have a positive effect on performance (Richter, 1976, p. 11). Most states pursue local government capacity building as an IGM strategy, particularly in improving their ability to handle finances, personnel, general management, and community and economic development (Florestano and Mirando, 1981).

Policy Management. This approach came into prominence a decade ago, when it was defined as "the identification of needs, analysis of options, selection of programs, and allocation of resources on a jurisdictionwide basis" (Study Committee on Policy Management Assistance, 1975, p. 701). Interest in policy management stems from the needs for state and local officials to manage their jurisdictions as a whole by making conceptual and operational sense of the maze of functional, vertically structured programs and to ensure that the programs are meeting community needs. It has also been a federal government strategy for linking disparate domestic agency leaders (Gage, 1984).

Local governments often manage multiple state and federal grants and tax incentives toward the goal of community economic development. For example, the City of Kokomo, Indiana, used state-authorized bonding authority, a state tax abatement program for new businesses, federal housing grants, and federal historic preservation grants to develop its downtown. The tools of policy management include cross-program planning, problem-area policy development, problem-oriented resource allocation, and strategies for cross-program service delivery (Agranoff and Pattakos, 1978, pp. 263–264).

Bargaining. The need to settle differences due to differing interests is inherent in IGM. Ingram (1977) was one of the first analysts to identify bargaining as an IGM approach in her study of water quality programs. She concluded that federal grants do not necesarily buy compliance but create the opportunity for bargaining. The different parties have their weapons. Grantors and regulators have the power of law, money, and expertise, whereas grantees and regulated parties have the countervailing powers of numbers, political strategy, information, and, most important, control over execution. As a result, both grantors and grantees share the common program interest but want to serve their jurisdictions' best interests, thus bringing on conflict.

Buntz and Radin (1983, p. 406) write that conflict over aims can be functional in IGM and that the development of management strategies to deal with disputes is important. The intergovernmental system sometimes involves necessary conflict arising from structural conditions (national versus state goals), process events (political changes), environmental events or conditions (fiscal changes or new national initiatives), and events or conditions internal to jurisdictions (personnel changes or unique state needs). Buntz and Radin go on to suggest six possible conflict-management strategies that can be adapted to IGM, ranging from reformulation of respective interests to realignment of the forces underlying the conflict.

Bargaining in IGM is best known through use of the negotiated investment strategy (Kunde, 1979). Under the rubric of general community and economic development, three cities—Columbus, Ohio; Gary, Indiana; and St. Paul, Minnesota—initiated changes that were bargained through by the three levels of government until a set of package agreements was developed. The steps followed in Columbus to change four federal-state-local human services grants were as follows: (1) framing the specific issues by local human services interests; (2) carrying the identified issues to the local negotiating team and forwarding them to state and federal teams; (3) receiving initial federal and state responses to the local position; (4) negotiating and synthesizing the active range of issues to be dealt with; (5) setting agendas (some issues were dropped because of their complexity, while others were easily settled by administrative interpretation); (6) negotiating the remaining issues on a tripartite basis, including checking proposed decisions with respective higher authorities; and (7) developing an agreement that could be signed by all parties (Agranoff, 1986). Negotiated changes led to reduced local taxes, program waivers, new grant dollars, and fund reallocations.

Bargaining is a common IGM practice when parties representing two distinct jurisdictions who agree on the intent of a program need to settle core differences. Administrators use their respective positions to recognize conflicting and common interests, but they focus on issues in which one unit's gain is perceived to be tied to another's loss (Brown, 1983, p. 223).

Problem Solving. Problem solving is most commonly used when inherent differences are not so apparent or significant and require less formalized means of resolution. Interorganizational problem solving brings representatives together in circumstances dominated by issues in which common interests are perceived as more important than conflicting interests. It involves perceptions of common concern, relatively open exchange of information, and search for and selection of alternatives that benefit all parties (Brown, 1983, p. 224). Although problem solving is less well known than bargaining, it is a management approach that emanates from creative leadership and decision making (Kepner and Tregoe, 1965; Simon, 1977) and conflict management (Lawrence and Lorsch, 1967).

Problem-solving solutions are oriented to making adjustments that focus directly on issues. Agranoff (1986) concludes that parties were able to solve many multijurisdictional issues by convening, identifying and reaching agreement on the nature of problems, searching for and forging joint solutions, and implementing decisions through joint action. Most solutions were basic program accommodations, reciprocal tasks, or adjustments made to intergovernmental grant programs within requirements and standards, although they were shaped to local needs. They almost always turned out to involve very routine matters that rarely caused conflict once jurisdictional representatives had discussed them while focusing on specific problems.

Bardach (1977, p. 274) refers to "fixing" as a type of problem solving, particularly when actors take "means adjusting certain elements of the games." This type of fixing involves "lending a helping hand," "imposing a new set of priorities," "setting political forces in motion," and "trying to rewrite local zoning ordinances." Radin and others' (1981) evaluation of a federal-state experiment concluded that many of the program adjustments desired by state officials did not necessarily require the seeking of formal waivers, as had been anticipated. Numerous issues were resolved by discussion and agreement on mutually satisfactory solutions, through joint administrative action, or merely by federal administrative interpretation. The need for such mutual accommodations is inevitable, according to Elmore (1982, p. 23), when policy implementation relies on different organizations, variegated authority, expertise, and task proximity, necessitating "specialized problem-solving capabilities farther down the chain of authority."

Other techniques are also available to manage minor differences. One common method is conferencing, in which governmental actors meet to discuss common problems, exchange information, and develop resolutions and agreements on policy questions of mutual interest. For example, the Environmental Protection Agency regularly conducts conferences with state officials on standards and enforcement procedures.

Another means is the preapplication process. Prospective grantees attempt to avoid more serious conflicts by submitting informal drafts of their proposals for purposes of identifying potential trouble spots and avoiding rejection by grantors. States have found this to be a useful technique with consolidation plans (Radin and others, 1981). Waivers, or formal approvals to change program regulations, are often preceded by preapplication processes.

One very common means of difference resolution is the process of discussing and seeking administrative interpretations and reaching mutual understandings. Such transactions are common in IGM, since respective interests in making programs work constitute common denominators, and because contacts are ongoing. Seeking interpretations is in many ways a cooperative activity, as well as a difference-resolution process.

Cooperative Management. These transactions involve some form of agreement between jurisdictions. Several varieties of cooperative management exist. At the most basic level are informal cooperation and unwritten agreements by officials to engage in some activity. The contract involves the delivery of service by one unit of government for another on a payment basis. Joint service agreements, or parallel actions, are agreements between two or more governments for the joint planning, financing, and delivery of services. The compact, or cooperative agreement, is a formal agreement under which two or more governments undertake certain mutual obligations. Service transfers involve the permanent transfer of responsibility for a service from a governmental unit to another entity, either another government or a private organization (Henderson, 1984, p. 1; Martin, 1963, pp. 302–307).

Intergovernmental cooperative action goes back to the mid-nineteenth century, but its visibility and popularity began about three decades ago. Before 1954, a number of local governments had received more than one service from another government. In that year, the city of Lakewood, California, contracted to have all municipal services provided by Los Angeles County (Zimmerman, 1973, p. 3). Most cities in that county contract to have all or most services provided by the county or by other cities; some cities are themselves service producers for other cities (Lakefish, 1971). The federal government engages in a number of cooperative agreements with states, such as the interstate Cooperative Health Statistics System, in which vital records are maintained by states but are part of a national network operated by the federal government. Joint purchases, pooled liability, and group employee benefit packages are other examples of cooperative management.

Research on intergovernmental agreements suggests that such activity is extensive. One study of cities with fewer than twenty-five thousand inhabitants revealed that 58 percent received services from other units and private firms, but most agreements were limited in scope and involved only a single service. Jails and detention houses, police training, street lighting, refuse collection, libraries, planning, engineering services, electric supply, solid waste disposal, water supply, crime laboratory, and animal control services were the most frequently cited areas of exchange (Zimmerman, 1973, p. 11). Henderson's (1984) survey of cities and counties revealed similar patterns; 52 percent of cities and counties reported some involvement in intergovernmental service contracts, 55 percent had entered into joint service agreements, and 40 percent had been involved in service transfers. Generally, the larger the jurisdiction, the more likely it was to engage in one of these cooperative ventures. The most frequently purchased, transferred, or jointly operated services were public works and utilities, public safety and corrections, health and welfare, finance, and general government. The most frequent reasons for engaging in all three types of ventures were to achieve economies of scale, to organize more logically beyond a jurisdiction's boundaries, and to eliminate duplication.

The literature on cooperative IGM provides many suggestions for approaching these ventures. For example, Newland (1983, p. 92) suggests that alternative service delivery should be assessed according to eight criteria: cost of the government service, financial cost to citizens, choice available to clients, quality and effectiveness of service, potential distributional effects, service continuity disruption, feasibility and ease of implementation, and potential overall impact. Others provide guides to contracting and joint purchasing (see Lakefish, 1971, pp. 7–8).

System Changes. The final category of IGM approaches involves the use of politics and policies to change intergovernmental routines directly or indirectly. This approach is familiar in that a legal change often alters working relationships between governments. System changes include lobbying, the use of intergovernmental organizations, legal reforms, and process revisions.

Intergovernmental lobbying has increased as a result of growth in programs. Lobbying involves a number of dimensions. First are the efforts by national associations of state and local officials to articulate the need for federal action, to urge the use of certain grant and regulatory instruments to accomplish national purposes, and to support the renewal and perhaps the redesign of existing programs. Second, spokespersons for regions seek their fair shares of federal resources. Third, lobbyists represent special interests at the policymaking stage, advocating for components of program design that affect the concerns of their clientele. Fourth, special-interest lobbyists become involved at the policy implementation stage, through administrative hearings, conferences, and direct contacts, in the attempt to influence routine procedures related to specific programs. Fifth, lobbyists representing general government interests attempt to influence general procedures related to intergovernmental transactions, such as those that concern rules, guidelines, and interpretations. Sixth, state and local officials, as well as legislators at all levels of government, regularly lobby state and federal administrators regarding the specifics of grant and regulatory programs. The prevalence of intergovernmental lobbying has added a new dimension to IGM and IGR (Hale and Palley, 1981, pp. 16–18; Stenberg, 1980, p. 31).

Intergovernmental organizations exist to identify members' mutual concerns, to advocate for those concerns, and to manage research and other activities cooperatively. Such organizations include state regional organizations, councils of governments, mayors' and managers' compacts, and elected officials' organizations. These organizations deal with problems of scale that arise when functions or problems spill over jurisdictional boundaries (Derthick, 1974, p. 12). As IGM instruments, these organizations provide a wide range of activities, from the mutual design of laws and administrative procedures to the execution of programs on a cross-jurisdictional basis.

Legal reform is designed to make the process of working out routines easier by altering elements of the framework under which such affairs are conducted. For example, Congress has facilitated grants management through the Joint Funding Simplification Act of 1974. The act enables grantees to draw on resources from more than one agency, program, or appropriation for large-scale projects, so long as they meet individual grant requirements. A recent unsuccessful attempt at this approach was the Reagan administration's program to reach closure by swapping programs, making some entirely state and local (education, highways) and others national (health financing). The conversion of categorical grants to nine new block grants in 1981 involved a broad, sweeping reform. Conversion facilitates recipients' management by increasing their discretion and decreasing their administrative burdens.

Process revision is a more direct approach. Revision encompasses a variety of attempts to ease the managerial processes of intergovernmental assistance, without necessarily changing the legal structure of grants programs. These activities have received the greatest prominence at the federal level. They have included such measures as mandatory notification of state and local chief executives, a series of Office of Management and Budget circulars that streamline or rationalize grants management, experiments with joint federal agencies in grant review and funding, authorizations to waive program requirements that impede operations, decentralization of federal decision making and federal government regionalization, and the use of federal regional councils (Shapek, 1981, pp. 33–55). This approach has not been so central in the 1980s as in the 1970s. To a certain degree, it has been negated by block grants, deregulation, and more flexible categorical grants, but process revision still remains. For example, the Medicaid waiver program, under Section 2176 of the Omnibus Budget and Reconciliation Act of 1981, allows states to seek waivers to provide Medicaid-reimbursable home and community-based services to eligible recipients—the elderly, the developmentally disabled, and the chronically mentally ill—who otherwise would require nursing homes or intermediate care facilities (Agranoff and Pattakos, 1984, pp. 76–77).

Summary

By definition, IGM must focus on ordinary actions of officials as they work through the existing system of grants and regulations. A great deal of attention is focused on dramatic events: A city refuses to accept a formula grant because of the cost of compliance; a state loses 5 percent of its welfare grant because of an audit exception; a group of child care providers protests a new set of standards.

While these actions constitute one means of defining the workings of the system, they are overshadowed by thousands of routine transactions. The negotiation of a city's development bond, the adjustment of a grant to serve homeless migrants, and the administrative approval to dig a series of drainage ditches and install sewers are also definitive IGM transactions, although they rarely hit the newspapers or come to the attention of politicians.

Both types of intergovernmental problems are resolved by hidden but protracted processes that lead to jurisdictionally satisfying mutual agreements. These adjustments are based on what appears to be politically and technically reasonable and within the general scope of statutory intent. IGM is thus a ubiquitous process of solution seeking by means of interdependent exchanges of resources between government organizations. IGM's distinctiveness lies in its governmental, interorganizational, and managerial nature.

References

Advisory Commission on Intergovernmental Relations. *Improving Federal Grants Management.* Washington, D.C.: Advisory Commission on Intergovernmental Relations, 1977.

Advisory Commission on Intergovernmental Relations. *The Question of State Government Capability.* Washington, D.C.: Advisory Commission on Intergovernmental Relations, 1985.

Agranoff, R. *Intergovernmental Management: Human Services Problem Solving in Six Metropolitan Areas.* Albany: State University of New York Press, 1986.

Agranoff, R. "SSBG Planning and Participation Processes: Are the States Becoming Stronger Partners?" *Publius,* 1987, *17* (3), 111–129.

Agranoff, R., and Lindsay, V. A. "Intergovernmental Management: Perspectives from Human Services Problem-Solving at the Local Level." *Public Administration Review,* 1983, *43* (3), 227–237.

Agranoff, R., and Pattakos, A. N. "Human Services Policy Management: A Role for University Institutes." *Midwest Review of Public Administration,* 1978, *12* (4), 257–270.

Agranoff, R., and Pattakos, A. N. "Intergovernmental Management: Federal Changes, State Responses, and New State Initiatives." *Publius,* 1984, *14* (3), 49–84.

Agranoff, R., and Pattakos, A. N. "Local Government Human Services." *Baseline Data Report,* 1985, *17* (4), 1–20.

Aldrich, H., and Whetten, D. A. "Organization Sets, Action-Sets, and Networks." In P. Nystrom and W. Starbuck (eds.), *Handbook of Organization Design.* Vol. 2. New York: Oxford University Press, 1981.

Anderson, W. F. "Representing the Community with Other Governments." In W. F. Anderson, C. A. Newland, and R. J. Stillman (eds.), *The Effective Local Government Manager.* Washington, D.C.: International City Management Association, 1983.

Bardach, E. *The Implementation Game: What Happens After a Bill Becomes a Law.* Cambridge, Mass.: MIT Press, 1977.

Brown, L. D. *Managing Conflict at Organizational Interfaces.* Reading, Mass.: Addison-Wesley, 1983.

Buntz, C. G., and Radin, B. A. "Managing Intergovernmental Conflict: The Case of Human Services." *Public Administration Review,* 1983, *131* (5), 403–410.

Derthick, M. *The Influence of Federal Grants: Public Assistance in Massachusetts.* Cambridge, Mass.: Harvard University Press, 1970.

Derthick, M. *Between State and Nation: Regional Organization of the United States.* Washington, D.C.: Brookings Institution, 1974.

Derthick, M. *Uncontrollable Spending for Social Service Grants.* Washington, D.C.: Brookings Institution, 1975.

Elmore, R. F. "Backward Mapping: Implementation Research and Policy Decisions." In W. Williams and others, *Studying Implementation: Methodological and Administrative Issues.* Chatham, N.J.: Chatham House, 1982.

Florestano, P. S., and Mirando, V. L. *The States and the Metropolis.* New York: Marcel Dekker, 1981.

Gage, R. W. "Federal Regional Councils: Networking Organizations for Policy Management in the Intergovernmental System." *Public Administration Review,* 1984, *44,* 134–145.

Hale, G. E., and Palley, M. L. *The Politics of Federal Grants.* Washington, D.C.: Congressional Quarterly Press, 1981.

Henderson, L. M. "Intergovernmental Service Arrangements and the Transfer of Functions." *Baseline Data Report,* 1984, *16* (6).

Honadle, B. W. "A Capacity-Building Framework: A Search for Concept and Purpose." *Public Administration Review,* 1981, *41* (5), 575–580.

Howitt, A. M. *Managing Federalism: Studies in Intergovernmental Relations.* Washington, D.C.: Congressional Quarterly Press, 1984.

Ingram, H. "Policy Implementation Through Bargaining: The Case of Federal Grants-in-Aid." *Public Policy,* 1977, *25,* 22–53.

Jennings, E. T., and others. *From Nation to States: The Small Cities Community Development Block Grant Program.* Albany: State University of New York Press, 1986.

Kepner, C. H., and Tregoe, B. B. *The Rational Manager.* New York: McGraw-Hill, 1965.

Kettl, D. F. *The Regulation of American Federalism.* Baltimore, Md.: Johns Hopkins University Press, 1987.

Kunde, J. "As in the Past, the Cities Propose: Under NIS They Help Dispose." *Nation's Cities,* Nov. 26, 1979, pp. 4–9.

Lakefish, R. *Purchasing Through Intergovernmental Agreements.* Washington, D.C.: Management Information Service, International City Management Association, 1971.

Lawrence, P. R., and Lorsch, J. W. *Organization and Environment.* Cambridge, Mass.: Harvard University Press, 1967.

Lorenz, P. H. "The Politics of Fund Raising Through Grantsmanship in the Human Services." *Public Administration Review,* 1982, *42* (3), 244–251.

Mandell, M. P. "Intergovernmental Management." *Public Administration Times,* Dec. 15, 1979, pp. 2, 6.

Mandell, M. P. "Intergovernmental Management in Interorganizational Networks: A Revised Perspective." *International Journal of Public Administration,* 1988a, *11* (4), 393–416.

Mandell, M. P. "Organizational Networking: Collective Organizational Strategies." In J. Rabin, G. T. Miller, and W. B. Hildreth (eds.), *Handbook on Strategic Management.* New York: Marcel Dekker, 1988b.

Martin, R. C. *Metropolis in Transition: Local Government Adaptation to Changing Urban Needs.* Washington, D.C.: U.S. Government Printing Office, 1963.

Massey, J., and Straussman, J. D. "Another Look at the Mandate Issue: Are Conditions of Aid Really So Burdensome?" *Public Administration Review,* 1985, *45* (2), 292–300.

Newland, C. A. "Managing for Effectiveness, Efficiency and Economy." In W. F. Anderson, C. A. Newland, and R. J. Stillman (eds.), *The Effective Local Government Manager.* Washington, D.C.: International City Management Association, 1983.

Peterson, P. E., Rabe, B. G., and Wong, K. K. *When Federalism Works.* Washington, D.C.: Brookings Institution, 1986.

Pressman, J. L. *Federal Programs and City Politics: The Dynamics of the Aid Process in Oakland.* Berkeley: University of California Press, 1973.

Pressman, J. L., and Wildavsky, A. *Implementation.* Berkeley: University of California Press, 1973.

Radin, B. A. *Implementation, Change and the Federal Bureaucracy.* New York: Teachers College Press, 1977.

Radin, B. A., and others. *Planning Reform Demonstration Project Evaluation.* Washington, D.C.: U.S. Department of Health and Human Services, 1981.

Reagan, M. D. *Regulation: The Politics of Policy.* Boston: Little, Brown, 1987.

Reagan, M. D., and Sanzone, J. G. *The New Federalism.* (2nd ed.) New York: Oxford University Press, 1981.

Richter, A. J. "Federal Grants Management: The City and County View." *Urban Data Service,* 1976, *8* (10), 1–13.

Rosenthal, S. R. "New Directions in Evaluating Intergovernmental Programs." *Public Administration Review,* 1984, *44* (6), 469–476.

Rubin, H. J. "The Meshing Organization as a Catalyst for Municipal Coordination." *Administration and Society,* 1984, *16* (2), 215–238.

Shapek, R. L. *Managing Federalism: Evolution and Development of the Grants-in-Aid System.* Charlottsville, Va.: Community Collaborators, 1981.

Simon, H. A. *The New Science of Management Decision.* Englewood Cliffs, N. J.: Prentice-Hall, 1977.

Stenberg, C. W. "Federalism in Transition: 1959–79." In Advisory Commission on Intergovernmental Relations (ed.), *The Future of Federalism in the 1980's.* Washington, D.C.: Advisory Commission on Intergovernmental Relations, 1980.

Study Committee on Policy Management Assistance. "Executive Summary." *Public Administration Review,* 1975, *35,* 700–705.

Thompson, F. J. *Health Policy and the Bureaucracy: Politics and Implementation.* Cambridge, Mass.: MIT Press, 1981.

Whetten, D. A. "An Introduction to Research in Interorganizational Relations." *Journal of Higher Education,* 1981, *52,* 1–28.

Wright, D. S. *Understanding Intergovernmental Relations.* (2nd ed.) Belmont, Calif.: Brooks/Cole, 1982.

Wright, D. S. "Managing the Intergovernmental Scene: The Changing Dramas of Federalism, Intergovernmental Relations and Intergovernmental Management." In W. Eddy (ed.), The *Handbook of Organization Management.* New York: Marcel Dekker, 1983.

Zimmerman, J. F. "Intergovernmental Services Agreements for Smaller Municipalities." *Urban Data Service,* 1973, *5* (1), 1–12.

Dave Ulrich
Robert E. Quinn
Kim S. Cameron

11

Designing Effective Organizational Systems

An administrator in a federal agency recently confided to us that although he enjoyed his job, he had begun thinking more seriously about early retirement. He said that his managerial responsibilities had been more taxing in recent years than during his entire twenty-five years in the civil service. He noted that pressures for performance and accountability had increased, that scrutiny of and demands on his budget had grown, that legislative direction seemed more volatile and less predictable, that a continual flow of new programs and directives confronted him, that employees were less likely to respond to traditional organizational authority, and that all this made him wonder whether he could respond appropriately or whether it was even worth it. Our friend is not alone.

Public and private administrators alike have experienced a decade of enormous change—rapid and unpredictable legislative changes, technological innovations, and transitions in the composition of the work force. Managing in the face of increasing and continual change requires administrators to reexamine and redefine their assumptions and practices. This chapter examines the underlying causes of the increasing rate of change, suggests that traditional assumptions may need to be modified, and offers some guidelines for administrators attempting to design effective organizational systems in the face of increasing change.

Increasing Pressures for Change

The 1980s have been characterized as a decade of transformation (Huber, 1984). In all sectors of the economy, organizations are being rocked with change. During the last fifteen years, for example, 40 percent of the

Fortune 500 companies ceased to exist as independent, public firms through mergers, acquisitions, divestitures, and leveraged buyouts. In a seven-year period (1980–1987), merger and acquisition activity rose from $30 billion to $185 billion. In the public sector, similar pressures for change exist. Agencies at all levels of government reflect constant societal and technological change, new laws, increased fiscal constraint, and increased activity on the part of political interest groups. In the last decade, the U.S. Postal Service has been forced to compete with such private firms as United Parcel Service and Federal Express. Agencies like NASA, while under constant demand to justify basic mission and control expenses, have had to respond to major jolts, such as the Challenger disaster. Others, like the Federal Aviation Administration, have experienced sequential or simultaneous events, such as the controller strike, airline deregulation, and increased passenger demand, with fewer resources.

Before this decade of rapid change, administrators could focus much of their attention on maintaining stability and continuity in reporting relationships, program design and delivery, and agency objectives. In a world of continual change, administrators encounter complex and paradoxical demands. At the same time that they must maintain stability and continuity, they must also foster adaptability and temporariness. Designing effective organizations in a time of change involves paradoxical demands for engendering the capability of responding to change while maintaining stability and predictable service delivery.

As administrators recognize the increasing rate of change, they also need to identify new strategies for dealing with the turbulence. Guidance for designing effective organizations in a decade of change may come from two fields of research: the literature on organizational effectiveness (OE) and on organizational design. In the last few years, theory and research on OE have evolved toward a more complex view of defining good organizational performance. Because the organizational design literature takes these dynamic, transforming environmental conditions into account, it provides guidance for changing conditions. We shall suggest that the integration of these two literatures provides an alternative view of how to effectively design an organization in an age of transformation. This brief review of OE and organizational design literature provides a conceptual framework for designing effective organizational systems and points toward actions that may increase the ability to adapt to changing conditions.

Organizational Effectiveness and Design

To design effective organizations, one has traditionally started by determining the criteria of effective organizations and then devised organizational systems and procedures consistent with those criteria. Early organizational scholars identified *internal efficiency* as the dominant criterion of effective organizations. Weber (1946), Barnard ([1938] 1968), and other scholars emphasized that organizations need to maintain internal operating efficiency to be effective. Chandler (1962, 1977) chronicled organizational designs on the basis of the criteria of internal efficiency. Following principles of organization suggested by Fayol (1949) and Gulick and Urwick (1937), administrators paid attention to span of control, chain of command, authority, policies, and rules to ensure coordination and efficiency of internal work processes. For the first eighty years of industrialization, public and private organizational designs were dominated by this efficiency criterion. As these organizations grew, internal efficiency became the dominant issue.

In the early 1960s, however, organizational researchers began to recognize what most executives knew—that internal operating efficiency had to be balanced with the external demands on the organization. *Responsiveness* supplanted internal efficiency as the overriding criterion of effective organizations. Organizational scholars began to examine organizational environments and to suggest that organizational designs had to match criteria established by the environment. Burns and Stalker (1961), Lawrence and Lorsch (1967), and Emery and Trist (1965) suggested arraying environments along a continuum ranging from *simplistic, certain, and stable* to *complex, uncertain, and dynamic*. Organizational designs should be aligned to these environmental contingencies (Hellriegel and Slocum, 1973; Duncan, 1972). Mechanistic organizations, being more hierarchically structured with rules and policies, narrow span of control, and clear reporting relationships, were purported to operate more effectively in simplistic, certain, and stable environments, whereas organic organizations—those with loosely coupled systems (Weick, 1976), more decentralized control over operations, and control through values rather than rules (Ouchi, 1980)—were argued to perform better in complex, uncertain, and dynamic environments. Following this contingency view, a number of alternative approaches that match designs and environments have been proposed (Nadler and Tushman, 1980; Galbraith, 1977; Schoonhoven, 1981; Drazin and Van de Ven, 1985). The logic of these approaches is straightforward: Environmental conditions set parameters and determine criteria for OE, and organizational systems and processes are designed to fulfill these criteria so that effective performance results.

Integrating Models of Organization

In the last decade, it has become apparent that focusing merely on external criteria of effectiveness, or on internal efficiency, is not functional. As environments have become turbulent, understanding the definition and criteria of effective organization has also become more complex. One recent approach to this increasing complexity of the criteria of OE was Quinn's (1988) "competing values" approach to organizational effectiveness. His approach asserts that OE requires a multiple rather than a unitary perspective and that effective organizations must satisfy a complex set of changing demands or competing values.

The model in Figure 11.1 describes how individuals evaluate the performance of an organization. Its dimensions were derived inductively by analysis of similarity ratings given to a comprehensive set of effectiveness criteria by organizational scientists (Quinn and Rohrbaugh, 1983). These criteria clustered together to produce a theoretical model based on two main dimensions.

These two axes, placed perpendicular to each other, create four quadrants. Both axes focus on organizational and management orientations. The vertical axis ranges from *flexibility* to *control*. The horizontal axis ranges from an *internal focus* to an *external focus*. Each quadrant in the framework incorporates one of four major models of OE prominent in the literature: the *human relations model* (upper left), the *open systems model* (upper right), the *rational goal model* (lower right), and the *internal process model* (lower left). The human relations model, for example (Likert, 1967; Argyris, 1962), stresses such effectiveness criteria as cohesion, morale, and human resource development. The open systems model (Yuchtman and Seashore, 1967; Pfeffer and Salancik, 1978) stresses such criteria as flexibility, growth, resource acquisition, and external support. The rational goal model (Steers, 1976) stresses such criteria as planning, goal accomplishment, productivity, and competitiveness. The internal process model (Weber, 1946) is represented by information management, monitoring, stability, and control.

The framework of Figure 11.1, called the *competing values model*, implies that these four models of OE have conceptually coherent relationships with one another. For example, each model has a polar opposite. The human relations model, defined by the flexibility/internal quadrant, stands in contrast to the rational goal model, defined by the control/external quadrant. The open systems model, defined by the flexibility/external quadrant, runs counter to the internal process model, defined by the control/internal quadrant. Parallels among the models are also important. The human relations and open systems models share an emphasis on flexibility. The open systems and rational goal models are both grounded in an external focus. The rational goal and internal process models share an emphasis on control. The internal process and human relations models share an internal focus.

Cameron (1986) argued that as environmental conditions become more turbulent and complex, criteria of effectiveness become more paradoxical. As executives who struggle with competing and at times conflicting demands realize, organizations are often expected to embrace and pursue simultaneously all the criteria illustrated in Figure 11.1. Therein lies the major contribution of the competing values model: It captures the competing and paradoxical nature of the OE criteria in high-performing organizations.

If competing values drive organizational effectiveness, they also must drive approaches to organizational design. Unfortunately, many or most approaches to designing effective organizations have emphasized one model or approach to the exclusion of others (Astley and Van de Ven, 1983). For executives to design more effective organizational systems, guidelines for organizational design need to incorporate paradoxical and competing criteria.

Figure 11.1. Competing Values Framework.

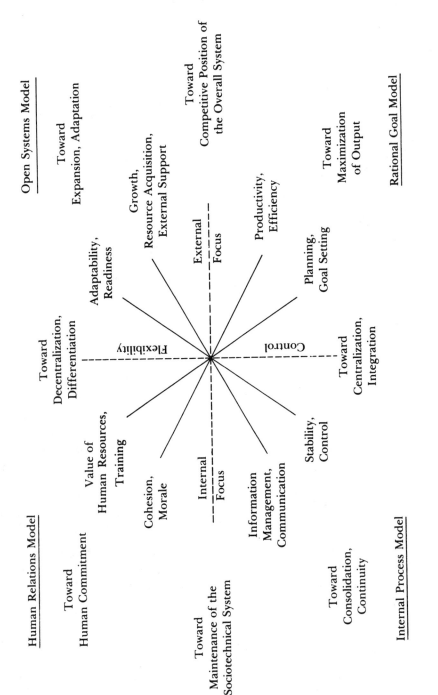

Source: Quinn, 1988, p. 48.

In the following sections, we discuss practical guidelines for designing organizations that incorporate paradoxical attributes. Whereas these guidelines are based on an extensive literature relating to organizational design, we emphasize the practical guidelines that are derived from them. We use our own extensive research in the redesign of the Federal Aviation Administration (FAA) to illustrate several of these guidelines.

More Effective Systems

Effectively designing an organization that deals with turbulence and paradox requires administrators to understand how to create a shared mindset among employees, how to control the behavior of employees, and how to assign accountability and responsibility.

Shared Mindset. To respond to rapidly changing and conflicting environmental demands, administrators need to adapt their managerial assumptions and organizational practices to the conditions of turbulence and paradox. When the environment is relatively stable, organizations may adapt management by objectives to motivate and focus employee attention. In turbulent environments, however, when objectives may be outdated before they can be accomplished, management by mindset may be needed.

Recent theory and research in cognitive psychology (Guidano, 1987) suggest that as individuals mature, they develop personal identity. This personal identity remains relatively stable in the face of changing environmental conditions. At the core of personal identity is a set of tacit assumptions that individuals have about how the world around them operates. Using these assumptions, individuals filter and process information, make decisions, and allocate time to particular activities. Likewise, organizations have identities or mindsets. Based on a set of shared assumptions about how the organization operates, organizational mindsets focus employees' attention, generate employees' commitment to key activities, and generate an organization's capability of responding to change. When a mindset focused on change exists in each member of the organization, the organization is more likely to adapt to changing conditions.

Step 1: Assess the current mindset and identify the one required. Administrators have the responsibility of evaluating existing organizational mindsets and adapting them to changing external conditions. Current mindsets can be seen in how employees spend time, make decisions, interact with each other, and interact with outside users of agencies' services. To design new mindsets, administrators need to specify the underlying assumptions that should permeate employees' thinking. In a turbulent environment, these assumptions may include the following: (1) organizational change is a constant; (2) organizational design is a process, not an outcome; and (3) successful organizational systems must meet simultaneous and competing demands. Some employees may already operate on these assumptions, but administrators have the responsibility of implanting these assumptions into all employees' mindsets.

Helping individuals acquire the mindset that change must become a way of life is fostered by a knowledge of past managerial practices and their incongruence with current conditions, as well as by an understanding of the reasons for changes made in the actual organizational design. In the FAA, administrators had to learn new management styles to interact with a completely new work force consisting of newly hired air traffic controllers. An initial step in the reeducation process was making sure that the administrators understood their current managerial styles and the potential negative consequences of those styles in the new situation. In training programs, FAA managers learned from feedback with subordinates how their current management styles were perceived. They explored the implications of particular management styles on both organizational and employee goals. They learned conceptual and practical elements of new managerial behaviors via role plays, videotapes, and observation. By helping individual managers learn flexibility in their managerial styles, the FAA administrators began to adopt a new mindset that focused on responding to and managing change (Ulrich, 1985).

Managing a process implies that organizational design occurs continually and that reporting relationships, span of control, organizational charts, and chain of command are merely by-products of a continuous dynamic decision-making process characterized by negotiations, trade-offs, compromises, and power plays. These traditional design characteristics, therefore, are better conceptualized as process outcomes rather than as fixed, steady-state attributes whereby an ideal solution is attained. To focus on the process of organizational design requires that attention shift from ends to means. The end, or structure of the organization, is not the most important consideration in turbulent environments. Rather, the processes put in place to those ends should become the primary focus of attention in organizational design. Administrators attempting to create new mindsets may focus more time on structuring the ongoing process of organizational design than on formalizing reporting relationships and organizational charts.

Administrators often recognize two primary outcomes of organizational design: efficiency and responsiveness (Prahalad and Doz, 1987). *Efficiency* focuses on centralization and tight coordination of an organization's activities. *Responsiveness* focuses on being close to customers, legislators, and other constituents outside the organization.

Many organizations experience continual pendulum swings between being centralized and decentralized. When efficiency criteria override responsiveness, organizations become more centralized, with headquarters staff making more decisions, and with tighter controls being established at the top. When responsiveness criteria dominate, organizations become more decentralized through the establishment of smaller units, regional centers, participative decision making, or other local control systems. Headquarters staff may expand or shrink, depending on where the arc of the pendulum exists at a particular time.

Administrators designing effective organizational systems in turbulent environments must identify and work toward a third option, that of being efficient and responsive simultaneously. This loosely coupled design (Weick, 1976) implies that administrators balance complex and, at times, competing processes and outcomes as they seek to accomplish multiple goals. The design is at the same time loose, or decentralized and responsive, and coupled, or centralized and efficient. Pressures for efficiency result when fewer resources exist to meet increasing demands for services. Pressures for responsiveness derive from public agencies' being in "glass houses" where their services are continually reviewed and assessed by legislatures and citizens. Both efficiency (to reduce the cost of delivery services) and responsiveness (to assess which services are most critical to the public and deliver them in a first-class manner) must compose the mindset that administrators instill in employees.

Step 2: Use institutional practices to instill a mindset. Once core assumptions for a mindset are identified, administrators may use a variety of practices to instill it. Selection systems—who is hired and promoted—not only move individuals with particular mindsets into key positions but also tell other employees what is valued for organizational success. Development programs offer administrators opportunities to share information and establish the foundations for new mindsets. Performance management systems—appraisal and rewards—focus employees' attention on particular behaviors and outcomes. This focus may instill a new mindset. Communication of key values through speeches, videos, brochures, meetings, newsletters, and other means may be used to establish a mindset among employees. These institutional practices (selection, development, performance management, communication) may be used by administrators to create a focused mindset among employees.

To illustrate the importance of a mindset and the use of institutional practices for establishing it, we turn to the FAA in the early 1980s. When the FAA faced labor problems in August 1981, administrators realized that the mindset of controllers was counter to the perceived goals of the agency. As a result, they began to change the mindset by firing over eleven thousand controllers and beginning a massive effort to hire new controllers who not only had technical skills but could also bring a new mindset to the work force. At the heart of the new mindset were the core values of adapting to continually changing conditions, gaining continual commitment to agency performance from all employees, and meeting safety standards in all activities.

Upon hiring the controllers, enormous resources were dedicated not only to controller training but also to management training. The Management Training Center was established in Lawton, Oklahoma, with the explicit mission of upgrading managerial competence in the agency. A major portion of the management development work focused on understanding and instilling in managers a common set of values. Managers were then asked to communicate these values to all FAA employees through workshops, meetings, discussions, reward systems, and example.

In addition, the agency worked to balance competing efficiency and responsiveness demands. Maintaining effective operations—defined as safe separation of aircraft and continued operation of the air traffic system—

had to be accomplished through a more efficient and productive organization and work force (leaner staffs and less overhead). Activities to increase efficiency (such as use of computer systems, changes in reporting relationships, planning processes, and management surveys and training) received increased attention and resources. Simultaneously, programs that responded to constituents of the air traffic system were launched to bring representatives of the airlines together to work on flight schedules, to work with civic leaders to upgrade airport facilities to handle more traffic, and to communicate with passengers about how the system was responding to increased demand. Had the agency focused exclusively on either internal efficiency or external responsiveness, it would not have responded to the turbulent environment.

Controlling Behavior. Administrators have the responsibility of focusing employees' attention on activities that are most central to the goals of the organization. Controlling employees' behavior means devising organizational systems that encourage and reinforce employees for spending time and behaving in ways consistent with organizational goals. Several alternatives are available for helping this to happen. For example, the Internal Revenue Service organized regional service centers to focus employees' behavior on the needs of particular localities. NASA's organization, by allocating increasing resources to space exploration and less to space research, reinforced space-exploration goals and behaviors of employees. In the Comprehensive Employment and Training Act (CETA) programs of the 1970s, the goal was to integrate federal employment programs with local needs. The organization and allocation of resources and responsibility to city and metropolitan CETA offices reinforced this desired outcome.

To control behavior, administrators need to set goals and objectives for their organizations. Clear organizational direction enables administrators to identify what employees should contribute for organizational success. Once goals are defined, administrators can choose which types of control mechanisms best focus individual behavior and attention on goals: market, bureaucracy, or clan controls (Ouchi, 1980; Williamson, 1975, 1979).

Market controls occur when employees are offered explicit incentives for accomplishing clearly articulated standards. Employees' behaviors and attitudes are shaped by the organizational practices of setting goals and reinforcing goals through rewards. When clear performance expectations can be established and monitored, when employees' performance can be directly linked to organizational outcomes, and when the organization focuses on short-term transactions, then administrators can use market systems of control.

Bureaucratic controls occur when the organization establishes rules and procedures to govern employees' behavior. Employees' attitudes and behaviors may be governed by policies, rules, and reporting relationships. In situations where performance standards can be monitored closely through personal inspection, and where employees lack the long-term professional competence to perform without monitoring, administrators can rely on policies and rules to govern behavior.

Clan controls occur when employees' behavior is shaped by a common set of values or norms. Common organizational values derive from selection, training, communication, and reinforcement. Controlling employees' behavior through development of shared values works when long-term contracts exist between employees and employers. Over time, employees learn the norms and expectations of employers, and employers learn to trust employees to act in accordance with the expected values. Clan controls also operate effectively with professional employees in ambiguous job settings. Professional employees, who have been socialized, selected, and developed to perform professional tasks, govern themselves because of personal and collegial commitment. Public administrators whose professionally trained employees perform ambiguous, nonmeasurable tasks can best govern behavior through the development of shared values.

Thus, administrators can cope with change and paradox by designing organizations to control the behavior of employees. As summarized in Table 11.1, guidelines exist for using market, bureaucracy, or clan controls (Ulrich, 1983). By selecting the right control systems, administrators foster the meeting of multiple and paradoxical effectiveness criteria.

Acountability and Responsibility. To operate dynamic, integrated organizations, administrators must establish processes to allocate responsibility and accountability, so that efficiency and responsiveness result. The process (deciding how to allocate responsibility) is more important than the outcome (reporting relationships, organizational chart), because in a continually changing environment, no conclusive or ideal organizational design will be attained. If a stable process can be established for reallocating accountability, the costs of continually reorganizing are reduced over time. Some version of the following four steps can be used to establish a process for ongoing reorganization.

Step 1: Specify key tasks that need to be accomplished. Key tasks are critical to the organization's accomplishment of its mission. Identification of key tasks forces reexamination of the duties an organization performs. It also encourages a discussion of why some tasks are performed. In the FAA, for example, a discussion by a regional management team exposed that some tasks (for example, meetings and reports) were not contributing to the accomplishment of the mission of the agency but still consumed extensive resources. Questioning about the key tasks for the region made clear whether activities should be expanded or reduced.

Step 2: Define options about where tasks can be done. After the specification of key tasks, options can be identified about where the tasks can be accomplished. The options can often be arrayed along a continuum, from headquarters to the smallest local unit:

- Headquarters: Tasks can be performed by a central staff at the federal, state, or local level.
- Region: Tasks can be performed regionally perhaps in a few states (for federal programs), counties (for state programs), or wards (for municipalities).

Table 11.1. Situations for Governance Mechanisms.

	Means of Governing Behavior	*Organizational Characteristics*	*Task Characteristics*	*Individual Characteristics*
Market governance	Explicit incentives	Clear goals Short-term transactions	Measurable Link individual performance to organizational outcomes	Short-term goals
Bureaucratic governance	Rules and procedures	Stable systems	Performance standards easy to monitor	Lack of long-term professional competence
Clan	Values or norms	Long-term transactions	Individual performance difficult to measure	Self-monitoring Professional

- District: Tasks can be performed in districts, in a state (for a federal program) or city (for a state program).
- Branch: Tasks can be performed at the local level, in a county office (for a federal program) or a ward or neighborhood office (for a state program).
- Outside: Tasks can be subcontracted through competitive bidding to outside contractors.

By specifying the key tasks and the options for where they can be performed, administrators can create a responsibility matrix to represent how work will be allocated. One axis of the matrix includes the key tasks; the other includes the locations where those tasks will be accomplished. The primary challenge of allocating responsibility is to make sure that for each cell in this matrix, decisions are made that allocate responsibility so that key tasks can be accomplished both efficiently and effectively. The responsibility matrix frames the organizational design process to allow ongoing choices about which components of the organization will be centralized or decentralized.

Step 3: Assign tasks to specific locations. In discussing each cell of the responsibility matrix, administrators help clarify roles and assign accountability and responsibility. What level of the organization will set *policy* for the particular task? What levels need to be *consulted* before particular activities? What level will have primary responsibility for *implementing* the task? What level will *monitor* task completion according to specified standards?

The discussion that occurs in setting these four roles becomes the most important component of the process for assigning responsibility. Defining current practices and debating desired practices in each cell of the responsibility matrix allow administrators to clarify accountability and responsibility, create more effective organizational designs, and focus employees' mindsets.

Step 4: Prepare reporting relationships and organizational charts on the basis of the discussion of Step 3. After discussing the responsibility matrix, administrators must clarify reporting relationships. The organizational chart becomes a by-product of an ongoing discussion. Through these discussions, roles and responsibilities are clarified, and individuals recognize their specific contributions to the organization and how those contributions fit with others.

This four-step process ensures that discussion about organizational design focuses on the process of establishing reporting relationships, and not on the organizational chart. It allows for change to occur continually in organizational design by revisiting these decisions regularly as conditions change.

Summary

Our main argument in this chapter is that organizational design must begin to account for turbulence and paradox. Because organizational effectiveness is inherently paradoxical (Cameron, 1986), the competing values model (see Figure 11.1) has been an important addition to our understanding of the contradictory criteria pursued by organizations. Because organizations pursue paradoxical criteria and develop paradoxical attributes, administrators working to design more effective organizational systems must focus on processes more than on outcomes.

Administrators who wish to develop more effective organizational processes must make informed choices about instilling organizational mindsets, establishing control systems, and instituting processes for allocating accountability and responsibility. As administrators acquire competence in managing these organizational processes, they design effective organizational systems. Thus, career administrators may find the increasing rate of change less a reason for retirement than a reason for renewal.

References

Argyris, C. *Interpersonal Competence and Organizational Effectiveness.* Homewood, Ill.: Dorsey, 1962.

Astley, W. G., and Van de Ven, A. H. "Central Perspectives and Debates in Organization Theory." *Administrative Science Quarterly,* 1983, *28,* 245–273.

Barnard, C. *The Functions of the Executive.* Cambridge, Mass.: Harvard University Press, 1968. (Originally published 1938.)

Burns, T., and Stalker, G. M. *The Management of Innovation.* London: Tavistock, 1961.

Cameron, K. "Effectiveness as Paradox." *Management Science,* 1986, *32,* 539–553.

Chandler, A. *Strategy and Structure: Chapters in the History of American Industrial Enterprise.* Cambridge, Mass.: MIT Press, 1962.

Chandler, A. *The Visible Hand: The Managerial Revolution in American Business.* Cambridge, Mass.: Harvard University Press, 1977.

Drazin, R., and Van de Ven, A. H. "Alternative Forms of Fit in Contingency Theory." *Administrative Science Quarterly,* 1985, *30,* 514–539.

Duncan, R. B. "Characteristics of Organizational Environments and Perceived Environmental Uncertainty." *Administrative Science Quarterly,* 1972, *17,* 313–327.

Emery, F. E., and Trist, E. L. "The Causal Texture of Organization Environments." *Human Relations,* 1965, *18,* 21–32.

Fayol, H. *General and Industrial Management.* New York: Pitman, 1949.

Galbraith, J. R. *Organization Design.* Reading, Mass.: Addison-Wesley, 1977.

Guidano, V. F. *Complexity of the Self.* New York: Guilford Press, 1987.

Gulick, L. H., and Urwick, L. F. (eds.). *Papers on the Science of Administration.* New York: Institute of Public Administration, Columbia University, 1937.

Hellriegel, D., and Slocum, J. W., Jr. "Organization Design: A Contingency Approach." *Business Horizons,* 1973, *16,* 59–68.

Huber, G. P. "The Nature and Design of Postindustrial Organizations." *Management Science,* 1984, *30* (8), 928–951.

Lawrence, P. R., and Lorsch, J. W. *Organization and Environment.* Cambridge, Mass.: Harvard University Press, 1967.

Likert, R. *The Human Organization: Its Management and Value.* New York: McGraw-Hill, 1967.

Nadler, D. A., and Tushman, M. L. "A Model for Diagnosing Organizational Behavior: Applying a Congruence Perspective." *Organizational Dynamics,* 1980, *9* (2), 35–51.

Ouchi, W. G. "Markets, Bureaucracies, and Clans." *Administrative Science Quarterly,* 1980, *25,* 129–141.

Pfeffer, J., and Salancik, G. R. *The External Control of Organizations: A Resource-Dependence Perspective.* New York: Harper & Row, 1978.

Prahalad, C. K., and Doz, Y. I. *The Multinational Mission.* New York: Free Press, 1987.

Quinn, R. E. *Beyond Rational Management: Mastering the Paradoxes and Competing Demands of High Performance.* San Francisco: Jossey-Bass, 1988.

Quinn, R. E., and Rohrbaugh, J. "A Spatial Model of Effectiveness Criteria: Toward a Competing Values Approach to Organizational Analysis." *Management Science,* 1983, *29* (3), 363–377.

Schoonhoven, C. "Problems with Contingency Theory: Testing Assumptions Hidden Within the Language of Contingency Theory." *Administrative Science Quarterly,* 1981, *26,* 349–377.

Steers, R. "When Is an Organization Effective: A Process Approach to Understanding Effectiveness." *Organizational Dynamics,* 1976, *5* (2), 50–63.

Ulrich, D. "Governing Transactions: A Framework for Cooperative Strategy." *Human Resource Mangement,* 1983, *22,* 23–39.

Ulrich, D. "Federal Aviation Administration Management: Myth Versus Reality." *MTS Digest,* 1985, *4,* 7–11.

Weber, M. *From Max Weber: Essays in Sociology.* (H. H. Gerth and C. W. Mills, trans.) New York: Oxford University Press, 1946.

Weick, K. "Education Systems as Loosely Coupled Systems." *Administrative Science Quarterly,* 1976, *21,* 1–19.

Williamson, O. E. *Markets and Hierarchies.* New York: Free Press, 1975.

Williamson, O. E. "Transaction-Cost Economics: The Governance of Contractual Relations." *Journal of Law and Economics,* 1979, *22,* 233–261.

Yuchtman, E., and Seashore, S. E. "A System Resource Approach to Organizational Effectiveness." *American Sociological Review,* 1967, *32,* 891–903.

12

Douglas C. Eadie

Building the Capacity for Strategic Management

The now widespread and rapidly growing interest in the use of strategic management techniques in public organizations is easily understood. For one thing, strategic techniques fill a clear niche in the "planning" market, as public organizations attempt to cope with incredible environmental complexity, as well as accelerating and often bewildering change.

Traditional long-range planning techniques cannot fill this planning vacuum. Typically projecting the present into the future, on the dangerous assumption of continuing environmental stability, formal long-range planning has not served public organizations well in an ever less predictable world. Indeed, the illusion of control that heavily documented long-range planning can generate among the unwary may leave an organization less capable of coping with change than if it does no long-range planning at all.

Another reason for the growing appetite for strategic management techniques is the widespread dissatisfaction and frustration of public and nonprofit policymakers (such as city council and board members) with their leadership roles in formulating their organizations' policy agendas. Theoretically, formal planning serves as the vehicle for policy bodies to make policy-level decisions. In practice, however, such decisions have often been mere ritualistic confirmation of decisions already made. This disparity between promise and reality, not surprisingly, has produced strong critics of planning among policy body members who are accustomed to exerting strong influence on the world around them.

This planning vacuum is slowly being filled, as public and nonprofit organizations around the country successfully design and implement strategic management applications. There is a growing body of literature that documents successful applications, and spreading knowledge of these success stories will surely increase the demand for strategic management techniques sharply in coming years (Bryson, 1988; Bryson and Roering, 1987; Eadie, 1983, 1985; Sorkin, Ferris, and Hudak, 1984).

Despite the obvious need, practitioners interested in applying strategic management techniques to their organizations are well advised to proceed cautiously. Strategic management is no panacea, any more than such predecessors as the planning/programming/budgeting systems (PPBS), zero-based budgeting (ZBB), and management by objectives (MBO) were. Enthusiasm for these powerful new techniques must be tempered by the reality that they are not simple to apply and that significant costs are involved. Otherwise, the cure can very well be deadlier than the disease.

Further complicating the lives of interested practitioners is the fact that the field of strategic management is rapidly changing, and there is no such thing as "the" strategic management process or "the" strategic plan. Rather, there are numerous methodological variations on the broad strategic planning and management theme, and each of these variations is associated with different outcomes, the least of which may be a formal, comprehensive strategic plan. Practitioners must also realize that their organizations' planning needs and capabilities vary greatly, and that particular strategic planning and management applications must be tailored to these unique needs and capabilities if they are to succeed (Bryson, 1988; Eadie, 1987).

This chapter's principal objective is to provide public and nonprofit policymakers and managers with practical advice for using strategic management techniques in their organizations. The chapter draws on reports of actual experience. It is not about the production of strategic planning documents per se. Rather, the question being addressed is how public and nonprofit organizations can strengthen their capability to cope with environmental complexity and change. After describing the broad strategic management logic, with emphasis on a significant variation on the theme *strategic issue management,* the chapter concentrates on the *design process,* by which particular organizations tailor the techniques to their specific situations. Discussion of three important issues then follows: the role of policy bodies in strategic issue management, and how their strategic leadership can be strengthened; the tie of annual budget preparation to strategic issue management, and how to enhance the strategic content of annual budgeting; and the role of the management team in strategic issue management, and how that process can simultaneously benefit from and strengthen teamwork.

The Strategic Field

Purpose. The strategic management process might best be thought of as a broad management logic—a theme with many possible specific variations in practice. The overall purpose is to establish and maintain a balance between an organization and its external environment, such that the organization's resources are put to the best feasible use in capitalizing on opportunities and addressing threats.

Strategic management is, then, primarily a change vehicle by which an organization fashions and implements strategies to ensure that balance is maintained. The vehicle becomes more critical—and yields a higher return to the organization—during a time of significant environmental change that calls the organization's priorities and programs into question. Strategic management is not basically a vehicle for refining activities and controlling costs, both of which the annual budgeting process excels at.

A Changing Field. The past few years have seen significant growth in strategic planning theory, drawing on rapidly accumulating experience. Indeed, the term *strategic management* is commonly used these days to describe a broader concept than the original *strategic planning.* Two closely related developments are particularly important: a bias toward action, and a focus on the human element in strategic management (Bryson and Roering, 1987; Eadie, 1986, 1987; Gluck, 1985).

In the early years of strategic planning, the field was captivated by the analytical techniques involved in formulating strategies, and it was biased toward the production of formal, comprehensive strategic plans (Olsen and Eadie, 1982). Subsequent experience showed that strategy formulation was only half the battle and that just as much, if not more, attention had to be paid to the task of implementation if the process was to be effective over the long run (Gluck, 1985; Tichy, 1983; Nutt and Backoff, 1987). It has also been recognized that in the process of preparing elaborate documentation, an organization might actually be distracted from the main business of making strategic decisions. In some circumstances, the rapidity of environmental change militates against the production of formal plans at all. Effective strategic management, in this case, may mean people around a table making decisions on the basis of the best information that can be brought to bear (Gluck, 1985; Mintzberg, 1987).

Strategies are formulated and implemented by people, and success on both fronts is heavily dependent on developing the human resources of an organization—far more than, for example, on developing an organization's computer capability. Senior management teams are now commonly involved in fashioning the strategies that they must implement, not only because better strategies result from diversity of knowledge and opinions but also because ownership and commitment are natural partners. We also now recognize that people learn to manage strategically, and that training in the techniques can facilitate that learning.

Diverse Applications. Strategies come in all shapes and sizes. The strategic management logic can be put to many uses, depending on the desired outcomes and the planning organization's capabilities. Over the past decade or so, three major types of applications have emerged: statewide or communitywide visionary applications; comprehensive, departmentally based applications; and the more selective strategic issue management approach (Bryson and Roering, 1987).

Statewide or communitywide applications of the logic have been attempted throughout the country—for example, in the Ohio state government and in such cities as Cleveland, Dallas, San Antonio, and San Francisco. These more global applications are typically very visionary, in the sense that they articulate broad goals and strategies that encompass both the public and the private sectors and numerous organizations. Such applications tend to involve extensive citizen participation, and implementation of strategies depends on a high degree of interorganizational cooperation and coordination (Sorkin, Ferris, and Hudak, 1984).

Comprehensive, departmentally based strategic management applications are what most people think of as strategic long-range planning. Taking this approach, the departments in a government or other public organization annually or biennially update their environmental scans and formulate their strategic goals and plans, which are then reviewed and compiled into a single strategic plan for the organization. Under the "umbrella" theory, this long-range plan serves as a kind of anteroom to annual operational planning and budget preparation.

The comprehensive departmental approach has been severely and often fairly criticized because the volume of paper generated and processed tends to work against the very decision-making and organizational change that it is intended to achieve. In effect, ritual overwhelms substance. Another serious deficiency is that a bottom-up approach to strategy formulation tends both to miss the broader picture and to fail to identify issues cutting across departments.

A more selective version of the comprehensive departmental application has steadily gained popularity as its utility has been demonstrated. Strategic issue management, as it is usually known, focuses on the identification and selection of strategic issues, which are addressed through strategy formulation. Eschewing the comprehensive "supermarket" approach, strategic issue management applications have succeeded because of their selectivity, which enhances their manageability. Because of demonstrated utility to organizations of all sizes and resource levels, the remainder of this chapter will focus on strategic issue management (Bryson, 1988; Bryson and Roering, 1987; Eadie, 1985, 1986, 1987).

Elements of Strategic Issue Management

Strategic issue management involves four basic elements: confirmation of organizational mission, identification and selection of strategic issues, formulation of strategy, and implementation of strategy. Precisely how each of the elements is handled by a particular organization is a matter of design—tailoring the logic to specific situations—which is examined in detail in the next section.

Confirmation of Organizational Mission. An organization's mission is a statement of basic purposes that distinguishes it from other organizations. Whatever its form—a terse description of its reason for being, or a listing of major goals or functions—the mission establishes the legitimate boundaries of organizational activity. In light of their fundamental nature, missions do not require annual or biennial updating. Rather, they are reconsidered as circumstances dictate.

Circumstances that signal the need to consider an organization's mission often occur when the environment in which the organization functions changes dramatically and when the organization experiences significant changes in leadership at the level of the policy body or the executive staff. Environmental change (such as the Great Depression or, more recently, the AIDS epidemic) can force an organization to reconsider the limits of its activities. Certainly, the New Deal represented a sweeping change in mission for the federal government, and the AIDS crisis is forcing many governments to move beyond their traditional service boundaries. Less dramatically, the election of several new members to a board or a city council can erode the consensus on basic purposes that is essential to orderly government.

More often than not, only a pause to consider organizational mission is required at the outset of strategic issue management. Perhaps a more formal statement is drafted, reflecting the existing consensus; but searching examination is seldom required. Nevertheless, to proceed with strategic issue management without clear consensus on basic purposes can jeopardize the process.

Identification and Selection of Strategic Issues. These are identified through a searching examination of an organization's environment, in the context of its stated mission. A strategic issue may be thought of as a significant question about an organization's products or services, usually in the form of an opportunity to do something different or a threat to be countered. While issues sometimes fall into neat functional or departmental categories, many cut across established organizational and programmatic units. These are the ones that tend to fall through the cracks and to catch an organization off guard.

An organization's environment is examined through what is known as *environmental scanning,* which involves identifying, collecting, and analyzing information pertinent to the planning organization's mission. A local government, for example, will need to collect a wide range of information— fiscal, economic, demographic, physical, social, cultural, and political. A planning department within a local government, by contrast, will, in formulating its own organizational strategy, want to examine a narrower, more internal environment, including its relationship with the mayor's office and the city council and the expectations and opinions of department heads, for example.

Scanning techniques can be as elaborate and expensive as organizational needs and resources dictate. At the more expensive end of the spectrum would be original research, such as opinion surveys; at the other end would be the use of already collected information, such as census reports. Although it is orderly and convenient to perform environmental scanning cyclically—say, the annual production of a trends-and-conditions document—in times of rapid environmental change an organization will be better served by continuous environmental scanning.

Whatever the form of the scan, and however it is produced, the ultimate utility of the process depends on creative analysis of the information, in order to identify strategic issues. Experience has demonstrated that such analysis is most effective if done as a collective activity involving, say, all department heads with, if feasible, members of the policy body (board or council). The department heads and city council in a local government, for example, might spend a day together at a retreat, reviewing trends and conditions and identifying what appear to be the critical issues facing the government. Even though prior staff analysis can be useful, having a diverse, senior-level group around the table for an extended time is essential to dealing with a complex, dynamic environment that can be understood only if viewed from different perspectives.

Selecting the issues that comprise an organization's strategic agenda is an essential step. Otherwise, there is danger of the kind of organizational paralysis associated with "supermarket" planning. In this regard, there is probably no better criterion for choice than cost. Put simply, what is the likely cost that will be incurred if the planning organization does not begin to address a particular issue now? Cost might be measured in terms of human suffering (for example, if AIDS is not effectively addressed now) or dollars (to rebuild bridges and roads that have deteriorated because infrastructure has not been addressed as a strategic issue).

Formulation of Strategy. The next step is to formulate strategies to address the issues that have been selected. A strategy will consist of change targets, with associated implementation plans. For example, a large urban community college identified as one of its strategic issues the opportunity to contribute to the community's economic development by training displaced workers for new jobs. To address this issue, it selected a target—creation of a high-tech training center separate from the mainline campuses—and formulated a detailed three-year plan to develop the center, consisting of financial, architectural, and educational plans (Cuyahoga Community College, 1984). A county government employment and training department selected as a strategic issue the need to strengthen ties to the local economic development corporation and identified several practical initiatives to address the issue (Eadie, Rose, and Bellow, 1988).

Interdepartmental task forces can be useful vehicles for strategy formulation. In identifying and selecting targets and formulating implementation plans, such task forces will basically apply a cost-benefit logic. Possible targets to address an issue are identified, the costs (financial, technical, political) of implementation are assessed, and targets are selected to produce the most impact on the issue at an affordable cost. Selection obviously requires that an organization's actual and potential resources be assessed. Organizational resources are basically its people (numbers, skills, attitudes), its financial capacity (cash on hand, revenues expected, borrowing and taxing power), and its technologies (computer capability, processes of production or service delivery).

Implementation of Strategy. Successful implementation of strategy depends on the following key factors:

- Policy body and chief executive leadership and firm commitment, both to the outcomes sought and to the costs that must be incurred
- Formal inclusion of the costs of implementation in the budget
- Careful management of implementation through a formal structure and process, including adequate staff direction and support, and regular collective monitoring by senior management staff of progress based on performance information

Role of the Planning Office. An organization's planning office can play a critical role in the implementation of strategic issue management. One obvious responsibility is to assist in environmental scanning, since planners are often skilled in scanning and have already collected much of the required information. The planning office might also assume project management and coordination, guiding strategic management from design through implementation. Whether this stronger role makes sense will depend on a number of factors, including the record of the office in project management, the staff's facilitation skills, and the relationshp with the chief executive officer.

Design of Applications

The Design Contribution. Design serves an essential twofold purpose in the process of applying strategic issue management. First, through design, the planning organization ensures that its particular application of strategic issue management techniques will produce the specific outcomes that the organization wants. Second, the organization determines that it is capable of managing the application of the logic it has selected.

For some reason, the design of strategic issue management applications has only recently begun to receive the attention it deserves in public sector literature, despite a long history of failed expectations in the planning arena (Bryson and Roering, 1988; Eadie, 1987). A strategic issue management design consists of the following major elements:

- A clear statement of the outcomes to be achieved from strategic issue management
- A detailed description of the technical process to be followed, the structure through which it is to be carried out, and the roles and responsibilities

of major actors (Who will produce the environmental scan, and how will it be reviewed in the process of identifying issues? Will task forces be used to formulate strategies? Who will comprise the task forces? Will there be a staff project manager to oversee the process?)

- A cost analysis, detailing the time and out-of-pocket costs that are likely to be incurred during the application, including the cost of required consulting assistance
- A work plan, setting forth a schedule of major events

Outcomes. The basic outcome of strategic issue management is strategies to address identified strategic issues, but strategic issue management is a sturdier beast, whose broad back can carry more baggage than that. Public and nonprofit organizations have considerable choice in deciding what they want to achieve through the process. If these choices are not made explicitly, however, as part of the initial design activity, they are unlikely to be achieved. Three examples will demonstrate the point.

First, strategic issue management application can be designed to strengthen the policy body–executive relationship, as well as to address strategic issues. If strengthening the relationship is a high priority, particular attention will be paid to policy body involvement and to policy body–executive interaction. Special care might be taken in structuring the policy body's work sessions and in developing materials that will facilitate its participation.

Second, strengthened public relations can result from a carefully crafted application. For example, the environmental scan can easily be turned into community "road shows" that present trends-and-conditions briefings for neighborhood groups, service clubs, and the like.

Third, senior management's staff development objectives can also be served through strategic issue management, if the process is appropriately designed. For example, presentation of the environmental scan to a city council might be shared by several or all department heads, who might also critique each other's presentation styles before the council's work session. The design might also place greater emphasis on staff training as part of the application, providing staff the opportunity to become familiar with the theory, as well as to participate in the process.

Development of the Design. There are strong reasons for the policy body and the chief executive to work closely together in developing the design for the strategic issue management process, especially in local government and nonprofit organizations. In federal and state government, the arm's-length, often adversarial relationship between the executive and legislative branches may make such design collaboration unrealistic. Without involvement in specifying desired outcomes and working out implementation details, a policy body will surely feel less ownership of the process and consequently will be less likely to support paying the costs, including time.

The following cooperative approach to design is based on a number of real-life consulting experiences. At a one-day work session—in a retreat setting, with a professional facilitator—the policy body and the chief executive are oriented to the strategic issue management logic. They determine the outcomes they want the process to achieve and reach agreement on the role that the policy body is to play in the process and on the time that will be committed to playing it. Major financial costs for such items as consultants and survey research are identified and agreed to in the work session. Following this session, the chief executive and senior management staff meet for a day to develop the detailed work plan, which is reviewed with the policy body.

Capability. The strategic issue management design—the outcomes to be achieved and the process to be followed—must be realistic, in the sense that the planning organization has or can build the capability required to carry out the design. Otherwise, the organization is guilty of that cardinal sin of management: wishful thinking. The old adage ''Better to have tried and failed than not to have tried at all'' may be a useful guide in some spheres, but certainly not in the realm of management. Failed experiments in management damage credibility and rightly anger participants who have wasted precious time and energy.

The preeminent and highly practical result of good design is manageability, which means that the organization can achieve what it has set out to achieve. The factors that should be taken into account in assessing organizational capability will include human resources, organizational climate, and competing organizational demands.

Human Resources. People make or break strategic issue management applications, and so they deserve an especially close look during the design phase. In the first place, staff time is needed to carry out the several steps, from environmental scanning to strategy formulation. But time alone means little. The planning organization must also frankly assess the quality of the time that can be committed to strategic issue management. Staff planning and management skills should be assessed, as should the pertinent experience of staff. A staff that has participated little in planning, or whose planning experience has been confined to a fiscally oriented budget-preparation process, will be less well prepared to support a strategic issue management application than a staff that has been actively and productively involved in long-range planning. Likewise, a staff that has little history of collective activity will not be well prepared for the intensive teamwork required by strategic issue management. Of course, staff can be developed and can learn through experience. The point is that staff development and on-the-job training must be factored into the design as constraints and costs, and the time required for preparatory activities must be added to the work plan.

Bryson and Roering (1988) have concluded that the keys to successful strategic issue management are influential process sponsors and process champions, the former to lend legitimacy to the process and the latter to manage the process itself. Examples of critical process sponsors are city councils, mayors, and city managers.

Organizational Climate. Climate is also a constraint on strategic management applications, and required changes in climate must be factored into the design as a cost. Attitudes are an important facet of climate. A senior management staff that has recently been involved in a failed planning experiment will not be carried away by enthusiasm at the thought of another. If creativity, initiative, and innovation have not been encouraged and rewarded in the past, staff will see little apparent reason for creative involvement. Staff who have worked with an authoritarian chief executive for some time will not easily participate in the kind of freewheeling debate that is characteristic of high-quality strategizing. If planning has received little respect from the policy body, staff can hardly be expected to become enthusiastic strategists overnight.

Competing Demands. Organizations do not implement strategic issue management in a vacuum; there is always competition for resources, especially for time. Therefore, the design should both identify and assess likely competitors and build in the flexibility required to cope with inevitable surprises. In state government, for example, a gubernatorial reelection campaign is guaranteed to preoccupy all political appointees for the six months before the election. To move forward with a strategic issue management process during this period would be an exercise in futility. In local government, if a tax issue is on the ballot and is being hotly contested, senior staff can be expected to devote considerable time and energy to the levy campaign and will have much less to give to strategic issue management.

The state of what might be called the *managerial infrastructure* can also compete with strategic issue management. The infrastructure comprises the basic administrative and service delivery systems of the organization—for example, on the administrative support side, financial management, budget preparation and management, computing, and, on the service side, such visible operations as garbage collection and police and fire protection in local government.

The point is that if one or more of these basic systems is seriously deficient, a public organization will have no choice but to fix it, and the time, attention, and other resources required to do so are likely to reduce the commitment to the strategic issue management application. Indeed, the need for system repair may be so great that the strategic issue management application is best deferred until the problems have been remedied.

The Policy Body's Involvement

The involvement of policy bodies—city and county councils and other legislative bodies, and nonprofit boards—in planning is a thorny issue. Seriously frayed policy body–executive relationships are frequently seen in the failure to address this issue effectively. There are several reasons why public organizations find the question difficult to address. There is a natural tension between the policy and executive functions, which by their very nature tend to be adversarial. This natural tension may have been exacerbated in recent years by the appearance of a more assertive breed of policy body member—well educated, expecting to play a strong role in directing the organization, and impatient with barriers to playing that role. There may also be an absence of clear guidelines for the division of labor and for policy body-executive team building. Despite the revered golden rule that councils and boards should make policy and administrators should carry it out, the distinctions between policy and administration are anything but clear in practice (Eadie, 1986; Neal, 1986; Svara, 1985). Finally, public administrators may be inadequately prepared. Their technically oriented education and training tend to make them insensitive to the needs of policy bodies and unnecessarily defensive in protecting administrative prerogatives. Ample proof may be found in the budget-preparation processes of many public and nonprofit organizations. Despite budget's being touted as the preeminent policy tool, all too many boards and councils carry out their leadership role by thumbing through a fat, finished document—surely the most trivial possible application of the policy formulation art.

Strategic issue management provides ample opportunity for the creative, policy-level involvement of boards and councils. The outcomes of such involvement include not only higher-quality planning but also a strengthened policy body–executive relationship that can serve as a "line of credit" to draw on in other areas of organizational management. The first obvious opportunity is in the design stage of a strategic management application, when the policy body can be actively involved in identifying outcomes and making the commitment to pay the price, principally in their time.

Another major opportunity for creative involvement is in the review of the environmental scan and the identification of strategic issues. Also, of course, when task forces have developed strategies to address identified issues, the policy body should be involved in reviewing and approving them.

The reader should be warned that it may be difficult to convince all policy body members to attend the initial design session, and that a sales pitch may be in order. In this event, it is crucial that the policy body members see the upcoming process in their own terms—not as a neutral "good government" step, but as a means to enhance their influence in the organization and to become identified publicly as leaders in modern management (through, say, presenting the environmental scan to neighborhood groups).

Enhancing the Budget Process

Budgeting is basically a very effective incremental negotiation process, and it does quite well the job of refining and adusting operating programs and controlling organizational costs. The frustration of the policy body that attempts to exert influence on the total process is inevitable, since the great majority of organizational resources are already allocated to ongoing programs, making the budget process anything but a vehicle for dramatic policy-making.

Nevertheless, the potential of budgeting as a policymaking tool can be more fully tapped through the application of strategic issue management. In the first place, the overall review of trends and conditions, and the identification of intersecting issues, can be timed to serve as a prelude (and backdrop) to budget preparation. Beyond this, the budget process can be formally opened with a policy body–senior management work session at which department heads can present detailed scans of their own unique environments and can analyze implications for the organization. Moreover, the policy body and assembled staff can reach agreement on the budgetary issues that will receive special attention, both in budget preparation and in the policy body's review of the submitted budget.

The application of strategic issue management techniques to the budget process creates, in effect, two different budget streams or agendas that operate concurrently: (1) the traditional stream, which involves the normal incremental negotiation over adjustments in line-item allocations to existing programs, and (2) the strategic budget agenda, which focuses on strategies to address issues in which the policy body has expressed strong interest. Keep in mind that these strategic issues may not involve major expenditures. The point is to select—on the margin, so to speak—areas of the budget where there is latitude for change and for the policy body to exert influence on that change, however modest it may be.

Examples from real life may help to make the point. One city council I worked with chose revenue enhancement, via the community recreation center, as a budgetary strategic issue. Another chose police department accreditation. A school board with which I worked identified a number of issues, including minority recruitment and public communications and relations. In light of the many well-intended but failed attempts to reform the tried-and-true object-of-expenditure budget process, to maintain the basic incremental process while simultaneously lifting up and managing a marginal change agenda has a certain practical beauty. As observed earlier, it is surely better to achieve modest concrete results than to have high-flown expectations dashed.

Management Team Building

The greater senior management's collective involvement in environmental scanning, issue identification, strategy formulation, and management of implementation, the more likely it is that the strategic issue management process will be successful. Management team building is a requirement for effective strategic issue management, but strengthened management teams are also a result of the process (Bolt, 1985; Eadie and Steinbacher, 1985; Lenz and Lyles, 1986; Robinson and Eadie, 1986; Shea and Guzzo, 1987).

Unlike approaches to staff development that take managers away from the workplace and put them through exercises divorced from the real work they do, strategic issue management builds teams through complex, important, and demanding organizational work. Rather than scaling a cliff or engaging in sensitivity exercises at a weekend retreat, management team members develop such skills as identifying issues, preparing for and participating in policy body–staff work sessions, and formulating strategies.

While doing this critical organizational work, management team members are also building an ongoing process that will make it possible for their participation to continue, thus marrying organizational and staff development in the same process. This is in clear contrast to the disillusionment that can result when enthusiastic managers return from their weekend in the wild only to discover that the proverbial "salt mine" awaits them Monday morning. How fast the warm glow from the scaled cliff or the forded stream can wear off!

Summary

Strategic issue management techniques hold real promise for public and nonprofit management. They provide a practical and affordable tool, not only to cope with environmental change but also to strengthen the role of policy bodies and their working relationships with senior staff, to upgrade the annual budget process, and to build more cohesive management teams. The promise can be most fully realized through development of a detailed application design that spells out the desired outcomes, the work plan to be followed, and the costs to be incurred.

References

Bolt, J. F. "Tailor Executive Development to Strategy." *Harvard Business Review,* 1985, *63,* 168–176.

Bryson, J. M. "A Strategic Planning Process for Public and Non-Profit Organizations." *Long Range Planning,* 1988, *21,* 73–81.

Bryson, J. M., and Roering, W. D. "Applying Private-Sector Strategic Planning in the Public Sector." *Journal of the American Planning Association,* 1987, *53,* 9–22.

Bryson, J. M., and Roering, W. D. *The Initiation of Strategic Planning by Governments.* Minneapolis: Strategic Management Research Center, University of Minnesota, 1988.

Cuyahoga Community College. *A Report to the Community.* Cleveland, Ohio: Cuyahoga Community College, 1984.

Eadie, D. C. "Putting a Powerful Tool to Practical Use: The Application of Strategic Planning in the Public Sector." *Public Administration Review,* 1983, *43,* 447–452.

Eadie, D. C. "Strategic Agenda Management: A Powerful Tool for Government." *National Civic Review,* 1985, *74,* 15–20.

Eadie, D. C. *Strategic Issue Management: Improving the Council-Manager Relationship.* Washington, D.C.: International City Management Association, 1986.

Eadie, D. C. "Strategic Issue Management: Building an Organization's Strategic Capability." *Economic Development Commentary,* 1987, *11,* 18–21.

Eadie, D. C., Rose, S. D., and Bellow, N. J. "One Job Training Program's Plan for the Future." *County News,* 1988, *20,* 22–23.

Eadie, D. C., and Steinbacher, R. "Strategic Agenda Management: A Marriage of Organizational Development and Strategic Planning." *Public Administration Review,* 1985, *45,* 424–430.

Gluck, F. W. "A Fresh Look at Strategic Management." *Journal of Business Strategy,* 1985, *6,* 4–21.

Lenz, R. T., and Lyles, M. A. "Managing Human Problems in Strategic Planning Systems." *Journal of Business Strategy,* 1986, *6,* 57–66.

Mintzberg, H. "Crafting Strategy." *Harvard Business Review,* 1987, *65,* 66–77.

Neal, J. E. "Managers and Councilmembers: Comparing Their Political Attitudes." *Public Management,* 1986, *68,* 13–14.

Nutt, P. C., and Backoff, R. W. "A Strategic Management Process for Public and Third-Sector Organizations." *Journal of the American Planning Association,* 1987, *53,* 44–57.

Olsen, J. B., and Eadie, D. C. *The Game Plan: Governance with Foresight.* Washington, D.C.: Council of State Planning and Policy Agencies, 1982.

Robinson, R. V., and Eadie, D. C. "Building the Senior Management Team Through Team Issue Management." Washington, D.C.: International City Management Association, 1986.

Shea, G. P., and Guzzo, R. A. "Group Effectiveness: What Really Matters?" *Sloan Management Review,* 1987, *28,* 25–32.

Sorkin, D. L., Ferris, N. B., and Hudak, J. *Strategies for Cities and Counties: A Strategic Planning Guide.* Washington, D.C.: Public Technology, 1984.

Svara, J. H. "Dichotomy and Duality: Reconceptualizing the Relationship Between Policy and Administration in Council-Manager Cities." *Public Administration Review,* 1985, *45,* 221–232.

Tichy, N. M. *Managing Strategic Change.* New York: Wiley, 1983.

Part Three

Strengthening Relationships with Legislatures, Elected and Appointed Officials, and Citizens

In a democratic political system, public administrators are one node in an extensive network of relationships. Citizens, legislators, elected executives, and political appointees share membership in the network with public administrators. Because the role of public administrators is circumscribed by democratic norms and institutions, each member of the network exercises a legitimate claim to the attention and loyalty of the public administrator. One response to the demands of these multiple claimants is for the public administrator to withdraw to avoid offending any of the other network members. The public administrator's role is not simply to coexist, however, but to serve each of these actors. Part Three probes how public administrators can achieve this goal by strengthening relationships with government's many publics.

      The nature of the relationships between the public administrator and "significant others" creates a high potential for alienation among the involved actors. Location in the executive branch can estrange the public administrator from legislators because of resentment and fear of the control that legislators exercise over programs, budgets, and other significant aspects of an administrator's life. Citizens may be perceived as nuisances who conceivably usurp the roles of legislators and elected executives and generate unacceptable inefficiencies. Even elected and appointed officials are not immune to becoming part of an "us-them" syndrome. In some cases, the antagonism reflects the administrator's reciprocation for the lack of respect and trust shown by elected and appointed officials. In other instances, it is the administrator's mechanism for guarding turf and protecting programs won in hard-fought battles.

Nevertheless, the public administrator's alienation from environmental actors is not inevitable, and the relationships can be managed for constructive results. In working to strengthen relationships, public administrators must begin by accepting the legitimate role of each constituency with whom they interact. Without recognition of the legitimate roles of legislators, elected and appointed officials, and citizens, no progress can be made toward developing mature, constructive relationships with these groups.

Good relationships between public administrators and other network members can be self-perpetuating. Mature relationships between a public administrator and various constituencies are essential sources of power—not over others, but with and through others. Citizens, legislators, and executives who perceive that they are empowered, not controlled, by public administrators are more likely to respond to their advice and counsel. Thus, many possibilities that are foreclosed by antagonistic relationships with these groups become realizable. The trust and the confidence that are outgrowths of mature relationships with legislators, elected and appointed officials, and citizens enhance the public administrator's ability to effectively play the role of arbiter and representative.

Citizens, legislators, and elected and appointed officials are the sources of public administrators' legitimacy and the beneficiaries of public administrators' performance. Part Three shows how strengthening relationships with these groups can ensure legitimacy while it enhances performance.

13

Roger L. Sperry

Developing Effective Relations with Legislatures

Legislative bodies in the United States play unique and ever growing roles in governance. The U.S. Congress has been characterized as "the First Branch of Government" because of its extensive constitutional powers (Fisher, 1981). Legislators, by virtue of their status as the people's elected representatives, are seen as the formulators of public policies; administrators are the agents of implementation.

Even though formally preeminent among equals, some say the role of the legislature in administration is already too large, but public administrators who ignore or attempt to ride roughshod over legislatures or city councils do so at their own peril. Administrators who lack understanding of the legislative process or the skills needed to deal effectively with legislative bodies have less chance of attaining their program goals.

History has taught that government leaders and managers can take numerous approaches to success on Capitol Hill or at the State House, but certain fundamental requirements exist. These include an understanding of the legislature's central place as an institution of representative government, an understanding of the legislative process, the ability to present a program and build necessary alliances, an understanding of the need to provide and obtain good information, and a facility for avoiding disaster. At a more human level, these requirements include the ability to listen and communicate effectively, develop trust, and follow through on promises. Because public administrators at all levels of government are responsible to elected officials, the people's representatives deserve the attention, understanding, and commitment of public administrators everywhere.

This chapter explores the dimensions of the executive-legislative relationship by describing the evolution and growth of legislative bodies, listing the key actors in the process and the roles they play, and summarizing the basic elements of the process. This description is followed by a brief discussion of the unique relationship that has developed between the president and the Congress of the United States. Next, some insights and advice are provided on some basic elements of establishing good relationships with legislatures. Finally, the chapter touches on several points associated with the somewhat more intimate manager-council relationship at the local level.

Evolution and Growth of Legislative Bodies

The role of legislatures in American governance has waxed and waned over the nation's two-hundred-year history. The first national government, established under the Articles of Confederation, was little more than the Congress itself. The executive branch, as we know it today, did not exist: Power was too fractionated and decentralized, and effective governance was impossible. This situation led to the creation of the Constitution, the three coequal branches of government, and the sharing—or separation—of powers among the branches.

Who Has the Power to Control Events? Dominance of the legislative branch over the executive, or vice versa, has varied with the times. In the last twenty-five years or so, the federal government has shifted from an era dominated by the executive branch in the 1960s to legislative ascendancy brought on by the Vietnam War and Watergate in the 1970s to a revitalization of the presidency in the early 1980s and, finally, to a return toward more coequal status as the Reagan presidency drew to a close.

In Congress, power has been decentralized as a result of post-Watergate reforms, but staff resources have grown markedly, especially during the 1970s, after the expansion of domestic programs and their attendant bureaucracies during the 1960s. The national legislature has also extended its reach—and to an ever finer level of detail—into more and more activities that used to be the exclusive province of the executive branch. At the same time, the last several presidents have used the mass media to appeal directly to the people for enactment of their programs. While some successes have been achieved at both ends of Pennsylvania Avenue, these developments have also led to greater hostility, lower trust, and a stalemate on major policy issues, both foreign and domestic.

With fifty state legislatures and thousands of local governments, it is harder to generalize about recent developments. Many of the trends associated with the evolution of the U.S. Congress are also evident in state legislatures. Their sessions are growing longer, campaign costs are rising, staffs are growing, automation is taking hold, and the division of activities along party lines is more evident. According to Pound (1986), "The increase in legislative capacity and function has paralleled the overall growth in state governments' responsibilities and functions, but the state legislatures have been more affected by change than any other governmental institution" (p. 76). For public administrators at the state level, this means that legislatures have—and are exercising—greater interest and capacity to influence and control program operations.

The Changed Environment. As a first step in developing effective relationships, public administrators need an understanding of the environment in which legislators function. Several years ago, a senior congressman said, upon his retirement, "Congress just isn't a fun place to work anymore." Others, no doubt, share his sentiments. These may be some of the reasons why.

1. Demands have increased, while resources have remained constant. Despite the large increase in staff and other resources during the 1970s, there has been little or no growth in recent years. Nevertheless, the volume of mail, the number of hours spent in session, the number of roll call votes, and the number and complexity of the issues with which individual congressmen are expected to be conversant have all grown proportionally, if not exponentially.
2. There are longer hours, with less control of the agenda. Congressional sessions, once confined to the spring and summer months, now routinely run the whole year. There are more late-night and weekend sessions. (One U.S. Senate meeting in 1986 ended at 5:27 A.M.)
3. There are increased requirements for fund raising. Campaign finance requirements have grown exponentially in the last decade. In 1986, the California race for the U.S. Senate cost each candidate over $12 million. According to Senate majority leader Robert Byrd, the Senate cannot take roll call votes on Mondays and Fridays because of the growing fund-raising demands (stated in briefing on Senate bill attended by the author, February 1988).
4. The dominance of television is a factor. Both houses of Congress have televised sessions. Excerpts from debates are available to the networks, and members of Congress spend increasing amounts of their time appearing on local and national programs. The advent of satellite technology makes direct reporting from Washington available to local news stations.
5. The growth of special-interest groups must be considered. Thousands of organizations, using ever more sophisticated methods to influence the legislature, have come to dominate some public policy issues. The use of political action committees and grass-roots lobbying efforts increases the pressure on legislators.

It all adds up to a more visible, more politically charged environment for legislators to conduct the people's business in. Public administrators who depend on legislatures for authorization of their programs and approval of their budgets must appreciate and, to a greater or lesser extent, function in this same environment.

Key Actors and the Roles They Play

The term *public administrator* covers a wide variety of individuals and positions in government. The roles of such individuals vary widely, depending on the positions they occupy and, to a lesser extent, on the level of government. Nearly all public administrators are affected by the actions of legislators, but only a relatively small proportion of them actually have much interaction with the legislatures. Here are a few who do.

Heads of Government. These are the individuals who usually set the tone for relationships with legislatures. Taking large and small actions at this level will shape an administration's relationshp with the legislature. Recent presidents have had their ups and downs with Congress, partly because they have seen Congress as an obstacle to implementation of their programs. A few have lost sight of the symbiotic relationship between Congress and the executive agencies. Both branches are implicated in the growth and direction of government. Conflict between the president and Congress affects not only the president's programs but also relationships at the department and agency levels.

Agency Heads. These are the individuals who, on a day-to-day basis, have the most opportunity to influence relationships with legislatures. They must take an active interest in cultivating good relationships right from the start. Such interest means getting personally acquainted with key legislators, responding promptly to various requests made by legislators (provided that they are legitimate and that agency heads have the capacity to respond), and maintaining some flexibility in integrating the goals of agencies with the needs of and points of view expressed by legislators.

Legislative Liaisons. Nearly all government organizations of any size need individuals or units to serve as go-betweens. The task of legislative liaisons is to maintain constant contact with legislatures, monitor developments affecting agencies, advise agency heads and senior officials on appropriate legislative strategies, respond to legislative requests for information and assistance, and represent agencies in negotiations on pertinent legislation. Nevertheless, this is distinctly a staff function. Decisions affecting program policies or operations belong to agency heads and program officials. In some cases, these officials also play key roles in maintaining relations. Legislative liaison officers who develop close relations with legislators or key staff must also resist the temptation to "go native," that is, to become more sympathetic to legislators' needs than to those of their own organizations.

Budget Officers. In terms of organizational survival, probably no units are more important than budget offices in dealing with legislatures. Whatever the visibility and urgency of various policy issues before a legislature, exercise of the "power of the purse" necessarily ranks highest in the bureaucratic order of priorities. This means that agency budget officers must be able to get along with legislatures, especially appropriations committees. Often there is a direct relationship between budget offices and appropriations committees, and if the former cannot regularly satisfy the needs of the latter, there is little that agency heads or legislative liaisons can do to ensure that budgets are adequately funded.

Program Officials. Most of the time, contact between program officials and a legislature is relatively infrequent. Contacts are often concentrated on presentation of an agency's budget request or on legislation authorizing the agency's programs. Program officials occasionally become involved in oversight hearings or investigations. Here is where a program official's relative lack of sophistication about the legislative process can be potentially most harmful. The willingness of program officials to take the time to understand how the legislative process works, as well as their ability to communicate effectively with legislators under a variety of circumstances, will make a lot of difference in how well their programs fare.

The Unique Relationship Between the President and Congress

At the federal level, the quality and productivity of relationships between the executive and the legislative branches are determined largely by how well the president and Congress are getting along. The same can be said at the state level. For most of the past twenty-five years or so, at least one house of Congress has been controlled by the Democrats, while the White House has been mostly in the hands of Republicans. This fact, combined with the traumas of Vietnam and Watergate (and, more recently, the Iran-Contra hearings and the budget deficit), has made the task of maintaining good relationships more than a modest challenge: Sometimes it is an unachievable task.

Such relationships are a complex mixture of political ideology, program initiatives, budget proposals, personnel appointments, and hundreds of small transactions involving the perquisites of office and favors for constituents. Numerous actors are involved in the process, including various White House policy staffs, the Office of Management and Budget (OMB), congressional liaison offices in the White House, and public agencies themselves. Savvy presidents have also involved various elements of Congress in both policy formulation and execution. The president has a number of opportunities to present his program, including the State of the Union message, his budget, individual legislative proposals, and nominations for office. Especially since the establishment of a formal budget timetable in 1974, presentation of and congressional action on the president's programs have followed a temporal rhythm that culminates in a flurry of activity, not unlike that at the end of a state legislature's session, around the start of the fiscal year, on October 1.

Recent years have witnessed especially intense end-of-session skirmishes over the budget, including a "budget summit" following the October
1987 stock market crash. Congress has rolled all thirteen appropriations bills
into a single "continuing resolution," providing more than $500 billion in
spending authority. Spawned by the Gramm-Rudman-Hollings law (which
mandates set annual reductions in the deficit) and by the congressional-
executive impasse over tax increases and spending levels, these omnibus bills
have altered the distribution of power between Congress and the president
and have intensified efforts to establish a line-item veto for the president.
In 1988, Congress, for the first time in many years, enacted appropriations
in thirteen individual bills by October 1. There is no guarantee, however,
that the omnibus bill cycle has been broken.

Officials at the program level probably spend more time coping with
activities on Capitol Hill and at the policy level of their own departments,
of OMB, and of the White House than they do developing and propounding
their own legislative initiatives. Independent budgeting and analytical capabilities on Capitol Hill, heavy reliance on budget reconciliation and other
omnibus bills, and growth of the White House staff have all made development
of the president's legislative program much more of a top-down process. Nevertheless, shepherding appropriations requests, obtaining program authorizations, and responding to constituents' routine problems are still responsibilities
that fall mostly on the shoulders of program managers.

Basic Elements of the Legislative Process

Legislatures act through three basic mechanisms—the legislative process, the budget process, and oversight activities. (A fourth activity, which
occurs largely outside the formal legislative processes, has become increasingly important—constituent service.) Each of these three major elements
will be described briefly in the context of the public administrator's typical
role, and, as we shall see, consideration of constituent service also yields
a useful perspective on public administration.

The Legislative Process. Legislation authorizes the conduct of government programs and establishes the boundaries and functions of government
organizations. Legislators introduce and act on the bills that become law,
but often it is the head of government who sets the legislative agenda and
provides the leadership to bring about the enactment of major programs.
The sweeping tax-reduction bill enacted by Congress in 1981 was labeled
after its two primary sponsors, Congressman Jack Kemp and Senator William
V. Roth, Jr., but the basic tenets of this law had been a central theme of
Ronald Reagan's 1980 campaign for the presidency. His support was essential
in securing enactment. So, too, is the leadership of public administrators
in senior positions in creating and maintaining the legislative bases of public
programs.

The Budget Process. For at least the past half-century, the president, governors, and mayors have been the initiators of the budget process, through presentation of financial plans at the beginnings of legislative sessions. More recently, Congress and many state legislatures have developed their own capabilities for evaluating and reaching decisions on budgetary matters. Congress, with the help of the Congressional Budget Office and the General Accounting Office (GAO), now creates its own budget each year, and the president's budget is simply the starting point of a long and complex process that ends many months later. The Gramm-Rudman-Hollings law has set parameters for the budget deficit and evoked huge, omnibus spending bills—the so-called continuing resolution and reconciliation bills—that have fundamentally changed the process by which spending decisions are made, as well as the determination of who makes them.

The intricacies and details of the budget process, especially at the national level, are well beyond the scope of this chapter. It is important to note, however, that budgeting has become a practice of statecraft with unique procedures, terminology, and relationships among players. Members of Congress, in addition to having to cope with the arcane intricacies of budgeting, find that the process has become all-consuming, leaving little time for other legislation and oversight. Thus, budgeting has become both the realm of specialists and a preoccupation. Public administrators who believe that they can function effectively here, with only a casual acquaintance with the process, place themselves at a substantial disadvantage.

Oversight Activities. Legislators often see themselves as watchdogs of the public purse and guardians of the public trust. At the national level, each congressional committee is formally required to continuously oversee the programs under its jurisdiction, and many committees have established oversight subcommittees whose sole responsibility is to perform this task. In addition, each house of Congress has a government operations committee whose primary task is oversight. These committees' efforts are supplemented by those of the auditors, evaluators, and investigators in the GAO, as well as by the efforts of a multitude of investigative reporters working for the newspapers and television networks.

Committee members past and present, such as Harry S. Truman, John Moss, Jack Brooks, John Dingell, John McClellan, and Sam Ervin, have developed national reputations through high-visibility oversight investigations. Television and the other mass media provide platforms for these activities and can make the names of politicians household words almost overnight. What is less appreciated is that public administrators can benefit from legislative oversight of their programs. It is the rare administrator who has the personality or the television presence of a George Shultz or a Paul Volcker, but exposure of problems in program implementation, especially those beyond the reach of program administrators, can educate

committee members and create support for needed changes through legislative action.

Basic Elements of Establishing Good Relationships

Functioning effectively with a legislature requires a solid understanding of the legislative process, an ability to develop and present a sound
legislative program, and a willingness to work with legislators and their staffs
as legitimate actors in the process of governance. At the federal and state
levels, the branches of government are separate and coequal, and the perspectives and goals of administrators and legislators often are quite different.
Little gets accomplished, however, without shared respect and a willingness
to compromise.

Understanding the Legislative Process. The public administrator's knowledge
base necessarily starts with an understanding of the formal legislative process, the one the civics books teach us. Bills are introduced, hearings are
held, committees report the bills, votes are taken in the two houses, conference committees resolve the differences, and the legislation is forwarded
to the president or the governor for his or her signature. Most administrators are familiar with these basic elements.

If only life were that simple! These days, Congress enacts relatively
few individual bills that deal with single issues. This is an era of continuing
resolutions and omnibus legislation. The process has become so complex,
and the conflicting interests so intense, that (at least at the national level)
little more than imperative legislation, such as appropriations bills and debt
ceiling extensions, actually becomes law. Such bills, as a result, have become
the "Christmas trees" onto which other bills are attached, bills that otherwise would be blocked from final passage. In Congress, one of the largest
such "Christmas trees" is that annual reconciliation bill, required by the
1974 Congressional Budget Act, to bring total spending in line with the
amounts authorized by the congressional budget resolution. This reconciliation bill typically amends dozens of existing laws to change taxing or spending
authorizations. It also provides a vehicle to make other changes that otherwise would not survive the process.

What this means is that the process is not as straightforward as the
textbooks describe it. When omnibus bills are used, at least two (and sometimes several) committees are involved in each house. Getting to know the
principal actors and maintaining an ability to influence events throughout
the process become quite a challenge. While the resort to omnibus bills is
not as prevalent at the state and local levels, the practice of attaching one
piece of legislation to another to facilitate its passage is not the exclusive
province of the federal government.

All of this means two things to public administrators. First, some time
and effort are required to gain sufficient understanding of the legislative

process. Second, some specialization is required to enhance the chances of success. This means ensuring that the organization has access to people who work regularly with the legislature (such as people in the legislative liaison and budget offices), who can facilitate contacts with the right people and help ensure that public administrators' interests get the proper attention throughout the many steps in the process.

Through a Legislator's Eyes. In dealing with legislatures, it helps to try to understand how the world looks to them. Public administrators all know that these people are where they are because they were elected to office, but what does that really mean? It means that if a legislator is to remain in office—and nearly all aspire to do so—he or she must be responsive to constituents. He or she must listen and respond to their demands and assist in solving their problems with government. It also means that his or her focus is on the home district or state, rather than on the problems of administration in the state capital or in Washington. In U.S. House speaker Tip O'Neill's father's words, "All politics is local" (O'Neill, 1987, p. 26).

This perspective may be inconsistent at times with the needs of rational, efficient government, but public administrators need to understand it if they are dealing with legislatures. Helping legislators respond to constituents' needs in ways that are not inconsistent with legitimate program objectives can go a long way toward facilitating good relationships and moving needed legislation forward.

Developing and Presenting Legislative Programs

The need for a public administrator to develop a legislative program will vary widely, depending on the circumstances. Some organizations are quite stable, and they have permanent legislation on the books authorizing their programs. In such cases, the only requirement may be annual approval of the budget. The programs of other organizations may require periodic or even annual authorization. This situation requires more frequent appearances before legislative committees, and there is more opportunity not only to reshape programs through amendments but also to have others tailor programs to their own liking.

Legislative activity is also influenced by the chief executive. If a governor or a president is elected on a conservative platform, few legislative proposals may be put forward. More activist politicians as heads of government may want to submit numerous proposals to "get government moving again."

Developing Legislative Proposals. This task involves processes internal to the executive branches of governments, which are beyond the scope of this chapter. Nevertheless, we can state that such processes are a necessary first step before formal submission to a legislature. Generally, proposals submitted before or early in the term of a legislature stand a much better chance of getting a fair hearing than those submitted later. Whatever the complexity and length of this process, the key is to ensure that development of proposals begins soon enough for timely submission.

Even before a formal proposal is submitted, or before the public administrator is very far along in the process of developing it, meetings should be held with potential sponsors and with the chairpersons of the committees that have jurisdiction, or with their senior staffs. Getting their input and including provisions they may want will facilitate favorable consideration. Testing the climate for the proposal before it is submitted may also save a lot of work, if it is found that there is little likelihood of its passing.

After submission of the proposal and its introduction, committees may ask agencies and other interested parties for written reports on the bill, but the next step usually is the committee hearing. Much has been written and said about how to prepare and present good testimony. This is a critical point in the process, the one where legislation most often runs into trouble—some of it avoidable—whatever the merits of that legislation.

Program managers, or their legislative representatives, should know well in advance of the hearing who are the responsible committee staff persons. If opportunity permits, they should be ready to work closely with these staff persons in preparing for the hearing, if so requested. Preparation includes supplying a list of potential witnesses and offering written questions to be asked at the hearing. Contact with these staff persons may also allow advance perusal of their prepared questions. The more that is known in advance about how the hearing will be conducted and what is on the minds of the committee members, the better the chances for a successful outcome.

Presenting Effective Testimony. There is probably no more potentially traumatic activity associated with legislation than making a formal statement before a congressional committee, a state legislative committee, or a city council. But administrators should consider it an opportunity. If the witness knows what he or she is talking about, acts in a professional manner, and provides honest and forthright responses to members' questions, the chances of coming out ahead are quite good. Here are some ideas that may help.

1. Prepare as brief a written statement as possible, long on facts and generally short on rhetoric. If the statement is longer than five or six pages, prepare a summary or highlight sections that in total can be presented in ten minutes or less.
2. Make the formal statement as clear as possible. Use charts, if necessary, but make sure they are large enough for members to see and simple enough for them to understand quickly.
3. Master the subject matter as much as time permits. Ask for backup materials, including any relevant legislation and statements of other witnesses, if available.

4. Get copies of audit reports relevant to the hearing topic, and be prepared to respond to any criticisms of or recommendations on the programs for which the witness is responsible.

5. Read the newspaper the day before and the morning of the hearing, with an eye to any articles about the hearing or to stories about related events that may come up at the hearing.

6. Have a last-minute meeting with staff to go over late-breaking developments.

7. Arrive before the hearing starts, and say hello to the committee members and other witnesses. Make sure the members have the prepared statement and any supporting materials.

8. Pay special attention to the chairperson's opening statement—it often reflects his or her personal interests—and listen to the statements of other witnesses for potentially useful comments.

9. Follow the chairperson's instructions on presenting the testimony, and offer to summarize the statement before beginning.

10. Have as few supporting witnesses at the table as possible. Those at the table should be persons who are likely to be needed to answer questions.

11. Provide straightforward answers to questions, but also use questions as opportunities to make points that support the prepared testimony.

12. Admit mistakes if they have been made, and concentrate on highlighting the corrective actions being taken.

13. If presenting the positions of higher authorities, be willing to characterize them as such, if asked. Respond truthfully if asked for personal views (this is generally good advice, but local customs prevail, of course).

14. Finally, remember that if one takes away all the fancy trappings of the hearing room, the committee staff lining the back wall, the klieg lights, the cameras, and the audience, what is left is a group of people sitting at a table and seeking information that will help them perform their jobs and maybe get reelected. If administrators are seen as helpful in those tasks and professional in their approach, the rest should proceed rather well.

Follow-up. After hearings are completed, committee members and staff, particularly the latter, will go over the testimony and any amendments proposed by witnesses. They also must decide whether to move legislation to a committee vote. Generally, this process entails informal meetings or other means of feeling out committee members. This is a process largely internal to the committee, but the program manager or legislative liaison should try to stay in touch and be ready to offer any additional information or other assistance the committee needs to get ready for a vote on the bill. Sometimes, one or more meetings between the agency head and the committee chairperson or other committee members may be necessary to clear up questions and work out compromise language or amendments.

If the committee votes to approve the bill and report it to the floor, the process of information exchange and negotiation continues throughout the vote by the full legislative body and the conference committee. As noted earlier, other committees may get involved, particularly if the bill becomes part of a larger package. The potential permutations are too many to describe fully here; suffice it to say that the best course for the program manager is to stay in touch and as much on top of the situation as possible, giving due deference to the prerogatives of the legislative body to act without what it sees as undue outside influence from an executive agency.

Knowing the Rules Against Executive Agency Lobbying

Although active involvement of the type described here will enhance the chances for success in most circumstances, it is important to be aware of any limits or restrictions on lobbying by executive agency officials. At the federal level, *lobbying* has been defined by the Supreme Court as "direct communication with members of Congress on pending or proposed legislation." Two types of laws restrict executive agency lobbying: criminal statutes and appropriations act limitations. No one has been prosecuted under the criminal statute, even though it has been on the books for nearly seventy years. Generally, the statute has been construed to apply to indirect or grassroots lobbying (U.S. General Accounting Office, 1984). According to GAO, the laws are regarded as unclear and difficult to enforce.

Nevertheless, an unduly aggressive campaign on behalf of legislation can be cause for embarrassment. The Department of Energy was recently taken to task by GAO for orchestrating extensive lobbying by a private firm and nuclear weapons scientists against a possible congressional ban on nuclear tests (Smith, 1987). The department supported the use of employees from two national weapons laboratories to conduct more than one hundred briefings for members of Congress and their staffs. Some of the members so briefed had Department of Energy facilities in their home districts.

The legislation in question passed the House but was defeated in the Senate. The department's lobbying rules had been amended to exempt such briefings by hired contractors from the restrictions, and a provision was included in the department's appropriation bill that maintains this exemption. Nevertheless, GAO and committee staff members expressed concern about this practice, and unfavorable publicity resulted from the incident.

Although no one is likely to go to jail for this or any similar incident, lobbying campaigns orchestrated by executive officials risk eliciting strong reactions from committee members and staff who might otherwise be neutral to or supportive of legislation.

One thing that legislators find particularly objectionable is surreptitious action by agencies to generate pressure from constituents and campaign contributors. As long as there is activity in legislatures that affects program outcomes—and there is more, now that legislatures are becoming more involved in operational details—public administrators will be employing whatever legal means are available to affect such outcomes, including consultations with sympathetic outside groups. The question that must be weighed, however, is how far the administrator can go before he or she is perceived as exercising undue influence on the legislative process.

Legislative Relationships at the Local Level

For city and county governments, the basic guidelines for establishing and maintaining good relationships are the same. They include having good communications, knowledge of how the legislative process works, personal acquaintance with legislators, and good information and assistance. At this level, however, issues affect citizens personally—property values, children's welfare, and the tranquility of neighborhoods. Personality conflicts can be more intense among the sometimes amateur politicians who serve on city councils, and these conflicts will hinder rational communication and problem solving.

In recent years, city managers, whether in council-manager or mayor-council forms of government, have found themselves spending more time and giving greater weight to activities that include council relationships. According to a recent study by Newell and Ammons (1987), chief executives and their principal assistants reported spending about one-fourth to one-third of their time in a "policy role." More than half of the city managers and more than a third of the mayors who responded to a survey questionnaire designated the policy (and council relations) role as "most important."

Also at the local level, governments are not so formally organized according to the separation-of-powers doctrine. Lines of authority between the executive and the legislative "branches" are not so neat, if they exist at all, and the confusion is frequently compounded by a mixture of quasi-public authorities, independent boards and commissions, special-purpose districts, and the like. Civil service merit systems similar to the federal government's are not so commonplace; therefore, legislators and others become more involved in who gets which jobs in city departments.

Relationships between administrators and councils of legislators may be somewhat more confrontational and emotional in these circumstances, and they may exist in a framework that is less neatly defined. This fact makes it harder to abide by a single set of guidelines for good relationships. Each situation needs to be carefully evaluated in determining which techniques will work best. Perhaps the most that can be said is that administrators who seek constructive relationships, and a process that seeks to solve problems on the basis of merit, are most likely to survive, if not prosper.

Summary

This chapter has attempted to describe the legislative process and to suggest some behavior patterns that will enhance public administrators' chances of achieving their program objectives by working more effectively with legislatures—federal, state, and local. This executive-legislative relationship is often difficult, at best, and if recent experience at the national level is a guide, the challenge of nurturing this relationship is growing.

A reversal of the trend toward greater involvement in program policy and operations by legislatures is also highly unlikely in the near future. Therefore, program managers will need to sharpen their communicative skills and increase their willingness to share power, if government is to remain an effective means for meeting people's needs. Not all would agree: Consider the confrontational styles of some recent presidents, governors, and mayors. Nevertheless, legislatures have their "ace in the hole"—the power of the purse. As a result, they can obstruct an administrator's program just as easily as they can cooperate in implementing it. In the long run, the sharing of power, and not its separate exercise, is our best hope for the future.

References

Fisher, L. *The Politics of Shared Power: Congress and the Executive.* Washington, D.C.: Congressional Quarterly Press, 1981.

Newell, C., and Ammons, D. N. "Role Emphasis of City Managers and Other Executives." *Public Administration Review,* 1987, *47* (3), 246–253.

O'Neill, T. P., Jr. *Man of the House.* New York: Random House, 1987.

Pound, W. T. "The State Legislatures." In W. T. Pound (ed.), *The Book of the States.* Lexington, Ky.: Council of State Governments, 1986.

Smith, H. J. "DOE Violated Rules on Lobbying, GAO Says." *Washington Post,* Oct. 8, 1987, p. A-16.

U.S. General Accounting Office. *No Strong Indication That Restrictions on Executive Branch Lobbying Should Be Expanded.* Washington, D.C.: U.S. General Accounting Office, 1984.

14

Thomas P. Lauth

Responding to Elected and Appointed Officials

Many public administrators work closely with elected executives or top political appointees. The working relationship between political executives and career administrators is likely to be characterized by both conflict and cooperation. The potential for conflict arises from the different orientations of political appointees and career administrators.

Political appointees, almost by definition, do not regard government service as a permanent career. Chief executives at all levels of government have terms of office that do not exceed four years, and their tenure in office usually does not exceed eight years. Their political appointees often do not serve with them for the entire period. Political appointees are also likely to identify with the policy priorities of the elected executive and may even have a psychological investment in the success of that executive.

In contrast, career administrators are likely to view government service as lifelong work and to consider the life cycle of programs and policies in time frames that extend well beyond the term of office of a particular elected executive.

In order to promote effective governmental action under these circumstances, it is necessary to minimize the negative aspects of conflict and to maximize the opportunities for cooperative action between political appointees and career administrators. Of course, conflict is not always dysfunctional, as when it occurs over matters of high principle, and cooperation is not invariably functional, as when cooptation elevates special privilege over the public interest or acquiescence condones violations of the public

Note: The author thanks Robert F. Durant and Hal G. Rainey for their valuable suggestions for improvements in an earlier version of this chapter.

193

trust. On balance, however, the goal of effective government is likely to be served best when the relationship between political executives and career administrators is one of limited conflict within a cooperative environment.

This chapter examines the relationship between political executives and career administrators from three perspectives. First, the theoretical justification for political control and direction of administration will be considered. Second, some empirical evidence regarding the nature of the relationship during the past two decades will be reviewed in an effort to identify propositions that might serve as guides for administrative action. Third, suggestions for administrative practice will be presented.

Public Administration and Democratic Theory

Political control of administration is an essential element of democratic governance. It is the means of linking public administration to the political will of the society (Mainzer, 1973, p. 68). In the executive branch, this means that elected executives and their political appointees are expected to direct and control the policy activities of agencies and administrators. That expectation stems from the constitution or charter that delineates governmental powers and responsibilities, and it is grounded in democratic theory, which designates citizens as the sovereigns (Appleby, 1962) and elected officials as their representatives. In a very fundamental way, public administrators work for their clients. They not only have the responsibility to serve their clients but also are ultimately employed by them. Political control of administration begins with popular control of elected officials and extends through the direction and control of agencies and administrators by officials acting on behalf of the chief executive. This hierarchical arrangement of democratic control, running from the people through their representatives to successive levels of administrative organization, is commonly known as *overhead democracy* (Redford, 1969, p. 70). Of course, elected executives are not the only political actors who attempt to influence career administrators. Legislatures, courts, interest groups, political parties, administrators at other levels of government, and other executive-branch agencies also attempt to affect the actions of career administrators. Nevertheless, because the primary focus of this chapter is the interactions between elected and appointed executives and career administrators, relationships with other political actors will be outside our immediate concern.

If the electoral connection between popular will and administrative actions is to be effective, it must be reflected in executive leadership of administration. A central tenet of public administration theory has been the desirability of a strong executive who exerts managerial direction and control over the agencies of the executive branch (Kaufman, 1956, p. 1062; Sundquist, 1974, pp. 453–455). Although victory in an election confers on a chief executive the authority to govern, his or her ability to govern is likely to depend very much on the skillfulness with which the agencies of the executive branch can be penetrated. Chief executives, no matter how extensive their formal powers (budget, appointment and removal, veto, and tenure in office), generally operate in a system of fragmented and shared powers, in which they are dependent on the cooperation of others, such as legislatures, other elected executive-branch officials (in the states and at the local level), and career administrators, to achieve their objectives.

Executives' efforts to penetrate the bureaucracy are essential to popular control of administration, but they are also potentially threatening to merit principles and professional values. Kaufman (1956) has noted the continuing struggle in American public administration to minimize the impact of narrow partisan interests on neutral professional competence in administration while at the same time seeking to maximize the political responsiveness and accountability of administrators to the elected representatives of the people. The primary mechanism for attempting to check partisan intrusion into administration and increase the technical and professional competence of administrators has been the merit system of personnel selection and promotion. Merit systems aim at the establishment of continuity, institutionalized knowledge, technical competence, and impartiality in government administration. The spoils system of personnel selection aided chief executives in that the functions of government were performed by individuals who were sympathetic to the policy objectives of the chief executives. Nevertheless, the excesses of that system led to the removal of most government jobs from spoilsmanship and retained only a small number of top-level positions to be filled by executive appointment (Pfiffner, 1987).

Now, elected officials and political appointees interact in the formulation and implementation of government policies with career administrators, who bring to that relationship a tradition of professional management skill and competence. Although there are essential differences between the realms of politics and career administration, the reality of their interdependence (Newland, 1983, p. 19) in the formulation and implementation of policies has been recognized for a long time (Appleby, 1949). The central issue concerning the role of career administrators in a modern democracy is not whether it is appropriate for them to participate in policymaking (their technical expertise and discretionary authority guarantee that they will) but rather to what extent they participate and whether their participation thwarts the will of elected officials. The issue is not whether elected and appointed executive-branch officials have the right to intervene in administration to promote responsiveness (clearly they do) but rather to what extent their politicization of administration threatens the professional values of career administrators, to the detriment of effective government action. In this connection, Mainzer (1973, p. 68) has written that "bureaucracy isolated from politics is not for democratic tastes; a bureaucracy servile to politics offends the concepts of objectivity and equal treatment and is unlikely to do the necessary work of government."

Politics and Administration: The Empirical Evidence

A number of studies in recent years have examined the relationships among elected officials, political appointees, and career administrators. These studies proceed from two premises. First, not only do elected and appointed officials seek to penetrate the career service in an effort to make administration responsive to the policy goals and objectives of elected officials, but it is also entirely appropriate and desirable that they do so. Second, the classical model of a career service that is hierarchically directed and politically neutral in its policy preferences does not accurately depict the world in which modern public administrators operate. In agencies, administrators seek to influence the formulation and implementation of policies, and they seek to protect their programs from chief executives' direction, through external alliances with legislators, interest groups (Abney and Lauth, 1982), the media, and other agencies. Having accepted these premises, the research has focused on the extent of political intervention in administration, the nature of career service responsiveness to political officials, and the conditions under which elected officials, political appointees, and career administrators can engage in cooperative action.

A common theme found in the recent literature on relationships between elected and appointed executives and career administrators involves new executives' perceptions of the career service. At best, the career service is seen as being made up of individuals who are so closely associated with existing programs and the policy goals of previous administrations that they will be reluctant partners in the tasks of governing. At worst, the career service is seen as ideologically hostile to the incoming administration and inclined to resist or even sabotage its efforts to redirect the course of government policies. There is certainly some justification for these perceptions. Career administrators have often attended the birth of programs, have become committed to and identified with them, and are understandably reluctant to see them change—especially if change means that a program will be sharply curtailed or eliminated. They may also believe that policy changes are morally or managerially wrongheaded because they are likely to result in social inequities or organizational inefficiencies. Still, significant problems of electoral accountability must be overcome, if a chief executive representing short-term political forces faces a long-term career service that is unresponsive to his or her policy objectives.

The efforts by Presidents Richard Nixon and Ronald Reagan to bring about major shifts in the programs and activities of domestic agencies have frequently been the focus of public administration research. Nevertheless, the first important change of national party control in the post–World War II era occurred as a result of the election of 1952. When the Eisenhower administration entered office in 1953, it found relatively few positions available that could be filled at top levels of the government by partisan supporters of the new administration. To gain some leverage over a career service that had served Democratic administrations for the previous twenty years, the president created, by executive order, a Schedule C for positions of a policy and confidential nature. This enabled the president to increase the number of appointments available to him and to penetrate the federal bureaucracy through the appointment of individuals sympathetic to the policy objectives of his presidency.

Similarly, the Nixon administration sought to gain some leverage over a career service that had served two previous Democratic administrations during a period of great domestic program expansion. After a relatively unsuccessful series of efforts early in his first term to bring about domestic policy changes through legislative action, President Nixon shifted from a legislative to a managerial strategy in an attempt to bring about those changes (Nathan, 1975). He attempted to alter the line between policy and administration, according to Nathan, by simultaneously placing loyal supporters in key line positions in the domestic agencies and centralizing policy decision making in the White House. In addition to politicizing line agencies, the Nixon administration seriously eroded the tradition of neutral competence found in such agencies as the Office of Management and Budget (OMB). He introduced a new layer of politically appointed officials who superseded the career division chiefs as heads of the principal examining divisions of that agency. The result, Heclo (1975, p. 87) argues, "was to identify OMB more as a member of the president's own political family and less as a broker supplying an independent analytic service to every president." That politicization severely damaged OMB's future ability to serve the institutionalized presidency as a neutral professional staff (Berman, 1979).

How accurate were the Nixon administration's suspicions that the federal career service was filled with partisan opponents of its domestic policy initiatives? Aberbach and Rockman (1976) identified a federal career bureaucracy that contained very little Republican representation, as well as administrators (particularly in social service agencies) who were "ideologically hostile" to many of the courses of action pursued by the Nixon administration in the field of social policy. They concluded that the federal bureaucracy was "not fertile soil in which to plant the most conservative of the Nixon administration's social policies" (p. 467). The Nixon administration's efforts to politicize key domestic agencies through changes in personnel were intended to offset what was perceived from the White House as the career service's opposition to the president's domestic policy initiatives.

Extending this line of research, Cole and Caputo (1979) reported that the Nixon strategy of placing partisan loyalists in key administrative positions gradually had its intended effect. They found that individuals selected for top administrative positions during the Nixon years were more likely to be Republicans and to favor President Nixon's goals and objectives than those individuals selected before his administration. This was true, they report, not only of political appointees (as would be expected) but also of career executives. In contrast to the Aberbach and Rockman (1976) findings, which were based on data drawn in 1970 (near the beginning of the Nixon administration), Cole and Caputo found that in 1976 administrators who identified themselves politically as independents resembled Republicans in their attitudes. Aberbach and Rockman (1976) had found political independents to resemble Democrats in their political attitudes. Cole and Caputo concluded (p. 412) that the body of politically independent career executives had become a "potential reservoir" of support of a conservative president. The Cole and Caputo research suggests that President Nixon was to this extent successful in his management control strategy.

These pieces of research suggest that chief executives' efforts to influence the top levels of administration, through the appointment of policy and partisan supporters to key noncareer and top-level career positions, can have measurable influence on bureaucratic responsiveness, but only after a lapse of time. In the span of one administration, the number of senior-level appointments is probably too small to have a more extensive impact. In this connection, Heclo (1977, p. 214) argues that no matter how many political appointees an administration makes, the total will not be enough; short of a massive reversion to spoils, no administration can place enough loyalists in government positions to make a difference on that basis alone. This argument underscores the vital role played by career administrators, who, because of their commitment to the public service, are usually willing to respond to political leaders of both major parties. Heclo contends that political executives must work cooperatively with career administrators, if they are to be successful in accomplishing their objectives.

Randall (1979) reports that the Nixon administration was able to have a discernible influence on welfare policy. He argues that the new management-oriented officials appointed to the federal welfare agencies in the Nixon years were able to use reorganization, monitoring, and evaluation to bring about a more "restrictive, sometimes punitive" welfare policy. Randall perceives federalism, rather than bureaucratic intransigence, to have been the principal impediment faced by the Nixon administration in its efforts to redirect welfare policy. State welfare systems, in Randall's view, turned out to be more formidable barriers to the administration than the federal welfare bureaucracy was. These findings, Randall argues (p. 809), call into question the conventional views about the limits to presidential control of policy.

In the 1980s, President Reagan has continued the trend toward an administrative presidency. Moe (1985) contends not only that Reagan continued a historical trend toward politicization and centralization within the executive branch but also that, as the result of his efforts, he can be regarded as the most administratively influential president of the modern period.

If the Nixon administration's efforts to penetrate the career service were thought to be aggressive, the Reagan administration's efforts have been criticized as excessive. Unlike the Nixon administration, the Reagan administration selected from the outset cabinet and subcabinet members whose views were highly compatible with those of the president. The administration came to office distrustful of career administrators. It increased the number of political executives and exerted strong White House control over their appointments (Pfiffner, 1987, p. 57). The president demonstrated a great deal of interest in lower-level appointments within the executive branch, such as Schedule C and Senior Executive Service appointments (Nathan, 1983, p. 76), and many important administrative positions were filled on the basis of partisan and personal loyalties (Newland, 1983, p. 1). Efforts were made to separate policy issues from administrative areas and to exclude career administrators from policy-level decisions (Newland, 1983; Pfiffner, 1987). In addition, appointees were urged to take advantage of opportunities to transfer and remove career officials who were perceived to be unsympathetic to the administration's objectives (Nathan, 1983, p. 77).

Several observers have argued that although it is appropriate and desirable for political appointees to attempt to influence decisions of career administrators, the Reagan administration's efforts in this regard have been excessive and have created an imbalance in the relationship between the values of political direction and control of administration, on the one hand, and neutral competence in administration, on the other. Pfiffner (1985, 1987) argues that distrust of the career service has been misplaced and the effectiveness of government is endangered by the unprecedented number of politically inexperienced appointees found in the Reagan administration. Newland (1984, p. 167) argues that the "gradual politicization and deinstitutionalization of the Executive Office of the President since the late 1960s has culminated under Reagan in an unprecedented partisan presidential system that reaches from the White House to deep into agency operating levels." Paul Volcker (Tolchin, 1988), commenting on the recent trend of more political appointments and fewer career appointments at upper levels of the federal bureaucracy, noted that top posts in federal agencies currently go to presidential political aides who helped in the campaign, but who lacked the ability to assume top-echelon posts in the new administration.

Perhaps the most direct defense of the Reagan administration's strategy for getting control of the federal career bureaucracy is found in an essay by Sanera (1984), which rejects the concept of neutral competence as a guiding principle for political appointees and argues that appointees should take full advantage of the opportunities available to them to bring about policy changes on behalf of the administration they represent. The exchange between Sanera (1984) and Pfiffner (1985) is probably the most direct assessment of what is at stake in the debate over the proper balance between, on the one hand, the desire of elected executives and political appointees to direct and control the career service so as to bring about policy objectives and, on the other hand, a concern that the "neutrality" of the career service be protected so that it can serve an institutionalized executive, rather than the personal political agenda of a particular chief executive. Sanera's essay portrays the federal career executive as an obstructionist force that needs to be circumvented; Pfiffner denies the accuracy of the characterization and argues that such a negative tone about the motives and abilities of career administrators harms the morale and effectiveness of the career service.

Whatever the case with regard to the tone of the Reagan administration's efforts to penetrate the career service, how successful were those efforts? Lynn (1984) examined the performance of five Reagan appointees in an effort to evaluate their success in bringing about changes in core agency activities that were consistent with the Reagan administration's policy preferences. Lynn observed that success was not ensured by the mere appointment to key positions of individuals who shared the president's values. The appointees who were successful in bringing about changes that reflected the policy preferences of the president were those who had a clear plan for accomplishing their objectives and who communicated their plans effectively to agency personnel. They had favorable organizational structures and climates and good constituency relationships. They also had managerial skills, previous experience in government, and personalities that enabled them to work with career administrators.

Several conclusions can be drawn from Lynn's (1984) study. First, President Reagan's practice of appointing individuals sympathetic to his ideological stances and policy preferences seems to have served him well, but no matter how sympathetic an appointee is to the policy preferences of the chief executive, loyalty and willingness to take on the career administrators are not sufficient for success; management competence is also required. Second, despite claims that the Reagan administration's politicization of executive agencies has been not only excessive but also destructive of the career service's morale, the appointees in the five agencies Lynn examined did not cause widespread deterioration in the agencies' performance. Third, reliance on extensive subcabinet appointments to bring about policy changes through agency actions is an uncertain and time-consuming strategy. Because success in penetrating the bureaucracy depends on the abilities and skills of appointees, as well as on their ideological kinship with the chief executive, a substantial amount of time must be invested in learning about potential appointees. The greater the reliance on political appointees (rather than on career administrators) to direct policy changes, the greater the investment a new administration must make in talent selection.

Similarly, Ingraham's (1988) study of political transition in two federal agencies reports that the joint efforts of political and career executives were essential to achieving presidential policy objectives. In both cases, Ingraham reports, political executives built on "pockets of receptivity" in the career service and found the cooperation of careerists to have been critical to the success of their policy initiatives. Ingraham concludes that political appointees charged with achieving change should arrive at their agencies with clear policy objectives and should rapidly develop constructive working relationships with career service personnel.

Much of the research on this subject has focused on efforts by elected officials and political appointees to penetrate what is often perceived as a bureaucracy determined to resist the policy initiatives of political executives. That research is usually from the perspective of elected and appointed officials. In what is perhaps the most comprehensive study to date of the relationships between appointees and career administrators, Heclo (1977) gives the perspective of career administrators a more prominent place in his examination of the political-bureaucratic interface. He contends (p. 171) that the basis of career administrators' power vis-à-vis politically appointed executives is the services they can provide or withhold. Without denying that career administrators can subvert political leadership through noncompliance, he argues (p. 172) that administrators' power "does not typically derive from refusing to do what their superiors want." Instead, it derives from withholding positive help unless it is specifically requested. Heclo (pp. 173–176) gives examples of the kinds of valuable services that career administrators can provide if they choose to do so: providing political appointees with an orientation to an agency's structure, processes, current issues, and cast of characters; sharing knowledge about the intricacies of the agency's budget, personnel, and other facets; and supplying intelligence about the agency's allies and enemies. Career administrators also perform valuable services for political appointees when they help in the formulation of policy proposals, facilitate policy implementation, and disagree when they believe that contemplated courses of action are not in the best interests of the political appointees—a service that Heclo (pp. 176–180) calls "positive resistance."

Heclo characterizes successful relationships between politically appointed executives and career administrators as based on a strategy of conditional cooperation. Conditional cooperation is grounded neither in suspicion nor in trust; it makes cooperation conditional on performance (Heclo, 1977, p. 193). This arrangement makes it possible for political appointees to cooperate with career administrators who are open to cooperation and, at the same time, to deal in a different manner with administrators who are unsympathetic or resistant to the objectives of the incumbent administration. According to Heclo, the basis of conditional cooperation is to give career administrators a stake in the future performance of political appointees. The latter may use their access to higher-level officials on behalf of an agency. They may obtain important information otherwise not available to the agency. Moreover, they may promote the agency's interests against political appointees from other agencies (Heclo, 1977, pp. 196–197).

Most of the research that has addressed the relationships between elected officials and political appointees and career administrators has been based on federal evidence. Relatively few attempts have been made to examine these relationships as they operate at other levels of government.

A study of Minnesota, Pennsylvania, and South Carolina found that, despite some interstate differences, administrators and politicians in those states generally held rather low opinions of each other, and each group believed that it was not trusted or understood by its counterpart. These perceptions reportedly inhibited cooperation, interaction, and confidence (Spadaro, 1973).

In her study of the Sargent administration in Massachusetts, Weinberg (1977, p. 209) concludes that management, for elected chief executives, was usually characterized by sporadic intervention in agency affairs, often for short periods of time and usually in response to some sort of crisis. Some agencies, she reports, required frequent attention because they had large budgets and employed large numbers of people; others got considerable attention because of the governor's interest in their missions. Some agencies received attention only because they had become involved in some sort of crisis, while still others required and received little or no attention. Weinberg notes (p. 227) that how accountable an agency is to a governor is not always the appropriate question to ask in seeking to determine how well it serves a public purpose. She acknowledges that all agencies need to be accountable to the political system, but she contends that an agency need not be directly accountable to the governor all the time in order to fulfill its public purpose.

In their national study of state administration, Abney and Lauth (1983) learned from the responses of state agency heads that governors did not dominate state administration. In that study, governors were found to be more active as managers than as policy leaders, and they were most likely to interact with administrators in departments that came within the purview of their appointment powers. In this connection, plural executives make the chief executive's direction and control of agencies more difficult, but it is not entirely clear whether agencies fare better or worse in state policy decisions when they have elected heads. One study of budgeting (Lauth, 1984) concluded that the method of selecting an agency head was not systematically related to the agency's budget success. Agencies with elected heads are simultaneously more independent of the chief executive and less likely to be supported and protected by the executive.

Roberts (1988) reports that, since 1970, more than half the states have moved in the direction of increasing the number of exempt managers. Although states vary in how far down the hierarchy exempt appointments exist, the effect of this shift has been to give elected and appointed administrators more personnel discretion to bring about cooperation, loyalty, and responsiveness. Roberts reports that in some states and agencies, exempt managers behave more like political officials, while in others they act more like career civil servants. In states where positions have been converted from career to exempt, incumbents are made more vulnerable to political leadership, but few firings have occurred because, at the program level, the experience of incumbents is too valuable for political officials to sacrifice. The positive effect of exempt status is an increase in responsiveness and cooperation, but the negative risk is discouragement of creativity, initiative, and program advocacy.

Guides for Administrative Practice

Several generalizations emerge from the literature, and these can guide administrative practice for elected executives, political appointees, and career administrators.

1. The goal of overhead democracy is served when the elected executive and his or her political appointees are able to penetrate the career service and cause it to be responsive to the policy preferences that were expressed through the electoral process. Research suggests that chief executives who take advantage of their appointment prerogatives are able to increase managerial control over the career service and obtain its cooperation in working for their own policy goals and objectives. More is not necessarily better when it comes to appointments, however. Attempting to fill as many positions as possible with partisan loyalists has at least two negative consequences: It will require a great deal of staff time and attention that might be better used for programmatic matters, and it may result in the selection of marginally capable individuals whose primary attribute is partisanship but whose managerial abilities and program knowledge are either weak or unknown to those who appoint them. Such personnel are not likely to serve the cause of good governance very well. Newly elected administrations may do better to devote time and attention to finding ways of engaging in cooperative efforts with both the career-oriented political appointees who have served previous administrations and top-level career administrators.

2. Political appointees should not assume that career administrators will be hostile or uncooperative. Expectations tend to influence behavior. By expecting the worst, political appointees are likely to get less than the best efforts from career administrators. Professional career administrators who are dedicated to the value of neutral competence in public service should be given the opportunity to demonstrate that value to a new administration. Individuals in some agencies or policy areas may resist change and will need to be dealt with. Nevertheless, a systematic effort to exclude or circumvent, rather than involve or work through, career administrators is likely to be counterproductive and to bring about the kinds of opposition and resistance that some political appointees expect to encounter from the outset.

3. Political appointees should look for what Ingraham (1988) has called ''pockets of receptivity'' in the career service. If they cannot obtain agreement on their objectives from everybody, they should look for individuals who share their interests. If they cannot get agreement on everything, they should search for areas of agreement and seek to make the most of them. Career administrators are more likely to respond to requests for cooperation than to hierarchical directives.

4. The research suggests that new administrations are most effective in achieving their objectives when incoming political appointees have well-defined priorities, which they clearly articulate to career administrators at

the outset. Political appointees should communicate their objectives and strategies to career administrators during the transition phase of the new administration.

5. The difference in the time perspectives of political appointees and career administrators has frequently been cited as an impediment to successful relationships. Political appointees who view government service as a short-term venture may not be able or willing to invest in the development of the kinds of relationships with career administrators that are necessary to achieve program objectives. Political appointees should understand that effective working relationships with key career administrators will require commitment of time and resources. They should plan to serve for at least one full term with their chief executive.

6. The role orientations of political appointees and career administrators are likely to be different. The former are agents of elected officials and, as such, are often motivated to bring about policy changes or innovations, and to do so in the short term. The latter are likely to have professional, rather than politically driven, agendas, and they tend to have long-term views of program accomplishments. These differences may breed suspicion and inhibit cooperation. To overcome these differences, political appointees responsible for agencies' performance should consider the use of team-building and conflict-resolution activities, such as retreats and other communication vehicles that are regarded as enlightened management practices in the private sector.

7. Political appointees, especially those new to government, should anticipate the complexity of government. Unlike the private sector, where organizational goals tend to be relatively clear and where the responsibility for goal setting resides in a small number of individuals, the public sector has goals that are frequently unspecified and sometimes conflicting. This usually does not mean that career administrators do not know their jobs, but it probably means that a particular agency has multiple goals and is operating in an environment where competing interests make conflicting demands. Political appointees should have both a tolerance for ambiguity and an understanding of the political environment of public organizations.

8. Career administrators must recognize that the efforts of an elected executive or a political appointee to redirect or change an agency's priorities are legitimate, within reasonable limits, and that career administrators have a professional obligation to carry out legitimate policy decisions, despite personal preferences. The mission of a career service is to provide institutionalized knowledge and expertise to a succession of administrations, and career administrators are expected to serve administrations that are at variance with their own preferences. They should also be positive and open to new administrations, to dispel the expectations of political appointees new to government of encountering hostility and resistance to the policy initiatives of a new administration.

9. Career administrators can use their contacts with politically ap-

pointed or elected executives as opportunities to educate them about agencies' program needs and about the services they can offer. When career administrators help in this way, they usually also help themselves and their agencies by building a basis of future cooperation. Because of the different orientations of political appointees and career administrators, conflict is inevitable, but there are also numerous opportunities for what Heclo (1977, p. 193) has called "conditional cooperation." Career administrators must be mindful of those opportunities and use them to their advantage whenever possible.

10. Ingraham and Ban (1988) have recently argued that the relationship between career administrators and political appointees should not be characterized by attempts to achieve the narrow objectives of political control or dominance of professional expertise. Rather, it should demonstrate the joint effort to achieve broadly based social goals in the public interest. In what Ingraham and Ban call the "public service model" of these relationships, mutual respect for the skills, values, and perspectives that each party brings to the enterprise of governance can lead to cooperative efforts to serve the public interest. This model should guide the actions of political appointees and career administrators alike.

Summary

Because governance is a political process and agencies are participants in that process, no easy separation between politics and administration is possible. Nevertheless, the goals of efficiency in management, professionalism in service delivery, and rationality in decision making are most likely to be met by a career service that is protected in its day-to-day activities from excessive amounts of political influence. It is the joint responsibility of politically appointed and elected executives and career administrators to work for a public administration that is responsive and accountable but not excessively politicized.

References

Aberbach, J. D., and Rockman, B. A. "Clashing Beliefs Within the Executive Branch: The Nixon Administration Bureaucracy." *American Political Science Review,* 1976, *70,* 456–468.

Abney, G., and Lauth, T. P. "The Tasks of State Administrators: Management or External Relations." *American Review of Public Administration,* 1982, *16,* 171–184.

Abney, G., and Lauth, T. P. "The Governor as Chief Administrator." *Public Administration Review,* 1983, *43,* 40–49.

Appleby, P. H. *Policy and Administration.* University: University of Alabama Press, 1949.

Appleby, P. H. *Citizens as Sovereigns.* Syracuse, N.Y.: Syracuse University Press, 1962.

Berman, L. *The Office of Management and Budget and the Presidency, 1921–1979*. Princeton, N.J.: Princeton University Press, 1979.

Cole, R. L., and Caputo, D. A. "Presidential Control of the Senior Civil Service: Assessing the Strategies of the Nixon Years." *American Political Science Review*, 1979, *73*, 399–413.

Heclo, H. "OMB and the Presidency: The Problem of 'Neutral Competence.'" *The Public Interest*, 1975, Number 38, 80–98.

Heclo, H. *A Government of Strangers: Executive Politics in Washington*. Washington, D.C.: Brookings Institution, 1977.

Ingraham, P. W. "Transition and Policy Change in Washington." *Public Productivity Review*, 1988, *12*, 61–72.

Ingraham, P. W., and Ban, C. "Politics and Merit: Can They Meet in a Public Service Model?" *Review of Public Personnel Administration*, 1988, *8*, 7–19.

Kaufman, H. "Emerging Conflicts in the Doctrines of Public Administration." *American Political Science Review*, 1956, *50*, 1057–1073.

Lauth, T. P. "Methods of Agency Head Selection and Gubernatorial Influence over Agency Appropriations." *Public Administration Quarterly*, 1984, *7*, 396–409.

Lynn, L. E., Jr. "The Reagan Administration and the Renitent Bureaucracy." In L. M. Salamon and M. S. Lund (eds.), *The Reagan Presidency and the Governing of America*. Washington, D.C.: Urban Institute Press, 1984.

Mainzer, L. C. *Political Bureaucracy*. Glenview, Ill.: Scott, Foresman, 1973.

Moe, T. M. "The Politicized Presidency." In J. E. Chubb and P. E. Peterson (eds.), *The New Directions in American Politics*. Washington, D.C.: Brookings Institution, 1985.

Nathan, R. P. *The Plot That Failed: Nixon and the Administrative Presidency*. New York: Wiley, 1975.

Nathan, R. P. *The Administrative Presidency*. New York: Wiley, 1983.

Newland, C. A. "A Mid-Term Appraisal—The Reagan Presidency: Limited Government and Political Administration." *Public Administration Review*, 1983, *43*, 1–21.

Newland, C. A. "Executive Office Policy Apparatus: Enforcing the Reagan Agenda." In L. M. Salamon and M. S. Lund (eds.), *The Reagan Presidency and the Governing of America*. Washington, D.C.: Urban Institute Press, 1984.

Pfiffner, J. P. "Political Public Administration." *Public Administration Review*, 1985, *45*, 352–356.

Pfiffner, J. P. "Political Appointees and Career Executives: The Democracy-Bureaucracy Nexus in the Third Century." *Public Administration Review*, 1987, *47*, 57–65.

Randall, R. "Presidential Power Versus Bureaucratic Intransigence: The Influence of the Nixon Administration on Welfare Policy." *American Political Science Review*, 1979, *73*, 795–810.

Redford, E. S. *Democracy in the Administrative State.* New York: Oxford University Press, 1969.

Roberts, D. D. "A New Breed of Public Executive: Top-Level Exempt Managers in State Government." *Review of Public Personnel Administration,* 1988, *8,* 20–36.

Sanera, M. "Implementing the Mandate." In S. M. Butler, M. Sanera, and W. B. Weinrad (eds.), *Mandate for Leadership II: Continuing the Conservative Revolution.* Washington, D.C.: Heritage Foundation, 1984.

Spadaro, R. "Role Perceptions of Politicians Vis-à-Vis Public Administrators: Parameters for Public Policy." *Western Political Quarterly,* 1973, *26,* 717–725.

Sundquist, J. L. "Reflections on Watergate: Lessons for Public Administration." *Public Administration Review,* 1974, *34,* 453–461.

Tolchin, M. "Is the Quality of the Federal Work Force Deteriorating?" *New York Times,* Jan. 15, 1988, p. 24.

Weinberg, M. W. *Managing the State.* Cambridge, Mass.: MIT Press, 1977.

Jeffrey M. Berry
Kent E. Portney
Ken Thomson

15

Empowering and Involving Citizens

As government has become larger and seemingly more distant from those it serves, the challenge of how to make it open and accessible has grown more difficult. In the past few decades, agencies have responded to this challenge by trying a number of different ways of allowing citizens the opportunity to participate in policymaking by public administrators. Such activities have ranged from simply giving people a chance to comment on proposed regulations to actually reimbursing citizen groups for taking part in complex rulemaking proceedings.

Many of the efforts to incorporate citizens' views in agency policymaking have come under heavy criticism for being largely symbolic in nature, for serving as a means of pacifying opposition, or for simply being ineffective. To be truly empowered, citizens must be given more than just an opportunity to express their views, yet much of what passes for citizen participation often amounts to little more than a chance to put one's views on the record. Empowering citizens requires that channels for participation be easily accessible. It also means that participation is an effective means of influence—that is, participation is not merely symbolic or part of a cooptive process.

In this chapter, we will evaluate the efforts made in recent years to bring citizens into administrative policymaking. A starting point is to ask if the incentive systems that guide public administrators are compatible with public involvement programs. What are the reasons why administrators may object to citizen participation? Under what conditions might they favor it? Next, we will ask if rank-and-file citizens are better off working through lobbying groups than directing their efforts toward public involvement programs. Finally, we will examine prospects for improving citizen participation programs. What steps can be taken to enhance the role of citizens in bureaucratic policymaking?

Bureaucratic Behavior and Citizen Participation

When we think of citizen participation, we usually do so in the context of some form of electoral politics. We often think in terms of citizens' decisions on who will serve as governmental chief executives and legislators. We think less frequently about what role citizens should or do play in other areas of government. Over the years, however, criticism of government has led many scholars and administrators to think of ways of making bureaucracies more responsive by facilitating public participation in agencies' policymaking.

The development of ideas concerning citizen participation in the function of the bureaucracy has been something relatively new in administrative agencies. N. M. Rosenbaum (1978, pp. 45–46) contrasts traditional assumptions about how agencies become responsive with actual experiences: "Rejecting theories of public administration that claim that the 'public interest' as a whole can somehow be defined by 'neutral' and 'disinterested' bureaucrats, legislators have recognized that it is only through the clash and conflict of the full diversity of affected interests that a reasonable approximation of responsive policy can be developed."

In a sense, this approach to bureaucracy is an extension of pluralist notions of American democracy as applied to the legislative arena. Pluralist political scientists had long argued that democracy could best be achieved through the lobbying of Congress by a galaxy of advocacy groups representing the interests in this country. At roughly the same time, the scholarly field of public administration began to question assumptions about the efficacy of the orthodox (top-down) model of administrative responsiveness, in which voters elect officials to whom administrators report and are responsible. Scholars began to integrate the practical call for citizen involvement with a normative theoretical framework, often referred to as "the new public administration." This movement in the field crystallized ideas about the need for public bureaucracies to be responsive to their clients and about the use of public participation to help bring that about (Marini, 1971; Frederickson and Chandler, 1984).

Federally mandated citizen participation continued through the 1970s, with hundreds of programs mandating some form of citizen participation (Community Services Administration, 1978; Rudman and Ruffner, 1977). It was reinforced by enactment of the Federal Advisory Committee Act of 1972, which mandated citizen advisory boards throughout the federal bureaucracy and encouraged participation of organized interests. This trend continued until the inauguration of President Reagan in 1981.

In rather sweeping fashion, the Reagan administration pursued its policies under the belief that federally mandated citizen participation caused the bureaucracy to become unresponsive to officials elected by the people and that citizen participation therefore actually became antidemocratic. In a call for the return to the orthodox view of administrative responsiveness, the Reagan administration suggested that agencies had become responsive to clients and special interests in a way that was inconsistent with what the general citizenry wanted (Berry, 1981). In contrast, advocates of citizen participation argued that there is nothing antidemocratic about citizens working with agencies to fulfill the spirit and intent of the programs enacted by Congress. This debate continues today.

Perhaps the greatest challenge to mandated citizen participation comes from recognition of the tension between the empowering of citizens and the devolution of administrative power. Citizen participation is something about which many agency officials might be said to be less than enthusiastic. Indeed, the resistance of administrators to citizen participation is one of the most common explanations for the failure of citizen involvement programs to make much difference (Herbert, 1972; Kaufman, 1969). In perhaps the most critical description of this problem, W. A. Rosenbaum (1978, p. 86) asserts, "It has been almost axiomatic in the literature of [citizen] participation that a major impediment to broad and effective involvement in administrative procedure—perhaps the major obstacle—is bureaucratic resistance. In ways elegant, blunt, and brutal, bureaucrats are commonly blamed in participation literature for thwarting public involvement in agency proceedings."

Much of the literature to which Rosenbaum refers attributes this resistance to the assertion that administrators are "secretive, self-serving, non-imaginative, . . . deceitful, conservative, . . . professionally arrogant, politically protective of agency and career interests, parochial, and lazy" (p. 86). A broader perusal of the empirical literature on the role of administrators in promoting or impeding citizen participation provides a somewhat less pessimistic view. At least one study (Kweit and Kweit, 1980) sought to be perhaps a little more explicit in describing the reasons why public administrators, even if unfairly characterized by all these unflattering adjectives, would oppose and resist citizen participation. Kweit and Kweit argue that most administrative agencies develop bureaucratic norms of behavior, which tend to conflict with participatory norms. These authors state four premises that, they contend, motivate bureaucratic behavior in general:

- The application of value-neutral professional expertise to agency functions
- The need for regularity, routinization, and predictability
- The pursuit of efficiency
- The need for self-maintenance

For example, Kweit and Kweit point to the norm of pursuing efficiency, which sends administrators in search of the fastest and cheapest ways of getting things accomplished. The problem with citizen participation is that it almost necessarily opens up the administrative decision-making process to more people, which causes the process to take longer. Citizen participation, if pursued diligently, would require administrators to involve parties whose conflicting positions lead to the inability to make decisions, or to policy gridlock (Huntington, 1975). Since time is often money, administrators come to see citizen participation as inconsistent with the pursuit of efficiency.

The result of the discrepancy between bureaucratic and participatory norms, where they exist, is that administrators develop different modes for dealing with citizen participation. For example, they may attempt to insulate themselves from the part of the environment placing demands on them. Kweit and Kweit suggest that this is usually the least effective mode, since it often only postpones the inevitable. In some cases, insulation may make program implementation more costly and less efficient in the long run, thus inadvertently creating a conflict with the efficiency norms. Another mode administrators may develop is to establish participatory channels that, by their nature, are designed to serve a symbolic function: to make citizens believe they are having an influence, while bureaucratic behavior does not really change. This mode includes establishment of open meetings or public hearings, citizen advisory boards, and other commonly used participation techniques. Administrators may also seek some sort of cooperation with those who wish to participate. In this mode, citizens are able to exercise some influence over administrators, but it is accomplished informally, with no exchange of formal authority or responsibility. Finally, administrators may actually be coopted by citizen participants and may delegate some authority or responsibility to citizens.

Thus, it may seem that there are major administrative impediments to citizen participation. Yet there is evidence that when administrators do make the commitment to citizen participation, the participation experience can be both representative and responsive (Berry, Portney, Bablitch, and Mahoney, 1984). In other words, empowerment of citizens is at least in part dependent on the willingness of administrators to empower them. The challenge is to find out under what conditions administrators make such a commitment. On the pragmatic side, the challenge is to find ways that administrators who wish to develop citizen participation can do so without confronting the myriad problems that often result.

The idea of being able to determine the "effectiveness" (Rosener, 1978) of a citizen participation program is one of the more sticky issues in the literature. Most studies of citizen participation's effectiveness that attempt some form of balanced measurement of effectiveness point to the structure of the programs themselves. For example, it seems clear that participation programs tend to be more effective for participants and administrators when they provide for participants to be selected through some process that is perceived to be representative of a broader underlying population. A citywide participation program would be more likely to be effective if participants reflected the characteristics of the city with respect to neighborhoods, races, ethnic groups, or other clearly recognizable characteristics. Moreover, programs that actually involve citizens early in decision processes, rather than after decisions have already been made, tend to be perceived by participants as being much more fair (Mazmanian and Nienaber, 1979). A participation program that consists of a public hearing in which administrators present a fully developed plan or proposal for public response is likely to be less well received by citizens than a series of hearings in which participants provide input from the time of a proposal's inception.

Not all analyses have pointed to structural characteristics of the participation efforts themselves. Herbert (1972) and Kweit and Kweit (1980) identify some conditions under which administrators are likely to share common interests with citizen participants. Herbert, for example, suggests that the training of administrators, either through schooling or on-the-job experience, makes them unwilling to live with the inevitable conflict produced by citizen participation. In his words, the "greatest challenge to public administrators operating within a participatory environment will be identifying and balancing citizen needs and demands against the potentially conflicting demands and socio-emotional needs of public employees, elected officials, and administrative superiors" (p. 623). For Herbert, then, the condition that best explains the ability of administrators to cope with citizen participation involves whether they have developed the personal skills necessary for conflict management. Kweit and Kweit point to the idea that citizen participation must conform to or be consistent with the premises that motivate bureaucratic behavior. As they note (p. 666), "when citizens are perceived as conforming" to the bureaucratic decision-making process, and when the environment is "unstable," administrators will accept citizen participation. For example, when citizens become technical experts on programs, administrators may come to see citizens as credible sources of opposition and may seek to work with rather than against citizen advocates.

Common wisdom describes citizen participation as ineffective or nonexistent, but there are many instances when citizen participation is welcomed by administrators. Indeed, most administrators probably cultivate selective citizen support and activity around their programs, if only in a symbolic form. Moreover, agency officials often seek clienteles for their programs as a way of building political support to prevent budget reductions or reallocations, and this type of relationship may transcend the purely symbolic.

Many officials go beyond the selective involvement of citizens to more open and participatory operations. Such officials often come to realize that they cannot avoid potential conflict simply by excluding opposing parties from the decision process. In the long run, exclusion may make conflict greater and prolong its resolution. Consequently, many administrators believe that, in the long run, it is actually more efficient to anticipate and deal with potential conflict before it becomes debilitating.

Formal requirements for citizen participation in public agencies tell part of the story, but it is also true that various types of citizen participation have developed even without such mandates. One of these relates to the integration of citizens and agency employees in the delivery of public services, especially at the local level. This integration is commonly referred to as coproduction of public services. (See Chapter Thirty-Six for an in-depth discussion of coproduction.)

Although coproduction of services unquestionably involves citizen participation, it is not at all clear that such participation helps to make the respective agencies more responsive. In some cases, coproduction involves citizens in providing services for themselves, in lieu of having them provided by local agencies. Moreover, local agencies often are not particularly receptive to citizen involvement. In this sense, coproduction may not be greatly different from other types of citizen participation programs in that there tend to be strong incentives for administrators to resist intrusion into agencies' affairs.

Perhaps the most important lesson from service coproduction is that it is one way of integrating citizens' needs and interests with those of program administrators. Coproduction seems to work best when citizens cooperate with agency officials to help implement programs or policies for which the agency officials can take substantial credit. Coproduction, then, can be thought of as a way to help agency officials meet their goals while achieving the substantive results desired by citizens. In some instances, this is no small task, because administrators often see coproduction as a way of substituting volunteer (citizen) labor for their own professional expertise. Still, there are many examples of citizens and administrators successfully working together in service coproduction.

There are also times when citizen participation becomes integrated into agency management through emphasis on points of common interest. We have seen many local agencies begin to incorporate citizen participation into their operations. If citizen participation is a valuable goal for agencies, perhaps it ought to be included as an explicit goal, along with all the other performance measures. Participation goals can be integrated into an existing or developing performance evaluation system. For example, the goal of increasing the number and representativeness of citizen participants can be pursued through management by objectives (Portney, 1981). This has happened in St. Paul, Minnesota, where agency officials' interaction with neighborhood-based district council representatives is a delineated and rewarded activity.

Citizen Groups and Government

Since administrators are frequently reluctant to establish effective citizen participation programs, citizens who wish to influence agencies usually resort to traditional forms of administrative lobbying. To empower themselves, therefore, citizens have had to take the initiative and aggressively seek out administrators and ask them to hear their case. The problem with this approach is that it has been the province of citizen groups' most frequent adversary: business. For citizen groups, it is not simply a matter of choosing to imitate a successful approach of others. To accomplish their goals through lobbying, citizens must be well organized and adequately funded. Therein, of course, lies the rub: The problems of organizing a lobby capable of competing with business lead to calls for citizen participation programs.

Despite the greater difficulty that citizen groups face, in comparison to business and other kinds of lobbies, there has been an upsurge in the past twenty-five years in the number of such groups. Indeed, the growth in citizen group advocacy helped stimulate more business lobbying. On the national level, corporate public affairs offices have proliferated, and more trade associations are making Washington, D.C., their headquarters as lobbying becomes a more central organizational priority (Berry, 1984). Has the movement toward more lobbying given citizen groups real influence in government, or have business and other adversaries easily countered this effort by devoting more resources to political advocacy?

There is no precise way to estimate the growth of these groups' influence, but it is clear that in many policy areas citizen lobbies have had a significant impact on government decisions. Liberal public interest lobbies have played a major role in the enactment of much regulatory legislation since the mid 1960s. Air and water pollution laws have been strengthened because of environmental advocacy. The food stamp program and other nutritional efforts were created or expanded with considerable help from citizen groups. The birth of the Consumer Product Safety Commission and the revitalization of the Federal Trade Commission also reflect increased public interest lobbying. On the conservative side, right-to-life groups have pushed hard to restrict women's access to abortion.

As subgovernments decline and as broader and more open issue networks become more common, citizen groups contribute to the more adversarial nature of interest-group politics. There are few policy areas where quiet negotiations between one or two lobbyists and a congressional committee or an agency will settle matters. In one study of four different policy domains, between 65 percent and 85 percent of the lobbies identified regular interest-group adversaries (Salisbury, Heinz, Laumann, and Nelson, 1986). Part of this conflict comes from increased business competition and deregulation. The most common source of conflict, however, is between business and citizen groups (Schlozman and Tierney, 1986).

The increase in citizen groups raises two significant questions directly relevant to our concerns here. First, has this movement brought us considerably closer to a true pluralist democracy? Second, is this an effective way to empower citizens in bureaucratic policymaking? As noted earlier, democratic pluralism—a balancing of interests achieved through the advocacy efforts of all affected constituencies—has long been viewed as a desirable form of government. Can we now stop promoting pluralism through public involvement programs, because expanded citizen advocacy has achieved the same goals at the heart of those programs? It would be a mistake to believe that citizen groups alone can bring about the type of balance among relevant interests that a democratic system demands. Although they have broadened their representation in the policymaking process, citizen groups are not a perfect counterweight to lobbies from other sectors of society. They still form only a relatively small proportion of the interest-group community, and their financial resources are dwarfed by those available to business. Some policy areas, like the environment, are well covered by citizen groups, while others, such as antitrust or securities law, are not. Citizen groups are often ad hoc, reactive organizations fighting projects that are long under way. Some administrative proceedings, such as ratemaking by state or federal regulatory agencies, require expertise and financial resources that make it extremely difficult for citizen groups to participate.

National citizen groups make an important contribution to empowering individuals, but they are more representative than participatory. People can acquire greater confidence in their ability to influence government by observing their groups' roles in policymaking. When their groups appear to be having some impact, members will feel that they deserve some of the credit. Nevertheless, group membership alone is not enough to empower citizens. It has long been assumed that participation beyond a financial contribution will result in an even greater sense of empowerment, because only active involvement develops the political skills that ultimately will enable citizens to build a participatory democracy. On this score, national groups have been roundly criticized. McCann (1986, p. 170) argues that liberal "reformers have managed to mobilize voluntary support from millions of card-carrying members, but . . . they have actually engaged very few of these members as genuinely active participants in political life."

It is hardly surprising that national citizens' lobbies are not highly participatory organizations. This is true of most interest groups active in Washington politics. Sending a check once a year to a favorite group is all some people ever want to do, although others choose to become part of a group's network of activists who write letters and make phone calls when prompted by the Washington office. Local citizen groups are much more accessible to the rank and file who are interested in more direct involvement. Local groups tend to be highly participatory, since they depend heavily on volunteer labor to offset their lack of financial resources. The lack of professional staffs, however, disadvantages these groups in complex administrative proceedings. External funding could help state and local groups participate effectively in rulemaking and ratemaking actions (Gormley, 1983).

Clearly, national groups have worked well in representing their citizen constituents before government, but they have not fared so well at directly involving their members in the political process. Local and statewide groups are more participatory, but they have fewer of the resources necessary to an effective administrative lobby. At all levels of government, external funding and other mechanisms for ensuring adequate representation of chronically underrepresented interests are necessary. More broadly, imaginative public involvement programs that facilitate citizen participation at every level are needed to further empower the clients of administrative agencies.

Toward Effective Citizen Participation Programs

To achieve empowerment without creating a new distortion of the political balance, a clear understanding of the public interest must be reached. But what is this public interest, and how can it be determined in any situation?

One argument has it that the public interest is best represented when people vote for their officials. Any tinkering with that mandate only gets in the way of effective direction of the programs that benefit the majority of the public. Another argument has it that the self-defined public interest groups are the best watchdogs of the greater good. They can focus on particular issues within the broad electoral mandate, and they can articulate policies while displaying less monetary vested interest than any other political actors. Yet a third argument holds that the pluralistic amalgam of such groups, representing both public and special interests, is the most complete reflection of the public good available to us. It is not perfect, but no other solution incorporates the full richness of analysis and debate that pluralist discussion and lobbying can provide.

Each of these arguments has merit, but each also falls short. Voting provides the broadest possible mandate, but it unrealistically demands that a whole host of complex and time-dependent issues be resolved down to a single either-or choice once every four years. Are all voters so well informed that they can make such all-encompassing choices? And while public interest groups are often effective watchdogs that do alert the public to dangers, which public interest, advocated by which group, is the right one? What about people who have views very different from those of any of these groups (public opinion polls suggest that they are many): Are they part of the public whose interest is represented? Finally, the pluralist argument patches some of the holes in the public interest group dictum, yet it seems to create even greater distortions in other areas because of the vastly different resources among advocates of various positions. At times, the "each for each and none for all" philosophy inherent in pluralism can lead to endless negotiations and failure to achieve resolution or decisive action.

These considerations have led a number of recent observers to search "beyond adversary democracy," as Mansbridge (1983) put it in her book by that name. For Barber (1984), the search has led to a call for a "strong democratic community." Barber outlines the characteristics he believes such communities must seek, including a process of "strong democratic talk," which enables large numbers of people to articulate their interests, listen and persuade, set political agendas, explore mutual interests and affiliations, reformulate and reconceptualize plans and proposals, and engage in community building "as the creation of public interests, common goods, and active citizens" (p. 179). A key to progress in this direction seems to include participation, not only of organized groups but also of individual citizens, in a sustained, highly interactive process.

Mansbridge, Barber, and others who advocate this search recognize the long distance between where we are now and where their goals would lead us. In our own work, however, we have found that the beginnings of some of the features of a "strong democracy" already exist in such communities as St. Paul, Minnesota, Birmingham, Alabama, Portland, Oregon, and Dayton, Ohio. Each of these communities has developed its own style to fit its social, political, and economic circumstances.

St. Paul, for example, a city of 270,000, has created perhaps the most comprehensive citizen participation system anywhere in the country. Seventeen district councils each have specific responsibilities in zoning, housing, and development issues, and many have taken on other issues, from environmental pollution to home health care. Each council has the ability to hire and fire its own staff, has a small budget from the city, and has the opportunity, which several have taken, to raise substantial additional funding on its own. The Capital Improvement Budget Committee allows representatives from the neighborhoods to individually rate every capital proposal, whether from agencies or from neighborhoods, and propose final allocations to each. Regular neighborhood newspapers are a common feature of the communication between district councils and community residents.

A very different city—Dayton, Ohio—facing economic conditions that have caused many neighborhoods to lose more than half their residents in the last decade, uses its system of seven priority boards and eighty-two neighborhoods as an intrinsic feature of its performance-oriented bureaucracy. In this community of 194,000 people, all city agencies work under a detailed management-by-objectives system, and a key measure of agencies' success is whether the public likes the results. They had better, because every five years the city has to face an all-or-nothing public vote on the local income tax, the primary source of the city's revenues. Each priority board has at least three full-time staff members funded by the city, screened by the civil service and the city's neighborhood office, and formally hired by the priority board itself. Each board has a monthly session with representatives of each major city agency. Board residents make up a majority of the citywide committee that allocates Community Development Block Grant funds. Major city initiatives, from hazardous waste siting to employee residency requirements, are often brought to the priority boards for advice and neighborhood promotion.

In examining citizen participation programs at the community level during the last five or six years (a period when federal participation mandates have been substantially relaxed or altogether eliminated), we have found a type of plateau phenomenon at work. In communities where citizen participation was designed to meet only the minimum requirements of the federal government, participation efforts have generally fallen off dramatically as federal requirements have ended. In communities that had reached a substantially higher plateau, however, and that had developed strong internal justifications and standards for effective participation, the programs have continued to grow, even in the face of major budget cutbacks at both the federal and the local levels.

What characteristics make strong programs? Four factors seem essential to—in fact, seem almost to be a definition of—a serious participation effort:

1. *Effective Outreach.* A serious participation effort must attempt to provide a realistic opportunity for large numbers of the target population to participate. Low on this scale would be a single public hearing announced

in the legal notices of a local newspaper. High on the scale would be a series of meetings, mostly in the evening or on weekends, announced through radio, television, the newspaper, and door-to-door distribution of descriptive pamphlets.

2. *Equal Access.* A balanced participation effort must provide this opportunity to all citizens on an equal basis. A minimum effort here would be a blue-ribbon commission. A maximum effort might provide for neighborhood-based elections and open meetings, with small-group sessions stimulating input from a large number of people and building up in Delphi fashion to a near-consensus agreement. On a larger geographical scale, the effort might involve a tiered representative structure based on such natural communities.

3. *Significant Policy Impact.* To be more than appeasement, the participation effort must provide an effective avenue for participants to have significant impact on final policy decisions. At the low end, policymakers present the public with a single take-it-or-leave-it proposition. At the high end, citizens are involved from the beginning, and the consensus achieved in the participation process becomes the final policy.

4. *Enactable Policy.* A meaningful participation effort must address a specific government policy or program decision being made at the level corresponding to the participation effort. Low on this scale would be a citywide participation effort leading only to a proclamation of a particular goal. At the high end would be a citywide participation effort distributing the city's capital funds to specific projects, or a nationwide effort resulting in new Environmental Protection Agency regulations governing toxic waste production and cleanup.

Beyond these four basic factors, the particular participation effort needs to be tailored to the specific target population and to the problem at hand. Many participation approaches exist, from fishbowl planning and charettes to goal-setting efforts and funding of neighborhood-based processes. The best description of these approaches to date remains the two-volume set produced by the U.S. Department of Transportation (1976), including thirty-seven citizen participation techniques, with a clear analysis of applicability and detailed references for each.

Other patterns of success at the community level are beginning to emerge from ongoing research, including that of the National Citizen Participation Development Project, in which the authors are involved. Here are some preliminary conclusions:

1. The significant innovations for most major participation efforts have taken place in one large step, not gradually over time. The key structural elements established at the beginning of the program ten to fifteen years ago remain in place today.

2. Most successful participation efforts in urban areas are built on neigh-

borhoods, unlike many state and federal participation programs, which rely on areawide forums or committees.

3. In successful programs, the informal powers of the neighborhoods have far outweighed the formal powers they have been granted. In most cases, the formal ordinances provide only advisory power, not decision-making power, to the participation system, yet the practical operation essentially gives veto power over certain types of issues to carefully designed neighborhood-based structures.

4. City funding for neighborhood organizational development and for communication between the neighborhood organization and residents is an essential ingredient of a stable system. Neighborhood roles in hiring and firing neighborhood support staff, and neighborhood offices for such staff to work in, appear to be extremely important in generating a high degree of accountability.

5. Timing and flow of information from the city to neighborhood organizations are the most consistent feature of successful participation systems. This "early warning" system has substantially improved the effectiveness of many of the neighborhood groups in accomplishing their own objectives, particularly on development, traffic, and environmental issues.

6. Comprehensive planning with neighborhood organizations can have an enormous role in effective participation, particularly when linked with ongoing administrative action or legally actionable remedies.

7. Representativeness is crucial. In every city, questions have been raised about how representative neighborhood organizations are. Clear and accepted neighborhood boundaries, ability of the neighborhood to speak in a single voice, and open and visibly legitimate neighborhood processes have made the difference between neighborhoods that stand or fall under pressure.

8. Even the most successful participation systems are seldom able to integrate the participatory power of neighborhood processes with effective citizen roles on citywide issues and major economic development projects on a citywide scale. The "not in my backyard" problem remains largely unsolved on issues ranging from halfway houses to toxic waste disposal.

Summary

Our review of the literature, and our own ongoing research, suggest that citizen participation programs can work effectively but that there are substantial obstacles to success. Administrators often view such programs as impediments to efficient government or as platforms for opponents. Incentive structures do not typically reward agency officials for operating public involvement programs that give citizens real influence in the policymaking process. Elected officials can easily derail citizen participation programs that have not been institutionalized into agency operations.

Citizen participation will be most successful when it is adopted broadly within a community. When it becomes embedded in the political culture of a city, such as in St. Paul and Dayton, it changes the incentive structure for administrators and raises the costs for politicians who might prefer to weaken such programs. When neighborhoods expect to be consulted on projects or programs that affect them, and when citizens believe that city officials are willing to listen to and negotiate with them, it becomes very difficult politically to make the city less participatory. Only rarely, of course, do cities take citizen participation so seriously that it becomes part of the social and political fabric of the community, and on the national level, only isolated programs of the federal government have worked over an extended period.

It is not easy to prescribe a route that will lead to a broad institutionalization of citizen participation. It takes committed administrators led by visionary agency heads, and elected leaders who persist in supporting these programs over many years. Still, we think it is imperative to keep trying to establish citizen participation programs. When we examine the other means of trying to promote a truly democratic political process, it can only be concluded that citizen participation programs will complement those means and enhance the empowerment of citizens. Citizen participation has the potential to move us closer to the democratic ideal than we can come through elections and interest-group politics alone.

References

Barber, B. *Strong Democracy: Participatory Politics for a New Age.* Berkeley: University of California Press, 1984.

Berry, J. M. "Maximum Feasible Dismantlement." *Citizen Participation,* 1981, *3* (2), 3–5.

Berry, J. M. *The Interest Group Society.* Boston: Little, Brown, 1984.

Berry, J. M., Portney, K. E., Bablitch, M. B., and Mahoney, R. "Public Involvement in Administration: The Structural Determinants of Effective Citizen Participation." *Journal of Voluntary Action Research,* 1984, *13* (2), 7–23.

Community Services Administration. *Citizen Participation.* Washington, D.C.: Community Services Administration, 1978.

Frederickson, H. G., and Chandler, R. C. (eds.). "Citizenship and Public Administration." *Public Administration Review,* 1984, *44* (Special Issue).

Gormley, W. T. *The Politics of Public Utility Regulation.* Pittsburgh, Pa.: University of Pittsburgh Press, 1983.

Herbert, A. "Management Under Conditions of Decentralization and Citizen Participation." *Public Administration Review,* 1972, *32,* 622–633.

Huntington, S. P. "The Democratic Distemper." *Public Interest,* 1975, *41,* 9–38.

Kaufman, H. "Administrative Decentralization and Political Power." *Public Administration Review,* 1969, *29* (1), 3–15.

Kweit, R. W., and Kweit, M. "Bureaucratic Decision-Making: Impediments to Citizen Participation." *Polity,* 1980, *12* (4), 646–666.

McCann, M. W. *Taking Reform Seriously.* Ithaca, N.Y.: Cornell University Press, 1986.

Mansbridge, J. J. *Beyond Adversary Democracy.* (2nd ed.) Chicago: University of Chicago Press, 1983.

Marini, F. (ed.). *Toward a New Public Administration: The Minnowbrook Perspective.* Scranton, Pa.: Chandler Press, 1971.

Mazmanian, D. A., and Nienaber, J. *Can Organizations Change? Environmental Protection, Citizen Participation, and the Corps of Engineers.* Washington, D.C.: Brookings Institution, 1979.

Portney, K. E. "Management by Objectives: A Means to Effective Citizen Participation." *Citizen Participation,* 1981, *2* (5), 16–19.

Rosenbaum, N. M. "Citizen Participation and Democratic Theory." In S. Langton (ed.), *Citizen Participation in America.* Lexington, Mass.: Heath, 1978.

Rosenbaum, W. A. "Public Involvement as Reform and Ritual." In S. Langton (ed.), *Citizen Participation in America.* Lexington, Mass.: Heath, 1978, pp. 81–96.

Rosener, J. B. "Citizen Participation: Can We Measure Its Effectiveness?" *Public Administration Review,* 1978, *38,* 457–463.

Rudman, S., and Ruffner, D. *Citizen Participation, General Revenue Sharing, and the Municipal Budget Process.* Claremont, Calif.: Claremont Graduate School, 1977.

Salisbury, R. H., Heinz, J. P., Laumann, E. O., and Nelson, R. L. "Who Works with Whom?" Paper presented at the annual meeting of the American Political Science Association, Washington, D.C., Aug. 1986.

Schlozman, K. L., and Tierney, J. T. *Organized Interests and American Democracy.* New York: Harper & Row, 1986.

U.S. Department of Transportation. *Effective Citizen Participation in Transportation Planning.* 2 vols. Washington, D.C.: Socio-Economic Studies Division, Federal Highway Administration, U.S. Department of Transportation, 1976.

Part Four

Establishing Successful Policies and Programs

One of the key functions of government is making public policies, that is, establishing and monitoring rules for the conduct of public affairs. Making public policy is a continuous process, involving creation of agendas, analysis of alternative courses of action, implementation of decisions, and evaluation of outcomes. The public administrator is an important player throughout this process. Part Four explores the functional aspects of the policymaking process and how public administrators contribute to them.

Many of the early writings in public administration drew a sharp distinction between politics (policies or expressions of the state will) and administration (the execution of policies). As public administration has evolved, the policy-administration dichotomy has become recognized as inadequate for describing the complex role public administrators play in the policymaking process. It is inevitable in modern government that public administrators exercise discretion, and much of that discretion has political implications—that is, for who gets what, where, when, and how.

The activities of public administrators at various stages of the policy process illustrate the difficulty of divorcing politics from administration. During agenda setting, when problems are brought to the attention of governmental decision makers, public administrators influence agendas both directly and indirectly. They sometimes act as intermediaries in deciding how the finite attention of policymakers will be allocated. At the same time, public administrators influence the agenda by the problem-finding routines they develop, the networks of contacts they nurture, and the types of expertise they develop.

The penetration of political choices into policy analysis is obvious. Administrative choices about which options will receive thorough review, what standards they will be judged against, and who will be involved in the process are inherently political. The public administrator tempers the political nature of these decisions by sharing them with others and deferring to the expertise of others, but there is no way to stop the public administrator from playing a political role.

Policy implementation—that is, putting legislative decisions into operation—also involves much discretion. Public administrators typically seek to move public policies in legislatively mandated directions. They are seldom able to do so, however, according to definitive blueprints. Instead, they must often employ their own judgment about appropriate means, on the basis of their understanding of legislative intent.

As in the other phases of the policy process, struggle over values permeates policy evaluation. The success or the failure of a policy can turn on which criteria are selected for judging its contributions, what groups are sought out for their views, and when the evaluation is conducted.

As our understanding of the interface between politics and administration has evolved, so also has our substantive understanding of public policy processes. We have become more keenly aware of variations in the policy process over an idea's or a policy's life cycle, across different types of policies, and across political jurisdictions. The last twenty years have seen significant advances in the knowledge base and technologies necessary for improving policy results. Part Four provides answers to critical problems confronting policy managers.

16

Laurence J. O'Toole, Jr.

The Public Administrator's
Role in Setting
the Policy Agenda

To achieve their promise, systems of democratic government must take action: They must make and execute public policy. It is widely recognized that public administrators perform a number of tasks to contribute to this process. It may be less obvious, however, that such administrators can play key roles even as policy problems first attract the attention of government and are placed on its agenda for decision.

This chapter considers the public administrator's role in helping to set the policy agenda and is designed particularly to assist those who seek guidelines for effective administrative practice. Accordingly, the first section briefly summarizes some important analytical distinctions and relevant findings. The next section, which constitutes the bulk of the chapter, explicitly sketches some research-based guidelines for effective practice regarding agenda setting within the framework of democratic government. These guidelines emphasize tools and processes through which public administrators can contribute to the agenda-setting activity.

Agenda Setting and Administrators

Governments in the United States are often expected to address a staggering number and range of concerns, from nuclear power to nuclear medicine, from social security to locally provided social services, from sex edu-

Note: The author gratefully acknowledges the assistance of two colleagues, John Heilman and Gerald Johnson, in identifying relevant literatures and issues for consideration.

cation to gender equality. By almost any measure, public agendas seem to have grown tremendously, despite service cutbacks and tax reductions at all levels during the 1980s. As governments are pressured to deal with an increasing number of issues while being constrained by budgetary and political boundaries, the process of setting the public policy agenda becomes crucial. What is the agenda-setting process like? What is the role of the public administrator in this set of decisions? What can and should that role be? This mix of empirical and normative concerns lies at the heart of the analysis here.

In simplest terms, the agenda is the list of issues up for public consideration at a particular time. Thus, agendas are limited by calendars, politics, and the time and attention of policymakers, and they can change over time. Agenda setting is "the course by which issues are adopted for public consideration and, perhaps, remedy" (Nelson, 1984, p. 20).

This notion is misleading, however. It conveys the sense of a clear array that all can observe. There are really many policy agendas that together constitute the formal or governmental agenda (see Cobb and Elder, 1983, p. 86; Nelson, 1984, p. 20). The federal system provides substantial policy autonomy between national and state governments, and local units pursue diverse issues. Thus, Washington, D.C., may focus on monetary policy at the same time that Oklahoma considers revisions in its severance tax on oil and Tulsa debates municipal service cutbacks as a budget-balancing maneuver. Furthermore, it is rare to find a single government unanimously considering a common set of topics. The president may devote a huge portion of time to the modernization of conventional defense forces, while Congress largely ignores the issue in favor of proposals for national health insurance.

What roles do public administrators play in agenda setting? Numerous studies document involvement by administrators at crucial stages of the process. (Individual case studies include Crenson, 1971; Derthick, 1979; Fritschler, 1983; and Nelson, 1984. Systematic inquiry across multiple cases is reported in Heclo, 1974; Kirst, Meister, and Rowley, 1984; Light, 1982; and Polsby, 1984.) Sometimes administrative success in agenda setting in one locale spreads to others: Analyses of the diffusion of innovations across units of government have shed light on the complex processes by which governments and governmental administrators pick up ideas and become receptive to learning from each other (Rogers, 1983; see also Savage, 1985). Nevertheless, administrators do not typically dominate the agenda-setting process in every case and from beginning to end (Ripley and Franklin, 1986, p. 33). Thus, it is important to develop a more refined understanding of that process and of the administrator's role in it. To do so requires distinguishing systemic from routine agendas and explaining different elements or stages of the agenda-setting process.

The governmental agenda may contain matters from the list of larger societal concerns (the *systemic* agenda), or the items may derive from the ideas and even the standard procedures of government itself (the *routine* agenda). The degree of match or mismatch between the systemic and routine agendas can provide clues to the responsiveness of public settings and thus about whether, when, and how public administrators might become more active in affecting the content of the agenda in the government or in their own agencies.

At the broadest systemic level, as society continually considers various problems and issues, one usually expects and even desires public administrators to play a more secondary role. This is the presumption of democratic theory, which reserves the primary agenda-setting role at the systemic level to the people and their political representatives. The systemic agenda is nevertheless neither neutral nor perfectly representative of the interests of the larger public (Cobb and Elder, 1983, p. 85). Some problems, like income inequality, may be perceived as outside the proper scope of governmental attention, since the agenda-setting process can reflect the interests of more powerful segments in the political community (see Lindblom, 1980, pp. 119–121). It would be too simple to conclude, therefore, that it is clearly inappropriate for administrators to seek to influence the systemic agenda.

More routine processes of policy initiation, which consume significant amounts of time, deal with complicated technical matters, and focus especially on the development of feasible alternatives for policymakers, are more likely to involve administrators regularly in important roles (see Kingdon, 1984; Polsby, 1984; and Nelson, 1984). This is because professional administrators possess a relative abundance of certain resources—principally longevity, ideas and expertise, regular channels of contact within and among communities of policy specialists, and key positions in the structure of policymaking—that provide particular advantages under these contingencies.

An understanding of the administrator's role also requires one to distinguish analytically between two elements or phases of the process: one through which issues achieve positions on the governmental agenda, and another through which policy alternatives are fashioned to compete as possible responses to the issues. This distinction, developed by Kingdon (1984, pp. 32–37) in the most rigorous empirical study of agenda setting to date, helps one to see that administrators are more influential, with respect to elected officials and political appointees, in the latter aspect of the process than in the former.

It cannot be assumed, however, that this refinement is a well-accepted division of labor, nor should an administrator believe that the policy process regarding agenda setting is rational and linear, with politicians selecting issues and administrators and other experts then fashioning and sifting through alternatives to deal with the issues. One finding consistently expressed in recent studies of innovation and agenda setting is that action is necessarily much more haphazard. The principal metaphor employed is borrowed from organization theory: agenda setting as a "garbage can" (Cohen, March, and Olsen, 1972). Issues are constantly being defined and redefined as they compete for the interest of busy decision makers; alternatives are also constantly being produced and, especially, recycled through the system—often by participants in the process who have been proposing them for years. These issues and alternatives are mixed chaotically as they are dumped into the ''garbage can'' of the policy process (see Kingdon, 1984; Levine, 1985; Light, 1982; Polsby, 1984; Rogers, 1983; and Walker, 1981). The politically successful linking of policy problems to appropriate alternatives, therefore, cannot be assumed; it requires the participation of skillful policy entrepreneurs, who are often administrators.

Successful policy entrepreneurship on the part of administrators often requires in turn that contextual conditions be favorable. More specifically, the influence of the administrator in such an entrepreneurial role varies across time, governmental jurisdiction, and substantive policy sector. (The nature of these variations and how they can be taken into account in the practice of administration are detailed in the following section.)

In sum, then, the agenda-setting process is really a set of processes, and the administrative role is actually an amalgam of varying and complex roles. The level of public administrative influence, as well as the degree of legitimacy accorded such administrative efforts, varies with the aspect and context of agenda setting being examined. More than that generalization, however, the distinctions and research findings sketched above imply some fairly specific guidelines for effective practice in agenda setting.

Agenda Setting: Guidelines for Effective Practice

As the previous discussion indicates, the task of setting the public policy agenda is complex and multifaceted. What is known about this topic demonstrates that no simple set of prescriptions can possibly provide detailed guidance for effective practice to administrators of all types, at all levels, for all occasions. Furthermore, some difficult ethical and political questions attend any effort by public administrators to influence the course of governmental action. Thus, there is bound to be some disagreement with the specifics of any set of guidelines for effective practice. Still, the research summarized here does provide implications worth considering.

Effective administrative participation in agenda setting varies by context. This proposition specifically means the following things.

1. Public administrators should be prepared to play major roles in routine agenda setting. Administrative agencies often are at their most efficient in dealing with the manifold routines of government, and many administrative routines provide the triggers that can move items to the policy agenda.

Sometimes the triggering forces that place items on public agendas reach largely beyond the control of any individual or institution. In other circumstances, however, administrative activities and processes contribute quite directly to agenda setting. The use of social and technical indicators, for instance, has become a pervasive part of the policy setting and affects both the recognition and the definition of problems, as well as the shape of the governmental agenda. Such familiar items as the administratively reported national unemployment rate or the monthly cost of living index have been responsible for moving some issues and programs to the forefront of the policy process. Feedback—through happenstance, routine reports, active monitoring, or sophisticated policy evaluation—may also strongly influence public agendas (Kingdon, 1984, pp. 95–103). Many of these items have to do with the acquisition, use, and communication of data and analytical information, with technical matters, or with fairly complex governmental and social processes. Although activists and political leaders may well have perceptions and viewpoints about various items, administrators are a crucial source not only of information but also of issues suggested by this information. The AIDS epidemic, discovered by public health officials through regular mechanisms of disease reporting, illustrates how information from a mundane, standard administrative process can alert a policy community, and eventually the world, to a major issue.

If administrators are not sensitive to their roles in routine agenda setting, it may be that no one else is well situated to do so. Government and policymaking may thereby suffer seriously.

2. The process by which the systemic agenda is established is somewhat different. Accordingly, the role administrators can and should take for effective action is also different. Whereas administrators are unlikely to be the main actors here, they can fulfill important roles by stimulating and managing creativity in administrative institutions—for example, by recruiting and rewarding diversity among agency personnel, encouraging staff to interact among other professionals in the field as well as with interested outsiders, structuring organizational arrangements to provide incentives for the exercise of "voice" (Hirschman, 1970), avoiding (if possible) patterns that focus almost exclusively on dealing with current crises rather than on considering the needs of the future, and by acting as policy entrepreneurs within the constraints of democratic government.

Furthermore, when considering the systemic agenda, administrators can contribute to effective practice by being aware of the distinctive features, indeed the biases, of the standard policy and political processes: Neither the so-called mandates of political campaigns nor the persuasive efforts of organized interest groups should be uncritically allowed to shape the policy-relevant activities of administrative agencies. Different modes of tapping public opinion are likely to reach and elicit responses from different elements of the public, who have very different views about which issues and problems are worth pursuing vigorously.

Without seeking to usurp authority, then, or to supplant the crucial role of overtly political actors in the policy process, administrators can help contribute to the shape of the systemic agenda by using innovative methods to identify the views and concerns of citizens. Polls, surveys, interviews, deliberative group processes, hearings, and computer and telecommunications technologies can all be used sensitively by administrators who seek to develop a richer sense of the systemic agenda as it relates to the activities of their organization. Moreover, the information garnered through such channels can be directed, as appropriate, to others in the policy process as they deliberate and shape the governmental agenda.

3. Administrative roles and their effectiveness differ by time, jurisdiction, and substantive issue. Administrators should be sensitive to these variations and adapt strategy and tactics to these dimensions of context.

More specifically on the matter of time, broad cycles of innovation and retrenchment have been found to envelop those involved in agenda setting and to render various periods promising or inopportune (see Eyestone, 1978, pp. 28–30). The most skillful administrator may thus encounter nothing but frustration when seeking to place large, controversial issues on the government's agenda during a period of across-the-board cutbacks. On the contrary, interesting ideas were comparatively easy to add to the agenda during such periods as the Great Society years, before the Vietnam buildup (Sundquist, 1968). Furthermore, influence by administrators and other experts sometimes cannot be seen easily in the short term, yet over the longer haul, and with their assistance, policy-oriented learning may take place and affect the definition of problems and the agenda for action. For instance, one study of policy regarding land use in the Lake Tahoe region of Nevada and California documents such long-term changes (Sabatier, 1987).

Governmental jurisdictions matter as well. Research on diffusion of innovation suggests that jurisdictions and political cultures vary in their openness to ideas from professionals in policy communities, including public administrators (see Eyestone, 1977; Kirst, Meister, and Rowley, 1984; Savage, 1985; and Walker, 1981). Some evidence (Palumbo, 1988, p. 47) also indicates that administrative influence "is even more pronounced" in state and local government than at the federal level, since "most councilmembers, state representatives, and senators work only part time." Part of the emphasis here is on the comparative expertise, leadership, and entrepreneurial skill of key individuals, including administrators, in the processes of setting the agenda and defining the options for serious consideration. Thus, in relatively open and innovative settings where administrators are the most knowledgeable and skillful actors, their role and rate of success in agenda setting are likely to be correspondingly greater, as is their degree of responsibility for the size and shape of the overall agenda.

That the issue and how it is defined also make a difference is clear from a great deal of research (for example, Meier, 1987, pp. 82, 91–92, 98–99, 105). On the whole, an important conclusion is that the way issues are defined or portrayed affects who participates in the process of agenda setting, the levels of consensus or conflict that are provoked, and thereby the relative influence of various parties (Cobb and Elder, 1983, pp. 6–97). When policy issues are portrayed in stark terms (often through the use of political symbols), and when they focus on interpretations of events that engage or mobilize large numbers of people, agenda setting moves away from the quieter, narrower, and more technical realms of government in which administrators are typically most influential.

Despite variations, public administrators generally can enhance their role in agenda setting by doing the following things.

1. They can develop and refine problem-finding routines. Some agencies and officials have "routine 'problem-finding' activities" (Nelson, 1984, p. 33) as part of their mandate, whereas others are not officially required to do so. In either case, however, efforts to monitor current programs, policies, and jurisdictions for issues or nascent concerns can be made a part of standard processes and can enhance effectiveness during agenda setting.

2. They can develop systematic efforts to identify and articulate, in policy circles, the concerns and issues of the public. For agencies and programs designed to serve particular segments of the public (such as the poor, organized labor, business, and the elderly), administrators may incur a special obligation to represent these constituencies in agenda-setting activities.

3. They can create and refine contacts with groups of specialists external to the agency, including those outside of government. Research demonstrates the importance of participation in policy issue networks for effective involvement in agenda setting. Nevertheless, administrators heavily involved in professional circles and issue networks generally need to guard against being coopted or being induced to see things primarily from the standpoint of the experts. Matters apart from those of great concern to policy specialists may deserve a legitimate place on the governmental agenda (that is, the professional and governmental agendas are not identical), and administrators should not restrict their attention merely to the more circumscribed set. Even on such esoteric subjects as genetic experimentation, individuals far beyond the community of research scientists may have good reason to be heard. These individuals include ethical and religious leaders, public health officials and physicians, representatives of agricultural interests, members of organized labor, and citizens at large.

4. They can retain in-house research and policy monitoring capabilities, instead (for instance) of contracting such activities out to other institutions, if it is especially important for administrators and their agencies to be directly involved in the agenda-setting process. Building expertise and influence by using specialists outside the public unit can weaken an agency's own ability to contribute to the definition of policy issues and feasible alternatives. For instance, the U.S. Children's Bureau lost its ability to lead in agenda setting for child abuse by contracting for policy-relevant research, rather than directly managing its own effort (see Nelson, 1984).

5. They can concentrate agenda-setting efforts in substantive specialties close to the administrator's (and the agency's) legitimate jurisdiction and demonstrated achievement. The description of the policy process (presented earlier) shows the importance of persistence, expertise, position, and timing

to the success of agenda setting. Administrators are most likely to do well on these dimensions in their own areas of specialty. In addition, more esoteric and routine items can be handled on specialized agendas—for instance, the institutional agenda of an agency (see Kingdon, 1984, p. 195); there is not so much competition for space on these as on the systemic agenda, nor is there as much potential for conflict. Thus, the chance to move an item to agenda status, and thence to decision, is enhanced. Furthermore, the normative argument on behalf of administrative activism during agenda setting is strongest when administrators act in or near their own bailiwicks.

6. They can time agenda-setting efforts wisely. Research by Kingdon (1984) and others shows conclusively that specific policy or program ideas may lie dormant in the "garbage can" or the "policy primeval soup" for years or decades before they become salient beyond a small, specialized group of experts. Recognizing the onset of openings—"policy windows"—for agenda setting is essential to effective practice. Some opportunities, like reauthorization hearings or a change of administration, come along at predictable intervals. Others are considerably less predictable, like nuclear power plant accidents (which mobilize opponents of this form of energy production) or attempted assassinations of political leaders (which galvanize the supporters of stricter gun control). In either case, many actors will seek to take advantage of the opening, and the period during which the agenda is flexible is short. Therefore, administrators who want to make an impact on this phase of the policy process need more than a good cause and a bright idea. They need to refine their skills in timing and in adapting to the rhythms and texture of the political process.

7. They can iron out differences within the policy or the professional community before seeking agenda status at some broader level. To the extent that an approximation of unanimity can be achieved among the specialists, that particular definition of an issue and its resolution is likely to carry weight more broadly in the process of policymaking. Such was the case a few years ago, when regulatory policy specialists, especially those with economic training, developed a coherent, persuasive, and nearly unanimous position on the benefits of national deregulation in the airlines, trucking, and telecommunications industries; the result was a potent and ultimately successful impact on the agenda-setting and overall policy processes (Derthick and Quirk, 1985). This sort of activity is one aspect of the task of policy entrepreneurship.

8. They can administer the preparation and maintenance of feasible options for possible adoption. Items may acquire agenda status or move to prime consideration partially on the basis of whether there seem to be any feasible policy alternatives available to deal with the issues. One aspect of effective administrative practice in agenda setting, then, is to stimulate novel but potentially usable ideas, to help combine and recombine these with other proposals, and to incubate these fledgling or candidate policies until the time is right. The stimulating and managing of innovation and creativity are themselves a topic far too complex to cover in this chapter, but administrators

need to be aware of its importance for the agenda-setting process, and they should also encourage those in the bureaucracy to think comparatively, to look to other governments and even to nonpublic settings for hints about which questions are defined as issues and which kinds of policy alternatives are possible.

Incubation itself, a prime responsibility of public administrators, involves "mobilizing support, doing technical research on the effects of various levels of government activity, trying out a variety of alternative means to the same or similar ends, and indoctrinating a generation of experts in the need for effort" (Polsby, 1984, pp. 127–128). Thus, administrators take on significant responsibility for stimulating fresh ideas, adapting them as appropriate, and floating them at the times and in the places where they may have some chance of catching on.

9. They can perform the function of policy entrepreneur within their own specialties. Issues of great public salience, which have reached a prime place on the systemic agenda, may be dealt with by government, without great need for assistance from policy entrepreneurs. Nevertheless, when he or she is absolutely convinced of the gravity and timeliness of an issue that has not reached the systemic agenda, the administrator—possibly with others—may seek to place it there, sometimes through the use of symbols, which can potently attract attention to issues, and perhaps through adroit use of the media. Some administrative agencies have learned how to use the media quite effectively to help shape the policy agenda—for instance, regarding law enforcement and crime (see Jacob, 1984). Learning about the processes through which the media actually construct the news is an important step, if administrators are to use such communication channels to raise issues effectively in much broader arenas (see, for instance, Altheide, 1985).

In contrast, when issues or options need time for interest to build or for maturation, the administrator's role can be especially critical. In the fluid, confused, and decentralized world of policymaking, the bureaucratic resources of persistence, longevity, expertise, and strategic position can make the pivotal difference. As one astute analyst commented after a study of several diverse instances, the agenda-setting process "often gives the illusion that powerful rather than knowledgeable people are the inventors of public policy. The case studies suggest, however, that policy innovations tend to belong to people who take an interest in them" (Polsby, 1984, p. 172; see also Kingdon, 1984). Above all, policy entrepreneurs take an interest in a nascent policy. They foster it, they work to understand it, they view the process with an eye toward spotting or opening policy windows, they keep the matter circulating in the right places, they advocate, and they broker (Kingdon, 1984). They are well aware of the importance of politics and of the distribution of power, but they also understand the impact of a good idea skillfully crafted and presented (see Levine, 1985, p. 256).

Through all these efforts at effective participation in the process, administrators should remain acutely aware of the normative issues at stake. In democratic systems, such officials have a fundamental obligation to serve the public, rather than to assert their own personal agendas. Fulfilling this obligation can be difficult, once it is understood that administrators cannot simply abdicate a role in agenda setting but instead must sometimes play active roles in identifying issues, helping to develop alternatives, and moving appropriate policies to center stage at auspicious moments. The administrator is not an overtly political official, nor is he or she a partisan interest-group representative. Public administrators have an obligation not simply to obey and defend an existing set of bureaucratic rules but also to work on behalf of "the practice of democratic politics and the cause of effective public policy," especially within their fields of specialty (Burke, 1986, p. 42). If so, an active and assertive role for administrators in agenda setting becomes more defensible, justified, and necessary:

- The more biased or skewed the existing governmental agenda is, as compared to the systemic agenda (this is a matter that can and should be monitored by conscientious administrators)
- The more the issues seem generated by the bureaucratic routines and functions of government (that is, the more agenda-setting action seems called for by the administrator's formally established role)
- The less the administrator disguises his or her activities behind a veneer of ministerial behavior (that is, the more the administrator makes clear to others that he or she is actually seeking to influence rather than merely follow the agenda)
- The more that debate about key issues or alternatives is based on demonstrably false or dubious empirical premises (the expertise of administrators carries with it a special obligation to correct the agenda-setting record in such situations)
- The fewer alternative channels are available to those who are concerned about the issue and seeking access to the agenda
- The more powerless are those who seek such access

Summary

This analysis of the process of agenda setting for public policy reveals a complex set of considerations for administrators to evaluate. There are many agendas, and the activities involved in their development are not simply or easily summarized. Public administrators can assume varying roles in these different settings: assisting in the assessment and development of the systemic agenda, while playing a more active and decisive part in crafting the routine one; assuming a real although often not primary role in forcing issues into consideration, while exercising lead responsibility in developing and considering major alternatives for decision; and, throughout the mix of agenda-setting processes, acting frequently as policy entrepreneurs, while being bounded by the legitimate constraints of the democratic system.

From several considerations advanced in this chapter, workable guidelines for effective practice have been developed to help administrators as they consider the complexities of the agenda-setting role. In a process as disjointed and fascinatingly convoluted as this one, however, there can be no way to reduce the set of possible guidelines to a few simple maxims. Indeed, plain "dumb luck" often plays a decisive part in the success of some participants in the process (see, for example, Nelson, 1984, p. 44). Nevertheless, the considerations explored briefly in this chapter should enhance the overall effectiveness of public administrators who use the guidelines as part of a strategy to have a thoughtful impact.

References

Altheide, D. L. *Media Power*. Newbury Park, Calif.: Sage, 1985.

Burke, J. P. *Bureaucratic Responsibility*. Baltimore: Johns Hopkins University Press, 1986.

Cobb, R. W., and Elder, C. D. *Participation in American Politics: The Dynamics of Agenda-Building*. (2nd ed.) Baltimore: Johns Hopkins University Press, 1983.

Cohen, M., March, J., and Olsen, J. "A Garbage Can Model of Organizational Choice." *Administrative Science Quarterly*, 1972, *17*, 1–25.

Crenson, M. *The Un-Politics of Air Pollution*. Baltimore: Johns Hopkins University Press, 1971.

Derthick, M. *Policymaking for Social Security*. Washington, D.C.: Brookings Institution, 1979.

Derthick, M., and Quirk, P. J. *The Politics of Deregulation*. Washington, D.C.: Brookings Institution, 1985.

Eyestone, R. "Confusion, Diffusion, and Innovation." *American Political Science Review*, 1977, *71* (2), 441–447.

Eyestone, R. *From Social Issues to Public Policy*. New York: Wiley, 1978.

Fritschler, A. L. *Smoking and Politics: Policymaking and the Federal Bureaucracy*. (3rd ed.) Englewood Cliffs, N.J.: Prentice-Hall, 1983.

Heclo, H. *Modern Social Policies in Britain and Sweden: From Relief to Income Maintenance*. New Haven, Conn.: Yale University Press, 1974.

Hirschman, A. O. *Exit, Voice, and Loyalty*. Cambridge: Harvard University Press, 1970.

Jacob, H. *The Frustration of Policy: Response to Crime in American Cities*. Boston: Little, Brown, 1984.

Kingdon, J. W. *Agendas, Alternatives, and Public Policies*. Boston: Little, Brown, 1984.

Kirst, M. W., Meister, G., and Rowley, S. R. "Policy Issue Networks: Their Influence on State Policymaking." *Policy Studies Journal*, 1984, *13* (2), 247–263.

Levine, C. H. "Where Policy Comes From: Ideas, Innovations, and Agenda Choices." *Public Administration Review*, 1985, *45*, (1), 255–258.

Light, P. C. *The President's Agenda: Domestic Policy Choice from Kennedy to Carter (with Notes on Ronald Reagan).* Baltimore: Johns Hopkins University Press, 1982.

Lindblom, C. E. *The Policy-Making Process.* (2nd ed.) Englewood Cliffs, N.J.: Prentice-Hall, 1980.

Meier, K. J. *Politics and the Bureaucracy.* (2nd ed.) Monterey, Calif.: Brooks/Cole, 1987.

Nelson, B. J. *Making an Issue of Child Abuse: Political Agenda Setting for Social Problems.* Chicago: University of Chicago Press, 1984.

Palumbo, D. J. *Public Policy in America: Government in Action.* Englewood Cliffs, N.J.: Prentice-Hall, 1988.

Polsby, N. *Political Innovation in America: The Politics of Policy Initiation.* New Haven, Conn.: Yale University Press, 1984.

Ripley, R. B., and Franklin, G. A. *Policy Implementation and Bureaucracy.* (2nd ed.) Chicago: Dorsey Press, 1986.

Rogers, E. M. *Diffusion of Innovations.* (3rd ed.) New York: Free Press, 1983.

Sabatier, P. A. "Knowledge, Policy-Oriented Learning, and Policy Change: An Advocacy Coalition Framework." *Knowledge: Creation, Diffusion, Utilization,* 1987, *8* (4), 649–692.

Savage, R. L. "Diffusion Research Traditions and the Spread of Policy Innovations in a Federal System." *Publius,* 1985, *15* (4), 1–27.

Sundquist, J. L. *Politics and Policy: The Eisenhower, Kennedy, and Johnson Years.* Washington, D.C.: Brookings Institution, 1968.

Walker, J. L. "The Diffusion of Knowledge, Policy Communities, and Agenda Setting: The Relationship of Knowledge and Power." In J. E. Tropman, M. J. Dluhy, and R. M. Lind (eds.), *New Strategic Perspectives on Social Policy.* New York: Pergamon Press, 1981.

Peter W. House
Roger D. Shull

17

Effective Policy Analysis

This chapter is about the performance of policy analysis in the real world by civil servants in executive branches of federal, state, and local government, irrespective of their formal titles or organizational locations. It does not address policy goals, how to make policy, or specific analytical methods. The advice provided is generic, because specific recommendations would be outmoded by press time and inappropriate to any given situation. The thoughts are presented by two senior policy analysts who have served the federal government in many different positions and in many different agencies over the past twenty years. Over time, methods have changed phenomenally, but as the amount of available information and analytical capability has grown, politics (as it must in a democratic government) has always remained the supreme component.

If a policy analysis is defined as simply an estimate of what would happen if some governmental procedure were changed, then—regardless of their formal titles or organizational locations—most civil servants, from the lowest management level up, conduct policy analyses from time to time. In the 1980s, probably the most common question put to civil service administrators was ''What would happen if your budget were cut by 50 percent?'' An administrator's projection of what would happen to staff, and of how many and which public constituents would be hurt by the budget cut, is a perfect example of an analysis of a proposed budget policy. Staffs in regulatory agencies prepare policy analyses, called *regulatory impact analyses,* every time a new or revised standard is proposed. Such analyses address who would be helped, who would be hurt, how much it would cost, or how much it would save. Policy analyses range from a five-minute, back-of-the-envelope calculation to $100 million, decade-long research studies like the federal acid rain research effort. They always involve politics and, usually, some amount of quantitative analysis.

A common shortcoming of freshman policy analysts is lack of appreciation for the interaction of the political process with factual information and quantitative analyses. This chapter is intended to provide a bit of front-line experience for those who have studied policy analysis only from a theoretical perspective, or for those with no formal training who must prepare policy analyses as part of another occupation. It is written from a federal standpoint; and, according to our observations, the dominance of politics over analyses in critical policy decisions increases from federal to state to local levels of government.

The Politics of Policy Analysis

For the most part, policy analysis is a discretionary commodity. Some political executives may desire a lot of it. Others, particularly ideologues at the beginning of a new administration, may see no need for it at all; their chief mission is to implement the changes promised in the electoral campaign, and they see analysis as obstructionism or recalcitrance. If a newly appointed or elected executive does appreciate analytical advice, he or she may still view the civil service staff as proponents of the policies of the previous administration. Organizational survival for the policy group, in these cases, depends on how well analysts can demonstrate that their politically neutral, objective skills can be of even greater utility to the new administration than they were to the old.

The theoretical model of policy analysis represents review and evaluation of factual information provided by totally objective, apolitical, expert professionals to provide a firmer basis for politically valued actions. While perfect achievement of this paradigm is impossible, it is still a useful guiding perspective to guarantee one's survival as a government policy analyst. Civil service policy analysts, whose tenure spans politicians' reigns, cannot survive purely on the basis of their political behavior. The initial analysis process must be objective. Once the analytical results are available, they are considered in the context of a political template provided by the elected and appointed officials and producing a set of alternatives with different physical, social, economic, and political costs and benefits. Then, the elected or appointed officials judge the political importance (weights) of the various components of the analysis and choose politically optimal courses of action.

After a decision is made, the time comes to close ranks, cease internal debate, and produce a united front on the wisdom of the decision, with the policy analysts prudently keeping any opposing opinions to themselves. At this stage, the policy staff might be asked to prepare more detailed studies, to further illuminate the reasons for and effects of a particular choice. In the main, however, unless there is an obvious threat of immediate judicial appeal by one or another of the interest groups concerned with the issue, this is a waste of resources, because most issues cool off immediately after a decision is made.

There are two judges for the suitability of a politician's decisions: the press, for the short term, and the electorate, for the long term. Policy analysts have a special interest in seeing that their leader does not fail: Even though analysts may be civil servants with tenure, they become politically tainted in others' eyes and are often expected to perform a professional "suttee" and to self-destruct along with the politician they have served. If they wish to live on to serve other masters, they must make their analyses appear to be as factual, objective, balanced, and value-free as possible. The ability to conduct such an objective analysis, followed by preparation of politically motivated public documents for the policymaker, is the most difficult mental challenge for the policy analyst, requiring what some consider a controlled schizophrenia.

On occasion, the policy analyst may provide advice on politically relevant aspects of the analysis. One might suppose that the political appointee understands politics better than the civil-servant analyst does; but when a politician with limited relevant knowledge is appointed to lead a bureau where the analysts have many years of experience in political observation of their bureau's operation (a not uncommon occurrence), the opposite may be true. If such is the case, political knowledge can be communicated to the appointee (with due tact and humility) if the analyst is interested in his or her continued employment.

Problems emerge on the public policy agenda because of dramatic circumstances, such as a health or energy crisis, a serious accident, or a zealous press. A crisis raises the relevance of issues and typically attracts broad public attention. Consequently, elected and appointed officials often feel compelled to respond with visible measures to relieve perceived problems. The duty of the analyst is to place the emergent issue in a context meaningful to the decision level: how the issue surfaced, who else cares, what everyone else is doing, and what the organization has done in the past.

The hardest single part of the interaction between the analyst and the executive is the precise definition of the question to be addressed. Analysts and executives must develop a vocabulary that allows them to communicate effectively. Analysts should try to understand why the decision maker is involved in the issue, his or her perspectives on what is happening, and what the favored outcomes are. The analyst has a very real problem sorting the actual policy question from other issues introduced by other debate participants inside and outside the agency.

The political context of public sector decisions is continually varying. The analyst must frequently reevaluate the actors in and audience for the candidate issue, including higher or lower levels of government, private sector interests, public interest groups, nonprofit research organizations, and relevant individuals. Time constraints on real policy analyses seldom permit the leisure of canvassing all such groups for input. Experienced policy analysts learn which individuals or organizations are the richest sources of information. Private special-interest groups frequently take sides on an issue and are a good source of political information. Governmental statistical units and professional societies are good sources of numerical data.

Specification of the criteria for evaluation of policy alternatives should be done jointly with the policy official. Policy analysis texts commonly dwell on the mathematical analysis of costs, benefits, economic efficiency, and effectiveness criteria. Such analyses are a useful contribution to highly technical matters, such as setting environmental quality standards, but often a policy decision must be made too soon to permit gathering of enough data to conduct detailed analytical studies. In other cases, despite extensive available technical information, politics is almost completely in control—for example, in locating a new municipal waste landfill. Numerous social, economic, and political values are at stake with regard to policy decisions. Quantitative evaluations of policy alternatives typically emphasize costs, risks, and benefits and deal with the actual dollar costs of one alternative as compared to another. Public policies, however, affect economic sectors and political jurisdictions in different ways and cause political pressure. Consequently, analysts should attempt to measure the distributional impacts of an action—not whether there is a net benefit, but who wins and who loses, and which constituencies are of most concern to the official.

The real output of the policy analysis process is not necessarily neat, tidy policy options on paper. Rather, it is increased understanding of and confidence in decisions, which officials gain as a result of verbal and written exchanges of ideas with analysts. The analytical portions may be interlaced throughout and set in the context of accompanying descriptions. Form and content of written documents are a function of a specific issue and of what the official wants to see on paper. Frequently, unconfirmed judgments committed to print can come back to haunt the analyst, if documents get into the wrong hands.

Therefore, a substantial portion of the analysis may be given verbally, with no physical documentation. Because of time pressures, many policy analyses would fail any test of scientific validity. Policy analyses deal with issues for which the absolute truth will never be known until long after it makes any difference.

Characteristics of a Successful Policy Analyst

There is no one list of the required characteristics of a policy analyst with which everyone would agree. Those who have been policy analysts in the public and private sectors have varied credentials. Their success has depended on situations, personal relationships, and numerous other factors. The characteristics that follow are those that the authors have come to regard as generally relevant.

Technical Skills. Sophisticated quantitative techniques are typically not helpful in the vast majority of policy analyses. Nevertheless, analysts must be able to understand the basic principles of sophisticated techniques, because they will be forced to analyze and cross-examine quantitative analyses submitted by various policy proponents or opponents. The advent of the personal computer (PC) has added a new dimension to the technical skills required of analysts. The computer has been a principal tool of analysts for years. Until recently, however, the actual preparation of data and the running of programs were performed by technicians other than analysts. Today, sophisticated software packages and computers are ubiquitous, and the analyst who does not know how to use them to his or her advantage is outclassed. In fact, a small but growing number of policy officials use computers to perform their own analyses (David Stockman, former director of the federal Office of Management and Budget, is a notable example). Although it is possible to engage the aid of a computer technician, the pace, constrained by repetitive communication between analyst and technician, cannot possibly compete with that of a policy analyst fluent in computer skills. Armed with a computer and spreadsheet software, the analyst can attack a new set of data with a broad range of mathematical and statistical procedures, finding all possible implications and presenting them in high-quality graphics, typically in a period of time drastically shorter than it would have been a few years ago. While, in the 1970s, only two or three options might have been proposed, it is now often possible to reiterate analyses during several direct discussions with policymakers, simultaneously increasing background understanding of policy issues and reducing the required time, labor, and paperwork. PC analyses are particularly suited to budget allocation analyses, whose mathematics are simple sharing-and-totaling formulas, perhaps with simple statistical analyses. The growing capacity of computers, combined with the growing efficiency of system programmers, is making physical simulation modeling possible. If data availability and knowledge warrant such applications (as in air quality or transportation models, for example), multiple simulations can be conducted quickly and inexpensively and can add to the robustness of projected policy outcomes.

Multidisciplinarity. Policy analysis requires the integration of knowledge and methodology from many different fundamental disciplines, including the sciences, engineering, the arts, and the humanities. Although each discipline has a set of procedures applicable to policy analysis, an analysis limited to only one disciplinary perspective will render the analyst a loser in most policy debates, to the detriment of the official being served. The analyst should be prepared to borrow from numerous fields, combining the theoretical and the empirical in whatever fashion best fits.

Creativity. Policy issues are rarely amenable to straightforward analytical investigation. Often, the ideal data and information that could quickly delineate the issue are not available. At worst, no information is available. Analysts must be able to frame issues quickly into fundamental questions, explore related information from all conceivable sources, and provide at least some useful insights into issues in the short time typically available. There are many different perspectives from which to approach an issue. Analyses using one approach may detract from the political agenda, while the same set of facts, presented in a different but equally professional manner, may support the political agenda. Choosing one's methodology to affect apparent results borders on ethical issues, but most policy analysts consider it proper to support officials' agendas with any types of information that are not factually fraudulent. Lies are unethical; incomplete information is acceptable. Generally speaking, analysts can choose among the following approaches to enhance the acceptability of analyses:

- Facts versus principles
- Shares versus totals
- Rates versus totals
- Different definitions of populations
- Expanded versus condensed axes on graphs
- Lines versus bars versus pies on graphs
- Three-dimensional versus two-dimensional graphs
- Generalities and averages versus anecdotes
- Redefinition of the universe of comparison
- Inclusion or exclusion of certain historical periods
- Inclusion or exclusion of statistical outliers
- Analytical models versus statistical models

Clarity. No matter how brilliant an analysis, it is worthless if it is not presented to policymakers in a form that gets points across clearly and quickly. Presentations must also be repackaged for other actors in the debate. Different vocabularies are required for different audiences, in terms of both interest in the issue and technical training. During the 1970s, such technical agencies as the Department of Defense and NASA refined the art of presentation to a sophisticated level of skill, far beyond that of other agencies, by using groups of people whose sole function was to prepare studies, evaluations, and reports for policymakers. Today, with the PC and its attendant software packages, these special-purpose units are declining in size and importance, since analysts can prepare high-quality presentation graphs directly on computer screens. Presentation slides in advanced policy analysis offices are now simply computer screens displayed on large-screen monitors or projection television systems.

Poise. Policy analysis is part of an adversarial process. Lawyers learn early that knowledge of the law is only part of what they are expected to bring to the courtroom. Analysts learn a similar lesson about analysis. Although there is much classroom discussion of the quality of an analysis as part of issue resolution, quality is seldom of overriding importance. If the issue is really complex, several groups of analysts will have defined it from perspectives that put their positions in the best light. Opposing analysts and lobbyists will be making presentations, not only to their own leaders but also perhaps to one's own executive. The atmosphere in policy resolution meetings is often tense, and debate is heated. Unanticipated ideas emerge, and attacks on a proffered analysis may reveal its weaknesses. Panic is the worst response. Losing one's temper loses the argument. Thinking on one's feet is a necessity. Instant analysis, based on first-order approximations and best guesses, is the rule. To hesitate is to lose; sometimes one merely loses face, but often one loses the debate itself.

Expertise. It is important for analysts to have good understanding of the subjects under debate. An analyst's perceived competence and credibility fade rapidly when an opponent points out that the analysis violates a fundamental physical law or ignores a fact known to many others. The importance of fundamentally understanding issues and subjects becomes evident when an analyst first meets with a new political appointee. If the analyst does not have a firm grounding in the subject of interest of the politician, there is little hope that the official will have sufficient confidence to trust the analyst with anything of importance to his or her political career.

Political Savvy. Since public policymakers owe their positions to politics, and since the positions they advocate are functions of political postures, policy analysts must be politically sensitive. They must recognize when technical findings support or conflict with political objectives, so that the findings can be highlighted, recast, or camouflaged, as appropriate.

If an individual possessed all these characteristics, a policy analysis office could be staffed by that one individual. More likely, any individual will lack one or more of these attributes, and so people with complementary skills should be employed. Further, policy issues are characterized by the need for short-fused response. Consequently, the size of a policy analysis group is also partly determined by the demand for its output.

Technical Sophistication

Widespread use of personal computers by public sector staff at all levels of government is a reality. Because policy analysis groups necessarily depend on analytical skills, the presence of computer technology is fundamentally changing the way they operate. Changes differ by agency, staff personalities, and constituencies, but detailed quantitative policy analyses that took months to perform in the 1960s can now be executed in a matter of hours. A change of this magnitude clearly brings adjustments. For example, there is more time to experiment with alternative scenarios and to discuss them with policymakers before a decision is made. The availability of sophisticated techniques improves the sophistication and accuracy of individual analyses, but that does not necessarily mean that more complex or larger mathematical models will become any more useful than they were in the 1970s or that paradigms that lack the information for analysis (such as benefit or risk models) will be any more relevant. When the deadline for a decision depends on the period required to conduct a study, decisions will come much more quickly. The availability of powerful software and hardware to everyone in the policy community means that more effort will be spent on improving data, both in terms of data collection and in terms of matching data sets with other sources that purport to be measuring the same phenomena. It will also be easier for analysts to check the work of others involved in the policy discussion, to ensure that an adversarial position has indeed been based on claimed assumptions.

Two real-world situations that approach the hypothesized future of ubiquitous analytical capability demonstrate the limitations of numerical analyses. During the energy crisis, environmental protection remained a strong popular cause; head-to-head confrontation was the rule of the day. The technical portions of the many debates were relatively amenable to empiricism, being largely engineering questions. The administration was committed to switching as much of the country as possible to coal burning, as long as the switch was achieved in an environmentally responsible fashion. Millions of dollars were spent on developing data and analytical methods but, regardless of the amount of information mustered to address any one issue, neither side would accept the findings of the other. Consequently, a disproportionately large number of issues went to the president for decision.

A second example of the potential impact of sophisticated analysis involves what happened at the National Science Foundation (NSF) several years ago, during a public meeting of the National Science Board. The issue was the need for government assistance in the refurbishing and building of science buildings and laboratories. The NSF policy analysis group conducted a sophisticated statistical survey of a representative sample of NSF grantees and their administrators to find out how real the need actually was. Results showed that only a very few researchers' projects were constrained by inadequate facilities, and that many were housed in newly renovated spaces. When this finding was presented to the National Science Board, it was not well received, because the sentiment among many members was that financial aid for facilities was necessary. One member stated, "I don't care what the numbers say, we know there is a problem."

In both these cases, the existence of considerable factual information did little to settle the debate. If there had not been information, the issue would have been dealt with at the highest level necessary, as determined by the political sensitivity of the issue. When information was introduced, questions of a technical nature dropped out, and politics reigned anyway.

Efficient Use of Technical Analysis

When introduced to a new policy issue, an experienced analyst quickly performs a triage to determine whether technical analysis is mandatory, potentially helpful, or irrelevant. In many regulatory issues, detailed economic and social impact assessment is required by law. In some cases, however (as in federal health-based air quality standards), economic factors are legally excluded from consideration. Another class of issues—school prayer, capital punishment, care for the terminally ill, abortion—is so dominated by moral perspectives that even though numerical data are available, any analysis would be viewed as irrelevant or irreverent.

Once it is determined to conduct some type of analysis, delineation of the analysis is necessary. Available resources are, of course, the overriding determinant, but other considerations help in the determination of whether to commit additional major resources. Analytical procedures are best suited to technical issues; the more technical the issue, the greater the potential for a rich mine of information. Complex issues, affecting many jurisdictions and interest groups and involving many different technical factors (for example, the multistate acid rain issue), can be viewed as ideal candidates for detailed technical analysis. Ironically, complex issues are the least likely to be specified clearly enough to be credibly analyzed within reasonable time periods and financial resources. At the other extreme, single-variable issues (for example, tightening or loosening a long-standing safety standard) have the greatest potential of being clearly specified. They often permit detailed calculations and allow resources to be focused, rather than dispersed across several aspects. Because of these issues' potential specificity, sophisticated techniques can be used with reasonable expectation of analytical solutions. Information availability poses a dilemma for the analyst. On the one hand, the more information available, the greater the likelihood of producing a useful analysis; on the other hand, when extensive information makes executives think they fully understand an issue, they tend to have little patience with detailed analysis. If the issue is new or highly technical, the analyst's skills are exercised in finding surrogates for missing data or designing studies to gather necessary information.

Judgments are made all along the decision chain. The more important or controversial the issue, the higher up the chain judgment will go. The higher the level of the decision maker, the less time an analyst has to perform any kind of sophisticated analysis, and the greater the possibility that any analysis will be largely descriptive. Issues are so simplified that they are presented to policymakers only as essences, distilled to precise and stark contrasts. The top official expects that all insignificant factors have been purged from the issue, and what remains is a political judgment. In preparing such highly condensed briefing documents, analysts must use extreme caution against leaving out key factors that will have political repercussions later.

Throughout this chapter, policy analysis is presented as an art that is at best definable within a broad framework. Although structured, quantitative decision methods are usually inappropriate, demonstrated scientific facts are certainly a part of the decision process and may constitute the substantial evidence required by the judicial system to ensure that policy decisions are not arbitrary and capricious. If pushed too fast, however, and if not carefully conducted according to accepted methods, policy analysis can quickly become an unethical art, with the purveyor of information knowingly or otherwise bending, twisting, and shaping information to support or detract from particular policy options. The ethical analyst resists these temptations, leaving the final use of information up to the political executive who is accountable to the electorate.

Summary

This chapter is based on the experience of two senior policy analysts in the federal government. In the authors' observation of state and local organizations, however, it appears that the rules apply equally well to any organization, public or private, that is large enough to recognize the need for policy analysis or to establish a job category related to policy analysis. In this light, the following maxims are offered as shorthand guidance for surviving as a policy analyst in the real world.

1. Policy analysts must understand and appreciate the politics of their agencies and executives and understand the principles of the U.S. Constitution and other relevant charters.
2. In political issues, there is no right or best solution to a problem, only a winning answer.
3. Policy analyses must be delivered in time to be used in decisions; otherwise, they are worthless.
4. Policy analyses have many different forms, and analysts must be skillful at using them all.
5. Policy analysts must be able to present their results in vocabularies of many different levels of sophistication.
6. Policy analysts must understand and appreciate the contributions and methodologies of many different scientific and professional disciplines.
7. Policy analysts must understand the academic, scientific methods that may be used for some analyses, but they should also be extremely sensitive to the shortcomings of such methods and limit their applications accordingly.
8. Mathematical analyses cannot solve social problems, although, if properly used, such analyses can enlighten related issues.
9. In technical issues with extensive data bases, policy analysts must be personally competent in the use of microcomputer applications and state-of-the-art software.
10. Many policy issues are not analyzable; they are only debatable. In such cases, quantitative analysis is impossible, and the analyst's only role may be to help clarify the debate.
11. Survival as a career policy analyst requires intellectual flexibility, to allow adaptation to changing political superiors and changing social priorities.

References

Brewer, G. D., and deLeon, P. *The Foundations of Policy Analysis.* Homewood, Ill.: Dorsey Press, 1983.

Dunn, W. N. *Public Policy Analysis: An Introduction.* Englewood Cliffs, N.J.: Prentice-Hall, 1981.

House, P. W. *The Art of Public Policy Analysis.* Beverly Hills, Calif.: Sage, 1982.

House, P. W., and Shull, R. D. *Regulatory Reform: Politics and the Environment.* Lanham, Md.: University Press of America/Abt Books, 1985a.

House, P. W., and Shull, R. D. *Managing Research on Demand.* Lanham, Md.: University Press of America/Abt Books, 1985b.

House, P. W., and Shull, R. D. *The Rush to Policy: Using Analytic Techniques in Public Sector Decision Making.* New Brunswick, N.J.: Transaction Books, 1987.

Lynn, L. E., Jr. *Designing Public Policy: A Casebook on the Role of Policy Analysis.* Santa Monica, Calif.: Goodyear, 1980.

Taylor, T. W. (ed.). *Federal Public Policy: Personal Accounts of Ten Senior Civil Service Executives.* Mt. Airy, Md.: Lomond, 1984.

18

Walter Williams

Implementing Public Programs

A new law passes at the national, state, or local level. An agency head with the administrative authority to make major changes opts for an extensive policy shift that involves either field programs or an agency reorganization. Then what happens? Does the policy get put in place as desired by the legislators or the agency head? If not, what has occurred to block or modify the desired change? If successful, what factors in the institutional process were important in bringing about the desired change? These are the central questions of the implementation issue that focus on what happens after a decision is made.

Levin and Ferman (1985, p. 2) argue that "in the past two decades, implementation has become the single most problematic aspect of policymaking." During this period, implementation research has burgeoned. What does this body of literature offer those who implement programs and projects? Can the practitioners find sound advice from these fifteen to twenty years of effort? My answer is a qualified yes. In particular, the power of any guidelines based on current implementation knowledge is far greater for projects that deliver services directly than for large-scale programs that involve shared governance; some recent work in the latter area, however, shows promise for developing more useful guidelines.

Two central areas that dominate the implementation field are considered in this chapter: single projects that deliver such goods and services as education, job training, housing, and disaster protection; and programs that deliver goods and services in which two or more governments have managerial responsibilities. The latter area is labeled *shared governance,* and the usual case involves a federal agency and subnational governments. Im-

Note: The author is indebted to his colleague William Zumeta for helpful comments on an earlier draft of the chapter.

plementation efforts in agency reorganizations and intragovernmental regulation are not considered, but much of the material on project and program implementation is relevant to reorganization and regulatory efforts. After an initial section, which expands on the key implementation issues and makes two broad points about implementation results, the chapter discusses project and program implementation advice that may prove useful to practitioners.

The Implementation Issue

An example of a federal implementation effort will illustrate key implementation questions. The federal government has been involved in disaster policy for years, helping states that experience natural (for example, the eruption of Mount St. Helens) and manmade disasters (for example, the Three Mile Island nuclear accident) to respond immediately to catastrophes and recover from them over time. Recently there has been more concern about mitigation and preparedness efforts, to prevent and lessen losses rather than simply respond when disasters strike. At the federal level, these tasks fall to the Federal Emergency Management Agency (FEMA), which uses a number of regional offices to work with states. The states in turn work with localities, which are the governments that actually execute most of the federal and state disaster policies. FEMA's implementation charge was to induce the key actors to engage in a number of new mitigation and preparedness efforts. To do so successfully, FEMA had to mount an organizational effort that altered the behavior not only of persons in the agency itself (both at the headquarters—Washington, D.C.—and at the regional level) but also of people in state and local governments.

The federal government faces a long implementation process, with only indirect control over the localities that have final responsibility for executing the new mitigation and preparedness policies. What organizational processes, procedures, and sanctions can FEMA headquarters use to induce desired behavior in the regional offices? In turn, how can the regions get states to change in the preferred direction? What strategy can a state use to bring about desired changes in behavior at the local level, where services are actually delivered to citizens? An implementation strategy has to do mainly with organizational (behavioral) change efforts involving processes, procedures, and sanctions that ultimately must induce front-line workers to execute policy decisions as desired, if the strategy is to be successful.

Researchers in the last twenty years have asked such questions in a variety of programs, but predominantly in social service programs. Two broad points cut across both project and program implementation discussions. First, the biggest changes over twenty years in social service programs (and, to a lesser extent, in other policy areas) are the emergence of a vertical network of specialists whose careers depend on the programs, a network that thereby increases significantly both capacity for and commitment to federal objectives; the development of strong local policy infrastructures and networks; increase in the knowledge base about what does not work and, more important, what does; and the demise of grandiose views of rapid progress that typified the early Great Society period, views that have been replaced by lowered, more realistic expectations. Second, the most difficult task faced by implementers is to keep a balance between extremes (for example, neither too little nor too much planning) in a dynamic, multivariable setting.

Big Changes. Implementation studies, until recently, were essentially negative, showing difficulties and indicating mostly what not to do (which itself can be useful advice). Currently, a number of books and articles are more optimistic (Levin and Ferman, 1985; Peterson, Rabe, and Wong, 1986). Levin and Ferman's study of youth training projects had three critical findings. First was the increasing number of competent people with extended experience in the Great Society and post–Great Society manpower and education programs. The study found that project executives with direct experience did better in solving problems and dealing with implementation difficulties than those executives without such experience. Second was the emergence over time of local social policy infrastructures that included both stronger organizational structures and networks showing a convergence of local interests. Levin and Ferman (p. 97) argue that the notion of infrastructure emphasizes "the rich organizational, rather than merely personal, legacy that we found in [the cities studied]." Third was the development over time of useful knowledge about how to implement and operate projects as exemplified by successful models.

Peterson, Rabe, and Wong (1986, pp. xii, 6) began their research in 1979 on nine federal programs in education, health care, and housing, expecting combative federalism because so much of the earlier research pointed in this direction: "We had expected to see confusion and disarray, overregulation and conflict, discouragement and defeat. . . . Instead we found a [high] level of cooperation, competence, energy and seriousness on the part of federal, state, and local officials. . . . Our findings concerning the federal role are more optimistic than has been typical in previous studies."

Does that mean that shared governance works—federalism works—a finding that would contradict the earlier studies? That goes too far, but there has been real improvement in cooperation, commitment, and capacity over time. First, the social programs have matured. A longer time frame has produced relative implementation success in cases where there had been earlier failure in the short run (Kirst and Jung, 1982). Second, the unrealistic initial view—of both a short period for implementation success and striking, highly visible, positive results—has been toned down. Third, there has been real learning over time about how to develop programs and how to operate in complex organizational and programmatic networks. The knowledge base has expanded to include models both of projects that worked and of how successful managers operated.

Most important of all, the marginal professionals so prevalent in the early years were replaced by persons who had more skills, experience, and commitment and who saw the programs more realistically than their less competent counterparts of the Great Society and post–Great Society years. The so-called administrative generalists were replaced by substantive specialists who had acquired general managerial skills. Professional cadres had similar knowledge, and often similar goals. As Peterson, Rabe, and Wong (1986, p. 190) observe: "Local professionals . . . are likely to be as strongly identified with federal rules as is the Washington bureaucrat, and federal policy is implemented quite satisfactorily." Such statements notwithstanding, there continue to be conflicts over objectives among local, state, and federal officials, but professionalization has reduced them.

A number of people (Bardach and Kagan, 1982; Williams, 1980a) have stressed the critical need for greater competence. Such a development, as recorded not only in Peterson, Rabe, and Wong (1986) but also in Levin and Ferman (1985), is the most critical change of the past two decades. But there is a darker side to this development. While competent professional cadres are necessary for the success of social delivery programs, there is danger that the vertical network of professionals at all levels of government may both subvert the political process and turn goals more toward professional needs than toward programmatic objectives. A cabal of professionals may stress its own gains over program goals and may have the bureaucratic skills to subvert programs. Such subversion is the dark side of complex professional networks.

The Search for Balance. A central implementation problem is a viable balance that avoids extremes in a complex, dynamic environment. As you may recall, a young lady named Goldilocks, lost in the woods and hungry, stumbled upon the Three Bears' house, found the house unoccupied, and further discovered three bowls of porridge. Empirical testing showed that one bowl was too hot, the second was too cold, and the third was "just right."

Her lack of precision has not diminished her story for countless children, but if, as I believe, the Goldilocks phenomenon is found in many (probably most) of the public sector activities and functions that are of great interest to us, lack of measurement is a critical matter. Moreover, the implementation problem is much more difficult than the one that faced Goldilocks, because a person or an organization seeking the right amount of, say, planning cannot simply measure at one point in time, as Goldilocks did. The "just right" point must be sought in a process that involves numerous and often interdependent variables that interact over time. It may be possible in a given innovative setting to determine retrospectively where the optimum or, more realistically, reasonable level of planning is. Prospectively, it is useful to warn against either of the extremes, but the question remains: How much farther we can go with general advice (O'Toole, 1986; Sabatier, 1986)?

O'Toole (1986) points out that most of the literature is short on recommendations about successful implementations and long on descriptions, that advice too often has no empirical research base beyond a single case, and that advice frequently is contradictory. He warns (p. 200) that "recommendations often take a proverbial rather than a heuristic character . . . what [Herbert] Simon sought to communicate in his analysis of the 'proverbs of administration' [that occur in pairs]." What can be made of O'Toole's pessimism? First, the proverbial nature of many injunctions stems in part from the fact that neither of the extremes will work. Thus, the advice "plan ahead" can be carried too far and bog down the effort. But no planning also is bad. Second, part of the problem of the lack of usefulness of advice to practitioners may come from failure to package results properly or offer them in the right arenas. Third, if implementers await definitive research, they will be waiting a long time. This is hardly surprising. After all, in the much more developed area of management (administration), the literature offers no sure answers, either. Proverbs still dominate there, too. Management and implementation, in their dynamic aspects, are much too complex to yield precise recommendations for practitioners such as "Do this, under these circumstances, and have a 96 percent chance of success."

Projects

This section considers the single project or a small number of projects under the managerial control of a social service delivery organization, but there is reason to believe that this advice is also relevant to other services (May and Williams, 1986, pp. 171–181). In the latter case, a caveat is warranted on the possible unavailability of an experienced cadre of professionals and the lack of viable local infrastructures to support projects, because many of the programs outside the social services are newer (for example, the environmental programs of the 1970s) and because far less implementation research has been carried out on them.

What advice can be offered from available implementation research results, both to the director of a local multifunction social service delivery agency who seeks to hire a new project director and to that new director? The most critical advice for the agency director is to look for an individual with a good track record in the programmatic area of concern. This is nothing startling, but it is now advice that can be heeded, whereas not long ago it was advice to seek a nonexistent, or at least very scarce, commodity.

What traits or skills should the agency director look for in discussions with applicants and applicants' references, or with others who know the applicants? Key areas include applicants' flexibility; their orientations toward planning, information gathering, and information use; their views of the relationship between themselves and front-line workers (the discretion issue); and their capacity to be fixers or problem solvers. (These traits will be elaborated on in the advice to project directors, to which we now turn.)

1. *Keep projects relatively simple, and seek relevant models.* The "just right" design is likely to be more simple than complex. If successful models of similar projects are available, consider their usefulness, but it is well to keep in mind that successful models may be presented as if there have been no early problems and no need for creative error correction. Look for information on managerial process, not just on technical elements. Also, do not try to follow the model slavishly; rather, take account of specific factors in your setting that differ from the model. That is, even if the techniques and the approach of the model seem to fit perfectly, the cast of key actors will be different, and the actor relationships are likely to be far more important than the technical factors (Ellickson and Petersillia, 1983; Elmore, 1982; Levin and Ferman, 1985; Nathan, 1982; Weatherley and Lipsky, 1977).

2. *Plan ahead, but not beyond the available data, and involve key actors.* On the one hand, not planning can be fatal. It does not make much sense to avoid thinking about where one ought to go and how to get there. On the other hand, staying on the drawing board too long can stop all action. Just as bad is planning beyond the available numbers, so that all sorts of assumptions and proxies are used to bring elegance to a master plan that has a crumbling foundation. Planning is a process that lasts over the entire implementation process; it is not a one-time activity. Involve key actors, including persons in other organizations, in the early stages of the planning process. Do not make inclusion an exercise in which advice is solicited but not heeded. Rather, use the interaction both to try to generate good ideas and to create vested interest (ownership) in the project (Ellickson and Petersillia, 1983; Levine, 1972; Peters and Waterman, 1982).

3. *Error correction and flexibility are keys to implementation.* In any new project, expect errors. Much of your job will be to correct them. Looking ahead will not uncover each potential error, but scenarios and other devices may help you prevent or ameliorate errors and avoid pitfalls. Do not lock yourself in. Be experimental and be willing and able to pull back if you are going the wrong way. Experimentation does not imply formal, design-of-experiment methodologies, but rather the much softer notion of trying a new idea out on a small scale and observing how it works. Unlike the classic experimental approach, in which a basic tenet is to hold the design, the essence of the kind of experimentation being discussed is adaptability. Try it, and if it does not work, change it or fix it. Ellickson and Petersillia (1983, p. 41) set out this dynamic notion as follows: "This trial-and-error process typifies the implementation of successful innovations. Understanding which procedures are both feasible and effective rarely occurs at the outset. It requires experimenting with different methods, learning which ones work, and adapting them to the capacities and motivations of those who carry them out." Successful implementation needs a good problem solver and fixer (Bardach, 1977; Levin and Ferman, 1985). The project director, or someone close to him or her, needs to have a "fix it" mentality ready to attack problems, find answers, and push them through.

4. *Get the right information, and get it quickly.* Determine what kinds of information are needed, both to show problems and to indicate what can be done to correct them. Do not be too concerned with the kinds of internal and external validity spelled out in the experimentation literature. Get information however you can, and use it. Keep lines of communication open. Recognize that front-line workers probably know more about their jobs than you or anyone else. Get them involved, both for good ideas and for ownership. As in the planning process, do not elicit comments from front-line workers just for show (Ellickson and Petersillia, 1983; Peters and Waterman, 1982; Weatherley and Lipsky, 1977).

5. *Never forget that serving target groups is your main objective.* Be people-oriented. Keep your eyes on the point of service delivery. Recognize that staff discretion, for better or for worse, is a fact of life in any social service delivery project. Do not go overboard on rules to control your staff, because such rules usually do not work, and they create resentment. See if indirect means of control, such as internal competition, can keep people tied to good service delivery. As Williams (1980b, p. 17) has observed in discussing the implementation perspective: "The commitment and capacity of the final service delivery organization and . . . the individual persons who actually provide services are the central focus of the implementation perspective. Here the critical institutional investment must be made . . . that allows these organizations to exercise reasonable discretion in providing needed services at the point of delivery and to cope with the implementation of program changes."

Two final caveats. First, much of this advice concerns how to cope in a dynamic, uncertain process over time and may seem sterile when cast in static terms. For example, involving key actors likely will be a delicate task that requires good interpersonal skills and sensitivity. Knowing when there is enough but not too much planning is not a cut-and-dried exercise. Second, however good the advice, it will merely raise the probability of success, and we do not know by how much.

Shared Governance

The advice in this section is aimed both at headquarters federal executives and state officials responsible for implementing major programmatic policy changes, but far more research has been executed on the former than on the state officials. The advice also reflects the assumption of active governance by the federal or state funding source.

1. *Avoid a compliance mentality.* Since federal officials have limited control over the grants-in-aid to states and localities, what has passed for control in the field has often been a compliance (regulatory) mentality that concentrated primarily on procedural rather than substantive programmatic issues. No one argues that there should be no rules and regulations, since they can specifically set out goals and means of attaining them (national intent) and form the basis of determining whether what is being done is con-

sonant with what is desired. Checking on compliance can both clarify national intent, by straightening out ambiguous cases, and catch offenders. Local choices are not inherently better than national ones. At the same time, difficulties in crafting workable rules seem to grow geometrically with complexity. The problem can be stated simply: Because rulemakers cannot anticipate the future clearly enough or calculate the interplay of factors in a complex situation so as to determine the right rules, reasonable levels of discretion and judgment need to be encouraged.

2. *Stress staff competence.* Sound technical assistance is critical, and here the growing capacity at all levels is of great importance. Peterson, Rabe, and Wong (1986, p. 154) argue that "by the 1980s the federal role was transformed from *watchdog to consultant*" (emphasis added). These optimistic findings are important for the light they shed on a more cooperative federalism. At issue is why those charged with enforcing rules in the past became legalistic and demanded blind compliance, whatever the consequences. Bardach and Kagan (1982) underscore the importance of competence in their discussion of the "good inspector" (p. 128): "[A] critical ingredient is the capacity to be reasonable, to distinguish serious from nonserious violations, and to invest effort in the former. This capacity seems closely related to technical competence—an ability to provide technically persuasive explanations for regulatory requirements and to understand how the regulations affect production or managerial functions. Lack of technical competence is a likely corollary of legalistic enforcement." The incompetent inspector is "safe" if he or she slavishly follows the rules, without question or deviation.

3. *Get good information.* Information still is power and a central element of control; its importance is not at question. At issue is what is to be controlled, since control objectives dictate the nature of the information required. If federal and state officials want to ensure that grantees are going by the book and complying with the law, good procedural information may do the job. If the goal of control is more successful implementation or better program outcomes, a totally different set of information is needed. In such cases, federal and state managers need knowledge both of the local government decision-making and implementation processes and of the local dynamics at work in substantive areas funded under grants. The demand is for overlapping but distinct kinds of knowledge. One kind of information concerns how the implementation process works generally at the local level. A second kind has to do with the particular aspects of programmatic areas. In a poverty-oriented jobs program, for example, needed information would indicate how the local market works in general and how it works in particular for disadvantaged youth (Elmore, 1982).

The higher the level of the federal or state agency, the more the demand is for general knowledge and information about states and localities. In moving down the agency hierarchy to field offices (for example, federal regional offices), the need is for both general and specific knowledge and information. Field office staff need to know not only about how disadvantaged young people generally view work and status among their peers but also about the idiosyncratic features of a particular city. Without such information, how can federal and state officials interpret the behavior of grantee agencies (whether what is being done is likely to contribute to or detract from successful implementation) or offer technical assistance that might be useful (Williams, 1980a, pp. 214–226)?

3. *In the agency management strategy for grants-in-aid, have as a central objective increasing state and local commitment to agency goals and capacity to provide particular services and make needed discretionary judgments.* Several comments are needed about inducing grantee organizations to embrace agency objectives. First, the stronger and clearer the federal mandate, the more power the agency has to demand compliance and to expect commitment. That is, with a highly specific mandate, there should be less bargaining or maneuvering room for subnational governments (May and Williams, 1986). Second, at issue is a local commitment to someone else's objectives, which are not necessarily consonant with local objectives. Third, federal objectives are usually broad enough to accommodate a fair degree of variation in specific local objectives. Fourth, federal officials, especially those at the regional level, usually lack the power—the control—to force local commitment. Both local variability and federal weakness point toward the need for flexible bargaining and negotiations between agency staff and subnational officials and the need for positive incentives to gain local commitment (Williams, 1980a).

Commitment alone is not enough; competence is the other key factor. Of great interest is the finding of Ellickson and Petersilia (1983) that commitment and competence appear to interact:

> Unraveling which comes first, commitment or competence, is not an easy matter. Our observations in the field suggest that the two interact. Once they have agreed to participate, competent professionals are frequently committed to make a project work. And all the exemplary innovations in our sample recruited staff with relevant experience (though not necessarily higher educational degrees or knowledge of the criminal justice process). Nevertheless, we noted several instances where competent staff lost motivation and subsequently downgraded the quality of their work. These cases typically followed the loss of an enthusiastic project director or a decline in his motivation that was attributable to top leadership vacillation or hostility [p. 33].

Two points need to be stressed. First, the lesser power of the implementation guidelines for programs, as compared to projects, must not be lost sight of. There is simply far greater complexity, far more chance of "a slip 'twixt the cup and the lip." Second, the big change of greater field competence, and the emerging evidence of more cooperation at different government levels (fostered, it seems likely, by greater competence), inspire a bit more confidence in the advice. But, as good managers know, except for blind good luck, there is no substitute for their own competent, adaptive behavior in complex, interactive settings, where no rules are foolproof.

Summary

Implementation research has burgeoned in the last two decades. This chapter asks whether practitioners who must put major project and program changes in place can benefit from these results. The answer is a qualified yes. Three key points are discussed. First, the biggest changes over twenty years of service delivery programs are the dramatic growth in the numbers of experienced, competent personnel available to projects and programs; the development of strong local policy infrastructures and networks; the increase in the implementation knowledge base; and the demise of the unrealistic expectations that characterized the Great Society years. These changes are much more clear for social programs than for other policy areas. Second, the most formidable task confronting implementers is keeping a balance between extremes (for example, too little or too much discretion by front-line workers) in a dynamic multivariable setting. Third, although implementation can provide guidelines likely to increase the probability of implementation success, the power of these guidelines is much greater for projects than for large-scale programs whose governance is shared by two or more levels of government.

References

Bardach, E. *The Implementation Game: What Happens After a Bill Becomes a Law.* Cambridge, Mass.: MIT Press, 1977.

Bardach, E., and Kagan, R. A. *Going by the Book: The Problem of Regulatory Unreasonableness.* Philadelphia, Pa.: Temple University Press, 1982.

Ellickson, P., and Petersillia, J. *Implementing New Ideas in Criminal Justice.* Santa Monica, Calif.: Rand, 1983.

Elmore, R. F. "Backward Mapping: Implementation Research and Policy Decisions." In W. Williams and others, *Studying Implementation: Methodological and Administrative Issues.* Chatham, N.J.: Chatham House, 1982.

Kirst, M., and Jung, R. "The Utility of a Longitudinal Approach in Assessing Implementation: A Thirteen-Year View of Title I, ESEA." In W. Williams and others, *Studying Implementation: Methodological and Administrative Issues.* Chatham, N.J.: Chatham House, 1982.

Levin, M. A., and Ferman, B. *The Political Hand: Policy Implementation and Youth Employment Programs.* New York: Pergamon, 1985.

Levine, R. A. *Public Planning: Failure and Redirection.* New York: Basic Books, 1972.

May, P. J., and Williams, W. *Disaster Policy Implementation: Managing Programs Under Shared Governance.* New York: Plenum, 1986.

Nathan, R. P. "The Methodology for Field Network Evaluations." In W. Williams and others, *Studying Implementation: Methodological and Administrative Issues.* Chatham, N.J.: Chatham House, 1982.

O'Toole, L. J., Jr. "Policy Recommendations for Multi-Actor Implementation: An Assessment of the Field." *Journal of Public Policy,* 1986, *6* (2), 181–210.

Peters, T. J., and Waterman, R. H., Jr. *In Search of Excellence: Lessons from America's Best-Run Companies.* New York: Harper & Row, 1982.

Peterson, P. E., Rabe, B. G., and Wong, K. K. *When Federalism Works.* Washington, D.C.: Brookings Institution, 1986.

Sabatier, P. A. "Top-Down and Bottom-Up Approaches to Implementation Research: A Critical Analysis and Suggested Synthesis." *Journal of Public Policy,* 1986, *6* (1), 21–48.

Weatherley, R., and Lipsky, M. "Street-Level Bureaucrats and Institutional Innovation: Implementing Special-Education Reform." *Harvard Educational Review,* 1977, *17,* 171–197.

Williams, W. *Government by Agency: Lessons from the Social Program Grants-in-Aid Experience.* New York: Academic Press, 1980a.

Williams, W. *The Implementation Perspective.* Berkeley: University of California Press, 1980b.

19

Eleanor Chelimsky

Evaluating Public Programs

Although program evaluation has become quite generally accepted as an important part of policymaking, its application, practice, use, and advantages are not always well understood by public administrators. In many graduate schools of public administration today, for example, there are still few courses dedicated to program evaluation. Moreover, the requisite component skills of evaluation design (Hatry, Winnie, and Fisk, 1981; Rossi and Freeman, 1985) and quantitative/qualitative methods (Cook and Campbell, 1979; Patton, 1978) are also often not taught. As a result, public administrators at different levels of government may not be well prepared to use evaluation. Thus, they lose access to a major resource that can help them (1) ensure the quality of a new program by drawing on the lessons of the past for the program's design and specifications, (2) recognize, early on, various problems developing in an ongoing program's field operations, (3) prepare for administrative, legislative, or public challenges with regard to the worth of a new or established program, and (4) build in a cumulative cycle of program improvement by using the results of repeated evaluations.

Program evaluation is a way of bringing to public decision makers the available knowledge about a problem, about the relative effectiveness of past and current strategies for addressing or reducing that problem, and about the observed effectiveness of particular programs. Having this knowledge does three things. It reduces uncertainty and risk in decision making, enhances administrative accountability in a tangible manner, and considerably increases appropriate administrative control over a program. The decision maker is not, of course, the only one to benefit. The public gains, as knowledge accumulates and service improves (whether at the federal, state,

Note: The views and opinions expressed by the author are her own and should not be construed to be the policy or position of the General Accounting Office.

or local level), and government in general reaps the important reward, over the longer term, of improved taxpayer confidence in governmental operations.

How, then, should public decision makers, and public administrators in particular, seek to use program evaluation? Since it is not always obvious which types of public activities require which types of program evaluation, the question is really one of linking the information needs of these decision makers to the kinds of program evaluations most likely to address those needs.

But to raise this question is simultaneously to raise a subset of component questions. For example, what kinds of information needs can an evaluation be expected to satisfy? How do these needs differ for various sponsors? Who are the typical sponsors of evaluations, and what kinds of relationships, if any, exist among them? Should a public administrator, in sponsoring an evaluation, seek to produce information for himself or herself alone, or can many users be targeted by the same evaluation? Are all types of evaluations likely to be useful at different times to different sponsors, or are some information needs unique to particular functions, particular roles, and particular times, so that certain types of evaluations will be predictably more useful to some administrators than to others? In sum, given a variety of demands (that is, information needs stemming from a variety of sponsors performing a variety of public functions) and given also a variety in supply (that is, the different program evaluation types available to meet those different needs), how can an administrator know when he or she needs to sponsor an evaluation, and how can the most appropriate evaluation approach be linked to the specific information need?

This chapter addresses the questions of what the most common methods for evaluating public programs are and when they should be applied. It discusses the kinds of administrative purposes that evaluation can satisfy and presents an overview of often-used evaluation methods, along with their applications to those purposes. Also explored are the relationships between different types of functions and users, different types of information needs, different times in the life of a public program, and different types of evaluation studies. By looking both at the public administrator's need for evaluative information and at the supply of program evaluation types available to meet that need, the chapter focuses, not on the qualities and failures of the evaluation types or on the merits of the information needs, but rather on the link between evaluation and its use.

Administrative Purposes for Evaluation

Program evaluations serve both general audiences (such as the public or the media, often the ultimate users of many evaluations) and individual public decision makers who have particular information needs. These decision makers may be in the executive or the legislative branches of government, may work at the federal, state, or local level of government, may play management or policy roles with respect to public programs, and may need information from evaluation for three very broad but distinct kinds of purposes:

- For *policy formulation*—that is, to assess or justify the need for a new program and to design it optimally on the basis of past experience
- For *policy execution*—that is, to ensure that a program is implemented in the most cost-effective and technically competent way possible
- For *accountability* in public decision making—that is, to determine the effectiveness of an operating program and the need for its continuation, modification, or termination

These purposes have specific implications for the kinds of issues that evaluations may be asked to address. For example, the purpose of policy formulation, as it applies to new programs, may require information from evaluation that includes the following items.

1. Information on the problem (or threat) addressed by the program: How big is it? What are its frequency and direction? How is it changing?
2. Information on the results of past programs or related efforts that attempted to deal with the problem: Were those programs feasible? Were they successful? What difficulties did they encounter?
3. Information allowing the selection of one program over another: What are the likely comparative costs and benefits? What kinds of growth records were experienced?

The evaluative information required for policy execution, as it applies either to new or to existing programs, is quite different from that required for policy formulation. It includes the following items.

4. Information on program implementation: How operational is the program? How similar is it across sites? Does it conform to the policies and expectations formulated? How much does it cost? How do stakeholders feel about it? Are there major problems of service delivery or of error, fraud, and abuse?
5. Information on program management: What degree of control exists over expenditures? What are the qualifications and credentials of personnel? What is the allocation of resources? How is program information used in decision making?
6. Ongoing information on the current state of the problem or threat addressed by the program: Is the problem growing? Is it diminishing? Is it diminishing enough so that the program is no longer needed? Is it changing in terms of its significant characteristics?

The purpose of accountability, as it applies to both new and existing programs, requires still different information, including the following items.

7. Information on program outcomes or effects: What happened as a result of program implementation?
8. Information on the degree to which the program made or is making a difference: What change in the problem or threat has occurred that can be directly attributed to the program?
9. Information on the unexpected (and expected) effects of the program: Was a program of drug education to reduce drug abuse accompanied by an increase in the use of drugs?

These purposes have implications both for the kinds of issues evaluations may be asked to address and for the types of evaluation approaches that are likely to be needed, given those purposes. But, most important, these information needs must be understood in relation to the functions and roles of the decision makers who will sponsor the evaluations.

Functions and Roles of Evaluation Sponsors

Who are the typical governmental sponsors and users of evaluative information developed for the three policy purposes? How do their functions or roles differ? To whom do they report? Among the types of executive and legislative decision makers at different levels of government who need and use evaluative information to serve one or more of these purposes are the following six general groups.

In the executive branch, at the federal, state, or local level:

- Program managers
- Agency heads and top policymakers in an individual agency or department
- Central budget or policy authorities

In the legislative branch, at the federal and state level:

- Four legislative agencies at the federal level (the Congressional Research Service, the General Accounting Office, the Office of Technology Assessment, and the Congressional Budget Office) and budget and evaluation staff offices at the state level
- Legislative authorization, appropriations, and budget committees
- Oversight committees

Executive-branch program managers seek evaluative information to plan, implement, manage, and eventually modify their programs so as to make them as cost-effective as possible. They usually are personally accountable for this work to the heads of their branches or agencies or to one of an agency's top policymakers. Thus, the program manager must consider, along with his or her own needs, the views and needs of his or her boss in developing an evaluative approach. A program manager is always publicly accountable to some degree, however, and this is especially true at the local level.

The functions and roles of agency heads and other top policymakers require somewhat different types of evaluative information than do those of program managers. For example, a departmental secretary is less interested than a program manager in detailed program information. Instead, the secretary will need data to determine or justify the need for a new program, to assess the effectiveness of an operating program, or to review the need to continue or modify a program. This is because an agency's top managers are likely to have to report at more general levels on these matters, not only to the administration (for example, at the federal level, to the Office of Management and Budget [OMB] as well as to the policymaking Executive Office of the President; at the state level, to the governor's office; or at the local level, to the mayor's office) but also to the Congress or state legislature (through its authorization, appropriations, budget, and oversight committees) or to the municipal council.

With regard to staff from central administrative offices such as the OMB or governors' and mayors' staff offices, these decision makers—in their central budget and policy functions—may also look to evaluation to inform them about the effectiveness of programs or to help in decisions to continue, cut, or otherwise change them. Their accountability is to chief executive officers: the president, governors, mayors, or city and county managers.

In the legislative branch, authorization, appropriations, and budget committees use evaluation findings essentially as contributing information to program funding or refunding decisions. Oversight committees, in contrast, rely on evaluation not only to supply findings about executive-branch programs but also to bring information about how executive agencies are performing their various functions (such as personnel and resource management, for example, or the manner in which an agency has organized itself to conduct research or to ensure internal controls). Although all these four types of legislative committees may use evaluation findings produced by executive agencies in their negotiation and decision-making processes, they also rely on evaluation findings from independent sources, such as universities, consulting firms, and other groups. They may use those findings directly, through the work of legislative or budget and evaluation staff, or indirectly, through the proxy of one or another of the legislative agencies. At the federal level, the Congressional Research Service may, for example, report findings to congressional sponsors from a wide variety of evaluations in an issues paper for legislative use. The General Accounting Office, which has a congressional mandate to perform program evaluations, may report its own findings to Congress, analyze evaluation findings from many different sources to inform Congress, or critique methodological or other technical aspects of existing evaluations when findings conflict (or appear to conflict). The Office of Technology Assessment may use evaluation findings as a foundation from which to forecast technological impacts, and the Congressional Budget Office may use them as part of the empirical base on which to construct the likely outcomes of alternative economic policies. Legislative agencies are accountable to Congress or to state legislatures; legislatures, like the president, are accountable to the public via general elections.

These six different types of evaluation users have some purposes in common and some that are uniquely their own. As a result, there are some areas of need that they share and some that are distinct. Only a program manager or the General Accounting Office, for example, may need to receive fine-grained information on implementation and operational issues specific to one or two local sites in a large national program. Even though there may not be many audiences for this information, it may be crucial to the needs of those two users. Other kinds of evaluation findings—those on the effectiveness of programs, client satisfaction or frustration with programs, views of program stakeholders, trends in the problems addressed by programs, changes in the dimensions or focus of programs—are likely to be helpful to all users and may interest general audiences as well.

The degree of detail that users need from evaluative information will differ according to users' specific functions, purposes, and particular accountability. A member of Congress or of a state legislature, for example, may need to be aware only of the major findings of a program evaluation, whereas an agency head—who may be called on by the Office of Management and Budget, the mayor, the city council, the governor, the president, the Congress, or the state legislature to defend the program or explain the findings—will require much more detailed knowledge of the information produced. The basic information produced by an evaluation may be useful to several different audiences, but different versions of that information, presenting different levels of detail, may also be needed.

The question of the appropriateness of a particular evaluation to multiple users' needs is one that ought to be considered very carefully by decision makers and evaluators alike. Evaluations are so few, and the idea of serving several users with the same evaluation is so attractive, that a danger exists of distorting information inadvertently. Explicit statements about the objectives and limitations of an evaluation are needed to ensure that an evaluation performed, say, for an agency head's information (to learn the opinions of practitioners or stakeholders about a program) is not interpreted by a secondary user—the press, for example—as an evaluation of program effectiveness.

Further, the ability to serve multiple users is always constrained by the need for an evaluation to answer the precise questions posed by the primary user and by the need for the conclusiveness of the answers given to match that user's particular information need. For example, it is reasonable to undertake an expensive, large-scale effectiveness evaluation when research in the field is mature and when the primary user must have the most conclusive information possible. If an evaluation sponsor merely wants to develop some general information in an area where little currently exists, then less conclusive, less costly, and more easily collected information may be both appropriate and desirable.

Finally, there is an essential difference in purpose between evaluative information designed for sponsors in the executive branch and in the legislative branch. Decision makers in both branches may need evaluative evidence—on, say, the need for a new program—as part of their policy-making role (that is, their planning or authorizing function). They may need evidence of efficiency or effectiveness to support their accountability role in their administrative and legislative oversight processes. Nevertheless, only the executive branch is charged with program implementation, and so that branch has the greater need for evaluative information related to policy execution. As a result, executive-branch managers (and, to a lesser degree, agency heads) may often (and quite properly) be virtually the sole users of certain types of detailed evaluative information that supports decision making about program operations.

As a general rule, public administrators, in thinking about the eventual use of their evaluation products, should probably expect their work on program effectiveness and on the feasibility and logic of proposed new programs to be more valuable to a greater variety of secondary users than their work on program operations is.

Information needs are not only different for different users; they also differ between new and existing programs. The administrator of a new program needs planning information that would not typically be required for an existing program, but the administrator of an existing program needs effectiveness and other information on a periodic basis that can be obtained only when a program has been fully operational for some time.

Information needs are also affected by a program's dimensions, life cycle, and surrounding circumstances. In a new program, for example, it makes a difference, with regard to the evidence required to justify its need, whether the program is large or small, expensive or modest, controversial or consensual, presenting many unknowns or clearly feasible. A large and expensive program needs stronger evaluative justification than a small, modest one does because of accountability to the taxpayer. This is often important for programs (such as the MX missile or B1 bomber at the national level, or a major highway or housing program at state or local levels) that cost a great deal and whose logic and assumptions are typically subject to extensive debate—first within the executive branch, then in the legislature, and eventually in the press and among the public.

Even when a new program is small, however, it needs a very sound basis and rationale if it is notably controversial. A recent federal example was the Reagan administration's proposal to end the moratorium on the production of nerve gas and to begin augmenting the existing stockpile of unitary weapons with new "binary" weapons. The initial appropriations requested were small, as defense programs go; but emotions surrounding the issue of chemical warfare run high, the moratorium had existed for many years, and the administration's case for ending the moratorium and starting production on binary weapons was not supported by strong evidence. After five years of debate, Congress has continued to withhold approval for the production of new chemical weapons.

A proposed program whose scientific or technological feasibility is still unclear also needs to have sound logic and convincing presumptions of effectiveness behind it. When feasibility problems are real, they are sure to emerge in the debate over funding and should therefore be persuasively addressed in the program rationale. Nevertheless, it sometimes happens that an agency believes a new research program is needed and that the feasibility problems cannot be resolved without federal funds. Under those circumstances, the temptation can be very great to minimize the feasibility problems so as to obtain appropriations for the program. While this strategy may work over the short term, it tends to mislead policymakers, create overoptimistic expectations for the program, and give credence to a highly simplistic and really quite inaccurate view of the research process. In particular, when technical problems are minimized, the implication is that a low-risk, routine, regular process exists, in which research leads inexorably and effortlessly to production (Nichols, 1971).

One long-term effect of such oversimplification—for the research process, in its true nature, is nonlinear, iterative, idiosyncratic, and highly uncertain—will be some inevitably negative evaluation findings (that is, if evaluation mistakes a program's rhetoric for its real success criteria). This is because significant technical unknowns in a program mean that events may be unpredictable, and that major problems may arise in development or testing that will cost a lot of money and take a long time to solve.

The point here is that, to rationalize funding for a new program, oversimplifying and overpromising about what evidence is available can misfire badly. One result, just mentioned, is that evaluation findings for the program may be meaningless, if the program's objectives were overstated and unachievable from the start. Another result is that efforts to deal with evaluation failures (by modifying objectives or continuing to test and retest) can further prolong what may already have been a long development cycle. A third—and perhaps the most serious—result is that the credibility of the overpromisers inevitably suffers over the long term as, one after another, negative evaluation findings are produced for programs on which so very much had been staked.

There is a truly critical need for public administrators to obtain evaluative information in the policymaking process that generates new programs. This is especially important for new programs that are expensive or controversial and for those that present significant scientific or technical unknowns.

Evaluation Approaches

The Evaluation Research Society has identified six types of routinely conducted approaches to program evaluation (Evaluation Research Society Standards Committee, 1982). These are front-end analysis, evaluability assessment, process evaluation, effectiveness (or impact) evaluation, program and problem monitoring, and metaevaluation or evaluation synthesis. All these approaches have applications to the individual information needs already discussed.

Front-End Analysis. This approach involves evaluative work that is usually conducted before a decision to move ahead with a new program. As such, it is similar to planning and likely to be prospective in its overall orientation. Typically, front-end analysis primarily addresses policy formulation questions, using prior evaluation findings as well as extant data, to estimate program feasibility and likely effects. An example of this kind of work is an evaluation performed by the General Accounting Office before the introduction in Congress of legislation proposing service programs for pregnant teenagers (U.S. General Accounting Office, 1986).

Evaluability Assessment. This approach may be used to answer policy formulation questions. A program's assumptions are compared to its stated objectives, and questions are asked about the reasonableness of those assumptions and the likelihood that the projected program's activities can fulfill its objectives. Evaluability assessment is also used to answer policy execution questions by describing the characteristics of actual program implementation and comparing program objectives with existing program activities. Finally, this approach serves to determine the feasibility and usefulness of performing later full-scale evaluation of the program's effectiveness. If the determination is positive, this approach lays the groundwork for such an evaluation. In that sense, an evaluability assessment may be the first phase of a larger evaluation effort, which seeks to answer accountability questions. The focus of evaluability assessment may thus be retrospective, insofar as accountability or policy execution questions are involved, or prospective, when the questions relate to policy formulation. Evaluability assessments have been done in various agencies; the National Institute of Justice, for example, has been particularly active in performing them. An example of a study that uses this approach is Buchanan (1981). The focus of the study is retrospective; it looks at an operating program to see whether a full-scale effectiveness evaluation is feasible.

Process Evaluation. This is a form of evaluation that either stands alone or is developed in combination with another type. It is always retrospective. Alone, its purpose is usually to describe and analyze the processes of implemented program activities—management strategies, operations, costs, interactions among clients and practitioners, and so forth—so as to improve them. But a process evaluation used alone may also target cause-and-effect questions. In combination with another evaluation type (most often an effectiveness evaluation), its purposes may include helping to determine the design of the effectiveness evaluation or helping to explain its findings. In the first case, the process evaluation will precede the effectiveness evaluation; in the second, the two will be coordinated more or less simultaneously. Thus, the process evaluation addresses policy execution issues but also helps effectiveness evaluations to answer accountability questions. An example of a process evaluation that preceded an effectiveness evaluation is found in

Chelimsky and Dahmann (1980). This study used in-depth analysis of the functioning of prosecutors' offices to form the basis of the research design of the subsequent effectiveness evaluation. Yin (1981) focused on the factors that lead to the routinization of new practices in local governments, as an example of a process evaluation standing alone.

Effectiveness or Impact Evaluation. Like process evaluation, this evaluation approach is retrospective. It seeks to find out how well a program has been working. To do this, it must show that changes observed are in fact results of the program, rather than of other factors or forces. Therefore, the design for this kind of evaluation must include a basis for comparison that permits an understanding of what the conditions would have been in the absence of the program or in the presence of alternatives to the program. This, of course, is the quintessential accountability question ("What were the effects of the program?"), but it is also true that effectiveness evaluations are needed for policy execution as well. Findings from effectiveness evaluations of the past also figure prominently in policy formulation efforts, because they provide a sound basis for estimating likely effects of new and similar programs. An example of an effectiveness evaluation is a study (U.S. General Accounting Office, 1985) of the effects of 1981 legislative changes in the Aid to Families with Dependent Children (AFDC) program. The study showed that the changes did indeed reduce caseloads but that working mothers and their families who left the AFDC program underwent considerable privation to do so. An earlier impact evaluation worth noting is the well-known randomized experiment conducted by Kansas City's Police Department (Kelling, Pate, Dieckman, and Brown, 1974). This evaluation was instrumental in bringing about a change in the thinking of police chiefs all over America with regard to the value of preventive patrols, a policy brought into critical question by the study.

Program and Problem Monitoring. This evaluation approach is different from the others in that it is continuous, rather than a single-shot process. Its function is to inform on problem characteristics or to track program or problem progress (long-term or short-term) in several areas (for example, the size of or change in the problem addressed by the program, the program's compliance with policy, the changing spread or characteristics of service delivery, and so on). As such, it may address either policy formulation or policy execution purposes. However, the administrative data systems that develop around the program and problem monitoring effort can also be used to answer accountability types of questions via time-series analysis. The extent to which time-series analysis is possible, however, depends on the quality, completeness, and consistency, over time, of the data systems involved. An example of the use of monitoring data in evaluation is seen in a study (U.S. General Accounting Office, 1982) of the effectiveness of the Comprehensive Employment and Training Act program. Three types of monitoring data were used: data on participants' characteristics (to address targeting); financial reports (to address expenditures); and program status reports (to address both the mix of services and placement rates). These monitoring data were available from 1976 to 1980, with only minor definitional changes, and had been submitted by prime sponsors (local administering bodies) to the Department of Labor on a quarterly or yearly basis.

Metaevaluation or Evaluation Synthesis. This is a form of evaluation that reanalyzes findings from one or a number of evaluations to determine what has been learned about a policy or a program. Depending on the availability of evaluations and other empirical work, this approach can address many different evaluative questions, including those about the effectiveness of the program and about the extent of existing knowledge in a given program or problem area. As such, metaevaluation is highly versatile, capable of serving all three types of evaluation purposes: *accountability* and *policy formulation* (by reporting on what is known about program effectiveness) and *policy execution* (by informing on what is unknown and, hence, on what the research agenda for program implementation needs to include). Evaluation syntheses may be quantitative or qualitative. An example of quantitative work in which effect sizes could be combined is a study (U.S. General Accounting Office, 1984) of the Special Supplemental Program for Women, Infants and Children. An example of a qualitative evaluation synthesis is a study (U.S. General Accounting Office, 1987) of drinking-age laws and their impact on highway safety.

These six approaches constitute the everyday repertoire of program evaluation. They are, of course, far from being the only approaches, but it would be fair to say that they represent widespread agreement in the field with regard to common practice in program evaluation, and that they are relevant, in various degrees, to the needs of public administrators.

These degrees of relevance can be better understood if the public administration activities (discussed earlier in this chapter) that generate evaluative information needs are consolidated into five basic functions: planning and rationalizing a program and its evaluation, implementing and managing a program, justifying the effectiveness of program implementation and management, demonstrating the effectiveness of a program, and measuring ongoing problem or program progress. When these five functions are linked with the six program evaluation approaches just identified, we have a clearer idea of the ways in which public administrators can seek to use program evaluation (see Table 19.1).

Several points can be made about the links in Table 19.1. First, it is clear that monitoring data are useful for each of the five types of information needs, because of the versatility of these data. They can help establish the range and frequency of a problem (before it has even been decided to propose a program). They can inform on progress in implementing and managing the program. They can be used, in conjunction with other efforts,

Table 19.1. Links Between Program Evaluation Types and Sponsors' Activities and Information Needs.

Type of Activity Generating Evaluative Information Need	Six Types of Program Evaluations					
	Front-End Analysis	Evaluability Assessment	Process Evaluation	Effectiveness or Impact Evaluation	Program and Problem Monitoring	Metaevaluation or Evaluation Synthesis
Planning and rationalizing a program and its evaluation	X				X	X
Implementing and managing a program		X	X		X	
Justifying the effectiveness of program implementation and management			X	X	X	X
Demonstrating the effectiveness of a program	O	O	O	X	X	X
Measuring ongoing problem/ program progress	X			X	X	

X = fulfills the information need standing alone
O = fulfills the information need supplemented by other evaluation work

to determine the effectiveness of both the program as a whole (longitudinal administrative data can be critical here) and its implementation or management. Finally, they are the instrument of choice for maintaining a minimum level of awareness of ongoing progress, either in the program itself or in the problem it is intended to address.

Second, it appears from Table 19.1 that demonstrating the effectiveness of a program can involve all six types of evaluation, some of them used in conjunction with others. This crossover is probably related to the difficulty of establishing program effectiveness and to the usefulness of employing several different methods in the same evaluation (often called *triangulation*). One point to note here is that effectiveness evaluations are typically the most arduous, the lengthiest, and the most expensive to perform. A public administrator who needs information on the effectiveness of a program must consider the time and costs required to obtain that information. Still, it is also true that monitoring, front-end evaluations, and evaluability assessments standing alone cannot normally supply adequate evidence of effectiveness when conclusive information is needed.

Third, with regard to the three policy purposes discussed earlier, the table shows that all six types of evaluation serve the needs of accountability (as reflected in the demonstration of program effectiveness). Five types serve policy execution (implementing and managing a program and measuring ongoing progress). Only three serve the needs of policy formulation (planning and rationalizing a program). While front-end analysis, problem monitoring, and metaevaluation are powerful tools in support of policy formulation, not many of these evaluations are being performed in the executive branch these days, and the question does arise of whether executive-branch decision makers are giving adequate emphasis to the use of policy formulation evaluations, which can help in major ways to ensure the soundness of new programs and policies. When there is a lack of evaluations supporting policy formulation in the executive branch, the onus falls on legislative agencies and evaluation staff to fill the void. Unfortunately, the oversight needs for evaluative information at the federal level have now become overwhelming, and legislative agencies have been understaffed. This means that legislative information requirements to support proposals for new programs—for example, information on need, past efforts, feasibility, expected results, and structure— may well be one of the most significant areas needing reinforced attention by evaluation sponsors. The work takes on added difficulty when the new proposals are sizable and technically complex—the Strategic Defense Initiative, for example. Further, as these kinds of efforts account for more and more budget dollars, and as scientists and engineers continue to develop more sophisticated technology, it is clear that explanations, justifications, and supporting data for new programs will become critically important. Nevertheless, such data have been in extremely short supply, and programs have often been presented in terms of highly optimistic but dubious rationales. Thus, the need is even more pressing for stronger oversight of new programs and for sounder evaluative information, before programs are implemented.

Another reason why public administrators should pay more attention to sponsoring front-end analysis and to the analytical needs of policy formulation is that the benefits of early problem identification considerably outweigh its costs, especially from the taxpayer's point of view. Heading off a program, changing its objectives so that they are achievable, focusing its activities so that they are measurable and valid in terms of the program's goals—all these things are easier and a lot cheaper to do before a program is implemented than after it is well established and its actors and advocates are deeply entrenched. In sum, although the determination of program effects remains a primary activity of evaluation, it is just as important that evaluation produce sound information to be used before action on proposals for new programs. This is true in every branch and at every level of government.

Summary

This chapter has developed a framework linking the information needs of public decision makers, in different branches and at different levels of government, with six routine evaluation approaches. It was argued that a public administrator can best use the resources of program evaluation to meet information needs in five areas. Specific evaluation approaches were matched to these five information needs, examples were given of appropriate applications of each of these approaches, and the importance of strong front-end analysis for sound public administration was especially emphasized.

References

Buchanan, B. "The Senior Executive Service: How Can We Tell If It Works?" *Public Administration Review,* 1981, *41* (3), 349–358.

Chelimsky, E., and Dahmann, J. *Final Report of the Career Criminal Program National Evaluation.* MITRE Technical Report 80 W 35. McLean, Va.: MITRE Corporation, 1980.

Cook, T. D., and Campbell, D. T. *Quasi-Experimentation: Design and Analysis Issues for Field Settings.* Skokie, Ill.: Rand McNally, 1979.

Evaluation Research Society Standards Committee. "Evaluation Research Society Standards for Program Evaluation." In P. H. Rossi (ed.), *Standards for Evaluation Practice.* New Directions for Program Evaluation, no. 15. San Francisco: Jossey-Bass, 1982.

Hatry, H. P., Winnie, R. E., and Fisk, D. M. *Practical Program Evaluation for State and Local Governments.* (2nd ed.) Washington, D.C.: Urban Institute Press, 1981.

Kelling, G., Pate, T., Dieckman, D., and Brown, C. E. *The Kansas City Preventive Patrol Experiment.* Washington, D.C.: Police Foundation, Oct. 1974.

Nichols, R. "Mission-Oriented R&D." *Science,* 1971, *172,* 29–36.

Patton, M. Q. *Utilization Focused Evaluation.* Newbury Park, Calif.: Sage, 1978.

Rossi, P. H., and Freeman, H. E. *Evaluation: A Systematic Approach.* (3rd ed.) Newbury Park, Calif.: Sage, 1985.

U.S. General Accounting Office. *CETA Programs for Disadvantaged Adults— What Do We Know About Their Enrollees, Services, and Effectiveness?* GAO/ IPE-82-2. Washington, D.C.: U.S. General Accounting Office, 1982.

U.S. General Accounting Office. *WIC Evaluations Provide Some Favorable but No Conclusive Evidence on the Effects Expected for the Special Supplemental Program for Women, Infants, and Children.* GAO/PEMD-84-4. Washington, D.C.: U.S. General Accounting Office, 1984.

U.S. General Accounting Office. *An Evaluation of the 1981 AFDC Changes: Final Report.* GOA/PEMD-85-4. Washington, D.C.: U.S. General Accounting Office, 1985.

U.S. General Accounting Office. *Teenage Pregnancy: 500,000 Births a Year but Few Tested Programs.* GAO/PEMD-86-16BR. Washington, D.C.: U.S. General Accounting Office, 1986.

U.S. General Accounting Office. *Drinking-Age Laws: An Evaluation Synthesis of Their Impact on Highway Safety.* GAO/PEMD-87-10. Washington, D.C.: U.S. General Accounting Office, 1987.

Yin, R. K. "Life Histories of Innovations: How New Practices Become Routinized." *Public Administration Review,* 1981, *41* (1), 21–28.

Part Five

Effective Budgeting and Fiscal Administration

Public agencies need financial resources to pursue their missions and meet payrolls, but acquiring scare resources is only one problem public administrators face when managing financial affairs. Financial resources must be allocated among a wide range of competing interests, which share no simple yardstick for measuring their contributions to the public good. Part Five addresses the problems that public administrators confront when making choices about revenues and expenditures.

Budgeting and fiscal administration require the public administrator to resolve a variety of operational, managerial, and strategic issues. At the operational level, public administrators are concerned with the timetables and procedures used for budget development, with the reliability of accounting procedures, with secure methods of cash collection, and with proper methods of registering bonds. From the managerial perspective, administrators are concerned with how a budgeting system will help them make difficult choices among competing demands, with what types of incentives a budgeting system creates for efficient use of resources, with the types of budget information to collect, with the efficient methods of service delivery, with the design of particular revenue sources, and with the appropriate timing and size of bond issues. At the strategic level, public administrators are interested in how to acquire adequate revenues for specific activities or programs, in the soundness of the government's fiscal condition, in the proper mix of revenues, and in appropriate amounts of short- versus long-term debt.

Resolution of these operational, managerial, and strategic issues is not purely or even primarily a technical matter. Budgeting and fiscal administration are both technical and political processes. Decisions about trade-offs among programs and activities, the incidence of taxes, and schedules for paying for governmental services have significant political dimensions. The dual character of budgeting and fiscal administration is inescapable. Part Five offers guidance for coping with the technical and political problems of budgeting and fiscal administration.

20 *Glen Hahn Cope*

Budgeting Methods
for Public Programs

Everyone budgets. Individuals, private businesses, and governments all budget for their activities. Budgeting methods and the budgets themselves can be quite different, however. Family budgets may be informal and flexible, while budgets of major corporations can be extensive documents providing elaborate plans for future operations. Government budgets vary widely, as well. Some include detailed plans for expenditures over a one- or two-year period and elaborate measures of output or efficiency, while others include only a compilation of annual line-item appropriations by expenditure category. The common denominator of all public budgets, regardless of the size of the jurisdiction or its geographical location, is a statement of the planned expenditures and revenues for the coming year (or two, if it is a biennial budget).

Whether done by private individuals, major corporations, or government agencies, budgeting is a political process. It requires making trade-offs among desirable activities, since few governments, individuals, or companies have sufficient resources with which to do everything. The purpose of budgets and budgeting is to help decision makers determine which activities are most desirable and to allocate resources among them as efficiently as possible, although efficiency is not the only criterion for budget decision making. The types of information used and the level of detail included in the budget document can be quite different among governments, but the necessity for making difficult decisions about which activity receives more or less money, or none at all, is universal. As long as governments face constraints on their ability to raise revenues, they will need to budget and to make those political decisions, since wants will always exceed resources.

This chapter begins with a discussion of the operating and capital budget decision processes at all levels of government. Next, types of operating budget reforms will be discussed, including such budget formats as the planning-programming-budgeting system (PPB), zero-base budgeting (ZBB), and performance budgets. In the section that follows the one on reforms, capital budget presentations will be discussed. Next, legislative budget reforms and current practices will be described. Finally, the issue of improving budgetary decision making will be examined, in light of both history and current practice.

Budgeting as Political Decision Making

In essence, budgeting is the process of making political decisions about financial issues. Governments, like corporations and households, have to decide annually or biennially how much to spend and how much revenue from taxes, fees, and other sources they can expect to collect. Most state and local governments are required by constitutional, statutory, or municipal charter provisions to balance their operating budgets, that is, to have revenues at least as great as or greater than their expenditures for the year or biennium. This is one major difference between the federal government, which is allowed to have operating budget deficits, and most state and local governments, which are not. Another difference is that the federal budget includes a large number and dollar amount of grants and contracts, often providing for multiyear commitments, while state governments budget for fewer activities through grants (education is a primary state-local grant function, for example), and local governments are more often recipients of grants, although they do provide some of their services through contracts with private firms.

Budget procedures differ somewhat by type of government activity, because a different decision process may be required for a different type of expenditure. Typically, governments distinguish between capital and operating expenditures, for example. Capital expenditures include purchases of equipment, real estate and buildings, and other items that will have a useful life longer than one year. These usually are expensive items, which may take several years to plan, acquire, or construct. This type of expenditure fluctuates greatly from year to year, depending on the needs of the government. Operating expenditures, in contrast, are those that finance day-to-day activities during the budget period, including purchase of supplies that will be exhausted during that period, utilities, personnel expenses, and maintenance costs. These tend to be fairly stable from one year to the next, as long as governments continue to pursue the same activities. Some governments, including forty-two states and many localities, prepare their operating and capital budgets separately because of the differences in the types of decisions involved in each. This procedure allows them to take extra care when making long-term capital decisions, so as to avoid costly mistakes. Other governments, including the federal government, prepare only one budget, including both capital and operating expenditures. (Both capital and operating budget procedures, and issues of similarity and difference between them, are covered in this chapter.)

Budgets can also be distinguished according to the classification systems used to organize and prepare them. As is true of many modern decision tools, a budget can be developed and used in several different ways. Since around 1900 in the United States, a movement to reform budgeting has had an impact on all three levels of government. Initially, this movement pushed for the creation of a budget system, to replace the rather lax methods of approving expenditures and revenues then in use in U.S. governments. Eventually, after budgeting was firmly established as the appropriate procedure for financial decision making by governments, reformers began to propose different ways of presenting budgetary information, on the premise that the type of information presented and its format influenced the way decisions were made (Fenno, 1968). Budget classification—the way information on revenues and expenditures is structured for presentation to decision makers— became an important consideration for budget reformers and ordinary budget preparers. Burkhead (1956) identifies three major types of budget classifications in his classic work, *Government Budgeting.* These are *object of expenditure,* in which expenditures are classified by their accounting expenditure categories, such as salaries or office supplies; *organizational unit,* in which expenditures and revenues are divided according to the departments or bureaus whose activities they support; and *functional* or *program classification,* in which expenditures are grouped according to the ''broad programs the government is conducting, in terms of the economic or interest groups which are served'' (Burkhead, 1956, p. 113). Later budget reform techniques, developed mainly for operating budgets, built on these budget classification systems in devising new methods for presenting budgetary information. Several of the major budget reforms developed since 1900, and their influence on the budget decision process, are discussed in this chapter.

Operating Budget Cycle

Budgeting is a cyclical process. The budget cycle varies from government to government and between operating and capital budgets; but, in general, it tends to repeat every year (or two) in the same pattern of procedures, timing, and roles of major participants. Budget staffs (both legislative and executive) tend to work very hard during the phase of the cycle that is their responsibility and to do other work, if they are part-time budgeters, or to perform longer analyses and, in some cases, program evaluations at other times during the year, if they work full-time on the budget. Large executive departments at all levels of government may have their own budget staffs, while in smaller ones the budget is prepared by executive staff who also perform other duties. Similarly, in small local governments there may not be full-time budget staffs, while in large cities a budget office can have over fifty staff members (Cope, 1986). The cyclical nature of budgeting creates a fairly uniform schedule for budget staffs from year to year, although their actual activities and the results of their analyses vary considerably.

Operating budgets usually are prepared annually, although a number of state governments have biennial budgets. In either an annual or a biennial budget cycle, the process begins with a letter from the government's central budget office, giving information on the budget process timetable, forms to be completed, revenue projections for the budget year (where relevant), and particular policy concerns or emphases that should be considered during budget request preparation. The process proceeds with preparation of budget requests in the departments and agencies, reflecting their needs for the budget year. Departments and agencies then submit these to the central budget office for review. Meetings or hearings are often held by central budget staff to discuss departmental requests. After the review phase is complete, the budget document is prepared, to reflect budget priorities. This document, often accompanied by an appropriations bill (or ordinance), is submitted for legislative review and approval. The budget request preparation process is often an executive responsibility, although in some states and in some mayor-council cities, it is done by the legislative (council) staff. This executive decision process can take from three to ten months.

After receiving the budget document, either from the executive or from its own staff, the legislative body (city council, state legislature, Congress) also holds hearings in which agency staff (and, in many cases, citizens and affected interest groups) testify about their budget requests and planned activities that will require funding in the coming year or biennium. After the hearings, the legislature makes whatever changes it finds necessary and passes the budget and, where required, sends it to the executive for signature. Upon signature by the governor or president, or after final passage by a city council, the budget act becomes a law, which guides fiscal activity for the one- or two-year period of the budget. In the federal government this legislative decision process can take up to nine months or more, while in small local governments it may take only one to three months.

Capital Budget Cycle

Capital budget preparation is somewhat different from that of operating budgets. Capital improvement programs (CIPs), often the first step in the capital budgeting process, are usually developed by the jurisdiction's planning staff, not by its budget office. They are multiyear project lists, with design and cost information included for each proposed project. Projects proposed for inclusion in the CIP are analyzed and screened by the facilities planning staff according to such criteria as timing, cost, and, in local governments, compatibility with the master plan. This planning process results in development of a priority listing of capital projects, which is then reviewed and approved, usually with modifications, by the legislative body. This is why the first step in the capital budget process is usually performed by planners, not by the budget staff.

The second step of the capital budget process is a financial analysis to determine the jurisdiction's capacity to support the large expenditures necessary for construction of new facilities, major renovations, or purchases of major equipment. This analysis is concerned with two issues: the government's capability to repay and service bonds, if debt financing is proposed, and its capacity to raise revenue from current tax levels or to support (politically and economically) a tax increase for the purpose of capital financing. After resolution of these issues, the third step is preparation of the actual capital budget. Both the second and third steps are performed by budget staff. Because capital budgets are concerned with such long-range items, cost-benefit analysis, including analysis of the present values of costs and benefits from the project, provides important information for budget decision makers. Building a new civic center for a local government, for example, would require consideration not only of construction costs and financing arrangements but also of projected future revenues (discounted to present value), which could be used to service debt incurred for construction, as well as to pay for future operating costs. The final step in the capital budget process is coordination with the operating budget, if the two are prepared separately. Without coordination, major equipment (for example, a fire truck) could be purchased in the absence of necessary staff to operate it, or a building could be completed without funding for utilities to support it (Mikesell, 1986). Because of these different purposes and considerations, capital budgets often are presented in a different format from that of the operating budget.

In some cases, including that of the national government, capital budget requests are integrated with operating budget items, and no separate capital budget is prepared. In other cases, a separate capital budget is prepared, sometimes appropriating funds for three to six years, and sometimes appropriating one year's funding for an ongoing CIP. When the operating and capital budgets are separate, capital budget preparation may be done simultaneously with operating budget preparation, or it may be an entirely separate process with its own timetable. In the latter case, particular attention must be paid to coordinating the two processes, so that operating budget requirements made necessary by capital budget–financed activities are met.

The CIP development and capital budgeting process can take from three to twelve months, or even longer in major construction projects that require extensive preliminary studies before budget development. In the federal government, in many cases, capital expenditures are planned by agencies and authorized by Congress to cover multiyear periods, but each year's funding is part of the unified national budget.

Executive Budget Preparation

The executive budget preparation process is remarkably similar across all levels and types of governments. Most governments require their component departments or agencies to prepare budget requests for submission to the central (executive or legislative) budget office, which revises and compiles them into a coherent budget request package for legislative action. (Capital and operating budget requests may be prepared separately or together, depending on the way the CIP and capital budgets are handled in the jurisdiction.) This departmental and central budget office preparation process is of interest to many budget reformers, because at this stage of the process information is developed that can be useful both for improved budget decision making and, in some cases, for improved executive department management. Much of the literature on executive budgeting is concerned with how the agencies and the central budget office prepare their requests, what formats they use, and what information they include. While the types of budgets and the information they include vary widely among jurisdictions, there are several general categories of operating budget format, each including characteristic types of information, that historically have been used most often.

The most basic type of operating budget is presented in a line-item format, so called because the requested expenditures are classified by object-of-expenditure categories. Each line item of expenditure represents requested appropriations in that category for the agency. Line-item budgets present only the most basic information to decision makers. They are particularly useful for expenditure control and accounting system compatibility. The national budget uses line-item object-of-expenditure categories only in supplemental schedules, if at all, and most states also use object-of-expenditure classifications only as supplements or appendixes to their budget requests. About one-third of local governments use only line-item budget presentation formats, however, while 43 percent use object-of-expenditure schedules in conjunction with other information (Cope, 1986). The incidence of the line-item format as the only budget presentation seems to be rising in local governments, after a number of years of declining use (or use only as supplemental data). This rise may be explained by the increased computerization of budget and finance processes in local governments, and by the ease with which line-item budgets can be prepared with spreadsheet programs on microcomputers and linked directly to the computerized accounting system for immediate expenditure control.

The argument against line-item budgets is that when they are used alone, they do not present information on the activities, outputs, efficiency, effectiveness, or impact of the governmental activities funded through them. Historically, one of the first responses to this problem was the development of a format that incorporated additional information, using a functional or program classification system, while still retaining the object-of-expenditure data in summary form (and usually including full line-item information in a supplemental schedule). The performance budget, as it was called, emphasized efficiency in carrying out governmental activities, rather than just expenditure control. Performance budgets included measurements of agency workloads, outputs in relation to workloads, unit costs, and efficiency of agency performance. They usually included information on agency staff levels, which allowed computation of output per person or unit cost of performance when combined with workload, output, or cost data (Burkhead, 1956).

Performance budget formats are especially useful in local governments when city councils (and their constituents) are concerned with the efficiency of the government's operations, many of which can readily be measured quantitatively—for example, miles of streets paved, number of gallons of water treated, or cost per pothole filled. Performance budgets were criticized, however, because they did not provide the types of information that many decision makers wanted, such as whether objectives were attained and how particular activities affected their constituents. They are much more useful for management than for policy decision-making purposes (Lee and Johnson, 1983).

The third major type of budget format was the program budget. It was a versatile budgeting system, which emphasized achievements, goal attainment, and impacts of the activities of the program or agency. One of its most famous incarnations was the planning-programming-budgeting system (PPB), which began to be used in the Department of Defense in 1961. Based on the techniques of systems analysis, cybernetics, cost-benefit analysis, and operations research, PPB attempted to link long-range planning with annual budgeting and ongoing program evaluation.

Under PPB, a budget program structure was developed that did not necessarily have to follow the government's organizational chart. Instead, the budget was divided into programs, such as public safety, economic development, transportation, leisure and recreation, and education. In a PPB program structure, an individual department's activities might be found in several different budget programs, and some programs would contain elements from several departments.

A second major contribution of PPB was its use of operations research and cost-benefit analysis for quantitative evaluation of program expenditures and their impacts on society. PPB required inclusion of some measures of the need for programs and their components; measures of actual demand; data on program outputs; and measurement of the impact, in relation to program goals, of each activity. Rather than emphasizing efficiency and productivity, as in performance budgeting, PPB was concerned with attainment of the government's goals. Collecting this information required development of program evaluation units in many government departments and central budget offices, and often extensive training of departmental staff. Control of the budget process from the top, in a very centralized fashion, was a third characteristic of PPB, which, again, contrasted with the more bottom-up style of performance budgeting or line-item budgeting.

Although many governments tried it, PPB was criticized for the complexity of the measurements and evaluations it required in order to calculate program impacts, its centralized nature, and the requirement (in nearly all governments in which it was implemented) that a large central budget staff be maintained to perform the evaluations and cost-benefit analyses, write the program policy guidelines, and manage the process. An additional problem was that executive departments had to have similar staffs, all of them trained in PPB and evaluation, which took considerable resources, even in small jurisdictions.

PPB was also criticized because of its insensitivity to the political accountability needs of legislators reviewing the budget, since programs did not conform to departmental units. Program evaluations and measures of need, demand, output, and impact often did not address the political criteria on which legislators made their decisions (Schick, 1973). While it was an excellent device for providing objective program information, PPB failed to become a long-standing budget decision system because it did not present information in the way legislative decision makers needed and wanted it presented. Although it did not survive the change from the Johnson to the Nixon administration as a federal budget system, PPB was adapted and modified by state and local governments to meet their information needs. Therefore, in its modified forms, it had more influence on state and local budgeting than on federal budgeting, in the long run.

PPB was developed at a time of budget and program expansion at all levels of government, and its characteristics were well suited to that task. Several years later, at a time of government contraction, it was perhaps inevitable that a budgeting system would be developed to aid in cutback decisions. Introduced by President Jimmy Carter in 1977, zero-base budgeting (ZBB), like performance budgeting, was concerned with productivity and efficiency. It specifically required budget preparers to package their requests so that expenditure reductions could be made easily and be based on productivity improvements, whenever possible. It was developed as a private sector tool for cutting back (Phyrr, 1973), in sharp contrast to the program development emphasis of PPB. The building blocks of ZBB are budget decision packages, prepared by supervisors of individual organizational units. Decision packages are required to indicate alternative ways of accomplishing the purposes of units and to recommend the most efficient ones, a process that is intended to result in cost savings. Decision packages are ranked in priority order and sent up through the levels of an organization until all the decision packages, appropriately grouped and ranked, reach the executive. In some cases, summaries of the decision packages and their rankings, rather than all the packages themselves, are given to the chief executive, because of the large volume of paperwork this process generates. (Indeed, one of the major criticisms of ZBB has been that it generates too much paper.) Executive decisions on the budget are then made from the set of ranked decision packages.

ZBB was adopted by a number of state and local governments, where it evolved into a system in which budget decision packages were prepared at set percentage levels of the previous year's base budget amount. Priority rankings continued to be used, and the system was seen as useful for cutback decisions and productivity improvement (Schick and Hatry, 1982).

Although ZBB, in modified form, is still in use in some jurisdictions, it was discontinued in the national government when President Ronald Reagan took office.

Capital Budget Preparation

Three major issues in capital budgeting have been of concern to budget decision makers and scholars in the field: the types of expenditures eligible for inclusion as capital items, the question of whether capital budgets should be separate from operating budgets, and the types of financing appropriate for capital projects. The debate over the definition of a capital expenditure has arisen in response to proposals that expenditures for such purposes as education and training be considered capital projects, because they are essentially for long-term investments in human, rather than physical, capital. Opponents of this view (who outnumber proponents) concede that the products of such activities have long-term effects, but they argue that most of the expenditures are of a regularly recurring nature, easily divided into annual appropriations. Therefore, treating them in the same way as one-time or multiyear capital spending is unnecessary and inappropriate. In addition, separation of education expenditures, for example, from the operating budget could distort decision making in both the capital and operating budgets.

This viewpoint is related to the second issue: whether capital and operating budgets should be separate. The issue of capital and operating budget coordination is the major argument for combined budgets in state and local governments. Arguments for separation include the different nature of capital and operating expenditures, the destabilizing effect of large capital items on the annual operating budget, the potential long-range impacts of capital decisions, and the need for different types of analysis for decision making (for example, cost-benefit analysis, useful for capital projects, is usually unnecessary for operating activities). The federal budget combines both capital and operating activities in one unified budget. There are two major reasons for this practice. First, the federal government often uses capital construction projects as part of its fiscal policy measures to control unemployment and economic growth. Combining all aspects of the budget helps federal decision makers use the size of the budget and its deficit (or surplus, theoretically) for fiscal policy and precludes the possibility of two separate budgets having contradictory (or overly complementary) purposes. Second, the federal government is not required to have a balanced operating budget, as are most state and local governments. Therefore, it does not need to separate capital and operating expenditures in order for the former to be debt financed. Besides concerns about the different types of activities and decisions involved, this is a major reason for separation of capital and operating budgets in state and local governments. (The third major issue—types of financing systems— has been complicated by federal tax reform and changes in bond markets, among other things, and is beyond the scope of this chapter.)

Legislative Budget Review

Executive budget development has not been the only target of budget reformers eager to improve decision making. The legislative process, inherently political and often lengthy and cumbersome, has also been modified several times since 1900, especially at the federal level. The creation of the General Accounting Office by the Budget and Accounting Act of 1921; the establishment of the Congressional Budget Office, the House and Senate Budget Committees, and a new budget process and timetable by the Congressional Budget and Impoundment Control Act of 1974; and the establishment of a set of deficit-reduction targets with a timetable for balancing the federal budget for 1991 by the Balanced Budget and Emergency Deficit Reduction Act of 1985 (also known as Gramm-Rudman-Hollings)—all have contributed to the modification of congressional procedures for reviewing the president's proposed budget and deciding on the political priorities to be reflected in the appropriations that are passed. Even with the new procedures, Congress has had difficulty passing its appropriations bills by the beginning of the fiscal year (the federal fiscal year is October 1–September 30). As a result, Congress has resorted to the frequent use of continuing resolutions in recent years. The continuing resolution is an omnibus joint resolution passed by both houses of Congress that is signed (if it is not vetoed) by the president to become law. It traditionally was used for short periods, a few days or weeks, as a stopgap measure until the appropriations bill could be passed. Recently, it has replaced appropriations bills as a full-year funding device, used for political expediency. It is often criticized as a retrograde step, negating some of the gains in improved legislative decision making accomplished by the recent reforms.

State legislative budgeting, for the most part, resembles the typical legislative process, in which a legislature reviews the annual or biennial budget request prepared by the state agencies and by a state department of management and budget. There are several exceptions to this pattern, however. Texas uses a legislatively controlled process, in which the governor's budget usually is treated as an advisory policy document, and a legislatively prepared budget is the one really considered. Nebraska has a unicameral legislature, and so coordination between houses and the use of conference committees to resolve differences are unnecessary. A number of states have biennial budgets, in contrast to the national annual budget, and only Vermont does not have a constitutional or legal requirement that its budget be balanced. Another contrast to the national budget is many governors' ability to veto a line item in an appropriations bill while signing the rest of the bill into law. Although forty-three state governors (all except Indiana, Maine, Nevada, New Hampshire, North Carolina, Rhode Island, and Vermont) have this power, the president does not (LeLoup, 1986). Half the states use single appropriations bills, while the other twenty-five have multiple bills, like the national government (Mikesell, 1986).

Legislative budget decision making in local governments differs from both state and national government budgeting in several ways. First, local legislative bodies (city councils, commissions, town meetings) are unicameral. Second, the form of government used locally affects the role of the executive. Most local executives, whether elected, appointed, or plural, do not have veto power over the budgets that their councils, commissions, or town meetings produce; and, in most cases, the budget ordinances become law, as do other ordinances, upon final passage by the legislative bodies, without need of an executive's signature.

Impacts of Budget Reforms

Budget reform, both legislative and executive, has had significant impacts on capital and operating budgets. Many so-called budget reforms have been, in essence, budget fads, changes in the budget process that have not survived the administrations or individuals that proposed them. Nevertheless, some genuine improvements in budget decision making have been made as a result of budget reforms. PPB, for example, was a fad in the sense that it was not used in its pure form for very long, but some of the concepts it introduced to budgeting, such as cost-benefit analysis, program output and impact measurement, and evaluation, have continued to be used in some form by many governments that long ago abandoned the formal structure of PPB. ZBB, another mercurial fad, has nevertheless had a lasting influence by orienting budgeting toward consideration of multiple-level (including below-the-base) budget requests with priority rankings, which are still used by governments that no longer (or never did) prepare ZBB decision packages in a formal way.

The budget process remains inherently incremental and political, however, because governmental funding needs rarely change radically from year to year, and decisions on difficult trade-offs among competing uses of limited revenues ultimately can be made only through a political process. Improvements in executive budget preparation and legislative review and approval certainly make the process more rational and provide better and more timely information to decision makers. Whether actual decisions are different because of the types of information provided in budget requests is difficult to determine, since controlled experiments of actual legislative decision making are not feasible. Legislators do tend to make decisions on the basis of the information at hand, and so it can be inferred that if they are provided information on program outcomes or efficiency, they will consider it in their decisions. Whether it is outweighed by other political considerations depends on the individual circumstances, as well as on the preferences of the legislators and the perceived credibility of the information. The long-term impact of such budget fads as PPB and ZBB, then, probably can be summarized as the introduction of new or improved types of information into the budget decision process, kinds of information that have made the process more rational, although they have ultimately not changed its inherently political nature.

Given the staying power of incremental budget decision making at all levels of government, various budget reforms have had a lasting impact on the way public sector financial decisions are made. Budget classifications still tend to be either functional (programmatic) or organizational, with object-of-expenditure line-item detail available as an accountability tool. From PPB, many governments have adopted program evaluation for operating budgets and cost-benefit analysis for capital budgets. Both performance budgeting and PPB have contributed the concepts of performance and program outcome measures of the efficiency and impact of governmental activities. ZBB has given budget decision makers both the option of asking for budget requests at several different levels (above and below the previous year's base) and the concept of priority ranking as an aid to decision making in cutback situations. Budget directors, department managers, executives (elected or appointed), and legislators can use these reform techniques (and many others too numerous to summarize here) to develop their own governmental budget decision systems according to the political and informational needs of their jurisdictions. The result should be better budget decisions and, therefore, improved governmental service delivery at all levels of government.

Summary

Budgeting is a universal activity, but not a uniform one. This chapter has described both capital and operating budget systems at the local, state, and national levels of government. It has shown that diversity, rather than conformity to a universal budgeting ideal, is the rule in budgeting. There is no best way to budget, but there are numerous examples, historical and contemporary, of procedures and techniques that make the budget process more rational. These include performance budgeting, PPB, ZBB, and various legislative reforms. In practice, these methods were adapted to the needs of each jurisdiction, as budgeting has evolved from a technical, accounting-based process to a complex political decision-making method using computers and the latest quantitative and qualitative techniques. Capital budgets and operating budgets share many similarities but are often prepared separately, and capital budgets include different techniques, such as multiyear planning and cost-benefit analysis. The issues of separating or unifying capital and operating budgets, and the long-term impact of budget fads, were also discussed. These issues have not been resolved, and no absolute conclusions can be drawn from this chapter. The only indisputable conclusion that can be reached concerning governmental budgeting is that it is continuing to evolve and adapt, both to new technology and to political realities. Actual practice is often in advance of theoretical developments in governmental management and decision making, and budgeting is a prime example of that phenomenon.

References

Burkhead, J. *Government Budgeting.* New York: Wiley, 1956.

Cope, G. H. "Municipal Budgetary Practices." *Baseline Data Report,* 1986, *18* (3), 1–13.

Fenno, R. F. "The Impact of PPBS on the Congressional Appropriation Process." In R. L. Charland, K. Ganda, and M. Hugo (eds.), *Information Support, Program Budgeting, and the Congress.* New York: Chandler, 1968.

Lee, R. D., Jr., and Johnson, R. W. *Public Budgeting Systems.* (3rd ed.) Baltimore, Md.: University Park Press, 1983.

LeLoup, L. T. *Budgetary Politics.* (3rd ed.) Brunswick, Ohio: King's Court Communications, 1986.

Mikesell, J. L. *Fiscal Administration: Analysis and Applications for the Public Sector.* (2nd ed.) Homewood, Ill.: Dorsey Press, 1986.

Phyrr, P. *Zero-Base Budgeting: A Practical Management Tool for Evaluating Expenses.* New York: Wiley, 1973.

Schick, A. "A Death in the Bureaucracy: The Demise of Federal PPB." *Public Administration Review,* 1973, *33,* 146–156.

Schick, A., and Hatry, H. "Zero-Base Budgeting: The Manager's Budget." *Public Budgeting and Finance,* 1982, *2,* 72–89.

21

Jerry L. Mc Caffery

Strategies for Achieving Budgetary Goals

One of the myriad tasks that confront administrators is constructing and presenting budgets. Without budgets, programs cannot exist. Administrators are responsible for the formal calculation of what needs to be done to execute programs and how much it will cost. They may be responding to demands arising from the greater society. They may be directed by forms, time guidelines, and fiscal constraints from the central budget office, and their budget requests may be reviewed, changed, and legitimized by other participants in the executive branch, the legislature, and, recently, the courts (Straussman, 1986). In any case, theirs is the basic task of putting into a formal structure the numbers of clients and dollars, the intention to do more or less, and the desire to provide more or less government to society. They are guided, reviewed, and controlled by law, and their task is often complicated by growing entitlements, top-down budget routines, and fiscal shortfalls; but they have the basic data-producing function: building a budget, what Levine (1985, p. 256) calls specification of the technical alternatives of programs. Even when fiscal stress reduces available resources and constrains potential programs, the fundamental task remains. Schick (1988, p. 532) observes that budgeting under fiscal stress emphasizes control. He concludes that "back to basics budgeting does not need new procedures, but increased reliance on old ones." This chapter is about those old procedures.

Administrators cannot magically close deficits, invent new revenue sources, or make workloads vanish, but they do have a fiduciary responsibility to do well what they do have control over. Rubin (1985) described the impact of budget cutbacks on a group of federal agencies. She found that, rather than fighting the cutbacks with "end runs" to Congress, the agencies followed the president's directives, even to the point of cutting their own budgets. White (1985, p. 629) calls this reality "agencies as victims" and suggests that while agencies no longer dominate budgeting, they remain an important participant. Moreover, White says, the person responsible for the agency budget exists to budget. His or her values are likely to be conservative ones like efficiency, effectiveness, and performance, because he or she has many demands to satisfy. Moreover, those values are understood by and important to all other players in the system (p. 630).

This chapter examines how administrators cope with the task of building budgets. It examines budget presentation practices and suggests how administrators can profit from coming budget decisions. The perspective of this chapter is that of the practicing administrator, who must daily confront program realities and budgetary boundaries.

Patterns

Budgets are fixed, periodic events, with organizational cycles and legal roots. Administrators must respond to budget calendars. Not all administrators respond the same way, nor are they all similarly motivated. Economic analysis of bureaucracy has produced a picture of administrators as budget maximizers who gauge their own self-interest in terms of budget expansion. On the one hand, they expand their budgets because their tenure in office is determined by sponsors and clientele who expect them to maximize their budgets. On the other hand, they maximize their budgets because of the rewards it brings in terms of salary, power, reputation, and the other perquisites a "wealthy" organization can provide its workers. As a result, public sector budgets are larger than they ought to be. In response, administrative theorists argue that bureaucrats do not attempt to maximize utility for personal gain and survival; they do it because they are motivated by duty, by a picture of the good society, and by the desire to help attain that society.

Sigelman (1986), who summarized and tested this argument, concluded that the maximization of personal utility does not necessarily lead to maximized agency budgets. Using a survey of high-level state officials, Sigelman found that only about three or four of every ten officials called for budgetary expansion of more than 15 percent. Between 30 percent and 50 percent called for expansions of less than 10 percent for their own agencies. Sigelman concluded that this is not a portrait of the bureaucrat as budget expansionist. Moreover, those who called for expansion did so because they believed that all state functions ought to be increased. Those who scored high on professional commitment were more likely to advocate more growth, and those who spent more time with an agency's clientele were also more supportive of larger increases, as opposed to those who were less committed professionally and those who were more limited in their range of client contact.

Therefore, place in the organization counts, as do professional commitment and the concept of the state's role. Certainly, the picture of administrators asking for more money because they identify more closely with clientele or because they are more professionally committed is more appealing than that of administrators budgeting for new carpets or salary increases.

Historical research in budget patterns discloses that aggressive agencies tend to get more in the budget struggle than less aggressive agencies do (Sharkansky, 1968) and that the outcome of the budget struggle tends to be incremental (Wildavsky, 1964), although precisely what *incremental* means has been a topic of extensive debate (Bailey and O'Connor, 1975; Tucker, 1982). In Wildavsky's original study (1964, p. 14), more than half the increases were within 10 percent of the previous year's base, but this is an analysis of aggregate budget totals. Research into outcomes of agency patterns has shown great fluctuation within individual agency budgets (Natchez and Bupp, 1973; LeLoup and Moreland, 1978), as well as producing an investigation of the base by reviewers (Kamlet and Mowery, 1980; Gist, 1977; Lauth, 1987). Although budget patterns tend to show incremental growth in the aggregate, prudent administrators can expect base-probing questions as they present justification for budget needs. LeLoup and Moreland's (1978) study of budget trends in the U.S. Department of Agriculture is especially interesting, since it clearly demonstrates the range of intraagency behavior.

In general, the aggregate pattern is for agency budgets to grow at an incremental rate and for the jurisdiction's budget office to cut because resource requests exceed available resources. The legislature tends to cut more from the proposed budget, while mainly taking its cues from the executive budget. Wildavsky (1964) emphasized the relationship of the agencies to congressional committees, but recent research indicates that the Office of Management and Budget was more powerful than the agencies or Congress in determining the size of the agencies' annual increments (Kamlet and Mowery, 1980; Tomkin, 1983). This trend was intensified by David Stockman and his emphasis on an ideological budget driven by top-down decision procedures (Heclo, 1984; Wildavsky, 1988). Nonetheless, the budget process manifests relatively stable patterns in which agencies rely on code words and behavioral repertoires to get what they think they need.

Wildavsky (1964, p. 64) says that technical data supporting budget requests are not enough; what matters is how good a politician one is. A good politician cultivates a clientele to support his or her requests, develops other people's confidence in his or her work, and sharpens his or her skills in using strategies designed to present requirements in the most convincing fashion. Confidence involves trust. The complexity of the budget process dictates that some people must trust others, because they can check up on them only some of the time, and because no one can be an expert in everything. In a fascinating study of state budget outcomes, Duncombe and Kinney (1987) found that for agency officials in five western states, budget success was measured not by ability to get the largest amount or percentage appropriated, but rather by ability to meet current needs with a few improvements and, especially, by ability to maintain good relationships with the legislature and its budget staff and with the governor and the executive budget staff. These were also the top concerns of the executive and legislative budget staffs: getting enough to meet current needs while keeping interpersonal relationships intact. This is a reaffirmation of the need for confidence, trust, and competence in the budget process. Duncombe and Kinney suggest that their findings may have been distorted by the recent climate of fiscal scarcity in the states they surveyed. If this is true, however, it only makes their conclusions more important, for bad times are when the system has to work; in good times, organizational slack can overcome mistakes, misunderstandings, and misfits.

Contingent Strategies

Wildavsky (1964) identified a group of behaviors designed for reacting to the conditions of the moment—time, place, and circumstances. He called these behaviors *contingent strategies*. On a fundamental level, contingent strategies are ways of combining the perennial concerns of an organization with the language and perceptions of current events. Public organizations administer laws; they are not free to choose what they will do from an unlimited list of possibilities. Their needs often outrun their resources, and so they must choose. When they choose, they couch their choices in words that budget reviewers are used to hearing. This simplifies the transfer of information. Weiss (1982) submits that efficient decision makers sort through numerous alternatives to give serious attention to only one or two, and that new information is prefiltered through what has occurred before. Decision makers simplify by seeing a problem as another case of something seen before and already understood. Weiss also concludes that decision makers master repertoires of skills and use them in combinations appropriate to decisions at hand. In budgeting, such skills include contingent strategies.

Contingent strategies are the shorthand ways in which administrators tell budget reviewers what is happening in their programs. Contingent strategies are detailed explanations of causation. They are responses to organizational and environmental demands, comparable to private sector marketing strategies and tactics. The ubiquitous strategies of clientele, confidence, and competence establish the environment for belief, and the contingent strategies attempt to establish causation. They explain why the budget should be changed from one year to the next, in terms that the reviewer is used to hearing and comprehending.

Casual observation suggests that contingent strategies are agency-specific (not all agencies can make a profit) and change over time. Wildavsky (1975) examined types of justifications in the outdoor recreation budget from 1949 to 1969. Twelve different justification categories were discovered for 1949. The most frequent justifications were inadequacy of facilities and personnel and increased pressure from users. These two themes accounted for over half the justifications. In 1958, the largest single category was increased user pressure. In 1969, the total number of strategies tripled. User pressure was third, with two new strategies taking first and second place: enhancement of social, spiritual, and educational values, and alleviation of city problems. Wildavsky argues that these new justifications were a reflection of current social thought in 1969, but user pressure persisted for two decades as an explanatory budget strategy. This pattern illustrates the persistence of agency budget themes.

Grizzle (1986) found an integrating theme in budget decisions. Examining how budget format influenced budget review, she found that, irrespective of format, questions about management dominated discussion, even under program budget formats designed to produce questions geared to planning. Straussman's (1986) examination of the courts' role in the budget process depicts the courts as basically making workload-oriented management decisions—for example, rulings on prison staffing. The point here is that although the total repertoire of contingent strategies may seem unlimited, most such strategies cluster around whatever basic element of management is specific to an agency. For a tax department, it may be processing tax returns; for a fire department, putting out and preventing fires; for a social work department, caseload and clientele counseling. Each function has different imperatives, but budget people learn to connect them by speaking a universal language. Contingent strategies are part of that language.

Contingent Strategy Elements

This section explores some powerful contingent strategies and potential responses to them.

Workload. Workload justifications often are linked to historical statistics, demographic trends, and forecasts. Their logic is simple: Workload growth must be handled. ("Eight auditors did eighty thousand audits; our forecasts indicate we will have to do ninety thousand audits; therefore, we need one more auditor. Each auditor keeps one clerical position busy with typing, filing, or billing.") The logic is seemingly inescapable: To do what was done last year requires another person. Reviewers may argue that the administrator can find other ways to manage, or they may argue that funds are too scarce and, whatever the consequences, no new personnel will be authorized. Another variation of this theme is to tell the agency to decrease its workload by decreasing program intensity.

Profit. An administrator may argue that auditors generate revenues far in excess of their salaries. Reviewers may reject this appeal by arguing that simpler forms would increase voluntary compliance, thus allowing the auditors to concentrate on the real criminals. Making a profit is a good justification, but most government agencies do not make a profit and hence cannot use the strategy.

Spending to Save. At this point, an administrator may argue that spending on the audit function now will encourage people to pay promptly now (thus getting the money in on time) and discourage people from not paying in the future (thus guaranteeing future streams of revenues and avoiding costly crash-audit programs to catch up for the lack of auditing). This strategy is often employed in the areas of flood, fire, and forestation, where a dollar spent now will prevent the spending of many dollars in the future. Reviewers tend to like the logic of this kind of argument but not to buy it unless some clear documentation exists. Hardheaded reviewers often try to talk administrators into estimates of how soon savings will begin. The criterion is that the tighter the resource situation is, the sooner the savings should begin.

Equity. In this instance, an administrator may argue that the law requires all clientele be audited; hence, another auditor is needed to maintain compliance with the law and provide equity among taxpayers. This argument can be turned back if reviewers ask whether differences exist among returns, and whether ''no problem'' returns or simple documents can be sorted and processed quickly enough so that no additional people are needed but the dictates of the law are fulfilled. Another strategy is simply to change interpretation of a law. For example, when defense proponents argue that treaties obligate us to a certain level of spending, one response is to say that the treaties do bind us to such commitments but not to precise levels of spending, and that the commitments can be fulfilled with a cheaper mix.

Backlog. Backlogs are generally bad business, particularly if they are composed of critically ill people. In this case, someone is certain to ask what difference it will make if a backlog occurs in an audit function. The rejoinder ought to mention equity, profit, and money in the state's coffers. Again, someone may ask if the workload could not be sorted so that the backlog is composed of relatively harmless returns. Backlog and workload justifications tend to look alike in their written form, but the distinction between the two is very important for the analyst. A true workload increase will probably have to be met either with increased personnel or with a changed policy (barring a stunning managerial improvement). A backlog may be solved with temporary personnel, who cost less, can go on to other jobs, and do not constitute a permanent increase in the personnel budget. In the example tracked so far, a backlog will build up, and it probably will be solved only by permanent personnel or by a change in policy. Nevertheless, it is very important for the analyst to be able to distinguish between a backlog and a workload change. A backlog once taken care of may stay taken care of; thus, it would be inappropriate to use permanent resources to solve it. The practicing incrementalist is likely to use temporary measures, such as overtime and temporary help, before resorting to a less flexible solution. The reviewer does not want to give away something for nothing.

Crisis. There is good justification when a crisis exists. Polio was a public health crisis in the early 1950s, as AIDS is in the 1980s. Most agencies do not have crisis themes to present. When they do, they present reviewers with difficult choices. Unable to make a crisis vanish, reviewers can say the level of spending is too high to be usefully spent out or put to work in the fiscal period under consideration. Thus, another theme recurs: If the item is unbeatable, try to decrease the level of support. Crises, however, do exist: Kemp (1984) found that accidents and scandals had an important effect on regulatory policy and budgetary outcomes in three regulatory agencies.

Small Increase. Allusions to size may seem effective when the increase is small, compared to the total size of the budget, but professionals do not take this line of argument seriously. Increases are either justified or they are not. One who argues that an increase is small may be urged to absorb it.

High-Risk Strategies. In the late 1950s and early 1960s, "cutting the popular program," such as sports or kindergarten, was an effective threat for a school superintendent to make. In 1987, San Francisco's school district used a cut in the athletic program to its benefit. Fiscal necessity has seen such programs cut with seemingly little effect, but in the right circumstances this remains a powerful strategy. "All or nothing" is a powerful but limited strategy. The administrator who takes an all-or-nothing approach has to be prepared to live with the consequences of a "nothing" decision.

Mandates and Commitments. Federal and state levels of government have been fond, over the last two decades, of levying requirements on subordinate levels of government, not always with the necessary funding to accompany workloads. An administrator who has a mandate has a strong case, but reviewers can always argue the fiscal level of concurrence (again, complying with the letter of the mandate, if not with the spirit). Administrators who were persuasive in convincing their reviewers to buy into federal grants sometimes were surprised when the continuing costs for maintenance bills came due. Therefore, reviewers now must fully examine the total and continuing costs of grants.

This list of strategies is not meant to be conclusive. The point to remember is that while many strategies are generic and cross boundaries, others are very specific (health and human services agencies' strategies are oriented to saving lives, but not to making a profit; a tax department can claim to make a profit, but not to save lives). The administrator's challenge in developing and presenting a budget is to bring forth the most compelling themes and be able to deal with the dialogue that surrounds those themes in the political environment. The retrenchment literature is rich in crisis management insights (Levine, 1978; Behn, 1980), but Lewis (1984) found that cutback budgetary strategies did not appear significantly different from expansionary strategies. A further indication of the staying power of contingent strategies can be found in a close reading of Wildavsky (1988). Old friends appear: the wedge (p. 232), what they do affects what we do (p. 184), spend to save, all or nothing (p. 182), it's so small (p. 183). Many things have changed, however, and the federal process of the 1980s has been replete with rather transparent gimmicks, like moving payroll dates, funding for less than a full year, and choosing the base number most useful for one's policy position.

Presentation Strategies

Administrators must be able to present their positions effectively, whether in clear, concise prose or in budget hearings. Since the hearing is a crucial stage, rehearsing the budget presentation makes sense. Hearings take place both in administrative settings and in legislatures. Contact with the budget bureau will usually warn an agency about what the bureau's concerns are. It also makes sense to scout budget hearings, to see what kinds of things interest the budget committee. Contact with the committee or its staff is also useful in preparing for the hearing.

Veteran observers usually advise that the agency play it straight, not spring any surprises, give the committee some warning in advance of key issues, and make sure the department's position unrolls the way the documents sent to the committee predict, so that all are working from the same script. Veterans urge that the presenter be organized, that only a few people testify for the agency, and that testimony be choreographed, so that the agency will not look confused and the right things will get said at the right times. They recommend that budget people answer only the questions they are asked. Glittering generalities, ambiguous phrases, and pious references to the general welfare are seen as inappropriate. Clear, direct presentation of programs, supported by documentation of accomplishments and solid justification of changes from the base, is what is necessary. Mastering the budget means mastering detail; detail then allows for consideration of the policy that guides the budget.

What if all agencies followed this advice? Would budgets automatically increase? Should spending increase simply because administrators become effective budget advocates? Not necessarily, for equally effective analysts can sit on the other side of the table. Not only can they know and respond to arguments the agency makes, they may also have developed a budget system that helps them in their battle to satisfy needs and hold down spending, as do the many variants of zero-base budgeting.

Prescriptive Considerations

Administrators' perceptions of how to approach the budget decision vary. In one study, managers explained how they decided how much to ask for. Most took a textbook approach (Mc Caffery, 1987): They determined what needed to be done, decided on production objectives, estimated how it would be accomplished (staff, supporting expenses), found the cost factors, and then wrote budget justifications. Their budgets were driven by many of the conditions discussed earlier, including workload, mandates, and local fiscal conditions.

Others took a different approach, one suited to the context and to relational factors in the budget decision, rather than adopting linear thinking about what needed to be done. One administrator said that she knew hers was a pet project, and so she would get most of what she could justify. First, she tried to find out how much her reviewers had to distribute. Then she built a budget based on program needs but padded it somewhat, because she knew the person who was going to review it believed that administrators ask for more than they need. She decided that budget supplements were not too hard to get, and so if she did not get what she wanted in the main budget battle, she could get it as a supplement. Since the word *training* was popular that year, she wrote as much of her justification as she could around training.

What is remarkable here is the step-by-step isolation of the key variables of the process. These included the identification of the project as a pet project, an estimate of how much there was to get, the felt necessity to pad a little, and the feeling that supplements always were available. This administrator seemed relatively comfortable with the budget process, possibly because of the pet-project syndrome, or possibly because she believed she had the insight to operate the budget mechanism to her advantage.

Another participant in the Mc Caffery (1987) study said that his most effective budgetary strategy was to project himself into the role of his superiors. He said that he examined their environment and their philosophies, both personal and institutional. By that time, he had already decided what he needed. He then went through a process of building a case for all or part of what he needed, such that it made sense to his superiors from their point of view and was justified within their environment. He said, "I try to make sure that I give them reasons they will feel comfortable using if someone asks them why they approved my request" (p. 119). His principles included being honest in determining need (and avoiding the temptation to define what he needed by what it was safe to ask for), being honest with the request (and not scheming by asking for two dollars in order to get one), recognizing reviewers' authority and responsibility and right to say no, and not settling for a plain no. If a request was denied, he asked for alternatives, suggestions for a better way of accomplishing tasks, or reviewers' acceptance of the consequences of their denial.

This is valuable advice for the student of budgeting, as well as a wise caution to the veteran who is convinced of the compelling power of numerical arguments. The two administrators quoted here approached the budget decision as an ongoing situation. People who imitate them are likely to be less frustrated and more successful in the budget struggle than if they approach budgeting as a simple technical calculation, wherein clear answers produce victories based on workload measures or sophisticated cost-benefit analysis.

Where the line is drawn between giving reviewers what they can approve and recommending what is technically necessary is critical. If the budget maker does not tell the political decision maker what the model program should be, then all that is left to compromise over is what cost the public will accept, not what needs to be done. Certainly, one proper role of the civil servant is to ask for what is necessary and let elected politicians decide what to do, on the basis of their judgments of what the public will pay for and what it needs. Nevertheless, putting oneself in the place of one's superior is still a useful technique.

Summary

Administrators choose their budget profiles. Some will be aggressive and some will not. (Jones, 1986, mentions the difference between proactive and reactive strategies.) Some will be content to say to funding sources: "If this is what you want me to do, here is what I need." The more aggressive will attempt to specify what else needs to be done. Both types of administrators need basic budget skills. Technically, the budgeter must write good justifications, make accurate calculations, maintain interpersonal communications, and view the budget decision as an ongoing situation, rather than as a unique event. With the realization that the concept of the budget base is more ambiguous than had previously been realized, doing the numbers alone is no longer so easy (Wildavsky, 1988, p. 201; Albritton and Dran, 1987); but then, none of it is easy. Duncombe and Kinney (1987) have additional advice for budgeters, especially with respect to legislatures: Be absolutely honest, do not predict dire consequences if they are unlikely to happen, and maintain good relationships, even if that means being a team player. They also urge budgeters to try to get greater flexibility in the use of funds, and to "keep agency expenditures within appropriations if at all possible, carry out legislative intent, and manage budgets wisely" (p. 36). While this advice may seem less persuasive than "Buy low and sell high," it is the public sector's equivalent. Indeed, it is more than that, for following these injunctions will increase everyone's gain.

References

Albritton, R. B., and Dran, E. M. "Balanced Budgets and State Surpluses: The Politics of Budgeting in Illinois." *Public Administration Review*, 1987, *47*, 143–152.

Bailey, J. J., and O'Connor, R. J. "Operationalizing Incrementalism: Measuring the Muddles." *Public Administration Review*, 1975, *35*, 60–66.

Behn, R. "Leadership for Cutback Management: The Use of Corporate Strategy." *Public Administration Review*, 1980, *40* (6), 613–620.

Duncombe, S., and Kinney, R. "Agency Budget Success: How It Is Defined by Budget Officials in Five Western States." *Public Budgeting and Finance,* 1987, *7,* 24–37.

Gist, J. R. "'Increment' and 'Base' in the Congressional Appropriations Process." *American Journal of Political Science,* 1977, *21,* 341–354.

Grizzle, G. "Does Budget Format Really Govern the Actions of Budget-makers?" *Public Budgeting and Finance,* 1986, *6,* 60–70.

Heclo, H. "Executive Budget Making." In G. B. Mills and J. Palmer (eds.), *Federal Budget Policy in the 1980s.* Washington, D.C.: Urban Institute Press, 1984.

Jones, L. R. "Budget Deficits and Restraint Management in Western Provincial Governments." *American Review of Canadian Studies,* 1986, *16,* 279–291.

Kamlet, M. S., and Mowery, D. C. "The Budgetary Base in Federal Resource Allocation." *American Journal of Political Science,* 1980, *74,* 804–821.

Kemp, K. A. "Accidents, Scandals, and Political Support for Regulatory Agencies." *Journal of Politics,* 1984, *46,* 401–427.

Lauth, T. P. "Exploring the Budgetary Base in Georgia." *Public Budgeting and Finance,* 1987, *7,* 72–82.

LeLoup, L. T., and Moreland, W. B. "Agency Strategies and Executive Review: The Hidden Politics of Budgeting." *Public Administration Review,* 1978, *38,* 232–239.

Levine, C. H. "Organizational Decline and Cutback Management." *Public Administration Review,* 1978, *38,* 316–325.

Levine, C. H. "Where Policy Comes From: Ideas, Innovations, and Agenda Choices." *Public Administration Review,* 1985, *45* (1), 255–258.

Lewis, G. B. "Municipal Expenditures Through Thick and Thin." *Publius,* 1984, *14,* 31–40.

Mc Caffery, J. L. *Budgetmaster: A Budgeting Practicum.* Pacific Grove, Calif.: McCaffery, 1987.

Natchez, P. B., and Bupp, I. C. "Policy and Priority in the Budgetary Process." *American Political Science Review,* 1973, *67,* 951–963.

Rubin, I. S. *Shrinking the Federal Government: The Effect of Cutbacks on Five Federal Agencies.* New York: Longman, 1985.

Schick, A. "Micro-Budgetary Adaptations to Fiscal Stress in Industrialized Democracies." *Public Administration Review,* 1988, *48,* 523–533.

Sharkansky, I. "Agency Requests, Gubernatorial Support, and Budget Success in State Legislatures." *American Political Science Review,* 1968, *62,* 1220–1231.

Sigelman, L. "The Bureaucrat as Budget Maximizer: An Assumption Examined." *Public Budgeting and Finance,* 1986, *6,* 50–59.

Straussman, J. D. "Courts and Public Purse Strings: Have Portraits of Budgeting Missed Something?" *Public Administration Review,* 1986, *46,* 345–351.

Tomkin, S. L. "OMB Budget Examiner's Influence." *The Bureaucrat,* 1983, *12,* 43–47.

Tucker, H. J. "Incremental Budgeting: Myth or Model?" *Western Political Quarterly,* 1982, *35,* 327–338.

Weiss, J. "Coping with Complexity: An Experimental Study of Public Policy Decision Making." *Journal of Policy Analysis and Management,* 1982, *2,* 65–82.

White, J. "Much Ado About Everything: Making Sense of Federal Budgeting." *Public Administration Review,* 1985, *45,* 623–630.

Wildavsky, A. *The Politics of the Budgetary Process.* Boston: Little, Brown, 1964.

Wildavsky, A. *Budgeting: A Comparative Theory of Budgeting Processes.* Boston: Little, Brown, 1975.

Wildavsky, A. *The New Politics of the Budgetary Process.* Boston: Little, Brown, 1988.

22

Robert Berne

Accounting for Public Programs

In the fiscal crisis that marked the beginning of an extensive period of stress for governments in the United States, the failure of accounting systems was a key part of the problem. The Securities and Exchange Commission (1977, p. 7), which reviewed the factors contributing to New York City's fiscal crisis, reported, "The City's unsound accounting and reporting practices, and the system of internal accounting control . . . successfully obscured the City's real revenues, costs and financial position. Substantial weaknesses in the City's system of internal accounting control caused its financial information to be inherently unreliable. Many of the City's accounting practices were specifically designed to assist the City in its budget balancing exercises by prematurely recognizing revenues and postponing expenses to unrelated future periods. . . . These were significant factors which contributed to the City's financial difficulties and enabled it to borrow funds from the public which could not be supported by its sources of revenue."

This is not the first time that governmental accounting has been scrutinized as the result of a crisis. Some of the first systematic assessments of governmental accounting were produced shortly after 1900, in response to graft and corruption in government. The depression of the 1930s spurred the next wave of governmental accounting reform, which led to many of today's practices and standards. Over the past fifteen years, the fiscal problems and severe resource scarcity of governments have rekindled interest in governmental accounting.

Note: Helpful comments on earlier drafts were provided by James R. Fountain and James Conant.

During this most recent period, fiscal pressure has been caused by rapidly changing macroeconomic conditions, regional shifts in economic activity, the tax- and expenditure-limitation movement, cutbacks in federal spending, and a general conservative shift in attitudes regarding the role of government. In some cases, governmental fiscal crises have been compounded by poor financial management.

Since New York City's near bankruptcy, thousands of governments have reviewed and reformed their accounting systems, and standard setting in governmental accounting and financial reporting has been significantly restructured. Managers and policymakers in all segments of government routinely need to obtain and interpret accounting information, and external parties, such as citizens, creditors, and employee groups, must use accounting information to reach their objectives. Finally, the most recent focus on ethical issues also has an important connection with finance and accounting. In short, accounting information and the systems that provide it are now an integral part of governmental decision making.

This chapter is aimed at the user of accounting information, both inside and outside of government. The chapter presents some of the important components of governmental accounting, its current and potential uses, and several of the crucial issues facing governmental accounting in the future. Obviously, no single chapter is a substitute for the many book-length treatments of governmental accounting (Freeman, Shoulders, and Lynn, 1988; Hay, 1985; Henke, 1985).

The Structure of Governmental Accounting

Governments, like for-profit organizations, use accounting and financial reporting to systematically record and present financial and economic information. Reliable, accurate, and cost-effective accounting systems are part of sound management in the private and public sectors. But, just as governments differ from for-profit organizations in specific ways, so does governmental accounting have certain characteristics that distinguish it from for-profit accounting. The differences are important and continue to be so, but there are many similarities in accounting, and there is evidence that the gap between the two is narrowing somewhat.

Fund Accounting. One of the principal distinguishing characteristics of governmental accounting is the division of the governmental entity into separate units, or *funds,* for accounting purposes. Funds are separate fiscal and accounting entities that have developed because of the many outside restrictions that are placed on governmental activity. Thus, every government is composed of a set of funds, where each fund is a separate and independent entity for purposes of accounting and financial management.

Every government has its own set of funds, but there are regularities in the fund structures of all governments. Almost every government has a *general fund* that is used to account for any resources that are not restricted to other funds. For many governments, the general fund accounts for most of the primary operating functions and is often the largest, in terms of the dollar value of inflows and outflows.

Governments vary in their use of funds other than general funds. Governments whose revenue sources are legally restricted to specific purposes often account for these activities in *special revenue funds.* State and local governments often account for highway taxes or federal aid in special revenue funds, and a city that includes a school district may account for it as a special revenue fund. The acquisition of capital facilities is accounted for separately in *capital projects funds,* and the payment of the current year's principal and interest on general long-term debt is often accounted for in the *debt service fund.* The general, special revenue, capital projects, and debt service funds are known as *governmental funds* and include all activities except those found in proprietary and fiduciary funds. Governments have certain capital assets and long-term liabilities that are not included in any funds but instead are listed in *account groups.* Capital assets and long-term debt not used in proprietary activities are often listed in the *fixed-asset account* group and the *long-term debt account* group, respectively.

Proprietary funds are used to account for activities similar to those in the private sector. Often, user charges are an important revenue source for these activities, and they are managed with a break-even philosophy, even though they may require subsidies. When the activity generates a service or a product that is sold to the public, it is accounted for in an *enterprise fund;* when the service or product is provided to other parts of the government, an *internal service fund* is used. Examples of the former are public transit, recreation facilities, and utilities; examples of the latter are maintenance garages, computer facilities, and print shops.

When a government holds assets as a trustee, *fiduciary funds* are used. When the government holds these assets for short periods, such as when a county collects property taxes for a city, an *agency fund* is used. When the holding periods are longer, a *trust fund,* such as a pension fund, is appropriate.

Thus, virtually every government has a general fund and one or more of the other governmental funds (special revenue, capital projects, and debt service), account groups, proprietary funds (enterprise and internal service), and fiduciary funds (agency and trust funds). Sound practice calls for the establishment and reporting of the minimum number of funds that satisfies legal requirements and effective financial management. Fund proliferation can be inefficient in its inflexibility and complexity.

Basis of Accounting and Measurement Focus. The accounting system of each fund keeps track of the fund's stock of resources at a single point in time, as well as of the flow of resources into and out of the fund during a certain period of time (usually a fiscal year). Resources at a point in time include assets (what the fund owns) and liabilities (what the fund owes). The difference between a fund's assets and its liabilities is the fund equity that includes the fund balance. This relationship *(assets = liabilities + fund equity)* is the governmental accounting equation that always holds true for every fund. Over time, resources that flow into a fund and thus increase the fund's equity are typically revenues, and resource outflows that decrease the fund's equity are usually either expenditures (for governmental funds) or expenses (for proprietary funds).

Although the accounting system records the funds' stocks and flows according to these broad concepts, significant variation may exist in the precise definition of stocks and flows of specific funds for any particular government. In governmental accounting, the issue of what should be measured in a fund is treated as the *measurement focus,* and the question of when transactions are recorded in the accounting system is the *basis of accounting.* In theory and practice, the measurement focus and basis of accounting are closely related, and both concepts have been the subjects of intense scrutiny over the past few years (Governmental Accounting Standards Board, 1985a).

In for-profit accounting, the measurement focus (flow of economic resources) and the basis of accounting (accrual) are similar across the vast majority of firms, and one objective of these practices is the measurement of profit. In governmental accounting, the measurement focus and basis of accounting used in the for-profit sector are typically found only in proprietary funds. Because the measurement of profit is not a goal appropriate to governments, the measurement focus and basis of accounting used by many governments, especially in their governmental funds, have differed significantly from the for-profit conventions.

For most of this century, the measurement focus of governmental funds has been based on the belief that the accounting system should portray the government's raising of current financial resources to provide services. At the risk of oversimplification, it can be said that the purpose was to show the resources that were spent and the resources available for spending. With this emphasis on financial rather than economic resources, along with a basis of accounting that sometimes used elements of cash rather than the accrual basis of accounting (known as *modified accrual*), governmental funds treat certain transactions, many of which have implications that extend beyond a fiscal year, differently from the way they would be treated if they occurred in a proprietary fund or in a for-profit organization.

Several examples of the differences in the measurement focus and basis of accounting between governmental and proprietary funds (and, thus, between governmental and for-profit organizations) should help clarify this distinction. With the measurement focus in governmental funds based on the flow of financial rather than economic resources, such items as land, buildings, and equipment are treated as flows only when they lead to cash transactions, usually upon acquisition. Thus, the purchase of a building by a for-profit firm would not reduce the firm's equity, and the building would be treated as an asset and depreciated over time. In a governmental fund, by contrast, the purchase of a building would be treated as a reduction in the fund balance (often as an expenditure of a capital projects fund), and the building would not be treated as an asset of a fund (but might be included in an account group). In a related manner, the principal on outstanding debt in governmental funds is not included as a liability (but may be listed in an account group), and the payment of principal on long-term debt reduces the fund equity (usually as an expenditure of a debt service fund). In a for-profit organization, by contrast, the payment of debt principal would reduce a liability (long-term debt outstanding) and would not reduce the firm's equity.

There are also differences between governmental funds and for-profit firms in the basis of accounting, which determines when a flow has taken place. For example, some governmental funds do not accrue taxes, such as income and sales taxes, where the amount of the tax is not determined until after collection. To summarize the importance of the measurement focus/basis of accounting issue, we can say that the actual practices used by a government must be examined carefully by users inside and outside of the organization. The notes to a government's financial statement should explain the measurement focus and the basis of accounting used by a government's fund. (These issues will be discussed again later in this chapter, when future trends in standard setting are assessed.)

Financial Statements. The primary vehicle for presenting accounting information to users is the financial statement. The financial statement is more than a technical or legal requirement. As noted by the Governmental Accounting Standards Board (1987, p. ii), ''Financial reporting plays a major role in fulfilling government's duty to be publicly accountable in a democratic society. Public accountability is based on the belief that the taxpayer has a 'right to know,' a right to receive openly declared facts that may lead to public debate by the citizens and their elected representatives. Use of financial reporting by citizens and legislative and oversight officials to assess accountability is pervasive.''

Most governments issue annual financial reports that include financial statements for each fund, as well as notes, supplemental accounting data, and statistical information. In addition, almost all governments prepare accounting reports for the use of their own managers and policymakers. Because of their public nature and the standards that surround them, annual financial reports receive considerable attention in governmental accounting. In this part of the chapter, some of the most salient features of these reports are reviewed; internal reports will be discussed in the next section.

While each governmental financial report is unique, almost all reports have certain common elements, including a transmittal letter, an auditor's letter, financial statements that disclose information on each major fund or fund type, and notes to the financial statements (Municipal Finance Officers Association, 1980; Tierney and Calder, 1986). In addition, many annual reports include statistical sections that contain more detailed information on funds and such nonaccounting items as assessed value of property and demographics.

The financial statement that presents the resources at a point in time (assets, liabilities, and fund balances or retained earnings) is the *balance sheet*. Typically, a balance sheet is presented for each fund or fund type (sometimes in a combined form, where all funds are displayed in a single table). An example of balance sheets for a fictitious government with five funds is displayed in Table 22.1. This fictitious government has four governmental funds and one proprietary fund (an enterprise fund for the public transit system). Because the measurement focus and the basis of accounting are almost always different for governmental and proprietary funds, the balance sheets are not comparable, even if they are displayed in a single table, as in Table 22.1. For example, fixed assets and long-term debt are included in the proprietary fund balance sheet but not in the governmental funds, where they would be listed separately in account groups (not shown in Table 22.1).

Table 22.1. Balance Sheet, Beginning of Fiscal Year (Thousands of Dollars).

	General Fund	Federal Aid Fund	Debt Service Fund	Capital Projects Fund	Public Transit Fund
Assets					
Cash	$ 720	$ 235	$1,007	$4,296	$ 67
Taxes receivable	1,622	—	760	—	—
Aid receivable	—	964	—	207	—
Due from other funds	—	—	429	721	—
Fixed assets (net of depreciation)	—	—	—	—	11,380
Total Assets	$2,342	$1,199	$2,196	$5,224	$11,447
Liabilities					
Salaries payable	$ 329	$ 276	$ —	$ 131	$ 419
Accounts payable	255	52	—	301	449
Due to other funds	1,150	—	—	—	—
Revenue bonds payable	—	—	—	—	6,854
Total Liabilities	$1,734	$ 328	$ —	$ 432	$ 7,722
Fund Equity					
Contributed capital	$ —	$ —	$ —	$ —	$ 2,500
Fund balance	608	871	2,196	4,792	—
Retained earnings	—	—	—	—	1,255
Total Fund Equity	$ 608	871	2,196	4,792	3,725
Total Liabilities and Fund Equities	$2,342	$1,199	$2,196	$5,224	$11,447

Note: This simplified balance sheet does not include the general fixed-asset and general long-term debt account groups or a "Total" column. Notes to these financial statements are also excluded.

For a governmental fund, the statement that discloses flows of resources (revenues and expenditures) and their effect on the fund's equity is the *statement of revenues, expenditures, and changes in fund balances.* Table 22.2 is such a statement for the governmental funds of the fictitious government. Certain flows, such as interfund transfers and receipt of proceeds from general obligation bonds, are recorded as other sources or uses of financing, not as revenues or expenditures, but the effect on the fund balance of the other sources and uses is the same as for revenues and expenditures. Although an example is not shown for the fictitious government, most governments present more detailed *statements of revenues and expenditures, with comparisons of budgeted and actual figures,* for funds that operate with formally adopted budgets (usually general and special revenue funds).

Table 22.2. Statement of Revenues, Expenditures, and Changes in Fund Balances: Year Ended June 30, 199? (Thousands of Dollars).

	General Fund	Federal Aid Fund	Debt Service Fund	Capital Projects Fund
Revenues				
Taxes	$ 14,621	$ —	$ 1,043	$ —
Intergovernmental aid	485	2,070	—	75
Charges for service	179	—	—	—
Licenses and fees	88	—	—	—
Miscellaneous revenues	125	—	—	—
Total Revenues	$ 15,498	$2,070	$ 1,043	$ 75
Expenditures				
Current				
General government	$ 2,371	$ 428	—	—
Public safety	4,810	697	—	—
Public works	3,155	1,264	—	—
Social services	824	42	—	—
Recreation	358	—	—	—
Capital projects	—	—	—	$ 4,421
Debt service				
Principal	—	—	$ 1,450	—
Interest	—	—	1,249	—
Total Expenditures	$ 11,518	$2,431	$ 2,699	$ 4,421
Excess of Revenues Over (Under) Expenditures	$ 3,980	$ (361)	$(1,656)	$(4,346)
Other Financing Sources (Uses)				
Proceeds of general obligation bonds	—	—	—	$ 1,000
Operating transfers in	—	—	$ 1,500	2,400
Operating transfers out	$ (3,900)	—	—	—
Excess of Revenues and Other Sources Over (Under) Expenditures and Other Uses	80	(361)	(156)	(946)
Fund Balance, Beginning of Fiscal Year	608	871	2,196	4,792
Fund Balance, End of Fiscal Year	$ 688	$ 510	$ 2,040	$ 3,846

For proprietary funds, the statement that presents resource flows is the *statement of revenues, expenses, and changes in retained earnings,* and an example is presented in Table 22.3. With the measurement focus/basis of accounting used in proprietary funds, depreciation is an expense, but the principal paid on outstanding debt is not; therefore, the latter does not affect retained earnings. A financial statement also usually includes a *statement of changes in financial position* (not shown here) for all proprietary funds, which assesses in detail the funds' changes in cash or working capital.

The statements just described form the core of a government's financial statements that are presented in an annual financial report. A critical part of these financial statements, found in virtually all annual reports, is the notes to financial statements. These notes are essential. They are usually required for proper interpretation of financial statements, and they typically disclose the government's significant accounting policies (such as basis of accounting, entity definition, and revenue recognition), long-term debt and debt service, changes in fixed assets, interfund transfers, receivables and payables, pension obligations, and other information.

Standard Setting in Governmental Accounting. Throughout this overview of governmental accounting, typical or usual practices have been described. A useful question is how standards are set in governmental accounting that

Table 22.3. Statement of Revenues, Expenses, and Changes in Retained Earnings: Year Ended June 30, 199? (Thousands of Dollars).

	Public Transit Fund
Operating Revenues	
Charges for services	$4,251
Total Operating Revenues	4,251
Operating Expenses	
Personal services	1,582
Contractual services	890
Materials and supplies	396
Utilities	784
Depreciation	674
Total Operating Expenses	4,326
Operating Income (Loss)	(75)
Nonoperating Revenue (Expenses)	
Interest revenue	39
Interest expense	(588)
Total Nonoperating Revenues (Expenses)	(549)
Net Income	(624)
Retained Earnings, Beginning of Fiscal Year	1,255
Retained Earnings, End of Fiscal Year	631

lead to these patterns of practice. Without standards to guide the accounting practices of governments, the interpretation of governmental accounting information would be virtually impossible. Before 1984, several organizations were involved in governmental accounting standard setting, including the American Institute of Certified Public Accountants, the Financial Accounting Standards Board, and the National Committee on Governmental Accounting, which was the most prominent. For a variety of reasons, including questions of legitimacy, commitment, representativeness, and funding, this situation was both unsatisfactory and, at times, controversial. It was compounded by the severe fiscal crises of the late 1970s, in which accounting problems were partly to blame, and by a series of conceptual and empirical reports that were critical of governmental accounting practices (Coopers & Lybrand, 1976; Davidson and others, 1977; Anthony, 1978).

While the need for change had been recognized for some time, the road to reform was not an easy one (Chan, 1985). The newly formed Governmental Accounting Standards Board (GASB) began in 1984, as a unit of the Financial Accounting Foundation (Governmental Accounting Standards Board, 1985b, p. xiii), "to promulgate standards of financial accounting and reporting with respect to activities and transactions of state and local government entities." The GASB more than merely replaces the National Committee on Governmental Accounting, since it has a full-time staff and budget. Moreover, its founding ended some of the jurisdictional disputes among contending organizations: Henceforth, the GASB was at the top of the standard-setting hierarchy. Since 1984, the GASB has produced several important statements that have significantly changed governmental accounting standards, and it has undertaken a substantial research agenda to support its work. The GASB has introduced a new level of energy, thoughtfulness, and rigor to standard setting in governmental accounting, and these should be factors in its scheduled review in 1989.

Alternative Uses and Users of Governmental Accounting

There are times when the intricacies of governmental accounting overshadow the fact that accounting systems are designed to help a diverse set of users as they strive toward government's important goals. Governmental accounting would be a failure if it affected only accountants. On the contrary, many of the key aspects of governmental accounting now under review by the GASB and others are shaped by the needs of nonaccountant users. In fact, the accounting system can be viewed as a component of financial decision making, which itself is a critical facet of management and policy. This part of the chapter uses a simple framework comprising, first, the financial decision makers who use accounting information and, second, the objectives of these government decision makers, to help explain the roles (both actual and potential) that governmental accounting plays in public management and policymaking.

In government, there is a long list of individuals and groups who use accounting information to support their objectives. Government managers at all levels of organizations, who are responsible for the operations of government, are important internal users of accounting information. Jones, Scott, Kimbro, and Ingram (1985, p. 24), in a recent research review, identify a diverse group of external users of accounting information, including "external management and oversight bodies; taxpayers, voters and other citizenry; investors and creditors; grantors and other voluntary resource providers; customers; employee and labor groups; regulatory bodies; vendors; public-interest groups; and independent auditors." Each of these groups is involved in its own decision-making processes that have significant financial components, and each group has a legitimate need for the government's accounting information. Since internal managers have substantially greater access to the government's accounting information, the discussion in this section separates internal from external users. This division, useful for discussion, recognizes that internal and external users are sometimes interested in the same issue, and that external users are diverse.

Government has numerous objectives, and three of its ideal objectives are closely linked to accounting and finance: efficiency, effectiveness, and equity. *Efficiency* refers to the least-cost use of resources in the production and delivery of output, and *effectiveness* is the measurement of goal accomplishment. *Equity,* in this context, refers to the fair distribution of outputs across different groups and across time. Efficiency, cost-effectiveness, and equity criteria are integral to government's objectives, and their implementation requires accounting information. Two other ideal objectives support service delivery: *management control,* which has a significant financial and accounting component (Anthony and Young, 1984), and *sound financial condition* (Berne and Schramm, 1986).

A six-part framework, based on internal and external users and on objectives related to these five ideal attributes, can be used to explore the alternative purposes of accounting information in government. This framework, and examples of accounting-related questions for each of its six parts, are presented in Table 22.4. (It should be noted that accountability is often listed as a separate goal of government. In this discussion, however, accountability provides a critical rationale for the inclusion of external users in the framework; thus, accountability objectives are met by the provision of information to external groups.)

Internal Control. Governments monitor and control their activities by a variety of means. Most governments have highly prescribed internal control mechanisms, where the accounting system plays a critical role in conjunction with the budget. Legal compliance is one component of a control system. In many cases, the budget approval process creates a series of legal directives for the government to follow, and the accounting system is often designed to ensure such behavior. In most cases, individual funds and accounts are

Table 22.4. Examples of Accounting-Related Questions Posed by
Financial Decision Makers.

Objectives of Financial Decision Makers	Financial Decision Makers	
	Internal	External
Control	Are expenditures being charged to the proper accounts? Do records of investments match the physical instruments on deposit?	Are expenditures being made according to budget? How do revenues compare with forecasts? Are contracts being let in an appropriate manner?
Efficient, effective, and equitable resource allocation	Should a service be produced by the government, or should it be contracted for? Is a new method of delivering a service cost-effective?	How do the costs per unit of output of the services provided by the government compare to other, similar governments, or over time? Are all groups receiving appropriate levels of service?
Maintenance of a sound financial condition	What are the surpluses or deficits of the various funds of the government, on an actual and a forecast basis? How should the capital program be financed?	What is the risk that the government's debt service payments will not be made in a timely fashion? How sound is the financing for the government's pension system?

established, and detailed procedures are designed to identify and stop unauthorized expenditures. The accounting system is often structured so that the level of control varies with the level of the organization. For example, a line manager may have unlimited authority to spend on specific expenditure categories, up to a prescribed amount, while a department manager may have authority to shift funds among categories. Regardless of the specific configuration, the accounting system is used extensively to ensure legal compliance.

The accounting system has the potential to go beyond the legal or budgetary compliance found in most governments. A significant part of governmental operations is devoted to the production and distribution of services; and, with the severe resource constraints facing governments, controlling the cost of these operations is essential. In many cases, a financial accounting system (such as the one described earlier in this chapter) cannot satisfactorily support operational cost control, and a managerial or cost accounting system is required. Such a system is commonplace in many for-profit organizations, but is only now beginning to be used in governments (Oatman, 1979; Kelley, 1984). A cost accounting system records the dollar value of the resources (or inputs) used to produce a good or a specific service (or output), and it often distinguishes among different types of inputs (current versus capital or personnel versus nonpersonnel costs), as well as between direct and indirect costs. For example, the costs per lane-mile to pave highways, per unit to rehabilitate housing, or per patient to treat a disease could be determined by a cost accounting system.

Variance analysis is an effective cost-control technique for services where input quantities vary with outputs in a sytematic manner (Finkler, 1982). Using the cost accounting system and established standards for unit prices of inputs and input-output ratios for a specific activity, variance analysis assesses which operations are out of control and helps trace the control problem to input purchase prices or to the quantity of inputs used to produce the outputs. Suppose, for example, a county's street repairing operation is costing more than expected. Variance analysis can help determine whether the overrun is due to labor or to material expenditures. Moreover, where materials are concerned, variance analysis can be used to assess whether the paving material is more costly than was expected, or whether more of the material is being used than was planned. This technique supports a "management by exception" approach to cost control.

External Control. Unlike for-profit organizations, governments have a diverse set of external groups for whom aspects of control are legitimate concerns. The financial statements, described above, that present actual revenues, expenditures, and comparisons with the budget are key in meeting the needs of external users in this area. Jones, Scott, Kimbro, and Ingram (1985, pp. 38–39) found that comparisons of actual figures with the original budget and with the modified budget, along with narrative explanations of variances, are extremely useful to investors, legislative and oversight groups, and citizens' groups, the three external users included in their study. Actual practices reflect this user demand, since a recent survey (Ingram and Robbins, 1987) found that among cities, counties, and school districts, the statements that compare budgeted and actual figures are presented in over 90 percent of cases for amended budgets and in over 75 percent of cases for original budgets.

Even with this high level of disclosure, questions can be raised about the quality of accountability provided by governments in this area. For many governments, even though a budget may be available to external groups in considerable detail, comparisons of budgeted and actual figures are often presented in highly aggregated form. In addition, many governments use different accounting conventions for their budgets and financial statements, and sometimes even different categories of revenues and expenditures (Green, 1987). Ingram and Robbins (1987) found that narrative explanations of key differences between budgeted and actual figures, and the reasons for significant overspending or underspending, were reported in only a little over half the cases they studied.

There are other aspects of external control where accounting information is important. External groups are often concerned with the taxing, contracting, purchasing, and personnel policies of governments, and financial disclosures regarding past practices in these areas rely heavily on accounting systems.

Internal Resource Allocation. Being able to spend the budgeted amount is necessary but not sufficient for acceptable performance. The need to raise and spend money efficiently, effectively, and equitably is a paramount concern of governmental managers. In many cases, the financial accounting system is not designed to support decisions in this area and thus must be supplemented by information on costs, either from a cost accounting system or from special studies. Unfortunately, many governmental managers who are responsible for particular activities do not have access to accounting information in the proper form for many of the key questions they must address.

The first prerequisite for many decisions in this area is the organization of accounting information by activity or program. Most operational decisions that involve efficiency and effectiveness need information at this level, rather than at the more aggregate departmental level. If a typical government accounting system has activity or program data, these are often not in the proper format, because of the fund structure or the use of expenditures (which ignore certain costs) rather than expenses. Even when information from a cost accounting system is available, additional analysis is often required. In the case of contracts, for example, one issue to address is an estimate of the incremental costs that will be incurred with governmental production, compared to the contracting method; or, if a break-even analysis is being performed, fixed and variable costs must be identified. For most governments, greater availability and analysis of cost information will improve decisions on resource allocation.

In decisions on resource allocation, accounting information needs to be combined with other variables, which often have their own measurement difficulties. For example, output measurement must be concerned with quality, service accomplishments must deal with goal definition, and equity issues incorporate a series of difficult value judgments. Whenever additional information, on accounting or other topics, is needed for a decision, costs should be compared between information generation and potential benefits of the decision. Information costs should not be ignored, particularly in areas where measurement is not straightforward.

External Resource Allocation. In most cases, society cannot rely on markets to ensure the efficiency and effectiveness of governmental operations. Moreover, equity is a governmental objective that has no counterpart in the private sector. As a result, numerous external groups monitor resource allocation in government, and they must rely on accounting information in that process. (Only some of the governments that have this information internally available provide it to external groups.)

The disclosure of efficiency and effectiveness information to external groups has been enhanced by the budgeting reforms of the last forty years.

Budgets are public documents, and recent budgeting trends, with their tendency to focus on activities and associated expenditures or costs, have increased the availability of this information. In many budget presentations, actual results (based in part on an accounting system), rather than budgeted amounts, are used in efficiency and effectiveness measures. In some cases, the efficiency and effectiveness measures are presented as part of the government's budget, while in others a separate report on these aspects of government performance is produced. The budget of the City of Dayton, Ohio (1985), is an example of the former; the *Mayor's Management Report* produced by the City of New York (1985) is an example of the latter. This type of disclosure to external groups is now under study by the GASB, which hopes to determine whether standards for routine reporting of efficiency and effectiveness measures are feasible and desirable.

In most governments, information for assessing the equity of operations is unavailable to external groups, mostly because the basic information needed to measure equity is not generated on a regular basis. In many jurisdictions, one issue of concern to external groups is whether spending and services are equitable for different geographical areas or for population groups that vary by race and income. Conceptually, accounting information could be presented to help in the analysis of equity (defined in this way), but this procedure is not common. A separate issue is equity across time. The focus on expenditures in government can obscure the link between the generation that is paying for an asset and the one that is receiving its benefits. Analyses of equity almost always must rely on special data-gathering efforts, rather than on the routine reports of an accounting system.

Sound Internal Finances. Since the fiscal crises of the mid 1970s, maintenance of sound financial condition has been emphasized as a goal of government. Government managers and policymakers need to be aware of the myriad factors that affect governments' financial conditions. *Financial condition* is defined broadly here (Berne and Schramm, 1986, p. 5) as the government's ability "to meet . . . financial obligations as they come due, in both the short and the long run, while raising resources and providing public goods and services." According to this definition, financial condition has both a short-run and a long-run dimension, includes economic as well as financial resources, incorporates a multidimensional or multiconstituency concept, and takes implicit as well as explicit obligations into account. One way to implement such a definition is to measure the revenue, expenditure, debt, pension, and internal resource components of financial condition. Examples of measures in these areas include tax capacity, expenditure needs, debt burdens, unfunded pension obligations, and fund balances.

The information required for measuring financial condition, according to this broad definition, is quite extensive and includes (but is not limited to) accounting information. The interpretation of timely financial reports is an important first step in addressing financial condition. Cash flows are important short-run accounting data, and these are usually available to internal managers in cash statements and forecasts. In the intermediate run, the statement of revenues, expenditures, and changes in fund balances (described earlier) are also essential to the evaluation of financial condition. In the longer run, forecasts of revenues, expenditures, and surpluses and deficits are becoming more commonplace in governments (Bahl and Schroeder, 1984; Zorn, 1982) and often rely on accounting information.

The current structure of government accounting is not ideally suited to the measurement of some of the longer-run aspects of financial condition. In the area of fixed assets, generally accepted accounting standards for governments are particularly weak, and this weakness may also be reflected in the management of fixed assets and in capital programs more generally (Urban Institute, 1984; Leonard, 1985). In fact, a case can be made that one of the causes of the current "infrastructure crisis" is governments' poor accounting for fixed assets. Not only are fixed assets and depreciation excluded from most funds in governments; inadequate accounting for fixed assets is also one of the most frequently cited exceptions to generally accepted accounting principles.

Sound External Finances. Although a government manager has the primary responsibility for maintaining a government's financial health, others share this concern. Many external groups, such as investors, creditors, taxpayers, rating agencies, oversight bodies, and employee groups, have strong interest in a government's financial condition. These external groups rely on the government's disclosure of accounting and other finance information, but they also use information from other sources, such as the U.S. Bureau of the Census, the Department of Labor, and state-level economic and finance data sources.

Because government financial condition lacks absolutes and "bottom lines," the measurement of financial condition is largely a comparative process. In the assessment of financial condition, there is a tendency among internal managers to prefer time series analysis as a comparative base—that is, to ask whether a government is weaker or stronger than in the past. This tendency is illustrated by the International City Management Association (1986), whose handbooks on financial analysis use no cross-jurisdictional comparisons. That approach stands in sharp contrast to analyses by external evaluators and researchers wherein comparisons across jurisdictions are combined with time series analysis to measure financial condition. In comparing across jurisdictions, care must be exercised to ensure the comparability of data and that of the jurisdictions themselves.

Given heightened interest in assessing governments' financial condition, some governments are beginning to go beyond the disclosures normally provided by annual financial reports and are reporting measures that reflect broader concerns. For example, the City of Seattle (1985) regularly reports on forty measures of different aspects of its financial condition and makes recommendations based on the trends shown in these measures. The City of New York (1986) combines time series and cross-jurisdictional analysis to report on its financial condition.

Future Trends in Governmental Accounting

In contrast to many years of relative stability in governmental accounting, the current pace of change and self-examination is remarkably high, and the trend is toward increased sophistication of accounting systems and financial reporting. There are several significant current changes in financial accounting. The reassessment of the basis of accounting/measurement focus has led to the analysis of alternatives that formerly were unthinkable in governmental accounting. Although the standard for governmental funds is not equivalent to that found in a for-profit organization, the accrual of total financial resources, as a basis of accounting, is better suited to today's government than is the modified-accrual basis. Improved standards for the reporting of pension liabilities on the basis of a standardized methodology (Governmental Accounting Standards Board, 1986) is also an example of a reform that has increased the usefulness of financial reporting.

Unresolved issues in financial accounting and reporting are being actively debated in the profession. With the proliferation of authorities and revenue bond financing, the boundaries of the government, for financial reporting purposes (known as the entity issue in accounting), are often complex and open to question. When government consists of multiple funds and organizations, there is no single unified accounting report on the government that meets the external needs examined in this chapter. As discussed earlier, accounting for fixed assets is primitive in government, and there are many differences of opinion over how to remedy this situation. Finally, accountants have traditionally reported on a well-defined set of transactions, a set that has included neither efficiency and effectiveness measures nor many indicators of financial condition. The question here is whether governmental accounting should expand its role in these areas. In each of these cases, there are serious changes under consideration that have particular relevance to external users, but they affect internal managers also.

It is no coincidence that the new standard-setting organization, the GASB, was formed concurrently with the reemergence of many issues. The GASB has undertaken a research agenda of its own and fostered debate among users and preparers of accounting information. There is also evidence (Ingram and Robbins, 1987) that, over the past few years, governments' compliance with existing and generally accepted accounting standards has improved.

Changes in technology are tied to many improvements in governmental accounting. Finances were one of the first areas to be computerized, initially with mainframe information systems and more recently with mini- and microcomputers. These trends are likely to continue as users share technology, prices for hardware continue to decline, and software becomes more user-friendly. Information systems that link accounting and nonaccounting data, on-line accounting systems, and decision-support systems are no longer considered innovative in this area.

Another area where change is now beginning in earnest is costing. As the potential benefits of computerized systems are better understood, and as the incentives for efficiency and effectiveness in government are increased, cost-benefit calculations on the development of cost analyses and cost accounting systems should lead to greater implementation of this technology.

Summary

Resource scarcity has increased the importance of the financial information generated by accounting systems and expanded the pool of potential users of that information. This chapter presents an overview of the structure of governmental accounting systems, since their comprehensibility is a necessary precondition of their effective use. Internal and external users of accounting information are concerned with control, with efficient, effective, and equitable resource allocation, and with the maintenance of sound financial condition. Accounting information currently satisfies only some needs in these areas. Several important changes now under consideration are aimed at meeting users' needs. Governmental accounting systems do not always tell us what we would like to know, but they do tell us a great deal more than they once did.

References

Anthony, R. N. *Financial Accounting in Nonbusiness Organizations. An Exploratory Study of Conceptual Issues.* Stamford, Conn.: Financial Accounting Standards Board, 1978.

Anthony, R. N., and Young, D. W. *Management Control in Nonprofit Organizations.* (3rd ed.) Homewood Ill.: Irwin, 1984.

Bahl, R., and Schroeder, L. "Multi-Year Forecasting in Annual Budgeting." *Public Budgeting & Finance,* 1984, *4* (1), 3–13.

Berne, R., and Schramm, R. *The Financial Analysis of Governments.* Englewood Cliffs, N.J.: Prentice-Hall, 1986.

Chan, J. L. "The Birth of the Governmental Accounting Standards Board: How? Why? What Next?" In J. L. Chan (ed.), *Research in Governmental and Non-Profit Accounting.* Vol. 1. Greenwich, Conn.: JAI Press, 1985.

City of Dayton. *Annual Operating Budget.* Dayton, Ohio: City of Dayton, 1985.

City of New York. *Mayor's Management Report.* New York: City of New York, 1985.

City of New York. *City of New York, Comparative Analysis: Financial and Economic Indicators, Fiscal Year 1985.* New York: Office of the Comptroller, City of New York, 1986.

City of Seattle. *Financial Indicators Report.* Seattle, Wash.: City of Seattle, 1985.

Coopers & Lybrand. *Financial Disclosure Practices of the American Cities.* New York: Coopers & Lybrand, 1976.

Davidson, S., and others. *Financial Reporting by State and Local Government Units.* Chicago: Center for Management of Public and Nonprofit Enterprise, Graduate School of Business, University of Chicago, 1977.

Finkler, S. A. "The Pyramid Approach: Increasing the Usefulness of Flexible Budgeting." *Hospital Financial Management,* 1982, *12* (2), 30–39.

Freeman, R. J., Shoulders, C. D., and Lynn, E. S. *Governmental and Nonprofit Accounting: Theory and Practice.* (3rd ed.) Englewood Cliffs, N.J.: Prentice-Hall, 1988.

Governmental Accounting Standards Board. *An Analysis of Issues Related to Measurement Focus and Basis of Accounting—Governmental Funds.* Stamford, Conn.: Governmental Accounting Standards Board, 1985a.

Governmental Accounting Standards Board. *Codification of Governmental Accounting and Reporting Standards, as of November 1, 1984.* Stamford, Conn.: Governmental Accounting Standards Board and Government Accounting Research Foundation, 1985b.

Governmental Accounting Standards Board. *Disclosure of Pension Information by Public Employee Retirement Systems and State and Local Government Employers.* Stamford, Conn.: Governmental Accounting Standards Board, 1986.

Governmental Accounting Standards Board. *Objectives of Financial Reporting.* Stamford, Conn.: Governmental Accounting Standards Board, 1987.

Green, C. B. "The Use and Usefulness of Governmental Financial Reports: The Perspective of the Citizen-Taxpayer Organizations." In J. L. Chan (ed.), *Research in Governmental and Non-Profit Accounting.* Vol. 3, Part B. Greenwich, Conn.: JAI Press, 1987.

Hay, L. E. *Accounting for Governmental and Nonprofit Entities.* (7th ed.) Homewood, Ill.: Irwin, 1985.

Henke, E. O. *Introduction to Nonprofit Organization Accounting.* (2nd ed.) Boston, Mass.: Kent, 1985.

Ingram, R. W., and Robbins, W. A. *Financial Reporting Practices of Local Governments.* Stamford, Conn.: Governmental Accounting Standards Board, 1987.

International City Management Association. *Evaluating Financial Condition: A Handbook for Local Government.* (2nd ed.) Washington, D.C.: International City Management Association, 1986.

Jones, D. B., Scott, R. B., Kimbro, L., and Ingram, R. *The Needs of Users of Governmental Financial Reports.* Stamford, Conn.: Governmental Accounting Standards Board, 1985.

Kelley, J. L. *Costing Government Services: A Guide for Decision Making.* Washington, D.C.: Government Finance Research Center, Government Finance Officers Association, 1984.

Leonard, H. B. "Measuring and Reporting the Financial Condition of Public Organizations." In J. L. Chan (ed.), *Research in Governmental and Non-Profit Accounting.* Vol. 1. Greenwich, Conn.: JAI Press, 1985.

Municipal Finance Officers Association. *Governmental Accounting, Auditing, and Financial Reporting.* Chicago: Municipal Finance Officers Association, 1980.

Oatman, D. "It's Time for Productivity Accounting in Government." *Governmental Finance,* 1979, *8* (3), 9–14.

Securities and Exchange Commission. *Transactions in Securities of the City of New York.* Washington, D.C.: Subcommittee on Economic Stabilization of the Committee on Banking, Finance, and Urban Affairs, U.S. House of Representatives, 1977.

Tierney, C. E., and Calder, P. T. *Financial Reporting for American Cities and Counties, 1986.* New York: Elsevier, 1986.

Urban Institute. *Guides to Managing Urban Capital.* 6 vols. Washington, D.C.: Urban Institute Press, 1984.

Zorn, C. K. "Issues and Problems in Econometric Forecasting: Guidance for Local Revenue Forecasters." *Public Budgeting & Finance,* 1982, *2* (3), 100–110.

23

John L. Mikesell

Revenue Administration

Most government services cannot be self-financed. That is, services are not provided through buyer-seller interaction; payment is not required before an individual can receive a service. Because the consumer of the service cannot be made to pay directly for it, government must employ its coercive power to collect payments that, in the aggregate, finance its operations. Because there is no buyer-seller interaction, financing the cost of service is a planning decision, separate from choices about what services will be provided. That financing decision establishes who will bear the burden of shifting resources from private to public use. The options selected will influence both the funds available to the government and the social and economic impacts of that transfer on society.

Patterns of Government Revenue

Governments raise revenue for general spending from taxes, charges for services, and miscellaneous sources like sale or rental of property. These general revenues to government equalled $1,106.8 billion in fiscal 1986, including $578.5 billion in federal revenues, $294.9 billion in state revenues, and $233.4 billion in local revenues (U.S. Bureau of the Census, 1987, p. 2). Gross national product was $4,235 billion in 1986, and so government general revenues reflect claims on about one-fourth of gross national product (U.S. Department of Commerce, 1987, p. 5). Governments also collect revenue from monopoly enterprises like municipal utilities and state liquor stores ($47.2 billion in 1986), but much of this revenue simply covers the cost of the enterprises, leaving little to support general governmental functions. Similarly, the $361.5 billion of insurance trust revenue—revenues for the social security system, unemployment compensation, employee retirement, and so on—is not available for general government use. The focus here is on the revenue that a government raises itself for spending on general functions—*own-source general revenue,* in public finance terminology.

Taxes. Taxes constitute around three-quarters of general revenue. The share is slightly higher for federal and state governments (82 percent and 77 percent, respectively) and slightly lower for local governments (62 percent). The three levels of government have fallen into an uneasy separation by tax source. The federal government dominates the income base, state governments dominate the consumption base, and, almost by default, local governments dominate the property base.

The federal government collects 60 percent of its own-source general revenue from the individual income tax, over 80 percent of all individual income tax collected by all levels of government. Because the federal government also levies tax on corporate income (slightly more than 10 percent of its own-source general revenue) and finances its massive social insurance trust system from payroll taxes and similar special income taxes, its dominance of the income base is indeed substantial. The major federal income tax reductions of the early 1980s did not change that domination.

Separation is not complete: States raised almost 30 percent of their own-source general revenue from individual and corporate income taxes (forty states levy broad individual income taxes, and forty-five states tax corporate net income) (Advisory Commission on Intergovernmental Relations, 1978, pp. 66, 67, 86–88), and local governments collected almost 4 percent of own-source general revenue from income taxes. Several states receive more revenue from income taxes than from any other tax. Furthermore, income taxes are likely to become more important in state and local revenue systems. Because the federal Tax Reform Act of 1986 preserved deductibility of state and local income taxes while ending deductibility of sales taxes, state and local governments can reduce the net cost of their taxes by switching to income from sales taxes. That should eventually bend state and local tax policy toward heavier use of the income tax.

Taxes on sales, general and selective, are the largest state tax source. Forty-five states have general sales taxes. All states have selective excise taxes, normally on motor fuel, cigarettes, and alcoholic beverages, plus some other items (Advisory Commission on Intergovernmental Relations, 1978, pp. 89, 97, 98), but state governments collect almost twice as much revenue from the general tax as from the whole array of selective excises. States frequently permit local governments to levy selective or general sales taxes, often piggybacked onto similar state taxes. Local general sales taxes produced almost 7 percent of local own-source general revenue, second only to the property tax in yield; local selective excise taxes generated almost 3 percent. The federal government makes trivial use of the sales base. It collects no general sales tax (an anomaly among central governments of developed countries) and only minor amounts from customs duties and selective excise taxes.

Taxes on property holdings yielded almost three-quarters of local government tax revenue. Despite the passage in California of Proposition

13 in 1978, and despite other actions in the revolt against the property tax and continual attacks on the tax by scholars, politicians, and the media, the property tax share of local government taxes is now only about 5 percentage points below its level a decade ago. The property tax has great staying power, probably because it permits more local autonomy than other taxes do.

Charges. Current charges reflect prices established in the political process; although conditions of service cost and customer reaction are not without influence, political choices by executive and legislative bodies dominate the interaction of buyers and sellers when governments sell services. Payments by customers, not taxpayers, constitute considerably less than 15 percent of the government's own-source general revenue but more than 20 percent of local revenue. Postal service and education charges dominate the smaller federal and state percentages (43.9 percent for the postal service and 59.8 percent for education). Local charge revenue is more broadly spread. Substantial shares come from the operation of hospitals (33.4 percent), sewerage systems (15.8 percent), and education (13.4 percent). Greater use of charges is tantalizing, because of popular resistance to taxes and some feeling that greater use of market concepts might improve government operations. Formidable barriers to the expanded use of charges include technical questions in designing and enforcing charges and agencies' reluctance to limit free access to government services.

Miscellaneous Revenue. Miscellaneous general revenue encompasses several special flows largely outside the topic at hand, including interest from government deposits, special assessments, and sales of surplus property. The category also includes net state lottery proceeds ($4.7 billion in fiscal 1986), only 1.6 percent of states' own-source general revenue. These games of chance, which somewhat more than half the states operate, provide entertainment but small revenue. Other public monopolies include publicly owned utilities (electric power, water, and the like) and publicly operated liquor stores. Their gross revenue of $44.8 billion contributes relatively little to the operation of general government.

Criteria for Tax Policy

Taxes are compulsory payments to government. They purchase no particular services and are neither prices paid for services nor contributions to government. Government coercion is used to extract the funds that provide public services. This situation contrasts with that of voluntary payment in market exchanges.

Break and Pechman (1975, p. 4) summarize the fundamental principle of tax policy: "The primary goal of taxation is to transfer control of resources from one group in the society to another and to do so in ways that do not jeopardize, and may even facilitate, the attainment of other economic goals." Governments must purchase resources to provide services. Taxes reduce private purchasing power and, hence, private claims on resources. Tax revenues finance government purchase of resources and complete the shifting of resources from private to public use. Tax policy should strive to accomplish that shift with the least harm to the economy and to society.

Criteria for analyzing a tax policy include the policy's capacity to generate revenue, its equity, its economic effects, and collectability of taxes. Counting votes on tax questions is, however, characteristic of neither sound revenue analysis nor fiscal leadership. Because an individual's payment of a particular tax ordinarily has no effect on whether a public service is available for that person's enjoyment, most people would prefer to have taxes paid by others. Recall Senator Long's principle of tax policy: "Don't tax you, don't tax me, tax that fellow behind the tree" (Reese, 1978, p. 199). Thus, public opinion seldom constitutes a criterion for revenue choices. Nevertheless, opinion may help identify approaches to revenue changes, and public opinion can be marshalled to stimulate legislative action; popular opinion about the unfairness of the federal income tax (Advisory Commission on Intergovernmental Relations, 1987, p. 5) certainly assisted passage of the 1986 tax reform.

Revenue Generation. Taxes may be levied for nonrevenue purposes— for example, taxes imposed at punitively high rates to constrain undesirable activity, or applied to monitor activity—but revenue is normally the objective. A tax is therefore normally undesirable unless it can raise meaningful revenue at a socially acceptable rate.

Any tax base has a maximum yield, and yield increases as the rate applied to that base increases, but not in direct proportion to the rate increase. Above some rate, further rate increases so discourage the taxed activity, or so encourage the activity to enter the underground economy, that collections decline. For example, it would be foolish to accept a cigarette tax to finance primary and secondary education in the state: The relatively small base would disappear into bootleg ventures when the necessary large rate was applied. Political or legal limits are more likely to constrain rates before this economic limit, but revenue policy must recognize the finite revenue prospects from each tax base. In general, large financing tasks are better handled by large tax bases. High rates on smaller bases are likely to create economic distortions and to discriminate against individuals or firms who must pay.

The revenue-yield criterion has dynamic as well as static, or absolute, dimensions. The tax may contribute to short-term budget balancing through stability in recession, and it may facilitate long-term stability by increasing rapidly enough to accommodate public spending demands driven by economic growth and development.

State and local governments are particularly sensitive to dramatic declines in the tax base. Because such units normally must balance their operating budgets, the responsiveness to recession and expansion that can act as an important macroeconomic stabilizer for the federal government can devastate these governments. Among the major tax sources, taxes on corporate profits and retail sales show considerable sensitivity to national economic cycles. Real property taxes show virtually no such sensitivity. Individual income taxes are in an intermediate position (Mikesell, 1984; Carnevale, 1986). The need for stability provides a strong reason for basing local revenue structures on property taxes. Governments with greater capacity to deal with deficits may rely more heavily on fluctuation-sensitive taxes.

The second dynamic element of revenue yield is responsiveness to economic growth. The demand for most government services grows at least as rapidly as the economy does, and, for many services, it grows even more rapidly. Unless the revenue base also grows, a government must either continually increase its statutory tax rates or choke off services. The revenue elasticity of tax bases (a coefficient that estimates the percentage increase in a base that results from a 1 percent increase in economic activity) varies widely. General sales taxes usually have elasticities of about 1.0; in other words, an increase in economic activity of 1.0 percent can be expected to increase the sales tax base by about 1.0 percent. Personal income taxes have elasticities averaging around 1.75 (an increase in economic activity of 1.0 percent would increase the base by about 1.75 percent) (Advisory Commission on Intergovernmental Relations, 1978, p. 254). Elasticities of property taxes depend critically on base assessment practices but are well below 1.0 (Mikesell, 1978). Major selective excise elasticities usually are well below 1.0 (Advisory Commission on Intergovernmental Relations, 1978, p. 254; Bowman and Mikesell, 1983). Governments that rely heavily on sources of low elasticity will face continual problems in responding to service demands.

Equity. How should the cost of government be distributed? Two philosophies dominate: Cost should be borne according to the benefits individuals receive from public service; and cost should be allocated according to individual ability to bear it. The focus of analysis is on individuals, because they ultimately must bear the cost of a tax on a business. Business taxes end up as higher prices to customers, lower payments to suppliers, or lower returns to owners; customers, suppliers, and owners are all ultimately individuals.

The benefits-received approach is a quasi-market approach. Individuals pay if and only if they benefit from a service. The approach prevents the oversupply of public service that can result when individuals receive service without bearing full cost, as well as the undersupply that can result when individuals must pay more than the value of the services they expect to receive. This approach prevents some in society from benefiting at the expense of others, because only beneficiaries must pay, and they pay in proportion to the benefits they receive.

The primary problem with the benefits-received philosophy is in its application. First, there is no method for establishing the individual benefit received from a particular public service, and without knowledge of what share of total benefits from a service an individual receives, there is no basis for allocating the cost of that service to the beneficiary. Second, many government programs are designed to help low-income families, to redistribute affluence, and a tax system based on market exchange would undo that transfer. Thus, measurement problems and redistribution motives severely limit the use of benefit-received principles. Only taxes on motor fuel are regularly defended on this basis: A tax on motor fuel divides the cost of highway provision among the primary beneficiaries, the consumers of the fuel that is used on those highways.

The ability-to-pay principle seeks to assign tax shares on taxbearing capacity, both horizontally and vertically. Horizontal equity demands that taxpayers with equal affluence pay equal tax. Among the reasons why a tax may fail this test are administrative problems (the property tax assessment system often places radically different tax bills on different properties of equivalent value), taxpayers' tastes (a tax on soft drinks burdens only their consumers), and compliance tactics (shrewd tax advisers may cut tax liability for some). The 1986 federal tax reform sought, with modest success, to achieve "more nearly equal treatment of taxpayers with similar incomes . . . by eliminating many of the deductions, exemptions, and credits which provide special tax reductions for some taxpayers" (Kiefer and Nelson, 1986, p. 193). Discovery of such inequities can be an important stimulus for reform.

Vertical equity considers the relative tax burdens paid by individuals in different economic circumstances. Most would argue that people with more capacity should pay more tax; but that argument does not guide tax policy, because virtually every tax extracts more from more affluent individuals. The issue is the intended redistributional effect of the tax: How should the tax alter the economic status of people with more affluence relative to people with less? If the tax is progressive (that is, tax paid as a fraction of total affluence rises with affluence), then the tax redistributes income from high-affluence to low-affluence individuals. If the tax is regressive (that is, tax paid as a fraction of total affluence falls with affluence), then the tax redistributes income from low-affluence to high-affluence individuals. If the tax is proportional (that is, tax paid as a fraction of affluence is constant across affluence classes), then the tax will not redistribute at all.

The distributional question is one of choice; no body of knowledge establishes the best pattern (Blum and Kalven, 1953). Regressivity has few political champions, even though several major taxes are generally regressive. The choice between proportionality and progressivity is less clear. Some argue that the tax system should aggressively redistribute income, and others argue that the tax system should leave redistribution to direct expenditure or income-transfer programs.

How equitably do the major taxes treat individuals of different economic status? Because the answer hinges on identifying those whose economic position is worsened by the tax (not simply those who write checks to a government), attention must be paid to product price or factor income changes that may shift the tax burden away from the entity bearing the initial impact. Unfortunately, tracing that shifting pattern can be complex, and there remains reasonable doubt about most modern taxes (Pechman, 1985; Feldstein, 1987; Davies, 1971; Browning, 1985; Due, 1986; Aaron, 1975). The combined tax systems in the United States are proportional to slightly progressive, with progressivity in the federal system being reduced by regressivity in state and local systems (Pechman, 1987, p. 6).

Economic Effects. A tax should be neutral, distorting economic activity as little as possible. Unfortunately, taxes almost always create differences in after-tax returns that were not present in before-tax returns. A tax may distort the choice between work and leisure through high marginal rates on income. It may induce convoluted business operations and stimulate purchases in low-excise-tax havens, or it may discourage investment in capital goods, for instance. Individuals and businesses can be expected to respond to any tax that unbalances the comparative return that can be earned among two or more competing activities by choosing the activity with the higher net return; that imbalance causes an economic loss to society. Considerable analytical attention has been directed toward identifying an optimal tax structure, one that minimizes this economic loss (Sandmo, 1976; Ballard, Shoven, and Whalley, 1985). The questions have not been resolved, but much of the discussion leading to the 1986 federal tax reform did focus on the need to reduce the economic distortions created by the tax system and on the need to create a "level playing field" (Auerbach, 1987, p. 80).

Some, however, seek to use the tax system to bend the market, to alter private behavior in a socially desirable fashion. For example, the special provisions for individual retirement accounts are intended to encourage private saving for retirement. Because the revenue loss associated with preferences tends to be hidden and not subject to the continual review characteristic of direct appropriations, most observers argue against the use of tax systems for nonrevenue purposes. Taxes also can be designed to penalize undesirable actions. The federal "gas guzzler" tax, for example, attempts to induce fuel economy in new vehicles (and, in an important sense, any revenue produced by this tax represents a failure of the tax to achieve its basic objective). There is general consensus that taxes ought not to do economic harm, even if they do not stimulate desirable economic behavior.

Collectability. A tax must generate revenue at reasonable cost to society. Collection resources in themselves provide no social return; hence, they should be kept to the lowest level consistent with satisfactory and equitable compliance. Collection costs include both the cost of administration incurred by the government (costs showing up in government budgets) and the cost of compliance incurred by the taxpayer (fees paid to tax preparers and record keepers, and the effort exerted by the taxpayer in filing). Both cost components use resources, and so attention cannot be limited to either element alone. Federal estimates of return-filing effort (U.S. Office of Management and Budget, 1985) appear not to shape discussions of tax policy.

The need to control compliance costs was recognized as early as 1776, when Adam Smith's *Wealth of Nations* was originally published (Smith, [1776] 1937). Two of Smith's canons of taxation are as follows: "The tax which each individual is bound to pay ought to be certain, and not arbitrary. The time of payment, the manner of payment, the quantity to be paid, ought all to be clear and plain to the contributor, and to every other person. . . . Every tax ought to be levied at the time, or in the manner, in which it is most likely to be convenient for the contributor to pay it" (pp. 778–779). A reasonably certain and conveniently collectable tax—a simple tax, in recent discussions—should reduce compliance expenses and improve general compliance. Unfortunately, a tax that is simple (a poll tax or a head tax may be the simplest) may fail to be equitable (a poll tax takes account of neither taxbearing capacity nor receipt of public services), and so a balance is required. But the quest for a simple, convenient, and certain tax is legitimate. Recent research finds the compliance costs of income taxes, both federal and state, to be from 5 to 7 percent of revenue collected (Slemrod and Sorum, 1984). Other major taxes probably have lower compliance costs; real property taxes, for example, are taxpayer-passive, assigning virtually all collection functions to public officials, and sales taxes make heavy use of vendor systems already in place for nontax reasons (Due and Mikesell, 1983, pp. 327–328).

Administrative costs for individual taxes usually can be measured only imprecisely, because most revenue agencies face nonrevenue responsibilities and administer interrelated bundles of taxes, thus creating impossible problems in allocation of costs jointly attributable to several activities. The pattern is clear, however: Broad-based taxes are administered at less than 1.0 percent of revenue collected (Mikesell, 1986b, pp. 354–355). The Internal Revenue Service reports an overall cost of $0.48 per $100 collected in 1985 (Fratanduono, 1986, Table 22). Good-quality property tax administration, a standard seldom achieved, requires closer to 1.5 percent of collections (Welch, 1973, p. 50). Of course, collection costs for property taxes are almost entirely administrative, while there are substantial compliance costs for the other taxes.

Revenue Management: Yield and Equitable Enforcement. Steuerle (1986, p. 1) notes: "Taxes, like most costs, are undesirable in and of themselves. They are justified only by the benefits and services they finance." This revenue is vital, but revenue management operates with dual objectives. According to Penniman (1980, p. 173), "The tax official's service can be generalized only in terms of the value of the revenue he collects for the operation of all government and in the fairness with which he collects such revenue within the state's tax framework." The revenue administrator must focus on both revenue collected and the fairness with which that revenue is being collected.

Tax collection combines government administration and taxpayers' compliance. The particular combination of efforts depends on whether the taxpayers' role is active or passive (Mikesell, 1974). Taxpayer-passive taxes require minimal compliance effort from taxpayers. The typical real property tax, a passive tax, includes record maintenance, property value estimation, computation of tax bills, and delinquency control as direct administrative tasks. The tax requires no direct involvement by the property holder. Administration, not voluntary compliance by the taxpayer, is the key for such a tax.

Taxpayer-active taxes place substantial responsibility on the taxpayer, who "must supply all relevant information, compute the tax base, calculate the tax, and pay the tax, or some installment of it, when he files his return" (Shoup, 1969, p. 430). The federal individual income tax, a taxpayer-active tax, places record keeping, computation, and filing responsibilities on taxpayers or their agents. Administration for such taxes aims to foster voluntary tax compliance by protecting honest taxpayers from the low-cost advantage that would be held by dishonest competitors, and by establishing a creditable belief that evaders will be found, thus making voluntary compliance a reasonable decision.

Assessment. The critical element for the real property tax, the major passive tax in the United States, is assessment of property parcels, that is, the valuation of land and structures for tax purposes. The property tax base must be estimated for each taxable parcel in a way that produces consistent treatment of all entities. The task is not simple, particularly because assessing officers seldom have resources comparable to those of private appraisers doing similar work. Nevertheless, failure to achieve consistent and uniform assessment ensures that the property tax will treat many property holders unfairly.

Several studies (Bowman and Butcher, 1986; Geraci and Plourde, 1976; Bowman and Mikesell, 1978) have examined the elements that help produce uniform property tax assessments. The evidence generally suggests that uniformity is improved when assessments are legally intended to be a high fraction, ideally 100 percent, of current market value; when the effective property tax rate is high; when there is a formal property tax relief program; when tax maps are used to help locate and value properties; and when assessments are done annually. Assessment is not a simple task. Because it must be done for many parcels simultaneously to retain a uniform standard, and because the work encompasses many different types of property (houses, agricultural land and structures, commercial and industrial properties, undeveloped land), the function requires professional assessors, computer technology, and a property tax law that does not interfere with the quest for uniformity.

Cash Collection and Return Accounting

A major concern of the revenue system is cash collection and return accounting—precise record keeping of payments, and immediate control of cash remittances for government use (Penniman, 1980, chap. 5; Due and Mikesell, 1983, pp. 162–167). An accurate accounting of receipts ensures that later enforcement efforts are properly directed and that taxpayers cannot dodge collection (by claiming that "the check is in the mail" or that the return has been lost in processing). While speed is important to maintain current records, accuracy and completeness are somewhat more critical. Control of cash remittance should nevertheless be undertaken with utmost speed: Checks in transit do not benefit the government, and so the government should seek to gain control over funds as quickly as possible. Several governments use decentralized lockbox collection systems, sometimes operated under bank contracts, to accelerate check deposits. A few have authorized electronic funds transfers for even more speed. Because the basic collection function is almost the same as for a major bank or a credit card company, business experience and expertise, and even private contracting, may be helpful if confidentiality of data can be preserved.

Delinquency Control. This function must be closely linked to collection and accounting (Penniman, 1980, chap. 6; Due and Mikesell, 1983, chap. 7). An important output from taxpayer accounting is a listing of entities from whom expected returns have not been received. Contact with suspected delinquents, often by telephone, clears up a high percentage of cases. The same process is also often used to deal with uncollectable checks.

Audits. Analysts emphasize the significance of audits to achieving voluntary compliance: "The auditing of the taxpayer's books is the usual means whereby respect for the tax service in finding and punishing evasion is developed. On the effectiveness of this function hinges the percentage of tax evasion that each country will have" (Nowak, 1970, p. 68). Analysis of tax administration has presumed taxpayers' rational choice between the expected gain from evasion and the expected gain from substantial compliance (presuming no ethical aversion to gain from tax evasion). Revenue authorities influence that choice, changing the net expected gain from evasion by adjusting penalty rates and the probability of detection. Holland (1984, p. 334) notes that tax administrators' objectives include the desire both "to 'equalize' the degree of underreporting among the various sources" (equalization of degree of dishonesty or equity) and "to minimize the total amount not reported" (revenue maximization). If there were no costs to consider, these objectives would converge, because collection of all liabilities would cause zero error rates for all taxpayers. But administrative resources do have a cost. The cost of pursuing some liability in the quest for revenue maximization would exceed the revenue involved, and so not all uncollected liabilities are worth pursuing. This means that authorities can either maximize revenue or equalize error rates; they cannot do both.

Evidence shows the power of audits to induce voluntary compliance with the tax law. Witte and Woodbury (1985) show the importance of audit coverage on total tax compliance, with revenue impact extending beyond the collections directly recovered from audits. Mikesell (1985) found a similar result for state sales taxes. Both studies indicate the importance of audits for inducing voluntary compliance and clearly show the importance of selecting accounts for audit on the basis of impact on total compliance, rather than simply on the basis of direct audit recovery.

Enforcement. The final element in tax administration is enforcement, the application of sanctions to violators. The basic taxpayer calculus on compliance or evasion may be influenced by the use of higher penalties to reduce the expected gain from evasion, provided that the likelihood of detection (largely determined by audit coverage) is unchanged. Consistent and meaningful penalties and enforcement remedies, including tax sales, liens, closing of businesses, and the like, are a necessary part of collection. Taxes are not voluntary contributions; they raise money by coercion, even if compliance is induced from voluntary self-interest. The voluntary compliance rate has been estimated by the Internal Revenue Service at 91.8 percent for the federal individual income tax. Although that rate is high, it does mean that $24.8 billion in tax goes unreported. The compliance rate is lower for individual business income (73.7 percent) than for other individual income (93.4 percent) and, most important, the aggregate rate has fallen from 94.3 percent in 1965 (Fratanduono, 1986, p. 16).

In recent years, a number of states have conducted brief periods of amnesty to allow evaders to report and pay previously unpaid taxes without incurring criminal sanction or civil penalties (Mikesell, 1986a). These amnesties were generally conducted in a manner that did not harm honest taxpayers and did add some new filers to the system. Most programs were accompanied by radical increases in penalties for nonpayment, and more resources were devoted to enforcement after the amnesty period.

Considerations About Nontax Revenue

Governments normally obtain their revenue from taxes. The power to finance by coercion allows governments to supersede the financial constraints of exchange, and governments should specialize in providing desirable goods that are not capable of being financed by sales. Nevertheless, there are a few conditions under which a government may sell services to any willing buyer, and individuals may choose to purchase or decline them.

User charges—prices determined by political interaction, rather than by market forces—apply to government services that are closely related to a public good or to important governmental concerns. Examples include prices charged by police for special monitoring of security alarm systems (this service is linked to communication networks needed to provide general public safety), admission fees to municipal swimming pools (pools often are in open playground areas and are associated with recreation services), and tuition to state universities (this service is linked to the desire for an educated citizenry). Each service is closely linked to an important public function, but each one provides special returns to a select and identifiable group (Mushkin, 1972). Government monopoly revenue results from exclusive sale of a good or a service that has no connection with any necessary public service. Examples include revenue from municipal utilities, state liquor stores, and state lotteries. (Private entities often provide the same services in other locales.)

User Charges. Charges may apply to a service only when people can be excluded from its benefits. Otherwise, rational people would choose to benefit from the purchases made by others. Because purchase of the service is voluntary, individual demand can be measured according to whether consumers choose to buy it.

User charges may improve resource allocation, equity, and revenue. They can help administrators determine the needs and interests of the public because they require consumers to register willingness to bear the cost of a service. Without a charge, administrators know only how many people value the service enough to use it when it is provided free. There is no comparison between value and cost.

User charges can improve the overall equity of service finance between those who use special facilities and those who do not. With general revenue financing, the general public subsidizes users, regardless of their socioeconomic position. A user charge causes those who use a facility most heavily to pay more than others. That seems more equitable than forcing all to contribute, regardless of their use. User charges will, however, reduce the accessibility of services to low-income clients. If there are no unobtrusive ways of providing reduced-cost (or free) service to those with low income, the service in question is not a good candidate for user charges. But pointing to the poor is not a general reason for failure to charge the rich for individualized service.

Most services that governments provide cannot be offered through market sales, so service provision should not be based on sales revenues. If user charges are levied simply for revenue, then there is a grave question of whether the activities so financed ought to be governmental functions at all. At the same time, charge revenue can be a useful adjunct to taxes for support of public services. Such revenue is helpful, but policy ought not to be heavily based on it.

Government Enterprises. Governments have considerable power to sell goods and services, but such enterprise is the exception in the United States.

The trend is toward privatization of public entities, not publicization of private entities. Furthermore, the tendency is to handle situations that are immune to competitive pressure through regulation of a private provider, not through ownership by government.

Some government enterprises can be characterized as natural monopolies. According to Blair and Kaserman (1985, p. 34), "A natural monopoly exists when the forces of competition cause all firms but one to leave the industry. This is a result of the interaction between technological conditions that require large scale for efficient production and demand conditions that make one firm of minimum efficient size approximately sufficient to supply the entire market at a price that covers full cost." In such circumstances, governments typically limit the market to one regulated firm, but some governments have created monopoly firms—for example, with transit and distribution operations for water, electricity, or gas (at state and local levels) or with the U.S. Postal Service at the national level.

Sometimes utility profits subsidize civil government operations, but the days of "tax-free towns" supported by utility profits generally have been ended by the increase in operating costs. Indeed, subsidization often runs from the civil unit to the utility. Other governments may seek low service prices, possibly for political appeal or to support services seen as important to economic development or to certain segments of society (transit for the elderly, for instance). They may also seek to prevent "cream skimming," as when private firms serve only lucrative portions of markets, but there does appear to be a trend toward privatization of some such functions.

Two other widespread government enterprises, unrelated to natural monopolies, are state liquor stores and state lotteries. Both enterprises sell private goods. In neither case do profits from the operation yield substantial support to government, although revenue is probably the primary objective for both operations. There is some regulatory motive involved with liquor store operation, and lotteries undoubtedly are operated by states because of the unsavory elements allegedly associated with commerical gambling (Mikesell and Zorn, 1986). Private operations subject to taxation could probably be substituted in both areas.

Summary

Governments must rely on taxes because most services that governments provide cannot be sold to raise revenue. While user charges (prices that governments charge for service) may impose the cost of services on those directly benefiting from them, their scope is limited, because most public services have public effects, and many have redistributional objectives. Taxes promise to remain the principal revenue source for government functions and should be designed to be equitable, productive, devoid of adverse economic effects, and collectable at reasonable cost to society.

References

Aaron, H. J. *Who Pays the Property Tax: A New View.* Washington, D.C.: Brookings Institution, 1975.

Advisory Commission on Intergovernmental Relations. *Significant Features of Fiscal Federalism, 1976–77.* Vol. 2: *Revenue and Debt.* Washington, D.C.: U.S. Government Printing Office, 1978.

Advisory Commission on Intergovernmental Relations. *Changing Public Attitudes on Governments and Taxes, 1987.* Washington, D.C.: Advisory Commission on Intergovernmental Relations, 1987.

Auerbach, A. J. "The Tax Reform Act of 1986 and the Cost of Capital." *Journal of Economic Perspective,* 1987, *1,* 73–86.

Ballard, C., Shoven, C. B., and Whalley, J. "General Equilibrium Computations of the Marginal Welfare Costs of Taxes in the United States." *American Economic Review,* 1985, *75,* 128–138.

Blair, R. D., and Kaserman, D. L. *Antitrust Economics.* Homewood, Ill.: Irwin, 1985.

Blum, W. J., and Kalven, H., Jr. *The Uneasy Case for Progressive Taxation.* Chicago: University of Chicago Press, 1953.

Bowman, J. H., and Butcher, W. A. "Institutional Remedies and the Uniform Assessment of Property: An Update and Extension." *National Tax Journal,* 1986, *39,* 157–170.

Bowman, J. H., and Mikesell, J. L. "Uniform Assessment of Property: Returns from Institutional Remedies." *National Tax Journal,* 1978, *31,* 137–152.

Bowman, J. H., and Mikesell, J. L. "Recent Changes in State Gasoline Taxation: An Analysis of Structure and Rates." *National Tax Journal,* 1983, *35,* 163–182.

Break, G. F., and Pechman, J. A. *Federal Tax Reform: The Impossible Dream?* Washington, D.C.: Brookings Institution, 1975.

Browning, E. K. "Tax Incidence, Indirect Taxes, and Transfers." *National Tax Journal,* 1985, *38,* 524–534.

Carnevale, J. T. "Sensitivity of Corporate Income Tax Revenues to the Business Cycle." *Federal-State-Local Fiscal Relations: Technical Papers.* Vol. 2. Washington, D.C.: U.S. Government Printing Office, 1986.

Davies, D. "Clothing Exemptions and Sales Tax Regressivity." *American Economic Review,* 1971, *61,* 187–189.

Due, J. F. "Tax Incidence, Indirect Taxes, and Transfers—A Comment." *National Tax Journal,* 1986, *39,* 539–540.

Due, J. F. and Mikesell, J. L. *Sales Taxation: State and Local Structure and Administration.* Baltimore, Md.: Johns Hopkins University Press, 1983.

Feldstein, M. *The Effects of Taxation on Capital Accumulation.* Chicago: University of Chicago Press, 1987.

Fratanduono, R. J. "Trends in Voluntary Compliance of Taxpayers Filing

Individual Tax Returns." In *Trend Analysis and Related Statistics: 1986 Update.* Washington, D.C.: Internal Revenue Service, U.S. Department of the Treasury, 1986.

Geraci, V. J., and Plourde, J. L. "The Determinants of Uniform Property Tax Assessments." *Assessors Journal,* 1976, *11,* 235–251.

Holland, D. M. "Measuring and Combatting Tax Evasion." In H. Hanusch (ed.), *Public Finance and the Quest for Efficiency.* Detroit: Wayne State University Press, 1984.

Kiefer, D. W., and Nelson, S. "Distributed Effects of Federal Tax Reform." In *Proceedings of the Seventy-ninth Annual Conference on Taxation of the National Tax Association–Tax Institute of America.* Columbus, Ohio: National Tax Association–Tax Institute of America, 1986.

Mikesell, J. L. "Administration and the Public Revenue System: A View of Tax Administration." *Public Administration Reveiw,* 1974, *34,* 615–624.

Mikesell, J. L. "Property Tax Assessment Practices and Income Elasticities." *Public Finance Quarterly,* 1978, *6,* 53–65.

Mikesell, J. L. "The Cyclical Sensitivity of State and Local Taxes." *Public Budgeting and Finance,* 1984, *4,* 32–39.

Mikesell, J. L. "Audits and the Tax Base." *Western Tax Review,* 1985, *6,* 86–114.

Mikesell, J. L. "Amnesties for State Tax Evaders: The Nature of and Response to Recent Programs." *National Tax Journal,* 1986a, *39,* 507–526.

Mikesell, J. L. *Fiscal Administration: Analysis and Applications for the Public Sector.* (2nd ed.) Homewood, Ill.: Dorsey Press, 1986b.

Mikesell, J. L., and Zorn, C. K. "State Lotteries as Fiscal Savior or Fiscal Fraud." *Public Administration Review,* 1986, *44,* 311–320.

Mushkin, S. (ed.). *Public Prices for Public Products.* Washington, D.C.: Urban Land Institute, 1972.

Nowak, N. D. *Tax Administration in Theory and Practice.* New York: Praeger, 1970.

Pechman, J. A. *Who Paid the Taxes, 1966–85.* Washington, D.C.: Brookings Institution, 1985.

Pechman, J. A. *Federal Tax Policy.* (5th ed.) Washington, D.C.: Brookings Institution, 1987.

Penniman, C. *State Income Taxation.* Baltimore, Md.: Johns Hopkins University Press, 1980.

Reese, T. J. "The Thoughts of Chairman Long, Part I: The Politics of Taxation." *Tax Notes,* 1978, *6,* 195–199.

Sandmo, A. "Optimal Taxation—An Introduction to the Literature." *Journal of Public Economics,* 1976, *6,* 37–54.

Shoup, C. *Public Finance.* Chicago: Aldine, 1969.

Slemrod, J., and Sorum, N. "The Compliance Cost of the U.S. Individual Income Tax System." *National Tax Journal,* 1984, *37,* 461–474.

Smith, A. *An Inquiry into the Nature and Cause of the Wealth of Nations.* New York: Random House, 1937. (Originally published 1776.)

Steuerle, E. C. *Who Should Pay for Collecting Taxes?* Washington, D.C.: American Enterprise Institute for Public Policy Research, 1986.

U.S. Bureau of the Census. *Government Finances in 1985–86.* Series GF86, no. 5. Washington, D.C.: U.S. Government Printing Office, 1987.

U.S. Department of Commerce. "National Income and Product Accounts Tables." *Survey of Current Business,* 1987, *67,* 5–18.

U.S. Office of Management and Budget. *Information Collection Budget of the United States Government, Fiscal Year 1985.* Washington, D.C.: U.S. Office of Management and Budget, 1985.

Welch, R. B. "Characteristics and Feasibility of High-Quality Assessment Administration." In International Association of Assessing Officers, *Property Tax Reform.* Chicago: International Association of Assessing Officers, 1973.

Witte, A. D., and Woodbury, D. F. "The Effect of Tax Laws and Tax Administration on Tax Compliance: The Case of the United States Individual Income Tax." *National Tax Journal,* 1985, *38,* 1–14.

24

Robert L. Bland
Chilik Yu

Acquiring and Repaying Debt

This chapter discusses the preferred procedures for acquiring and repaying debt in state and local governments. Because of the flexibility state and local governments have in entering the bond market, debt administration at these levels of government critically depends on the manager's skill at planning and timing the sale of bonds. In addition, the bulk of research on debt administration is directed at these levels of government, rather than at the national government.

As used in this chapter, the term *state and local governments* includes organizations eligible under the U.S. Internal Revenue Code to issue tax-exempt securities. This exemption distinguishes state and local securities from those of other issuers, such as the national government and private corporations, and represents a significant in-kind subsidy from the national government. Because of the tax exemption, investors are willing to accept lower interest rates on these securities, and issuers realize substantial savings in debt service expenditures. For example, between 1966 and 1985, the ratio of tax-exempt to taxable interest rates generally fell in the 65 percent to 75 percent range (Petersen, 1987). This implies that the federal exemption enabled state and local governments to reduce their interest costs by approximately 30 percent. Given the current volume of interest payments by state and local governments, this represents a $17 billion annual subsidy from the federal treasury to state and local governments (Petersen, 1987).

One of the goals in debt administration is to obtain funds at the lowest possible cost. Two types of costs are associated with acquiring debt: flotation costs and interest cost (Fischer, Forbes, and Petersen, 1980). Flotation costs are associated with marketing and underwriting (or reselling) government securities. State and local governments usually sell their securities to an underwriter (or wholesaler) who in turn resells the securities, usually at a profit, to households and institutional investors. Flotation costs include the underwriter's spread or profit margin. They also include the costs for conducting a bond election, publishing the notice of a bond sale, printing bonds, obtaining a bond rating, and the fees for the services of legal and technical advisers to the sale.

The topics discussed in this chapter are grouped according to debt administration's three interrelated phases: planning the bond sale, designing and selling the bond issue, and administering repayment of outstanding debt. The following section discusses the first phase of the debt administration cycle and provides evidence from research on strategies for minimizing the cost of marketing debt.

Planning the Sale of Debt

Planning the bond sale requires the finance officer to decide on the type of debt to issue, the amount and maturity structure of the issue, the method for selling the securities, and the selection of outside advisers, if any, to assist in the sale. The manager's goal in this phase is to negotiate terms for the sale that are the least burdensome to the jurisdiction yet appealing to underwriters and investors.

Types of Debt. Tax-exempt debt is classified as either short-term debt or long-term debt, depending on the length to final maturity for the issue. Short-term securities, called *notes,* have maturities of less than one year and are normally issued to meet cash flow needs. These securities include revenue anticipation notes (RANs), tax anticipation notes (TANs), grant anticipation notes (GANs), tax and revenue anticipation notes (TRANs), and bond anticipation notes (BANs). Each receives its name from the source of funds used to repay the short-term obligation once it matures.

Bonds, or long-term debt, have maturities greater than one year and are sold to finance capital improvements. Unlike most corporate issues, which are usually composed of bonds with a single maturity (term bonds), most municipal bonds have serial maturities, with principal and interest repaid in annual installments over the life of the issue. For example, a city may issue $20 million in debt, with $1 million maturing annually in the sixth through the fifteenth years from the date of issue and $2 million maturing annually in the sixteenth through twentieth years. Serial bonds attract a wider range of investors, who have varying maturity preferences, and this broader appeal enhances the demand for municipals.

Under normal market conditions, the shorter the length to maturity, the lower the interest rate on the bond. Bonds with longer maturities incur higher interest rates, because there is a greater risk for investors that interest rates in the market may turn upward. The unusually high interest rates on longer-term debt during the past decade prompted issuers to use more short-term debt in order to take advantage of lower interest rates.

Although short-term debt lowers interest cost, repeated entry into the market in order to roll over short-term obligations results in increased flotation costs. There is also no assurance that the market will allow an issuer to repeatedly roll over its short-term debt. Experience has shown that excessive reliance on such debt can lead to illiquidity and to a greater risk of precipitating a financial crisis, like New York City's in 1975, when New York was unable to refinance the short-term debt it had accumulated over the years (Petersen, 1980).

Types of Repayment Pledges. Municipal debt is also classified according to the type of revenue pledged as the source of repayment. A general obligation (GO) pledge represents a commitment by the issuer to use all available sources of revenue and taxing powers to repay outstanding securities. Thus, the issuer pledges its full faith and credit to the repayment of qualifying bonds. Because of this unconditional pledge, voter approval is usually required by state law for the issuance of GO debt.

By contrast, a revenue bond represents a limited pledge of resources to repay qualifying debt. Usually, revenue bonds are issued to finance a revenue-producing project, such as a hospital, dormitory, toll road, or water treatment facility. Only revenues earned from these projects are pledged to repay outstanding obligations. Because of the limited pledge, revenue bonds incur interest costs that average about 6 percent higher than comparable GO debt (Gurwitz, 1983–84). Revenue bonds also incur higher flotation costs (Fischer, Forbes, and Petersen, 1980), but they have the advantage of not requiring voter approval for their issuance, in most cases, and they promote economic efficiency to the extent that user fees, rather than general revenues, are employed to repay the debt.

Probably the most significant transformations in the bond market over the past fifteen years have been the steady decline in the relative amount of GO debt issued, and the corresponding increase in the amount of revenue debt sold. Whereas, in the early 1970s, GO debt represented 60 percent of the volume, by 1986, 62 percent of the new-issue volume was revenue debt (Bond Buyer, 1987). The increased volume of enterprise-related debt issued by public authorities, combined with taxpayer-imposed restrictions on the issuance of GO debt, accounts for this shift.

Some repayment pledges represent variations on GO and revenue debt. For example, limited or special tax bonds are repaid solely from the revenues of a particular tax, such as a state gasoline tax (Moody's Investors Service, 1987). While these bonds are similar to GOs, since the proceeds are used for governmental purposes, they are not a general obligation of the issuer.

Another variation is the "moral obligation" bond, which is a revenue bond typically issued by a state authority that bears the state legislature's moral commitment to meet any shortfall in payments by the authority. The state has no legal obligation to honor its moral commitment, however.

A third variation is the double-barrel pledge. Although a general obligation of the issuer (the first barrel), bonds of this type are also secured by a particular revenue source, such as gasoline taxes (the second barrel), and are repaid from this dedicated revenue source (Lamb and Rappaport, 1987). Bonds bearing a double-barrel pledge should incur lower interest costs than comparable issues bearing just a general obligation pledge.

Determining the Proper Issue Size. In most cases, state and local governments have flexibility in determining the amount of debt to sell, particularly long-term obligations. They can bundle their various capital needs into a larger bond issue by delaying entry into the market. Fischer, Forbes, and Petersen (1980) found that flotation costs declined as issue size increased, as a result of the economies of scale from marketing larger issues.

Other studies have found a U-shaped relationship between issue size and interest cost (Benson, Kidwell, Koch, and Rogowski, 1981; Kidwell and Rogowski, 1983). Bonds of larger, better-known issuers have an active secondary market, where they can be traded after their initial sale. This increased liquidity improves the marketability of the issue in the primary market, which means lower interest costs. Beyond some point, however, larger issues become more difficult to underwrite, as investors seek to diversify their portfolios. For example, Kidwell and Rogowski (1983) found that issue sizes of $60 million (in 1972 dollars) incurred the lowest interest costs. At some point, marketability declines and interest costs increase, as issue size increases.

Bland (1984) found a joint effect between issue size and frequency of entry into the bond market by an issuer. The greatest savings occurred for issuers who bundled their capital needs into issue sizes of at least $40 million (1976 dollars) and deferred entry into the market to once every eight years. Deferral by more than eight years does not result in any significant savings in interest costs.

Methods of Sale. Issuers of municipal debt rarely deal directly with investors, preferring instead to sell their bonds directly to an underwriting syndicate, which in turn unbundles the bonds for resale to investors. Underwriters may be either commercial banks or investment banking firms. Underwriting is done through a syndicate or group of underwriters who form a temporary association to raise sufficient capital to purchase an issue. The larger the issue, the greater the number of firms coming together to form the syndicate.

Two methods of sale are used by issuers to bring debt to market: competitive bidding and negotiation. Competitive bidding involves a public auction at which a bond issue is sold to the syndicate submitting the lowest bid for interest cost. In contrast, negotiation involves an issuer who negotiates a sale price directly with a preselected syndicate. In recent years, negotiation has been the preferred method of sale, particularly for revenue bonds. Negotiated sales represented about 82 percent of the $204 billion in municipal bonds sold in 1985 and about 75 percent of the $143 billion sold in 1986 (Bond Buyer, 1987).

A hotly debated issue related to the method of sale is the ineligibility of commercial banks to underwrite revenue bonds. The Glass-Steagall Act of 1933 precludes commercial banks from underwriting most types of revenue bond issues. Opponents of this policy argue that excluding commercial banks reduces competition by reducing the number of bidders, which increases the cost to issuers (Petersen, 1980). One study (Cagan, 1978) concluded that if banks had been eligible to underwrite revenue bonds, issuers would have realized savings in interest costs equal to 1.5 percent of the total principal in revenue debt issued in 1977. Proponents of the exclusion argue that it is designed to protect banks from buying more risky types of debt and to protect smaller investment banks from being driven out of business by larger commercial banks. Another study (Bierwag, Kaufman, and Leonard, 1984) found that commercial banks' ineligibility had no statistically significant effect on interest cost.

Several studies have found that bonds sold through negotiation incur higher interest costs than comparable issues sold through competitive bidding. It is generally assumed that the absence of competition among underwriters in a negotiated sale drives up interest costs. Braswell, Nosari, and Summers (1983) found about an 18 basis point spread between negotiated and competively sold issues, but some research has shown that market conditions affect differences in interest cost between the two methods of sale (Hays, Kidwell, and Marr, 1984). During stable market conditions, competitive issues sold for 13 basis points lower than negotiated issues, on the average, but during unstable periods, negotiated issues sold for up to 32 basis points lower than competitive issues receiving fewer than three bids from underwriting syndicates, and 19 basis points lower than competitive issues receiving three or more bids. In unstable market conditions, negotiation has the advantage, because of the underwriter's ability to obtain buy orders from investors during the presale period.

Bland (1985) found that when the previous market experience of negotiators was taken into account, debt sold by local governments that were experienced at negotiation incurred interest costs comparable to the interest costs of debt sold by competitive bidding, but inexperienced or infrequent issuers incurred higher interest costs when selling their debt through negotiation. Roden and Bland (1986) found that issuers' sophistication at negotiating explained the decline in interest costs for issues sold through negotiation.

With negotiation, the issuer has greater flexibility in timing the sale. Once announced, a competitive sale date cannot be changed easily, unless the issuer is willing to cancel the sale. By contrast, the timing of a negotiated sale can be postponed if the market for municipals appears crowded or if interest rates in the market take an upward turn.

Finally, research has shown that the degree of competition (represented by the number of syndicates submitting bids for an issue) and the intensity of underwriters' search for investors (indicated by the dispersion of bids) are inversely related to interest cost (Benson, 1979). Nevertheless, the marginal effect of additional bids on interest cost declines as the number of bids increases, so that the second bid lowers interest cost more than the seventh (Kessel, 1971). Numerous other studies have demonstrated the favorable and sizable effect of increased underwriting competition on interest cost. For issuers, the implication is obvious: Encourage as many bids as possible by widely advertising the sale and offering terms that are attractive to investors.

One related issue involves the measure usually used to select the lowest bid for interest cost at competitive sales: a simple interest measure known as *net interest cost* (NIC). NIC does not take the time value of money into consideration; thus, NIC may lead to the selection of a bid with a higher interest cost than one in which a time discounted measure has been used. Experts recommend using *true interest cost* (TIC) or *present-value interest cost* (PIC) as the basis of awarding bids; both methods take the time value of money into consideration (Hopewell and Kaufman, 1974). Despite this admonition, tradition and computational simplicity have combined to make NIC the standard measure for awarding contracts in the industry.

A few municipal issuers have experimented with a third method: selling small-issue bonds (minibonds) directly to investors, without the aid of an underwriter. In 1985, Germantown, Tennessee, sold its entire issue of $2 million in "citizen bonds" directly to local residents. The sale was accomplished with no current bond rating, no prospectus, no underwriter, and the publication of one advertisement announcing the sale (Canary, 1986). The bonds were sold in $500 denominations, rather than in the usual $5,000 denominations used by underwriters, and were limited to $25,000 per person. The entire $2 million issue was sold in just one week. Citizen bonds do not signal the demise of underwriters, but direct marketing offers a cost-effective alternative for issuers seeking small amounts of capital.

Outside Advisers. Successfully selling a bond issue requires technical expertise in two critical areas: assuring investors that federal and state laws relating to the sale have been properly observed, and designing the bond issue so that it will appeal to a wide array of investors.

Bond counsel provides an opinion approving the bond as a legally binding obligation of the issuer. For tax-exempt bonds, the opinion also certifies that interest income from the bond qualifies for federal and state tax exemption under statutes currently in force or anticipated. Bond counsel is almost always a law firm that specializes in reviewing the legality of municipal bonds. Without an approving opinion from a respected and well-known bond counsel, even the most valid issue may not be marketable.

In principle, bond counsel assumes a position of neutrality between investors and issuers, even though counsel is selected and compensated by the issuer (Moak, 1982). In fact, counsel works with the issuer to ensure that legally defensible procedures are followed and that an accurate official statement is prepared. After reviewing all documentation associated with the bond sale, counsel prepares a written opinion stating the legality of the issue. This opinion is included in the bond certificate.

The financial adviser provides the issuer with technical advice on designing the terms of the issue, making presentations to bond-rating agencies, and securing the services of a paying agent or trustee (Moak, 1982, p. 136). In general, the financial adviser provides services unavailable from in-house personnel. For smaller issuers, the financial adviser is indispensable. For larger issuers with qualified in-house personnel, or issuers in states (such as North Carolina) where the state provides extensive financial advisory services, an outside adviser may be necessary only when the issue is for an unusual purpose or has complex repayment provisions.

Designing and Selling the Bond Issue

In this phase, the debt administrator seeks to obtain the lowest possible interest rate for an issue, given current market conditions. The administrative tasks include obtaining a bond rating, preparing the disclosure statement, deciding whether to purchase outside credit enhancement, and choosing among an array of creative repayment features to include with the issue.

Rating Municipal Debt. Probably the most significant determinant of an issue's interest cost is its rating. A credit rating provides investors with an objective measure of an issue's credit quality. It also provides public officials with an independent appraisal of their government's relative standing in the investment world. Some even use the rating for political purposes—for example, as an indication of the quality of management or of a jurisdiction's business climate.

A rating seeks to answer a simple question for lenders: What is the probability of the timely repayment of principal and interest on this obligation? A rating is initiated upon application and payment of a fee by the issuer. Two private firms rate most of the debt coming to market—Moody's Investors Service and Standard & Poor's Corporation (S&P's). GO debt is rated according to the issuer's overall creditworthiness and applies to all that issuer's outstanding GO debt. A rating for revenue debt takes into consideration the stability of the revenue stream dedicated to repaying the bonds and applies only to the particular issue.

Each firm uses symbols to indicate its appraisal of creditworthiness. For bonds, Moody's uses Aaa, Aa, A, Baa, Ba, B, and below to indicate the best to poorest quality. S&P's uses AAA, AA, A, BBB, BB, B, and below to indicate its credit appraisal. For bonds in categories Aa and below, Moody's differentiates among stronger credits within a given category by assigning a 1 to the rating, such as Aa-1 or A-1. S&P's uses a plus (+) or minus (–) sign to indicate stronger or weaker credits within a rating category. Both firms rate short-term debt, too. Moody's rates notes as MIG1, MIG2, MIG3, or MIG4 to indicate the best to poorest quality. S&P's uses a three-point scale—SP-1, SP-2, SP-3—to indicate strong, satisfactory, and speculative grade notes.

Rating agencies first look to an issuer's previous debt service record for an indication of its willingness to make timely payments on the pending bond issue. For GO bonds, the two rating agencies consider four basic factors in making a rating decision: an issuer's debt management practices, economic base, finances, and management capacity (Lamb and Rappaport, 1987). When evaluating debt practices, rating agencies give particular attention to existing debt service levels, but they also consider the nature of the repayment pledge in the proposed issue and the issuer's future debt needs. Their evaluation of the issuer's economic condition takes into consideration trends in population and income growth, diversity and growth in the tax base, sales activity, and employment diversity in the jurisdiction. An assessment of the jurisdiction's financial condition includes an examination of its accounting and financial reporting practices, of its sources of revenues and expenditures, and of the trends in its annual operating statements and fund balances. Finally, assessment of the management capacity of the issuer includes making a determination of the degree of organizational autonomy, the ability of officials to make timely and sound financial decisions, and the capacity of the jurisdiction to provide the range and level of services it has assumed.

Ratings for revenue bonds rely more on the financial viability of the enterprise benefiting from the debt process. Particular consideration is given to the debt-coverage ratio—the ratio of expected net operating revenues to debt service payments. This ratio should be between 1.10 and 1.75 (Lamb and Rappaport, 1987). Rating agencies also give close scrutiny to the legal protections for investors, including the rate covenant and the level of reserves to be maintained in the debt service fund.

In the case of ratings for notes, both agencies claim that an issuer's rating for short-term debt has no direct relationship to its rating for long-term debt (Moody's Investors Service, 1987; Standard & Poor's Corporation, 1986). Research confirms this claim. Ratings for notes give primary consideration to factors affecting an issuer's liquidity and cash flow projections (Raman, 1986).

As a result of its informational value for investors and particularly for households, a rating directly affects the interest cost of the issue. One reason is that a rating determines an issue's marketability. Federally chartered financial institutions are limited to investing in investment-grade bonds, that is, issues bearing a Baa or BBB rating or a higher one. Most tax-exempt mutual funds and unit investment trusts (currently the largest group of investors in municipals) also have charter provisions limiting their purchases to securities with at least an A rating from one of the rating agencies (Adams, 1985). Thus, issues with ratings at or below investment grade face a limited market and can expect to incur much higher interest costs as a result.

Another reason for the influence of ratings on interest costs is that, because of the municipal bond market's inefficiency, timely financial information on issuers is unavailable or only slowly disseminated (Ingram, Brooks, and Copeland, 1983; Reeve and Herring, 1986). Ratings convey a significant amount of information to investors; in many cases, they provide the sole means whereby investors form an opinion of a bond's worth.

About 30 percent of the municipal issues coming to market in a typical year are unrated (Reeve and Herring, 1986). It is widely assumed that unrated bonds incur interest rates comparable to or higher than Baa-rated issues, but Reeve and Herring found some market segmentation for unrated issues, with issues under $1 million incurring interest rates 10 basis points lower than the rates for Baa-rated issues, while larger unrated issues were priced at 30 basis points higher than Baa-rated issues, on the average. Larger issues apparently remain unrated because of low quality, whereas smaller issues go unrated because of the relatively high cost and low benefits expected from a rating.

A sizable body of research has sought to replicate the bond ratings of Moody's and S&P's statistically, through such techniques as multiple-discriminant analysis (Adams, 1985; Parry, 1983; Aronson and Marsden, 1980). Using a small number of financial and socioeconomic variables, these studies seek to identify the most important factors determining an issuer's rating. For example, Aronson and Marsden (1980) found that the proportion of a city's population that is black is the most important determinant of a rating. This line of research is of questionable value, however, because it assumes a degree of "scientificness" in the rating process that the rating agencies themselves do not claim.

One bond issue does not necessarily receive the same rating from both of the major firms. A study of corporate bonds found that the two agencies disagreed 58 percent of the time (Perry, 1985). Although similar criteria are used by the two agencies in making rating decisions, disagreement occurs because each weights the factors going into the decision differently. For example, in rating GO bonds, Moody's places greater weight on debt factors, and S&P's places greater weight on the issuer's economic base (Lamb and Rappaport, 1987). Nevertheless, deciding on a rating is still a matter of judgment.

Disclosure Practices. As a result of several highly publicized defaults by major issuers of municipal debt during the past decade, investors now expect more complete and timely disclosure of material information from issuers. The official statement provides important information on an issuer's ability to repay its debt. This document summarizes all the pertinent facts about the financial condition of the issuer or about the project benefiting from the debt proceeds and the repayment terms of the proposed issue.

In an effort to bring more consistency to the format and content of official statements, the Government Finance Officers Association (1988) has published guidelines for their preparation. About one month before the planned date of sale, the issuer publishes a preliminary official statement, commonly referred to as a "red herring" because of the red ink used on the front page, cautioning readers of the preliminary nature of the statement (Lamb and Rappaport, 1987). This statement describes the purpose of the issue and the security backing the bonds, provides a summary of the issuer's audited financial report, and gives any other information relevant to the offering. Once the issue is sold, the terms of the sale are incorporated into the final official statement.

Credit Enhancement. Uncertainty in the bond market during the past decade, brought on by well-publicized defaults and record high interest rates, has prompted a "flight to quality" among investors. This preference for higher-rated securities has compelled debt managers to pursue credit enhancement through strategies designed to increase the investment appeal of their bonds. Credit enhancement is of three general types: private bond insurance, standby letters of credit (LOCs), and various state-funded programs for assisting local governments in the bond market. As much as one-third of the bonds now coming to market bear some form of credit enhancement (Bland and Yu, 1987).

Private bond insurance is the best-known and most widely used form of credit assistance. The insurer guarantees holders of insured bonds that in the event of a default by the borrower, the insurance company will repay outstanding obligations. The insurance is purchased by the issuer at the point of sale and is irrevocable for the life of the issue. The premium is usually paid out of the proceeds of the bond sale and averages about 0.8 percent of the *sum* of the principal and interest for the issue (Bland, 1987). Insured bonds bear the credit rating of the insurer (usually an Aaa or AAA rating), rather than the rating of the issuer. The enhanced credit rating presumably lowers the interest cost to the issuer, as a result of the issue's increased marketability with investors.

Two studies have found, however, that insured bonds sell at interest rates comparable to A-rated issues, not Aaa-rated ones (Bland, 1987; Bland and Yu, 1987). Research has also shown that savings in interest costs from insurance depend on the issuer's underlying credit rating, with the greatest benefit from insurance going to issuers with the lowest underlying ratings (Bland and Yu, 1987). Unfortunately, as a result of profit-maximization pressures, insurers tend to restrict their coverage to higher-rated issues, because of their lower claims-paying potential.

An LOC, the second approach to credit enhancement, is a commitment by a bank to provide funds to bondholders in the event that the issuer is unable to meet maturing obligations. Both rating agencies rate LOC-backed debt on the basis of the bank's ability to pay, without regard to the issuer's creditworthiness (Moody's Investors Service, 1987; Standard and Poor's Corporation, 1986). The issuer is required to reimburse the bank for any amount drawn on the LOC, because banks are prohibited from guaranteeing the debt of another entity (Kim and Stover, 1987). LOCs are usually limited to maturities of five years or less. One study found that although LOCs reduce interest costs, the savings are negligible when compared with the cost of the LOC (Kim and Stover, 1987).

Unlike the first two approaches, the third approach to credit enhancement is available in the public sector and assumes three general forms: state credit guarantees, state payment of debt service, and state financial intermediation (Forbes and Petersen, 1983). With a state guarantee program, repayment of local debt is legally guaranteed by the state in the event of default by the local issuer. The state's backing may be an unfunded commitment in the form of a full-faith-and-credit pledge (such as New Hampshire's guarantee of certain school bonds), or it may be a collateralized commitment in which earmarked revenues are pledged to satisfy local debt payments in default. The best-known collateralized guarantee is the Texas School Bond Guarantee Program. The $5 billion in assets of the state's Permanent School Fund are pledged as collateral for bonds issued by school districts with ratings of A or lower. Research indicates that these guaranteed bonds sell at interest rates between those of A-1 and Aa-rated bonds, thereby lowering interest costs to virtually all participants (Bland, 1987).

In the case of state payment of debt service, state grants-in-aid, otherwise earmarked for use by a local government, are used to ensure timely payment of the issuer's debt service. For example, the New Jersey state treasurer regularly withholds a sufficient amount of state aid to cover each school district's debt service payments. Payment is made by the state directly to the paying agent or trustee. In Indiana, however, the state treasurer disburses earmarked state aid to the designated paying agent only in the event of a default by a school corporation. Research indicates that a state credit guarantee is the most cost-effective measure for lowering interest cost (Bland and Yu, 1988).

In the case of state financial intermediation, a state agency or authority serves as a financing conduit on behalf of local governments, in some cases making a moral pledge to repay defaulted obligations of participating local governments. State bond banks are the best-known example. A bond bank enables small, relatively unknown local governments in a state to pool their long-term issues. The bank then sells the pooled issue in its name on behalf of the participating governments (Kidwell and Rogowski, 1983; Cole and Millar, 1982). Bond banks lower flotation costs because of the economies of marketing a single pooled issue, rather than several small issues. Interest costs are lowered because most bond banks receive a rating one grade lower than the state's GO debt rating, which represents a credit upgrade for most participating local governments.

Creative Approaches to the Design of Debt Issues. To reduce interest costs and attract more investors, issuers in recent years have developed a number of creative provisions for repaying borrowed funds. These include put-option bonds, variable-rate securities, and zero coupon bonds.

Traditionally, municipal bonds contain a call provision, giving the issuer the right to redeem bonds within a specified number of years before the bonds' maturity. With a call provision, an issuer can remove burdensome covenant restrictions or reduce debt service expenditures by refunding the debt, if current market interest rates decline significantly below the rates on outstanding bonds (Kidwell, 1975). All these advantages for issuers represent disadvantages for investors, however. As a result, bonds bearing a call provision usually incur higher interest costs.

The *put option* represents essentially a call provision capable of being exercised by the investor, rather than by the issuer. This option, also known as a *demand option* or *tender option,* gives investors the right to demand payment from the issuer at a price specified in the bond agreement and at a point prior to the bond's maturity. The option protects investors from being locked into a security with a yield lower than that available in the current market, but it increases the financial uncertainty for issuers because they must redeem bonds that have been tendered before maturity. The trade-off is that put-option bonds have lower yields, and that means lower interest costs for issuers.

Variable-rate securities—also known as *floating-rate, flexible-rate,* or *adjustable-rate securities*—are the most popular of the creative approaches. Variable-rate securities represented about 20 percent of the total municipal volume in 1985 and 13 percent in 1986 (Bond Buyer, 1987). Whereas the yield on traditional municipals is determined by fixed coupon rates at the point of issuance, yields on variable-rate securities are periodically adjusted to reflect changes in market interest rates. Variable-rate securities protect investors from investment loss when market interest rates rise. The issuer assumes the risk of adverse changes in market rates. The compensation is lower interest rates for borrowed funds, particularly when interest rates are high (Hamilton, 1983).

Unlike conventional municipal bonds, which usually pay interest semiannually, *zero coupon bonds* (ZCBs) do not pay periodic interest to investors. Rather, they sell at a deeply discounted price, compared to their face value at maturity. One advantage to ZCBs is that investors make smaller investments initially but receive full face value at a bond's maturity. This arrangement can mean a sizable return for investors. For example, an initial investment of $1,000 in a ZCB yielding 12.8 percent will have a face value of about $20,000 at maturity in twenty years (Forbes and Renshaw, 1983).

Other Factors Affecting Interest Cost. The interest cost of municipal debt is determined by many factors, some of which are beyond the immediate control of the issuer. These include aggregate supply and demand for municipal debt, federal and state tax policies, market interest rates, and regional market conditions.

The supply of municipal debt coming to market has increased tremendously over the past twenty years, peaking at $204 billion in long-term securities and $19 billion in short-term securities in 1985 (Bond Buyer, 1987). The volume of tax-exempt debt has increased as a result of expanded use of private-purpose financing, advance refunding, and issuers' seeking to earn arbitrage income. State and local governments increasingly function as financial intermediaries, issuing tax-exempt debt on behalf of private firms. By the end of 1985, about 28 percent of the outstanding municipal debt was for private purposes (Petersen, 1987). The use of industrial revenue bonds is the best-known example of this type of debt.

Advance refunding uses the proceeds from one bond issue (the refunding issue) to replace another outstanding bond issue (the refunded issue) before the refunded issue's date of callability or maturity. The primary advantage of advance refunding is the savings in interest cost that can be achieved when market rates have declined. Nevertheless, the Tax Reform Act of 1986 greatly restricts state and local issues eligible for advance refunding.

The term *arbitrage* refers to the practice of selling securities at a lower interest cost and then reinvesting the proceeds in securities that earn higher interest rates. Because of the federal tax exemption for most state and local securities, it is relatively easy for these issuers to earn arbitrage income. Again, however, the Tax Reform Act of 1986 markedly limits the opportunity to earn arbitrage income, since there is revenue lost to the federal treasury because of this practice.

On the demand side, three groups of investors dominate the municipal market: commercial banks, casualty insurance companies, and households. Throughout the 1960s and early 1970s, commercial banks bought most of the municipals being sold, but their demand for tax-exempt debt began to decline as other tax shelters beame available, and they began to give more emphasis to the liquidity of their portfolios (Petersen, 1980). Households (particularly those in higher income brackets) and mutual funds and trusts have picked up the slack, and now they represent the largest buyers of tax-exempt debt. The advantage of tax-exempt mutual funds and unit investment trusts is that investors can benefit from this tax shelter with a relatively small amount of capital. They also offer investors greater liquidity.

Federal and state tax policies directly affect the demand for municipal bonds and, thus, the interest costs issuers incur for their debt. The Tax Reform Act of 1986 is significant to state and local governments for its sweeping limitations on the types of debt now qualifying for tax exemption. Public-purpose debt remains exempt, although the conditions and qualifying purposes are more narrowly defined, but fewer private-purpose bonds now qualify for exemption. State and local governments will now be forced to issue more taxable bonds, increasing debt service costs to issuers (Petersen, 1987).

State tax treatment of interest income from municipals also varies (Kidwell, Koch, and Stock, 1984). Thirteen states and the District of Columbia either levy no income tax or exempt all municipal interest from state taxation. Thirty-one states exempt interest on all in-state issues but tax interest earned on out-of-state bonds. Finally, six states tax earnings on out-of-state issues but exempt some (although not all) in-state issues. Kidwell, Koch, and Stock (1984) found that for smaller issues (under $5 million), interest costs were lower in states taxing out-of-state bonds at higher rates than in-state securities. Discriminatory tax policies increase the demand for smaller in-state issues, which tend to be marketed locally rather than nationally.

Overall market conditions, as measured by the change in real gross national product (GNP) and market interest rates, have a significant effect on borrowing costs, too. Research has shown that municipal interest costs vary inversely with overall economic growth, as measured by changes in real GNP (Benson and Rogowski, 1978). Market interest rates at the point of sale also have an obvious impact on interest costs, making the timing of a sale critical to the minimizing of costs.

Some research also indicates that the market for municipals is segmented regionally. Issuers in states with large volumes of debt (New York and California, for example) appear to incur higher interest costs (Kaufman, 1976). Hendershott and Kidwell (1978) found that an increase in the relative supply of tax-exempt debt statewide drove up the interest rates of smaller in-state issues, compared to the national rates. Finally, regional factors may affect interest costs indirectly through credit ratings. Morse and Deely (1983) found some regional biases in bond ratings, with southern states underrated and Central Plains states overrated.

Administering Repayment of Outstanding Debt

In this, the final phase of the debt cycle, the debt manager seeks to ensure the timely disbursement of funds to investors. Administrative tasks include selecting a trustee to assist in meeting the issuer's obligations and selecting a method for handling registered bonds.

The Bond Trustee. Before closing a bond sale, the issuer, in consultation with the lead underwriter, selects a trustee or fiscal agent who represents the interests of investors during the closing and for the life of the issue. Although not required by law to do so, state and local governments usually designate a trustee as a matter of financial prudence. Commercial banks and trust companies usually serve in this capacity.

In the case of revenue bonds, the trustee performs the fiduciary function of holding the funds used in servicing the debt (DuBose and McFadden, 1983). This includes holding funds for debt service and debt service reserves, renewal and replacement funds for the project, and funds used through the construction phase of the project. Of equal importance, the trustee monitors compliance by the issuer with the covenants included in the revenue bond agreement, such as making certain that project fees or tolls are sufficient to provide the level of debt service coverage specified in the rate covenant.

For both GO and revenue bonds, the trustee often serves as paying agent, registrar, and transfer agent (DuBose and McFadden, 1983). As paying agent, the trustee functions as the financial conduit between the issuer and investors. Before the payment date, the debt manager must authorize the transfer of funds to the paying agent for payment of maturing interest and principal. The paying agent then distributes these funds to the bondholders of record. The debt manager must meet payment deadlines and avoid technical default on the outstanding debt; nothing destroys investors' confidence in an issuer faster than even the slightest delay in meeting a payment deadline.

Bond Registration. The Tax Equity and Fiscal Responsibility Act of 1982 requires that virtually all bonds issued by state and local governments have their ownership registered in order to retain their exemption from federal income taxes. Unlike a bearer bond, which is owned by whoever possesses it, a registered bond records the name of the owner on the bond certificate itself and on a bond register maintained by the registrar for the issue. In the event that the owner sells the bond, the old certificate must be cancelled and a new certificate issued in the new owner's name. The transfer agent serves as an intermediary between buyers and sellers in the secondary market. Usually the trustee performs this function, but occasionally this task is awarded to a firm specializing in this service. Alternatively, the issuers sometimes perform the transfers, and the registrar functions internally, rather than contracting for the transfers. The primary complication of the registration requirement is the increased complexity and cost it creates for the buying and selling of bonds in the secondary market. Issuers have three options for handling registered bonds: the use of bond certificates, a book-entry-only system, or certificate immobilization (Petersen and Buckley, 1983).

The most commonly used method, although it is declining in popularity, is the use of certificates, with the name of the registered owner printed on each bond. This approach appeals to investors who want tangible evidence of the security's existence. Of the three methods for handling bond registration, this is the most costly, because a new certificate must be issued each time the bond changes owners. In these cases, issuers incur significantly higher costs for printing, authentication, distribution, and documentation. Investors incur higher costs because of the delay whenever certificates are reregistered. This method will continue to decline in popularity, although it will probably remain the standard for smaller issues that are traded only infrequently in the secondary market.

The book-entry-only method was introduced in the late 1960s to eliminate the use and disadvantages of certificates. With the book-entry-only method, no bond certificates are printed or distributed by the issuer. Records of ownership are maintained as bookkeeping entries on computerized records. In lieu of a transfer agent, a securities depository maintains a computerized directory of bond owners and records transfers of ownership as bookkeeping changes (Petersen and Buckley, 1983). The buyer receives a confirmation statement of the acquisition, rather than a certificate. The depository's member banks and investment firms periodically provide the investor with an account statement that indicates the number and value of bonds owned.

A securities depository is a nonprofit clearinghouse established to provide custodial and book-entry services for securities dealers, brokers, and commercial banks (Petersen and Buckley, 1983). The cost of operating the depository is paid by member institutions. The depository usually holds a "global certificate" in trust for each maturity in the issue, and depository members and their customers essentially purchase portions of the global bond.

With the book-entry-only method, an issuer incurs no costs for printing or registering bond certificates, no costs for transfer agents' fees, and significantly reduced costs for distributing payments for principal and interest. For example, the Depository Trust Company of New York (1987) estimates that for a $10 million issue, these services would cost about $37,000 if individual certificates were used, but only $145 if a book-entry-only system were used. As investors gain confidence in certificateless securities, the book-entry-only option will become the principal method for handling registered tax-exempt bonds.

The third approach to handling registered bonds is certificate immobilization. This approach is essentially the book-entry-only system, with some certificates available for investors who want them (Hutton Public Finance Group, 1984). A transfer agent serves as the intermediary among investors seeking to trade or sell their certificates, but most of the issue is available only in book-entry form, with a depository handling transfers of ownership through its computerized records. This approach lowers costs as the portion of immobilized certificates in an issue increases.

Summary

Administering the acquisition and repayment of debt by state and local governments is a monumental financial responsibility. The new debt acquired by state and local governments in 1986 alone was equivalent to 30 percent of all general revenue received that same year by those governments. Debt administration is also a technically complex responsibility. This chapter has summarized what research and practice have shown to be the preferred policies and procedures for administering government debt. Topics in the chapter were grouped around the three phases of debt administration: planning the bond sale, designing and selling the bond issue, and administering repayment of outstanding debt. The administrator's goal in the first phase is to negotiate terms that are the least burdensome to the jurisdiction yet the most appealing to investors. In the second phase, the debt administrator seeks to obtain the lowest possible interest rate for the issue, given current market conditions. In the final phase, the administrator ensures the timely repayment of obligations to investors and the preservation of the issuer's credibility in the investment market.

References

Adams, W. "Modeling the Bond Raters: Improving the Ability to Predict Bond Ratings." *Municipal Finance Journal*, 1985, 6, 7–17.

Aronson, J. R., and Marsden, J. R. "Duplicating Moody's Municipal Credit Ratings." *Public Finance Quarterly*, 1980, *8*, 97–106.

Benson, E. D. "The Search for Information by Underwriters and Its Impact on Municipal Interest Cost." *Journal of Finance*, 1979, *34*, 871–885.

Benson, E. D., Kidwell, D. S., Koch, T. W., and Rogowski, R. J. "Systematic Variation in Yield Spreads for Tax-Exempt General Obligation Bonds." *Journal of Financial and Quantitative Analysis*, 1981, *16*, 685–702.

Benson, E. D., and Rogowski, R. J. "The Cyclical Behavior of Risk Spreads on New Municipal Issues." *Journal of Money, Credit, and Banking*, 1978, *10*, 348–362.

Bierwag, G. O., Kaufman, G. G., and Leonard, P. H. "Interest Rate Effects of Commercial Bank Underwriting of Municipal Revenue Bonds." *Journal of Banking and Finance*, 1984, *8*, 35–50.

Bland, R. L. "The Interest Savings from Optimizing Issue Size and Frequency of Participation in the Municipal Bond Market." *Public Budgeting & Finance*, 1984, *4*, 53–59.

Bland, R. L. "The Interest Cost Savings from Experience in the Municipal Bond Market." *Public Administration Review*, 1985, *45*, 233–237.

Bland, R. L. "The Interest Cost Savings from Municipal Bond Insurance: The Implications for Privatization." *Journal of Policy Analysis and Management*, 1987, *6*, 207–219.

Bland, R. L., and Yu, C. "Municipal Bond Insurance: An Assessment of Its Effectiveness at Lowering Interest Costs." *Government Finance Review*, 1987, *3*, 23–26.

Bland, R. L., and Yu, C. "State Aid for Public Schools: A Comparison of the Cost-Effectiveness of Five State Programs." *Journal of Education Finance*, 1988, *13*, 460–476.

Bond Buyer. *The Bond Buyer 1987 Yearbook*. New York: The Bond Buyer, 1987.

Braswell, R. C., Nosari, B. E., and Summers, D. L. "A Comparison of the True Interest Costs of Competitive and Negotiated Underwritings in the Municipal Bond Market." *Journal of Money, Credit, and Banking*, 1983, *15*, 102–106.

Cagan, P. "The Interest Saving to States and Municipalities from Bank Eligibility to Underwrite All Nonindustrial Municipal Bonds." *Governmental Finance*, 1978, *7*, 40–48.

Canary, H. W. "Germantown's Capital Appreciation Citizen Bonds Sell Like Hotcakes." *Government Finance Review*, 1986, *2*, 7–10.

Cole, C. W., and Millar, J. A. "The Impact of Municipal Bond Banking on Municipal Interest Costs." *Financial Management*, 1982, *11*, 70–76.

Depository Trust Company. *Book-Entry-Only Municipals: An Idea Whose Time Has Come*. New York: Depository Trust Company, 1987.

DuBose, W. P., and McFadden, J. F. "The Role of the Municipal Bond Trustee." In F. J. Fabozzi and others (eds.), *The Municipal Bond Handbook*. Vol. 1. Homewood, Ill.: Irwin, 1983.

Fischer, P. J., Forbes, R. W., and Petersen, J. E. "Risk and Return in the Choice of Revenue Bond Financing." *Governmental Finance,* 1980, *9,* 9–13.

Forbes, R. W., and Petersen, J. E. "State Credit Assistance to Local Governments." In J. E. Petersen and W. C. Hough (eds.), *Creative Capital Financing for State and Local Government.* Chicago: Government Finance Officers Association, 1983.

Forbes, R. W., and Renshaw, E. "Tax-Exempt Zero Coupon Bonds." In J. E. Petersen and W. C. Hough (eds.), *Creative Capital Financing for State and Local Government.* Chicago: Government Finance Officers Association, 1983.

Government Finance Officers Association. *Disclosure Guidelines for State and Local Government Securities.* Chicago: Government Finance Officers Association, 1988.

Gurwitz, A. S. "Twelve Improvements in the Municipal Credit System." *Federal Reserve Bank of New York Quarterly Review,* 1983–84, *8,* 14–25.

Hamilton, R. "The World Turned Upside Down: The Contemporary Revolution in State and Local Government Capital Financing." *Public Administration Review,* 1983, *43,* 22–31.

Hays, P. A., Kidwell, D. S., and Marr, M. W. "The Effect of Market Uncertainty on Negotiated and Competitively Underwritten Public Utility Bonds." *Financial Review,* 1984, *19,* 339–350.

Hendershott, P. A., and Kidwell, D. S. "The Impact of Relative Security Supplies." *Journal of Money, Credit, and Banking,* 1978, *10,* 337–347.

Hopewell, M. H., and Kaufman, G. G. "Costs to Municipalities of Selling Bonds by NIC." *National Tax Journal,* 1974, *27,* 531–542.

Hutton Public Finance Group. *Public Finance Directory and Resource Guide.* New York: Hutton Public Finance Group, 1984.

Ingram, R. W., Brooks, L. D., and Copeland, R. M. "The Information Content of Municipal Bond Rating Changes: A Note." *Journal of Finance,* 1983, *38,* 997–1003.

Kaufman, G. G. "State and Regional Effects on the Interest Cost of Municipal Bonds in the United States." *Local Finance,* June 1976, pp. 19–23.

Kessel, R. "A Study of the Effects of Competition in the Tax-Exempt Bond Market." *Journal of Political Economy,* 1971, *79,* 706–738.

Kidwell, D. S. "Call Provisions and Their Effect on Municipal Bond Issues." *Governmental Finance,* 1975, *4,* 28–32.

Kidwell, D. S., Koch, T. W., and Stock, D. R. "The Impact of State Income Taxes on Municipal Borrowing Costs." *National Tax Journal,* 1984, *37,* 551–561.

Kidwell, D. S., and Rogowski, R. J. "Bond Banks: A State Assistance Program That Helps Reduce New Issue Borrowing Costs." *Public Administration Review,* 1983, *43,* 108–113.

Kim, J., and Stover, R. D. "The Role of Bank Letters of Credit in Corporate Tax-Exempt Financing." *Financial Management,* 1987, *16,* 31–37.

Lamb, R. and Rappaport, S. P. *Municipal Bonds.* (2nd ed.) New York: McGraw-Hill, 1987.

Moak, L. L. *Municipal Bonds: Planning, Sale, and Administration*. Chicago: Government Finance Officers Association, 1982.

Moody's Investors Service. *Moody's on Municipals: An Introduction to Issuing Debt*. New York: Moody's Investors Service, 1987.

Morse, D., and Deely, C. "Regional Differences in Municipal Bond Ratings." *Financial Analysts Journal*, 1983, *39*, 54–59.

Parry, R. W. "Moody's Analytical Overview of 25 Leading U.S. Cities—Revisited." *Public Finance Quarterly*, 1983, *11*, 79–93.

Perry, L. G. "The Effect of Bond Rating Agencies on Bond Rating Models." *Journal of Financial Research*, 1985, *8*, 307–315.

Petersen, J. E. "State and Local Government Debt Policy and Management." In J. E. Petersen and C. L. Spain (eds.), *Essays in Public Finance and Financial Management: State and Local Perspectives*. Chatham, N.J.: Chatham House, 1980.

Petersen, J. E. *Tax-Exempts and Tax Reform: Assessing the Consequences of the Tax Reform Act of 1986 for the Municipal Securities Market*. Washington, D.C.: Government Finance Research Center, 1987.

Petersen, J. E., and Buckley, M. P. *A Guide to Registered Municipal Securities*. Chicago: Government Finance Officers Association, 1983.

Raman, K. "Assessing Credit Risk on Municipal Short-Term Debt." *Advances in Accounting*, 1986, *3*, 171–180.

Reeve, J. M., and Herring, H. C. "An Examination of Nonrated Municipal Bonds." *Journal of Economics and Business*, 1986, *38*, 65–76.

Roden, P. F., and Bland, R. L. "Issuer Sophistication and Underpricing in the Negotiated Municipal Bond Market." *Journal of Financial Research*, 1986, *9*, 163–170.

Standard & Poor's Corporation. *Debt Rating Criteria*. New York: Standard & Poor's Corporation, 1986.

Part Six

Managing Human Resources

Human resources comprise another type of resource essential to governmental and quasi-governmental organizations. Human resources encompass the entire mix of the capabilities (knowledge, skills, values, commitment, aptitudes, and abilities) of the people who work for government. Public administrators must strive to bring together the right mix of these capabilities to accomplish their missions. Part Six addresses how public administrators can facilitate the accomplishment of their missions by managing human resources effectively.

In most governmental jurisdictions, public administrators manage human resources under civil service provisions, systems of rules and procedures covering personnel practices. Civil service systems buffer public administrators from arbitrary political interference, but the requirements may entail sacrifices of flexibility and managerial discretion. Public administrators must manage human resources to achieve simultaneous ends: the objectives associated with civil service systems, and with the human resource requirements of their missions.

Beyond the constraints of civil service requirements, public agencies carry special obligations in managing human resources, because of agencies' visibility in our society and their potential influence on legitimating political choices. Government is frequently expected to be an incubator for social change, a model for other sectors of the economy, and a redistributor of opportunities and wealth. These expectations are manifest, for example, in government's leadership with respect to comparable worth policies, equal employment laws, and employment and training programs. Although special demands on government organizations are consistent with the nature of our political system and, perhaps, inevitable, these considerations do nothing to lessen the difficulty of public administrators' obligations.

In the context of civil service constraints and special social obligations, the public administrator employs a variety of tools for managing human resources. Compensation is one of the most versatile tools, because it can have significant consequences for the attraction, retention, and motivation of employees. Limitations in formal monetary reward systems, however, lead the public administrator to draw on informal systems as well. The administrator must also look to a variety of developmental tools, among them performance appraisal, discipline, training, coaching, and mentoring, to help human resources reach their potential and meet the needs of organizations.

Acquiring, developing, and maintaining sufficient human resources to fulfill agencies' missions depends on knowledge of laws and institutional rules, an understanding of human behavior, and the ability to maneuver in the unique institutional niche that public administrators inhabit. Part Six provides lessons about how public administrators can meet the human resource needs of their organizations.

25

Frank J. Thompson

Managing Within Civil Service Systems

Effective public administrators typically possess an understanding of and a knack for human resource management. They create or exploit opportunities to shape practices of position determination—the creation and allocation of formal roles within agencies (for example, job design and classification). They often prove adroit at shaping human resources flows—recruitment, promotion, transfer, demotion, removal. They creatively use performance appraisal, processes through which managers acquire and interpret information concerning the activities of subordinates. They strive to motivate and socialize employees by structuring incentives and providing training to instill certain knowledge, perceptions, and values.

In managing human resources, public administrators tend to operate within civil service systems. These systems refer to the formal structures of authoritative rules that govern personnel practices in government programs and activities. Some public managers in very small jurisdictions do not, in any meaningful sense, manage human resources in the context of these systems, but in most local governments of any size, and certainly at the state and federal levels, civil service systems markedly influence the day-to-day management of personnel.

Reformers of various stripes have not underestimated the importance of civil service systems. The struggle against the spoils politics of the late nineteenth century evoked intense feelings and impassioned rhetoric (Kaufman, 1965). The Pendleton Act of 1883 forged the basic template for the spread of merit systems throughout the country. It established the Civil Service Commission, buffered from the direct authority of the president and

Note: The author thanks Carolyn Ban, James Perry, and Norma Riccucci for their helpful comments.

Congress. It called for "open, competitive examinations" of a "practical" character to test the fitness of persons to "discharge the duties of the service" (Thompson, 1979, p. 16). It forbade the discharge of employees for failing to make political contributions and helped implant the notion that civil servants would lose their jobs only for reasons of incompetence. Subsequent developments, in the early part of the twentieth century, encouraged the spread of formal classification and pay plans. Under the surveillance of civil service commissions, rules governing the discharge, transfer, and promotion of employees proliferated. Pockets of patronage persisted, but by the 1960s, merit systems had spread to all levels of government (Sorauf, 1960).

The new merit systems spawned their own discontents. Criticism has emerged in various forms throughout this century. In part a response to the ferment generated by the civil rights movement, the castigation of these systems became particularly pronounced in the 1970s. A study sponsored by Ralph Nader referred to federal personnel practices as *The Spoiled System* (Vaughn, 1975). Two top administrators (Savas and Ginsburg, 1979) in New York City government suggested that the city's personnel practices were "meritless" (p. 215). They claimed that the city's civil service system produced "mindless bureaucracies that appear to function for the convenience of their staffs rather than the public" (p. 221). They concluded that the city's personnel system had developed "rigor mortis"; it had "been warped and distorted to the point where it can do hardly anything at all" (p. 224). Discontent with civil service systems also found expression in the common view that public organizations lack the efficiency and effectiveness of their counterparts in the private sector. This belief fueled the privatization initiatives of the 1980s, which, among other things, urged that government's work be arranged through contracts with the private sector (Savas, 1982).

Most people who have spent any time working in the public sector sense that the criticisms of civil service systems are often excessive. Effective human resource management does occur in public agencies. Nevertheless, expressions of discontent with civil service systems occur with enough regularity to demand attention. This chapter explores three factors that frequently spawn criticism of these systems: competing values, uncertainty, and political culture. It suggests some implications of these factors for those who work in civil service systems and for those who would reform them.

Competing Values

Certain core values compete for expression in civil service systems. Typologies of these values vary. One analysis, for instance, points to four basic values, and another points to fourteen (Klingner and Nalbandian, 1985; Elliott, 1985). Drawing on these and related discussions, one can make a strong case for focusing on five basic values: instrumental goals, merit, political responsiveness, social equity, and employee rights and well-being. At times, the perceived performance of civil service systems with respect to any one of these values has prompted discontent to simmer and, less frequently, to boil over into a reform initiative.

Five Core Values. Civil service systems can facilitate or impede the efforts of public managers to accomplish *instrumental goals*—economy (cost containment), efficiency (as expressed by the ratio of output to cost), and effectiveness (achievement of program goals). In cities with political machines, the absence of merit systems has often forced public managers to put up with many marginally skilled or incompetent employees. This situation has heightened the risk that city agencies would be inefficient and ineffective.

More recent criticism holds that civil service systems impede instrumental achievement by undermining managerial discretion. Some analysts see the restrictive character of government's personnel systems as the critical difference between managing in public and private organizations (Downs and Larkey, 1986, p. 46). The rules embedded in civil service systems presumably hamstring managers, who would otherwise use discretion over personnel decisions to enhance the efficiency and effectiveness of agencies' operations. Nowhere can one find a more piercing expression of this view than in a report released by the National Academy of Public Administration (1983). In reviewing federal personnel practices, the report noted that the *Federal Personnel Manual* has 8,814 pages, and that the personnel system "does not seem to work very well for anybody." According to the report, "executives and managers feel almost totally divorced from what should be one of their most important systems" (p. 37). The report called for substantial deregulation of government managers and stressed that the U.S. Office of Personnel Management should delegate more authority to line departments.

Among other effects, restrictions on managerial discretion allegedly make it more difficult to motivate employees. Observing practices in New York City, Savas and Ginsburg (1979, p. 220) charged that promotion tests robbed managers of opportunities to motivate subordinates; they further asserted that "the knowledge that it is almost impossible to penalize or discharge the barely competent or even incompetent permanent employee" is "demoralizing for supervisors" (p. 220). At the state level, a survey (Elling, 1986) of top executives found 30 percent who indicated that they faced serious or very serious problems in disciplining or dismissing inept employees. These observations, from all levels of government, echo a common theme: that the rules of civil service dampen motivation because they weaken relationships between performance, on the one hand, and pay, promotion, disciplinary actions, and firing, on the other (Rainey, Trout, and Blunt, 1986, p. 53). In a related vein, Golembiewski (1979, p. 138) focuses on job design and description in arguing that civil service systems "fail to respond to the need to facilitate the management of work by increasing supervisory power." Excessively constraining rules march hand in hand with the charge that much of public personnel administration represents the triumph of technique over purpose (Sayre, 1979).

Merit is a second core value. Meritocratic norms have deep roots in the classic, liberal tradition of the United States. In the case of personnel, they emphasize that rewards ought to go to the most competent individuals— those with the best records of or potential for achievement. A sense of society as a market, where individuals compete and prizes go to the most adroit, undergirds this view. Therefore, strong sentiment and legal requirements often insist that public managers hire the most competent people from pools of eligible applicants. More recently, various policies have called for managers to allocate pay increases to the most meritorious performers.

While civil service systems often promote merit ideals, the 1960s and the 1970s witnessed countless accusations that these systems left much to be desired in this regard. Recruitment policies, in particular, came under fire. Hiring practices in the past had clearly excluded many well-qualified applicants on the grounds of race and sex. Moreover, very few civil service tests had been strictly validated (proved predictive) via scientific research. Thus, in reviewing the situation in New York City, Savas and Ginsburg (1979, p. 217) noted that out of four hundred civil service examinations, "not a single case could be found where the validity of a written test . . . was ever proven." Moreover, merit hiring practices sometimes had unanticipated consequences. In New York City, delays between the scoring of tests and the actual hiring of individuals produced a situation in which candidates with low passing grades were more likely to be hired than those with higher marks.

The value of *political responsiveness* asserts that the preferences of elected officials and their appointeees ought to weigh heavily in personnel management. The civil service reform movement of the late nineteenth century grew up in an effort to reduce the weight assigned to one form of political responsiveness, that associated with spoils systems. Spoils aimed primarily at maintaining the electoral coalition that had allowed politicians to stay in office by providing patronage in the routine, lower-level jobs of government. The institutions spawned by civil service reform made the practice of such patronage more difficult. Written tests for employment, quite aside from their capacity to predict the best person for a job, made it harder (although by no means impossible) for elected officials to practice patronage. "Independent" civil service commissions served a similar function. While some manifestations of low-level patronage politics persist (Johnston, 1979; Wolfinger, 1972), the spoils system is not a major rallying point for reform in the current era. For instance, one survey of over eight hundred state executives found that only 5 percent viewed patronage in filling positions as a serious problem (Elling, 1986, p. 76).

In another sense, however, issues of political responsiveness remain on the front burner. The rise of the administrative state presents perplexing issues of accountability and control in a democracy. How can the elected representatives of the people ensure that government administrators remain sensitive to their concerns and not become autonomous power holders? More specifically, what role should personnel administration play in the quest for such responsiveness? In this regard, top policy jobs in the bureaucracy tend to be a central target of concern, as elected officials strive to place loyal people in strategically sensitive positions. In contrast to discussions of spoils politics, the issue becomes one of using personnel administration as a vehicle for governance, rather than as a means of building electoral machinery or rewarding the party faithful.

Civil service systems take heat from both sides of the fence on this issue. Some observers worry that these systems have helped spawn bureaucracies that are the "new machines," largely unresponsive and unaccountable centers of power (Lowi, 1969, pp. 200-201). In this regard, Nathan (1983, pp. 1, 7) argues that it is "desirable . . . for political chief executives to seek to exert greater managerial influence over the bureaucracy." He believes that the discretion wielded by the bureaucracy remains too vast and technical to be understood by ordinary citizens. The president, as a popularly elected official, must do his utmost to ensure that management tasks "be performed by partisans." Others note that the presence of these partisans need not precipitate widespread deterioration in agencies' performance or be inconsistent with "open, trusting, and participative approaches to agency management" (Lynn, 1984, p. 360).

Civil service systems can, however, tip the balance too far in the direction of this form of political responsiveness. Democracy requires not only responsiveness but also nonpartisan technical competence and respect for law among public managers. In this regard, some observers criticize civil service systems for facilitating too much political responsiveness (Rosen, 1986; Newland, 1983). They see many top political appointees as transient birds of passage, who all too frequently possess minimal qualifications for the jobs they hold and whose zealotry can lead to an administration that departs from both the spirit and the letter of the law. These observers note how heavy emphasis on political responsiveness can yield declining appreciation of career civil servants' professional expertise. In turn, morale among these civil servants may plummet, and turnover may increase. Administrative capacity thereby diminishes. These observers hold that civil servants, within the bounds set by law, will usually attempt to be responsive to their political masters. Civil servants understand that a political executive who goes too far in seeking to control personnel processes may paradoxically wind up with administrators who are unresponsive—not because they lack loyalty, but because they lack the skill to carry out the executive's wishes.

Social equity concerns the uses of government employment practices to help groups who are deemed disadvantaged or potentially disadvantaged. One variation on this concern involves the declaration that certain characteristics of groups are off limits in personnel decisions, an action that helps protect these groups from adverse discrimination. Job applicants, for instance, generally enjoy the right not to be discriminated against on the basis of being Catholic or fifty years old. Another version of this commitment to social

equity goes beyond protection to representation. In this regard, various affirmative action plans have urged government officials to seek out and hire
women and minorities. Other groups, such as veterans and the handicapped,
have also received preferential treatment in the name of social equity.

Social equity concerns are sometimes at the heart of the criticisms and
legal actions directed against civil service systems. Protected groups, such
as women and minorities, frequently complain that the practices embedded
in these systems continue to perpetuate injustice. Others complain because
civil service systems do not officially recognize their characteristics as deserving of protection or proactive treatment. Hence, gay rights leaders charge
that civil service systems permit discrimination against gay and lesbian applicants and employees. From another perspective, white male job applicants
sporadically complain of not having obtained employment or promotion
because of so-called reverse discrimination.

Employee rights and well-being also constitute a salient value in civil service systems. A pervasive norm, buttressed in many instances by law and
regulation, asserts that an individual enjoys certain substantive and procedural rights as an employee of an organization. These rights increase to
the degree that four conditions, among others, hold. First, they expand to
the extent that rules limit the reasons for which executives can take actions
(firing, demotion) perceived as adverse to employee interests. For instance,
laws often constrain public executives from punishing subordinates for
engaging in certain activities off the job, such as contributing money to
political campaigns. Second, employee rights grow as the procedures (for
example, appeals systems) for taking adverse action become more elaborate
and place a greater burden of proof on executives. Third, employee rights
loom larger when employees with more seniority in an agency enjoy greater
protection from adverse action than employees with less seniority. Fourth,
employee rights grow as formal procedures require executives to consult or
bargain with official representatives of subordinates (say, union leaders) over
a broader scope of issues. Beyond these formal safeguards, the notion of
employee well-being implies a concern with the quality of work life. Work
that provides employees with psychological gratification and promotes their
physical well-being goes to the heart of this concern.

Some criticize civil service systems for being excessively deferential
with respect to employee rights. Among other things, employees are allegedly
too hard to fire or lay off. Seniority, critics claim, receives excessive weight
in decisions. Skirmishes over these and related issues erupt sporadically. Other
critics, however, charge that civil service systems fail to demonstrate sufficient respect for employee rights and well-being. For instance, concern over
drug use and AIDS in the 1980s has fueled debate over employee rights to
control who can monitor their physical condition. Guidelines issued by President Reagan required federal agencies to test designated employees for mari-
juana and cocaine use. The guidelines permitted employees to provide urine

samples without observation, unless agency officials believed that subordinates would alter or substitute samples. To guard against such "cheating," the guidelines recommended such steps as the use of bluing agents in the toilet water at testing sites, to prevent employees from diluting their samples. Union leaders denounced the plan as "tidy-bowl justice" and a violation of the constitutional rights of employees (Laurent, 1987, pp. 1, 18).

Still others have criticized civil service systems for perceived failures to permit employees greater involvement in and psychological gratification from work. For example, Golembiewski (1979) notes the tendency of civil service systems to impede job enlargement, thereby thwarting employees' sense of control over their jobs.

The Optimal Mix. These five core values of the personnel arena have several implications for those who seek to assess civil service systems and the practices of human resource managers. In some instances, a given personnel practice does not serve any of the core values well. In other cases, a practice may promote all of them.

Assessment becomes more complex when, as is often the case, personnel practices involve trade-offs among the core values. Consider, for instance, a small step that certain federal agencies have taken in recognition of the growing number of dual-career families. With the rise in the number of families in which both spouses work, persuading employees to relocate geographically can become a severe problem. Government agencies that depend on such relocation have attempted to cope with the problem by modifying personnel rules. In 1987, for instance, both the U.S. Navy and the U.S. Army adopted policies that gave spouses employment preference under certain conditions. When these military organizations transfer personnel to new duty stations, guidelines call for spouses to be hired ahead of other applicants in certain federal positions within commuting distance (Pursell, 1987, p. 17). This practice may well contribute to military effectiveness, but it stands in tension with the merit principle. It could give rise to a situation in which the spouses of military personnel obtain available jobs, even though other job applicants are more qualified.

The presence of trade-offs means that civil service systems run the risk of being "damned if they do and damned if they don't." In essence, discontent springs from the inability to forge a consensus on the appropriate weight to be assigned to particular values—to define the optimal mix of achievement on the various dimensions. This inability to reach consensus means that reform movements often contain the seeds of new discontent and assume a cyclical pattern. When some reformers succeed in causing civil service systems to increase their emphasis on certain values (for example, more political responsiveness), they prompt others to seek change on behalf of other core concerns (merit, for example, or instrumental goals) (Rosenbloom, 1986).

Uncertainty

Uncertainty permeates much of human resource management. To be sure, designers of civil service systems, and those who manage within them, sometimes know exactly what they want to do and how to do it, but on many other occasions, they lack pertinent information. Some uncertainty stems from difficulties in calibrating the performance of these systems in terms of the five core values. The degree to which civil service systems foster efficiency, effectiveness, or merit, for instance, seldom proves easy to measure. Of all the core values, those related to social equity can most readily be gauged. For example, one can compute the percentage of women and minorities occupying certain positions or scoring well in selection processes. In general, however, those who seek to evaluate civil service systems do not enjoy the luxury of baseball aficionados, who can examine a bevy of statistics that reveal much about performance.

Ambiguity also tends to characterize the means of achieving certain personnel values. For instance, the move by many governments to apply merit pay systems to many of its managers does not rest on a body of highly credible scientific evidence; to the contrary, one can find very few rigorous studies that shed much light on the efficacy of such systems (Perry, 1986). Others highlight the problem of means-ends uncertainty more generally. In this regard, McGregor (1985, pp. 44, 49, 51) notes that "federal managers themselves do not have the data that would demonstrate the adequacy or inadequacy of their own [personnel] practices." Therefore, personnel techniques remain divorced from the goals of strategic management. The same observation applies to many state and local agencies. Uncertainty about the implications of personnel practices has driven observers to extreme positions at times. Noting the problems of constructing valid written tests, one analysis suggests that "random selection may become a viable alternative to the quagmire of employee selection device validation. By definition, it gives an equal opportunity to all applicants" (Couturier and Schick, 1983, p. 323). The incompetent would presumably be screened out during their probationary periods.

What are the implications of uncertainty for discontent with civil service systems? The limits to understanding of cause-effect relations mean that the prospects for error are substantial in any effort to improve the systems. Practices hypothesized to accomplish certain objectives may do nothing of the sort, or the epiphenomena generated may prove surprising and distressing. Note that uncertainty typically exists even if one seeks to promote only one value (for example, merit). Matters become even more complex when one expects a given reform to foster simultaneous improvement in terms of several of the core personnel values. Furthermore, the complexities of evaluating the performance of civil service systems make learning from past reform efforts difficult. Hence, uncertainty can breed discontent by creating a sense that attempts to improve civil service systems seldom work.

To be sure, uncertainty may mitigate discontent and dampen conflict under some circumstances. Ignorance of the trade-offs implicit in a reform proposal can sometimes lubricate the wheels of change. Proponents of a reform can insist that it will promote one of the core personnel values, at no cost to any of the others. Those making this claim are often quite sincere and, in some cases, correct. But in other instances, trade-offs do exist, and reformers benefit from the fact that the costs of their proposals to other core values remain hazy. Ambiguity may also ameliorate discontent by giving administrators and elected officials wide latitude to interpret the performance of civil service systems and efforts to reform them. In the absence of hard evidence, they can define victory politically; they can claim that the system performs well, or that a particular reform has worked wonders. In essence, uncertainty may fuel optimistic subjective judgments (see March and Olsen, 1983, p. 290). Over time, however, potent forces often lead observers to resolve uncertainty on the side of skepticism. These forces have deep roots in the nation's political culture.

Political Culture

One major strain of the political culture of the United States encourages criticism of public agencies and, by implication, civil service systems. This cultural strain tends to tout the virtues of private enterprise, of running government like a business. The rhetoric of political campaigns, as well as the tendency of the press to play up bureaucratic foibles, fuels negative stereotypes of public agencies (Goodsell, 1985, p. 150). Thus, a substantial majority of people in the United States believe that the federal government hires too many people, and that these personnel do not have to work as hard as those employed in the private sector. Most people believe that government wastes a lot of money (Downs and Larkey, 1986, pp. 9-11). While the public expresses more positive sentiments about particular agencies and programs, many people adhere to the "grand myth" that inefficiency and ineffectiveness permeate the public sector (Goodsell, 1985). This cultural strain has fueled interest in contracting out many government functions to private enterprise.

Hence, much discontent with civil service systems probably has less to do with the specifics of their performance than with stereotypes of government's incapacity. Given this cultural bias, people may discount, ignore, or disregard evidence of accomplishment by civil service systems. When, as is more likely to be the case, considerable uncertainty clouds the particular achievements of these systems, people can easily resolve ambiguity on the side of pessimism.

A skeptical political culture, biased toward the techniques of business, means that some personnel reforms take life as much because they cater to these biases as because they stand some chance of promoting core personnel values. For instance, while merit pay motivates better performance under some circumstances (for example, in routine, nonmanagerial jobs), much evidence suggests that serious problems accompany efforts to develop and implement such plans in the public sector. In this regard, Perry (1986, p. 67) concludes that "requiring a public organization's compensation system to harness pay for motivating short-term managerial performance is not realistic." Another study (Cohen and Murnane, 1985) of merit pay in public schools argues that the effort to distinguish between good and very good performance through merit pay systems tends to exacerbate dysfunctional tensions. This study found that school systems where merit pay plans survived tended to manipulate the awards so as to minimize provocations; for instance, they would keep the differences among awards small or would pass them out to nearly everyone (pp. 7, 23, 28). Others have also expressed doubts about the merits of merit pay (Rainey, Trout, and Blunt, 1986; Downs and Larkey, 1986; U.S. General Accounting Office, 1987).

While study after study suggests the limits of merit pay, the practice remains popular with the public. Among other things, it squares with notions that government ought to be run more like a business. In the words of Donald Devine, former director of the U.S. Office of Personnel Management, "automatic increases," rather than those based on merit pay, are "something we can't justify to the private sector. It's the kind of thing that's given federal employees a bad name" (U.S. House Committee on Post Office and Civil Service, 1983, p. 563). At the local level, Cohen and Murnane (1985, p. 23) suggest that in many school districts merit play plans "seem to have been most useful for their political symbolism"; the plans "broadcast different messages at the same time"; they "seemed to tell teachers that their work was valued while telling elected officials and constituents that management was taking a tough line with the hired help"; they "helped school administrators to justify spending money on education to their boards"; and they "helped both boards and administrators to make the same argument to their communities." Hence, placating the political culture may do much more to account for some reforms than any evidence that the change will, in and of itself, directly promote any of the core personnel values. Some of the appeal of "scientific" techniques in personnel administration springs from a similar source (Elliott, 1985, pp. 140–141).

Implications for Practice

Multiple values, uncertainty, and the political culture present major challenges to those who seek to improve civil service systems and to those who manage within them. These challenges are far from insurmountable. Designers of civil service systems, as well as human resource managers, have demonstrated great ingenuity in the past and will no doubt continue to do so in the future. In dealing with these challenges, policymakers and practitioners should keep certain central propositions (among others) in mind.

First, those involved in the personnel arena need to look for reinforcing situations and to interpret reform as a quest for a better set of problems.

Some civil service rules and human resource practices do not serve any of the core values very well. In other instances, sharp trade-offs exist, where to promote one value (say, efficiency) leads to less achievement of another (say, political responsiveness). But trade-offs are not always present. A key task for civil service reformers and public managers is to seek opportunities to promote several core values simultaneously or, at a minimum, to foster achievement of one value at no cost to another.

Thus, participants in the personnel arena need to be open to the possibility of trade-offs but not to assume them. For instance, conventional wisdom holds that too much job security weakens prospects for the achievement of efficiency and effectiveness. In the private sector, however, some organizations have taken to emphasizing employment security on the grounds that the benefits of a stable work force outweigh the financial gains from layoffs. This view holds that job security not only is consistent with the pursuit of human civilization but also enhances productivity (Bolt, 1983). In a similar vein, efficiency may be ill served by vigorous efforts to appraise performance and fire the incompetent. While in a narrow sense such a practice would serve meritocratic norms, it could ultimately create a dog-eat-dog work culture that would erode employees' motivation, loyalty, and productivity. Showing respect for employee rights, even to the point of retaining some subordinates who have "lost their stuff," may ultimately spawn greater efficiency and effectiveness than a meritocratically driven commitment to organizational Darwinism (Goode, 1967).

While scanning the environment for reinforcing opportunities, participants in the personnel arena must be sensitive to cycles, to the prospect that change may well lead to better achievement with respect to one value while fueling new concern about others. Reform is better seen as a quest for a better set of problems than as a solution. One strives for a more optimal mix of achievement among the core values, while recognizing that no one system can provide complete satisfaction once and for all.

Second, participants in the personnel arena need to get in the habit of treating action as a complex hypothesis. Given the uncertainty about the achievements of civil service systems and many human resource technologies, officials need to view personnel practices and reforms as tentative: If one does A and B, then one expects X, Y, and Z to follow; officials then need to be alert to information that can shed light on the validity of the hypothesis. Such a cognitive orientation helps guard against dogma and overcommitment. It encourages a genuinely evaluative outlook and can help inoculate the personnel arena against such pathologies as the triumph of technique over purpose. It can encourage those involved in personnel administration to be vigilant in seeking out opportunities to experiment, reflect, debug, and retest, to be more open to information or explanations that run counter to expectations.

The tendency to treat action as a hypothesis should not undermine a sense of complexity. Thinking of a practice or a reform as hypothetical can become a pitfall, if it encourages those involved to impute excessive orderliness to personnel processes. Neat and simple assumptions about uni-lateral or unidirectional (as distinct from reciprocal) causation can help managers simplify their worlds. Simplification can enable them to act, rather than be overwhelmed by complexity, but they need to be aware of the limits of these simplified models of reality and to recognize the likelihood of unan-ticipated outcomes (Weick, 1979, pp. 86, 261).

The concept of action as a complex hypothesis leads naturally to a third proposition: Policymakers should encourage more systematic and rigorous research related to public personnel administration, but attempts at such uncertainty reduction ought not to be viewed naively. As those who drafted the Civil Service Reform Act of 1978 understood, there is a critical need to advance empirical research in public personnel administration. Thus, Title VI of the law called for the U.S. Office of Personnel Management to conduct research, create demonstration projects, and disseminate the results of this initiative to the public. Others have called for better information systems, which would facilitate assessment of personnel practices (McGregor, 1985, pp. 58–59).

Important as additional research is, one must guard against approach-ing it naively. Better information should foster the more sophisticated testing of hypotheses and should contribute to learning, but it is no panacea. More information will not abolish tension among advocates of different core per-sonnel values; it may even exacerbate conflict, as the stakes involved in a given personnel practice or reform become clearer. Thus, more research will not give a "technical fix" to those involved in major decisions about civil service systems. Consequently, they will need to hone the skills required to manage conflict and the politics of organizational life (Yates, 1985). Fur-thermore, the complexities of the subject, and the limits of the methodologies of social science, mean that much uncertainty will remain, even in the face of expanded research initiatives (Lindblom and Cohen, 1979). Those operat-ing in the personnel arena will need to sustain the capacity for action and commitment in the face of considerable ambiguity about the efficacy of their actions. They will need to juggle a scientific temperament with the ability to take a leap of faith.

Those committed to improving civil service systems must also guard against assumptions that research findings will "sell themselves." The per-vasive biases of the political culture about the inferiority of administration in the public sector mean that officials need to consider how to translate and communicate research findings for and to opinion leaders (for example, the media and politicians). Strategies for disseminating findings to practitioners of public personnel administration also deserve attention, since practitioners have often ignored or failed to act on the conclusions of researchers.

Fourth, faced with a negative political culture, participants in the public personnel arena need to guard against defeatism and to work toward changing that culture. The term *defeatism* refers to a kind of inferiority complex, whereby human resource managers take too limited a view of what can be accomplished. They come to believe in stereotypes about the impossibility of creative human resource management in civil service systems. As a result, they become less creative. Fortunately, most human resource managers in the public sector do not appear to have succumbed to defeatism, but participants in the personnel arena should remain vigilant in resisting this pathology. In this regard, the International Personnel Management Association, other associations of human resource professionals, and more general groups (such as the American Society for Public Administration) need to clarify the limited empirical foundation for claims of the private sector's superiority. They need to educate the public and combat negative stereotypes (Goodsell, 1985). As part of this process, scholars and others should seek out, explore, and develop case materials illustrating excellence in public personnel management. The point is not, of course, to gloss over problems engendered by civil service systems, but to promote a view more consistent with the available evidence.

Finally, those concerned with human resource management in public programs need to expand their focus across the boundaries of government. Public agencies frequently rely on other governmental or private organizations to implement their programs. This pervasive use of administration by proxy raises an intriguing question for human resource specialists: What personnel regulations should a sponsoring government impose on those implementing its programs? A clear precedent exists for regulating certain human resource practices of grantees and contractors. For instance, the professionalization of state and local government personnel stemmed in part from merit system requirements promulgated by the federal government under the Social Security Act of 1935 (Derthick, 1970). In a similar vein, the U.S. Office of Federal Contract Compliance imposed certain affirmative action requirements on private firms that had contracts with the federal government. Drawing on these and related precedents, should government impose human resource requirements on grantees and contractors? Or should it deregulate them? The answers to these and related questions will do much to shape the mix of core personnel values represented in public programs. Those who design and manage within civil service systems need to address these questions explicitly.

Summary

This chapter has pointed to three major factors that impinge on civil service systems and on the practice of human resource management: multiple values, uncertainty, and political culture. However inappropriately, these factors often encourage discontent with civil service systems. Criticism sometimes springs from trade-offs among core personnel values, and from the inability to forge a consensus on the appropriate mix of values. Uncertainty can also spark discontent. It heightens the risk that reform initiatives will yield unanticipated and undesirable consequences or otherwise fail. The absence of crisp indicators of achievement with regard to most of the core values opens the door to the possibility that outsiders will see problems even where none exist. A political culture skeptical about the public sector's performance increases the prospects that pessimism will take root and that officials will pursue practices that are alleged to produce benefits in the private sector but that stand little chance of yielding desirable results for public personnel management.

In meeting these and related challenges, participants in the personnel arena need to search for alternatives that minimize trade-offs and to view reform as the quest for a better set of problems. They need to treat action as a complex hypothesis and encourage more evaluative research, but they should not assume that such research can eradicate ambiguity or provide a "technical fix" for human resource management. Those involved in the public personnel arena also need to guard against defeatism and to work with other professional groups to combat negative stereotypes. Finally, they should adopt a more comprehensive perspective on civil service systems, one that acknowledges the growing pervasiveness of administration by proxy.

References

Bolt, J. F. "Job Security: Its Time Has Come." *Harvard Business Review,* 1983, *61,* 115–123.

Cohen, D. K., and Murnane, R. J. "The Merits of Merit Pay." *The Public Interest,* 1985, *80,* 3–30.

Couturier, J. J., and Schick, R. P. "The Second Century of Civil Service Reform: An Agenda for the 1980s." In S. W. Hays and R. C. Kearney (eds.), *Public Personnel Administration: Problems and Prospects.* Englewood Cliffs, N.J.: Prentice-Hall, 1983.

Derthick, M. *The Influence of Federal Grants: Public Assistance in Massachusetts.* Cambridge, Mass.: Harvard University Press, 1970.

Downs, G. W., and Larkey, P. D. *The Search for Government Efficiency.* New York: Random House, 1986.

Elling, R. C. "Civil Service, Collective Bargaining, and Personnel-Related Impediments to Effective State Management." *Review of Public Personnel Administration,* 1986, *6,* 73–93.

Elliott, R. H. *Public Personnel Administration: A Values Perspective.* Reston, Va.: Reston, 1985.

Golembiewski, R. T. "Civil Service and Managing Work: Some Unintended Consequences." In F. J. Thompson (ed.), *Classics of Public Personnel Policy.* Oak Park, Ill.: Moore Publishing, 1979.

Goode, W. J. "The Protection of the Inept." *American Sociological Review,* 1967, *32,* 5–19.

Goodsell, C. T. *The Case for Bureaucracy.* (2nd ed.) Chatham, N.J.: Chatham House, 1985.

Johnston, M. "Patrons and Clients, Jobs and Machines: A Case Study of the Uses of Patronage." *American Political Science Review,* 1979, *73,* 385–398.

Kaufman, H. "The Growth of the Federal Personnel System." In W. S. Sayre (ed.), *The Federal Government Service*. Englewood Cliffs, N.J.: Prentice-Hall, 1965.

Klingner, D. E., and Nalbandian, J. *Public Personnel Management*. Englewood Cliffs, N.J.: Prentice-Hall, 1985.

Laurent, A. "Drug Guidelines Complete." *Federal Times*, Mar. 2, 1987, pp. 1, 18.

Lindblom, C. E., and Cohen, D. K. *Usable Knowledge*. New Haven, Conn.: Yale University Press, 1979.

Lowi, T. J. *The End of Liberalism*. New York: Norton, 1969.

Lynn, L. E., Jr. "The Reagan Administration and the Renitent Bureaucracy." In L. M. Salamon and M. S. Lund (eds.), *The Reagan Presidency and the Governing of America*. Washington, D.C.: Urban Institute Press, 1984.

McGregor, E. B., Jr. "The Grace Commission's Challenge to Public Personnel Administration." In C. H. Levine (ed.), *The Unfinished Agenda for Civil Service Reform: Implications of the Grace Commission Report*. Washington, D.C.: Brookings Institution, 1985.

March, J. G., and Olsen, J. B. "What Administrative Reorganization Tells Us About Governing." *American Political Science Review*, 1983, *77*, 281-296.

Nathan, R. P. *The Administrative Presidency*. New York: Wiley, 1983.

National Academy of Public Administration. *Revitalizing Federal Management: Managers and Their Overburdened Systems*. Washington, D.C.: National Academy of Public Administration, 1983.

Newland, C. A. "A Mid-Term Appraisal—The Reagan Presidency: Limited Government and Political Administration." *Public Administration Review*, 1983, *43*, 1-21.

Perry, J. L. "Merit Pay Systems in the Public Sector: The Case for a Failure of Theory." *Review of Public Personnel Administration*, 1986, *7*, 57-69.

Pursell, R. "Navy Helping Spouses Find Federal Jobs." *Federal Times*, Aug. 24, 1987, p. 17.

Rainey, H. G., Trout, C., and Blunt, B. "Reward Expectancies and Other Work-Related Attitudes in Public and Private Organizations: A Review and Extension." *Review of Public Personnel Administration*, 1986, *6*, 50-72.

Rosen, B. "Crises in the U.S. Civil Service." *Public Administration Review*, 1986, *46*, 207-214.

Rosenbloom, D. H. "A Theory of Public Personnel Reforms." In F. S. Lane (ed.), *Current Issues in Public Administration*. New York: St. Martin's Press, 1986.

Savas, E. S. *Privatizing the Public Sector: How to Shrink Government*. Chatham, N.J.: Chatham House, 1982.

Savas, E. S., and Ginsburg, S. G. "The Civil Service: A Meritless System?" In F. J. Thompson (ed.), *Classics of Public Personnel Policy*. Oak Park, Ill.: Moore Publishing, 1979.

Sayre, W. S. "The Triumph of Techniques over Purpose." In F. J. Thompson (ed.), *Classics of Public Personnel Policy*. Oak Park, Ill.: Moore Publishing, 1979.

Sorauf, F. J. "The Silent Revolution in Patronage." *Public Administration Review*, 1960, *20*, 28–34.

Thompson, F. J. (ed.). *Classics of Public Personnel Policy*. Oak Park, Ill.: Moore Publishing, 1979.

U.S. General Accounting Office. *Pay for Performance: Implementation of the Performance Management and Recognition System*. Washington, D.C.: U.S. General Accounting Office, 1987.

U.S. House Committee on Post Office and Civil Service. *Civil Service Oversight*. Washington, D.C.: U.S. Government Printing Office, 1983.

Vaughn, R. G. *The Spoiled System*. New York: Charter House, 1975.

Weick, K. *The Social Psychology of Organizing*. Reading, Mass.: Addison-Wesley, 1979.

Wolfinger, R. E. "Why Political Machines Have Not Withered Away and Other Revisionist Thoughts." *Journal of Politics*, 1972, *34*, 365–398.

Yates, D., Jr. *The Politics of Management: Exploring the Inner Workings of Public and Private Organizations*. San Francisco: Jossey-Bass, 1985.

Charles A. Pounian
Jeffrey J. Fuller

26

Compensating Public Employees

The objective of a compensation program for a public agency should be to support the mission of the agency through the enhancement of the recruitment, retention, and motivation of qualified employees. Traditional governmental personnel systems have often focused on a different objective: limiting the role of managers in making appointments or fixing salaries.

Personnel systems based on civil service practices generally have left managers with very limited discretion in most critical personnel decision making, including compensation. The typical pattern provides for a step pay plan, with a designated starting salary and increases based on longevity, supplemented by cost-of-living adjustments. Any links to recruitment, performance appraisals, or other aspects of the human resources system are often lacking. The human resources program of a public agency should be directed at support of the purpose for which the agency was created—the public services determined necessary through the political process. Therefore, the success of a compensation program for a public agency can best be judged by the degree to which the program facilitates better service to the public.

Criteria for a Successful Compensation Program

An effective compensation program must be based on a clearly communicated policy and should have the following characteristics (Rock, 1984).

Internally Equitable. The program should ensure that salaries reflect the relative value of each job to the agency and should recognize job content and pay relationships among the various positions and job families.

375

Externally Competitive. Salaries should be realistic in relation to other employees competing for needed personnel. There should be an awareness of the impact of labor market factors on compensation and benefit schedules and on the ability to attract and retain qualified employees.

Supportive of Sound Administrative Actions. Guidelines and controls should permit effective salary program management, provide the capability to recognize different levels of performance and tenure, and be responsive to any changes in the organization. The program should be flexible and supportive during any reorganization.

Easily Communicated. The principles and procedures of the program should be understood by employees and should enhance their view of the program as fair and competitive.

In Legal Compliance. The program must be cognizant of federal laws that affect compensation practices, such as the Equal Pay Act, Title VII of the Civil Rights Act, the Age Discrimination in Employment Act, and the Fair Labor Standards Act, as well as relevant state and local laws.

Program Elements Defined

Some of the basic elements of a compensation program should be defined to provide a common understanding. These elements include the following.

Classification of Positions. Positions are grouped into classes or jobs. All the positions in a class or job have similar duties and responsibilities and are of the same relative value to the organization. All positions in the same class or job may be treated on the same basis for a variety of personnel actions, such as selection, promotion, compensation, and training.

Job Evaluation. There is systematic review of a job (class of positions) to determine its value to the organization for purposes of compensation and other administrative actions. The worth of a job may be determined by any of several systems, to be described later.

Base Compensation. The annual salary of an employee, including deductions, is the base compensation.

Total Remuneration. This is the full monetary value provided to an employee. It includes base compensation plus the value of all benefits provided to the employee (for example, health insurance, pension, and disability).

Salary Administration. The collective rules and systems that govern the delivery of compensation to employees—through base compensation, incentive pay (such as bonuses), and benefits—are referred to as *salary administration.*

Developing Effective Compensation Programs

Unless the organization is on the drawing board and not yet operational, it will already have some form of compensation plan in place. All compensation programs share the same goals: to attract, retain, and motivate qualified employees for the organization. The question is this: Does the current pay program meet the organization's objectives for internal equity, external competitiveness, legal compliance, and ease of administration? There are several indicators of the quality of the existing pay program. The most important of these are the following:

Turnover. Is the organization losing qualified employees to other employers? How high is the turnover, expressed as a percentage of full-time employees?

Vacancies. When job openings occur, do pay ranges make it difficult to get qualified candidates to accept employment offers? How long do positions remain vacant?

Tenure. Do employees stay in their jobs longer than is expected or desirable from the standpoint of organizational vitality?

Survey Data. In reviews of survey data, do salaries appear to be too high or too low?

These are rough indicators that must be carefully interpreted and used only in the preliminary assessment of the health of a compensation program. Where possible, multiple data sources should be used, to increase confidence in the findings. Furthermore, the indicators must be interpreted in the context of the organization's strategic direction. High turnover and low market position may be desirable in an agency whose size is diminishing because of decreasing service demands or decreased funding. The same indicators in a fast-growing agency would probably be disastrous.

A governmental agency should conduct a formal review of its compensation practices whenever there is uncertainty about the pay program's effectiveness. A comprehensive review process requires six steps:

1. Describe each unique class of positions or jobs.
2. Establish a hierarchy of jobs on the basis of their relative value to the organization.

3. Analyze internal equity.
4. Analyze external competitiveness.
5. Develop a compensation philosophy.
6. Link the compensation plan to human resources strategy.

Describing Jobs

An effective compensation program depends on a thorough understanding of job content and requirements. This information is used to establish the relationship between jobs, on the basis of their value to the organization, for comparison with similar jobs in the employment marketplace and for performance management. A variety of methods are used to collect information on job content, including observation of work, interviews, and position-description questionnaires. Each method or combination of methods is appropriate under certain circumstances but not in others. Position-description questionnaires are expeditious and cost-effective for positions where job content is easily understood and position incumbents can communicate effectively in writing. Direct observation of work by trained job analysts can be used effectively to capture job content of positions where work is repetitious. To further understanding of managerial jobs, or of individual contributors' positions when these are highly technical, job content information should be collected by a skilled interviewer. Regardless of the data-collection method chosen, the result should be a description of each job, which specifies the following elements.

Why the Job Exists. Its general function and primary objective should be defined, as well as important results that the incumbent must achieve in order to be considered a competent performer.

The Job's Nature and Scope. This element includes the environment in which the job operates, its place in the organizational structure, its dependence on other jobs and functions, its major duties and responsibilities, and its basic challenges.

Key Dimensions. These include, for example, operating budgets, number of employees, number of cases handled per year, and number of client contacts.

Freedom to Act. This element concerns the nature and source of control that limits the incumbent's ability to make final decisions and take action.

Position descriptions prepared by job analysts must be approved by incumbents and reviewed for accuracy and completeness by supervisors, to ensure common understanding of jobs' key elements.

Establishing a Job Hierarchy

To establish internal equity, some basis must be found for determining the relative size differences among jobs in an organization.

Job size refers to a position's relative value in an organization: Larger jobs have greater internal value to the organization than smaller jobs do. It is important to understand that job size is established by job design, not by the performance of the job holder. Many governmental agencies define fairness in terms of compensable factors and use methodologies for job evaluation that determine the size of jobs. All such evaluation programs are based on the analysis of job content and typically use position descriptions as source documents that establish positions' nature and scope, as well as their requirements for the following factors:

- Specialized knowledge and skills (however acquired) needed for job performance, including education and experience
- Managerial skills
- Human relations skills in supervisory positions or in interactions with others
- Degree of definition of directions and variety of challenges in solving problems
- Accountability and answerability for action, as measured by freedom to act and influence results.

These kinds of factors may be defined in different terms, depending on the system being applied. The four methods of job evaluation most commonly used in the public sector are whole-job ranking, job classification, point systems, and factor comparison.

Whole-job ranking is the simplest of the four methods. Jobs are ranked from highest to lowest, without regard for individual compensable elements, focusing rather on the overall value of each job relative to others.

Job classification defines a series of job classes by qualitatively describing levels of skill, effort, and responsibility in a class specification. Jobs are then fitted into the classes provided. (This method, as well as the first, is considered *nonquantitative* because it does not produce quantitative measures of compensable factors.)

Point systems measure jobs by using factors that have been divided into several quantitative levels of difficulty. Points are assigned to each difficulty level, and each of the factors is weighted. A single number is obtained, which represents the evaluated job content for each position.

Factor comparison, like whole-job ranking, makes job-to-job comparisons, but factor comparison takes into account several aspects of job difficulty, including intellectual requirements, skills, responsibilities, and working conditions. Factors are assigned weights, and each job is ranked on each factor.

Quantitative rankings are produced through multiplication of the rank on each factor by the factor weight.

Whole-job ranking programs typically suffer credibility problems, because ranking decisions cannot easily be explained to employees. Job classification has been used widely in governmental agencies because it is relatively inexpensive. Nevertheless, many view job classification as inflexible, imprecise, and unresponsive to changes in job design and organizational structure. Point systems and factor comparison are used by most major corporations and are gaining popularity in many state and local governments.

Regardless of the job evaluation system an organization uses, the resultant job hierarchy is a snapshot of the organization at any given time. Organizations, and therefore jobs, are dynamic. Changes in public policy, service levels, technology, and programs may cause changes in the structure of an organization and in the way jobs are designed.

Internal Equity

In general, one would expect people holding jobs of greater value to an organization to be paid more than people holding jobs of lesser value. Once a job hierarchy has been established, internal pay relationships can be analyzed and their appropriateness determined.

This analysis considers three questions. First, are employees in larger jobs actually paid more than those in smaller jobs? Second, how are people in job families or market groups (engineers, accountants, chemists, and clerical workers) paid relative to one another? For instance, does the organization pay a premium to people in some job groups? If it does, then the organization should determine whether the premium is a response to market factors or to organizational values. Third, are salaries paid within an appropriate range, given the performance, experience, and qualifications of incumbents? While an organization's pay practice may be internally equitable, it may also restrict the organization's ability to compete in the salary market. Internal equity must be tempered with external competitiveness.

In some cases, internal equity and external competitiveness clearly conflict. A clear example is that of a public hospital, where a medical director reports to a chief executive officer (CEO). If internal equity were the only issue, compensation would be based on reporting relationships. The CEO is responsible for the entire hospital, including the work of the medical director, and therefore would be paid more. Nevertheless, the labor market for physicians is such that a medical director must be at a higher pay level, so that the hospital can attract and retain people of competence. If, in contrast, we maintain an internally equitable relationship between the two positions, by allowing the medical director's salary to be established at a competitive level in the physicians' market and paying the CEO at yet a higher rate (to reflect the reporting relationship), other problems arise. The raising of the CEO's salary affects his or her position's relationship with all subordinate positions: Either the salaries of other persons reporting to the CEO are raised out of proportion to the outside market, or the CEO will be paid disproportionately well, as compared to other key personnel (aside from the medical director). As a general principle, it is good to balance internal equity and external competitiveness, but it is necessary to adjust to the labor market in order to obtain the services of those persons necessary to the achievement of goals.

The criteria used to establish a compensation program should be easily communicated to employees and easily understood. A governmental agency that takes a positive approach to compensation will develop a statement of philosophy—for example, ''The salary and benefits provided by the agency are for the purpose of attracting, motivating, and retaining competent employees to provide services at a level established by the City Council. Specific salary and benefit levels will be determined on the basis of internal equity, external competitiveness, and fiscal ability. The target rate is the median of the public sector market for cities between fifty thousand and seventy-five thousand population in the Midwest.''

Assessing External Competitiveness

The first step in assessing the external competitiveness of an organization's pay practice is to define the marketplaces in which the organization competes for talent. Organizations must understand where employees are hired from, and where they go when they leave. Most organizations compete in a variety of employment markets. Nonexempt employees (those covered by the provisions of the Fair Labor Standards Act), such as clerical and maintenance workers, may be hired from local markets, while professional employees and department heads are recruited on a regional or national basis. Some positions or job families are found only in other governmental agencies, while others (for example, data processing, engineering, and health care positions) must be recruited from a broader marketplace, including both the public and the private sectors. Once employment markets are identified, salary surveys provide the data necessary for comparisons. The three common types of salary surveys involve title match, demographic control, and job evaluation.

The *title match* survey is the most common approach. Typically, the survey states a title and provides a brief description of the position being surveyed. Respondents determine whether they have a match and, if so, provide the data for their organizations. Title match surveys provide the most inexpensive approach to compensation but are usually poor data sources. Title match ignores major differences in organizational size and structure, as well as differences in the primary accountability of individual incumbents.

Demographic control surveys attempt to counteract this problem by taking into account key demographic variables, such as population, revenues, number of employees, and geographical location.

A greater degree of precision in comparing salary practices to external marketplaces can be achieved by surveys based on *job evaluation*. This process applies a measurement methodology to each position included in the survey. The content of each job, for each participating organization, is evaluated according to the common factors of the methodology. These factors recognize critical differences between specific organizations and jobs, differences that other survey approaches tend to ignore. On the basis of job size and salary as variables, scattergrams can be constructed, and salary practice lines can be obtained by means of linear regression.

On the basis of comparing its current pay practices with those of the market, an organization can determine where it wants to pay. This decision should take into consideration the organization's employment needs, its access to human resources, its ability to pay, its willingness to pay, the current status of its internal equity, and its pay practice relative to appropriate external marketplaces.

When considering the internal equity of current pay practices, the organization must analyze pay relationships between market groups, as well as across a broad spectrum of job content. For example, how are office and clerical employees paid relative to blue-collar workers in jobs of similar size within the organization? What is the relationship between the annual take-home pay of high-level nonsupervisory employees and first-line supervisors? The resulting pay plan should reflect a balance between the organization's desire for internal equity, on the one hand, and market demands, on the other.

Careful analysis of internal equity and external competitiveness, coupled with an articulated compensation philosophy, should result in a series of pay ranges designed to meet the organization's human resources objectives. Movement through those salary ranges should be based on compensable factors that support the achievement of organization goals and objectives.

Issues Affecting Program Management

There are many similarities between compensation practices in the private sector and in government, and all signs indicate that the areas of difference are diminishing. There are, however, some issues that affect public agencies differently. The most important differences are related to sources of funding (for public agencies, the taxpayers), public debate of budgets and compensation plans (with news media coverage), and requirements of various laws that affect public bodies.

A number of key issues (with varying degrees of similarity to issues in the private sector) affect public agencies. These issues are not discrete; they overlap, and they include the following.

Collective Bargaining. In the past quarter-century, an increasing number of public agencies have entered into collective bargaining agreements with many of their employees. This practice has varying effects, but it often affects salary schedules, cost-of-living increases, and other aspects of compensation programs. Collective bargaining also indirectly affects compensation practices for management employees and others not covered by contracts. For example, in dealing with the compensation of management employees, it is difficult not to at least match any gains in salary or benefits granted to employees who are covered under collective bargaining contracts.

Executive Compensation. Because of many factors, public executives, with very few exceptions, are paid less than their counterparts in the private sector. Compensation is often limited by the salary of the elected official to whom an executive reports. This limitation very often causes competent persons in key jobs to leave the public sector for more lucrative fields. In some cases, special pay schedules have been developed to respond to this issue. Where compensation of executives is concerned, it is not possible to respond to every initiative in the private sector. Nevertheless, additional efforts must be made to attract the most capable candidates available for these important assignments.

Compression of Salaries. Salaries of public executives and managers are below those of their private sector counterparts. Nonmanagement salaries, however, tend to reflect the market because of collective bargaining and greater public acceptance of public/private equity for these positions. The combination of artificially low salaries for top managers (relative to a broad managerial marketplace) and fully market-competitive pay for nonmanagerial employees compresses the salaries in between these levels. Therefore, as jobs get larger, pay differentials between job levels tend to get smaller. As a result, promotional increases are often quite small and lack the desired motivational effects. Also, because of overtime, nonexempt employees often approach or surpass supervisors in total income. Compression is a particularly persistent and difficult problem to solve in the public sector.

Pay for Performance. Private organizations have often used forms of incentive pay. In recent years, public bodies have recognized that some link between job performance and pay is needed to produce the most effective and efficient results. For example, step increases could be linked with performance appraisals or with provision of bonuses for outstanding performance.

Total Remuneration. Very often, the rationale for keeping salaries of public employees below market levels is based on what is assumed to be a rich benefits package—for example, pensions, sick leave, holidays, plus the security associated with public employment. This assumption should be tested through appropriate survey techniques. Given the changing nature of private sector benefits, this assumption may be erroneous. Surveys conducted by governmental agencies should make comparisons of the total remuneration of employees—base compensation plus the value of benefits—to be sure of the total competitive situation. This information can also be the basis of communicating important information to employees concerning total remuneration.

Fairness. While public and private sector employers alike have the responsibility to comply with federal laws, governmental agencies are more likely to attract attention if they are charged with noncompliance. Moreover, government should take a leadership role in ensuring fair treatment of employees. The issue is very simple: Employment decisions, including decisions on compensation, should be based on the ability of an employee to perform the work, not on factors extraneous to work (such as age, sex, race, and national origin). Many employers, including governments, had policies based on discrimination (for example, women custodial workers were paid less than men) when such policies were not illegal. They are now illegal, and they have always been a foolish use of human resources.

Also related to fairness is the issue of comparable worth. The basis of the Equal Pay Act is well accepted in law and in practice. If two people in the same agency are doing substantially the same work, they should be paid on the same basis. The theory of comparable worth states that if there are two dissimilar positions of comparable value to the same organization, they should be paid on the same basis. Many state governments have funded studies of comparable worth. Some collective bargaining agreements provide for some classes of positions, filled predominantly by women, to be given additional increments based on comparable worth. The issue of comparable worth is one that will continue to receive attention in the years ahead. At this time, there is no clear-cut answer, nor is there general acceptance of the issue's validity, as there is of the issue of equal pay for equal work.

Implications for Effective Practice

There is no one best way to establish a compensation program. A wide variety of successful programs exist throughout the country at various levels of government. A successful program depends on a number of factors related to a jurisdiction, such as number and kinds of positions, laws, the nature of the personnel system, labor market considerations, the local economy, and the history of the compensation program.

Regardless of the specific aspects of the program—type of classification system, structure of compensation plan, or clarity of compensation policy—there are several required steps to safeguard the development of a sound program.

Get Good Data. The data obtained must be relevant to the issue at hand: the development of an appropriate compensation program responsive to the needs of the agency. This means getting good information by which to evaluate jobs. The employee and his or her supervisor must play an active role in the gathering of the data. The data should be verified by job analysts, at least on a sample basis. In conducting labor market surveys, the other employers selected for a survey must be competitors in the same labor market, employers viewed as similar in nature (for example, county governments with budgets of fifty million to one hundred million) or reflective of a national or regional trend. Clearly, the more specifically the data relate to the recruitment and retention of employees in the local market, the better the data and the conclusions that are reached. In many cases, good data can be obtained from the U.S. Bureau of Labor Statistics, other governmental agencies, or such consortia as municipal leagues, and these data will limit the need for special surveys. Such sources should be checked as possible means to obtain good data and cut costs.

Analyze Data Carefully. The analysis of the available data is critical to the development of sound recommendations that are clear and provide a basis of action. There must be adherence to the criteria established for whatever system has been adopted, in order to maintain a fair, consistent program. The conclusions and recommendations that are reached should be congruent with the objectives set forth for the program: internal equity, external competitiveness, compliance with appropriate laws, fair and consistent administration, and ease of communicability to employees. The presentation of the data in a manner that is easy to understand is vital to the acceptance of the recommendations. The analysis should be presented, as simply and directly as possible, in graphic form to enhance understanding. The analysis of internal equity should clearly describe the hierarchy of jobs and the bases of the conclusions that have been reached. The analysis of external competitiveness should clearly indicate the relationship of compensation practices to the defined competition. All analysis should be conducted with presentation to policymakers clearly in mind.

Present Options to Policymakers. The installation of the program must be coordinated with the budgetary process and must receive necessary legislative and executive approval before it can be established. All these steps must be carefully calculated in order to ensure a smooth transition.

A preliminary report on options should be developed for presentation to policymakers, the appointed and elected officials who must assume the responsibility for the administrative and financial ramifications of programs. Decision makers should be given all necessary information concerning available options and the positive and negative consequences of each one. It is particularly important to prepare cost analyses of the different options.

The responsibility of the human resources staff is to ease the burden of policymakers by providing all necessary data and analyses to facilitate decision making. Thoroughness will provide a greater chance of implementing a compensation program that will help the governmental body provide good services to its citizens.

Plan Communications. Good communications with employees concerning compensation are vital to effective administration of the program. Perhaps nothing is more detrimental to the adoption of an effective program than suspicion and rumor. The way to counter suspicion and rumor is through forthright communication on a timely basis. This is most critical at two points: at the inception of a study of the system, and at the time new policies are adopted and about to be implemented.

Needless to say, the management team must be apprised of all aspects of the program before employees are informed. The management team should play a significant role in the communication process, if only as a channel to employees. It is imperative that the management team understand the changes and be able to respond correctly to questions or refer questions to a central source.

All personnel responsible for decision making, or for processing personnel actions affected by the compensation program, should be thoroughly briefed about any changes in policy or practice. In all cases, there should be a single source for answers to questions that develop during implementation. The need for good communications does not cease when a program is implemented. Any time a significant change is made, it is essential that a plan be developed for communicating with employees.

Investment in Administration

A pay program, like any other system, requires time and attention. For the program to be effective over the long term, elected and appointed officials must work to ensure that it stays on track and supports the policy and management needs of the government. All too often, governmental bodies spend tens of thousands of dollars on pay programs, and the only maintenance offered is in annual salary adjustments given at budget time.

Governments that recognize pay programs as the foundation of human resources investment understand that pay programs must adapt over time. Changes in work methods, technology, and structure all affect organizational relationships and may require changes in how people are paid.

As an organization changes, so do people. They leave, and their replacements need to understand the workings of their new employers. New employees develop new skills and interests and become more valuable to operations, taking on larger jobs.

If pay is tied to performance, then there needs to be ongoing training in how the two are linked. Supervisors need to be able to work with employees in improving performance. This is a learned skill, which needs expert assistance if the pay and performance link is to be successful.

Finally, there must be a constant awareness that labor markets are dynamic—that supply and demand for various kinds of employees will change over time. For example, computer programmers are in much greater supply now than they were ten years ago; nurses, in contrast, who were plentiful ten years ago, are now in very short supply. Changes in governmental agencies, whether reflective of expansion or contraction, are also factors that the compensation program must accommodate.

Once a program is in place, it must be able to respond to change and to support the mission of the organization. A well-developed and soundly administered compensation program will accomplish its purpose through better public service and, consequently, a public better served.

Summary

The ability of a public sector agency to recruit, retain, and motivate competent employees is directly related to the nature of its compensation program. Traditional systems have limited the role and effectiveness of government managers in compensation administration. Carefully developed and well-administered compensation programs enhance the probability of an agency's achievement of the organizational mission through a more competent and motivated work force. Therefore, the installation of such programs is critical to effective human resources management.

An effective compensation program must be internally equitable, competitive in the external labor market, supportive of sound administrative practices, easily communicated, and in legal compliance.

Job information, including accurate job descriptions, is essential to the development and implementation of sound compensation programs. Such information provides the basis of establishing a job hierarchy through job evaluation. The application of a sound methodology for job evaluation will ensure a fair reward system, based on the value of jobs to the organization, and provide the basis of an analysis of pay relationships to determine internal equity. These evaluations are also used in making comparisons with the external labor market to determine competitiveness with other employers.

There is no one best way to establish a compensation program or to make adjustments to existing programs. Regardless of the methodology applied, it must be based on good data and on careful analysis of those data. Once this is done, recommendations for action can be presented in a comprehensive manner to policymakers for their consideration.

A compensation system requires time and attention. It cannot be considered static. It must be responsive to the changing needs of an agency and to changes in the outside labor market.

Finally, any successful compensation program must have a strong communications component. Employees need to understand the program and, in particular, how it rewards them for good performance.

References

Rock, M. L. (ed.). *Handbook of Wage and Salary Administration.* (2nd ed.) New York: McGraw-Hill, 1984.

27

Wilbur C. Rich

Appraising Employee Performance

The effective use of performance appraisals remains one of the most difficult aspects of human resources management. Public managers at all levels of government have had to grapple with the uncertainty of the process, the unreliability of instruments, and the unrealistic expectations of elected and appointed officials. Rice (1985) has called performance review the job nobody likes; the dreadful work must be done, however. Overcoming the anxiety of an evaluation encounter is never easy for the supervisor or the subordinate. The timing always seems wrong, and the accuracy is suspect. Yet employees must be assessed for selection, promotion, transfer, and job assignments. The problem arises when one attempts to conceptualize or capture a series of events, impressions, and observations in a formal document. Considerable research, improvements in instrument construction, and legal protections for employees still leave a variety of questions concerning the efficacy of the appraisal process itself.

This chapter answers questions about when subordinates should be judged, by whom, and how often. It also reviews the issues of bias, rater abuse, and employee participation. In offering some insights into the recurrent problems of performance appraisal, it discusses theories of effective practice and their implications for public management.

In a seminal article on performance appraisal, McGregor (1957, p. 90), the late management analyst, expressed his uneasiness about the appraisal process: "Managers are uncomfortable when they are put in the position of 'playing God.'" Understandably, managers will resist this role in the appraisal process. Overcoming such resistance requires placing the major responsibility for goal setting on subordinates, rather than on supervisors.

By focusing attention on the development of subordinates, managers will relieve the anxiety of the process and facilitate a more constructive relationship.

Since McGregor's article, many other writers have supported the notion of transforming the evaluation encounter into a developmental experience. Under this scheme, managers become coaches rather than judges. Few public managers have taken this advice, either because they do not have the same control over the process as their private sector counterparts do or because they adhere to the old school ("Theory X" management) of using appraisals as rewards and punishment. Whatever the reason, the appraisal process in the public sector has become more controversial, fragmented, and confusing. Consequently, the evaluation encounter remains adversarial.

Growing apprehension about performance appraisal systems seems to be a reaction to the increased reliance on results for making human resources decisions. Renewed interest in productivity, coupled with fiscal uncertainty, has prompted a closer look at employees. Before an actual evaluation begins, a manager must ask some preliminary questions: What is expected of civil servants? Do they understand what is expected of them? What do they expect of themselves? Is there a conflict between their expectations and those of the organization? These preparatory questions are essential to the performance appraisal process and to what can be called the norm of effective practice and presentation.

Norms of Effective Practice

As the significance of performance appraisal grows, so does the demand for clearer definitions of supervisor-subordinate relations. Supervisors are expected to adhere to a norm of effective practice—that is, to organize the task of assessment in a fair, efficient, and effective manner. Conversely, subordinates are also expected to adhere to a norm of effective presentation—that is, to complete and display assigned work in a timely, measurable, and acceptable manner. The term *display* is used here in its broadest sense. For example, subordinates are obligated to allow the supervisor to examine, count, and otherwise evaluate the work performed. Without these norms, performance appraisal would be neither useful nor meaningful.

The maintenance of these norms is required to avoid role stress and ambiguity. Each participant in performance appraisal must understand the implicit boundaries for acceptable performance. It is a two-way street, involving rules of reciprocity.

To meet the norms of effective practice and presentation, performance appraisal should do the following things:

- Be job-related and job-specific, measuring the task performed and being tailored to the job examined
- Measure only observable behavior

- Conform to acceptable standards of clarity in wording (ambiguity and vagueness compromise the instrument)
- Avoid subjective and personal references (words such as *sincerity* and *commitment* should not be used unless these characteristics can be measured)
- Be attempted only after a concerted effort to communicate performance standards to employees
- Be attempted only after rater training has been completed
- Be scheduled at convenient intervals
- Be documented and supported with collaborating evidence
- Be validated and updated regularly
- Maximize employee participation

These rules of conduct go beyond the formal obligations of union contracts and employee manuals. They are found at the core of the microdynamics that characterize human relations. It is this interaction that reinforces the legitimacy of the appraisal process.

Specifically, the norms of effective practice and presentation require some method of participative appraisal, including consultation between the supervisor and subordinates throughout the process; reliable and continuous training for raters, in order to avoid abuse and error; and a nondiscriminatory implementation process, with a commitment to unbiased evaluation. Meeting any of these requirements entails creating the appropriate environment and attitudes.

Perils of Selecting Appraisal Instruments

Performance appraisals are of two types: formal and informal. Although these types are not mutually exclusive, they are often treated separately. Informal evaluation of employees may involve simple supervision by managers. Formal evaluations are usually more elaborate and binding. Supervisors are expected to know the strengths and weaknesses of their subordinates, regardless of whether there is a formal evaluation process.

The selection of an instrument, perhaps the most important part of performance appraisal, requires thoughtful consideration of factors ranging from operating costs to the organization's overall readiness for the system. Convenience and simplicity should never be the guiding principle of instrument selection. In other words, effective practice and presentation require consultation of the participants. The choice of a particular instrument should be justified and defended by the participants; otherwise, the cooperative and facilitative environment will be difficult, if not impossible, to create. Employees should be involved in writing the rationale for and the evaluation of the instrument.

Instruments can be divided into two basic types: trait-oriented and behavior-oriented. The trait-oriented scales range from simple checklists, used to evaluate low-level jobs, to management by objectives, used to evaluate professional and managerial employees. Regardless of the choice of instrument, the standard of effective practice must be met.

The graphic scale, the most widely used instrument, can meet the requirements of job relatedness, but care must be taken that trait labels are not abstract. Trait labels, such as *reliability* and *initiative,* are usually followed with short descriptive statements. Such an instrument also provides explanations of job factors and of the performance levels used for rating. Brief and understandable explanations enhance the rating process. A supervisor is simply required to mark the line or box that best describes the employee. Anything so simple must have problems, however, and this instrument does. Words used in rating categories and for job factors may be vague and ambiguous, and they should not mean simply what the supervisor wants them to mean. There must be some shared meaning between rater and ratees. Without this agreement, the traits are meaningless.

Despite these problems, trait-oriented scales continue to have fans. Users apparently like their simplicity and pure subjectivity. Citing Landy and Farr (1980), who claim that thirty years of research have failed to develop a better instrument than graphic scales, Allen (1983) lauds these scales as efficient and effective. In his study of firefighters in Mobile, Alabama, he found no differences in scores of blacks and whites; he also found a reduction in leniency bias. Murphy and Constans (1987, p. 577) support claims of objectivity for graphic scales. They assert that "behaviorally oriented scales are not always more objective than trait scales or graphic scales."

Employee participation is also a hallmark of behavior-oriented scales. Critical incident technique (CIT) and behaviorally anchored rating scales (BARS) require consultation among participants to create wording. The whole process of scale development is consistent with effective practice and presentation. Nevertheless, bias appears when the group relies too heavily on current or recent events to formulate examples of unacceptable behavioral criteria. The negative side of the ledger tends to get the most attention in the construction process.

BARS assume that employees can give accurate descriptions of effective and ineffective behavior or performance. Standards emerge from group discussions of critical incidents in the workplace. After a series of sessions, a scale is developed for each job dimension. This type of measuring device is especially useful in multirater situations. If there is a high level of interrater agreement, the scale is assumed to measure what it was designed to measure. BARS are an excellent vehicle for training and evaluating production personnel from different departments.

The current performance appraisal of choice for professional and managerial personnel is management by objectives (MBO). Borrowed from the private sector, MBO incorporates most of the features of participatory management. Some scholars have called MBO the triumph of "Theory Y" in the workplace. With its focus on joint goal setting by supervisors and subordinates, it allows maximum employee input. Aside from a rather elaborate process of consultation, there is also a schedule for periodic review and revision of goals. At the end of the project or review cycle, superiors and subordinates review the results of the collaboration and plan the next project or set of goals. Designed to improve communication, planning, and self-actualization, MBO is results-oriented, rather than performance-centered. The rater concentrates on completed items and on progress toward agreed-on goals. Although it is recommended for managerial and professional employees, MBO is limited because it is individual-specific. This tailor-made approach has its problems, because it is impossible to compare one employee with another.

How to Ensure That Results Reflect Intentions

Implementation of performance appraisal programs creates new problems. Government managers are increasingly required to employ performance appraisal as the key element in merit pay decisions and promotions. Since the government employs large numbers of educated workers, and since public law requires that workers understand the process, there is little conflict over the objectives of performance appraisal, yet there are problems of implementation. The use of performance appraisal to make merit pay decisions has come under attack or has been questioned by a series of scholars (Pearce and Perry, 1983; Siegel, 1987). Perry (1986) raised questions about the accuracy of the supervisory ratings used in the federal government. His research suggests that managers do not obtain the level of information and observation necessary to complete the more sophisticated and subjective BARS.

In an important symposium on performance appraisal and merit pay (Gabris, 1987), researchers were not sanguine about the appraisal process. They questioned the goals of the process and whether the wrong values (for example, competition for monetary reward) were being introduced into the public workplace. They claimed that employees' motivation can be improved in better and less costly ways.

Effective practice and presentation can eliminate some of the implementation problems of performance appraisal, but these efforts may be offset by external forces, such as court rulings and political leadership, which play a major role in the entire appraisal process. Regardless of the level of government, agencies' decisions about performance appraisal systems are made in a policy environment that includes legal, political, organizational, and psychometric dimensions. The various dimensions of performance appraisal are linked in a symbiotic social system. Any change in one dimension can cause change in another. Performance appraisal, like most human resources management policy, does not stand alone.

Age, Race, and Gender Controversies

Affirmative action law has had a profound social impact on public sector agencies. Transformation of this once white- and male-dominated environment has been slow but has created considerable controversy. The entry of minority groups and women into the workplace in unfamiliar roles has created some questions about performance ratings. Will these newcomers be treated differently or the same as white males? In other words, will they be given preferential treatment at rating time, as many were at hiring?

The empirical research on race and performance appraisals is extensive but inconclusive. In an early study by Flaugher, Campbell, and Pike (1969), white and black supervisors were asked to rate subordinates of both races. Black subordinates were rated higher than their white counterparts by black supervisors. A later study by Bigoness (1976) found that raters tended to inflate ratings of blacks when whites' and blacks' performances were equally low, but they gave equivalent ratings to high-performing workers of both races. These studies were done in the laboratory, but they show that race is an important variable in evaluations. In field studies (for example, Schmitt and Hill, 1977), black female employees received lower ratings when raters were white males. Landy and Farr (1980) reviewed the performance appraisal literature and found that ratees tended to receive higher ratings from raters of the same race.

There is also research that contradicts these studies. Wendelken and Inn (1981) suggest that the race factors found in laboratory experiments were minimized in the field. In a recent review of the literature, Kraiger and Ford (1985, p. 62) concluded that "no firm conclusions can be reached regarding the extent to which results found are due to rater bias or ratee performance. Rather, the evidence suggests that differential ratings are more likely due to some combination of bias and performance difference." These two authors, apparently realizing their vulnerability on this issue, immediately issued a caution and quasi-disclaimer: They suggested that readers look to other social sciences for answers to the continuing disparities between white and black workers' performance.

Gender presents some of the same problems as race discrimination but also includes different ones. When women began entering the managerial occupation groups, and particularly when they managed mixed-sex groups of subordinates, researchers expected to find differences in the way women perceived the rating process. Lovrich and Jones (1983), however, found that women and men perceived the performance process in the same way. Nevertheless, many women assert that there is a continuing pattern of disparate treatment in performance appraisal. They claim that their work often receives less credit in the workplace than that of their male counterparts. Indeed, there still remain some negative stereotypes about women workers.

Kanter's (1977) observations about the role of women in corporations (for example, women in supervisory or leadership positions were treated as exceptions and were never really accepted by male counterparts) probably also hold for large public organizations. If Kanter is correct, then one should expect women to overcompensate by being particularly tough raters. This tendency should show up in their evaluation of other women and of identifiably weak male subordinates. Nevertheless, few research data support this stereotype.

Despite recent improvements in occupational mobility, female subordinates continue to litigate their performance appraisals. In cases where performance appraisal determines merit pay and promotions, women believe that a pattern of subtle discrimination continues. Some maintain that in order to get an outstanding review, a woman must be an overachiever, while males receive such ratings on the basis of fewer accomplishments. Whether these perceptions can hold up to longitudinal statistical analysis is not certain, but they do affect women's attitudes toward male raters.

In recent years, age discrimination has become a factor in performance appraisal. Employees are living and working longer. Rhodes (1983) found that there was widespread belief that age affects performance. Many older workers, particularly those whose capacity remains high, claim that they receive low ratings when ratings are linked to merit pay: The higher wages go to younger workers, to keep them in organizations. Other older workers maintain that young supervisors treat them differently and exaggerate their mistakes. They also claim that young workers are assigned jobs that allow them to appear as "rising stars." Conversely, younger workers believe that leniency inflates the productivity of older workers. Indeed, Waldman and Avolio (1986), using meta-analysis of existing data on age discrimination, found only a slight tendency to give lower ratings to older employees. This phenomenon did not occur in professional organizations, however. In a highly competitive environment, intergenerational conflicts may influence ratings and perceptions of fairness. The problem with comparing young workers to older ones is that the accumulated boredom of senior workers is often confused with poor attitude.

The courts have entered the performance appraisal arena through the door of race and gender discrimination. Human resources administrators have been alerted to such terms as *disparate treatment* and *disparate impact*. The courts have created a vast body of case law on the subject of performance appraisal. They have insisted that appraisal instruments be job-related and validated. They have also looked askance at any attempt to rely solely on informal appraisal systems.

The courts have also accepted cases involving so-called reverse discrimination. In *Planells* v. *Howard University* (1984), the court found that black administrators used different and more stringent criteria to evaluate white professors than the criteria used in evaluating blacks for reappointment. In *Cleverly* v. *Western Electric Co.* (1979), an otherwise lawful appraisal system was used to discriminate against an older worker. An organization cannot use performance appraisal to terminate an older worker if she or he has been productive. In *Nord* v. *U.S. Steel Corp.* (1985), the court found that a woman who had been receiving exemplary performance appraisals was rated lower after she applied for a promotion. The courts will not tolerate this type of subterfuge. They have also attempted to ferret out the use of a subjective appraisal system to mask the bigotry of supervisors.

Psychometric Dimensions: Tuning of the Process

From a psychometric point of view, legal prescriptions and restrictions present a challenge, if not an impediment, to valid and reliable instruments. Psychologists who study performance appraisals wish to develop a science of evaluation. Accordingly, they concentrate on the mechanics of the measurement process, rather than on policy debates. Personnel and psychology journals report on research in validation, rater behavior, and rater training results. They debate the causes of distribution errors, halo effects, leniency, and central tendency. Although their findings have yielded insights about the nature of supervisor-subordinate dynamics, the controversy over instruments and the rater training process has not ended; researchers usually issue disclaimers regarding the generalizability of their findings, yet the fine-tuning continues. We know now that distribution errors can haunt most instruments.

Kane and Lawler (1979) propose a distributional measurement system, a statistical approach (behavioral discrimination scales) to alleviate rampant rating inflation. These researchers propose forcing raters to make differentiations among ratees. Few practicing raters have taken their advice, and rating inflation continues to distort many evaluation systems. Why? Ilgen and Feldman (1983) proffer a possible explanation, pointing out that ratings have been too closely linked to continued employment. The norm is that if a person is not doing a good job, he or she should be terminated. In most cases, employees are not terminated and are given acceptable ratings, because supervisors are unwilling to admit errors in hiring and in not having terminated poorly performing employees during a probationary period. The other cause for inflation is supervisors' use of higher ratings to suggest that they are managing productive units and that employee development programs are successful.

In public organizations, the incentive for rating inflation lies in the "hassle factor." The less distribution, the less hassle (politically and organizationally) one receives from higher management and employee organizations. Regardless of its cause, fine-tuning of the system has not eliminated the practice of inflation.

Trait-oriented performance appraisals are considered suspect, but Murphy and Constans (1987, p. 575) conclude that "when BARS contained incidents that had actually been observed by the rater, but that were not representative of a ratee's performance, performance ratings were biased in the direction of those unrepresentative anchors." BARS are often poorly designed and contain biased anchors. Collaborative systems, such as BARS and MBO, have also been under attack as time-consuming and biased toward certain types of jobs. In the case of BARS, separate scales are necessary for each job category. Since they are job-specific, BARS are not very transferable from one organizational unit to another.

The research on raters, although rigorous, is indecisive. Training can reduce but not eliminate the halo effect, leniency, and recency in ratings. We also know that intelligence and attitudes affect rating accuracy. What we do not know is how to prevent the influence of personal friendships, informal groupings, and power relationships from distorting the process. Psychologists tell us to rely on organizational leadership to solve these problems.

Organizational Dimensions

Organizational dynamics can determine the success or failure of a rating system. Ilgen and Feldman (1983) found that a rater's observational opportunities act as a contextual limit on the rating process. In some organizations, supervisors simply do not have the opportunity to observe workers and make informed judgments. Aside from supervisors' other duties, the nature of the workplace precludes their observations of workers' natural work cycles. Simple, routine tasks are easy to observe and evaluate; complex ones are not. In addition, it is difficult to observe a worker separately from his or her work group. One is forced to make comparisons. Since most individuals work in groups, one must be aware that group dynamics may be affected by ratings of individuals. Accordingly, a rater may be influenced by the need to maintain group harmony, rather than to differentiate between employees. Brinkerhoff and Kanter (1980) believe that group dynamics can militate against ''rate busters'' and keep workers' performance within the norm. In such cases, meaningful distributions are inhibited.

In public organizations, workplace groups play a role in the development of an employee's ''work reputation.'' It is not uncommon for supervisors to defer to these groups before making final ratings of individuals. This process, called *consultation with fellow workers,* accords considerable influence to workplace groups. The reason for the continuation of this practice is that workers do not begrudge ratings inflation for weak members, so long as their own ratings are not affected.

Organizational dynamics are also affected by the relative openness of a particular organization. Since agencies differ in their priorities, constituencies, histories, and leadership, their approaches to effective practice and presentation in an appraisal process also differ. Agencies that by tradition are open organizations seem to manage participatory appraisal better than closed organizations do. In relatively closed agencies, any carefully developed appraisal process is doomed if it is perceived as a threat to the internal dynamics of the organization.

The climate of an organization also affects attitudes toward the training of raters. The attention paid by the organization to this matter will determine raters' attitudes toward the training process itself. If the organization invests in rater training, which can be expensive, then it will improve raters' skills.

Operating costs are another factor. The more money invested in the system, the greater the chance that the appraisal process will operate effectively.

One cannot expect to invest in the front end of the process (instrument selection) but not in the end product (employee development). In other words, the cost of implementation should be incorporated into the budgetary process.

Finally, a responsible organization will create opportunities for employee feedback, which should yield information about the ongoing appraisal process. Such feedback allows the organization to make adjustments throughout the rating cycle. Keeping all the involved groups informed about adjustments enhances the political dimensions of the process.

The Political Dimension

Probst (1931, p. 148) observed, "To rate or not to rate is no longer the question. The vital thing is how to rate—how to rate accurately, easily, without prejudice, and without arousing antagonisms." The politics of human resources management suggests that the choice of a performance appraisal instrument, as well as the process itself, involves negotiations among interest groups. These groups include the central human resources management staff, line supervisors, employee unions, and informal employee groups. The choices within organizations are whether to impose a standardized form or to allow decentralized units to develop a task-specific one, whether to centralize or decentralize training of raters, and whether to use ouside consultants or in-house staff to conduct rater training and the development of instruments. Each of these decisions may involve different constituencies. Since so much of what happens in organizations involves status and power, weak groups do not fare well in the rating process.

In addition, administrative regulations regarding performance appraisal must also take legislative intent, as well as political objectives, into account. If politicians maintain an interest in the process, agency leaders will also maintain an interest in monitoring the work of their subordinates. Conversely, if politicians do not follow up on the progress of the system, it will not be given the kind of administrative priority it deserves. Good administrative practice flows from good politics.

The most effective performance appraisal system may be the one that is least disruptive of power relationships in the agency. Brinkerhoff and Kanter (1980) remind us that one's position on ratings may be determined by one's place in the organization. In other words, one's attitude toward the process may be related to one's perception of power relationships in the organization. The high-ranking organizational member can safely avoid the process. Meeting the norms of effective practice and presentation is enhanced by political acumen, flexibility, and feasibility. Political sensitivity in the selection and implementation process does not mean that the choice of rating systems must be a purely political decision; rather, the choice should conform to the political environment of the user.

Schmidt (1980) has suggested that psychologists' reliance on small samples precludes any meaningful empirical validation of instruments. He advocates the use of informed group estimates of validity. Some public administration scholars recoil at this suggestion, because introducing more joint decision making among actors creates more opportunity for politicization.

An equally difficult problem is the cost of installing and maintaining performance appraisal. Can a public agency afford the time to develop an effective system? If time is found, can the system survive the high turnover and policy shifts of public life? Consider the claims of Patten (1982), a leading advocate of MBO. According to Patten, MBO works best if performance obectives are linked to clearly stated organizational missions, the process is voluntary, and the process is synchronized with budget realities. In addition, Patten advocates extensive training of managers and a trial period of up to five years. Unfortunately, public agencies do not operate that way. Five years may include several budgets, as well as new leadership and missions. To survive, public organizations have learned to live with changing and ambiguous missions. There is plenty of evidence that budget realities in the public sector will continue to be characterized by permanent uncertainty. These uncertainties, however, have not slowed the transfer of the MBO process to government agencies. Ammons and Rodriguez (1986) surveyed 122 major cities and found that MBO alone was used by 35 percent but that only a small percentage of time (5 percent per person year) was spent on the process.

Although performance appraisal analysts remain optimistic about a bias-free instrument, they are pessimistic about the human element of appraisal. They share Nalbandian's (1981) adage that evaluations would work very well, if only people were not involved. Nevertheless, people will continue to be involved, and uncertainties will continue to frustrate and challenge the imagination of researchers, raters, and ratees.

Summary

Every organization must find its own way to an effective performance appraisal. This chapter has offered a discussion of the factors that inhibit and enhance effective performance appraisal, arriving at these factors by analyzing the roles and objectives of actors who influence performance appraisal policy. None of these actors, either working alone or in concert, can solve all the problems of performance appraisals. Nevertheless, reducing the isolation of these actors and their inputs can help organizations manage, if not solve, some of the difficulties of the process.

This review of the literature suggests, along with the norms of effective practice and presentation, the following points.

1. The introduction and maintenance of a performance appraisal system require a total organizational commitment.
2. The content of a performance appraisal should come from the bottom up, not from the top down. Raters and ratees alike should be involved in initial planning for the process.

3. Job analysis, written standards, and rater training are essential to the entire appraisal process. The courts will support any organization that puts forth good effort in this regard.
4. The individual being rated has a right to know not only the purpose of this process but also the links between job element and measurement factors.
5. Individuals who fare poorly in performance ratings should be accorded counseling, a second opinion (in special cases), and a formal appeal mechanism before any serious action is taken.
6. As demonstrated in several articles written by psychologists, the results of research on performance appraisal are inconclusive. When race, age, and gender are involved, the advice is to be vigilant and treat all complaints seriously.
7. Selecting the appropriate instrument and rater training are the first steps in a long journey of implementation. The success of the journey depends on sound organizational leadership, employee involvement, and supportive elected officials.

Flawless performance appraisals are challenges to human creativity. We may not reach our goal of errorless evaluations, but we can create conditions that will allow every individual to develop and produce to his or her full potential.

References

Allen, L. "Evaluating Firefighters' Performance." *Psychological Report,* 1983, *53,* 1219-1122.

Ammons, D. N., and Rodriguez, A. "Appraisal Practice for Upper Management in City Government." *Public Administration Review,* 1986, *46,* 461-467.

Bigoness, W. J. "Effects of Applicants' Sex, Race, and Performance on Employers." *Journal of Applied Psychology,* 1976, *4,* 145-150.

Brinkerhoff, D., and Kanter, R. M. "Appraising the Performance of Performance Appraisals." *Sloan Management Review,* 1980, *21,* 3-13.

Cleverly v. *Western Electric Co.,* 594 F.2d 638 (8th Cir. 1979).

Flaugher, R. L., Campbell, J. T., and Pike, L. W. *Ethnic Group Membership as a Moderator of Supervisors' Ratings.* ETS Bulletin PR-69-5. Princeton, N.J.: Educational Testing Service, 1969.

Gabris, G. T. (ed.). "Why Merit Pay Plans Are Not Working: A Search for Alternative Pay Plans in the Public Sector—A Symposium." *Review of Public Personnel Administration,* 1987, *7,* 1-94.

Ilgen, D., and Feldman, J. M. "Performance Appraisal: A Process Focus." In L. L. Cummings (ed.), *Research in Organizational Behavior.* Vol. 5. Greenwich, Conn.: JAI Press, 1983.

Kane, J. S., and Lawler, E. E. "Performance Appraisal Effectiveness: Its Assessments and Determinants." In B. Staw (ed.), *Research in Organizational Behavior.* Vol. 1. Greenwich, Conn.: JAI Press, 1979.

Kanter, R. M. *Men and Women of the Corporations.* New York: Basic Books, 1977.

Kraiger, K., and Ford, J. K. "Meta-Analysis of Ratee Effects in Performance Ratings." *Journal of Applied Psychology,* 1985, *70* (1), 56–65.

Landy, F. J., and Farr, J. K. "Performance Rating." *Psychology Bulletin,* 1980, *87,* 72–107.

Lovrich, N. P., and Jones, C. "Affirmative Action, Women Managers, and Performance Appraisal: Simultaneous Movement in Conflicting Directions." *Review of Public Personnel Administration,* 1983, *3,* 3–20.

McGregor, D. "An Uneasy Look at Performance Appraisal." *Harvard Business Review,* 1957, *35,* 89–94.

Murphy, K. R., and Constans, J. I. "Behavior Anchors as a Source of Bias Rating." *Journal of Applied Psychology,* 1987, *72,* 573–577.

Nalbandian, J. "Performance Appraisal: If Only People Were Not Involved." *Public Administration Review,* 1981, *41,* 392–396.

Nord v. *U.S. Steel Corp.,* 758 F.2d 1462 (11th Cir. 1985).

Patten, T. H. *A Manager's Guide to Performance Appraisal.* New York: Free Press, 1982.

Pearce, J. L., and Perry, J. L. "Federal Merit Pay: A Longitudinal Analysis." *Public Administration Review,* 1983, *43,* 315–325.

Perry, J. L. "Merit Pay Systems in the Public Sector: The Case for a Failure of Theory." *Review of Public Personnel Administration,* 1986, *7,* 57–69.

Planells v. *Howard University,* 32 FEP Cases 336 (D.D.C. 1984).

Probst, J. B. "Substituting Precision for Guesswork in Personnel Efficiency Record." *National Municipal Review,* 1931, *20,* 143–148.

Rhodes, S. R. "Age-Related Differences in Work Attitudes and Behavior: A Review of Conceptual Analysis." *Psychological Bulletin,* 1983, *92,* 328–367.

Rice, B. "Performance Reviews: The Job Nobody Likes." *Psychology Today,* 1985, *19,* 30–36.

Schmidt, F. C. "The Future of Criterion-Based Validity." *Personnel Psychology,* 1980, *33,* 44–60.

Schmitt, N., and Hill, T. "Sex and Race Composition of Assessment Centers as a Determinant of Peer and Assessor Rating." *Journal of Applied Psychology,* 1977, *62,* 261–264.

Siegel, G. B. "The Jury Is Still Out on Merit Pay in Government." *Review of Public Personnel Administration,* 1987, *7,* 3–15.

Waldman, D. A., and Avolio, B. J. "A Meta-Analysis of Age Difference in Job Performance." *Journal of Applied Psychology,* 1986, *71,* 33–38.

Wendelken, D. J., and Inn, A. "Nonperformance Influences on Performance: A Laboratory Phenomenon." *Journal of Applied Psychology,* 1981, *66,* 149–158.

28

Jone L. Pearce

Rewarding
Successful Performance

Is it particularly difficult to reward employees' performance in public organizations? Here it will forcefully be suggested that this assumption is false, that managers in or out of government have powerful informal rewards at their command. Certainly, there are important differences in the formal personnel and pay policies between government and smaller businesses. Clearly, most employees in businesses are not subject to the variety of goals and constituents that often occur in public organizations; yet it will be suggested here that dwelling on the limitations of normal procedures and external links is the leading contributor to the neglect of rewarding good performance in government. In public organizations, the expectation that performance in itself cannot be rewarded leads to few rewards for good performance, a classic self-fulfilling hypothesis.

The chapter begins with an analysis of the limitations of formal policies for effectively rewarding performance. This is followed by an argument for the use of informal systems to reward performance, with special attention to the strengths and limitations of this approach. Finally, the chapter concludes with specific steps that individual managers and policymakers alike can take to implement effective informal procedures to reward good performance.

The Attraction of Formal Reward Systems

Formal systems to reward performance have a long history in public administration. For example, the civil service tradition of competitive examinations rewards educational attainments. Nevertheless, these traditional public sector definitions of *merit* as knowledge or intelligence have been supplanted in recent years by policies designed to formally reward current job performance, today's concept of merit. Formal pay-for-performance programs, such as merit pay and performance-based bonuses, have become increasingly popular among U.S. managers in both the private and public sectors. For example, a study by the American Productivity Center and American Compensation Association reported that bonuses are an increasing proportion of take-home pay for all ranks in private business (Yoshihara, 1987). Similarly, the Federal Civil Service Reform Act of 1978 had several provisions for the mandatory rewarding of performance: bonuses for the highest-level executives, and merit pay tied to individual goal achievement for middle-level managers (Pearce and Perry, 1983).

Despite the intuitive appeal of such efforts to formally reward performance, their effectiveness in both sectors has always been limited. These formal programs simply have not been effective in consistently and equitably rewarding good performance for any but the simplest jobs. The difficulties in the private sector have long been noted (Meyer, 1975; Thompson and Dalton, 1970; Whyte, 1955). More recently, this author reported the results of a longitudinal study of the merit pay provisions of the Federal Civil Service Reform Act, suggesting that these formal systems were not effectively rewarding performance. For example, Pearce and Perry (1983) found that managers in five federal agencies believed that their pay was less merit-based under the new formal system; Pearce, Stevenson, and Perry (1985) reported that tying pay to goals did not result in increased measured performance (despite the fact that pay was now directly tied to these measures); and Pearce and Porter (1986) discovered that these formal performance measurement systems had a significant and sustained negative impact on the attitudes of scientists and engineers formally rated as "average" in NASA and in a U.S. Department of Defense agency, with no concomitant increase in the attitudes of those formally labeled "above average." That formal programs to reward performance rarely work as intended is a virtual truism among compensation professionals in both the private and public sectors, and there are several reasons why formal programs cannot be relied on to reward performance effectively.

Most important, formal systems are constrained. Whenever formal rewards are disbursed, care must be taken to develop procedures that safeguard employees, managers, the organization, and equity itself. Particularly with pay, the need to pay the market wage for each job and various requirements to maintain internal equity across departments and hierarchical levels result in proportionately small amounts retained for merit raises and bonuses. Employees depend on their incomes, and anything affecting such an important area of their lives receives intense scrutiny. For example, when performance-contingent pay was mandated for the Social Security Administration's managers, its executives decided to tie pay raises to the performance measures they had been using for years to evaluate the quality and quantity of work performed by these managers' offices. The executives felt fortunate that they did not have to develop new, untested measures; they had been evaluating managers on these statistics for decades. Yet once pay was tied to them, the numerous inequities in this measurement system were raised. Certain offices would always rate poorly, simply because their clientele had more complex problems (for example, document translations). Further, one manager produced a list of how each measure could be "cooked," which he distributed so that all managers would at least have access to the same "expertise" (and, incidentally, to embarrass the executives into changing the merit pay measurement system). This imperfect measurement system had been accepted, even serving as a source of pride, until formal rewards were directly tied to it.

These constraints exist for all organizations; but in the public sector, pay has the additional burden of being awarded in the "political fishbowl," which tends to place a low ceiling on the amount of overall pay, as well as on the size of a bonus or raise given at any one time (see Pearce, 1987, for an extended discussion of the limitations of formal pay-for-performance systems).

Additional complexities result from the difficulty of developing comprehensive measures of desired performance for any but the simplest jobs. Further, even when reasonable measures of job performance are developed (usually at great effort and expense), they are vulnerable to any significant change, such as a change in the environment or in political leadership. For example, the government of Orange County, California, has a department responsible for the production of the economic and demographic statistics and forecasts that are used by business and municipal planners. Therefore, a formal measurement system for them would include the timely and accurate production of these reports. Yet this department must also respond to requests for special analyses from the elected board of supervisors. Sometimes these special projects are so large and important (very recently, the department had to produce an analysis of the fiscal impact of a ballot initiative to slow the growth of development in the county) that they result in the delayed production of routine reports. A formal reward system that would lead the department's analysts to neglect important work simply because it was unexpected (or, more likely, would punish them for being responsive to the organization's needs) would clearly be dysfunctional.

Finally, one of the attractions of pay as a reward has always been its power of appeal to so many (after all, that is why people are working). Yet this attraction is in practice a false one. Certainly, one could get behavior change if one removed an employee's entire salary, but that is not what is really at stake in pay-for-performance plans. The amount of money at stake is often painfully small, particularly in public organizations operating in the "political fishbowl." For many employees, it is insulting to consider that others think that they, respected professionals, could be expected to jump for such small sums. Merit pay plans in industry, as well as in public organizations, are frequently interpreted by employees as reflecting a lack of respect for them and their work, and this perception can be considerably more powerful as a punishment than the few hundred dollars offered as the reward (Thompson and Dalton, 1970; Pearce and Perry, 1983). It is not that these employees, as an expression of some sort of personality trait, do not value money so much as that the structure of these formal programs leads the programs to be interpreted as a slap in the face, rather than as an opportunity to obtain something of value. This interpretation of merit pay plans influences whether formal programs will be effective, short of the massive infusion of money that is virtually impossible in public settings. The inability to control employees' interpretations drives formal policymakers to distraction.

Thus, the power of formal systems to reward individual employees' performance is limited in all but the simplest organizational settings. It is not that the systems could not work if they were adequately funded, based on a comprehensive measurement of performance, and implemented in organizations that experienced no significant changes; it is just that these conditions virtually never occur for the kinds of complex tasks and shifting political environments characteristic of most governmental organizations. Hence, one encounters the typical pessimism about rewarding performance in public organizations.

This pessimism is misplaced, however. What has been ignored is the fact that such formal systems have always had a limited role in organizations. Even in a business with much greater freedom to implement such performance reward systems, they often play only a modest role in rewarding performance (Meyer, 1975). The conversion of merit pay to seniority pay by practicing managers is certainly not confined to government (Medoff and Abraham, 1981). In fact, effective managers in any sector have always recognized that the formal rewards at their command are never sufficient. Effective managers have discovered how to build a system of informal rewards that extends their influence beyond the meager resources provided by their formal systems.

This need for managers to build and cultivate a store of informal means for influencing subordinates' (or peers' or supervisors') actions has long been recognized, if not clearly articulated. Barnard ([1938] 1968) reminded supervisors that they were dependent on the "cooperation" of their subordinates and provided specific suggestions for ensuring that cooperation: for example, clear and compatible orders that are consistent both with the goals of the organization and with the recipients' personal goals.

After the experience of World War II, this reliance on informal rewards was called *leadership*, with massive resources dedicated to research seeking to distinguish effective from ineffective supervisors in a single organization (who therefore worked with identical access to formal rewards). This work has culminated in a store of knowledge about how supervisors can be more effective in influencing the actions of others, which forms the basis of the practical suggestions offered at the end of this chapter.

The Strengths and Limitations of Informal Rewards

Informal rewards are simply those that are not formally mandated by an organization. All of us have access to rewards for those with whom we work in organizations. Most employees and, certainly, all managers are interdependent; we depend on the cooperation and willing assistance of dozens of others to accomplish our jobs. The manager of a department may ask a compensation analyst how to make a case for a higher salary for a needed civil engineer who has another job offer, at a considerably larger salary. That analyst can do the minimum, or he or she can make a genuine, creative effort to help this department manager. A clerical worker may look over and see that a new co-worker is struggling to do a task that she does not yet understand. She can ignore the novice, considering her to be the supervisor's problem, or she can go over, assist her, and show her the effective way to do that particular task. We all benefit from colleagues who make an effort to be considerate and pleasant, and we suffer from working closely with someone who is cold or abusive. All of us in organizations depend on thousands of small acts by others that cannot be dictated from above.

Thus, we all have available to us numerous informal means of rewarding performance or any other actions on which we depend. Supervisors, in particular, can and do use subordinates' dependence on them for the myriad little things that can make work easier.

Supervisors assign work or special projects. They can closely monitor a subordinate, or they can grant considerable autonomy. Dansereau, Graen, and Haga (1975, p. 46) report that supervisors do not treat all subordinates identically; rather, they establish "leadership exchanges" (influence without authority) with a select subset of subordinates.

Informal rewards are not solely the province of supervisors; they arise wherever interdependence does. Equally, they cannot be mandated by the hierarchy. Supervisors, however, often have a broader array of informal resources at their command. Supervisors act as intermediaries for their subordinates. They often control access to other individuals and information inside the organization, and they have responsibilities for task assignments, as well as the (often informal) ability to recommend or not recommend a subordinate for promotion or transfer. They can provide expense-paid attendance at conferences, assist in preparing professional publications, or provide public recognition (for example, through a city council resolution for meritorious employees).

Although these potential informal rewards are numerous, the rest of this discussion will analyze one powerful reward that is particularly well suited to use in public organizations: bestowal of esteem and respect. This reward is particularly useful with a professional and highly skilled work force and in the constrained legal environments that are characteristic of public organizations. Many public managers supervise employees who have strong professional or craft loyalties—for example, employees in urban planning, social welfare, civil engineering, forestry, specialized ship mechanics, aeronautics, teaching, soil chemistry, economic development, and so on. In these circumstances, supervisors are expected to be experts in these specialties and often represent the specialties to others, both inside and outside the group. They are in a position to build on professionals' own self-respect by embodying specialty-based characteristics for their colleagues and subordinates. Thus, professional respect is an appropriate reward for good performance of professional duties. It is a reward that seems to fit naturally with the desired behavior of good job performance.

Even in circumstances where they do not represent particular professions, supervisors usually can and do represent the mission of a department or an agency. Public organizations are all engaged in a form of public service, and managers are particularly well placed to represent these ideals. If private sector managers believe that they can rally their employees behind the value of producing consumer electronic appliances (as Matshushita Corporation does), it seems that public managers should be able to do so with inherently more attractive missions.

Further, most public managers operate in a very constrained legal environment. It would be both inappropriate and inadvisable for them to make concrete entitlements contingent on job performance. Nevertheless, one's respect for others is not owned by elected officials or by the taxpayers, nor is it covered in any labor-management agreement. No one is entitled to it; it is bestowed or withheld on the basis of one's own judgment. No one was ever sued or ever became the object of a grievance because he or she did not bestow respect equally or on the basis of objective criteria.

In addition, there is no upper limit on the amount of respect that can be bestowed. It is not something that must be hoarded and handed out only sparingly. Further, since it is not perceived as a punishment, it does not have negative reactivity; it is not divisive and demotivating. Rather, it can contribute to collegial solidarity and enhance self-esteem.

Thus, respect has several advantages as an informal reward for performance. First, it is appropriate and flows as a natural consequence from behavior (good performance) and from the supervisor's role as representative of the profession or department. It is not artificially attached. Second, like all informal rewards, it is flexible—there is no upper limit on the amount to be distributed, and there are no legal requirements to be met in its bestowal. The supervisor has complete autonomy in its use. Finally, it builds rather than destroys departmental esteem and morale.

There are, however, certain limitations to this particular informal reward, shared by most informal rewards. First, respect must be earned; it cannot be mandated. No one can say, "You must value my respect." Individuals want the esteem and respect of those whose standards and personal characteristics they themselves value. As a practical matter, the actions that deserve respect in each profession or craft are particular to each one and cannot be suggested here. Thoughtful reflection by any member of a guild, however, would probably lead to a clearer understanding of such actions and characteristics. What can be provided in this chapter is a brief description (in the next section) of concrete actions that can help managers earn respect as managers.

Further limitations derive from the fact that informal rewards cannot be mandated from the top of the organization. This particular limitation seems to have symbolic implications that are particularly difficult for public organizations. First, it involves open acknowledgment of the incomplete control exercised in all large organizations by the top executives and their assistants. This lack of control has been acknowledged by economists and organization theorists as "control loss" (Williamson, 1967), yet public organizations, in particular, seem unwilling to acknowledge it. The moral and values-based nature of their missions no doubt makes it difficult to be cavalier about possible inequities and inconsistencies across their diverse operations. Nevertheless, the needs of employees and managers are too often sacrificed to dysfunctional general rules and procedures, which serve purposes more symbolic than practical. The Federal Civil Service Reform Act's provisions concerning pay for performance were one example of this unfortunate approach to management.

Thus, the recognition of the importance of informal rewards implies greater importance placed on the skills and abilities of managers. Rather than leaning on formal policies to shield and support incompetent managers, policymakers in public organizations can provide greater support for managerial training. Recognition of the importance of informal rewards in managing performance necessarily implies that those at the top of the hierarchy can no longer feel as if they have accomplished something simply by decreeing a new rule.

There is a final limitation, which is rather more a limiting condition. Informal rewards, like all rewards, must be valued by their recipient, or else they are not effective. One of the implicit attractions of formal rewards has been the assumption that they are powerful, yet this is a spurious advantage: The amount of money actually contingent on performance is rarely enough in public organizations to act as a powerful reward.

With informal rewards, everyone is forced to acknowledge that different rewards will be attractive to different individuals. Discretion in the use of informal rewards necessarily devolves to supervisors, who know their subordinates. The use of informal rewards requires greater managerial autonomy and responsibility. Supervisors always have been the ones with the best information about what would work with their own people, and the use of informal rewards openly acknowledges this reality.

Implementing Informal Rewards

It is one thing to state the obvious: that informal rewards can be attractive motivators in organizations. It is quite another to detail how they can be harnessed. Introduced here are several concrete steps that managers can take to earn the respect of their subordinates for their abilities as managers. The following discussion is an adaptation of the excellent text by Sayles (1979), and the interested reader is advised to consult that work for additional practical guidance in the craft of managing.

Sayles was concerned with effective leadership, and not necessarily with informal rewards. Nevertheless, his insights into the limitations of "carrots and sticks" (threats and punishments) led him to provide a detailed discussion of how managers can become more influential, without relying on these formal tools. Several of his ideas are particularly appropriate to helping public managers earn respect for their managerial abilities. These ideas concern the importance of continuous interaction, the building of legitimacy by increments, and the necessity of representation and buffering.

Management researchers have long noted that managers spend their time in a string of continuous interaction, in encounters of very small duration. For example, Mintzberg (1973) reports an average interaction of nine minutes for his sample of chief executives. Sayles (1979) argues that these interactions are important, both for the information they provide about subordinates and their work and for their ability to spark motivation.

First, managers are respected if they have organizational knowledge (what Wilensky, 1967, called "organizational intelligence"), and managers who do not know what is going on will not merit respect as managers. Managers serve an informational role in organizations (Galbraith, 1977). They are freed from hands-on task performance, so that they are able to move around and gather information that improves decision quality. In addition to learning more about work, managers in continuous interaction with their subordinates will understand them better, understand what they do or do not value. With frequent, balanced contact, subordinates learn that their problems are understood, and they find it easier to discuss work-related issues. In addition, contact itself can be motivating. People seem to need contact with others, and contact with high-status individuals seems to be even more attractive (Hurwitz, Zander, and Hymovitch, 1960). Relationships depend on contact.

Second, managers need to build legitimacy for their leadership incrementally. When working with such subtle processes as respect, managers need to be sure that their respect is in fact valued before they can assume that it will be effective. Sayles (1979) suggests that managers never want to give a "command" that they think may not be obeyed, since insubordination is devastating to a manager's credibility. Shrewd managers learn to build authority through small, incremental requests. Similarly, it is important to understand how the bestowal of an informal (or formal) reward will be received or interpreted.

Symbolic rewards, like respect, are particularly vulnerable to interpretation. Individuals either individually or collectively decide whether certain symbolic rewards are valuable or ludicrous. This indeterminate quality of symbolic rewards has led such theorists as Etzioni (1975) to argue that symbolic rewards are too weak and uncertain to be used as effective organizational controls. Here, it is suggested that managers are giving up a potentially valuable resource if they ignore the power of symbolic rewards. Rewards like respect are less subject to withering satire than are such symbols as badges and titles, since we all want to be respected. Certainly, however, care in preparing and understanding the social interpretive setting for symbolic rewards through incremental trials is critical.

Finally, one of Sayles's (1979) most important contributions has been his emphasis on the importance of representation and buffering, or upward and lateral influence, in subordinates' judgments of their managers. Pelz (1952) demonstrates that the best predictor of subordinates' satisfaction with supervision is the perceived "power" of their supervisors: Whether a supervisor can obtain resources for the department and protect subordinates from disruptive interference is more important than whether the supervisor is considerate. Managers are in the middle, mediating between levels; they are not photocopy machines for commands from on high. As Sayles (1979, p. 38) suggests, "Respected, admired leaders are those [who] deal profitably with outsiders and bring back benefits and protection."

Particularly in public organizations, managers seem prone to adopt a helpless, "cynical bureaucrat" pose: "Of course it is a stupid requirement, but the mayor's office wants us to do it." One of the most critical areas in which public managers can earn the respect of their employees is in successful management of the bureaucracy. Nothing is more demoralizing than to have a supervisor who passively acquiesces to any whim coming from outside the unit; yet, surprisingly, managers frequently fall into this trap. Often it is because they do not yet understand others outside the unit and how their requests can be modified. Sometimes it is because they do not want to be seen as ogres, and so responsibility is assigned elsewhere. It is usually easy to do this in public organizations, since responsibility is so fragmented by design. Nevertheless, this passive supervisor can create severe problems for subordinates and is actively creating an image of powerlessness and uselessness.

How can managers more effectively manage those above and lateral to them? According to Pfeffer and Salancik (1978), units that provide critical resources or services to the organization gain relative power. Thus, solving others' problems is a useful strategy. In any complex organization, there are other managers and professionals who have problems and needs of their own. Discovering these and then making oneself useful to others can help to earn respect for oneself and one's unit. Passive and cynical accommodation and surreptitious resistance are signs of powerlessness, which will scarcely engender respect.

Finally, there is a role for high-level policymakers in assisting their managers to reward performance with informal rewards. What is most important is that policymakers realize that they cannot mandate the effective use of informal rewards; these depend on the skills and relationships of individual managers. With delegation, supported by strong training and audit programs, policymakers can replace policies that attempt to "micromanage" all features of their organizations. Effective training in the identification and implementation of effective informal rewards is both possible and desirable. Too often, what is labeled *management training* is no more than a survey of formal systemic requirements—the proper way to fill out forms—interlaced with warnings that are intended to prevent lawsuits. Managers also need to learn the craft of managing.

Since delegation must be accompanied by controls, audits can replace rulemaking as the primary vehicle to support effective organizations. Audits have the dual advantage of being cheaper, since fewer auditors than analysts are needed to design programs, review implementation, and give permission for exceptions. Further, auditing is also more effective, since local managers are not mired in elaborate rules but can experiment with ideas that meet their unique needs.

Summary

Effective managers, in both the public and the private sectors, have always supplemented their formal resources with informal ones. Why, then, is there the presumption that the weaknesses of formal reward systems in public organizations would necessarily lead to an inability to reward performance at all? Powerful informal systems are used in public organizations, yet they have not received the prominence they deserve in writings on public administration. This chapter is intended to restore some balance to this literature and to help practicing managers articulate what they have often observed and probably practiced. This rudimentary introduction to the practical implementation of informal rewards for performance could probably be embellished and enriched by effective managers in virtually every public jurisdiction. The most practical suggestion of all would be for readers to make copies of this chapter, give the copies to groups of managers, and ask them to use the chapter as a basis of sharing their own reactions, ideas, and practices. That is where the real knowledge is.

References

Barnard, C. *The Functions of the Executive.* Cambridge, Mass.: Harvard University Press, 1968. (Originally published 1938.)

Dansereau, F., Jr., Graen, G., and Haga, W. J. "A Vertical Dyad Linkage Approach to Leadership Within Formal Organizations." *Organizational Behavior and Human Performance,* 1975, *13,* 46–78.

Etzioni, A. *A Comparative Analysis of Complex Organizations.* (Rev. ed.) New York: Free Press, 1975.

Galbraith, J. R. *Organization Design.* Reading, Mass.: Addison-Wesley, 1977.

Hurwitz, J. I., Zander, A., and Hymovitch, B. "Some Effects of Power on the Relations Among Group Members." In D. Cartwright and A. Zander (eds.), *Group Dynamics*. New York: Harper & Row, 1960.

Medoff, J. L., and Abraham, K. G. "Are Those Paid More Really More Productive? The Case of Experience." *Journal of Human Resources*, 1981, *16*, 186–216.

Meyer, H. H. "The Pay-for-Performance Dilemma." *Organizational Dynamics*, 1975, *3*, 55–61.

Mintzberg, H. *The Nature of Managerial Work*. New York: Harper & Row, 1973.

Pearce, J. L. "Why Merit Pay Doesn't Work: Implications from Organization Theory." In D. B. Balkin and L. R. Gomez-Mejia (eds.), *New Perspectives on Compensation*. Englewood Cliffs, N. J.: Prentice-Hall, 1987.

Pearce, J. L., and Perry, J. L. "Federal Merit Pay: A Longitudinal Analysis." *Public Administration Review*, 1983, *43*, 315–325.

Pearce, J. L., and Porter, L. W. "Employee Responses to Formal Performance Appraisal Feedback." *Journal of Applied Psychology*, 1986, *71*, 211–218.

Pearce, J. L., Stevenson, W. B., and Perry, J. L. "Managerial Compensation Based on Organizational Performance: A Time Series Analysis of the Impact of Merit Pay." *Academy of Management Journal*, 1985, *28*, 269–278.

Pelz, D. C. "Influence: A Key to Effective Leadership in the First-Line Supervisor." *Personnel*, 1952, *29*, 209–217.

Pfeffer, J., and Salancik, G. R. *The External Control of Organizations: A Resource-Dependence Perspective*. New York: Harper & Row, 1978.

Sayles, L. R. *Leadership*. New York: McGraw-Hill, 1979.

Thompson, P. H., and Dalton, G. W. "Performance Appraisal: Managers, Beware." *Harvard Business Review*, 1970, *48* (1), 149–157.

Whyte, W. F. *Money and Motivation: An Analysis of Incentives in Industry*. New York: Harper & Row, 1955.

Wilensky, H. L. *Organizational Intelligence: Knowledge and Policy in Government and Industry*. New York: Basic Books, 1967.

Williamson, O. E. "Hierarchical Control and Optimum Firm Size." *Journal of Political Economy*, 1967, *75*, 123–138.

Yoshihara, N. "Performance Pay: New Trend Has Its Rewards." *Los Angeles Times*, Apr. 12, 1987.

29

Nicholas P. Lovrich

Managing Poor Performers

A very common complaint heard from public service supervisors and managers relates to the occasional "bad apples" found among otherwise worthy and underappreciated subordinates. In the course of an administrative career in government, it is very likely that one will encounter a persistently poorly performing subordinate, one whose position in the merit system is almost certain to provide ample job protections, and whose interest in job security is likely to be the concern of an employees' representative organization (Ban, Goldenber, and Mazzotto, 1982; Hildreth, Miller, and Rabin, 1984). It is also likely that the manager saddled with such an employee will spend an inordinate amount of time thinking about, worrying over, and coping with (or, as is commonly the case, feeling guilty about avoiding dealing with) the troublesome situation. In so doing, however, an administrator's effectiveness in reinforcing and recognizing the accomplishments of productive employees is seriously weakened.

While this situation is common in organizations of all sorts, public and private, and is found at all levels of government, there is surprisingly little written about the problems of managing such employees (Morgenroth and Morgenroth, 1986). The scholars and the self-conscious practitioners who have labored to perfect our knowledge of the practice of organizational management have quite correctly focused their attention on those management policies and practices that work for most people. Arguments over whether a directive ("Theory X") or a more self-actualization–oriented management philosophy ("Theory Y") is the more appropriate are always fought out on the battleground of the greatest degree of applicability to the greatest proportion of employees (Lovrich, 1985). Similarly, the utility of more narrowly drawn personnel practices—such as merit pay, flexible work schedules, quality circles, and team building—is usually debated in the same way: For what proportion of my employees will this practice bring me benefit (Kilmann, 1984)? Virtually no attention is given to the question of how useful

a personnel practice may be in the handling of one's very own "bad apple"—
a question that, moreover, may be of great concern to supervisors and
managers faced with the difficult job of managing poor performers (see,
however, the interesting attempt in Weiss, 1980, pp. 211–222).

What underlies the virtual avoidance of this problem in the supervision and management literature is the great difficulty in dealing with what
psychologists term *individual differences* (Staw, Ball, and Clausen, 1986). Persons in a given society are subjected to a ubiquitous and shared process of
socialization into society's mores and values. Nevertheless, specific individuals
exhibit a wide range of adaptation to that commonly experienced process.
Consequently, a considerable variety of personalities is the unavoidable outcome of multitudes of individuals in a given society maturing into adulthood
(Sherman, Smith, and Mansfield, 1986). The particular individual differences
that concern the supervisor or manager are the aspects of individual personality that are related to job performance and that cause some people to
perform at unacceptably low levels in workplaces that contain satisfactory
incentives to high performance for nearly all other employees.

Hirsch (1985) has noted, for example, that the application of the Myers-
Briggs psychological predisposition inventory in organizational settings
typically produces a wide variety of personality types, whose dissimilarities
can be viewed either as a weakness or as a strength. While it is relatively
easy to agree that, in theory, all employees—including the "bad apples"—can
contribute valuable insights on how work can best be accomplished, in practice, the poor performers tend to be persons we would rather avoid than
engage in serious dialogue. While this disinclination to confront the challenge
of dealing with persistent poor performance is understandable on the part
of the busy supervisor or manager, the disinclination of students of management to deal with this common problem stems from the considerable complexity of the remedies to be developed.

Just as the inevitability of individual differences in personalities makes
it likely that virtually all public sector supervisors or managers will confront
the challenge of a persistently poor performer at some point in their administrative careers, it is also likely that no two poor-performer problems are
identical, either in origin or with respect to appropriate remedy (Zemke,
1987). In fact, individual differences among poor performers are extensive,
making it very difficult for students of administration to prescribe a uniform
remedy for the troubled supervisor or manager (Lees-Haley, 1986; Leap
and Crino, 1986). While the guiding figures in organization theory and
management boldly advocate the virtues of "management by objectives"
(Odiorne, 1965), "job enrichment" (Herzberg, 1966), or "organizational
development" (Campbell and Dunnette, 1968) for adoption in a wide range
of settings for a broad range of employees, they scarcely take up the issue
of how best to deal with recalcitrant, low-productivity employees.

What follows is an attempt to help fill this void in our public management literature. The foregoing discussion should serve to highlight the fact

that the management of the poor performer is indeed an important subject of administrative concern. Moreover, it should be clear why this problem is almost certain to occur (and likely to recur) in the administrative careers of the readers of this volume. In addition, it should also be evident why supervisors and managers tend to avoid such problems, and why students of management tend to avoid discussion of this problem in their usual scholarship and professional training. The following section represents a modest attempt at providing the reader with a typology of the most common kinds of poor performers encountered. In addition, the next-to-last section of this chapter contains suggestions for how poor performers can be diagnosed and managed.

A Typology of Poor Performers

A commonplace observation in the study of epistemology (the study of what constitutes knowledge) is that "appropriate classification is the first step toward scientific understanding" (Jurkovich, 1974). In the case of poor performers, the wide range of individual differences in personality predispositions evident among these people guarantees that no single approach is likely to work out in every situation. Such simplistic prescriptions as "crack the whip" or "show great compassion" or "set a good example" or "rotate employees through a series of jobs" are unlikely to improve very many undesirable circumstances, although any one of these prescriptions might be exactly what one particular type of poor performer might require.

Fortunately, a good start on the problem of identifying the most common types of poor performers is available in the work of Bramson (1981). Bramson correctly argues that the kinds of difficult people he identifies act the way they do because of their fundamental personality predispositions, and he appropriately advises that supervisors and managers cannot hope to change an employee's basic personality. What Bramson does advise is the development of managerial techniques for "coping" with personality orientations that, without appropriate direction, result in seriously deficient performance. The following list of seven types of difficult persons draws heavily on Bramson's work, but it also reflects the knowledge gained from the present author's twenty years of administrative experience with government personnel problems in agencies of federal, state, and local government.

The Time Bomb. During our careers, most of us have encountered employees who are inclined to make scenes or fly off the handle or go a little crazy or make a big fuss if they are placed under pressure (Leap and Crino, 1986). The proverbial wisdom of letting sleeping dogs lie is the norm usually applied to such persons, and supervisors and employees alike generally tend to avoid or even ostracize such employees (Orenstein, 1987). Most of us do not mind such persons too much if they do their work well enough, but quite often these persons perform at levels considerably below what might reasonably be expected. When managers ask supervisors about an employee like this, and about what they are doing to improve his or her poor performance, supervisors generally respond by noting either that the absence of outbursts of uncontrolled behavior is itself a great accomplishment or that any failings the unit may have are attributable to the often convenient "scapegoat" employee (Dalton and Thomas, 1979).

The Wet Blanket. While the time bomb tends to remain on the fringes of her or his organizational unit and generally revolves in his or her own personal protected space, the wet blankets like to be part of everything that goes on in the group. Typically, these employees feel slighted if they are not included in decision processes or group activities, but their typical behavior in group settings is to cast a negativistic pall on the questions being discussed. Comments like "That's not in the cards" or "It'll never work" or "I can see a lot of problems with that" or "Think of all the things that might go wrong" are the common stock of such persons. Therefore, managers who are innovators or risk takers tend to exclude persons of this negative outlook from important discussions of ideas for change. The wet blankets tend to feel resentment of such exclusion by "infernal optimists," a resentment that both feeds their negativism and even leads to their efforts to "prove everybody wrong" by undercutting change initiatives.

The Isolate. Somewhat less common than the first two types of problem employees are the isolates, or highly private persons. These employees typically do their jobs well enough, in the technical sense, but do very poorly in the sense of performing the key function of facilitating intraorganizational communications. For example, an isolated employee may be an excellent gardener who is maintaining a city recreation area in fine condition but who is totally unaware that the park grounds are being used as the primary exchange point for drug sales to teenagers. Such an employee initiates few conversations with clients or colleagues, and her or his responses to others' attempts to communicate are generally of short duration and lacking in interest for continued exchange. These employees tend to take great satisfaction and pride in their work (defined in their own narrow sense) and consider all the personal and social aspects of work to be largely irrelevant "noise" in their environment, which must be endured with some pain and quiet resentment. They tend to be left out of work unit discussions but, unlike the wet blankets, they are quite pleased to be left alone to "tend their own little gardens" (Lasch, 1979, pp. 43–48).

There is a sacred right to privacy in the United States, a right that has been read into the several amendments to the U.S. Constitution that are designed to ensure Americans' protection from undue intervention by government into their personal affairs. For some Americans, that right extends to the workplace. It entails the maintenance of a sphere of private concerns at work, a private sphere that relegates all other matters to nonconcern

(Kaplan, 1976, pp. 179–196). This definition of one's work world may cause few problems in a job requiring little communication with others. Imagine, however, doctors and nurses who operate in their own private worlds while treating a lowly patient. How much quality in treatment is lost if these professionals do not exchange information, feelings, and insights pertinent to the work of caring for this patient? Imagine as well a client who depends on several offices or officials to accomplish the filing of permits or the registration of entitlements. How much will the quality of service to this client suffer from the lack of informal contacts, open communications, and willingness to share confidence among persons and offices in government? To the extent that such communications are important to client services or professional attention to the public welfare, it is often important to deal with the problems posed by isolated employees.

The Really Nice Person. Another type of problem employee encountered from time to time is one who, by virtue of personality, appearance, friendships, or some combination of these factors, is very much liked by others. Although his or her performance is far below par, such an employee is seen as being "too nice" to sanction. The desire to be highly charitable to some and not charitable to other, less "nice" persons can derive from any number of origins. Highly popular persons, handsome or attractive individuals, older persons, and very generous and caring people are the most likely to receive this kind of special consideration. Most of us can remember the incompetent but caring and loving teacher, the lovable but ineffective coach, the considerate and friendly secretary who could not type, and the jovial mechanic with ten hungry kids to feed who could never quite figure out how to get the broken motor pool vehicles back into service. Supervisors who have to deal with clients who complain about the work done by such persons tend to invent excuses for the inadequacies of these employees, and they reason that they have done so properly because these persons have "other qualities" that compensate in some way for their poor performance (Crawford, Thomas, and Fink, 1980).

In many circumstances, people who benefit from the "really nice person" reputation do become competent in their jobs, but their jobs have been reduced to fewer (and easier) responsibilities than they ought to be shouldering for their level of compensation or status. The secretary who cannot type is given more "other duties as assigned," and the teacher who cannot teach is made responsible for curriculum review, new textbook selection, or similar nonstudent contact. This sort of creative adaptation is frequently done with good results; but, as often as not, these modifications in work assignments lead to problems. When one engineer does not pull his or her own weight in the design shop, others have to pick up the pace just to stay even with the work flow. Similarly, when the worst teachers are pampered, the better teachers are inclined to wonder whether their dedication to duty is not a bit foolish.

The Excuse Maker. Another sort of common problem for supervisors is the employee who has all the answers. While such an employee often falls short of reasonable expectations in performance, his or her ability to come up with convincing excuses seems unlimited. Untimely personal illnesses, frequent occurrence of a series of unlikely disadvantageous events, mysteriously lost documents or records, reports on the failings of others to coordinate or cooperate as anticipated, promises of better results in the future—all these ''lines'' serve as excuses and allowances for inadequate outcomes. Since a general social norm dictates that one does not ''kick a guy when he's down'' and that one ought to help out a person who is ''down on his luck,'' there is a natural tendency at first to accept these excuses, without much questioning. The more sensitive the supervisor or manager, the more likely that the excuse maker will gain both time in service and the job protections such service provides.

Sooner or later, of course, the excuses begin to mount, and the credibility of the excuse maker comes into doubt. The supervisor with an employee of this type tends to go through a predictable developmental process in the formulation of an attitude toward the problem employee (Guy, 1984). At first, the inclination is to be sympathetic. Next, the feeling of having been deceived leads to a toughening of attitude. Finally, the failure to elicit a positive reaction to tough talk and threats typically leads to one of three unfortunate ultimate courses of action: trying to get the person to resign by taking him or her to task for every minor failing, trying to get the problem employee to trim down his or her work to a modest level of assured and predictable outcomes, or becoming resigned to the need to pass on the excuses of this troublesome employee to managers higher up and to clients affected by the employee's work.

The Loose Cannon. Most readers will recall hearing about employees who in most respects are quite competent but whose very enthusiasm for their work causes them to raise problems for their managers or clients. Strictly speaking, they are seldom considered poor performers, but their behavior can be at least as damaging as that of the other types of problem employees. The overzealous police officer whose sense of mission leads to the writing of many citations for trivial infractions, the well-intentioned social worker whose compassion for the needy causes her or him to be too susceptible to the con games of the most devious clients, employees whose commitment to work is so profound that they work such long hours that their own health is damaged—these are all examples of the loose cannon.

Common to all these loose cannons is the failure of judgment. Dedication to the goals of the organization is a good thing, of course, but excessive or misdirected enthusiasm can do much harm to those goals over the long run. In many cases, loose cannons mistakenly assume that their own enthusiasm is shared by others, and they often make commitments for colleagues that put their peers on the spot. For some loose cannons, colleagues become the worst enemies, persons whose commitment to duty seems less than it ought to be (Friedman and Rosenman, 1974).

Loose cannons are often called crusaders for their causes, and they are frequently the prime sources of inside information for the press and attentive publics of one sort or another. The many polite fictions and myths that keep any organization going are, for the loose cannons, often the very targets of their criticisms. Normally hidden facts—that contingency plans for unlikely developments are highly dated, that some employees lack important elements of skill or knowledge, that an important deadline for a grant program was overlooked, or that in the long run good hard work will be rewarded by public support or clients' appreciation—are likely to be brought into question at the most inappropriate times by loose cannons.

Supervisors attempting to deal with such employees generally begin by according them great trust and support, but they end up trying to find ways to corral the energies of their crusaders. At first, efforts are designed to keep crusaders from doing damage to the organization and organizational morale. In the case of ambitious crusaders, managers often seek out information on opportunities for employment elsewhere and try to convince loose cannons that there are more dedicated and able agencies in other jurisdictions that could really use their talents to the fullest.

The Employee with Paralysis of Indecision. The last type of problem employee is one who is competent in most respects, particularly under normal circumstances, wherein the behavior required of her or him has been clearly identified, and standards for performance are broadly understood. Difficulties arise for these problem employees when independent judgment is required or when inventive solutions to problems or critical incidents must be developed (Flanagan, 1954). What should be done when there is a client who does not fit the normal pattern? What should be said when two equally valid claims are made on a single indivisible resource? How much work should go into the preparation of a report on a new problem that requires an agency's attention? The most common location for these problem employees is among supervisors. Their position is a function of the ''Peter Principle,'' whereby a person who is perfectly competent in one job gains promotion to a position requiring different skills and abilities (Peter and Hull, 1969). In most civil service systems, the practice of promotion from within is a well-established tradition, and the promotion of persons who are unfit for supervisory roles is more common than we might prefer.

Whereas the loose cannon is inclined to get the agency into trouble from an excess of enthusiasm, the employee who suffers from paralysis of indecision is liable to cause problems as a consequence of a fundamental lack of confidence. How to decide matters of interpretative policy? How to know which applicant for agency resources is the most deserving? How to know when enough time has been spent on an open-ended task? These sorts of questions are the kinds of concerns that plague the indecisive, and they can lead to severe problems when excessive fear of making mistakes (perfectionism) compounds the indecisiveness of those who lack self-confidence.

Managers generally tend to keep their distance from the business of their supervisors, and they are unlikely to take note of problems until serious concerns come to their attention. Managers are often interested in delegating some decisions to their lower-level administrative associates in order to build their experience, confidence, and abilities. For most supervisors, this delegation is welcomed. For the supervisor lacking in confidence, delegation often occasions a new crisis in self-appraisal.

These seven types of problem employees do not constitute, of course, a comprehensive listing. The descriptions probably bring to mind varied images of actual difficult employees, but they may also lead one to recall yet other types of problem employees. What can be said about effective methods for understanding and managing them? The following section deals with that question in some detail.

Identification and Management of Problem Employees

The difficulties created for supervisors and managers by problem employees are very difficult to deal with under any circumstances, but they are particularly troublesome in the context of public sector tenure of service and civil service job protections (Wheeler and Kochan, 1980). Part of the difficulty derives from the fact that there are so many different types of problem employees, and no single effective approach to dealing with them is likely.

Nevertheless, it is possible to outline some essential considerations that can be profitably investigated to improve one's management of problem employees. These considerations are germane to any and all of the types of problem employees already discussed, and they are fundamental to understanding how to deal with problem employees. Table 29.1 sets out two fundamental dimensions of concern and specifies the interrelationships between these dimensions.

One dimension of primary concern is the question of the inherent *ability* of the employee to do the work in question. Some kinds of problem employees are incapable of performing their duties, while others are quite able to do good work. In addition to the question of ability, these problem employees also differ in their *willingness* to change the behavior shown to be detrimental to organizational goals and objectives. Taken in combination, these two dimensions produce four basic types of problem employees: those who are unwilling to change their behavior and are unable to do their work; those who are unwilling to change their behavior, although they are capable of performing their work; those who are willing to change but unable to perform their jobs; and those who are both willing to change and able to do their work.

For each of these four combinations, Table 29.1 shows recommended courses of action for administrators. For example, the "really nice person"

**Table 29.1. Diagnostic Typology of Problem Employees and
Appropriate General Approaches for Managing Poor Performers.**

	Attitude Toward Change of Behavior	
Ability to Do the Work Required	Unwilling to Change	Willing to Change
Unable to Do the Work Required	The candidate for *discipline*	The candidate for *training*
Able to Do the Work Required	The candidate for *coaching*	The candidate for *mentoring*

DISCIPLINE	=	use of a combination of negative and positive sanctions to change behavior
TRAINING	=	use of focused learning experiences to impart new job-related skills
COACHING	=	use of intensive supervisory attention to develop appropriate attitudes toward job performance
MENTORING	=	use of senior, experienced employees to help junior or problem employees to acquire good judgment on the job

is a good candidate for *training;* that is, such a person is very likely to express a willingness to change, but he or she lacks the ability to perform at higher levels. The value of that employee to an agency would probably be enhanced if he or she were provided training that was specifically designed to improve present performance or teach new and necessary tasks that others in the agency have not mastered.

Similarly, problem employees who can do their work and are willing to change their inappropriate behavior—for example, indecisive employees—may respond to mentoring. Mentoring encourages professional or occupational maturation by passing on lessons acquired from experience. The intention is to help someone who lacks judgment develop it in his or her own work (Ouchi, 1981, p. 21; Odiorne, 1984, pp. 130–142). The mentor is normally the superior, or a senior person who possesses the reputation of exercising good judgment in his or her own work.

The loose cannon is often able to perform tasks and is often willing (even too willing) to change. Matching a loose cannon with an agency's respected, well-placed senior person can often give the loose cannon a good sense of how to balance the need for personal dedication with the need for organizational success (Albrecht, 1988).

When a problem employee is able to do the work but is unwilling to change, *coaching* is probably a fruitful approach to management (Ward and Sandvold, 1963; Zajonc and Brickman, 1969). In the case of the isolate, for example, a dedicated effort by a supervisor or a manager to involve the otherwise competent employee more fully in the social communication network—facilitating the formation of relationships, assigning joint projects and collaborative undertakings, taking an interest in the person's affairs—should net considerable benefits to agency performance. In the case of the wet blanket, the coaching that often nets benefits entails the purposeful assignment of responsibility. "Eternal critics" often can be taught the utility of optimism in the process of having to try to make something that they control a success.

Finally, in those most difficult cases, when problem employees are incapable of doing their jobs and are also unwilling to admit the need for change, the recommendation is for the careful use of progressive *discipline*. Excuse makers, for example, eventually find that their views are no longer given credibility, even when they actually deserve respect. An experience with "positive discipline" (Cavanaugh, 1982), entailing paid time off to think about how to accomplish the needed change in behavior as a first step, could allow an excuse maker to begin again with a clean slate; his or her word would be taken at face value by the supervisor, and the excuse maker would promise to deal truthfully with supervisors and colleagues alike (Bryant, 1984; Campbell, Fleming, and Grote, 1985; Redeker, 1985). Positive results have been reported with even the most recalcitrant public employees in settings where positive discipline has been tried (Riccucci and Wheeler, 1987).

Summary

This chapter has reviewed the literature on problem employees, developing two strong themes. First, the sparse attention that has been given to this area highlights the wisdom of a positive approach to troubled or troublesome employees. The natural tendency of organizations is to require the Procrustean fitting of diverse personalities into the confines of a uniform work environment (Aredal, 1986). Quite probably, a number of poorly performing employees would be capable of quite excellent performance if one or another type of accommodation could be made to allow for their uniqueness. Second, human failings being what they are, negative perceptions, perhaps mistakenly formed early on, could predetermine negative reactions to some employees and beget the negative behavior already expected. Such unfortunate self-fulfilling prophecies are indeed common in social interactions (Jones, 1977), particularly in organizations. Given these considerations, it is wise practice for administrators to give their more difficult employees every fair chance to succeed.

This line of argument, so much in evidence in the literature, is very much reinforced by the state of the law governing the treatment of public employees. As a general rule, decisions that adversely affect employees' interests can now be challenged effectively by employees, to a degree never before known. Meeting such challenges requires documented evidence that efforts were made in good faith to assist employees to succeed in their jobs (Macleod, 1986). Training, mentoring, coaching, and positive discipline would all constitute such evidence—provided, of course, that these efforts were conducted in the genuine belief that a troubled employee is owed a fair chance to prove her or his ability to succeed on the job.

References

Albrecht, T. "For the Manager: Gaining Compliance from Key Subordinates." *Pacific Northwest Executive,* 1988, *4,* 23-25.

Aredal, A. "Procrustes: A Modern Management Pattern Found in a Classical Myth." *Journal of Management,* 1986, *12,* 403-414.

Ban, C., Goldenber, E., and Mazzotto, T. "Firing the Unproductive Employee: Will Civil Service Reform Make a Difference?" *Review of Public Personnel Administration,* 1982, *2,* 87-100.

Bramson, R. M. *Coping with Difficult People.* New York: Doubleday, 1981.

Bryant, A. W. "Replacing Punitive Discipline with a Positive Approach." *Personnel Administrator,* 1984, *29,* 79.

Campbell, D. N., Fleming, R. L., and Grote, R. C. "Discipline Without Punishment—At Last!" *Harvard Business Review,* 1985, *63,* 170.

Campbell, J. P., and Dunnette, M. D. "Effectiveness of T-Group Experiences in Managerial Training and Development." *Psychological Bulletin,* 1968, *70,* 73-104.

Cavanaugh, H. A. "The Power of Positive Discipline." *Electrical World,* 1982, *196,* 57.

Crawford, K., Thomas, E., and Fink, J. "Pygmalion at Sea: Improving Work Effectiveness of Low Performers." *Journal of Applied Behavioral Science,* 1980, *16* (4), 482-505.

Dalton, D. R., and Thomas, E. D. "Turnover Turned Over: An Expanded and Positive Perspective." *Academy of Management Journal,* 1979, *22,* 225-235.

Flanagan, J. C. "The Critical Incident Technique." *Psychological Bulletin,* 1954, *51,* 327-358.

Friedman, M., and Rosenman, R. H. *Type A Behavior and Your Heart.* Greenwich, Conn.: Fawcett Publications, 1974.

Guy, M. E. "Passages Through Organizations: Old Dogs and New Tricks." *Group Organization Studies,* 1984, *9* (4), 467-479.

Herzberg, F. *Work and the Nature of Man.* Cleveland, Ohio: World Publishing, 1966.

Hildreth, W. B., Miller, G. J., and Rabin, J. "The Liability of Public Executives: Implications for Practice in Personnel Administration." In B. Bozeman and J. Straussman (eds.), *New Directions in Public Administration.* Monterey, Calif.: Brooks/Cole, 1984.

Hirsch, S. K. *Using the Myers-Briggs Type Indicator in Organizations.* Palo Alto, Calif.: Consulting Psychologists Press, 1985.

Jones, R. *Self-Fulfilling Prophecies: Social, Psychological, and Physiological Effects of Expectancies.* New York: Wiley, 1977.

Jurkovich, R. "A Core Typology of Organizational Environments." *Administrative Science Quarterly,* 1974, *19,* 380-394.

Kaplan, M. A. *Alienation and Identification.* New York: Free Press, 1976.

Kilmann, R. *Beyond the Quick Fix: Managing Five Tracks to Organizational Success.* San Francisco: Jossey-Bass, 1984.

Lasch, C. *The Culture of Narcissism: American Life in an Age of Diminishing Expectations*. New York: Warner Books, 1979.

Leap, T. L., and Crino, M. D. "How to Deal with Bizarre Employee Behavior." *Harvard Business Review*, 1986, *65*, 18–20, 22.

Lees-Haley, P. R. "How to Direct Malingerers in the Workplace." *Personnel Journal*, 1986, *65*, 106–110.

Lovrich, N. P. "The Dangers of Participative Management: A Test of Unexamined Assumptions Concerning Employee Involvement." *Review of Public Personnel Administration*, 1985, *5*, 9–25.

Macleod, J. S. "Avoiding Disciplinary Problems." *Employment Relations Today*, 1986, *13*, 219–223.

Morgenroth, W. M., and Morgenroth, R. L. "Handling the Difficult Employee." *Business and Economic Review*, 1986, *32*, 12–16.

Odiorne, G. *Management by Objectives*. New York: Pitman, 1965.

Odiorne, G. *Strategic Management of Human Resources: A Portfolio Approach*. San Francisco: Jossey-Bass, 1984.

Orenstein, M. W. "Violent Employees." *Management*, 1987, *6* (4), 33–35.

Ouchi, W. G. *Theory Z: How American Business Can Meet the Japanese Challenge*. Reading, Mass.: Addison-Wesley, 1981.

Peter, L. J., and Hull, R. *The Peter Principle: Why Things Always Go Wrong*. New York: Morrow, 1969.

Redeker, J. R. "Discipline: The Nonpunitive Approach Works by Design." *Personnel*, 1985, *62*, 7–14.

Riccucci, N. M., and Wheeler, G. R. "Positive Employee Performance: An Innovative Approach to Employee Discipline." *Review of Public Personnel Administration*, 1987, *7*, 49–63.

Sherman, J. D., Smith, H. L., and Mansfield, E. R. "The Impact of Emergent Network Structure on Organizational Socialization." *Journal of Applied Behavioral Science*, 1986, *22* (1), 53–63.

Staw, B. W., Ball, N. E., and Clausen, J. A. "The Dispositional Approach to Job Attitudes: A Lifetime Longitudinal Test." *Administrative Science Quarterly*, 1986, *31*, 56–77.

Ward, W., and Sandvold, K. "Performance Expectancy as a Determinant of Actual Performance: A Partial Replication." *Journal of Abnormal and Social Psychology*, 1963, *67*, 293–295.

Weiss, H. H. *Supervisor's Standard Reference Handbook*. Englewood Cliffs, N.J.: Prentice-Hall, 1980.

Wheeler, H., and Kochan, T. "Unions and Public Sector Supervisors: The Case of Fire Fighters." In M. Levine (ed.), *Public Personnel Management: Readings, Cases, and Contingency Plans*. Salt Lake City, Utah: Brighton, 1980.

Zajonc, R., and Brickman, P. "Expectancy and Feedback as Independent Factors in Task Performance." *Journal of Personality and Social Psychology*, 1969, *11*, 148–156.

Zemke, R. "Working with Jerks." *Training: The Magazine of Human Resources Development*, 1987, *24*, 27–38.

30

Loretta R. Flanders

Developing Executive and Managerial Talent

Management is generally recognized as one of the most, if not the most, critical occupations in today's organizations. Currently, most major public and private organizations support management development activities to help meet their need for high-quality managerial talent. The degree of support varies, but the trend is toward the view that "there has to be systematic work on the supply, development, and the skills of tomorrow's management. It cannot be left to luck or chance" (Drucker, 1973, p. 421).

Management development can be broadly defined as the processes and methods through which individuals acquire or enhance the knowledge, skills, and characteristics needed for effective performance of managerial responsibilities in a given organizational setting. A *setting* includes such variables as type of organization (public or private, production or research and development, and so on) and management level (executive, middle, or supervisory), which affect what is expected of a manager and thus the content of management development.

As measured by professional publications and reputation, most of the innovation and advancement in management development practices, and in their underlying theories, has occurred in or for private sector organizations. Until very recently, management development was often not even mentioned in textbooks on public personnel administration. For example, while the texts by Stahl (1983) and Nigro and Nigro (1981) have chapters dealing with training, they have no specific references to management development. A more recent text (Shafritz, Hyde, and Rosenbloom, 1986) shows a change in approach: *Human resources development* is one of six organizing subparts of the book, and it includes a chapter that gives considerable attention to management development.

There has been a growing concern with the status and development of public sector career managers (for example, see Brock, 1984, p. 223). Indicative of this concern has been the increase in separate executive personnel systems since 1978. In that year, Congress established the federal government's Senior Executive Service (SES). For the first time, executive development for and within the highest ranks of the federal career service was required by law. Four states—California, Minnesota, Oregon, and Wisconsin—had executive personnel systems before SES, and eight more states have established SES-type systems since 1978. According to Sherwood and Breyer (1987, p. 412), "developing individuals to their full potential as leaders" is one of the major functions of these state executive personnel systems.

This chapter covers current generic (applicable to the public and private sectors alike) and government-specific management development practices and issues. The presentation includes an overview of the scope and major types of management development processes and methods; guidelines for making management development choices; an analysis of the scope of responsibility of career managers and of public management by experts, since scope affects both the content and the implementation of management development; and a review of federal, state, and local government approaches to management development.

Processes and Methods

The content and the emphases of management development programs for public and private sector managers will differ somewhat, but most development processes and methods are applicable to both sectors. This section provides an overview of the scope and types of processes and methods, new and old, that are currently being used in management development. Processes range from unplanned, seat-of-the-pants learning on the job by individuals to multifaceted, systematic, organizationally supported programs for the development of the management team. The indispensable element of establishing and maintaining the latter type of program is top-level management support.

Organizational processes for management development include at least some of the following components:

- Provisions for involving line management
- A professional human resources development and training staff under a high-level executive
- Management career paths and succession planning
- Early identification of managerial talent, to promote those deemed to have executive potential
- Planned use of job assignments as a developmental tool
- Formal training courses

- A management competency model
- Formal means for assessing the management capabilities and development needs of individuals and the organization
- Individual development plans
- Encouragement of self-development activities

Three of the better sources on systematic approaches to management development are Braham (1987), Schulze (1986), and Digman (1978). Management development methods include on-the-job learning, education, training, and self-paced learning.

The first category, on-the-job learning, offers an incredibly rich and diverse array of learning and developmental opportunities, including networking inside and outside the organization; coaching, counseling, and mentoring by one's supervisor or another manager; rotational, acting, committee, and task force assignments; feedback from performance appraisals and from other sources, such as peers and employees; participation in team-building activities; day-to-day problem solving; and observation of good and bad managers and management techniques.

The second category, management education, for both the public and the private sectors, frequently takes the form of academic degree programs, such as those leading to master's degrees in public and business administration. By nature and purpose, they are generally theoretical and conceptual, typically relying heavily on seminars and lectures (although case studies and simulations are used to a great extent in some programs). Many universities also provide educational programs of shorter duration for senior managers and executives (for example, Harvard's Senior Executive Fellows Program).

The third category, training, generally is focused on job-related behaviors, attitudes, and issues or on skills building. Even though technology has produced a new set of training methods (including computer-based training, teleconferencing, and interactive videodiscs), classroom training predominates by up to 95 percent. As Broadwell (1987, p. 383) observes, "It is easy to do classroom instruction, for all one has to do is find a room, assemble an instructor and students, and have all the ingredients for carrying on instruction—not necessarily the *best* instruction, but instruction nevertheless." The continuum of methods used in classroom training for managers ranges from "dog and pony shows" (programs of expert speakers, where participants are largely passive recipients of information) to techniques that feature greater involvement of participants (such as case studies, role playing, games, simulations, and assessment and feedback instruments) to highly participative group techniques (including groups for counseling and therapy) (Cooke, 1987, p. 432). With respect to computer-based training for middle managers and executives, a particularly exciting development is the use of complex games and simulations aimed at helping participants acquire or enhance such capabilities as broad perspective and strategic thinking. These types of skills and characteristics are among the most difficult to deal with in a training context.

The fourth category of development methods consists of self-paced learning approaches. These may take the form of correspondence courses, programmed instruction, or a variety of techniques in which individual self-paced learning tools are integrated with work being performed on the job or in classrooms.

Guidelines

Given the number and variety of processes and methods in use for developing managerial skills, how should organizations use their limited resources for management development? What is the best developmental approach for the individual interested in getting into or advancing in a management career? In view of organizational and individual differences, there are no absolute answers to such questions; therefore, guidelines that reflect commonalities provide the best solution.

In identifying such guidelines, the target population for management development provides the starting point. This population, in public and private organizations alike, primarily consists of adults with full-time jobs and recognized experience as technical experts in such nonmanagerial specialties as science, teaching, and accounting. (Because of the special demands of management in the public sector, the issue of using technical experts as managers is explored in some detail later in this chapter.) Theory and research on adult learning, career orientations and motivations, types of learning objectives, self-knowledge and self-assessment, and management provide the substantive basis for guidelines on management development.

Andragogy, or the "art and science of helping adults learn" (Knowles, 1987, pp. 170–175), rests on adults' needs "to be self-directing . . . to know or to be able to do in order to perform more effectively . . . and [to] enter into a learning experience with a task-centered (or problem-centered or life-centered) orientation to learning." These propositions have significant implications for designing and selecting development experiences to enhance managerial capabilities.

Research findings on career orientations and motivations, in conjunction with studies of self-knowledge and types of learning objectives, underscore the importance of attention to understanding one's strengths, weaknesses, and preferences with respect to a management position. Schein (1978, 1982), one of the first to investigate career motivations and orientations, talks in terms of people having "career anchors." He has identified a variety of such anchors, which concern managerial issues, technical specialties, security, autonomy, entrepreneurship, service or dedication (to a cause, a client group, or an ideology), challenge, and life-style. Each of these career anchors consists of somewhat different self-perceived talents, abilities, motives, needs, attitudes, and values, which significantly affect occupational choice and job satisfaction.

The importance of self-knowledge—in the sense of awareness of one's own values, strengths, weaknesses, feelings, impact on others, and other attributes—is a growing theme in management development. Self-knowledge has been proposed as one of five broad types of learning objectives to be used in designing and selecting development experiences; the other four objectives concern cognitive, affective, interpersonal, and psychomotor issues (Huczynski, 1983).

Kaplan, Drath, and Kofodimos (1985) provide a good in-depth treatment, particularly for top managers, of the need to provide opportunities for structured introspection and self-assessment. One combination of assessment tools that has worked well for the U.S. Office of Personnel Management and several other federal agencies is the Myers-Briggs Type Indicator (MBTI) and the Management Excellence Inventory (MEI). These instruments provide different but complementary types of information. The MBTI, a widely used self-assessment instrument, provides insights into personal preferences, values, and orientations and into how these affect decision making and behavior. A useful summary of the background and uses of the Myers-Briggs tool is provided by Rush (1987).

The MEI (Flanders and Utterback, 1985) is a questionnaire on job tasks, skills, and behaviors. It is designed for self-assessment and/or supervisory assessment of an individual. The results give information on these tasks, skills, and behaviors in terms of their relative importance to a job and in terms of an individual's management strengths and developmental needs. The MEI is based on the Management Excellence Framework (MEF), developed for the federal government (U.S. Office of Personnel Management, 1985c). Both the MEF and the MEI have proved adaptable to other government settings, including New York City, the Michigan Judicial Institute, and the government of Indonesia. Transferability of the MEF and the MEI is facilitated by an IBM-compatible microcomputer-based software system that analyzes responses to the questionnaire and produces a series of individual and group reports. This software is available through the National Technical Information Service (U.S. Office of Personnel Management, 1987).

The five guidelines that follow draw on research into the nature of management responsibilities, knowledge, skills, and characteristics. In the development context, management level—executive, managerial, or supervisory—is particularly important. In general terms, management responsibilities and skills, at all levels, can be described in the same terms, but they differ in importance and in specifics by level (U.S. Office of Personnel Management, 1985c; Katz, 1974). In other words, "What will get you promoted at one level will get you killed at another" (Fox, 1980, p. 46). These guidelines, based on characteristics of target populations and on theory and research from various fields, are presented as an aid in choosing among the many options for management development.

1. Recognize that the individual must be open to new information and willing to engage in self-development before effective learning can occur. "Management development must be self-development. The organization can provide training opportunities but they will only be effective if the individual manager is motivated to take advantage of them" (Schulze, 1986, pp. 23–25).
2. Use on-the-job activities as the primary vehicle for management development.
3. Select learning methods appropriate for specified learning objectives, but, as much as possible, use practical, job-related training that actively involves the participants in the learning process.
4. Pay particular attention to key career transitions in management—entry and movement from one level to another.
5. Use an approach that involves assessment of multifaceted individual strengths and needs as a means of accomplishing several goals: assisting the individual to understand how management roles and responsibilities differ from those of the specialist or individual performer; linking individual and organizational management development goals and plans; and getting a better return on investment in training or education programs by supporting those that are needed most.

Career Managers: Responsibilities and Expertise

The content and program emphases of management development should be grounded in job responsibilities and in the knowledge, skills, and characteristics needed to do a job effectively. In our constitutional, democratic system, government, business, and industry serve different purposes and have very different organizational power structures. A long-standing issue in public administration is the degree of possible transferability of the large body of private sector management theory, principles, and practices to the public sector. "It is not an accident that the National Association of Schools of Public Affairs *and* Administration is so named. The compound labeling reflects a schism at the philosophical core of education for the public service. In considerable degree it comes down to the importance that attaches to the word 'public'" (Sherwood, 1983, p. 50).

Bowman and Plant (1982) represent the view that considers *public* the operative term in public administration. Nevertheless, as illustrated by the controversy and heated rhetoric generated by changes and proposed changes made during the Reagan administration, there are significantly different views of what the public service or the public good is, and of the role of career civil servants in pursuing it. For example, some commentators hold that "primacy should be placed on the word 'administration.' They are concerned that leaders in government, as in the private sector, have the capacity to make things happen" (Sherwood, 1983, p. 51).

Graham and Hays (1986, pp. vii, 4) take a synthesizing and balancing approach to this issue: "Public administrators have many purely managerial responsibilities that must coexist with their political and public service orientations . . . in a much more demanding institutional environment [than that of their private sector counterparts]." This environment is a system of government with checks and balances and fragmented decision authority for policy and expenditures. It is also a system in which career service managers are subordinate to appointed and elected officials but responsible for staying within constitutional boundaries, even though their political bosses may sometimes make demands to the contrary.

To these three public management responsibilities—"pure" management, responsiveness and accountability to political officials, and public service orientation—a fourth responsibility can be added. Public administration theorists would label it *neutral competence,* but most career public managers would probably call it *maintenance of technical or program expertise.* Thus, the typical public manager is faced with carrying out a complex, diverse, and often contradictory set of responsibilities.

Given the paths by which people advance to managerial positions in government, there is no guarantee that they will be competent managers (Allison, 1980, p. 37). In relation to the total population of several hundred thousand public managers, there are very few who have broad, generalist perspectives and understanding of the public service. The most identifiable of these few (even though they are not career civil servants per se) are city managers (Newland, 1980, p. 3). City managers are the exception, however. For the majority of public managers, management is a second, and often a secondary, profession. Most individuals, before having been promoted into management positions in government organizations, were successful accountants, computer programmers, engineers, lawyers, physicians, police officers, personnel specialists, scientists, social workers, teachers, and so on down the list of most occupational specialties (see Misler, 1986, p. 390).

The degree of specialization in the career service of the federal government is evident in the job classification system for white-collar employees. There are 22 broad occupational groups, which are subdivided into 443 different job series (U.S. Office of Personnel Management, 1985a). In the federal civil service, with a few exceptions, all jobs designated as supervisory or managerial, including those at the highest SES level, have program-area job series designations. Mosher (1982, p. 3) identifies the fundamental reason for concern about public management by experts: "The kinds of decisions and actions these officials take depend upon their capabilities, their orientations, and their values; and these attributes depend heavily upon their backgrounds, their training and education, and their current associations." For the most part, the orientations, values, and training and education provided in many professions do not offer a good foundation for carrying out or even understanding public management responsibilities. This shortcoming is well illustrated by Krembs (1983, pp. 36–38), who catalogues the problems of technical specialists promoted to management jobs. Moreover, such problems cannot be solved by one-shot development experiences upon entry into a first management position. As Bayton and Chapman (1972, p. 1) found, "the transformation from specialist to manager is a continuing process."

Overall, management development in the public sector is generally going to be more difficult than in the private sector, for several reasons: the scope and diversity of the public manager's responsibilities; the presence of so many specialists in management positions, coupled with relatively rigid personnel rules and procedures that perpetuate this situation (Heisel, 1980); and political leadership. Long-term development efforts supported by government agencies—particularly efforts that require substantial expenditures or staff—are difficult to establish and maintain. Political executives have policy and program agendas to accomplish in a very short time, and, given their roots in specialized professional fields, many high-level career executives simply do not see the need for such efforts.

Management Development in the Public Sector

If the situation in state and local governments is similar to that in the federal government, then there is much more organizationally supported management development going on in states and localities than the small number of professional publications seems to indicate. (The tendency in government is to produce in-house reports and other documents, such as policy statements, which are not widely disseminated, and the demise of the Intergovernmental Personnel Act assistance and information-sharing activities, in the early 1980s, only exacerbated this situation.) Although there are great variations among federal agencies, the creation of the SES and the establishment of SES candidate development programs have stimulated management development in the federal government. In states that have instituted executive personnel systems, however, this has not been the case (Sherwood and Breyer, 1987).

Perhaps state and local governments place more emphasis on first-line supervisors and middle managers, given the preponderance of direct service delivery. Certainly, articles on the major types of state and local management development activities—training needs assessments and formal training and educational courses—deal with supervisors and middle managers (see Swierczek and Carmichael, 1985; Hilliard, 1986; Misler, 1986; Bernick, Kindley, and Pettit, 1984).

Two particularly noteworthy management training efforts at the state level are the certified public manager (CPM) programs and New York's Public Service Training Program. Georgia initiated the first CPM program in 1976 (Henning and Wilson, 1979). Within a few years, the National Certified Public Manager Consortium of states was established. As of early 1988, the consortium had five accredited programs (in Arizona, Florida, Georgia, Louisiana, and New Jersey), and three other states (Alabama, North Carolina, and Oklahoma) had programs under development. Nine additional states are associate members, on the basis of their commitment to instituting CPM programs.

In general, certified public manager programs follow the Georgia model, in which there is a series of six job-related management courses. The courses parallel the management continuum, from supervisory to senior levels, and are delivered in association with state university systems, usually through some government institute. In contrast to most management training, the CPM programs rigorously test participants' competence (Henning and Wilson, 1979).

New York's Public Service Training Program, begun in 1983, also features a systematic approach to courses. It is organized around a competing-values framework of leadership and includes two practical, skills-based curricula—one on supervision, which deals with individual performance factors, and the other on administration, which emphasizes organizational performance factors (Faerman, Quinn, and Thompson, 1987). The funding arrangement for the program is highly unusual and provides an alternative to standard budget and policy processes for allocating scarce resources. Funding for the Public Service Training Program is provided for in the bargaining agreement between the state and the bargaining unit for professional, scientific, and technical employees (Faerman, Quinn, and Thompson, 1987).

The federal government seems generally to support a wider array of management development activities than most states and localities do. In addition to formal training and education, these activities include research on management competency models and multifaceted, comprehensive development programs. The federal programs, while they share a number of courses, are individualized for each participant on the basis of initial assessments and the use of mentors, senior advisers, and developmental work assignments.

Organizationally supported management development in the federal government occurs at two and often at three levels: interagency, agency, and subagency. At the interagency level, the U.S. Office of Personnel Management (OPM) has governmentwide policy and guidance responsibilities and has the authority to provide training and other assistance on a reimbursable basis for the agencies. It has operated a set of training centers, including the Federal Executive Institute, since the 1960s. Even though several thousand incumbent and would-be managers attend these training courses every year, the bulk of management training is done through the agencies, with contractors, universities, and in-house staff. Some agencies also have their own management training centers.

Since 1978, OPM's management development policy emphasis has been on promoting systematic development programs rather than individual training courses in the agencies. A few agencies, such as the Internal Revenue Service, already had such programs in place and served as models for policy revision, the most recent of which occurred in 1985 (U.S. Office of Personnel Management, 1985b). Among the major features of this policy, which envisions the establishment of an integrated human resources management system, are the following:

- Use of a common competency base for the development of supervisors, managers, and executives
- Assessment of individual and organizational management development needs
- Use of Executive Resources Boards, composed of career and noncareer executives, to manage the development system
- Incorporation of a variety of learning methods, including coaching, rotational assignments, special work projects, and formal training
- Evaluation of program and individual success in terms of such factors as cost and performance
- Integration of management development with agencies' other personnel management programs (recruitment, position management, and so on).

To date, the most ambitious agency effort to place management development in the context of human resources management is the Environmental Protection Agency's Framework for Achieving Management Excellence program.

Summary

This chapter was designed to further management development in the public sector by providing a review of the diverse processes and methods of developing managerial skill that are currently being used in the public and private sectors. These include on-the-job activities, complex computer simulations, and management succession planning, among other methods. The chapter also identified guidelines for choices of management development activities. These guidelines can be summarized as emphasizing organizational support for practical, skills-based training, structured assessment opportunities, and other methods that complement, assist, and stimulate self-development. Two features of public sector management that significantly affect management development were discussed: the special and complex nature of the career public manager's responsibilities, and the preponderance of technical experts in managerial positions. These and other factors interact to make organizationally supported management development more difficult in the public sector than in the private sector. Finally, the chapter offered a summary of recent and current management development efforts in federal, state, and local governments. Systematic, up-to-date approaches to management development (in particular, skills-based training and competency-based assessment) exist in the public as well as in the private sector, and while they may not be the norm, at least they are a trend.

References

Allison, G., Jr. "Public and Private Management: Are They Fundamentally Alike in All Unimportant Respects?" In *Public Management Research Agendas: Integrating the Sponsor, Producer and User.* Washington, D.C.: U.S. Office of Personnel Management, 1980.

Bayton, J. A., and Chapman, R. L. *Transformation of Scientists and Engineers into Managers.* Washington, D.C.: National Aeronautics and Space Administration, 1972.

Bernick, E. L., Kindley, R., and Pettit, K. K. "The Structure of Training Courses and the Effects of Hierarchy." *Public Personnel Management,* 1984, *13* (2), 109–119.

Bowman, J. S., and Plant, J. F. "Institutional Problems of Public Administration Programs: A House Without a Home." In T. Vocino and R. Heimovics (eds.), *Public Administration Education in Transition.* New York: Marcel Dekker, 1982.

Braham, J. "Cultivating Tomorrow's Executives: How Do GE and IBM Grow All That Talent?" *Industry Week,* 1987, *234* (2), 35–38.

Broadwell, M. M. "Classroom Instruction." In R. L. Craig (ed.), *Training and Development Handbook.* (3rd ed.) New York: McGraw-Hill, 1987.

Brock, J. *Managing People in Public Agencies: Personnel and Labor Relations.* Boston: Little, Brown, 1984.

Cooke, P. "Role Playing." In R. L. Craig (ed.), *Training and Development Handbook.* (3rd ed.) New York: McGraw-Hill, 1987.

Digman, L. A. "How Well-Managed Organizations Develop Their Executives." *Organizational Dynamics,* 1978, *7* (2), 63–79.

Drucker, P. F. *Management: Tasks, Responsibilities, Practices.* New York: Harper & Row, 1973.

Faerman, S. R., Quinn, R. E., and Thompson, M. P. "Bridging Management Practice and Theory: New York State's Public Service Training Program." *Public Administration Review,* 1987, *47* (4), 310–319.

Flanders, L. R., and Utterback, D. "The Management Excellence Inventory: A Tool for Management Development." *Public Administration Review,* 1985, *45* (3), 403–410.

Fox, J. *Trapped in the Organization: (Fox's Fixations).* Los Angeles: Price/Stern/Sloan, 1980.

Graham, C. B., Jr., and Hays, S. W. *Managing the Public Organization.* Washington, D.C.: C. Q. Press, 1986.

Heisel, W. D. "A Nonbureaucratic View of Management Development." *Public Personnel Management,* 1980, *9* (2), 94–98.

Henning, K. K., and Wilson, L. D. "The Georgia Certified Public Manager (C.P.M.) Program." *Southern Review of Public Administration,* 1979, *2* (4), 424–435.

Hilliard, C. L. "Management Development at Work in Texas." *Public Personnel Management,* 1986, *15* (4), 377–381.

Huczynski, A. *Encyclopedia of Management Development Methods.* Aldershot, England: Gower, 1983.

Kaplan, R. E., Drath, W. H., and Kofodimos, J. R. *High Hurdles: The Challenge of Executive Self-Development.* Technical Report no. 25. Greensboro, N.C.: Center for Creative Leadership, 1985.

Katz, R. L. "Skills of an Effective Administrator." *Harvard Business Review,* 1974, *52,* 90–102.

Knowles, M. S. "Adult Learning." In R. L. Craig (ed.), *Training and Development Handbook.* (3rd ed.) New York: McGraw-Hill, 1987.

Krembs, P. "Making Managers of Technical Gurus." *Training and Development Journal,* 1983, *37* (9), 36–41.

Misler, D. I. "Management Development and More: Contracting Out Makes It Possible." *Public Personnel Management,* 1986, *15* (4), 389–393.

Mosher, F. C. *Democracy and the Public Service.* (2nd ed.) New York: Oxford University Press, 1982.

Newland, C. A. "Professional Public Executives and Public Administration Agendas." In C. A. Newland (ed.), *Professional Public Executives.* Washington, D.C.: American Society for Public Administration, 1980.

Nigro, F. A., and Nigro, L. G. *The New Public Personnel Administration.* (2nd ed.) Itasca, Ill.: Peacock, 1981.

Rush, H.M.F. "The Behavioral Sciences." In R. L. Craig (ed.), *Training and Development Handbook.* (3rd ed.) New York: McGraw-Hill, 1987.

Schein, E. H. *Career Dynamics: Matching Individual and Organization Needs.* Reading, Mass.: Addison-Wesley, 1978.

Schein, E. H. *Individuals and Careers.* Technical Report no. 19. Washington, D.C.: Office of Naval Research, 1982.

Schulze, G. L. "Management Development." In J. J. Famularo (ed.), *Handbook of Human Resources Administration.* (2nd ed.) New York: McGraw-Hill, 1986.

Shafritz, J. M., Hyde, A. C., and Rosenbloom, D. H. *Personnel Management in Government: Politics and Process.* New York: Marcel Dekker, 1986.

Sherwood, F. P. "The Education and Training of Public Managers." In W. B. Eddy (ed.), *Handbook of Organization Management.* New York: Marcel Dekker, 1983.

Sherwood, F. P., and Breyer, L. J. "Executive Personnel Systems in the States." *Public Administration Review,* 1987, *47* (3), 410–416.

Stahl, O. G. *Public Personnel Administration.* (8th ed.) New York: Harper & Row, 1983.

Swierczek, F. W., and Carmichael, L. "Assessing Training Needs: A Skills Approach." *Public Personnel Management,* 1985, *14* (3), 259–274.

U.S. Office of Personnel Management. *Federal Civilian Workforce Statistics: Occupations of Federal White-Collar and Blue-Collar Workers.* Washington, D.C.: U.S. Office of Personnel Management, 1985a.

U.S. Office of Personnel Management. *Federal Personnel Manual Chapter 412: Executive, Manager, and Supervisory Development.* Washington, D.C.: U.S. Office of Personnel Management, 1985b.

U.S. Office of Personnel Management. *The Management Excellence Framework: A Competency-Based Model of Effective Performance for Federal Managers.* Washington, D.C.: U.S. Office of Personnel Management, 1985c.

U.S. Office of Personnel Management. *Management Excellence Inventory Software System (MEISS) and Supporting Materials.* Washington, D.C.: U.S. Office of Personnel Management, 1987.

31

John Thomas Delaney
Raymond D. Horton

Managing Relations with Organized Employees

Labor's contribution varies from service to service and across levels of government in the American system of public administration; but, overall, it dominates the other factors that administrators manage in order to produce public services. While underappreciated, human resources management occupies an important position in the hierarchy of public management functions. Human resources management policies and practices exert a substantial impact on the cost and level of public services. An otherwise well-managed government—one with appropriate revenues, facilities, and policies—will find it difficult to provide acceptable services at acceptable costs if its work force is poorly managed.

Managing employees who have the right to organize and to bargain collectively is a relatively new experience in the public sector, but in the past three decades it has become an important component of human resources management. Today, more than 40 percent of the American public work force is covered by collective bargaining contracts that stipulate employment terms (Lewin, Feuille, Kochan, and Delaney, 1988), and in many state and local governments, collective bargaining is nearly synonymous with human resources management because virtually the entire work force is unionized.

The transition to negotiated determination of the employment relationship has required public officials to devise formal policies to regulate collective bargaining, and informal policies to organize the behavior of public managers therein. In the absence of bargaining experience, initial public policy drew heavily on the conventional wisdom that public sector bargaining

Note: The authors are grateful to Peter Feuille, Jim Kuhn, and Donna Sockell for their helpful comments.

was essentially different from bargaining in the private sector (Wellington and Winter, 1971). Proponents of that view assumed that public managers, not subject to the same competitive pressures as their counterparts in firms, would be soft bargainers when contested by economically and politically powerful unions. As a result, regulatory policies and managerial strategies appropriate to the private sector, such as permitting (or taking) strikes, were deemed inappropriate to the public sector. Public officials were thought to need additional protection if they were to protect the public interest in collective bargaining.

But what if the conventional wisdom is wrong? What if it understates the role of competition in government and thus overstates the power of organized employees? More important, what if the regulatory policies, and related managerial practices, contribute to union power? In other words, we ask whether some policies and practices are counterproductive. If the objective of public administrators is to protect the public interest, then aspects of the regulation and management of collective bargaining may need to be altered. In this chapter, we explore these issues in the following manner.

First, we examine the conventional view of public sector bargaining, as well as our own view, which embraces different assumptions. Next, we illustrate our thesis by examining several important aspects of public sector bargaining, including management organization for bargaining, the scope of bargaining, and the management of bargaining impasses. Finally, we summarize our arguments and identify some issues we hope will be considered by administrators and scholars concerned with management of unionized public employees.

Assumptions About Public Sector Bargaining

For the purposes of this chapter, we define *modern* public sector labor relations to be the collective bargaining relationship between public managers (including elected officials) and organized employees. (This definition necessarily excludes many aspects of the larger human resources management system in government.) A full-scale review would include all public employees, not just organized employees, and all decision-making processes that determine the terms and conditions of public employment, not just collective bargaining.

The Development of Public Sector Unionism. In 1960, relatively few public employees belonged to unions or were covered by collective bargaining agreements. Unionism grew rapidly in the 1960s, however, following President John F. Kennedy's 1962 executive order granting limited bargaining rights to federal employees. It continued to expand rapidly through the mid 1970s, as many states provided bargaining rights to their employees and, in many cases, to local government employees as well (Freeman, 1986). The expansion of unionization among public employees has slowed in the past decade or so, but by the mid 1980s, 43 percent of public employees were covered by collective bargaining agreements (Gifford, 1986), and thirty-seven states had enacted collective bargaining laws covering state and local employees.

Although variations exist across governments in the specific rules that govern bargaining, the legal environment in most jurisdictions encourages American public employees to unionize. In fact, unionism and bargaining have become institutionalized in the public sector. As a result, it is appropriate to examine the conventional wisdom on public sector unionism in light of three decades of bargaining experience.

The Conventional Wisdom. Wellington and Winter's (1971) classic study of public sector bargaining provides a widely accepted articulation of the conventional view. Published amidst the takeoff period of public sector unionization and bargaining, the volume provided both a provocative exposition of potential differences between private and public sector bargaining and policy recommendations for students and practitioners. Clearly, Wellington and Winter were concerned about the practice of collective bargaining in government. Their study outlined the theoretical basis of their concern and proposed a set of policies designed to make the most of what they believed was an inherently bad situation. Over time, this view has shaped public sector bargaining legislation and management strategies.

Although our brief summary does not do it justice, their core argument is that public and private organizations are different—not totally, but basically—because of their different proximity to competition. Wellington and Winter noted that not all firms are subject to perfect competition, nor are all governments impervious to market forces, but they clearly located the two sectors differently on the competition-monopoly spectrum.

Wellington and Winter drew on accepted theories of economics and political science to support their thesis that public employees would exercise inordinate power in collective bargaining. For instance, they argued that governments monopolize essential services, which makes demand for many public services relatively inelastic or insensitive to price changes. Inelastic demand reduces the effect of the wage-employment trade-off in government relative to the private sector, where the trade-off typically is seen as constraining union bargaining power.

In addition, Wellington and Winter offered a noneconomic rationale for the "inordinate power" thesis: Government decisions are based on political considerations, whereby organized interest groups have more influence over official policy and behavior than unorganized groups do. Public officials may understand that other interests are traded to pay higher wages, but the public at large may not. Accordingly, public officials are held to be unduly responsive to organized employees, behaving more like politicians than managers in collective bargaining. This would be particularly true if organized public employees enjoyed the same rights as their private sector counterparts, including the right to withhold their labor. The consumers of state and local government services, or the public, would supposedly offer precious little support to public officials in the face of a strike threat, particularly if it involved essential services.

The policy implications of the "inordinate power" thesis were relatively straightforward to Wellington and Winter: If it is not too late, then resist collective bargaining; but if bargaining is inevitable, then do not transplant the private regulatory scheme wholesale into the public sector. Restrict the scope of bargaining and prohibit strikes; granting the right to strike would only increase the already formidable power of organized public employees, and defining the scope of bargaining broadly would only increase the number of issues on which excessive union power could be brought to bear.

Although Wellington and Winter's arguments were speculative, they were generally accepted and expanded by other scholars (C. W. Summers, 1974; R. S. Summers, 1976). Further, some early experiences with public sector bargaining seemed to support Wellington and Winter's thesis. During the 1960s, public payrolls increased, both absolutely and relatively, with respect to private sector payrolls, reflecting gains in both the volume and the price of labor. Moreover, there was some evidence that these gains were correlated positively with unionization (Ehrenberg and Goldstein, 1975). In addition, the scope of bargaining tended to expand beyond economic issues, formal limits notwithstanding, and to encompass what were considered managerial prerogatives (Feuille, Delaney, and Hendricks, 1985; Valletta and Freeman, 1986). Finally, and despite widespread legal prohibitions, public employees' strikes increased, sometimes even involving services thought to be essential to the safety and health of the populace (Lewin, 1986). In short, evidence demonstrated that public officials were having a difficult time dealing with unionized employees, and it suggested that the public might be suffering the consequences.

Another View. Because almost two decades have passed since the publication of Wellington and Winter's book, it is appropriate to ask whether accumulated evidence supports the conventional wisdom. We believe, on the basis of emerging evidence, that the "inordinate power" thesis of public sector bargaining is overstated. To us, the power of organized employees is situational, not inherent. Competitive pressures do exist in government, and they may induce public managers to behave less like politicians and more like private sector managers are presumed to behave in collective bargaining.

This perspective assumes that both private and public sector bargaining is heavily influenced by the settings in which it occurs. Political and economic variables affect the nature and outcomes of labor-management relations in government, just as they do in the private sector. The officials of a government may be soft bargainers for a time (as negotiators in the American auto, tire, steel, and meatpacking industries once were), but changing organizational and environmental circumstances may alter their behavior. Thus, neither the demand for public services nor the demands of organized public employees fully explain managers' behavior in collective bargaining.

Certainly, this perspective is supported by longitudinal analyses of collective bargaining in single governments (Horton, 1986; Katz, 1979). In New York City, for example, an economic crisis became a fiscal crisis in the mid 1970s, and the resulting reconfiguration of political relationships changed the collective bargaining process and decisions. The rules of the game stayed essentially unchanged, but public officials were better able to integrate their political and managerial roles. Organized employees found their wage and employment goals harder to realize, formal and informal work rules were renegotiated, and strikes and recourse to arbitration declined in number and importance, respectively.

Comparative data analysis on three decades of public sector bargaining also provides some support for the view that organized employees' power is situational, rather than inherent. In general, public employment and public employees' compensation have risen less rapidly since the mid 1970s, and there is evidence that public officials, with public support, have used the bargaining process to regain productivity givebacks previously negotiated away (Lewin, 1986). The evidence suggests that the bargaining power of organized employees varies across time and depends on economic and political circumstances.

Assumptions and Policy in Three Areas

If the conventional wisdom on public sector bargaining is wrong or at least overstated, then it is appropriate to consider whether policies derived from that so-called wisdom actually serve the public. We shall do so by examining three broad questions: Who should represent management in collective bargaining? Over what issues should the parties be permitted to bargain? In the event of bargaining impasses, how should disputes be resolved?

Management Organization for Bargaining. Since the inception of public sector bargaining, the conventional perspective has assumed that the decentralized or fragmented nature of public management is a problem. This assumption reflects the view that private bargaining and public bargaining are different. Collective bargaining in the private sector, the argument goes, may produce rational outcomes because it involves bilateral bargaining between one labor adversary and one management adversary. Further, it is considered to be unimportant whether the chief executive officer of the firm is directly involved in negotiations. The executive's agents—professional negotiators—speak for management and thus provide a chain of command that links management's organizational goals and bargaining behavior.

In public sector bargaining, however, management is seen as fragmented and often unable to present a united front. This condition is seen as the inevitable result of the underlying features of American public administration. Constitutionally, the separation-of-powers doctrine encourages horizontal fragmentation of authority among officials of the same government and invites legislators and executives to compete in determining the terms and conditions of public employment. The principle of federalism adds a vertical dimension to fragmentation, particularly in local government. In the event that mayors or city managers are able to orchestrate a united bargaining front within their own governments, state and federal officials may intervene with different policies, designed to protect their own roles in local government.

Politically, the conventional argument goes, these constitutional conditions strengthen the hand of unionized public employees. The nature of governmental decision making, coupled with the influence of public employee unions over the election and appointment of officials at all levels of government, provides union leaders the opportunity to circumvent management negotiators who will not yield to their demands. This option also allows unions to circumvent the bargaining process and achieve additional benefits in other, nonbargaining decision forums.

To the extent that management authority in bargaining can be centralized, or made to conform more closely to the private model, unions' bargaining power is thought to be constrained. In this vein, Wellington and Winter (1971, p. 128) advised policymakers to "carefully define the governmental employer and, in so doing, severely curb or eliminate the role of each governmental body save one." Generally speaking, analysts have recommended that the responsibility for collective bargaining be focused on the chief executive, although the actual conduct of collective bargaining should be the responsibility of professional negotiators. Policy and practice have tended to move in this direction. In local and state governments, the executive branch has tended to displace the legislative branch, and in the executive branch, professional negotiators have displaced budget officials, personnel administrators, and line managers (Burton, 1972; Derber, 1979).

While the trend clearly has been toward greater centralization of management authority in the conduct of bargaining, the dominant view is that public sector bargaining remains a multilateral rather than bilateral process, wherein unions characteristically are able to negotiate the terms and conditions of their employment with more than one employer (Kochan, 1974). The explanation for this characteristic is that the inherent political and constitutional characteristics of American government combine to defeat the requirement of centralized management authority.

Without quarreling with the conclusion that public sector bargaining is best characterized as a multilateral process, we ask whether the causes and consequences of the phenomenon are fully understood. Specifically, is fragmented management solely a function of inherent constitutional and political variables, or does it also reflect policy choices regarding other aspects of public sector bargaining, which are based on the assumption that unions have inordinate bargaining power?

Our view, which we shall develop in greater detail, is that the assumption of inordinate union power has contributed to the development of policies that exacerbate the fragmentation of management authority. As Wellington and Winter (1971, p. 128) warned, "A check in the form of budget approval by the legislature, where the executive is the employer, or in some cases by direct voter approval, may be necessary to curb the power of the unions." Notwithstanding Wellington and Winter's call for centralized authority, these approval mechanisms work against centralized authority, just as policies do that restrict the scope of bargaining and prohibit strikes.

The Scope of Bargaining. How broad should the scope of public sector bargaining be? The debate over this question has reflected the tension between maintaining management control over the terms and conditions of public employment and providing unionized employees with a voice in the establishment of those terms. Not surprisingly, the conventional wisdom has recommended—and public administrators generally have favored—a narrow bargaining scope, while unionized public employees have sought a broad bargaining scope.

While the scope-of-bargaining issue has received considerable attention in the literature (see Weitzman, 1975), the focus has been on how bargaining issues should be classified, rather than on the impact of bargaining scope on the conduct and outcomes of bargaining. Many public sector jurisdictions have adopted the private sector practice of classifying issues as mandatory, permissive, and illegal. Mandatory issues are those that must be negotiated, if either party desires. Illegal issues may not be included in collective bargaining agreements. Permissive issues may be negotiated, if both parties choose.

Public policy generally has reflected the assumption that the scope of bargaining in government should be narrower than in the private sector, although, within that general rule, considerable variation occurs across jurisdictions. As noted earlier, the federal government prohibits wage bargaining altogether, whereas virtually every state with a collective bargaining law either permits or requires wage bargaining (Valletta and Freeman, 1986). State practice, however, varies considerably concerning nonwage (or noneconomic) bargaining. Some states, like Pennsylvania, have defined the scope of bargaining broadly (as in the National Labor Relations Act, which requires bargaining over wages, hours, and other terms and conditions of employment); others, like Nevada, specify clearly which issues may be negotiated.

In most states, however, the formal definition of bargaining scope for nonwage issues is ambiguous. The result is that the scope of bargaining is determined on a case-by-case basis, either by agencies specifically designated to administer collective bargaining or by state courts. For instance, the New Jersey Supreme Court has concluded that bargaining is permissible only over issues explicitly mandated by state law, a decision that set aside contract clauses covering a broad range of issues. While most states employ a looser standard than New Jersey does, the scope of public sector bargaining in general remains narrower than in the private sector.

Although there has been little systematic study of the effect of differences in bargaining scope on bargaining outcomes, some research does suggest that unions are able to negotiate contracts more favorable to themselves when the scope of bargaining is broad rather than narrow (Feuille, Delaney, and Hendricks, 1985). At first glance, this observation appears to validate the underlying policy presumption in favor of limiting the scope of bargaining. Consider, however, some of the advantages that might result from a more expansive definition of mandatory bargaining.

In our view, a narrow scope of bargaining is likely to reduce policy innovation and to produce contradictions between collective bargaining and other human resources management policies. Empirical studies have demonstrated that public sector bargaining forces unions to trade employment for wages (Freeman, 1986). This evidence implies, other things being equal, reduced public services absent offsetting gains in labor productivity. Labor productivity may increase for a number of reasons, however, including a higher-quality work force or better management of the work force or both. Consider the ability of government to capitalize on the trade of employment for compensation when the scope of bargaining is limited to wages or other components of compensation. Will existing civil service policies governing recruitment, appointment, and promotion of public employees permit higher pay to be translated into a more qualified work force? Will existing agency "work rules" permit increased labor productivity?

The answer to these questions, in our view, is not necessarily: In contrast to the assumption of those who would restrict the scope of bargaining, we see little evidence that managers actually control other facets of human resources management. Remember that civil service and agency management systems predate collective bargaining and reflect long-standing accommodations with public employees. Thus, opening those systems by broadening the scope of bargaining may provide public officials the opportunity to trade higher wages for changes in nonwage aspects of human resources management, which would increase productivity and result in more effective service delivery.

Further, a narrow scope of bargaining creates incentives for unions to circumvent negotiations. As a result, unions may be able to achieve goals unavailable through collective bargaining, without having to provide a "quid pro quo" for their gains. A broader bargaining scope can provide more bargaining trade-offs, especially if public managers negotiate purposively and aggressively.

There are other reasons for expanding the scope of bargaining that we believe are important. One problem with multilateral bargaining in government is that it provides public officials with the means of ducking responsibility for their behavior. As we noted earlier, limiting the scope of bargaining helps ensure that management's authority is divided or fragmented. This fragmentation makes it easier for elected officials to pass the blame for unfavorable outcomes to someone else. Similarly, a limited scope of bargaining offers union leaders the same dodge with respect to their constituents. In general, political democracy and union democracy are best served by a tightening of the responsibility-accountability relationship between elected leaders and their constituents. Broadening the scope of bargaining in government would help keep the heat on those who are in the kitchen.

Finally, formal changes in the definition of bargaining scope would minimize the divisive impact of after-the-fact judicial decisions (see Befort, 1985). Such decisions foster instability and hostility in public sector labor relations. Moreover, the possibility of such decisions forces unions to negotiate solely over mandatory bargaining issues, even when unions and employers alike want to bargain over nonmandatory issues. No rational union will trade concessions on mandatory issues for contract provisions covering permissive issues, if there is a possibility that a court will invalidate those provisions.

The Management of Bargaining Impasses. There is no guarantee, of course, that collective bargaining will lead to collective agreement. In the private sector, generally speaking, employee strikes are accepted strategies in the event of deadlocks in bargaining. In the public sector, however, the fear of strikes has led many states to prohibit them and to devise alternative procedures—compulsory arbitration, in particular—for the resolution of bargaining impasses.

While the prohibition of strikes and the substitution of compulsory arbitration are the dominant policy choices, there is increasing diversity across jurisdictions (see Valletta and Freeman, 1986). Currently, thirty-eight states explicitly prohibit strikes by certain public employees, and compulsory arbitration laws cover public sector occupations (usually "essential service" employees) in twenty-one states and in the District of Columbia. Eleven states, however, now permit strikes by "nonessential" workers (Delaney and Feuille, 1987; Valletta and Freeman, 1986). No federal employees are permitted to strike, and compulsory arbitration is specified only for postal employees.

The emerging policy diversity at the state level provides a laboratory for assessing alternative approaches to the regulation and management of bargaining deadlocks. In general, research suggests the following propositions. First, and most obvious, prohibitions against strikes deter but do not prevent them (Ichniowski, 1982; Olson, Stern, Najita, and Weisberger, 1981). In other words, the enactment of strike prohibitions and penalties does not guarantee the absence of strikes. Second, compulsory arbitration is the most effective insurance against strikes (Feuille, 1979; Lester, 1984). Less powerful alternatives, such as fact finding and mediation, are less likely than arbitration to reduce the incidence of strikes. Third, conventional forms of compulsory arbitration tend to chill collective bargaining by discouraging concessions during negotiations (Feuille, 1979). Thus, there is a trade-off between the general goal of achieving negotiated settlements, on the one hand, and substituting compulsory arbitration for strikes, on the other. Fourth, final-offer arbitration (whereby arbitrators must choose between one or another "last best offer") has less of a chilling effect on bargaining than conventional arbitration policies do (Delaney, Feuille, and Hendricks, 1986). The reason, apparently, is the parties' increased uncertainty when arbitrators are not permitted to "split the difference" between the parties' positions. The literature suggests that final-offer arbitration provides the best means of facilitating negotiated settlements while prohibiting strikes.

Should public employees' strikes be prohibited in the first place? In general, we believe not. Two arguments underlie this position. First, a democracy should strive toward equal protection in at least some basic ways, which should include the right to withhold labor. Exceptions to the rule are justified only when they involve clear and present danger to a community. In such a case, injunctive relief can be available to protect the commonweal. Second, management can win strikes. Prohibitions against public employees' strikes remove a potent weapon from management's bargaining arsenal— the ability to take a strike. For these reasons, we believe that the policy presumption should be for the right to strike, and the burden of proof should be on those who would abridge that right.

The conventional wisdom has been that the right to strike should not be extended to public employees because they could capitalize on the (presumed) inelasticity of demand for public services by withholding their labor. This notion, originally explicated by Wellington and Winter (1971) but still widely held, assigns public sector bargaining one nature and private sector bargaining another. Managers in the private sector are able to take strikes and lock out their employees, but public managers supposedly must be protected from such tactics. Therefore, the idea goes, better to have an arsenal of third-party alternatives leading up to binding arbitration—better, presumably, for the public.

This logic is suspect. How are public officials and the public necessarily in a bind if a group of workers strikes? The immediate effect of a strike is to free up money for other purposes, since public revenues typically are not affected by strikes. Moreover, the savings that result from not having to pay strikers add up each day, while the service costs may not increase so tangibly or may even be reduced if others (such as managerial employees) provide services in the interim. The logic of the situation suggests that it is the strikers, not management, who are in a bind—unless, of course, managers are prohibited by law from being so stringent in their behavior.

What does experience tell us about the nature and consequences of public employee strikes? First, it is difficult to argue that public employees' strikes threaten catastrophic consequences. There have been nearly 5,000 such strikes since the late 1960s (many occurring in states that have legalized them), including 245 police strikes (Delaney and Feuille, 1987). Many caused public inconvenience, no doubt, but the evidence suggests that only a handful of these 5,000 posed a serious threat to public safety or health (Feuille, 1979).

It is unlikely that so many such strikes would be tolerated if their results were truly catastrophic. Second, experience suggests that government can win as well as lose strikes. The public—to whom elected officials should be responsive—does not always demand that strikes be settled at any price; that is, "labor peace" is not the only coin of the political realm. When citizens support elected officials (as they did in San Francisco in 1975), the balance of bargaining power shifts to management (Katz, 1979). Management then has a better chance to use collective bargaining for public purposes—provided, of course, that the scope of bargaining has not been excessively abridged from fear of inherent union power.

Summary and Implications

Nearly three decades of experience and research can be brought to bear on the practice of managing unionized public workers who are entitled to bargain collectively over the terms and conditions of their employment. Although organized workers have not displaced unorganized workers, collective bargaining in the public sector is here to stay, and it will remain the focal point of human resources management in many state and local governments.

Those who introduced collective bargaining into government relied on policy cues derived from experience in the private sector and filtered through a core assumption: that public and private organizations are different in ways that produce weak management in government and strong management in firms. Accordingly, the prevailing policies that govern public sector bargaining include rules designed to protect public administrators from the inherently inordinate bargaining power of unions. We believe, however, that the gathering evidence suggests that power in public sector bargaining is situational, not inherent. This belief implies certain things about how public officials should regulate and manage the bargaining process.

One implication of our analysis is that policymakers should consider changing some of the basic rules of the game. Legalizing strikes (or at least changing arbitration procedures to some variant of the final-offer model) and broadening the scope of bargaining are two components of this "deregulation" scheme. By *deregulation,* we mean a process of permitting those who must manage collective bargaining to engage in a somewhat broader set of strategies for negotiating appropriate wages and determining how wage policy affects other managerial issues. Our confidence in the effect of lifting or easing the protective shield of no-strike laws, and of restricted bargaining scope, reflects our understanding that power in public sector bargaining is situational. If public employees are not inherently powerful, then there are situations in which public officials can use collective bargaining to advance their interests. While changing the rules of the game would help public officials capitalize on their opportunities at the bargaining table, improvements in managerial performance need not await formal deregulation. Managers can manage the current process better.

One aspect of improved management involves minimization of fragmented management. The structure of American federalism makes it difficult for chief executives at the state level and, particularly, at the local level to make collective bargaining the sole decision center for the resolution of labor-management conflicts. Nevertheless, it does not prevent an actual centralization of management in collective bargaining. What is required is a prebargaining bargaining process, whereby negotiators, budget and personnel officials, line managers, and (not least) chief executives negotiate an integrated set of management goals or collective bargaining demands. The resolution of conflict among a diverse group of overhead and line managers, each of whom had important stakes in collective bargaining, would strengthen the executive's hand in negotiations and probably reduce the incentives for legislators to provide unions the proverbial "second bite at the apple."

Once an administration has defined its collective bargaining goals and developed an inclusive set of bargaining demands, the next challenge is to realize them through hard bargaining. Management of the bargaining process itself has tended over time to fall under the egis of professional negotiations, but the prebargaining process implies that nonprofessionals should have a continuing role in collective bargaining. The budget director, for example, may be better equipped than a labor negotiator to explain to union representatives why management seeks to reduce the wages of a given bargaining unit. The commissioner of an agency may be better equipped to explain why management seeks to reduce staffing for a given function by substituting capital for labor. The top personnel official may be better able to explain why management seeks to upgrade the quality of employees in a given title by permitting lateral entry. In short, there is no reason why officialdom cannot assume a more forceful role in bargaining. Some demands, like modification of the civil service system, may lie outside the formal scope of bargaining; but it cannot weaken management's bargaining power to remind union representatives that management is considering some tactics of its own.

Hard bargaining is likely to increase labor-management conflict, but this is not necessarily undesirable. An issue that a union leader believes is worth fighting for is likely to be an important management issue as well. If labor and management are unable to resolve their conflicting interests through bargaining, then government officials need to manage bargaining impasses. In the event that bargaining deadlocks are resolved by such peaceful impasse-resolution procedures as arbitration, management needs to present its case well. To the extent that public officials have developed a coherent set of demands before bargaining begins, the preparation and presentation of management's case in arbitration are made easier.

In the event of a strike (and whether it is legal or not makes little difference), more than strong-willed management is required. When the provision of labor is interrupted, public officials need to respond in time-honored ways: enlisting the support of the press and other opinion leaders; convincing the public that the costs of a proposed settlement outweigh the benefits and enlisting public cooperation in reducing demand for the service; and continuing to provide the service, in scaled-down fashion, by drawing on other providers (including management and supervisory officials, other governments, and volunteers, if need be).

Because the officials of American governments will continue to face financial and human resources management problems in the future, we feel that the public sector bargaining process should be less insulated. Bargainers should be forced to address difficult problems like productivity improvement, unfunded pension liabilities, and poor service delivery. Traditional regulatory approaches that reflect the "inordinate union power" thesis make it difficult for managers to do so. In our view, it is time to consider less traditional approaches that would help managers use collective bargaining for their own purposes. Finally, even without changes in public policy, public managers can achieve better bargaining outcomes by casting aside the conventional wisdom and bargaining more aggressively.

References

Befort, S. F. "Public Sector Bargaining: Fiscal Crisis and Unilateral Change." *University of Minnesota Law Review,* 1985, *69,* 1221–1275.

Burton, J. F., Jr. "Local Government Bargaining and Management Structure." *Industrial Relations,* 1972, *11* (2), 123–140.

Delaney, J. T., and Feuille, P. "Police." In D. B. Lipsky and C. B. Donn (eds.), *Collective Bargaining in American Industry.* Lexington, Mass.: Heath, 1987.

Delaney, J. T., Feuille, P., and Hendricks, W. "The Regulation of Bargaining Disputes: A Cost-Benefit Analysis of Interest Arbitration in the Public Sector." In D. B. Lipsky and D. Lewin (eds.), *Advances in Industrial and Labor Relations.* Greenwich, Conn.: JAI Press, 1986.

Derber, M. "Management Organization for Collective Bargaining in the Public Sector." In B. Aaron, J. R. Grodin, and J. L. Stern (eds.), *Public-Sector Bargaining.* Washington, D.C.: Bureau of National Affairs, 1979.

Ehrenberg, R. G., and Goldstein, G. S. "A Model of Public Sector Wage Determination." *Journal of Urban Economics,* 1975, *2,* 223–245.

Feuille, P. "Selected Benefits and Costs of Compulsory Arbitration." *Industrial and Labor Relations Review,* 1979, *33* (1), 64–76.

Feuille, P., Delaney, J. T., and Hendricks, W. "The Impact of Interest Arbitration on Police Contracts." *Industrial Relations,* 1985, *24* (2), 161–181.

Freeman, R. B. "Unionism Comes to the Public Sector." *Journal of Economic Literature,* 1986, *24* (1), 41–86.

Gifford, C. D. (ed.). *Directory of U.S. Labor Organizations: 1986–87 Edition.* Washington, D.C.: Bureau of National Affairs, 1986.

Horton, R. D. "Fiscal Stress and Labor Power." In Industrial Relations Research Association, *Proceedings of the Thirty-eighth Annual Meeting.* Madison, Wis.: Industrial Relations Research Association, 1986.

Ichniowski, C. "Arbitration and Police Bargaining: Prescription for the Blue Flu." *Industrial Relations,* 1982, *21* (2), 149–166.

Katz, H. C. "Municipal Pay Determination: The Case of San Francisco." *Industrial Relations,* 1979, *18* (1), 44–58.

Kochan, T. A. "A Theory of Multilateral Collective Bargaining in City Governments." *Industrial and Labor Relations Review,* 1974, *27* (4), 525–542.

Lester, R. A. *Labor Arbitration in State and Local Government.* Princeton, N.J.: Industrial Relations Section, Princeton University, 1984.

Lewin, D. "Public Employee Unionism in the 1980s: An Analysis of Transformation." In S. M. Lipset (ed.), *Unions in Transition.* San Francisco: Institute for Contemporary Studies, 1986.

Lewin, D., Feuille, P., Kochan, T. A., and Delaney, J. T. *Public Sector Labor Relations.* Lexington, Mass.: Heath, 1988.

Olson, C. A., Stern, J. L., Najita, J. M., and Weisberger, J. M. *Strikes and Strike Penalties in the Public Sector.* Final Report to the Labor-Management Services Administration. Washington, D.C.: U.S. Department of Labor, 1981.

Summers, C. W. "Public Employee Bargaining: A Political Perspective." *Yale Law Journal,* 1974, *83,* 1156–1200.

Summers, R. S. *Collective Bargaining and Public Benefit Conferral: A Jurisprudential Critique.* Ithaca: Institute of Public Employment, New York State School of Industrial and Labor Relations, 1976.

Valletta, R. G., and Freeman, R. B. "The NBER Public Sector Collective Bargaining Law Data Set." Unpublished manuscript, 1986.

Weitzman, J. *The Scope of Bargaining in Public Employment.* New York: Praeger, 1975.

Wellington, H. H., and Winter, R. K. *The Unions and the Cities.* Washington, D.C.: Brookings Institution, 1971.

32   *Grace Hall Saltzstein*

Enhancing Equal Employment Opportunity

The role of government in ensuring and expanding equal employment opportunity (EEO) has evolved gradually. Major policy provisions—beginning with President Roosevelt's 1941 executive order barring discrimination by defense contractors and including the Civil Rights Act of 1964 and its amendment of 1972, the Age Discrimination Act of 1967 and its amendment of 1978, and regulations issued by the U.S. Department of Health, Education, and Welfare in 1977 regarding employment testing of disabled persons—have increased the number of protected groups and expanded the scope of prohibited actions. Federal government discrimination provisions were extended to state and local governments in 1972, while legislative and administrative actions at both the national and the state levels of government, coupled with considerable judicial activity in this area, have further enlarged the scope and complexity of requirements.

As these developments have occurred, there has been a shift, both in law and in judicial interpretation, from a singular emphasis on neutral employment practices to affirmative action (AA), which seeks to redress previous injustices. Yet disagreements about the proper definition and focus of EEO and AA remain embedded in legislation, administrative implementation, and judicial interpretation. As Rosenbloom (1984) notes, there is a lack of clarity in EEO policy concerning whether EEO requires nondiscrimination, equalization of opportunity, or equalization of representation. Which standard is adopted has a marked impact on both the choice of policies used to implement it and the likelihood of finding that any given policy works. Thus, public administrators today find themselves facing myriad requirements for color-, gender-, age-, and disability-blind approaches to hiring and promotion, as well as requirements to alter presumably neutral institu-

451

tional patterns and practices that perpetuate previous inequities. Nevertheless, administrators are provided little guidance toward how to advance equity in the workplace.

Because analysts also disagree on how to assess the impact of EEO (parity in job representation at a single point in time? improvement in employment representation? lack of disparate impact?), there have been few straightforward assessments of the effect of EEO processes on equity, and policy studies have provided administrators little guidance concerning what works (Rosenbloom, 1984). To begin to understand what works in enhancing employment opportunity, we must turn to a wide variety of research, in different disciplines, to delineate the status of protected groups in employment, the nature of the barriers to their employment, and the success of various efforts to open employment opportunities to these groups. Because so little research has been done on many of the groups covered by EEO protections, we shall focus on these issues as they pertain to selected groups of employees only. Studies by labor economists on wage discrimination, and by sociologists on occupational status differentials, are especially useful in highlighting differences between white males and minorities or women in employment and in delineating some of the aggregate-level causes of such differences.

Employment Status of Minorities and Women

Numerous studies show blacks, especially black males, to be markedly disadvantaged in employment. They have lower wages, lower levels of occupational status, and dramatically higher levels of unemployment than do whites with equivalent skills, education, and personal characteristics (Parcel and Mueller, 1983). Further, while some of these differences have declined over the years for some segments of the work force (for example, occupational status differentials between college-educated blacks and whites), a considerable amount of inequality has endured (Welch, 1981). At the aggregate level, such differences are at least partially attributable to lower levels of educational attainment for blacks, to lower rates of return (in terms of wages or occupational status) for black investments in education, and to the crowding of blacks into less desirable occupational positions, in which they ''are less likely to be engaged in complex work and are more likely to perform work involving physical activities in unpleasant environments'' (Parcel and Mueller, 1983, p. 278).

Studies of the relative occupational status of Hispanic Americans find them lagging behind Anglos on most measures of occupational attainment but faring better than blacks. In the aggregate, the primary handicaps faced by Hispanic Americans appear to be consequences of lower average levels of education, lower average ages, lower rates of Hispanic female work force participation, and larger numbers of immigrants or individuals who lack fluency in English. Like blacks, Hispanic Americans receive lower occupational rates of return for the education they do possess, although the actual rates of return vary, depending on the ethnic origin of the group examined (Mexican American, Puerto Rican, Cuban, and so on). Hispanic Americans in general, however, appear to enjoy higher rates of return for education and experience than blacks do.

Some evidence suggests that Native Americans and Asian Americans also are handicapped in the workplace, although the problems they face differ considerably. Native Americans suffer occupational problems similar to those of Hispanic Americans or blacks, partly because of similar problems with education, experience, and access. Asian Americans, in contrast, have average education and training levels that are superior to those of virtually all other groups, yet they do not always obtain the occupational returns that such attainment should warrant.

Female employment is characterized by considerable segregation, both by occupational categories and within occupations in firms (Waldman and McEaddy, 1974). Women are crowded into a relatively small number of occupations, which are dominated by women, require traditionally female social skills (for example, nurturing), and rarely require physical activity. Further, these positions are characterized by occupational ladders that have fewer opportunities for advancement, are harder to climb, and pay lower wages at every step, relative to comparable male-dominated occupational categories. All these problems have come to be linked with proposals for comparable worth. Both in female-dominated occupations and in more integrated occupational sectors, women are much more likely than men to occupy the lower rungs of the occupational ladder. Evidence suggests, then, that the primary cause of sex inequalities in employment is that women fail to "obtain equivalent returns for the resources [education, training, and so on] they do possess" (Parcel and Mueller, 1983, p. 279). In addition, male-female occupational disparities are even greater for minority females.

Analysts disagree about the size of the population of disabled and older workers and about the current employment status of either group. Whether they define older workers as those over age fifty or those over age sixty-five, analysts agree that the number of older persons who work is increasing, and that numerous trends point to even larger increases in the future. At the same time, there is clear evidence that older employees are discriminated against in hiring, training, promotion, and job evaluations (Rosen and Jerdee, 1976), largely on the basis of frequently erroneous, negative stereotypes. Similarly, while analysts disagree about the precise extent of work-force participation of the mentally and physically handicapped (see Koestler, 1978; Bowe, 1985), they do agree that more extensive work-force participation of the disabled is limited by negative stereotyping on the part of employers, as well as by institutional factors (such as inadequate transportation or architectural barriers) that act as barriers to employment of the disabled.

Public Sector Employment

Studies indicate that many protected groups fare better in public employment than in private employment (Rumberger, 1983; Dometrius and Sigelman, 1984). As recently as 1980, public employment accounted for a disproportionate share of female employment, especially in regard to the employment of female college graduates (Rumberger, 1983). A comparison of state and local governments to private employers (Dometrius and Sigelman, 1984) found that women and blacks, but not Hispanics, were better represented in public than in private employment. In addition, census data indicate that wage inequities are less pronounced in public employment than in private employment (again, except in the case of Hispanics, whose public and private wage rates are the same).

Despite the generally more positive record of the public sector as an employer of minorities and women, inequities are still evident. Blacks, Hispanics, and women at all levels of government are overrepresented in clerical or menial positions and underrepresented in supervisory, managerial, and professional positions (Lewis, 1986; Cayer and Sigelman, 1980). White males have higher job grades, and higher salaries, than do minorities and women with comparable backgrounds (Grandjean, 1981). At all levels of government, minorities and women are clustered in certain kinds of positions and in certain kinds of agencies, and they are virtually excluded from others. Hence, female and minority employment in the public sector exhibits many of the same features that characterize private sector employment, although the aggregate results are somewhat more equitable, in most cases.

Occupational Sorting

There is well-documented evidence of substantial disparities in the employment status of various groups relative to white males. Not all the disparity can be explained by measurable differences in job-related skills and abilities. Research indicates that these disparities are produced in a complex environment in which various types of job aspirants are sorted into different occupational levels and spheres of responsibility. To delineate the barriers to equal employment opportunity for various groups, we must first understand the processes by which current (and less than equitable) occupational sorting is achieved. While there is considerable disagreement on the reasons behind current patterns (see Blau and Jusenius, 1976; Parcel and Mueller, 1983), analysts agree that supply (premarket discrimination) and demand (postmarket discrimination) factors play a part. Supply, or premarket, discrimination takes place before the worker has entered the marketplace. It shapes the "human capital" (training, education) that workers bring to the marketplace, while demand, or postmarket, discrimination takes place within firms and occupations.

Supply Discrimination. Supply influences that appear to have impacts on the occupational status of minorities, women, the aged, and the disabled include both remote and immediate factors. Cultural factors have a profound impact on the kinds of socialization toward work experienced by different groups, on the attitudes various groups bring to the workplace, on the attitudes held by others in the workplace regarding particular groups, and on the kinds of stresses and role strains that will be felt by various groups or individuals who seek to reconcile their occupational and their personal role requirements. Females' participation in the work force, for example, is strongly influenced by the attitudes of women and those around them regarding women's role in the family, the desirability and suitability of various kinds of education and employment for women, and assumptions about females' performance characteristics and inherent abilities (Blau and Jusenius, 1976). Similarly, social and cultural factors strongly influence the structure of the educational system and employment training systems, as well as the access of various groups to such systems and the nature of their experiences within them (Feagin and Feagin, 1978), all of which shape the human capital that groups have to offer in the workplace.

Location-specific factors also influence the supply side of the employment equation. Regional or local demographics have an impact on the availability of certain types of workers, while such factors as unemployment rates or the availability of the jobs desired or preferred by various groups affect the success of specific organizations in attracting and retaining different categories of workers (Parcel and Mueller, 1983). Community characteristics can affect participation rates and workers' reliability by their effect on the sheer physical accessibility of places of employment and on the nature of the support system provided to various types of workers. For example, the location of public places of employment in communities, coupled with the nature of residential segregation of minority groups and the viability of public transit systems, can exert a profound influence on minorities' interest in public employment and work attendance, while the amount, types, and locations of child care facilities in communities influence the availability of mothers to the work force.

From this perspective, it is clear that the supply side of the employment equation, which is commonly thought of as the sum of an individual's choices regarding education, training, experience, and so on, is influenced in numerous ways by social, cultural, and political forces. Further, public employers in many cases could exert considerable influence on some of these factors over the long term and could use their awareness of such constraints to devise programs that would increase the supply of targeted groups, even in the short term (through changes in recruiting strategies, for example).

Demand Discrimination. Supply discrimination is obviously important and can be influenced, to varying degrees, by the actions of employers. Evidence suggests, however, that a considerable amount of discrimination takes place within firms and occupations and is hence more readily influenced and altered by the direct actions of employers. Consequently, these forms of discrimination are usually of more immediate interest to those concerned with achieving equal employment opportunity. Discrimination within organizations can be both informal (functioning outside the formal rules and structures) and institutional (embedded in the operating rules and procedures), with research indicating that both forms of discrimination are significant in organizations.

Informal discrimination is evident when seemingly objective rules or requirements are differentially applied to minorities or women. For example, particular levels of education and experience may call for a particular grade or salary level in terms of the formal salary system, yet informal practice may function consistently to discount women's qualifications, so that female employees are always brought in at the bottom of any applicable salary range, while men are offered the maximum salary within that range. Significant amounts of informal discrimination have been documented in organizations; thus, improvements in minority and female occupational status can be achieved through the overcoming of such biases, even in the absence of changes in formal organizational rules or procedures.

The extent to which such informal barriers can be counteracted depends at least partly on other characteristics of an organization. For example, informal discrimination can be counteracted more easily in rapidly growing organizations or in those with high turnover, but it appears to be more difficult to overcome where more restrictive civil service systems operate or where public employees' unions are strong. A minority or female mayor or chief executive is liable to demand and get better representation of minorities or women in the organization, regardless of the formal rules and procedures, as are any top- or midlevel officials committed to affirmative action. Administrators functioning in a climate supportive of AA may be able to accomplish quite a bit, without changing formal routines.

Where the organizational climate is not so supportive of AA, administrators may have more difficulty overcoming informal barriers and may act more effectively by focusing on employment barriers embedded in organizational structures, rules, and procedures. In that regard, certain common mechanisms are implicated in employment inequities. Analysts argue that the type of occupational segregation and internal workplace crowding so characteristic of female and minority employment is made possible by the presence and operation of internal labor markets in many organizations (Doeringer and Piore, 1971). Organizations having such internal labor markets are divided into numerous occupational clusters, with specific mobility ladders associated with each one, and movement across clusters is constrained by structural features of the organizations. Moreover, there is a sharp separation between the top and bottom levels of most white-collar positions, with separate and distinct channels of access to each level. Thus, to a substantial degree, employees' prospects within an organization are structured by their entry-level assignments, and discrimination in entry-level assignments can ensure discrimination at all levels of the organization, because those assigned to less desirable job tracks will have difficulty ever moving out of them.

Key characteristics of internal labor markets are evident in many public organizations, with their separate career lines and institutionalized promotion ladders. Further, evidence suggests that these systems have contributed to sex and race segregation in public employment. The formal mechanisms most frequently identified as barriers to females, minorities, and disabled and aged persons include a wide range of entrance requirements and procedures, as well as rules specifying employment preference for other categories of applicants. Barriers to advancement include the formal structure of the upward mobility system, the operation of benefit and seniority systems that limit mobility, and the entire range of techniques for preparing and evaluating applicants for promotion.

The recruitment process has been a major focus of concern in combating discrimination and is consequently a major element of EEO/AA programs (U.S. Equal Employment Opportunity Commission, 1979; Backoff and Rainey, 1977). Recruitment has been expanded, in many cases, to include job advertising in specialized publications targeted at specific groups; school visits and special youth programs (for police cadets, for example); and the use of mixed-sex and mixed-race recruitment teams; yet recruitment still appears to be a problem in many areas. Informal, friends-and-neighbors recruiting continues as a major mechanism for many public sector career lines and clearly serves to limit female and minority representation in the hiring pool. This appears to be especially true in recruiting both women and minorities for jobs from which they traditionally have been excluded (for example, see Roos and Reskin, 1984, on recruiting women for nontraditional employment).

In terms of general employment levels, recruitment appears to be a much less significant barrier to minority and female employment than the presence of discrimination or bias in the process of selecting employees from any single applicant pool. The entire process of screening any given applicant pool for employment purposes in the public sector has been subject to intense criticism for considerable time. Critics have argued that "the excessively rigid procedures for entering and advancing in most merit systems have long been recognized as being hindrances to effective management practices" (Shafritz, 1975, p. 3), as being impediments to attainment of merit (Savas and Ginsburg, 1973), and as being barriers to equity in employment (Backoff and Rainey, 1977). Legal proscriptions against reliance on anything that can be shown to be a systemic barrier to the employment of protected groups, as well as the requirement that all screening tests shown to have an adverse impact be job-related, have led to close scrutiny of civil service rules and procedures, many of which (it has been charged) "themselves constitute systemic barriers to minorities and women" (U.S. Equal Employment Opportunity Commission, 1979).

Application forms (which, in the public sector, are frequently long and complex and require extensive documentary data) can be daunting to poorly educated or unsophisticated applicants (who are overrepresented in certain target groups). While complex application forms may be an appropriate screening device for jobs requiring high levels of education, incomplete or unclear applications have been used to reject job candidates for routine jobs as well, with an unwarranted, disproportionate impact on particular groups (see Cohen, 1973, in regard to police background forms).

There have been considerable changes in the number and types of preemployment requirements used to screen public sector job applicants, but some requirements continue to be used, frequently with a disparate impact on some group of applicants. For example, many municipal governments impose preemployment residency requirements of varying duration on applicants (which can and often are intended to work to the advantage of minority applicants in central cities and to their disadvantage in suburbs), while police departments' common requirements for swimming skills and possession of a valid driver's license have a disparate effect on central-city minorities (Maher, 1984). Education, training, experience, and age requirements in nontraditional areas may perpetuate previous discrimination in women's access to such experiences (Roos and Reskin, 1984). In many cases, such requirements may not be related to important elements of job behavior; or, if they are, they represent skills that could be learned easily on the job. The validity of various physical requirements has been criticized for similar reasons (see Maher, 1984, on police departments' physical ability tests).

While selection devices of all kinds have been subject to legal scrutiny, written ability tests attracted some of the earliest attention and strongest criticism. After considerable research, it has been demonstrated that written ability tests can be valid predictors of job performance in many cases (see Hunter and Schmidt, 1982, for a thorough analysis). They do not appear to disadvantage women, yet they continue to have an adverse impact on many minority groups (blacks, Hispanics, and Native Americans in particular). Further, considerable alteration in test procedures is necessary for disabled applicants (see Nester, 1984, for a thorough review).

The issue of testing has been further complicated by confusion about whether fairness in testing requires equality of opportunity or equality of results. The issue remains controversial, and considerable ambivalence is evident in the demands of minority groups (who sometimes fear that pursuing equality of results may serve to discount actual minority accomplishment), in administrative requirements, and in legal restrictions. Partly because of uncertainty about what is acceptable in testing, many organizations have looked for alternatives to standardized written tests of ability for screening applicants.

Among the more common alternatives to written tests are personality and interest tests, unassembled exams (structured, scored evaluations of applicants' backgrounds), biodata blanks (structured scoring of candidates' backgrounds or life-history data), work sample testing (typing or dictation tests, for example), assessment centers (use of a variety of assessment modes), and employment interviews. When assessed on the basis of validity, adverse impact, administrative feasibility, and acceptability to applicants, however, few of these alternatives fare well (see Davey, 1984, p. 365). While personality and interest factors "are generally considered to be more important determinants of job success than are basic intellectual abilities," existing attempts to test such factors demonstrate low levels of validity and of retest reliability. Davey's summary indicates that unassembled exams and assessment centers appear to have fewer adverse impacts and to be valid, but only for specific types of positions (jobs requiring specialized backgrounds, in the former case, and managerial positions, in the latter). In addition, neither can be used with large numbers of applicants because of costs and the amount of time required. Biodata blanks score high on validity but are expensive to validate, have high adverse impact, and encounter resistance, because so much of the material included is highly personal and appears to be only weakly job-related. Bona fide work samples have high content validity, if properly developed and scored, but the evidence regarding adverse impact is not clear at this point, and such tests are not appropriate for large groups.

Employment interviews may be "the most invalid part of the selection process" (Dresang, 1984, p. 221), yet they continue to be widely used in the personnel process. As Davey (1984, p. 366) notes, interviews may have greater or lesser adverse impact than written tests: Because scoring is more flexible and interviews "do not typically assess the same sort of abstract intellectual processes that ability tests do," minority candidates may do better in interviews than on written tests. Nevertheless, a danger exists that bias on the part of the interviewer can bias the ratings that are provided. That danger appears to be minimized, however, through the use of structured oral exams administered by panels of interviewers, which may include female or minority members.

Of the major alternatives to standardized written ability tests, then, a few appear to be superior for certain kinds of jobs, but none provides a clear alternative to written exams for large numbers of candidates applying for general entry-level positions. Hence, jurisdictions have sought to redesign tests or to use them differently, in the hope of reducing the demonstrated adverse impacts of standard written ability tests for general positions. Without actually altering their tests, some jurisdictions have used preexam tutoring to provide minority candidates with test-taking skills. Such tutoring then appears to lead to higher scores on subsequent civil service exams (Panzarella, 1986). In other cases, organizations have sought to change actual test designs. Experiments with test design suggest the possibility of eliminating subtests or individual test items that have adverse impact, without reducing overall test validity; but efforts to identify and eliminate culturally biased test items have not been so successful (Davey, 1984). In some cases, written ability tests have been combined with or supplemented by alternative test forms, to provide more balanced assessments.

Some analysts have argued that different scoring procedures, such as pass-fail scoring or the use of limited numbers of categories (for example, *high, medium, low*), could also reduce the disadvantage suffered by minorities on written tests, but there is fairly convincing evidence that such scoring schemes require a substantial trade-off in terms of validity (Hunter and Schmidt, 1982).

Scoring questions are inextricably joined to questions regarding certification procedures. Once applicants have been evaluated and ranked according to their skills and abilities, they usually must be certified as eligible for hire. When veterans' preference systems provide extra points to applicants who are veterans, many women and other, nonveteran target groups may have a harder time reaching the top ranks of a given civil service register. Because of the subjectivity of the scoring process and the fact that a single point in the final score can mean a difference of several hundred places on an eligibility list, EEO advocates have been loath to accept either finely graduated scoring systems or widely used certification rules, which seek to advance merit by restricting hiring agents' choices to the single top-ranking applicant or to the top three.

In some jurisdictions, agencies have been able to hire lower-scoring minorities or women through judicious use of "emergency" or "provisional" appointments (DiPrete and Soule, 1986). In some cases, jurisdictions have eliminated veterans' preference or have reduced its restrictiveness. Still other jurisdictions have moved to broader certification schemes (West, 1984), such as a rule of ranks, which allows selection of any applicants within certain specified ranks (the top 10 percent, for example), or even a rule of the list, which allows selection of any of those ranked as eligible; yet reliance on restrictive certification schemes remains fairly widespread (Stein, 1987). Hunter and Schmidt (1982) demonstrate that the optimal mix of racial balance and productivity is best served by hiring on the basis of ability (as indicated by scores on cognitive ability tests), with quotas; that is, separate lists of minority and majority scores would be compiled, and officials would hire equal numbers from the top down within each group, until the desired number of new hires was obtained. This approach has been adopted by a number of jurisdictions in the form of a "3 + 3" certification rule, whereby the top three scorers from each list are certified for hire. In this fashion, Davey (1984, p. 372) argues, "the merit system and affirmative action seem to have found a way to coexist."

In addition to the barriers posed by individual components of the selection process, the time needed to complete it has been identified as a hindrance, not only to hiring the most qualified (Savas and Ginsburg, 1973) but also to hiring minorities (Cohen, 1973). Because many minority applicants are poor and unemployed or underemployed, few can afford to wait what may amount to a year and a half from the initial application to the first day on the job. The lag time between application and appointment varies considerably across jurisdictions, and evidence suggests that jurisdictions that reduce lag time can ensure that a somewhat higher percentage of minorities will remain in the pool at the time of appointment.

Nevertheless, the slow pace of minority and female advancement in the public sector suggests that simply increasing entry into organizations is not sufficient. Gains are needed in terms of advancement and promotion, as well as in terms of retention. There is considerable evidence of harassment, sabotage, and social segregation of women and minorities who move into positions from which they formerly were excluded, leading to higher rates of exit from such employment (see Roos and Reskin, 1984, on women; Gazell, 1974, on minorities in police work). Even in the absence of overt hostility, disadvantaged groups find it more difficult to get the kind of mentoring needed to develop and pursue effective strategies for advancement, because they tend to be excluded from the social networks in the workplace and are denied access to training programs. Similarly, disadvantaged groups and others have criticized performance appraisal systems for relying on inadequate qualifications standards and ratings criteria, for undervaluing the job demands and working conditions of traditionally female jobs (Eyde, 1983), and for showing evaluator bias in the promotion process (Roos and Reskin, 1984; Thomsen, 1978).

Because of these problems, reforms have focused on a wide variety of structural and attitudinal efforts. DiPrete and Soule (1986, p. 296) chart improvement in minority and female representation in upper-level entry-grade positions following adoption of "policies for the identification of talent, the identification of barriers to mobility, the creation of bridge positions to surmount these barriers, and the use of on-the-job training to make up for deficiencies in the qualifications of potentially capable lower-level employees." Research consistently reveals biases and stereotyped thinking throughout the employment and advancement processes, especially in regard to nontraditional employment of various groups. Therefore, additional, concerted efforts must be made to ensure that biases and stereotyped thinking do not enter into the selection of entrants to professional career ladders, evaluations of promotability of employees, or assessments of job performance in supervisory positions (Roos and Reskin, 1984). In some cases, significant gains in the representation of disadvantaged groups at the top levels of a public agency may be achieved only through major changes in the structure and operation of internal labor markets, such as changes in rules of seniority, alteration of career ladders to allow transfers across occupational channels, and job redesign and reevaluation to allow more opportunities for supervisory experience and to give more credit for potentially relevant current job responsibilities.

EEO/AA Programs. Many of the changes implicit in the preceding discussion can be achieved in the absence of a formal program to promote EEO/AA. Most jurisdictions, however, have sought to develop such programs, in order to provide an organizational locus of responsibility for EEO and, presumably, to do a better job of enhancing employment opportunity. Fairly substantial variation continues in the form and operation of such programs, and it is certainly expected that some programs are more effective than others.

Still, little is known definitively about any substantive impacts of EEO programs. As Rosenbloom (1984) notes, there are many "pre- versus post-adoption of EEO" analyses of target group representation, but these are primarily suggestive about which (if any) specific features of EEO programs have made a difference. Other studies have looked at participants' perceptions of program effectiveness, while many analyses of EEO/AA program characteristics and features simply assume that such programs matter in terms of employment outcomes.

Nevertheless, a variety of fairly consistent conclusions about which formal and informal features of EEO/AA programs matter have emerged from existing research. First, several careful, well-developed studies clearly indicate a strong positive link between goals and actual rates of change (Hunter and Schmidt, 1982; Leonard, 1985). However controversial such goal setting remains, techniques for developing reasonable, realistic goals do exist (see Ledvinka and Hildreth, 1984, for example), and organizations that adopt clear, specific goals based on careful analyses of actual labor market characteristics, for various types of groups for various jobs, are much more likely than those that do not to actually increase their employment of such target groups.

Virtually all analyses assert the importance of organizational commitment to EEO, although evidence behind that assertion is somewhat limited. Generally, commitment is presumed to be demonstrated by clear assertions of top-level support for a program, by location of the program in a high-visibility spot, and by provision of operational authority and resources commensurate with program responsibilities (Hitt and Keats, 1984; Marino, 1980). EEO programs or units clearly must be able to exert some real authority over personnel procedures or actions in the rest of an organization if they are to have any impact.

Because it is difficult to ensure sufficient influence for EEO units, analysts assert a need for the internalization of EEO throughout the organization. Some would achieve this through program interventions aimed at increasing knowledge of and attitudinal support for EEO requirements (Stewart, 1980); others stress the importance of policy and procedural changes to enhance EEO, coupled with programs to monitor and supervise progress throughout the organization (Hitt and Keats, 1984; Stewart, 1980).

Conclusions

In looking at both the public and the private sectors, we see continued pervasive barriers to equal workplace participation of women, minorities, and aged and disabled persons. All these groups have been subject to occupational segregation in lower-paying and less prestigious positions as a consequence of the interaction of social, cultural, and institutional processes. While the specific barriers to equal opportunity vary, depending on the group in question, informal and institutional barriers are significant in every case.

Further, because most informal barriers and many institutional barriers, such as employment policies and practices, have been shown to have only a tenuous link with merit, it has been and is possible to alter such practices to advance equal employment opportunity in the short run, without sacrificing quality.

Under the best of circumstances, however, existing EEO/AA interventions are associated with slow progress toward equal representation in the workplace (Feinberg, 1984), and analysts increasingly focus on what may be inherent incompatibilities between dominant models of work life and the personal lives and needs of many nontraditional employees. These traditional models of the organizational career are based on early schooling leading to entry-level positions that require long hours, travel, and relocation to work on a variety of demanding and challenging assignments. During this time, recruits are evaluated, and those assessed to have high potential are put on a fast track for advancement, while those who cannot or do not impress their superiors are left behind (Bailyn, 1982).

While the model is best applied to high-level positions, the assumptions behind it filter down to other positions as well. It is assumed that serious workers work full-time, are always available for extra assignments or overtime, will work on an on-call basis or with revolving shifts, and will accept promotions, with attendant increases in job demands, as needed by the organization. As Bailyn (1982, p. 47) notes, the demands of this model are so intense that it entails and virtually requires an extensive support system outside the workplace, resulting in what is virtually a ''two-person career.''

The model worked reasonably well, Bailyn argues, as long as such positions were held predominantly by men, who could curtail nonwork demands because of the presence of full-time housewives at home who provided the necessary support system. Now, however, changing social demographics and the increased diversity of the work force are associated with increased strain in meeting work demands.

Female employees must meet workplace demands while maintaining primary responsibility for running households. Employed mothers must handle both responsibilities and virtually the entire job of child rearing. Minorities confront the standard workplace demands, as well as numerous additional expectations to perform as minority role models, both in the organization and in the minority community. Elderly and disabled people often cannot or do not wish to work standard shifts on a full-time basis, or to travel to and from work at peak driving hours.

Employees facing such nontraditional strains between work and personal needs have encountered little social support or institutional flexibility. To date, most accommodations to such demands have been made by previously excluded workers anxious to get and keep good jobs. Institutions' attempts to lessen job demands are made only on a piecemeal basis, usually to accommodate valued employees who otherwise might quit. Yet changing organizational needs (such as the need for lifelong education to keep up with rapidly changing technology), heightened sensitivity to the dysfunctions of the traditional model (such as midcareer burnout or plateauing), and growing awareness of the burden of meeting the demands of the model, felt especially by minorities, mothers, older workers, and disabled workers, have led to a search for alternative models of work life.

Efforts to create social support systems for employees who are juggling multiple roles and to establish alternative models of work life constitute the next horizon of EEO/AA efforts. Employers committed to equal opportunity increasingly find themselves taking the lead in attempting to reduce their own employees' multiple burdens, by providing such things as child care benefits or services, "cafeteria" benefit plans to let employees choose the benefits that can help them meet their outside responsibilities, and job-hunting assistance for spouses of employees asked to relocate. Nevertheless, major reductions in the role strains and inequities experienced by nontraditional employees probably will be achieved only through widespread alteration of work structures and adoption of new models of work life. Thus, the needs for comparable worth, flextime, job sharing, nonpermanent employment, and part-time employment must be considered in the achievement of genuine equality of opportunity.

Summary

Women, minorities, and aged and disabled persons all suffer from numerous disadvantages in both the public and the private workplace. Not all these disadvantages can be explained by deficiencies in relevant education and skills. A considerable amount of the evident differentials in employment status between such groups and white males can be traced both to informal and to institutional barriers against equity in organizations, and any number of practices have been and can be developed to address such problems. Such changes, however necessary, are nevertheless clearly inadequate to resolve inequities in employment. Consequently, EEO/AA inevitably requires organizational and social changes, to provide a better fit between work life and personal life in an increasingly diverse work force.

References

Backoff, R. W., and Rainey, H. G. "Technology, Professionalization, Affirmative Action, and the Merit System." In C. H. Levine (ed.), *Managing Human Resources*. Newbury Park, Calif.: Sage, 1977.

Bailyn, L. "The Apprenticeship Model of Organizational Careers: A Response to Change in the Relation Between Work and Family." In P. A. Wallace (ed.), *Women in the Workplace*. Boston: Auburn House, 1982.

Blau, F. D., and Jusenius, C. L. "Economists' Approaches to Sex Segregation in the Labor Market: An Appraisal." In M. Blaxall and B. Reagan (eds.), *Women and the Workplace*. Chicago: University of Chicago Press, 1976.

Bowe, F. "Controlling the 'Uncontrollables.'" *American Behavioral Scientist,* 1985, *28,* 429–432.

Cayer, N. J., and Sigelman, L. "Minorities and Women in State and Local Government: 1973–1975." *Public Administration Review,* 1980, *40,* 443–450.

Cohen, B. "Minority Retention in the New York City Police Department." *Criminology,* 1973, *11,* 287–306.

Davey, B. W. "Personnel Testing and the Search for Alternatives." *Public Personnel Management Journal,* 1984, *13,* 361–374.

DiPrete, T. A., and Soule, W. T. "The Organization of Career Lines: Equal Employment Opportunity and Status Advancement in a Federal Bureaucracy." *American Sociological Review,* 1986, *51,* 295–309.

Doeringer, P. B., and Piore, M. J. *Internal Labor Markets and Manpower Analysis.* Lexington, Mass.: Heath, 1971.

Dometrius, N. C., and Sigelman, L. "Assessing Progress Toward Affirmative Action in State and Local Government: A New Benchmark." *Public Administration Review,* 1984, *44,* 241–246.

Dresang, D. L. *Public Personnel Management and Public Policy.* Boston: Little, Brown, 1984.

Eyde, L. D. "Evaluating Job Evaluation: Emerging Research Issues for Comparable Worth Analysis." *Public Personnel Management Journal,* 1983, *12,* 425–444.

Feagin, J. R., and Feagin, C. *Discrimination American Style.* Englewood Cliffs, N.J.: Prentice-Hall, 1978.

Feinberg, W. E. "At a Snail's Pace: Time to Equality in Simple Models of Affirmative Action Programs." *American Journal of Sociology,* 1984, *90,* 168–181.

Gazell, J. A. "The Attitudes of Nonwhite Police Personnel Toward Retention." *Police Law Quarterly,* 1974, *3,* 12–21.

Grandjean, B. D. "History and Career in a Bureaucratic Labor Market." *American Journal of Sociology,* 1981, *86,* 1057–1092.

Hitt, M. A., and Keats, B. W. "Empirical Identification of the Criteria for Effective Affirmative Action Programs." *Journal of Applied Behavioral Science,* 1984, *20,* 203–222.

Hunter, J. E., and Schmidt, F. L. "Ability Tests: Economic Benefits Versus the Issue of Fairness." *Industrial Relations,* 1982, *21,* 293–308.

Koestler, F. A. *Jobs for Handicapped Persons.* Washington, D. C.: U.S. Government Printing Office, 1978.

Ledvinka, J., and Hildreth, W. B. "Integrating Planned-Change Intervention and Computer Simulation Technology: The Case of Affirmative Action." *Journal of Applied Behavioral Science,* 1984, *20,* 125–140.

Leonard, J. S. "What Promises Are Worth: The Impact of Affirmative Action Goals." *Journal of Human Resources,* 1985, *20,* 3–20.

Lewis, G. S. "Race, Sex, and Supervisory Authority in Federal White-Collar Employment." *Public Administration Review,* 1986, *46,* 25–29.

Maher, P. T. "Police Physical Ability Tests: Can They Ever Be Valid?" *Public Personnel Management Journal,* 1984, *13,* 173–183.

Marino, K. E. "A Preliminary Investigation into the Behavioral Dimensions of Affirmative Action Compliance." *Journal of Applied Psychology,* 1980, *65,* 346–350.

Nester, M. A. "Employment Testing for Handicapped Persons." *Public Personnel Management Journal,* 1984, *13,* 417–434.

Panzarella, R. "The Impact of Tutoring Minority Recruits for Civil Service Exams for Police Officer Selection." *Review of Public Personnel Administration,* 1986, *6,* 59–77.

Parcel, T. L., and Mueller, C. W. *Ascription and Labor Markets.* New York: Academic Press, 1983.

Roos, P. A., and Reskin, B. F. "Institutional Factors Contributing to Sex Segregation in the Workplace." In B. F. Reskin (ed.), *Sex Segregation in the Workplace.* Washington, D.C.: National Academy Press, 1984.

Rosen, B., and Jerdee, T. H. "The Influence of Age Stereotypes on Managerial Decisions." *Journal of Applied Psychology,* 1976, *61,* 428–432.

Rosenbloom, D. H. "What Have Policy Studies Told Us About Affirmative Action and Where Can We Go from Here?" *Policy Studies Review,* 1984, *4,* 43–48.

Rumberger, W. *Social Mobility and Public Sector Employment.* Stanford, Calif.: Institute for Research on Educational Finance and Governance, School of Education, Stanford University, 1983.

Savas, E. S., and Ginsburg, S. G. "The Civil Service: A Meritless System?" *Public Interest,* 1973, *32,* 70–85.

Shafritz, J. M. *Public Personnel Management: The Heritage of Civil Service Reform.* New York: Praeger, 1975.

Stein, L. "Merit Systems and Political Influence: The Case of Local Government." *Public Administration Review,* 1987, *47,* 263–271.

Stewart, D. W. "Organizational Variables and Policy Impact: Equal Employment Opportunity." *Policy Studies Journal,* 1980, *8,* 870–878.

Thomsen, D. J. "Eliminating Pay Discrimination Caused by Job Evaluation." *Personnel,* 1978, *55,* 11–22.

U.S. Equal Employment Opportunity Commission. *Eliminating Discrimination in Employment: A Compelling National Priority.* Washington, D.C.: U.S. Government Printing Office, 1979.

Waldman, E., and McEaddy, B. J. "Where Women Work—An Analysis by Industry and Occupation." *Monthly Labor Review,* 1974, *97,* 3–14.

Welch, F. "Affirmative Action and Its Enforcement." *American Economic Association Papers and Proceedings,* 1981, *71,* 127–133.

West, J. P. "City Personnel Management Issues and Reforms." *Public Personnel Management Journal,* 1984, *13,* 317–334.

Part Seven

Improving Operations and Services

Public administration has many faces and therefore represents different things to different people. Some people identify public administration with making and implementing public policies. Others associate public administration most prominently with the maintenance of democratic governance. While these images are accurate, probably the most widespread image surrounding public administration involves government's role as service provider. From federal revenue agents to motor vehicle license examiners to local animal control officers to chemists in local water authorities, most public administrators are involved in delivering some type of service. Part Seven communicates methods and approaches for ensuring that government operations provide high-quality results.

Managing government operations involves the assessment, design, control, and adjustment of systems for producing goods and services. Assessment involves evaluating both the need for new services and the effectiveness of existing services. Performance measurement is a core assessment activity. Public administrators employ a variety of methods, including analysis of historical data, surveys of clients and other external experts, and physical measurement devices, to develop information about public services. Measuring performance permits public officials, citizens, and administrators to assess the quality, quantity, and efficiency of services.

Operations design encompasses decisions about systems for delivering services and about the allocation of responsibilities within those systems. In recent years, many innovations have been introduced into operations design. One of the most significant has been the proliferation of public enterprises in response to calls for greater competitiveness and efficiency. Another change has seen the role of clients expanded, so that many public services are now delivered through coproduction arrangements.

Actual operation and control of government production systems have also experienced many recent changes. With the most recent wave of interest in privatization, procurement has taken on renewed importance in most public organizations. The growth of computerized information systems has challenged public administrators to configure operating systems in response to opportunities and threats created by the development of this technology. Perhaps the most stable aspect of the operation and control of public production systems has been the continuing need for effective internal and external communications.

Adjustment involves the adaptation of operations to environmental, policy, or resource changes. As the environment for many public services has become less friendly in recent years, public administrators have been challenged to become adept at cutting services back. Such environmental changes tend to be cyclical, however, and to vary with the arena of government activity. Thus, a public administrator's repertoire of skills must include the capacity to direct the growth and rejuvenation of public services and to respond to hard times.

The delivery of services often involves ordinary routines of government, but the importance of these routines cannot be underestimated. Public trust and confidence in government depend as surely on the efficient and effective delivery of services as on the making of good policy. Part Seven offers insights for improving government operations and services.

33

Harry P. Hatry

Determining the Effectiveness of Government Services

This chapter is about performance measurement. This type of measurement is defined as the measuring, in some systematic and reasonably accurate way, the efficiency and effectiveness (quality) of government service or programs. The focus of this chapter is on program and organizational performance, not on the performance of individuals.

Recent History and Importance

In 1938, the International City Management Association (ICMA) published *Measuring Municipal Activities: A Survey of Suggested Criteria for Appraising Administration* (Ridley and Simon, 1938). This book was written by Clarence E. Ridley, then executive director of ICMA, and Herbert A. Simon, then an assistant professor of political science at the Illinois Institute of Technology. This was a pioneering work discussing the potential ways to measure the performance of a number of municipal services. After World War II, there was a movement toward performance budgeting. It emphasized measures of efficiency as expressed by the cost or number of hours per unit of output.

In the mid 1970s, ICMA again sponsored and participated in an examination of performance measurement of municipal services. This work, which focused on procedures for measuring the quality of municipal services, not their efficiency, was done with the Urban Institute and two local government participants: Nashville–Davison County (Tennessee) and the City of St. Petersburg (Florida) (Hatry and others, 1977). In recent years, ICMA has issued additional materials on performance measurement.

Also in the mid 1970s, the National Commission on Productivity sponsored probably the first effort focusing on performance measurement for state government services. The National Association of State Budget Officers and the Urban Institute undertook an examination of existing efficiency and effectiveness measurements used by state governments and, with the participation of the states of North Carolina, Wisconsin, and Michigan, undertook a series of projects to identify performance measures and data collection procedures for major state services (see, for example, Urban Institute, 1975).

In the 1970s, the National Commission on Productivity attempted to spur measurement of state and local government productivity by cosponsoring a number of productivity measurement projects. It made an important contribution by defining *productivity* as including both efficiency (relation of the amount of input to the amount of output) and effectiveness.

The federal government in the 1970s formed numerous program evaluation offices. Some such offices have also been established in state and local government agencies. The U.S. General Accounting Office (1972) issued its *Standards for Audit of Governmental Organizations, Programs, Activities, and Functions*. It established program results and economy and efficiency as legitimate elements of governmental auditing. This led some state and local governments to establish legislative offices to conduct performance evaluations (sometimes called *performance audits*), in addition to fiscal and compliance audits. These studies, both executive and legislative, focus primarily on one-time, in-depth studies of the effectiveness or efficiency of selected government programs. The studies attempted to assess the performance of individual programs, but in greater depth and more sporadically, sometimes using highly sophisticated statistical procedures in an effort to determine the extent to which a program actually caused the identified outcomes.

About the same time in the 1970s, the federal government sponsored a number of projects aimed at developing procedures whereby governments could regularly assess the outcomes of particular services, such as mental health, social services, physical health, crime control, fire, and transportation (funded by such federal agencies as the National Science Foundation, the U.S. Department of Health and Human Services, the National Institute of Justice, and the U.S. Department of Transportation). The mental health community, in particular, has had a long history of evaluation activity aimed at assessing the outcomes of various treatments. The National Institute of Mental Health sponsored a series of projects in the late 1970s to develop procedures for public agencies to use on an ongoing basis to assess performance of mental health services (see, for example, Windle, 1984).

At the same time, measurement technology has improved. Over the last decade or so, such tools as "scientific" sample surveys and "trained observer" ratings have begun to be used to obtain measurements of service quality. The development of powerful, inexpensive data-processing equipment (enabling analysts to record, collect, and analyze data quickly and accurately) has greatly increased the feasibility of measurement of both the quality and efficiency of government services.

An equally important development over the past decade is that government managers and public officials (elected as well as appointed) have become much more sensitized to the issue of accountability and the need to measure performance. One thoughtful author, discussing social service programs, stated that accountability for effectiveness is limited, because those who promote government programs believe in their intrinsic worth. He further noted that a "silent revolution" was occurring in public accountability (Carter, 1983). This same theme was promulgated by a former deputy secretary of one state's department of human resources (Benton, 1981). Both argued that, as a result of difficult economic conditions, administrators and legislators have been forced to ask what is happening to clients as a result of the programs that are funded by tax dollars. Another author, addressing local government services, argues that performance measurement is needed by officials to convince a "skeptical public that, given inflation and spending constraints, people are getting reasonable value for their tax dollars" (Epstein, 1984). All three authors emphasize that obtaining feedback on performance should be of considerable value to public agencies, even if they are not pressured by the public, by legislatures, or by tight fiscal constraints.

The growth of interest in performance measurement was also coaxed in part by such novelties as planning-programming-budgeting systems (PPBS); their toned-down variation, program budgeting; zero-based budgeting (ZBB); and the introduction of a new discipline, program evaluation. More recently, interest has been triggered by the fiscal containment movement, which has led to more concern over how to use very scarce dollars and thus to more focus on the need for justification of services and their levels.

In addition, some public officials began to experiment with internal motivational approaches, such as management by objectives (MBO) and performance contracts between chief executive officers and their department managers. These approaches attempt to motivate and hold managers accountable for their organizations' performance.

In the past decade, the movement toward pay for performance has stressed the need to assess managers' performance in order to provide more objective measures that can be used to help determine dollar rewards. Personnel departments, in parallel, have begun to push for better performance appraisal procedures that move away from appraising personal traits and instead stress more objective, behaviorally oriented performance results achieved by individual managers.

In recent years, a new and less recognized development is occurring: greatly increased public reporting of government performance by governments and, subsequently, much more reporting by the public media. For example, the U.S. Department of Health and Human Services has begun publicly reporting actual mortality rates for various categories of illness for each hospital participating in the Medicare program. These results are being reported along with estimates of the expected mortality rates of each of the hospitals, based on nationally estimated probabilities of death for patients similar in such characteristics as age, sex, and the presence of complicating conditions.

The U.S. Department of Education has indicated its intention of basing college and university accreditation in part on systematic measures of how much students are learning, such as performance on standardized tests or placement in jobs. Some states and individual campuses have been experimenting with such measures.

Also in recent years, there has been an explosion of publicly released data by school districts on academic test scores reported for individual schools and for different racial and ethnic groups. School systems are also beginning to determine and report dropout rates, as well as the results of local surveys of households on a variety of rating and opinion questions, sometimes patterned after the annual Gallup Poll survey on education. For example, since 1985, the education department of New York State has required school districts to publicly report school test results. The report that initiated this work stated, ''Public review and debate about student achievement has proven to be one of the most effective ways to develop the concern of parents and the public and to bring about action. . . . One of the most effective ways for drawing attention and involvement of communities and boards of education is to display trend information on pupil progress. The information itself is a powerful motivation to take action'' (New York State Department of Education, 1984). If we change the word ''pupil'' to ''client,'' this statement probably applies equally to most government programs, not only to elementary and secondary education.

The *Boston Globe,* in a unique effort in 1985, assigned a team of reporters to examine the city's performance in delivering services. Reporters undertook a series of ''trained observer'' ratings of the condition of city streets, parks, and playgrounds. They conducted a telephone survey of a sample of households, conducted a series of in-person interviews, and examined agency data. On the basis of their findings, the reporters generated a series of articles on government performance (Kaufman, Arnold, Frisby, and Witcher, 1985). This effort was followed a year later by that of a citizens' committee, which reviewed agencies' performance measurement systems (City of Boston, 1986). The city, responding to the committee's report, initiated a series of steps to strengthen performance measurement.

At the federal level, beginning in 1967, the U.S. Bureau of Labor Statistics has annually calculated and published productivity indexes for most federal agencies, covering about 70 percent of the executive-branch work force (U.S. Department of Labor, 1987). The indexes are used to show changes in the productivity of the various federal agencies. The productivity measure used is the ratio of the number of physical units of output to amount of employees' time applied. Federal agencies, however, vary greatly in the extent to which they regularly monitor their own levels of performance. Agencies that deal directly with the public, such as the Social Security Administration and the Internal Revenue Service, seem to have much more extensive performance tracking systems than other agencies do.

What does all the foregoing mean? Through the middle of the 1970s, performance measurement by public entities, such as state and local governments, was rare, and public reporting of such measurements was even rarer. Over the past decade, however, there has been an increasing amount of such measurement, accompanied by an increasing amount of public reporting of agency performance results. This is likely to have major consequences for the way in which public administrators do their business.

Data Sources and Procedures

Public agencies have used a number of sources and procedures for measuring performance. The principal sources and procedures are (1) analysis of agency records (perhaps after modifications to agency data-collection forms), (2) "trained observer" procedures, (3) citizen/client surveys, and (4) various physical measurement devices (see Hatry and others, 1977, for details on many of these procedures as they are applied to basic municipal services).

Analysis of Agency Records. This is the traditional source of information for performance measurement. It is the primary source for efficiency data, such as data on program costs and the number of units of physical output produced by a program (number of repairs, number of records processed, number of gallons of water treated, tons of garbage collected). With adequate cost accounting procedures, records can be used to yield efficiency and productivity measurements, such as various cost-per-unit-of-output measurements.

In some instances, agency records are the source of information on service quality and effectiveness. Examples include the number of reported crimes (as an indicator of successful crime prevention), the clearance rates for crimes that have been reported, the number of complaints related to particular government activities, and the quality of water after treatment by a water supply or wastewater treatment facility.

In recent years, as one measure of service quality, public agencies have made increased use of indicators of agencies' response time to customers' requests for services. Probably the most traditional example of service quality measures is response time to calls reporting fires and crimes. Governments have begun to apply measurements of response time to many public services, such as time to answer complaints, provide motor vehicle and driver's licenses, complete eligibility determinations, make welfare payments, complete housing and building inspections, and repair broken water mains or traffic lights.

Response-time data can be obtained from agency records, but government agencies may need to modify forms and procedures somewhat in order to record the times of initial requests and of completion of needed work.

"Trained Observer" Procedures. These are procedures in which observers are trained to rate some characteristic of a service, usually a physical char-

acteristic. For example, New York City and Charlotte, North Carolina, have undertaken regular ratings of street cleanliness, using a photographic rating scale. Such physical ratings have also been used to assess conditions of roads and bridges, to rate the condition of parks and playgrounds (and, thus, the quality of maintenance work), to rate the condition of traffic signs and signals, and to rate the condition of public buildings.

To make systematic ratings, employees, volunteers, or student interns are trained in the use of rating scales. The purpose is to establish objective, clear rating procedures, so that different trained observers making ratings at different points in time will give approximately the same ratings to particular conditions. The items to be rated during each reporting period should be selected in such a way that they are representative of the units to be rated. If an agency has resources to rate all streets and buildings, representativeness is not a problem. If resources are scarce and the number of units is large, the agency may find it more efficient to sample a portion of those units during each rating period. In this case, the agency needs to apply a sampling procedure that produces a representative set of units to be rated.

An attractive feature of such ratings of physical conditions is that the agency can map conditions, showing the relative extent of deficiencies in various parts of the jurisdiction (for example, by using various degrees of shading). A classic example of this is the maps that have been included in New York City's annual *Mayor's Management Report* (City of New York, 1988).

These procedures have also been used in human services to estimate extent of improvement in the condition of clients (for example, clients of developmental disability, mental health, and social services programs). Rating scales are established for various conditions that indicate clients' functioning and problem levels, relevant to particular types of clients. The observer rates each of these at intake and again at one or more times after the client has received services. The ratings are then compared to determine the percentage of clients whose condition improved (to various degrees).

The use of trained observers has been controversial. A particular bone of contention has been the use of clients' own case workers to make these ratings. If such ratings are used to evaluate the overall performance of units or programs (such as for future budget allocations) or as part of annual performance appraisals (and, to cite an even more extreme example, as part of pay-for-performance determinations), this procedure will have major creditability problems concerning the objectivity of the raters. Thus, when such procedures are used for performance measurement, it is desirable to use personnel who have no self-interest in the clients and programs being examined.

Citizen/Client Surveys. Surveys of households in a community, or of only those citizens who have been clients of a particular service or particular facility, can be used to obtain feedback on the quality of particular services. Clients, after all, are the recipients of most government services, and their ratings of government services should be of critical importance to public officials.

The use of standard survey techniques by state and local governments has increased considerably in recent years. Some states, for example, sponsor annual surveys (usually by state universities). Surveys can provide information on customers' perceptions of specific characteristics of service quality—such as the timeliness, adequacy, and dignity with which services are provided—by asking clients to rate each particular characteristic. Surveys can also obtain factual information, such as current unemployment rates (to help evaluate employment programs) and the percentage of households that use particular public services or facilities (such as parks, playgrounds, and public transit). Agency records can provide counts of the number of uses for activities for which access is controlled, but they are not very useful for counts of use of noncontrolled facilities, such as parks and playgrounds; in any case, they usually do not indicate how many different families use facilities or activities.

The current constraints on wider use of surveys are their cost and public officials' lack of familiarity with them. Also, some public administrators argue, administrators do not control the perceptions of their customers and should not be held accountable for customer ratings.

Nevertheless, surveys have become more practical in recent years and are likely to be increasingly used. For an agency that keeps records of the names, addresses, and telephone numbers of clients, it should be relatively easy to construct a short, reasonably well worded questionnaire and administer it by mail or telephone. Follow-ups of nonrespondents are likely to be needed, especially in the case of mailed questionnaires, in order to obtain adequate response rates (preferably over 50 percent).

When resources are quite limited, or when the number of clients or households is large, agencies can use random sampling to contact clients. Even samples of 100 or fewer clients or households can be informative, since the issues on which the surveys provide information seldom require high degrees of precision. Public administrators should realize that findings are likely to be far more valid if an agency obtains completed questionnaires from 100 clients out of perhaps 150 that it samples (a 67 percent return rate) than if it gets 1,000 returns from a mailing to 5,000 clients (only a 20 percent return rate).

Since most families have access to a telephone, telephone interviewing has become a quite acceptable approach. Attempts to interview people in person at their homes are expensive and unlikely to be practical for most governments, at least when interviews are conducted on a regular (a quarterly or even annual) basis. Mailed questionnaires are inexpensive, but if they do not provide for follow-up of nonrespondents, they are liable to yield inadequate response rates. The advent of microcomputers with standardized programs for tabulating and presenting the results of surveys means that information can be processed quickly and efficiently once returns have been received.

Regular multiservice surveys, such as have been undertaken by Dayton, Ohio, and Charlotte, North Carolina, permit survey costs to be spread   out among many services. Such surveys, repeated regularly, can be undertaken by outside contractors by telephone for perhaps only $10 to $15 per household—about $5,000 to $7,500 for a sample size of 500 (probably adequate for small and midsize local governments).

Physical Measurement Devices. These are used by some governments to measure selected physical outcomes of some services, such as air and water pollution levels and road conditions. For example, some state and local transportation agencies use "roughometers" or "ridemeters" that, when driven along roads, record vertical displacement accurately and thus give reliable measurements of road conditions.

Glaring Omission: Lack of Breakout Information

Performance measurement up to now has often suffered greatly from "aggregationitis." Most frequently, government agencies provide performance measurement data only for an overall program or service. An old story is that of the man who drowned in a lake whose average depth of water was only twelve inches. Aggregated data often hide the most useful information.

To be of maximum use to program officials, data for most performance measures should be disaggregated, or broken out, by relevant groupings. Data for some performance measures should be broken out for groups of clients served by each manager and supervisor (such as for clients of individual facilities and individual service districts and for each supervisor's own clients). Data for other measures should be broken out by various demographic characteristics of clients (such as residential area, age group, income group, and racial or ethnic group). The particular characteristics depend on the particular performance measure.

Another type of breakout is also often quite important: breaking out performance in terms of the level of difficulty of the incoming workload. Differences in workload difficulty can have major impacts on the costs and effectiveness of individual programs and services. If not explicitly considered, the performance data can be misleading. For example, outcomes may actually have improved for all categories of clients, but aggregate performance might indicate a deterioration in service effectiveness or efficiency in the performance period because a larger proportion of difficult-to-help clients came in for help, causing the aggregate data to look worse.

A classic example is the percentage of children available for adoption for whom adoptive parents are found. Adoption agencies almost universally find it much easier to place healthy white babies than older or minority children or those with physical or mental problems. Differences in the difficulty of the incoming workload will directly affect results in almost all services and programs. As another example, investigation cases assigned to police units with considerable evidence collected at the scene of the crime should produce higher solution rates than assigned cases that have fewer leads. Similarly, certain models of vehicles will be more prone to breakdowns and high gas consumption than others; thus, operating and maintenance costs per vehicle for those models should be distinguished from costs for others. The recent movement to report hospital mortality rates broken out by client difficulty characteristics and to report school test scores broken out by race and ethnicity and by school building are also examples of efforts to provide these breakouts.

Whenever possible, public agencies should categorize their incoming workloads by different levels of difficulty (perhaps grouping them into three, four, or five levels) and collect performance data on each category. Agencies should then track performance over time for each such category.

Appropriate breakouts will provide managers and other public officials with more precise information on the extent of success of their programs in different parts of jurisdictions and with different types of clients. This information can provide important clues to where problems must be addressed and where additional effort may be needed, and (when programs are successful) it may indicate possibilities for replicating success in other areas.

How Do We Know Whether Performance Is Good or Bad?

A key question for public administrators reviewing performance data is whether the current level of performance is good or bad, whether performance is improving or worsening, and to what extent. Administrators want and need some indication of the level of good performance, and they can obtain it by comparing the current level of performance to something else. Public agencies can make the following comparisons.

- Comparisons can be made to previous years' levels of performance. This is the most frequently used approach.
- Comparisons can also be made to targets set by the agency or agency managers for the performance period. This approach is particularly appropriate in agencies that use some form of management by objectives.
- Comparisons to similar data from similar jurisdictions can be made. This approach is useful only if there are reasonably comparable data for reasonably similar communities. Examples of such comparison data include traffic accident rates, air pollution levels (at least for major metropolitan areas), infant mortality rates, and illness rates.
- Comparisons can also be made to "engineered" work standards. Unfortunately, these are seldom available. When work standards have been established, usually for routine repetitive activities (particularly such activities as maintenance of roads, buildings, and government vehicles), comparisons of actual performance to the standards can be used to assess the productivity and efficiency of these operations.
- Comparisons to similar client groups or to other demographic groupings can be made. The level of performance achieved in one neighborhood or district, for example, can be used as a target level for others. Alternatively, the average performance in all parts of a community can be used

as the target to compare performance in each part of the jurisdiction.
- Finally, comparisons can be made across work groups. Performance on service quantity, quality, and efficiency can be compared among different police, fire, sanitation, or road maintenance districts. Similarly, performance can be compared among similar types of facilities serving similar types of clients, such as different mental health, parks and recreation, or correctional facilities.

Uses of Performance Measurement

Governments use performance measurements for the following principal purposes:

1. *To hold public officials accountable for performance on service quantity, quality, and efficiency,* and not solely for compliance with laws and adherence to budgets. This purpose has become increasingly important, as elected officials and the public have become more sophisticated and concerned and as finances have become more constrained.

2. *To motivate public employees.* A number of governments provide measurements of the performance of their personnel, especially managers, sometimes as part of management-by-objectives programs. Managers set targets for the forthcoming year. Progress during the year is assessed (such as on a quarterly basis and at the end of the year) against those targets.

Performance measurements are also beginning to be used more often as part of pay-for-performance plans, in order to document accomplishments. Pay-for-performance plans are increasingly applied to state and local governments, as well as to the federal government, with actual performance sometimes compared to goals and objectives on specific indicators as part of performance appraisal. Performance measurement is used less frequently as a basis for paying nonmanagerial personnel. For example, Detroit and Flint (Michigan) experimented with bonuses for crews collecting solid waste, on the basis of reductions in overtime and on such quality measures as completion of all routes on time and with no missed households. The states of North Carolina and Washington have provided bonuses to nonmanagerial workers for improving efficiency in the maintenance of roads.

3. *To monitor contractors.* As contracting has become more common, public agencies have become more concerned about performance. (Public agencies seem more inclined to measure the performance of contractors than that of their own personnel.) Ongoing monitoring of the quality of contractors' services is becoming more of a concern and is gaining more attention as the use of contracts expands. Agencies are beginning to include more requirements concerning quality of performance in contracts, rather than specifying only amount and types of inputs and physical products. Some contracts include financial incentives to contractors—bonuses for work that meets or exceeds performance targets, or penalties for work that is done poorly or not on schedule. Examples of strategies that have been used in these in-

centive contracts include measurement of the frequency of rework for contracted vehicle maintenance (with bonuses for staying below a targeted rework rate), awards for finishing road or bridge construction ahead of time (with bonuses for each day the work is finished early, and penalties for each day it is finished late), and payments based on the number of persons placed in jobs for a minimum period of time and at a wage at or above the minimum level. A contractor in Wisconsin's division of rehabilitation reported that the incentive contract had pressed the division's staff to focus on client outcomes much more than before. Employees made substantial changes in their time allocations, spending considerably more time out of the office working with prospective employers. The incentives also encouraged managers' attention to efficiency. The contractor pointed out, however, that some employees had problems adjusting to the need to generate income and had to be transferred to other activities (Hatry and Durman, 1985, pp. 19–20).

4. *To determine and justify budgets.* Performance measurement data can be used to aid funding allocations and justify requests to a legislative body. For example, information on the current condition of streets and bridges and reports of breaks in water mains have been used by public works agencies to develop and support capital replacement programs justifying maintenance for particular roads, bridges, or water mains.

5. *To encourage government personnel to focus on the needs of their customers.* This does not appear to have been a major explicit use thus far, but governments that focus on service quality (such as reducing response times to requests and complaints from citizens) and that use citizen surveys to rate services are implicitly encouraging government personnel to focus on such criteria.

6. *To guide improvements in public service.* This use is, in effect, the fundamental purpose of measuring service quality and efficiency. All the purposes already enumerated should lead ultimately toward improved service delivery.

To a great extent, however, governments across the United States, thus far, seem to put much more effort into measurement itself than they do into its use. Even when governments undertake substantive measurement, its usefulness is often stunted by lack of timeliness, poor presentation of data, lack of sufficient breakout of data, and managers' inexperience with performance data. In the long run, performance measurement can be justified only if it yields sufficient information to lead to significant service improvements, whether in service quality or efficiency.

Regular Versus Ad Hoc Feedback

Public agencies can decide to examine service performance on a regular basis or an ad hoc basis or both. Ad hoc studies are often called *program evaluations*. These are in-depth studies that assess the effectiveness of particular services or programs. Such studies attempt to determine whether a program has succeeded in its objectives, and to what extent. These studies can also be structured to identify ways to improve the service or program. Ad hoc program evaluations generally require substantial staff effort or outside contractors. Thus, agencies can do very few of these in any given year. With this approach to performance measurement, any individual service can probably be covered only once every several years at best. Regularly scheduled performance measurement is probably more useful to operational management. If conducted in a timely way and frequently enough, the process can provide many managers and supervisors with regular feedback that will allow them to identify problems, take action, and subsequently assess whether their actions have led to the improvements that were sought. Regularly scheduled performance measurement, however, is likely to be less helpful to administrators than in-depth program evaluations when it is a question of identifying the extent to which government action (rather than external factors) has caused the success or failure of a program.

Timing and Frequency of Measurement

The timeliness with which performance measurement data get back to public administrators is critical to the data's usefulness. Many current local and state government performance measurement systems were developed primarily to provide data for the budget process. Agencies often do not use the data except for budget preparation. Once-a-year measurements are unlikely to be very useful to public managers; more frequent feedback seems essential to help operational personnel.

The frequency of data collection and reporting will depend on specific performance measures. Some measurements are best done weekly; others are best done less often. Data on street cleanliness may be provided weekly or monthly, as in New York City; data on road conditions may be needed only on a quarterly basis.

Surveys of samples of households have been undertaken on a regular basis in recent years by a number of governments, to obtain feedback on quality of services. Most often, these surveys have been conducted annually or biennially. This is not a very timely schedule for program managers. One option is to break annual surveys into parts. For example, a quarter of the total year's sample might be surveyed every three months. The quarterly data will yield findings that are comparatively less precise, but the increased frequency of feedback is likely to be more useful to managers. Moreover, quarterly results can be expressed both cumulatively and quarterly and therefore permit more precision in later quarters.

Frequency is only one of the conditions of timeliness. Performance data should also be available as soon as possible after the reporting period, so that managers can act on the information while it is still fresh. In past years this has been a problem, because of dependence on mainframe central computers that sometimes broke down or were encumbered with more urgent duties (such as payrolls and accounting calculations). With recent breakthroughs in the technology for information processing, reports on data can be expected to become available within two weeks or even sooner—certainly, no more than a month after the end of the reporting period.

Problems in Performance Measurement

Thus far, this chapter has highlighted the merits of performance measurement for public administration. There are also important problems.

1. It costs money to track performance, and some of the most important data-collection procedures (such as citizen surveys and methods that rely on trained observers) are unfamiliar to many public agencies.
2. Performance measurement, even though major technical improvements have occurred in recent years, is far from perfect. We do not know of any perfect way to accurately measure all aspects of most services.
3. For most service effectiveness and efficiency measures, public agencies have only partial control over performance. Inevitably, external factors (the economy, the weather, and events in clients' lives) affect performance.
4. Performance information has almost universally been presented in aggregated form, which sacrifices a great deal of its potential usefulness.
5. Public administrators are often not familiar with or trained in the nature and use of performance measurements. Thus, when administrators are given poor or poorly presented data, they do not protest or seek improvements. When given reasonably good, well-presented data, they may not know how to use the information effectively.

Summary

Concern among elected officials, the public, and media over accountability and performance seems to have grown significantly in recent years and seems likely to continue to be strong. Some form of standards for reporting nonfinancial performance data is likely to be promulgated during the next decade, to reduce the likeliness of deceptive reporting by public bodies.

In addition, public administrators themselves are becoming more exposed to, and therefore more familiar with, performance measurement, both in their schooling and in their work. Recent efforts to break out performance data by key client or workload characteristics and by managerial responsibility units are likely to increase administrators' interest in performance data, as well as such data's usefulness.

Better technical tools seem to exist, including such procedures as ratings and surveys. Computer technology provides tabulations quickly, economically, and in detail.

Administrator interest in and use of such procedures as internal performance contracting, MBO, and pay-for-performance plans are growing. These should encourage continued growth and interest in regular performance measurement.

The federal government, as it has in the past, remains a major motivator of state and local governments to track performance. Although the federal government has been reducing its role in delivering services, it is likely to continue to apply pressure to achieve accountability when federal funds are involved.

Knowing how well one is doing is a basic need for administrators in all sectors of the economy, in the government no less than in the private sector. If one does not know what the score is, how can one tell whether changes or improvements are needed? If one does not know the score, how can one play the game?

References

Benton, W. "The Ethic of Intrinsic Goodness." Paper presented to the International Council on Social Welfare, Ontario, Canada, Aug. 1981.

Carter, R. K. *The Accountable Agency.* Newbury Park, Calif.: Sage, 1983.

City of Boston. *Mayor's Management Review Committee Final Report.* Boston: City of Boston, 1986.

City of New York, Office of the Mayor. *Mayor's Management Report.* New York: Mayor's Office of Operations, 1988.

Epstein, P. D. *Using Performance Measurement: A Guide to Improving Decisions, Performance, and Accountability.* New York: Van Nostrand Reinhold, 1984.

Hatry, H. P., and Durman, E. *Issues in Competitive Contracting for Social Services.* Falls Church, Va.: National Institute of Governmental Purchasing, 1985.

Hatry, H. P., and others. *How Effective Are Your Community Services? Procedures for Monitoring the Effectiveness of Municipal Services.* Washington, D.C.: Urban Institute Press and International City Management Association, 1977.

Kaufman, J., Arnold, D., Frisby, M., and Witcher, G. "City Services: Does Boston Deliver?" *Boston Globe,* June 16, 1985, p. 21.

New York State Department of Education. *Regents Action Plan to Improve Elementary and Secondary Education Results in New York.* Albany: New York State Department of Education, 1984.

Ridley, C. E., and Simon, H. A. *Measuring Municipal Activities: A Survey of Suggested Criteria for Appraising Administration.* Washington, D.C.: International City Management Association, 1938.

U.S. Department of Labor, Bureau of Labor Statistics. *Federal Government Productivity Summary Data: Fiscal Years 1967–86.* Washington, D.C.: Bureau of Labor Statistics, 1987.

U.S. General Accounting Office. *Standards for the Audit of Governmental Organizations, Programs, Activities, and Functions.* Washington, D.C.: U.S. Government Printing Office, 1972.

Urban Institute. *The Status of Productivity Measurement in State Government: An Initial Examination.* Washington, D.C.: Urban Institute Press, 1975.

Windle, C. *Program Performance Measurement: Demands, Technologies, and Dangers.* DHHS Publication no. ADM/84-1357. Washington, D.C.: U.S. Government Printing Office, 1984.

34

Annmarie Hauck Walsh
James Leigland

Designing and Managing the Procurement Process

Procurement, in the context of public administration, means purchase of goods and services by governments or public agencies from suppliers that are not part of the purchasing entity. Most government procurement consists of purchase from private firms—both investor-owned, profit-seeking companies and not-for-profit institutions. The federal government spends over $200 billion annually in the direct purchase of products and services from the private sector. In some city governments, more than one-third of annual budgets is spent on purchases and contracts.

While government procurement began with the purchase of standard goods and routine services, it grew rapidly during the Great Depression and World War II, in both volume and complexity. Privatization campaigns— in the 1930s, the 1950s, and the 1980s—have not cut into this growth, because they have generated more contracting than load shedding. The range of government contracting and purchasing is vast, encompassing research and development for weapons systems and traffic and dispatch systems, routine janitorial and custodial services, and the purchase of paper and cheese.

The purchase of goods and services from private entities in the United States is a market function, but government is not traditionally organized to function as a marketplace actor. The central challenge of designing and managing public procurement is to develop the capability of functioning effectively as a marketplace actor, within the constraints of legitimate due process for public action. Tensions between flexible business practice and prescribed administrative procedure are intrinsic.

Note: Research supporting this chapter was conducted by the Institute of Public Administration, New York.

In practice, private companies put less emphasis on formal competitive bidding, on documented procedures, and on constraining conflicts of interest than governments do. Private managers in a well-run company will be held to account for results. They have built-in incentives, backed up by corporate audit systems, to purchase goods that provide high value for the price, relative to available alternatives. They have built-in incentives to hire contractors and consultants who will accomplish high-quality jobs at competitive prices. The dimensions of accountability are related to results, including timeliness. Many private companies are not well run, of course, but the presumption is that mismanagement, bad bargaining, or collusion will eventually lead to dismissal or corporate failure (although they may survive unnoticed for some time). The effect of that presumption is that results are controlling in business, with less emphasis on process than is usually found in government.

In government, the manager is more often a permanent career public servant who must follow prescribed processes. Eventually, he or she, or political counterparts, may have to answer for results—in legislative hearings, in audit reports, in departmental reviews, or in the press. In the short run, however, government does not rely primarily on program results for accountability. Compared to business enterprises, government agencies are more bound to administrative due process, which encompasses statutorily established parameters, administrative regulations, and prior reviews by staff agencies.

Public procurement systems need balance between procedural accountability and flexibility to act successfully in the marketplace. Public managers involved in procurement must be able to analyze market sources for various goods and services, attract competitive suppliers, evaluate products and consultants, negotiate at arm's length, develop performance-oriented specifications, manage and monitor contracts, and resolve differences with dispatch. That is a tall order, when they must also meet procedural requirements that often include complex social and political goals; formal requirements for solicitation and low price bidding; splitting of business among small and local suppliers; submission of extensive data and affidavits by potential contractors and their principals; prior reviews by numerous agencies concerned with budget, legal boilerplate, fiscal administration, social policy, and intergovernmental relations; lengthy prepayment procedures; and detailed specifications on components of products or services (from the type of wood in a park bench to the width of snow shovels). Many of these requirements can be defended as being in the public interest. In contrast, there are common practices in the private sector that are not acceptable in government, including the exchange of gifts and entertaining, repeated use of one or a few contracting firms, heavy reliance on sole source negotiations, and the vesting of authority to award contracts in a single program manager.

In many governments, however, administrative due process has accumulated detail beyond the point of diminishing returns. That assertion can be documented by a glance at request-for-proposal documents and purchase regulations from federal, state, and local agencies. Over time, government procurement processes at all levels have a tendency to become increasingly complex and inflexible. "Regulations have proliferated, use of the competitive marketplace has declined, and standards of performance are lacking" (U.S. Executive Office of the President, 1986, p. 27). That observation, made of the federal government, applies to state and local government as well. As regulations proliferate, the procurement process may become an end in itself, although its real purpose is as a tool of program goals. In local government, it is not uncommon to find that well-intentioned program managers, who are skilled at circumventing formal procurement regulations, develop informal and undocumented systems in order to do their jobs. Procurement reform represents efforts to reverse those tendencies, in order to obtain the highest quality of services at fair and competitive prices, as well as to prevent misuse.

The State of the Art

There are widening areas of consensus about how to establish and maintain effective procurement systems in government. The state of the art in procurement reflects agreement among a broad range of procurement experts and practitioners on a variety of issues, agreement that is often divergent from existing practice and therefore creates agendas for reform (for example, Institute of Public Administration, 1987; National Academy of Public Administration, 1983; National Association of State Purchasing Officers, 1986b; Short, 1987).

Agreement about preferred practices tends to be general in scope; it does not extend to every aspect of procurement. There are some specific procurement procedures that most experts agree should or should not be used, but there are many other functions that must be tailored to the needs of individual jurisdictions or agencies. Common goals are to avoid favoritism or graft and to obtain improved value, productivity, and favorable benefit-cost ratio from the goods, services, and information acquired from outside government. Overall, there are five major themes that are common in procurement reform. They can be summarized as systems management, policy codification, documentation, competition, and professionalism.

First, there is substantial agreement on the need to develop managed systems that integrate centralized policy with decentralized operations. This emphasis seeks to move away from detailed controls and prior approvals by central staff agencies. The contract management system aims to develop a set of common objectives and process guidelines that would be operationally decentralized. Responsibility for effective procurement operations rests primarily with program managers, for complex contracts, and with procurement specialists, for purchasing. While program managers should have major influence on selection, monitoring, and evaluation of contractors and equipment, procurement specialists are key partners who provide checks and balances, specialized skills, and negotiating assistance.

Second, development and codification of contracting policy and procedures are needed nearly everywhere. There are wide efforts to consolidate, simplify, and express the rules of the game in a framework usable by both public managers and potential contractors. When regulations and procedures are clear, more firms may be attracted to compete for public business. Written policies should define the parameters of acceptable procedures flexibly enough to allow adaptation to the varying missions and sizes of individual agencies and programs. Policies should clarify the processes of competitive contract award that may be used. They should specify standards for prequalification and for sole-source contracting. They should also determine appropriate roles for negotiation, define conflicts of interest and administrative remedies, outline procedures for review and audit, and delineate payment procedures. In some cases, such efforts develop policies where none have existed. Other cases involve sorting through, simplifying, and making compatible a maze of existing statutory, regulatory, and informal rules.

Third, the importance of improved information and documentation in public procurement is widely endorsed. No matter what specific procedures are used, they should be described in writing and be publicly available. The roles and responsibilities of public officials should be clearly expressed. Procurement decisions should be recorded and accessible. To establish accountability, oversight agencies must be able to determine, after the fact, who made crucial decisions and why. This ability is essential to developing confidence in the processes of postaudit and review. That confidence is a prerequisite to reducing reliance on prior controls. Good documentation requires automated information systems in large government units. These are needed for several purposes: to permit efficient ordering and tracking of purchases and contracts, to facilitate investigation or postaudit, and, most important, to provide managers with convenient access to performance data and market information on various vendors and contractors.

Fourth, increasing competition in government procurement is a goal. For example, the Federal Competition in Contracting Act of 1984 increases competitive efforts within departments and narrows justifications for sole-source contracting. State and local governments need to increase their use of open solicitation of firms, to improve their handling of competitive technical proposals, and to streamline their payment and administration procedures, in order to attract more firms to compete for public business. Competition should not necessarily rely on the choice of low bids in price competition. For the vast majority of procurement expenditures, the weighing of technical, quality, and reliability factors is at least as important as the comparison of bids.

Finally, current views of procurement emphasize the growing importance of professionalization and training. The technical aspects of contracting and purchasing have become more complicated. Procurement officials increasingly need to carry out a wide range of technical tasks and bargaining efforts. They must be able to communicate and negotiate effectively with vendors of technical and innovative goods and services. They must deal with the political and managerial complexities of modern procurement systems. Their skills and internalization of professional standards, while not easy to attain, is the most effective safeguard against irregularity and graft. This body of normative notions has emerged from several sources, which are briefly described in the discussion that follows.

Private Sector Procurement. Business management literature reflects growing consensus on fundamental issues related to procurement, particularly standardization and professionalization. This is an outgrowth of efforts by corporations to use cost-effective procurement as an integral part of overall strategy to maintain competitive positions in the international marketplace. Procurement management is now widely studied and taught. A survey commissioned by the National Association of Purchasing Managers found that over two hundred colleges and universities offer courses in purchasing and materials management.

Many large, diversified companies have separated the function of purchasing policy from the function of purchasing operations. A general purchasing staff at company headquarters may establish guidelines, conduct research programs, coordinate purchasing activities, provide technical assistance to operating divisions, evaluate purchasing performance, and counsel top management regarding procurement. These management offices typically do not make personnel decisions, carry out buying, or approve discrete contracts (see Leenders, Fearon, and England, 1985). This model has had some influence on recommendations for government procurement.

Reorganization in the Federal Government. Attempts to improve procurement practices at the federal level have produced dozens of studies and reports, as well as hundreds of recommendations that indicate elements of preferred practice for government at every level. After assessing the cumbersome content and confused lines of authority that plagued federal procurement regulations, the Federal Commission on Governmental Procurement recommended in 1972 that procurement policymaking be distinguished from actual purchasing and contracting operations, and that the U.S. Office of Federal Procurement Policy (OFPP) be established in the U.S. Office of Management and Budget to consolidate the policy function.

OFPP was to be composed of a small number of ''seasoned procurement experts'' and would be independent of any agency having operational responsibility (for example, the General Services Administration or the Department of Defense). Created in 1974 and headed by a presidential appointee, OFPP began a process of study, recommendations, and reform that is still going on (although it has been slowed because OFPP is weaker than had been originally recommended, and it encounters some resistance from Congress, defense agencies, and other staff agencies).

OFPP's proposals for a uniform procurement management system, together with supporting proposals and studies, have provided the background for procurement reforms in state and local government. OFPP's "uniform system" is described in terms that are widely accepted: "*Uniform* does not imply centralized management of the procurement function, nor that everything will be procured the same way in every agency. It refers to the common management processes and objectives, and those policies, regulations and standards which apply government-wide. Within this broad framework, ample latitude is provided for business judgment, for unique agency requirements and for tailoring the procurement process to individual circumstances" (U.S. Office of Federal Procurement Policy, 1982, p. 5). OFPP's recommended system is being developed mainly through agency cooperation and executive order in a long-term, strategic process. Each agency designates a procurement executive to oversee development of the systems within it and to certify that these systems meet approved criteria. In addition, OFPP has assisted particular agencies in conducting detailed internal self-assessments.

Model Procurement Code for State and Local Governments. Developed under a grant from the U.S. Law Enforcement Assistance Administration, the Model Procurement Code was approved for publication by the American Bar Association (ABA) in 1979 (American Bar Association, 1979). Many procurement experts, including those associated with the National Association of State Purchasing Officials and the National Institute of Governmental Purchasing, maintain that the code represents the most comprehensive and consistent attempt to apply good-practice concepts in a usable manner. It is a model code, rather than a uniform one. It outlines options and is designed for adaptation to particular state and local circumstances. Detailed regulations for implementing the code were published by the ABA in 1980 (American Bar Association, 1980) (although they were never formally approved by the organization's policymaking branch).

The code, like federal recommendations, distinguishes procurement policy from procurement operations. The policy function is to be carried out by a central procurement policy office. While alternative locations are suggested, the preferred arrangement is a separate entity in the executive branch. The policy office can be headed by a board (with or without citizen members) or by a single official who reports to the chief executive. Staffing can be separate or can be provided by an existing staff agency, but not one with operating responsibility for procurement.

The procurement policy office would have broad authority to promulgate regulations governing the purchase of supplies, services, and construction. It would have the power to monitor and conduct postaudits, but it would have no authority over the award or administration of any particular contract or over any particular claim. Research on new methods, education, and training might be organized by the policy office.

Actual operations would be supervised by a chief procurement officer with specified qualifications (for example, at least five years' experience in public procurement). All powers and duties related to procurement, including construction contracting, would be transferred to the chief procurement officer, except those powers of the procurement policy office. (In large jurisdictions, chief procurement officers in each major agency are more feasible than a single central officer.) Subject to regulations, the procurement officer could delegate authority to any bureau or agency. This approach to decentralization could keep pace with the development of capabilities and systems within the various agencies.

The code also provides for an ethics commission, to delineate standards of ethical conduct, and for an administrative appeals board (or for use of existing agencies for these functions).

By late 1987, thirteen states and Guam had adopted legislation based on the model code, and legislation based on the code was under consideration in Illinois, Missouri, New Jersey, New York, and Pennsylvania (Del Duca, Falvey, and Adler, 1986, 1987). Over twenty local jurisdictions had adopted legislation incorporating elements of the code, including Kansas City, Washington, D.C., and Atlanta. Political subdivisions in South Carolina and Virginia have been required to adopt certain code provisions, as have all but "home rule" municipalities in New Mexico. In each case, the code has been adapted to local practices and experience, as the ABA intended. A variety of different organizational frameworks have resulted, embodying some aspects of the code more than others.

The National Association of State Purchasing Officers (NASPO). Beginning in 1961, NASPO has surveyed, discussed, and recommended procurement statutes, rules, and management practices, including a synthesis of the "best practices" in the fifty states with regard to the "purchase, management, and disposition of equipment, materials, supplies, and services" (National Association of State Purchasing Officers, 1986a, p. 11). NASPO stresses the importance of performance purchasing, an approach that emphasizes contracting for defined results. The terms of specifications in a contract or purchase order should focus on performance factors, rather than on design components or product contents; on overall costs of products and services, rather than on initial bids or prices; and on efforts to stimulate competition. Practices that unnecessarily limit competition—such as paperwork burdens that discourage small businesses, awarding of multiple contracts, and random rotation of bidders' lists—are strongly discouraged.

Performance purchasing calls for a more management-oriented approach to procurement than traditionally has been the case. Procurement operations should be organized systematically and must produce accurate and current data, so that purchasing and contracting of all kinds can be continuously reappraised, evaluated, and improved. Computerized procurement information systems are recommended as a cost-effective way of facilitating performance purchasing, and specialized training and professionalization programs are considered essential to the procurement work force.

NASPO contributed to the process that resulted in the ABA Model Procurement Code and, to a large extent, NASPO supports many aspects of the code, including its emphasis on more complete documentation of procurement activities and on the importance of price and cost analysis. Some differences do exist between the approach taken by the ABA, which relied heavily on federal procurement practices while developing the model code, and NASPO, which claims more sensitivity to state and local procurement needs. For example, NASPO supports centralized purchasing operations more strongly than the code does, recommends more vigilance concerning contractor collusion and anticompetitive practices, and argues that competitive sealed bidding can be used more broadly than the code recognizes, if appropriate evaluation criteria are included in the process.

Professionalization. All the major studies and organizations dealing with procurement improvement stress upgrading and professionalization of the work force. The first annual report, *Management of the United States Government* (U.S. Executive Office of the President, 1986), asserted that improving procurement personnel would be a major priority for the future.

With the increase in the volume of purchasing and in the technology of the goods and services involved comes the need for a skilled procurement work force and experienced career executives. Needs assessment and inventory, market research, cost and price analysis, design of performance specifications for complex equipment and services, management of diverse selection procedures—all these areas involve skills and time that few general managers may have. The U.S. Office of Federal Procurement Policy (1982, p. 37) stated the case thus: ''The proposed Federal procurement system includes a more responsible role for procurement personnel than they have generally exercised in the past. The system calls for more informed judgments about what is available in the marketplace, and about opportunities for competition. It calls for early participation by procurement personnel, as the Government's business manager, in the development of procurement strategies.''

Training opportunities have grown. Programs of certification are offered by the National Institute of Governmental Purchasing, the National Contract Management Association, and the National Association of Purchasing Managers. The Federal Acquisitions Institute maintains information on hundreds of accredited institutions that offer procurement courses. A number of jurisdictions across the country have developed specialized in-house training and certificate programs.

Federal, state and city agencies have a variety of ways of organizing so that program knowledge and procurement skills can interact. In the more centralized systems, most specialists and procurement executives are in central purchasing departments, but they specialize in various programs and line departments so that they remain familiar with program needs and work closely with program managers. In more decentralized systems, procurement specialists work in line departments and with counterparts in central policy offices. Combinations include matrixing procurement specialists from central agencies to line departments. In larger jurisdictions, the purchase of commonly used goods, services, and real estate may be centralized in procurement staff agencies, while contracting and specialized purchasing fall under program managers in line departments working with departmental procurement officers.

In decentralized contract systems, where operations may be handled mainly by program managers and midlevel administrators, highly trained and experienced procurement officers at the top of each agency (or small jurisdiction) can stimulate significant improvements by providing a source of checks and balances (strengthened in some jurisdictions by credentialing), technical assistance (through suggestions on selection strategies, performance specifications, quality assurance, market research, and conflict resolution), and information (including consolidated data on regulations, guidelines, and comparative experience with suppliers and contracting techniques).

Recommended reforms have generally included improving and clarifying position classifications for procurement managers and specialists, organizing career programs (including opportunities for training, rotation, and promotion), recruiting experienced individuals for management-level procurement positions, developing procurement internship programs, developing training plans, and establishing performance standards.

The State of Practice

Administrative Politics. The targets of reform or the characteristics of a state-of-the-art system may seem somewhat remote to many practitioners. Different perspectives on procurement are institutionalized in different agencies. Reconciliation of policy and practice is more a process of organizational bargaining than a result of study and systematic decision. There are some common sources of opposition to procurement reorganization, including legislative bodies that would like to continue controlling individual procurement decisions or regulations. Legislative control is defended as a necessary guard against graft and waste. Historically, political review of contracts has not eliminated irregularities or contributed a great deal to efficiency, but legislative bodies do determine the framework of organization, the basics of procurement policy, and relevant ethics provisions.

Budget goals are also sources of tension. Cost-effective procurement focuses on relatively long-range results: the sustainability of projects, the final cost (not the original bid), the quality of goods, and improvements in staffing and systems that could generate benefits and savings in the future. Short-term budget interests focus more on accepting low bids (despite perceived differences in quality or likely performance), holding down personnel upgrades, limiting hiring and training costs, deferring maintenance or repair, and restrictive pricing and payment procedures. Economy measures become dysfunctional when they discourage good firms from competing for government business or are outweighed by the costs of delay and poor results.

Effective procurement managers have to be prepared to persuade others— particularly comptrollers, personnel managers, and budget officials—when long-term savings can be achieved, and to negotiate the trade-offs between fiscal pressures and program goals.

The slow progress that has been made on federal procurement reform demonstrates the tension. The failure of federal officials to fully implement a system recommended in 1982 continues to be an issue (see Cushman, 1987). Several years were required to establish fifty procurement executives to certify programs in various agencies. Budget and personnel staffs opposed upgrading procurement staff (the U.S. Office of Personnel Management recommended downgrading some procurement positions). In 1983, Congress passed a bill strengthening the U.S. Office of Federal Procurement Policy (OFPP) and asserting its responsibility for drafting governmentwide regulations on procurement. But three years later, the U.S. Executive Office of the President (1986) asserted a plan to integrate OFPP into the U.S. Office of Management and Budget (presumably ending OFPP's separate mandate and structure). In another shift, the Executive Office report for 1988 stated that legislation would be offered to reauthorize OFPP and to expand its mandate to test new and innovative procurement concepts, giving it demonstration authority (U.S. Executive Office of the President, 1988).

The relationship between central procurement staffs and program managers in the field or in line agencies is also a continuing dynamic in public procurement. In many instances, the tendency of the program manager is toward a private sector model—seeking flexibility and discretion, and favoring sole-source or limited-competition solicitation methods. Apart from the dangers of favoritism, there are dangers of poor selection and of dependence on a small number of suppliers for parts or services. Nevertheless, pressures to increase competitiveness may seem cumbersome to program managers. The tendency of the central procurement agency may be more toward the control model, involving more administrative checks and, in some cases, more emphasis on price bidding. The danger of this approach is loss of quality control and timeliness. The tension can be constructive, if there is leadership at the policy level to set parameters and deal with disagreement.

There are also tensions between contractors and clients that are central to the procurement process. These begin with arm's-length bargaining. As in any market relationship, the interests of the two parties are not the same (despite the popularity of the term *public-private partnership*), but a deal can be struck at the point where interests overlap. Project monitoring, performance evaluation, product testing, change-order processing, inspection, and settlement of claims are some of the subsequent stages of negotiation and trade-off. In many cases, the project representative of government may be at a disadvantage by having less experience and technical expertise than the contractor's representative (this is one of the common problems that underlie the current emphasis on upgrading the work force).

The Decision to Buy. The extent to which services and utilities have been produced by government or purchased from the private sector has been subject to fluctuations that are linked to political philosophy, as well as to practical circumstances. Education, electricity, water supply, waste disposal, and transportation are examples of activities that include both private and public production and financing, mixes that have been shaped by fundamental political decisions. In the middle range of services are many in which the decision to use contracts is at least partly within procurement management. Some governments have defined frameworks for such decisions. These call for particular analyses of the relative costs of an agency's performing services itself or contracting for them. They encourage contracting, or they stimulate administrative units to assess their own productivity in comparison with estimated contractors' costs. The federal process (for example, OMB Memorandum A-76) has been charged with causing delays in letting contracts, but it has also been praised for stimulating improvements within bureaus. At least at the analytical level, the public agency can compete with potential contractors.

Most governments deal with these decisions haphazardly, with minimal analysis. Research indicates that cost savings from contracting are uncertain and difficult to predict (see Hatry, 1983). Public employees' unions tend to limit the contracting out of services that have traditionally been performed by government employees. Budget and staffing constraints make contracting for specialized services unquestionably necessary, but the ability to analyze the advantages and disadvantages of contracting in a given market and under particular circumstances is clearly a skill that procurement managers are increasingly called on to develop.

Contractor Selection Procedures. There are many different ways of selecting a contractor in public administration, with varying ranges of competition. Sole-source awards (accounting for more than half of federal purchase volume) are based on an agency's picking only one vendor or contractor and negotiating an agreement. It is controversial but defensible, if procurement managers handle it well and if there are rules for how and when it is used. Many times, one firm or supplier is clearly the only or the most qualified one to provide something, making sole-source procurement appropriate. Such a determination should be based on some form of market research (from telephone inquiries to formal surveys) or product testing. Most large jurisdictions require public announcement of sole-source purchases. Some cases highlight problems with the structure of the supplying industries. Near monopolies have developed in certain space and defense industries and in local asphalt industries, for example. There are many other cases in which procurement or program managers simply want to deal with a favored or familiar firm (which may lead to price creep, discrimination, or kickbacks).

Competitive modes of acquisition cover a wide range of techniques. The one considered most objective, and therefore widely favored in state and municipal regulations, is sealed price bidding. The job or purchase is advertised, all bids delivered are opened on the same date, and the low bidder is awarded the job. The process is seldom as simple as it sounds, however. Most jurisdictions call for some version of the ''lowest responsible bidder'' concept. In other words, procurement managers must have information and judgment to apply in order to discern an unrealistically low bid (which will lead to change orders during a project or to unsatisfactory performance) or to identify a company with inadequate qualifications or with faulty past performance. Management also must be on guard against bid rigging by a group of suppliers willing to rotate jobs or to share the market.

Prequalification is a process that may be used with bidding or with other competitive methods. Well-organized government units have forms and procedures for continuous prequalification of firms for jobs that are frequently contracted out. Bids or proposals may then be invited only from firms on the list. This process works best when there is open solicitation or vigorous outreach for firms and when evaluation techniques are thorough. Some governments use rotation of a randomly ordered prequalified list for routine supplies or services. This approach tends to eliminate competition and judgment about the quality and suitability of the supplier for the particular job, but some argue that it makes the job of the public manager easier.

Many other competitive methods of awarding contracts do not rely on price alone. Most of them use some version of a request for proposals (RFP). More complex than simple bidding, RFP processes are favored for acquisition of every product and service for which quality, innovativeness, compatibility, and experience are important. Procedural regulations usually govern how RFPs are drafted and how proposals are evaluated, but capacity to carry out the process is very uneven from agency to agency, at all levels of government. The most effective RFPs are explicit about the proposal format desired, the evaluation criteria, and the performance targets. When the criteria are clear, the subsequent award process can be audited. When the criteria are virtually nonexistent, the process can be little more than a cover for sole-source procurement.

There are many variations on RFP procedures. Proposals or prequalified firms may be ranked on a technical basis, without reference to price. Discussions may then be held with at least three firms, which may then be asked for submission of ''best and final'' offers. Alternatively, technical proposals may be ranked, and cost negotiations may proceed with only the top-ranked firm. The combination of technical judgment and negotiation requires skills that are critically short in government procurement. It also requires carefully stated policy guidelines and procedural regulations, so that public officials and potential contractors alike understand the rules of the game. In many state and local governments, such guidelines and regulations are so scattered and incomplete as to be of little use. (The same could be said about the federal government until recently.)

The Contract. There is enormous potential for improving procurement results. Managers can be encouraged to become expert at drafting contracts that emphasize performance and results, make monitoring and evaluation feasible, and make boilerplate comprehensible to the ordinary mortal. In some cases, contracts are drafted by lawyers (as is the norm in the federal government). In others, they are drafted by program managers and subjected to formal review by lawyers. In the vast majority of cases, they are a far cry from performance purchasing. Often the only resource a line manager has is to use language from a past contract, without information on how that contract worked in practice.

Ethics and Social Values

Procurement is increasingly a technical and managerial process; but, perhaps more than any other public administration function, it is crucially linked to ethics and social values. At the nexus of the public and private sectors, relationships range from partnership to conflict, with collusion possible at any point. Outright bribery, extortion, and fraud in procurement are relatively infrequent. They can be guarded against when there are internal checks and balances—more than one person or unit involved in a selection process—and professionalism in procurement management, unless political leaders move procurement decisions out of normal channels.

More difficult to control or even to recognize are corrupt practices on the part of vendors (bid rigging among vendors, using materials below specifications, making illegal arrangements with labor organizations, accepting kickbacks from subcontractors, and so forth). Some industry associations have established codes of conduct. National procurement associations have held workshops on how to prevent bid rigging. Some jurisdictions are trying to tie investigatory information into management information about contractor firms. In 1986, Congress enacted the Anti-Kickback Act, which provides civil and criminal penalties for violation of the prohibitions on kickbacks between subcontractors and contractors. Procurement managers still face a number of difficult questions, however. For example, should one eliminate a firm from a bidding list on the basis of informal information? on the basis of indictment without conviction? on the basis of personal ties? How can these actions be made compatible with principles of equitable treatment and open competition?

By far the most prevalent problems are in the gray area of conflict of interest. Conflict of interest is always present in human affairs: Individuals have complex interests, not all of which are identical to the interests of an organization. In public administration, the challenge is to keep conflicts of interest from damaging the values or interests of the public mission. In procurement, this generally requires conflict-of-interest provisions in law or administrative code and an ethics office or board from which individuals can seek advice in specific cases. The need for the latter arises from the fact that uncertainties always exist. The proof of uncertainties lies in the frequency with which people charged with acting on conflicts of interest stipulate the facts but maintain that they have done no wrong. May a manager who owns fifty shares of AT&T stock consider long-distance communications agreements? May an engineer resign from city government to join a consulting firm doing business with the city? May a businessman call a public manager to help solve a problem with city government? Is that call permissible in connection with economic development projects, but not concerning licensing? If there is a provision prohibiting the receipt of gifts except from one's immediate family, may a woman manager accept an engagement ring from someone who does business with the agency that employs her?

The movement toward coherent ethics codes and ethics advisory boards is fairly young in state and local government. While codes of ethics have existed in state law since early in this century, it was not until the early 1970s that the conflict-of-interest laws in their current form began to become commonplace. Spurred by a wide variety of scandals at the state and local levels, forty-five states enacted new conflict-of-interest provisions or drastically revised existing ones between 1974 and 1984. Many of these laws have undergone further revision to strengthen the provisions and their implementation. In most states, financial disclosure in one form or another is required to facilitate enforcement of the conflict-of-interest provisions. At the local level, interest in conflict-of-interest laws and financial disclosure laws has mounted in the 1980s, as local governments have become more involved in contracting for services and service delivery and as franchising has become an important part of local government activities and revenues.

Finally, the procurement process is loaded with rules and policies reflecting social values. Nondiscrimination and affirmative action policies are the most prevalent. Set-asides for small business, for minority business, and for local business are often required. Federal contracting procedures have been used to regulate the work week, to enforce wage standards, to strengthen environmental protection, to improve work safety, to target job development, and to limit purchases from certain foreign nations.

Procurement managers tend to argue that these requirements add costs and other problems to the process—that however worthy the objectives, periodic analysis of the impact of such regulations should be required. The issue is probably moot. Society will and should implement consensual values through its allocation of resources, and procurement does allocate resources. In any case, identifying costs attributable to applying social values would in itself be a slippery and costly undertaking, but procurement executives must be wisely alert to how social values are being applied, and they should be prepared to raise issues when and if the process becomes counterproductive.

Summary

The management of government purchasing and contracting should be a challenging career opportunity in coming years. It can make a significant contribution to the quality of government performance. Managers in this field are at the center of many technical, ethical, and social issues of importance. Policy and professionalism, development of decentralized management systems and improved information systems, upgrading skills in government—these are the continuing tasks of procurement organization. The public manager in this field must combine the best of public service with the energy of business.

Significant improvements in procurement policy and procedures are possible at all levels of government. Particularly in state and local governments, strengthening organization and management for contracting and procurement has great potential for improving the quality and timeliness of services and projects, for effecting savings, and for reducing the risk of scandal or graft. The degree of current consensus about some elements of good procurement practice is unusual in government. The elements seem practical, not dogmatic. They are emerging from experience, not from theory. They are designed by practitioners. Each aspect of procurement reform must be adapted to the political traditions and structures of each jurisdiction or agency. Certainly, what suits a city with a $5 billion annual contracting volume will be different from what suits a system that handles $100 million. Still, the directions seem clear to many commentators, and the changes undoubtedly will continue to be incremental and subject to adjustment.

References

American Bar Association. *Model Procurement Code for State and Local Governments*. Washington, D.C.: American Bar Association, 1979.

American Bar Association. *Model Procurement Code for State and Local Governments: Recommended Regulations.* Washington, D.C.: American Bar Association, 1980.

Cushman, J. H. "Purchasing Chief Expected to Quit at Defense Department." *New York Times,* Sept. 12, 1987, p. 1.

Del Duca, L. F., Falvey, P. J., and Adler, T. A. "State and Local Government Procurement: Developments in Legislation and Litigation." *Urban Lawyer,* 1986, *18* (2).

Del Duca, L. F., Falvey, P. J., and Adler, T. A. *Annotations to the Model Procurement Code for State and Local Governments.* Washington, D.C.: American Bar Association, 1987.

Hatry, H. P. *A Review of Private Approaches for the Delivery of Public Services.* Washington, D.C.: Urban Institute Press, 1983.

Institute of Public Administration. *Contracting in New York City Government: Final Report and Recommendations.* New York: Institute of Public Administration, 1987.

Leenders, M. R., Fearon, H. E., and England, W. B. *Purchasing and Materials Management.* (8th ed.) Homewood, Ill.: Irwin, 1985.

National Academy of Public Administration. *Revitalizing Federal Management: Managers and Their Overburdened Systems.* Washington, D.C.: National Academy of Public Administration, 1983.

National Association of State Purchasing Officers. *A Guide to Buying Professional and General Services.* Lexington, Ky.: Council of State Governments, 1986a.

National Association of State Purchasing Officers. *State and Local Government Purchasing.* (2nd ed.) Lexington, Ky.: Council of State Governments, 1986b.

Short, J. *The Contract Cookbook for Purchase of Services.* Lexington, Ky.: Council of State Governments, 1987.

U.S. Executive Office of the President. *Management of the United States Government: Fiscal Year 1986.* Washington, D.C.: Office of Management and Budget, 1986.

U.S. Executive Office of the President. *Management of the United States Government: Fiscal Year 1988.* Washington, D.C.: Office of Management and Budget, 1988.

U.S. Office of Federal Procurement Policy. *Proposal for a Uniform Federal Procurement System.* Washington, D.C.: U.S. Government Printing Office, 1982.

Hal G. Rainey
Barton Wechsler

35

Managing Government Corporations and Enterprises

In the United States, there have always been many hybrid or mixed forms of organization, which were neither strictly private nor fully governmental. Over the years, more and more public enterprises, government corporations, government-sponsored enterprises, public authorities, and similar hybrid organizations have been established to perform a wide variety of crucial functions. They run airports, seaports, hospitals, bridges, parks, railroads, electric utilities, and broadcasting and communication services. They provide funding for the building of schools, sewers, housing, and environmental protection facilities. There are now tens of thousands of such organizations in the United States (Walsh, 1978). Most of the state and local government debt in this country is issued by public corporations and authorities. In some other countries, state-owned enterprises or mixed enterprises account for most of the economic activity of the society. By one estimate, at least one-third of the world's gross product and one-half of the world's productive investment are accounted for by governmental corporations (Ruffat, 1983).

Recently, there has been increasing interest in these forms in the United States, due in part to growing skepticism about large government agencies and to an attraction to more privatized alternatives. Yet public enterprises have been proliferating for a long time, because they have been seen as a mechanism for bringing together governmental involvement in an important function with an organizational form that allows for more autonomy, flexibility, market control, and businesslike efficiency than is believed to be available from governmental bureaucracies.

This combination seriously complicates the management of public enterprises, however. While they are supposed to offer autonomy and efficiency, some of them are criticized as bastions of political patronage, pork-barrel politics, political meddling, and managerial inefficiency. In contrast, a highly efficient and profitable public enterprise may be criticized for overemphasizing its own profits at the expense of the public interest goals it is supposed to pursue.

Since public enterprise represents a purposeful mixing of governmental control with more private or market-based forms of organizational control, its promise is in drawing on the best aspects of both forms of control. Yet it should be expected that this will be more a delicate balancing act than a marriage made in heaven. All management involves confronting complex and conflicting values and objectives, but public enterprise puts the manager in a context where there is more intentional conflict among goals than in most other settings. In addition to the conflict of goals, it is common for officials who establish an enterprise to leave its goals very general and unclear. Still, careful reviews are showing that public enterprises often perform very well (Walsh, 1978; Aharoni, 1986) and that their performance ultimately depends on how they are governed and managed.

Effective management of these interesting hybrids is the main concern of this chapter. We will discuss the meaning of the term *public enterprise* and the sorts of organizations to which we are referring. We will briefly review the relevant theory and research. Then we will suggest major considerations and steps for officials and policymakers involved in the management of public enterprises, in the sense of establishing and governing them. Finally, we will offer suggestions about strategies and key issues for persons who are in executive positions within enterprises.

The Meaning of Public Enterprise

By *public enterprise,* we mean an organization that is operated under government auspices to produce products or services as generally specified or approved by government officials, but which is given more autonomy from governmental controls and oversight than are normal government agencies. A public enterprise is often required, or at least allowed, to obtain large proportions of its capital and operating revenue from sales, user charges, or private grants or donations. A public enterprise has a legal status as a corporate entity, which distinguishes it from regular government agencies. It will normally be exempted from certain governmental controls imposed on typical government agencies, such as civil service personnel rules, standard governmental audits, governmental purchasing and procurement rules, and the standard budgeting process for government agencies (Seidman, 1983).

We refer to these organizations—variously called *public enterprises, government corporations, state-owned enterprises, government-sponsored enterprises,* and *public authorities*—primarily as they exist in the United States. There is an extensive literature that contains examples and descriptions of these organizations (Musolf and Seidman, 1980; Musolf, 1983; Seidman, 1983; Seidman and Gilmour, 1986; Walsh, 1978; Aharoni, 1986). There is no standard nomenclature or typology for them, although there are authoritative discussions of some distinctions that policymakers have tried to make or that should be made (Seidman, 1983; Seidman and Gilmour, 1986). In fact, however, the literature shows that the names are often used interchangeably. When there is supposedly a difference between, say, a government corporation and a government-sponsored enterprise, the policies for creating such organizations have been so inconsistent that the two organizations may have similar characteristics or overlaps on major dimensions. Therefore, while there is immense diversity within this group of organizations, it is appropriate to refer to them as members of the same general set of public enterprises.

The discussion is also relevant to organizations that may be called *nonprofit private corporations* but clearly are operated under governmental auspices and policies. For example, a commission on advocacy for the mentally disabled may be formally organized as a private nonprofit corporation but funded through a federal program and established as a result of federal legislation. In the past, the U.S. Department of Labor has funded "private, nonprofit corporations," such as the Manpower Development Research Corporation, to serve as flexible, adaptive "staff arms" to labor officials (Orlans, 1980, p. 28). Much of the discussion will also apply to the numerous organizations that are privately operated for public service or for charitable purposes, even when they maintain a high degree of independence from government (Salamon, 1987). All these organizations face, to varying degrees, the problem of balancing their professional or technical effectiveness with external community or public accountability requirements and other public interest criteria.

Theory and Reality of Public Enterprise

This section deals with public enterprise from two standpoints: that of its theoretical foundations and that of research into the behavior and performance of public enterprises.

General Principles and Theoretical Bases. There is a great deal of writing on public enterprise, but there is little highly developed theory. Theory has not guided practice; rather, an attractive general idea and some very general principles have been widely applied on an ad hoc, inconsistent basis (Seidman, 1983), with scholars and experts laboring to assess rapid developments. The basic idea is simple: Establish an organization that pursues public purposes in a form that has more autonomy, flexibility, and self-support than typical public agencies do, and let economic markets (or other relatively private processes, such as charitable donations or competition among providers) play a major part in controlling it. In his 1948 budget message, President Truman stated a very general rationale for the use of government corporations, which is still cited as one of the most reasonable statements of basic principles. He said that the corporate form is suited to the administration of government programs that have a predominantly commercial character in that they are revenue-producing, at least potentially self-sustaining, and involve many businesslike transactions with the public. Such organizations often become attractive alternatives to policymakers when there are strong issues of public interest or political reasons that justify government's involvement in such commercial activity. Instances of this type often arise from natural monopolies, from fiscal monopolies, when organizations whose outputs can be exchanged on economic markets have highly significant components related to the public good or the public interest (as may be the case for certain logistics, communication, utility, or general economic development functions), and sometimes when there is simply strong political support for government to sustain such activities when the private market will not (Aharoni, 1986). Under these conditions, the public corporation is supposedly subject to more control by the organization's customers and therefore offers some degree of the desirable aspects of control by economic markets, such as more incentives for efficiency and innovativeness. The combination of governmental and market controls is supposedly a way of supplementing both forms of social control by combining them.

Public enterprise has also been regarded as a way of escaping some of the rigidities or dysfunctions of typical governmental administration (such as rigid constraints on funding patterns, personnel procedures, and auditing and budgeting processes), as well as a means of preventing political interference with the efficient performance of the enterprise. This has actually been the rationale for establishing as public corporations some organizations that have virtually no businesslike character. Similarly, public enterprise is also promoted as a way to decentralize government, allow for individual or local initiative, or allow localities to join in providing certain public services.

Another view of public enterprise sees it as a means of generating revenues for needed infrastructure development and (historically in the United States and especially in other, developing countries) as a means of marshaling resources for economic development. A Council of State Governments document once described state and local public authorities as indispensable vehicles for financing public services (Seidman, 1983). There are constitutional and other restrictions on state and local indebtedness; revenue bonds of autonomous bodies with separate legal status are not subject to these restrictions. Such organizations provide a way around the debt restrictions and therefore greater access to capital funding for government infrastructure and services. This is probably the most important single reason for the vast proliferation of state and local public authorities.

There is a recent trend toward promotion of a variety of relatively independent nonprofit arrangements, contracting arrangements, voluntary or charitable activities, and other means of reducing governmental control and costs, allowing for more relatively private initiative and control and improving efficiency in provision of public and social services (Salamon, 1987;

Savas, 1987; DeHoog, 1984). Not all of them are readily classified as public enterprise organizations, but they are often based on analogous hopes and assumptions. Recently, some of the arguments for them have been based on a strong ideological orientation against government and in favor of private business activities.

This makes it ironic that the few applications of highly developed academic theory to the concept of public enterprise have been by economists who express skepticism. Some economic theories, such as property rights theory, suggest that governmental corporations will not necessarily be highly efficient, since government retains ownership rights, and as a result managers are deprived of the incentives that would be available in private firms (Aharoni, 1986). Other theorists suggest that public enterprise will inherently and unavoidably be subject to political pressures to provide services in inefficient and inequitable ways (Lindsay, 1976).

Research on Public Enterprises' Behavior and Performance. Much of the research on the actual operations of public enterprises concentrates on countries other than the United States (Aharoni, 1986; Mazzolini, 1979). Almost all the research is based on general expert observation and description or on case studies, with emphasis on the politics and governance of these organizations. These studies find evidence of both good and bad outcomes. Many public enterprises have been quite successful at performing specific functions (Walsh, 1978) and at operating profitably (Aharoni, 1986). Advocates of contracting argue that there is substantial evidence that contracts and other quasi-public arrangements produce more efficient and effective service delivery (Savas, 1987).

In contrast, many state-owned enterprises and public corporations have suffered serious operating inefficiencies and losses (Aharoni, 1986). Analogies to the market and to private enterprise often turn out to be oversimplified or nonexistent. Walsh (1978), for example, points out that the bond market funding for many public corporations and authorities does not provide the flexibility that is available to private enterprises, which have multiple ways of raising capital; it faces public authorities with incentives to be more cautious in the projects for which they seek funding. Some observers argue that the trend toward contracting, under which many public enterprises are formed, frequently has been marked by serious abuse.

Experts repeatedly express concern that the lack of consistent theory and policy in the establishment of public enterprises contributes to administrative problems (Seidman, 1983; Walsh, 1978; Hackbart and Leigland, 1988). They depict the use of public enterprises of all kinds as haphazard, disorganized, and piecemeal. The organizations are often created with vague goals and missions and with little clarity about how they are to balance accountability for public purposes with attention to their own operating efficiency. These unclear policies sometimes mask more covert objectives on the part of policymakers. The flexibility conferred on an enterprise is sometimes criticized as a method of back-door spending by government, a tactic not readily recognized by the public. For example, the creation of public authorities as a means of evading state-level constitutional constraints on public spending is increasingly raising concerns about public accountability for governmental spending decisions (Walsh, 1978; Hackbart and Leigland, 1988).

Research on Managerial Behavior. Case observations of managerial behavior in public enterprises suggest that their autonomy is often not adequately controlled by competition or other private market forces and actually confers just enough independence to make these entities only loosely accountable to other public officials. Some common mechanisms, such as boards of directors, are said not to be very effective in controlling enterprises to make them responsive to the public interest or to external public authorities. A frequent complaint is that managers in many public enterprises behave like stereotypical bureaucrats, concerned primarily with their own perquisites and power and resistant to divulging information about their operations.

Not many theory-guided comparative studies of public enterprise managers systematically assess these general observations about managers' behavior. The existing studies of this sort concentrate on state-owned enterprise in countries other than the United States. They depict the managers as responding to conflicting pressures by emphasizing one set of goals over another. In a comparison of the strategic behavior found among managers of state-owned enterprises in fourteen countries, Zif (1981) found that some managers adopted a political orientation and emphasized low prices, sales over profits, the marshaling of political support for decisions, and vague goals; other managers adopted a business orientation, which emphasized the opposite of political priorities.

In Weaver's (1985) more elaborate framework, three types of strategic behavior are distinguished. First, managers may adopt a security orientation, in which they seek increased political support to ensure the survival of an enterprise. Second, they may adopt an autonomy strategy, which seeks to maximize managers' decision-making autonomy through profits and to reduce dependence on governmental funding. A third alternative is a public service strategy, which seeks to maximize contributions to social welfare by clarifying and implementing trade-offs among specific public service goals. A high degree of very visible government financial support tends to encourage a security strategy, while a lower degree of less visible support leads to an autonomy strategy. Encouraging a public service strategy is a major challenge, Weaver contends, because managers tend to prefer the other two strategies. More specific government subsidies for specified services and operations, as well as stronger and more centralized governmental control mechanisms, will be more likely to induce a public service strategy.

There have also been general studies of managerial roles and strategic decision processes, and these studies have included research on managers of hybrid or quasi-public organizations. Such studies have found that these managers are involved in a greater number of formal and informal meetings with external authorities and groups than private sector managers are (Mintzberg, 1973) and that the decision processes in their organizations are more sporadic and turbulent (Hickson and others, 1986). There is also a growing literature on managerial behavior in public and governmental organizations (Lynn, 1987), some of which pays attention to hybrid organizations (Perry and Rainey, 1988; Bozeman, 1987). Much of this literature emphasizes constraints on public management, which public enterprises should escape, to some degree, but it also suggests that public enterprise managers probably find themselves in relatively turbulent settings, with complex and conflicting external political pressures.

In sum, public enterprise faces both higher-level officials and enterprise managers with difficult problems of strategizing and balancing conflicting criteria and values. Overall, policies concerning the use and governance of public enterprise are in a state of some confusion, which in turn aggravates the problem of balancing the accountability of such enterprises against the need to allow them reasonable independence and flexibility. These conflicts in turn set the context for the managers of the enterprises themselves, who are sometimes characterized as a new class of administrator (Aharoni, 1986), positioned between the public and the private spheres and faced with particular challenges in responding to the demands of public accountability and of effective, self-reliant management.

Prescriptions for Managing Public Enterprises

The research on public enterprise shows that their management involves two levels. Most of the attention has been focused on what can be called the *policy level,* at which public officials charged with establishing, governing, and controlling public enterprises must make decisions about those processes. There has been less attention to the *managerial level,* at which the people responsible for actually running an organization must carry out their responsibilities. These levels are interrelated, obviously, but it is useful to consider the management issues at both of them. As we have said, this set of organizations is extremely diverse, and there are diametrically conflicting observations that apply to different circumstances. Nevertheless, the research, expert opinion, and policy developments we have reviewed suggest the value of attention to the following exhortations and suggestions.

Policy-Level Management

Pay Attention. Experts regard strong leadership from elected officials and other policymakers as essential to the effective management of public enterprises, yet they also worry that policymakers often seem to have little incentive to provide such leadership. More officials and participants in government need to devote more time and effort to the management of public enterprises.

Organize Information. Invest in improved collection and analysis of information by establishing and supporting this function in professional associations, government offices, commissions, and legislative committees. We are just beginning to learn how various jurisdictions and professional associations gather and use information about these organizations (Hackbart and Leigland, 1988). There is wide variation among states, localities, and professional associations in the way this responsibility is assigned and handled. There is a need for much more investment in developing common terminologies, knowledge of alternative models and practices, and evaluation of the effectiveness of various models.

Organize Financial Information. The spread of public enterprises has serious implications for governmental finance, which are not being adequately assessed (Hackbart and Leigland, 1988; Walsh, 1978). Many public authorities are established as ways around state debt limits, and the growth of public enterprises obviously increases general public debt. Defaults on debt by certain public authorities have drawn some states rapidly into efforts to shape up their policies. There is a serious need to assess the prospects for competition or crowding out among debtors, for general strains on the capacity to fund and manage debt within and among jurisdictions, and for other potential developments. Hackbart and Leigland (1988) found that 68 percent of the states that responded to their survey reported that a central office is assigned responsibility for monitoring the debt issues of public authorities; obviously, further development of such activities is needed. The growth of public enterprises raises many additional issues, such as how much is being spent in a given jurisdiction on a given policy or functional area, and with what effect. These sorts of issues should provide more and more incentives for attention to public enterprise management. (A default or the downgrading of a debt rating can focus the mind wonderfully!)

Organize Policy. Experts lament the haphazard nature of general policies concerning the establishment and governance of public enterprises, at all levels of government in the United States. We must invest in efforts to articulate the rationale and guidelines for the establishment of public enterprises. What are needed are consistent guidelines concerning the handling of exemptions from financial, personnel, and other controls; efforts to assess and develop appropriate legislation concerning the use of public enterprises; efforts to clarify policy responsibilities within the legislative and executive branches; and efforts to develop appropriate regulatory and oversight guidelines (for example, common auditing procedures and provisions for periodic reviews of the fiscal impact of public enterprises' proliferation) (Walsh, 1978; Hackbart and Leigland, 1988; Seidman, 1983). Any general standards or regulations, of course, must be designed so as to allow the autonomy that a public enterprise requires.

Provide Central Support and Technical Assistance. Higher levels of government can provide debt management assistance and other forms of support as a means of improving management, without imposing constraints on autonomy.

Clarify Goals. Policymakers commonly leave public interest goals, and their trade-offs with the other goals of an enterprise, vague or unspecified. Clarification is very difficult, and there are strong incentives to avoid it, but vagueness often contributes to problems, both in public accountability and in the operating efficiency of public enterprises. Some European countries have experimented with "program contracts" to reduce conflicts between policymakers and public enterprise managers over the goals and priorities of organizations (Aharoni, 1986). Experts in the United States urge more efforts of that sort as a means of enhancing public enterprises' performance and accountability (Walsh, 1978). Weaver (1985) argues that, without efforts at clarification, social service and public interest goals are the ones most likely to go unattended by managers.

Invest in Social Audits. For many enterprises, explicit studies of performance on public service or social criteria are one means of clarifying trade-offs with other performance goals (Walsh, 1978; Aharoni, 1986; Ruffat, 1983) and of enhancing accountability for public service goals.

Assess Alternatives for Governance Structures. There is now a literature on alternative arrangements for the governance of various forms of public enterprises (Walsh, 1978; Aharoni, 1986; Seidman, 1983). It addresses such issues as board composition and function, location of enterprises within governmental structures, and forms of control and apportionment of authority among controllers. The alternatives and variations are complex, and clear resolution and consensus are unlikely, but this material is available to support efforts to organize policies and to design or reform specific enterprises.

Organization-Level Management

Prepare for Politics. The hybrid nature of public enterprises requires managers to be particularly adept at dealing with the external political environment. Khandawalla says that effective public enterprise managers "learn to accept and manipulate levers of power in government and refuse to view their business and regulatory environment as unalterable by them" (Khandawalla, 1984, p. 183). Even highly privatized hybrids, such as private nonprofit service organizations operating on the basis of private donations, are likely to be drawn into the political arena in various ways. From the literature we have reviewed on the conflicting pressures that face public enterprise managers, we are learning the applicability of many suggestions.

Know the System. Obviously, a public enterprise manager must know or have staff members who know a good deal about the institutions and processes of government that are related to the enterprise. The relevant topics include legislative processes or structures; legal processes, including administrative law; regulatory agencies, central management agencies responsible for governmental personnel, purchasing, and budgeting; and other forms of institutional knowledge that effective public administrators normally have.

Prepare to Manage Complexity. Managers in all settings are now being exhorted to maintain a high tolerance for ambiguity and to learn to operate effectively in the turbulent and often paradoxical environment of contemporary management. The same is even more true for public enterprise managers, because they must deal with political conflicts, complex and conflicting goals, actual or attempted interventions, public scrutiny, and accountability for public goals. Managers of private nonprofits often face analogous complications: A board of a private charitable or social service organization made up of community volunteers can be devilishly unwieldy and particularly amateurish with regard to managing an organization.

Study "Garbage Can" Management. We are rapidly learning more about how managers respond to these conditions. The "garbage can" model, probably the most prominent current perspective on managerial decisions, stresses the ambiguous and chaotic nature of most important decision processes. The developers of this model offer tactical suggestions for managers in such contexts. For example, they suggest that managers must persist, facilitate participation by the opposition, overload the system with proposals, and interpret history by articulating a particular version of events (Peters, 1987). Additional advice is rapidly appearing, much of it published by Jossey-Bass, on how managers can contend with turbulence, complexity, and paradox through management of "dominant values" and "culture" in their organizations (Cohen and March, 1986; Peters, 1987). Clearly, the message about tolerance for ambiguity does not imply passiveness or indecisiveness. Aggressiveness and purposefulness are as indispensable as ever.

Prepare Your People for Politics. Given the inherent conflicts we have discussed, one challenge for many public enterprise managers will be to maintain staff morale and sense of direction in the face of political complexity. For example, the manager of a government-sponsored nonprofit housing finance corporation may decide to accede to pressure from a legislator to provide funding for a project that, on the basis of business or technical criteria, the staff does not support. Especially if the staff has been chosen on the basis of professional credentials and has little background in government, managers in such situations will need to articulate their own ethical and political rationales, the relationship of such decisions to larger and longer-term objectives, and the legitimacy of certain types of political responsiveness.

Empower Your People. The contemporary management literature is full of exhortations to managers to motivate people in their organizations by empowering them through delegation of responsibility. Government agencies are often observed to be weak on this point, because of heavy pressures for the strict accountability of top officials to political leaders. The public enterprise is purportedly designed to provide flexibility in the management of human resources. Use it.

Clarify Goals. Some political observers and "garbage can" modelers point out that there are sometimes reasons not to be too explicit about goals—for example, to maintain flexibility and avoid conflict. Yet taking this approach too far is harmful. Many experts on public enterprises argue that clarifying goals and the trade-offs among them is an essential challenge for public enterprise managers, which can help them contend with the inherent conflicts imposed on them (Walsh, 1978; Weaver, 1985). Pressing policymakers for clarification of public service goals can reduce conflict over subsequent decisions. Weaver (1985) describes how the Canadian National Railway established an unprofitable operation as a distinct organizational entity, to show policymakers some of the trade-offs being imposed on the company's efforts to operate profitably and autonomously. Public enterprise managers often have opportunities to influence enabling legislation or its revision. The commonplace vagueness of enabling legislation with regard to public service criteria and other goals provides leeway for managers to influence decisions on goals and their clarification. As already noted, social audits and operating contracts are additional ways of pressing controllers and policymakers to come to a reasonable consensus on goals and the trade-offs among them.

Conduct Strategic Planning. Another way of clarifying goals and priorities is strategic planning. Strategic planning is now widely used in business and government (Wechsler and Backoff, 1986), and there are numerous supports for it.

Employ Conflict Resolution and Consensus Building. For a public enterprise, goal clarification and strategic planning usually involve complex negotiations with diverse staff members, board members, external policymakers, and external interest groups. There is now extensive material on techniques for conflict management (Yates, 1985) and on group decision and communication processes (often as part of strategic management activities). Public enterprise managers need to be experts on such procedures.

Address the Balance Among Goals. Experts stress the choices among strategies based on political responsiveness, social service, and businesslike proficiency and operating autonomy. They observe that one of these goals usually predominates. If a public enterprise is actually going to fulfill the purpose for which its structure purportedly is designed, there must be a continual striving for the appropriate balance. Ruffat (1983) proposes a method for strategizing for, accounting for, and maximizing service, commercial, and financial objectives. Such conceptions and procedures should be employed in the strategic planning process and in its implementation. Aharoni (1986) provides a review of the approaches to clarifying goal trade-offs in state-owned enterprises in other countries.

Assess Autonomy and Discretion. It is often unclear just how much autonomy and discretion public enterprise managers actually have. Obviously, many factors influence this, but it often depends a great deal on the skill and aggressiveness of managers. Can you diversify or add or drop a particular function or service? Can your personnel system be linked with that of the parent government in certain useful ways (such as insurance and pension plans) while your organization maintains its autonomy in position classification and pay levels? Often, issues such as these are not entirely clear. There are particular "windows of opportunity" during the establishment of the organization or during periods of managerial turnover when managers can exert great influence over such provisions.

As part of planning and strategizing, seek to assess specific constraints and prospects for discretion in key areas where external governmental controls over the enterprise are often at issue. These include provisions for establishment and termination of the organization and its activities, mission and goal set, goods and services produced, geographical sphere of operations, clients served, personnel systems, executive appointments and appointments to boards, purchasing and procurement requirements, budgeting and auditing requirements, and financial resource levels and sources.

As Weaver (1985) points out, the level and nature of such constraints can be key determinants of the balance among goals. More constrained organizations are more likely to have to pursue strategies that stress building political support through political responsiveness.

Assess the Market or Service Delivery System. Obviously, there are major factors, other than governmental controls, in the operating context. These vary so widely among different types of public enterprises that they are beyond the scope of this chapter, but they include the assessment of such characteristics of the operating environment as market competition or monopoly, consumer and client demand, and costs of inputs and resources. Discussions of such factors in the environments of public enterprises that are engaged in commercial and manufacturing functions are increasingly available (Aharoni, 1986; Mazzolini, 1979; Weaver, 1985).

Summary

A public enterprise is an organization that delivers a governmental service or function but has legal status as a separate corporate entity, distinct from typical government agencies. It has more autonomy from governmental rules and controls than typical government agencies do. This form of organization is widespread and increasingly significant in the United States and in other countries.

The basic idea of public enterprise is to combine governmental accountability and control with a form of organization that is more flexible, efficient, politically independent, and self-sustaining than government agencies are normally thought to be. Yet the combination creates serious challenges for managing. How much should they be held accountable by political policymakers for serving general public or governmental goals? How much should they be allowed independence to perform their functions efficiently and profitably? There has been little clarity or consistency in the way these organizations are established and held accountable by external policymakers. Policymakers who are responsible for governing these organizations must devote more attention to organizing information about them, including financial information; organizing policies, including well-developed policies for creation, assessment, governance, and central support and technical assistance to them; and clarifying their goals and goal trade-offs.

Managers who actually run the organizations have to balance political accountability, social service, and business or technical effectiveness. They must deal effectively with the political environment by knowing the political system, preparing for management under turbulent conditions, preparing and empowering their employees for these conditions, striving to clarify goals and goal trade-offs (in part by pressing policymakers for clarification), employing strategic planning and conflict resolution and consensus-building techniques, and assessing and appropriately using their autonomy and discretion.

References

Aharoni, Y. *The Evolution and Management of State-Owned Enterprises.* Cambridge, Mass.: Ballinger, 1986.

Bozeman, B. *All Organizations Are Public: Bridging Public and Private Organizational Theories.* San Francisco: Jossey-Bass, 1987.

Cohen, M. D., and March, J. G. *Leadership and Ambiguity.* (2nd ed.) Boston: Harvard Business School Press, 1986.

DeHoog, R. H. *Contracting Out for Human Services.* Albany: State University of New York Press, 1984.

Hackbart, M., and Leigland, J. *State Debt Management Policies and Procedures.* Lexington: College of Business and Economics, University of Kentucky, 1988.

Hickson, D. J., and others. *Top Decisions: Strategic Decision Making in Organizations.* San Francisco: Jossey-Bass, 1986.

Khandawalla, P. N. "Some Lessons for the Management of Public Enterprises." *International Studies of Management and Organization,* 1984, *14,* 167–196.

Lindsay, C. "A Theory of Government Enterprise." *Journal of Political Economy,* 1976, *84,* 1061–1077.

Lynn, L. E., Jr. *Managing Public Policy.* Boston: Little, Brown, 1987.

Mazzolini, R. *Government Controlled Enterprises: International Strategic and Policy Decisions.* New York: Wiley, 1979.

Mintzberg, H. *The Nature of Managerial Work.* New York: Harper & Row, 1973.

Musolf, L. *Uncle Sam's Private, Profitseeking Corporations.* Lexington, Mass.: Lexington Books, 1983.

Musolf, L., and Seidman, H. "The Blurred Boundaries of Public Administration." *Public Administration Review,* 1980, *40,* 124–130.

Orlans, H. (ed.). *Nonprofit Organizations.* New York: Praeger, 1980.

Perry, J. L., and Rainey, H. "The Public-Private Distinction in Organization Theory: A Critique and Research Strategy." *Academy of Management Review,* 1988, *13,* 182–201.

Peters, T. J. "Symbols, Patterns, and Settings: An Optimistic Case for Getting Things Done." In J. Shafritz and J. Ott (eds.), *Classics of Organization Theory.* Chicago: Dorsey Press, 1987.

Ruffat, J. "Strategic Management of Public and Nonmarket Corporations." *Long-Range Planning,* 1983, *16,* 74–84.

Salamon, L. M. "Partners in Public Service: The Scope and Theory of Government-Nonprofit Relations." In W. W. Powell (ed.), *The Nonprofit Sector: A Research Handbook.* New Haven: Yale University Press, 1987.

Savas, E. *Privatization: The Key to Better Government.* Chatham, N.J.: Chatham House, 1987.

Seidman, H. "Public Enterprises in the United States." *Annals of Public and Cooperative Economy,* 1983, *54,* 3–18.

Seidman, H., and Gilmour, R. *Politics, Position, and Power: From the Positive to the Regulatory State.* (4th ed.) New York: Oxford University Press, 1986.

Walsh, A. H. *The Public's Business: The Politics and Practices of Government Corporations.* Cambridge, Mass.: MIT Press, 1978.

Weaver, R. "Government Policy and Public Enterprise Performance." Paper presented at the annual meeting of the American Political Science Association, New Orleans, 1985.

Wechsler, B., and Backoff, R. "Policy Making and Administration in State Agencies: Strategic Management Approaches." *Public Administration Review,* 1986, *46,* 321–328.

Yates, D., Jr. *The Politics of Management: Exploring the Inner Workings of Public and Private Organizations.* San Francisco: Jossey-Bass, 1985.

Zif, J. "Managerial Strategic Behavior in State-Owned Enterprises—Business and Political Orientations." *Management Science,* 1981, *27,* 1326–1339.

36   *Jeffrey L. Brudney*

Using Coproduction to Deliver Services

The 1980s have witnessed the flowering of a promising form of citizen participation in the affairs of public agencies: coproduction. Coproduction can be understood as a cooperative relationship between government, on the one hand, and citizens, neighborhood associations, community organizations, or client groups, on the other, for the delivery of public services. As students of participation can attest, relationships between these parties have not always been smooth, particularly at the local level. In many communities, early efforts to include citizens in public decision making employed top-down approaches initiated and controlled by municipal agencies, not to secure the benefits of cooperation but to win support and legitimacy for government decisions and programs. For example, the use of blue-ribbon committees of high-profile citizens as a participation device in urban renewal projects excluded representation of targeted areas, and as the effects of these projects became known, they produced protest and advocacy groups that turned officials and residents into adversaries, rather than partners. Too often, the inability of participants to effect change or wield influence through formal channels, such as public hearings, advisory boards, and citizen surveys, bred disillusionment, frustration, and conflict.

Although the Community Action Program established by the Economic Opportunity Act of 1964 and the 1966 Demonstration Cities and Metropolitan Development Act (the Model Cities program) deserve some of the credit for stimulating broader citizen involvement (Herman and Peroff, 1983), coproduction is largely a bottom-up, citizen-initiated reaction to the problems associated with the conventional modes of participation. It represents

Note: The author is grateful to John Clayton Thomas for his insightful comments and suggestions.

513

a movement by individual citizens, as well as neighborhood, community, and client groups, to gain greater control over the quality and amount of government services through direct activity in their design and especially their implementation. Yet the growth of this form is not solely a result of citizen impetus, for government agencies have demonstrated increasing interest. As budget cutbacks, coupled with mounting service demands, have pressed administrators at all levels to stretch resources, the possibility of using citizens as coproducers has emerged as an attractive option to build capacity and to reduce reliance on government (DeHoog, 1984). While citizens have always had a role in the service process, the coproduction approach is novel in conceiving of their participation as a systematic delivery mechanism.

This chapter focuses on the management of relationships with clients through the coproduction of services. It first elucidates the coproduction model of the agency-client relationship and differentiates it from the traditional model. The sections that follow elaborate the advantages of coproduction and treat difficulties in implementation. The chapter concludes with a discussion of strategies for increasing the application and effectiveness of coproduction of services.

The Coproduction Model

Sharp (1980) presents a cogent description of differences between the coproduction model and the traditional or dominant model of government service provision. In the dominant model, citizen participation consists of demanding, consuming, and evaluating services. As Rourke (1984) points out, public agencies may also mobilize clientele in the political process to support new or existing programs. Government officials are then held accountable for adequate performance in the delivery of services. To the degree that citizens participate in service production, their involvement is only incidental to the final result.

The coproduction model diverges significantly from the traditional conceptualization of the agency-clientele relationship. The primary point of departure is the blurring of the basic distinction between government service providers and citizen service consumers. From the standpoint of coproduction, government officials and citizens are jointly responsible for the design and implementation of services, and the activities of both affect the quality and scope of the services ultimately produced (hence, the appellation of the model). As Sharp (1980, p. 111) explains, "Here, the assumption is not that government officials perform *for* citizens, and therefore bear total responsibility for productivity improvements or the lack thereof; rather, the emphasis is upon service delivery as a joint venture, involving both citizens and government agents" (emphasis in original).

Several implications derive from the coproduction perspective. First, clients should be viewed not as passive recipients of services, but as potential contributors. The model encourages public officials to work with them to develop their capacities as coproducers (Sharp, 1980). Second, as opposed to traditional forms of citizen participation, which center on the input side of the service process (that is, on policy formulation and legitimation activities), coproduction is concerned principally with the output, or delivery, side. Although participation is valued throughout the service process, the model emphasizes client involvement in the creation and implementation stages. Third, for coproduction to be a viable option for service delivery, adversarial relationships between citizens and government agencies must give way to cooperation. Without this foundation, prospects for successful application of the model seem dim.

Thomas (1986) identifies a final distinction. In the dominant model, citizen participation is a political recourse aimed at influencing policy decisions; in the coproduction model, in contrast, it is a critical aspect of the administrative process. When services are coproduced, the involvement of clients becomes largely a management issue (and challenge) of eliciting and supporting their contributions to service delivery and integrating them with the efforts of regular personnel. Participation, thus, centers on service bureaucracies, rather than on elected officials. In Cincinnati, Thomas found that as mechanisms for community involvement took hold, neighborhood contacts gradually shifted from elected city council members and their meetings to appointed city administrators and municipal departments. The quality of these interactions also evinced movement away from traditional avenues of political redress, such as petitioning city hall, toward increased negotiation and cooperation with the municipal bureaucracy.

Citizen-agency collaboration in the production of services occurs at all levels of government. Most prevalent are the activities of neighborhood associations and community groups, which assist city governments in providing a variety of services, including public safety, fire protection, refuse collection, and area beautification. The Council of State Governments reports that by 1983, thirty-two states had organized offices to make greater use of citizens in service delivery, and forty-two states had established task forces to promote private sector initiatives in meeting community needs (Millard, 1983). At the federal level, the Department of Housing and Urban Development (HUD) and the Neighborhood Reinvestment Corporation underwrite several programs that depend on residents to rehabilitate, convert, and increase the stock of low-income housing and to manage multiple units (Bratt, 1987). Federal agencies also call on citizens to inform them of problems in the field. For example, Plant and Thompson (1986, p. 155) document how the Equal Employment Opportunity Commission (EEOC) relies on citizen "beneficiaries . . . as untrained inspectors who alert the agency to potential violations." Moreover, the EEOC does not undertake all resulting litigation but instead provides incentives to the private bar to become involved as coproducers of enforcement.

While the coproduction literature has devoted greatest attention to client self-help activities that augment those of the service bureaucracy, the model also embraces programs in which citizens work directly for government agencies as volunteers. A 1982 survey of the service-delivery practices of cities and counties found high levels of volunteer utilization in the social and human services. A minimum of 15 percent of the local governments reported using volunteers in cultural and arts programs (32 percent), museum operations (21 percent), recreation services (20 percent), programs for the elderly (18 percent), fire prevention and suppression (18 percent), emergency medical services (16 percent), and ambulance service (15 percent) (Valente and Manchester, 1984). Many of these efforts derive from statewide volunteer programs, which also include legal aid, public libraries, state tourism, and counseling for youthful offenders. The ACTION agency is responsible for promoting citizen volunteerism at the federal level. It houses a number of programs—for example, Volunteers in Service to America (VISTA), citizen participation and volunteer demonstration programs, and older American volunteer programs, such as the Retired Senior Volunteer Program (RSVP). Other volunteer programs are independent of ACTION. For example, since 1964, the U.S. Small Business Administration has used members of the business community to provide individual counseling and group training to aspiring and established entrepreneurs (Brudney, 1986).

Although several researchers have elaborated definitions of the coproduction concept (Ferris, 1984; Brudney and England, 1983; Warren, Harlow, and Rosentraub, 1983; Parks and others, 1981), none has gained universal acceptance. Nevertheless, scholars in the field would probably agree that coproduction is predicated on the active involvement of citizens or clients in the creation and delivery of public services, that this process is endemic to the provision of many services, and that it has been largely overlooked. The coproduction model enlarges the notion of citizen participation to encompass service production and emphasizes the cooperative possibilities of the client-agency relationship. The following section elaborates important benefits of this approach.

Advantages of Coproduction

Public agencies can realize four major benefits from coproduction: expansion of services, greater cost efficiency, promotion of citizenship, and increased governmental responsiveness to community needs and preferences.

Expanding Services. One of the chief advantages of coproduction is its potential to extend the scope of services. As a Virginia state senator commented on the establishment of a state office for citizen volunteerism, "We're not talking about saving money—we're talking about providing services with money we do not have" (quoted in Millard, 1983, p. 263). The basic argument is that the addition of citizens' inputs to those of government agencies increases the resources devoted to producing services and, thus, the level of service delivery that can be attained (Percy, 1984).

Most of the evidence on this point comes from the area of public safety and security, which has been the subject of the bulk of empirical research on coproduction. Scholars conclude that neighborhood associations, individual residents, and citizen volunteers extend conventional law enforcement services through such activities as neighborhood watches, citizen patrols, target hardening (for example, installation of door locks), and donations of labor to police departments (Sundeen and Siegel, 1986; Warren, Rosentraub, and Harlow, 1984). The situation is similar in other service domains. Citizens enhance educational services by helping to maintain school facilities, acting as aides in the classroom, and tutoring students. In the area of sanitation, neighborhood associations conduct cleanup campaigns and monitor local conditions.

In these core services, citizen participation supplements existing government capability. In other areas, citizens and clients produce services that lie beyond the reach of public resources. In Arvada, Colorado, for example, an army of over four hundred volunteers provides services that "might not be possible otherwise," according to the city director of human resources (Martin, 1982, p. 13); half this number work in the city center for the arts and humanities, a "department that could not have functioned without its volunteer staff." In the absence of participation by client groups, community organizations, and citizen volunteers in the production process, many communities would be hard pressed to maintain cultural, recreational, emergency medical, and library services.

Cost Efficiency. A second benefit of coproduction is its potential to achieve greater cost efficiencies in the delivery of services. While citizen coproducers are not a free resource to be used indiscriminately by government bureaucracies, application of the model typically offers a less expensive method to raise service outputs than conventional alternatives, such as expenditures for new technology or additional paid personnel.

The gains in productive capability that public agencies may realize as a result of coproduction seem well worth the monetary investment. Although economic data are lacking on the costs of all types of coproduction, examination of government volunteer programs gives some indication of this relationship. Research on the use of volunteers in public safety (Sundeen and Siegel, 1986), assistance to small businesses (Brudney, 1986), and general city services (Martin, 1982) establishes that these efforts are highly cost efficient. The economic valuation of the labor donated is typically several times greater than the total program costs for training, support, supervision, and the like.

While such results are often proffered as cost savings, the claim is misleading. The government organizations involved have not employed and would not employ this labor at its economically valued rate. Instead, this valuation represents the costs avoided by government agencies through the use of citizen coproducers in lieu of other methods to raise service outputs.

Actual cost savings depend on the substitution of citizen coproducers for government service agents. Because this substitution is limited by the technical nature of many services and by political considerations (such as opposition from public employees' unions), "it would seem that the greatest advantage of coproduction is not in using citizens to replace paid personnel, but rather in using citizens to assist service workers" (Percy, 1984, p. 437).

Promoting Citizenship. In addition to its potential economic benefits, coproduction fulfills classic democratic functions. The model helps to induce responsibility on the part of public officials, to communicate citizens' preferences, and to educate the citizenry (Wilson, 1981). Coproduction programs increase citizens' involvement in government, facilitate mutual understanding between participants and service agents, and foster a partnership orientation to public problems (Sharp, 1980). Levine (1984) links these characteristics to confidence in government, arguing that the approach encourages the restoration of trust in and support for public institutions. In sum, as Redburn and Cho (1984, p. 160) argue, by encouraging citizen participation in policy development and by generating cooperation and shared commitments in the community, coproduction "can be highly valuable . . . as a means of promoting citizenship."

Official Responsiveness. In several ways, coproduction can increase government's responsiveness to citizens' demands and preferences. First, through communication and contact with the individuals and groups engaged in coproduction, public officials have greater opportunity to learn firsthand about community needs, expectations, and evaluations of services. Second, citizen coproducers can assume the more mundane tasks of regular service workers, thus allowing them to devote more time, resources, and expertise to areas or cases that, in the absence of coproduction, would not receive sufficient attention. Such an arrangement can improve not only the responsiveness but also the effectiveness of services. Last, by contributing their labor to the production of certain services, citizens identify domains where greater quantity or quality is desired. Thus, coproduction provides relatively specific information to government officials regarding individuals' preferences for services and allows both parties to adjust the supply (Ferris, 1984).

Implementing Coproduction

The coproduction model offers an impressive array of benefits. Like other approaches to service delivery, however, it also encounters difficulties. In the implementation of coproduction programs, government officials and citizens will confront obstacles in five main areas: equity of service distributions, resistance from public employees, funding of coproduction, limitations on the applicability of the model, and potential for co-optation of citizens' interests.

Service Equity. The advantages to government agencies and clients yielded by coproduction stem from the increased participation of citizens fundamental to the model. If coproduction improves the level or the cost efficiency of services, for example, the reason is that some or all of the costs of production have been shifted to citizens (Brudney, 1985). Although these burdens are most often nonmonetary, the time, effort, and organizational skills necessary for involvement in service implementation nevertheless impose actual costs on citizens and client groups. The capacity to undertake these investments is not uniformly distributed but falls more heavily on lower socioeconomic neighborhoods and groups (Warren, Rosentraub, and Harlow, 1984). To the extent that these individuals lack the income, time, and skills to participate in coproduction programs, application of the model can exacerbate differences in quantity and quality of service, to their detriment.

Public Employees' Resistance. Public agencies have not always welcomed the participation of citizens in decision making. The reasons are not hard to find. Citizens' involvement may lengthen and complicate an already complex policy process, disrupt established organizational procedures and routines, and require novel restructuring of traditional, hierarchical government agencies. Public employees may perceive an increased role for citizens as a threat to their own authority and expertise, and they may resent working with nonprofessionals who lack similar background, training, and values. Coproduction can heighten these apprehensions by implicitly raising the prospect of citizens' substituting for paid personnel in some aspects of service delivery.

A survey of the attitudes of one group of public employees—police officers—toward citizen participation in two Texas cities (Fort Worth and Sherman) lends credence to possible antagonisms. Rosentraub and Warren (1987) found that these personnel most strongly supported activities normally expected as part of the responsibilities of citizenship (for example, reporting suspicious behavior), as well as those that did not involve collaboration with police (for example, installing a burglar alarm). They were far less amenable to coproductive activities based on direct work with citizens, such as neighborhood patrols. Rosentraub and Warren (1987, p. 88) conclude that the results offer a "somber view" for developing programs to involve citizens in service production: "For any of the more active or substantive forms of participation, a great deal of work will be required to avoid conflicts and misunderstandings."

Funding Coproduction. Just as coproductive activities are not without costs to citizens, they are also not free for service bureaucracies. Evidence from several studies suggests that the level of citizen participation achieved in service delivery is contingent on governmental support for coproduction programs. In an extension of the research on Fort Worth and Sherman, for example, Rosentraub, Warren, and Harlow (1983) found that the percentage of citizens who engraved their valuables with identification markings, and who attended meetings between community groups and the police, fell from 30 percent and 16 percent, respectively, to less than 1 percent in both instances, when the cities withdrew sponsorship of the programs. Similarly, a study of health planning agencies documented that, regardless of the size of their budgets and professional staffs, organizations that committed greater resources to consumer participation attained higher levels (Checkoway, O'Rourke, and Bull, 1984). Citizen involvement increased with the share of the budget allocated to these activities and with the proportion of staff members who had this function as a primary responsibility.

Thomas's (1986) examination of neighborhood organizations in Cincinnati underscores these findings. Coproduction proved a successful approach to the provision of recreational services only when the city granted a substantial subsidy to neighborhood community councils to operate facilities. When the subsidies proved insufficient in two neighborhoods, the recreation centers foundered. Thomas argues (p. 151), "More generally, years of public support of the community councils probably figure in *all* of their coproductive involvement" (emphasis in original). A newspaper series on New York's South Bronx makes a similar point regarding federal programs. According to a member of a community organization that had rehabilitated ten apartment buildings with federal mortgage guarantees, "Groups like ours can make a dent. But we're at a critical stage. We can take a dive if Congress does not come out with new programs to subsidize housing" (*Washington Post,* 1987, p. A8).

No guarantee exists, however, that governments coping with fiscal stress will make the necessary support available. At the local level, federal funding has been cut, and cities face other economic problems of their own. Attempts to divert money from traditional basic services to coproduction programs will further arouse the resentment of public employees' groups. Yet if support is not forthcoming, coproduction can degenerate into a retrenchment strategy to shift public responsibility for certain services to citizens, clients, or community groups, without adequate arrangements for service provision (Mattson, 1986; Brudney, 1985). Unilateral citizen action could be expected to fall far short of achieving the benefits attributed to the model.

Limitations to Applicability. Two sets of considerations appear to restrict the applicability of the coproduction model. First, communities differ in their capacity to coproduce services (Sundeen, 1985). The degree of social interaction, cohesion, and organization in a neighborhood or a city affects the capability of residents to engage in collective activities to enhance services (see Percy, 1984).

Second, the service areas open to citizen participation are restricted by the technical expertise that clients can bring to the production process. For example, none of the cities and counties polled in a survey of service delivery practices used citizens in such areas as street repair, code inspection and enforcement, or vehicle management and maintenance (Valente and Manchester, 1984). Ahlbrandt and Sumka (1983) analyzed grant applications from ninety-four cities. The applications were generated by a HUD demonstration project intended to encourage cities to enter into service partnerships with community-based organizations. In general, the cities used the organizations to provide peripheral or supplementary services, rather than using them to provide essential services. While public employees' resistance may be partly responsible for these limitations, they occur primarily because citizens lack professional expertise that they are both willing and able to devote to service production. In addition, some argue, volunteers may jeopardize the continuity of basic services (Thomas, 1986). Although training for coproducers could improve these conditions, the costs of significant training would detract from the economic benefits of the model.

Possible Co-optation. A final difficulty in the implementation of coproduction is the potential for co-optation of citizens' interests. Gittell's (1980) research on citizen groups' participation in education services in Atlanta, Boston, and Los Angeles offers the most prominent example. Her analysis suggests that government support of coproduction programs may ultimately distract community groups and organizations from adopting a policy focus. These groups generally responded to an agenda set by school professionals, narrowing their efforts from policy influence to service provision. To meet ongoing operational needs, the organizations grew preoccupied with funding and staffing, to the detriment of the policy and advocacy functions that formed their original purposes.

Government agencies may also use citizen participation instrumentally—for instance, to deflect blame for service problems, or to delegate responsibility for service delivery on the basis of employees' preferences or convenience (Brudney, 1985). A study of Georgia planning agencies found that citizens were given a strong role in decision making only when agencies stood to benefit from their participation (MacNair, Caldwell, and Pollane, 1983). Such practices jeopardize the goals of citizenship, service effectiveness, and efficiency envisioned by the model.

Increasing Application and Effectiveness

What steps can be taken to increase the application of coproduction while minimizing these problems in implementation? First, although scholars agree on the threat to distributional equity arising from coproduction—these programs may disproportionately reward individuals and groups in a better position to participate in them, such as whites and those with higher education and income—several possible remedies exist. These include the selective application of economic and other incentives to groups or neighborhoods judged high in need, the allocation of additional service resources and access to these areas, and the employment of neighborhood organizers (Brudney, 1984). Organizational restructuring of government agencies toward greater decentralization and outreach to communities may also prove effective (Clary, 1985; Percy, 1984). Because citizens' coproductive efforts vary with the level of government facilitation and support, these measures are important to avoiding an unduly regressive system of benefit distribution.

A second obstacle to successful implementation of coproduction is possible resistance from public employees' unions and line personnel. Despite the intentions of proponents—that citizen coproducers supplement, rather than replace, regular employees—the adversarial history of community involvement and the apprehensions aroused by conditions of fiscal stress make opposition a likely scenario. Perhaps the most effective approach here is educational programs for public administrators. In order to discourage manipulation of citizens' input, these programs should inculcate the value and legitimacy of participation. Equally important, they should stress the benefits that can accrue to employees. While the point is little discussed, application of the model can make the jobs of public employees more satisfying and stimulating—for example, by generating a pool of citizen labor with the potential to assume the mundane aspects of service delivery and expand governmental productivity. Moreover, participating groups and organizations can act as powerful allies in budget and other governmental processes essential to the welfare of an agency.

Thomas (1986, p. 151) calls public funding "the most serious limitation on coproduction." The research already reviewed here offers a cogent reminder to public managers that coproduction is not costless and that government support is essential to stimulate and sustain it. In some cases, the message will be heeded; in others, fiscal austerity will render funding problematic. This dilemma may lead to hard choices for officials, but the portents are not entirely negative. One of the most promising is the emergence of an applied literature on alternative methods for service production that urges practitioners to consider a range of options (for example, see Valente and Manchester, 1984). As a result, such novel forms as agreements with neighborhood organizations, use of volunteers, and self-help efforts, barely acknowledged only a decade ago, receive a greater hearing. In addition, privatization, which could displace government workers through contracting or the sale of public assets, engenders controversy that may actually work to the benefit of coproduction advocates: If fiscal stringency continues to force changes in the way services are provided, employees' groups presumably will find coproduction preferable to privatization. Nevertheless, for financially strapped governments, no pat answers exist.

Government agencies must confront additional limitations to coproduction. The prospects for successful implementation may indeed be strongest in socially cohesive communities, but public administrators should be prepared to undertake different types of activities to meet local conditions. Sundeen (1985) advises administrators to adopt a community development focus when the capacity for collective or individual participation in coproduction is most limited, a facilitator role in communities that have potential coproducers who require technical or other assistance, and a broker orientation when substantial citizen experience, motivation, and resources combine. Some evidence also suggests that changes in political structure—for example, toward formal representation of neighborhoods in city government—can promote coproduction across a variety of local circumstances (see Thomas, 1986).

The relatively low level of expertise that citizens can be expected to bring to the delivery of services presents a further restriction on coproduction. Nevertheless, while community-based groups and organizations lack the capacity to supplant government as direct providers of core services, this factor does not consign coproduction to nonessential service domains. On the contrary, instances of coproductive arrangements appear in the five major service areas identified by Valente and Manchester (1984) in a 1982 survey of cities and counties. Such arrangements were operating in public works and transportation, public safety, health and human services, parks and recreation, and support functions. Coproduction may be limited primarily to low-skilled contributions from citizens, but these are necessary and important, in peripheral as well as in core services.

A final concern is that public support of coproducing groups and organizations may create a dependence on government that will compromise the groups' autonomy to act as critics of existing policies and as proponents of new ones. Given the importance of funding to coproduction, some support must be provided; the alternative would be weaker organizations even less capable of assuming policy and advocacy functions, and perhaps even the demise of some organizations. Several funding strategies seem feasible for balancing support with autonomy. These include competitive programs to earn grant income and contractual arrangements for providing certain services. A coproducing group should be required to demonstrate some degree of organizational integrity—for example, through provisions to submit an application for public funding and to match at least a portion of the amount received.

Summary

Coproduction is the active participation of citizens and clients in the delivery of government services. The coproduction model places new demands on public administrators: to develop citizens' potential for contributing to services, to coordinate their inputs with those of regular personnel, and to resolve possible conflicts between employees and participants. In return, coproduction offers substantial advantages: expansion of services, increased cost efficiency, promotion of citizenship, and greater governmental responsiveness.

To take full advantage of these benefits, policymakers need to address the problems that may arise during implementation. Education programs will probably prove necessary, to overcome the resistance of public employees' unions and line personnel. Administrators may need to experiment with different role sets to stimulate and sustain the coproductive process. The possibility of service inequities resulting from the model calls for redistributive strategies. As in most service approaches, funding plays a crucial role, but total dependence on government should be avoided, to allow coproducing groups and organizations a measure of autonomy. Resolution of these difficulties is all the more important, so that the productive capacities of citizens and clients can be united with the efforts of government agencies in the delivery of services.

References

Ahlbrandt, R. S., and Sumka, H. J. "Neighborhood Organizations and the Coproduction of Public Services." *Journal of Urban Affairs,* 1983, *5* (3), 211-220.

Bratt, R. G. "The Role of Citizen-Initiated Programs in the Formulation of National Housing Policies." In J. Desario and S. Langton (eds.), *Citizen Participation in Public Decision Making.* New York: Greenwood, 1987.

Brudney, J. L. "Local Coproduction of Services and the Analysis of Municipal Productivity." *Urban Affairs Quarterly,* 1984, *19* (4), 465-484.

Brudney, J. L. "Coproduction: Issues in Implementation." *Administration & Society,* 1985, *17* (3), 243-256.

Brudney, J. L. "The SBA and SCORE: Coproducing Management Assistance Services." *Public Productivity Review,* 1986, *40,* 57-67.

Brudney, J. L., and England, R. E. "Toward a Definition of the Coproduction Concept." *Public Administration Review,* 1983, *43* (1), 59-65.

Checkoway, B., O'Rourke, T. W., and Bull, D. "Correlates of Consumer Participation in Health Planning Agencies: Findings and Implications from a National Survey." *Policy Studies Review,* 1984, *3* (2), 296-310.

Clary, B. B. "Designing Urban Bureaucracies for Coproduction." *State and Local Government Review,* 1985, *17* (3), 265-272.

DeHoog, R. H. "Theoretical Perspectives on Contracting Out for Services: Implementation Problems and Possibilities of Privatizing Public Services." In G. C. Edwards III (ed.), *Public Policy Implementation.* Greenwich, Conn.: JAI Press, 1984.

Ferris, J. M. "Coprovision: Citizen Time and Money Donations in Public Service Provision." *Public Administration Review,* 1984, *44* (4), 324-333.

Gittell, M. *Limits to Citizen Participation: The Decline of Community Organizations.* Newbury Park, Calif.: Sage, 1980.

Herman, R. D., and Peroff, N. C. "Public Management and the Third Sector: Neighborhood Organizations and Citizens Groups." In W. B. Eddy (ed.), *Handbook of Organization Management.* New York: Marcel Dekker, 1983.

Levine, C. H. "Citizenship and Service Delivery: The Promise of Coproduction." *Public Administration Review,* 1984, *44,* 178–189.

MacNair, R. H., Caldwell, R., and Pollane, L. "Citizen Participants in Public Bureaucracies: Foul-Weather Friends." *Administration & Society,* 1983, *14* (1), 507–524.

Martin, S. "The Arvada Volunteer Story." *Public Management,* 1982, *64* (10), 13–14.

Mattson, G. A. "The Promise of Citizen Coproduction: Some Persistent Issues." *Public Productivity Review,* 1986, *40,* 51–56.

Millard, S. "Voluntary Action and the States: The Other Alternative." *National Civic Review,* 1983, *72* (5), 262–269.

Parks, R. B., and others. "Consumers as Coproducers of Public Services: Some Economic and Institutional Considerations." *Policy Studies Review,* 1981, *9* (7), 1001–1011.

Percy, S. L. "Citizen Participation in the Coproduction of Urban Services." *Urban Affairs Quarterly,* 1984, *19* (4), 431–446.

Plant, J., and Thompson, F. J. "Deregulation, the Bureaucracy, and Employment Discrimination: The Case of the EEOC." In M. W. Combs and J. Gruhl (eds.), *Affirmative Action: Theory, Analysis, and Prospects.* London: McFarland, 1986.

Redburn, F. S., and Cho, Y. H. "Government's Responsibility for Citizenship and the Quality of Community Life." *Public Administration Review,* 1984, *44,* 158–161.

Rosentraub, M. S., and Warren, R. "Citizen Participation in the Production of Urban Services." *Public Productivity Review,* 1987, *41,* 75–89.

Rosentraub, M. S., Warren, R., and Harlow, K. S. *Service Providers, Citizens, and the Production of Urban Services: The Case of Police Officers and Coproduction.* Arlington: Institute of Urban Studies, University of Texas, 1983.

Rourke, F. E. *Bureaucracy, Politics, and Public Policy.* (3rd ed.) Boston: Little, Brown, 1984.

Sharp, E. B. "Toward a New Understanding of Urban Services and Citizen Participation: The Coproduction Concept." *Midwest Review of Public Administration,* 1980, *14* (2), 105–118.

Sundeen, R. A. "Coproduction and Communities: Implications for Local Administrators." *Administration & Society,* 1985, *16* (4), 387–402.

Sundeen, R. A., and Siegel, G. B. "The Uses of Volunteers by Police." *Journal of Police Science and Administration,* 1986, *14* (1), 49–61.

Thomas, J. C. *Between Citizen and City: Neighborhood Organizations and Urban Politics in Cincinnati.* Lawrence: University Press of Kansas, 1986.

Valente, C. F., and Manchester, L. D. *Rethinking Local Services: Examining Alternative Delivery Approaches.* Management Information Service Special Report, no. 12. Washington, D.C.: International City Management Association, 1984.

Warren, R., Harlow, K. S., and Rosentraub, M. S. "Citizen Participation in the Production of Services: Methodological and Policy Issues in Coproduction Research.'' *Southwestern Review of Management and Economics,* 1983, *2* (3), 41–55.

Warren, R., Rosentraub, M. S., and Harlow, K. S. ''Coproduction, Equity, and the Distribution of Safety.'' *Urban Affairs Quarterly,* 1984, *19* (4), 447–464.

Washington Post, Aug. 25, 1987, p. A8.

Wilson, R. K. ''Citizen Coproduction as a Mode of Participation: Conjectures and Models.'' *Journal of Urban Affairs,* 1981, *3* (4), 37–49.

37

Kenneth L. Kraemer

Managing Information Systems

The growing use of computerized information systems at all levels of government suggests that managing information systems should be an important topic for senior management. There are two factors that compel management attention to information systems. The first is the realization of the return on their investment; the second is the realization of the potential of information systems as a strategic resource. Despite the sizable investment in these systems and their strategic importance, however, many senior managers still avoid taking responsibility for computerized information systems, preferring to delegate responsibility to others. This chapter argues that all senior managers must take responsibility for managing information systems, and that some will want to take greater responsibility than others, depending on the strategic importance of these systems to the government. Moreover, it spells out various roles that senior managers can fulfill, as well as the contingencies that propel them toward these roles.

Four major trends in the government's use of computerized information systems are changing the way in which we think about the management of such systems. First is the widespread use of computing as a result of price/performance increases in the last twenty years. Departmental computing installations have sprung up in most government agencies, as minicomputers have helped to spread computing equipment, staff experts, and user experience. End-user computing has become commonplace with the advent of microcomputers. Today, most government professionals have microcomputers on their desks that are ten times more powerful and one hundred times less expensive than the mainframe computers of the late 1960s. This price/performance change has led to tremendous growth in the number of computers, in the number of computer users, and in the complexity of managing computer technology in government.

The second trend is the merging of information technologies. In the past, managing information systems was largely a matter of managing computer technology; but, since the 1980s, it has changed dramatically to include telecommunications and office automation as well. These technologies are not merely extensions of computer knowledge and expertise. They are dramatically different and bring whole new issues for the management of technology, such as dealing with technologies at different stages of development, merging the technologies and their related technical staffs, determining who should be in charge of the consolidated enterprise, and setting standards to achieve compatibility and connectivity among the technologies.

The third trend is the dramatic growth of government data banks. As government automation has continued apace in the interest of efficiency and economy, so has the accumulation of data about taxpayers, welfare recipients, veterans, students, and the unemployed. More important than the accumulation of data is the growing tendency to merge information in government data banks. The merging of information is most dramatic at the federal level, where files about a single individual can be merged from several different agencies, such as the Internal Revenue Service, Health and Human Services, and the Department of Labor. Moreover, the federal government is increasingly requiring state and local governments to match tax and welfare records in eligibility tests for social welfare benefits. These developments raise serious unresolved issues about the trade-off between the government's need to know and the individual's right to privacy.

The fourth trend is the rise of national information systems. In the past, most information systems were limited to the boundaries of a single agency or level of government. Beginning in the 1960s, however, the Federal Bureau of Investigation and the Law Enforcement Assistance Administration created the first national information system, linking law enforcement agencies at the federal, state, and local levels. Similar systems have been proposed for social services, employment, and taxation, and they raise the prospect that federal agencies will use these information systems to promulgate federal standards and to check on conformance with these standards, thereby interjecting the federal government into decisions that were previously state and local matters (Laudon, 1986).

Taken together, these four trends are significantly changing the meaning of effective practice in at least three ways. First, it is no longer sufficient to manage only computing. Computing must be integrated with the information technologies of telecommunications and office automation. Second, it is no longer sufficient to manage only the technology. The integration of computers with telecommunications and office automation requires managing three different kinds of technical staffs, those in data processing, telecommunications, and office automation. The challenge is to manage these staffs and to manage the changing relationships among these staffs, senior management, and department management. Third, it is no longer sufficient to be concerned only with technical efficiency in the management of information technology. The challenge is to balance technical with political considerations, efficiency with privacy, and power distribution with power reinforcement. How these challenges can be met is unclear. No established body of research and experience addresses these situations. There is knowledge from both research and experience, however, that can be brought to bear on managing information systems. This chapter seeks to organize that knowledge and to draw out its implications for improving management practice in public administration.

Findings About Effective Practice

Research and experience over the last several decades suggest nine general findings about the effective management of information systems (Kraemer and King, 1986). Some of these findings primarily relate to the technology and to arrangements for making it, whereas others are primarily behavioral and involve human and institutional relationships.

1. Effective practice requires new perspectives.
2. Information technologies require integration.
3. Policy and organization arrangements require integration to achieve technology integration.
4. Technical staffs require integration to reinforce technology and policy integration.
5. Advanced technologies increase the successful use of computing.
6. Managing relationships among senior management, users, and data-processing staff requires the definition of roles and responsibilities.
7. The sociotechnical interface is critical to effective computer use.
8. The growing computerization in government is not a threat to fundamental relationships among branches and levels of government.
9. The computer's threat to privacy needs monitoring, but the technology's greatest threat is its seductiveness.

New Perspectives. Until the mid 1970s, most approaches to effective practice with respect to computing centered on the rational management perspective in one form or another. Nevertheless, the work of various scholars (Laudon, 1974; Westin, 1971) showed rational management perspectives to be incomplete and brought political perspectives on computing to the forefront. More recent work has brought in the contingency perspective as an alternative to solely rational or political thinking about effective practice (Danziger, Dutton, Kling, and Kraemer, 1982; Dutton and Kraemer, 1977). The newer contingency perspectives have grown out of recent empirical research, which attempts to incorporate both rational and political perspectives. One recent theory—reinforcement politics—focuses on existing computing arrangements. Another, which focuses on states of computing management, considers changes in organizational computing.

Reinforcement politics argues that rational or political perspectives may be correct, depending on the character of the organization. Thus, decisions regarding computers may be controlled by a rational-managerial elite, a technocratic elite, or a pluralistic array of participants. Decision-making power over computing varies from setting to setting, with the dominance of particular groups contingent on the local political system and its specific configuration of dominant values, interests, and actors. Those who control the decision processes will operate to promote their own interests, and the resulting decisions will serve to enhance the position of those who represent the dominant political coalition. Thus, technological decisions will reinforce the power and influence of those actors and groups who already exercise substantial control over the authority structure and resources of the organization (Danziger, Dutton, Kling, and Kraemer, 1982).

Reinforcement politics further argues that the dominant political coalition need not directly control technological decisions. Rather, those groups that do directly control the technology will attempt to anticipate the values and interests of the dominant coalition and to serve it as a means of securing its cooperation and support (Dutton and Kraemer, 1977, 1978).

The theory of states of computing management is a change-oriented perspective, which is empirically grounded in the reinforcement politics perspective and posits that computing evolves directly and indirectly as a result of the actions of three types of management—senior management, department management, and information system (IS) management. The particular trajectory of computing in an organization is a function of which of these managements is in control of computing, and of whose interests are served by computing. In simplest terms, the theory defines three "pure" states of computing—service, control, and skill—and a "mix" state (Kraemer, King, Dunkle, and Lane, 1989).

In the *skill* state, IS management controls computerization and applies computing resources to technical interests. In the *service* state, departmental management controls computing, and the operational interests of these departments are served. In the *control* state, senior management controls computerization, and its broad managerial interests are served. The *mix* state exists in the absence of any of the three "pure" states. That is, the mix state encompasses any set of conditions where the level of control and the level of interests served do not directly correspond. There is no consistent link between the control over means and the particular ends sought in the mix state.

The practical significance of this theory is that the state of computing management in an organization is independent of particular information technologies or their states of development. It focuses on management action, whether direct or indirect, as the controllable driver of computing change, and it permits the identification of the current state of computing in an organization, as well as the prediction of the future trajectory of computing, given that state. Moreover, it shows how the trajectory of computing is governed by management action. This knowledge enables managers who wish to change the trajectory of computing in their organizations to gain insight into changing their behavior and thereby changing the trajectory.

Integration. Computing, telecommunications, and office automation grew up separately in organizations. When computing was introduced, in the 1950s, it was initially provided to finance or comptroller departments and eventually spread to other departments. Office automation was introduced in typing pools, and the pool concept has characterized its development until very recently. When word processors came along, in the 1970s, they were seen as extensions of typewriters, and they were provided in pooled arrangements, through general services or administrative services departments. In many instances, this pooled arrangement has persisted, even with the newest shared word processing–office automation systems. Until the 1980s, telecommunications was primarily a responsibility of the private phone companies. Most organizations had only one or a few people to oversee relations with the phone companies. With deregulation of the telephone industry, and its fragmenting effects on services and equipment, government agencies have had to take responsibility for their own telecommunications facilities and services, in order to reduce costs, provide integrated service, and simplify problems for users.

It has now become clear that the use and evolution of these technologies can no longer be allowed to proceed independently in organizations. Computing applications increasingly involve on-line, real-time communications capabilities among government offices within and across regions of the country. Office automation users have discovered the limitations of special-purpose word processors, whether they are shared or stand alone, and these users want general-purpose computing capabilities, with access to mainframe resources, shared data bases, and outside sources. Local telephone operations need data communications to be integrated with voice communications, in order to help them justify the costs and capabilities of new communications systems. All these technologies require integrated planning, management, and control for their physical integration.

Policy and Organizational Integration. As the need for integration of the technology has become apparent, so has the need to integrate the islands of technology within organizations. The physical integration of information technologies does not require consolidation of the various islands into a single organization. Nevertheless, it is no longer sufficient, from an organization-wide perspective, to simply allow each user group to make its own computing arrangements, because integration requires standardization and compatibility, and because the costs of integration require a broad base of use for economic feasibility. Thus, policy decisions must be made centrally, although implementation can be determined locally. User groups may operate their own computing facilities, but it has now become apparent that they must be brought under consolidated policy control, with respect both to technical and to managerial matters.

Studies of the centralization-decentralization issue have indicated that this remains the thorniest policy issue of computing, but they have also shown that the centralization of policy control is the critical component of the centralization-decentralization issue—that is, whether the physical location of computers, staff, or functions is centralized or decentralized is less important than whether policy control is centralized (King, 1983).

On balance, the studies have also indicated that centralization of computing is cheaper than decentralization, although there are costs of user responsiveness associated with the more distant and bureaucratic organization that usually results from giving anyone a monopoly over computing services. These studies also show, however, that the dollar and control costs of decentralization can easily outweigh the benefits of greater user responsiveness (Kraemer and King, 1981; King, 1983).

Integration of Technical Staffs. As information technologies become integrated within organizations, so will the technical staffs that plan, manage, and operate these technologies. Any of the three functions of data processing, office automation, and telecommunications may be host to the others. Most often, however, the technical staffs for office automation and telecommunications will be integrated with the data-processing function, rather than vice versa. This trend is apparent in both government and industry, and it is apparent even in organizations where the telecommunications budget far outstrips the data-processing budget.

The reason for the trend is straightforward: Data-processing staffs usually have some experience and competence in these other areas and therefore can assimilate them. Many data-processing units have had to support multisite installations requiring computer-to-computer communications. Most of the computer applications developed over the last ten years (or longer) have involved telecommunications components, in order to allow computer access from remote sites and field offices. In the process, data processing has had to deal with telephone companies' rate structures and has had to resolve such technical issues as getting terminals to communicate with computers over telephone lines, which were initially designed to handle voice and, more recently, to handle both voice and data. Thus, data-processing management and staff already have familiarity with the kinds of technical, economic, and managerial issues involved in telecommunications.

Similarly, many data-processing staffs have considerable familiarity with office automation. They have provided for communication between remote sites and learned how to handle the movement of words and data between sites. As word processing was developed for mainframes, they provided these capabilities throughout the organization and to remote sites through terminals. When stand-alone word processors were introduced, data-processing staffs frequently operated such centers or at least were among the first users. As electronic mail, shared word processing, and multifunction microcomputers have been introduced, they have been involved either as sole providers or as technical supports to other units. Thus, data-processing staffs have developed experience and competence with the technical, economic, and managerial issues involved in office automation.

Advanced Technologies. Empirical research shows that greater benefits from computing accrue to sites that use more advanced technology (Kraemer, Dutton, and Northrop, 1981). To some extent, this relationship is a function of their relatively greater experience, but it is clearly also a function of their keeping abreast of new technologies. This relationship is nicely illustrated by the microcomputers of the mid 1980s, which not only have greater capacity and reduced costs, compared to their mainframe predecessors, but are also easier to use and have more useful software available with them.

The research does not support slavish attempts to be at the leading edge of the technology's application. Most failures in computing come from failures in development of new applications or systems, rather than from failures in the equipment itself. Indeed, the low levels of computing development in some organizations can be directly attributed to one or more attempts to develop leading-edge computer applications. Such efforts are disastrous because they set back both the particular system and the entire development effort, demoralize users and data-processing staff, and create a crisis of confidence in data processing within the organization. Most organizations have experienced one such failure at some time or another, and they usually learn from it. Some organizations, however, seem prone to repeated failures because of overextension of their own and the technology's capabilities.

It is now clear that organizations are safest with mainstream technology that is available from well-established and reputable vendors, is used by similar organizations, and contains proved technical advances. For leading-edge technologies, it is best to experiment with small pilot applications in a limited sphere, in order to determine benefits, problems, and technical performance.

Definition of Roles and Responsibilities. Relationships between data-processing technology and users have always involved tension between data-processing dominance and user dominance. Because of microcomputers, the tension is greater today than perhaps ever before in the history of computing. The basic issue concerns who will control computing resources and priorities and, therefore, whose interests will be served by these resources. The issue is seldom framed that way, however. Usually it is framed in a more sanitary fashion, such as in terms of data processing's responsiveness to overall organizational interests versus its responsiveness to individual users' interests.

Users naturally want control over their own computing and want to develop their own computing resources and expertise. There are strong reasons for users to develop their own expertise. First, the backlog of development work in most data-processing organizations means that users frequently must wait several years for any major new system or system enhancement.

This backlog of development work, relative to staff resources, usually is large, on the order of two to three years. Second, as user organizations have developed more experience with computing, they have become more sophisticated, both in their understanding of their own needs and in their understanding of how those needs can be met by computing. In addition, user organizations are now employing people with considerable expertise both in computing and in their own functional specialties. They want to employ the technology both more broadly and more intensively, and they have at least some of the skills required to do so. Third, the protocols of dealing with a central computing system and of meeting organizationwide control standards can be very time-consuming, complex, and unnecessary. In contrast, a stand-alone system, purchased by a user organization and independent of the central system, can simplify work and permit less skilled staff to participate. It may require no major changes, particularly if one or more employees have had prior experience with the system.

There are also strong reasons for not allowing users to develop their own expertise and systems. First, user groups have a tendency to buy or develop systems tailored to fit their own very specific situations, when they could instead obtain more standard systems. This preference for tailored systems may lead to long-term maintenance problems and costs, as well as to inability to enhance the system. Second, with user development, there is often poor technology transfer between similar users, as well as failure to achieve leverage by sharing systems among similar parts of the organization or building one system on another. Third, when users develop their own systems, there is often poor documentation. This can create nightmares, both for the user organization and for data processing, when the person who developed the system and who is the sole source of expertise leaves an organization.

In summary, there are strong reasons for users to develop their own computing resources and expertise, but there are also strong reasons for controlling and channeling how users' expertise and computing resources are employed. How, then, can one sort out these issues and make decisions for a specific organization? The tension over control can be managed by establishing clear policies regarding users' domain, data processing's domain, and senior management's domain. The following guidelines stem more from experience than from research, but they are a useful starting point for discussions of relevant domains.

Broadly, the domain of data processing includes all policy decisions related to procurement, operation, and maintenance of the technology and its application. These include the following matters.

1. Identification of preferred hardware and software, and negotiation of volume contracts to gain vendor discounts.
2. Comparisons of internal development of systems versus outside purchases. This area requires procedures and standards for system evalua-

tion, project costing, project control, and system documentation. Procedures for mainframe and minicomputer systems should be distinguished from those for microcomputer systems.

3. Maintenance of an inventory of installed systems, systems in development, and planned systems (along with their priorities).

4. Development and maintenance of procedures related to mandatory telecommunication standards, standard classes of acquired equipment, standard languages for different classes of acquired equipment, standard application programs for different classes of acquired equipment, procedures for determining deviations from or exceptions to any of the foregoing standards, documentation procedures for different types of systems and an organizational data dictionary, and examination of systems developed by users or developed for them by outside vendors.

5. Identification and provision of staff career paths throughout the organization, including those in data processing, both in and among user departments.

6. Establishment of educational programs for end users.

7. Continuous review of applications to determine whether they should be redeveloped (adapted from McFarland and McKenney, 1983).

In their own domain, users should be assured that they will receive consistent, reliable, and useful services from data processing. Specifically, users should be permitted, at the very minimum, to do the following things.

1. Manage the user–data-processing interface to ensure that users' input is available and incorporated into decision making about computing. They should also participate in design and development teams, review system specifications before signoff, evaluate prototype systems, and participate in user advisory boards.

2. Evaluate the user staff resources needed to ensure satisfactory systems and services—for example, development of new systems, their operation once implemented, periodic training of staff in their use, and ongoing maintenance and enhancement.

3. Monitor the direct-service charges for data-processing services, the indirect costs of user staff resources for all systems, and the quantitative and qualitative benefits associated with systems, so that decision making about new systems and enhancements can be better informed.

4. Perform regular evaluations of data-processing services, including reliability and responsiveness of systems, security of data, suitability of applications, and responsiveness of data-processing staff (adapted from McFarland and McKenney, 1983).

At the minimum, senior management should play a significant role in ensuring that the foregoing policies are developed, that they are effectively implemented, and that they evolve appropriately over time. Senior management's domain may extend considerably beyond this minimum, however, depending on the role of information technology in the organization. This can be seen by examination of the "strategic grid," originally developed by Porter (1980) for thinking about strategic planning, but applied by McFarland and McKenney (1983) to information technology. It classifies the role of information technology in organizations as *production, support, turnaround,* or *strategic,* depending on the importance of current systems and future systems to the organization's performance. These four types are shown in Table 37.1.

Table 37.1. Roles of Information Systems in Organizations.

	Future Impact of Systems	
Low		**High**
Impact of Current Systems	Production	Turnaround
	Support	Strategic
High		

In the *production* role, information systems are not strategic; they are operational. They are concerned with efficient, timely production of services. Links between data processing and long-term organizational planning and strategy are not critical, but detailed operational planning, production scheduling, and capacity planning are absolutely critical.

In the *support* role, information systems are once again more operational than strategic. They are concerned with the support of operations, staff, and management but are not critical to any of these. Each can operate without critical dependence on data processing but may be assisted by information systems. Links between data processing and long-term planning and strategy are not critical, but responsiveness to ad hoc information requirements can be helpful. Senior management's involvement is also not critical.

In the *turnaround* role, information systems are not currently critical to organizational performance, but they are critical to organizational performance in the future. Information technology is a critical part of such major administrative reforms as reorganization, the introduction of new management systems, or services integration. Considerable planning is required for information technology, for how the technology will support the administrative reform, and for how the technology will be smoothly implemented. Considerable involvement by senior management is required.

In the *strategic* role, information systems are critical to the smooth functioning of the organization and to the achievement of organizational goals. They require strategic planning for information technology, close links between such planning and organizational strategic planning, and considerable involvement of senior management.

In summary, senior management's domain can be characterized by involvement that is either minimal or intense. In organizations where the role of information technology is that of production or support, it is not essential for there to be a close link between long-range planning and data processing or for senior management to be closely involved with data processing. It is sufficient if senior management ensures that policies for managing information technology are developed, implemented, and adapted to changing conditions. In organizations where the role of information technology is characterized as turnaround or strategic, it is critical that data-processing planning be closely tied to organizational planning and that senior management and top data-processing management be closely involved.

Sociotechnical Interface. There is clear evidence that the use of computer technology can enhance both the performance and the work environment of people in organizations (Danziger and Kraemer, 1986). Moreover, the characteristics of the technology, as well as of the users' relationships with the technology and the technologists, are critical determinants of the level of benefits derived from computing. Specifically, the research suggests five major conditions that seem to increase the contribution of computers and information systems to the work of end users.

1. The computer package is more decentralized, and so it is in the hands of the users. Decentralization increases both use of the technology and the benefits derived from its use.
2. The computing capacity is more developed, especially when it permits human-machine interaction. This finding, at the level of the end user, is consistent with the finding that cities with more advanced technology receive greater payoffs from its use. Moreover, it specifies desirable features of the technology, such as extensiveness, routinization, and resource support. The research shows that as more of these features are present, there are greater positive impacts on use, performance, and the work environment among end users.
3. Users have greater competency and experience with computing.
4. Computer experts are more responsive to the needs of users regarding the design and operation of computerized information systems.

5. Users routinely, rather than selectively, employ computers and information systems.

These findings have important implications for general managers. Managers can directly and indirectly influence the sociotechnical interface and end users' involvement with computing by controlling computer specialists and taking actions that enhance the computing competency of end users. There is much to be gained from firm managerial control of data-processing staff, so that their activities are highly responsive to the needs of end users for training, support, and applications whose design and use are explicitly tailored to serve their activities. Among the strategies to facilitate control, managers can oblige data-processing units to assign specific staff to user departments on a long-term basis, so that rich working relationships can develop and so that data-processing staff acquire greater sensitivity to the unique computing needs of particular user groups. In addition, managers can require, at regular intervals, systematic user evaluations of the quality of services they are receiving from the data-processing staff. Salary and status rewards for data-processing staff might be attached to such evaluations. Of equal importance are managerial actions to enhance the computing competency of end users. Organizational rewards, both material and symbolic, can be directed to individuals for levels of use, models of use, efficiency of use, and training and involvement. The desired level and nature of use must be defined by managers according to their conceptions of how computing can contribute most fully to organizational goals.

Computerization: No Threat to Constitutional Relationships. Two major nexes of the federal system are considered to be susceptible to disruption by computerization: relationships among the branches of the federal government, and relationships between the federal government and other governments in the federal system. The U.S. Constitution checks the central power of the national government by dividing it into three essentially equal and independent branches. The differential rate of computerization among the three branches, however, is considered by some to have the potential of undermining constitutional checks and balances by providing substantive, procedural, functional, or symbolic advantage to one or more branches (Burnham, 1983). Similarly, the construction of national information systems (such as those in criminal justice) and the growing linkage of federal, state, and local information systems (such as in the employment, tax, and welfare systems) are sometimes viewed as increasing the power of the national government and nationalizing, or at least delocalizing, state and local policies and programs (Laudon, 1986). To date, the research indicates that computers have had very little effect on either of these issues. Relationships among the branches of the federal government supersede the issues of computing and even the issues of relative information access. There is no effective way for one branch to gain a sustained monopoly on information, on the technology to handle it, on the expertise to manipulate it, or on the right to determine when it will be applied. Thus, computers' impact on constitutional checks and balances appears moot. Intergovernmental relations appear similarly unaffected by computerization, largely because the role that could be played by computer technology is subordinated to the existing constitutional definition of authorities and the political and practical nature of federal, state, and local interactions. There is not much potential for computer technology to change this arena except at the margins (Kraemer and King, 1987).

Privacy Threat Versus Seductiveness. The Constitution clearly intends to protect citizens from abuse by a monolithic government. Given the limitations on the separate branches and levels of government, computer use will not create a monolithic government. There is much greater ambiguity, however, surrounding the issue of whether duly elected representatives, working through appropriate constitutional mechanisms, will engender computer-dependent abuse of individual rights.

Most of the concern over this issue is expressed in the debate about computers, data banks, and personal privacy (Westin, 1985; Burnham, 1983; Laudon, 1986). The absence of empirical evaluation of government recordkeeping activities, and of widespread privacy invasions to cite as causes for immediate action, has the practical effect of making alarms over computers and the privacy issue largely ideological. Yet the potential for abusing the individual right to privacy is substantial and growing rapidly as a direct result of computer-based surveillance and action (Laudon, 1986). Computer matching and national information systems are currently directed toward perpetrators of crime and fraud, but they could be directed more broadly.

Computers are also related to broader concerns about how government ought to function. According to one view, computers form part of a demonic vision, an Orwellian nightmare in which autocrats eliminate democratic government and individual freedom through computerized surveillance. According to another, computers form part of a beatific vision of efficient, effective, and democratic government: Computers eliminate waste, fraud, and abuse, streamline the functions of government, and permit electronic voting and plebiscites. A less common view, orthogonal to these two, sees technology as a seductive force leading to complacency, in which liberty and freedom are given up to a benign and helpful social order facilitated by the technology. One either lives with the contradictions of the present or removes them with a technical solution. If American constitutional government is threatened by the application of computers, the threat does not come from weaknesses in the Constitution or in the government it shapes; rather, the threat comes from the failure to protect and defend constitutional rights to personal privacy and due process.

There is reason to believe that this may be happening, given the growing use of computers in mass social surveillance and in partisan political contests. For example, the concept of constitutional democracy depends on an informed electorate capable of discriminating among candidates on the basis of their overall strengths, yet the extensive use of television in campaigns has already decreased the quality of debate and reduced attention to the issues. Highly targeted, single-issue fund raising and campaigning, conducted through computer-assisted direct mail or targeted telephone solicitations, contribute to this trend. Thus, computerization can and probably will affect the political processes by which people are elected to public office. The threat is that people will be distracted from the issues or lulled into complacency.

Implications for Improving Practice

Management of information technology, like management generally, is still more an art than a science. Research and knowledge from practice suggest several implications for improving public administration practice with regard to the use and management of computing in organizations. The first implication is that rational management theories, by themselves, are an inadequate basis of understanding computing in organizations, how it evolves and changes, and how to manage it. Rational management must be accompanied by political perspectives and by evolution-oriented change theories. In particular, the states-of-computing management concept provides a useful guide to action.

The second implication is that computing itself is unevenly distributed in organizations and has particular effects as a result of that distribution and use. Computing is not apolitical, either in its distribution or in its effects. Current applications of computing in organizations, even with the advent of microcomputers and their relatively greater distribution, tend to be conservative. Generally, the distribution of microcomputers follows the distribution of mainframe resources, both across functions within government and across levels within organizational hierarchies. This distribution has tended to favor the dominant political coalition within organizations, regardless of the type of governmental form or structure. To the extent that there has been a discernible shift recently in relative advantage because of microcomputers, it appears to be in favor of staff professionals, particularly those who serve senior management in financial, budgeting, planning, personnel, and administrative matters. Thus, microcomputers currently appear to be further reinforcing the interests of the dominant coalition while also extending the influence of the staffs that serve it.

The third implication is that information technology is adapted by organizations to fit into the culture, practices, and goals of their members. This view underlies the states-of-computing management notion about how computing is introduced and managed in organizations. It is quite another thing to say that computing affects organizations by bringing about fundamental changes in their goals, structures, and behavior. This latter view underlies many projections of how information technology will change organizations in the future. Over time, both views will be correct, since organizations and technology are interactive. Technology is introduced into organizations and adapted to their objectives. Introduction and use bring changes to organizations, and change affects future efforts to adapt and use the technology, in an endless cycle of innovation and change that is marked by mutually interacting effects.

The fourth implication, which is consistent with the foregoing argument, is that the states-of-computing management concept has particular relevance to senior management. Top managers have a choice: They can permit computing to drift toward one or another of the states, or they can take control of computing and direct how it develops. In deciding to take control, they have two further alternatives: They can take control directly, or they can delegate control to someone else—either departmental management or data-processing management. (Of course, these choices largely depend on top managers' orientation toward information systems.)

Different management orientations are related to each of the states of computing management. In the service state, computing is viewed as a general-purpose tool for government departments, similar to other tools, like vehicles and communications. Thus, the organization's computing activity is primarily concerned with increasing departmental access to computing, user competence in computing, and applications that really serve operating department functions, on the grounds that departmental users can best apply computing to serve the organization's needs.

In the skill state, computing is viewed as a specialized support service, involving technical skills and technologies that undergo continual advances. Thus, the organization's computing activity is primarily concerned with keeping current with the state of the art, on the grounds that continued advances in technology provide improved capabilities for less money and thereby better serve government's needs.

In the control state, computing is viewed as a method for generating information to improve internal management and decision making. Thus, computing activity is primarily concerned with ensuring that management-level information is generated (as special applications or as part of the applications developed for the operating departments) on the grounds that increasing the available information for decision making best serves organizational needs.

Thus, each state displays a different orientation toward computing, and that orientation has consequences for how computing develops in an organization. Senior management can influence that trajectory by conscious choices that shape the states. For example, in the control-skill state, senior management places data processing in control of a data-processing unit but also makes it clear that the unit's management is to serve managerial interests. In the control-skill state, operational and technical interests are served, but only when these also serve managerial interests through the information, communication, or control capabilities they provide.

The fifth implication is that top managers should not presume that any of the states is necessarily preferable. Whether a particular state is ultimately beneficial depends on at least three factors: the fit of the state with the organizational environment, the costs and benefits of the state to senior management, and the adherence of the state to the larger organizational vision of computing. Obviously, the state must fit with the organizational environment. It is unreasonable to expect that the service state can exist in a highly centralized organization, because the service state assumes a highly decentralized organization, with substantial autonomy in the departments and minimal central control. Similarly, it is unreasonable to expect the skill state to exist in an organizational environment where technology and technologists are anathema. The control state, on the contrary, will do very nicely in centralized organizations.

Each of the states presents a different set of costs and benefits for managers. The skill state has the advantage of requiring little time and attention from senior management, because senior management turns over complete responsibility and authority for computing to data-processing management. It also has the advantage of not creating additional problems for senior management to deal with in the short term, because in the skill state both departmental and data-processing management tend to be relatively satisfied with computing arrangements, although for different reasons. Departmental managers are satisfied because data processing responds positively to most requests for new or enhanced applications. Data-processing managers are satisfied because growing user demands provide the needed rationale for continuous expansion of data processing's domain, equipment, and staff and, with these, its status as a department, as well as the status of its management. The skill state, however, has the potential disadvantages of high computing costs due to rampant technological virtuosity, problematic computing investments due to frivolous user applications, and opportunity costs due to failure to develop managerial and organizationwide applications.

Summary

Computers were introduced into government in the 1950s. They have initiated remarkable change. They have also shown remarkably dismal performance, compared to predictions and expectations. Computing has introduced a new administrative function into government. It has permeated nearly all functions and levels of government. It has required more investment of public resources (with uncertain outcomes), spawned technical staffs with a strong desire to maintain their monopoly on computing expertise, and become the expression of and heightened various tensions within public administration between centralization and decentralization, line and staff, and experts and generalists. At the same time, computing has failed to produce the decision-making benefits expected by senior managers, the staff reductions feared by employees, and the cost reductions hoped for by politicians. Nevertheless, it has been enthusiastically embraced, by users and nonusers alike.

The thirty-five-year history of computing is a brief one. Most technologies require fifty to a hundred years to be widely adopted and used. Computing is all the more enticing and frustrating because it is a general-purpose tool whose capabilities and possibilities are continually changing but all the while never quite measuring up to our expectations and hopes. What is clear is that the technology will be as widely distributed in organizations as telephones are. It is also clear that the functions of telephones, computers, word processors, and reproduction equipment will become increasingly integrated in single, multifunction workstations that, in order to be useful, will connect work groups and other subunits of governmental organizations, regardless of physical location.

Our knowledge about effective practice has grown markedly in the last fifteen years, as a result of empirical research and experience. Perhaps the greatest changes have been the introduction of political perspectives on computing use and the impact and the development of contingency theories for thinking about effective management of the technology. Equally important have been results that show the importance of advanced technology, the sociotechnical interface, and the growing need for the integration of data processing, telecommunications, and office automation.

The potential threats of computers and information technology remain just that—possibilities, rather than realities. The fact that the threats have not materialized is a function both of the failed promises of the technology and of the strength of our public institutions to adapt the technology to the constitutional, democratic framework of American government. The constitutional structure of the branches of government and the federal system appears strong enough to counter temporary imbalances that might result from differential computerization in any single branch or at any one level of government. Nevertheless, the threat to privacy posed by computerized matching of government data banks looms large, and it requires special vigilance. The prospect that our freedoms will be taken away appears less frightening than the prospect that we will give them up in exchange for the convenience and false sense of well-being provided by information technology.

References

Burnham, D. *The Rise of the Computer State*. New York: Random House, 1983.

Danziger, J. N., Dutton, W. H., Kling, R., and Kraemer, K. L. *Computers and Politics*. New York: Columbia University Press, 1982.

Danziger, J. N., and Kraemer, K. L. *People and Computers*. New York: Columbia University Press, 1986.

Dutton, W. H., and Kraemer, K. L. "Technology and Urban Management." *Administration and Society*, 1977, *9* (3), 304–340.

Dutton, W. H., and Kraemer, K. L. "Management Utilization of Computers in American Local Government." *Communications of the ACM*, 1978, *21* (3), 206–218.

King, J. L. "Centralized Versus Decentralized Computing: Organizational Considerations and Management Options." *Computing Surveys,* 1983, *15* (4), 1–31.

Kraemer, K. L., Dutton, W. H., and Northrop, A. *The Management of Information Systems.* New York: Columbia University Press, 1981.

Kraemer, K. L., and King, J. L. "Cost as a Social Impact of Telecommunications and Other Information Technologies." In M. Moss (ed.), *Telecommunications and Productivity.* New York: Addison-Wesley, 1981.

Kraemer, K. L., and King, J. L. "Computing and Public Organizations." *Public Administration Review,* 1986, *46,* 488–496.

Kraemer, K. L., and King, J. L. "Computers and the Constitution." *Public Administration Review,* 1987, *47* (1), 93–105.

Kraemer, K. L., King, J. L., Dunkle, D. E., and Lane, J. P. *Managing Information Systems: Change and Control in Organizational Computing.* San Francisco: Jossey-Bass, 1989.

Laudon, K. C. *Computers and Bureaucratic Reform.* New York: Wiley-Interscience, 1974.

Laudon, K. C. *Dossier Society.* New York: Columbia University Press, 1986.

McFarland, F. W., and McKenney, J. L. *Corporate Information Systems Management.* Cambridge, Mass.: Harvard University Press, 1983.

Porter, M. E. *Competitive Strategy.* New York: Free Press, 1980.

Westin, A. *Information Technology in a Democracy.* Cambridge, Mass.: Harvard University Press, 1971.

Westin, A. "Privacy, Technology, and Regulation." In D. P. Donnelly (ed.), *The Computer Culture.* Rutherford, N.J.: Fairleigh Dickinson University Press, 1985.

38

James L. Garnett

Effective Communications in Government

A public recreation superintendent sent a letter to social service agencies asking them to transfer "that incurable client, that nasty delinquent, or that lovable human vegetable" to a special recreation center. In the letter, the recreation superintendent asked, "Having trouble with all those extra whackos left over from last year's case load? County government sending you the sickies instead of throwing them behind bars where they belong?" ("Official Suspended . . . ," 1978, p. 8).

This misguided communication by a public administrator resulted in angry attacks from social services professionals and clients, making his work and the work of his agency more difficult. It also lost much-needed government credibility and cost the public administrator his job. On other occasions, breakdowns in communication have produced wrong votes in the United Nations and other bodies, confused and irritated taxpayers, and abetted the demise of public officials, even presidents. In the words of one commentator, "The president who can sell his ideas to other nations, to his own countrymen, and to the Congress is likely to succeed. The president who can't, won't" (Kilpatrick, 1981, p. 12).

According to Corson and Paul (1966, p. 50), "the program manager's accomplishment . . . depends largely on his ability to communicate with others—in writing and orally—to gather needed facts and views; to instill subordinates with the confidence that he understands the problems they are attempting to resolve and the programs they are engaged in; to persuade these subordinates of the wisdom of following and supporting his leadership; to sell his program to peers, bosses, interest groups, Congress, and the public; and to win the support of powerful and interested groups for his agency's programs."

The crucial nature of communicating effectively in order to manage is underscored by theorists who have recognized the centrality of communication for decision making and control (for example, Barnard, [1938] 1968; Katz and Kahn, 1966), and by practicing government managers who have ranked oral and written communication skills the most crucial for administrative success (Murray, 1976). One political commentator observed: "Government is only in part the art of politics. It is chiefly an exercise in the art of communication" (Kilpatrick, 1981, p. 12).

Although communicating pervades both government and business management, communicating in government has several important differences. First, a government has "*nodality*, . . . the property of being in the middle of an information or social network" (Hood, 1983, p. 4). Because of its legal regulatory and planning functions, and because it is the official voice of the people in a country, state, county, or city, government is typically at a communications nexus. Some businesses and citizens communicate with one another, but virtually all businesses, nonprofit organizations, and citizens communicate with government.

Moreover, communications to and especially from government typically carry messages of higher salience that affect people's standards of living, health, or safety. Because governments possess the powers to tax, regulate, incarcerate, or even kill, governmental communications often are more important and sensitive than most private sector communications. Therefore, the media and the public tend to scrutinize government more closely. Communications to and from government get wider and more visible attention than do similar, private sector messages. The "sickies" letter mentioned at the beginning of this chapter would have been less likely to be carried by the Associated Press if the author had not been a public servant. For these reasons—the official centrality of government and the high salience and visibility of governmental communications—such communications require special care.

This chapter explores the art and science of communication, concentrating on knowledge that can help public administrators manage more effectively. The following section addresses theories and research findings that can be applied for more effective practice. This knowledge comprises a synthesis of findings from behavioral and social science research, and it cites administrative experience on key elements of communicating with government's internal and external publics. Internal government communication deserves attention, because most public administrators and staff specialists spend most of their time writing or speaking to internal publics—colleagues, subordinates, superiors, and officials in other agencies or even in other governments. Communicating with government's external publics deserves attention as the means by which government informs and persuades its citizenry and learns about the opinions and needs of its many publics. The chapter concludes with a discussion of the implications for communicating practice and a summary.

Knowledge About Effective Practice:
Research-Based Guidelines for Communicating

Much knowledge has been accumulated through research on the way people behave individually, in groups, in organizations, and in masses. This knowledge has resulted from research in psychology, sociology, social psychology, cybernetics, political science, communication science, and other disciplines. Earlier research tended to be more sweeping in its generalizations for describing and prescribing communications behavior (Berelson and Steiner, 1969). Because much of the accumulated research on communication had different methods, subjects, situations, objectives, and research focuses, and because communication is a complex phenomenon, research results have often been divergent.

Some current scholars of communication science lament the dearth of broad, iron-clad generalizations that could guide communication behavior (Frandsen and Clement, 1984; Berger and Chafee, 1987). Certain findings have sufficient support, however, to serve as the basis for guidelines concerning the key elements of communicating: the *audience,* the *message,* and the *medium.* This section is organized around these key elements, in order to avoid repeating points that apply (with appropriate adjustments) to different audiences. Public administrators and other government professionals can use this existing knowledge to overcome or at least minimize communication barriers. The knowledge presented here can be applied to diverse government settings: intra- and interagency communication and communication with clients of government services and the general citizenry.

The difficulty of generalizing about a subject as complex as communication requires that this knowledge be applied carefully and intelligently. Research and experience in communicating have shown the importance of exercising a contingency approach to communication strategy: tailoring the message and the medium to the audiences and the goals to be achieved—to inform, persuade, or change behavior.

Knowledge About the Audience

Drawing on systems theory and information theory, a simplified description of the communication process involves a *source* (or sender) producing or *encoding* a *message* and then transmitting that message via a *medium* (or channel) to a *receiver* (or audience), who *decodes* the message and gives *feedback* about how well the message has been received (Arnold and Bowers, 1984). The designing and transmitting of messages usually get first and greatest attention, yet much evidence exists that the audience's receiving role is most crucial to communicating success (Frandsen and Clement, 1984; Gortner, Mahler, and Nicholson, 1987). Knowledge about intended and unintended audiences is necessary before one can craft a message. The following are key guidelines concerning audiences.

Audience Roles Affect Communication. Mathes and Stevenson (1976) found that an audience's role places it in one or more of three main types: immediate, primary, and secondary. *Immediate audiences* are the initial receivers of a message. They revise and transmit a message to other audiences or route it directly. Immediate audiences often include immediate superiors and peers; they may include reporters, when the latter serve as channels to reach other government officials, clients, or taxpayers.

Primary audiences are principal users who make key decisions and take actions based on a message. A message should be principally aimed at them. Primary receivers often include the heads of operating units and chief executives of agencies or departments. In the communication of public information, the general public or segments of the public are primary audiences. For example, smokers and potential smokers are the primary target audience in the surgeon general's media campaign against smoking.

Secondary audiences will probably use and affect a message and be affected by it, even though they are not the principal users. Secondary audiences often include staff specialists in the unit where the message originates, managers and staff specialists in related units, clients, and reporters. Recognizing secondary audiences can be more important than it might appear. While these people cannot affect decisions directly, they often can influence primary users or undermine decisions through faulty implementation. When a secondary audience is responsible for implementing decisions based on a message, a manager may need to use clearer language or include additional information that will be needed for secondary audiences to act appropriately. The recreation superintendent quoted at the beginning of this chapter failed to respect citizens, failed to analyze his primary audience correctly, and ignored potential secondary audiences—reporters and newspaper readers.

Some audiences play more than one role, complicating analysis. In many small, local government agencies, for example, the immediate audience is often the primary user as well. In large departments, many people act as channels for routing information. Sometimes these people are also part of the primary audience. Often they are part of both the secondary and the immediate audiences. For example, supervisors may have no direct decision-making power, but they must implement decisions that result from the information they route to decision makers.

Analyzing the role or roles an audience plays is crucial to knowing what the audience needs from the message, how much background and detail to include, what media to use, and so on. The success of public health information campaigns has been improved, for example, through the effective use of formative evaluations before and during an information campaign, to determine a target group's literacy level, health needs, life-style, communication preferences, and other relevant information (Rogers and Storey, 1987). As receivers, public administrators should inform people who communicate with them of their audience role, so that the senders can tailor their messages and media accordingly. (Often, managers say, "Write a memo to me, but tailor it to my boss, the primary audience.")

Faulty Assumptions About the Audience Cause Communication Problems. While all communications involve three elements—the source, the message, and the audience—many public administrators behave as if there were only two elements, the source and the message. Ignoring an audience's past, present, or future roles reveals a number of false assumptions, including the following ones.

1. The person addressed is the primary audience.
2. The audience is a group of specialists in our field.
3. The message has a finite period of use.
4. The author and the audience will both remain available for reference.
5. The audience is familiar with the assignment.
6. The audience has been involved in daily discussions of the material.
7. The audience awaits the message.
8. The audience has time to read or listen to our entire message (Mathes and Stevenson, 1976).
9. Only the intended target audience will get our message.
10. One style of writing or speaking is appropriate to all situations.

Public managers know from experience how risky any of these assumptions can be. A memo to a colleague that airs frustration over administrative red tape may end up on the desk of the bureau chief or appear in the *Washington Post.* A budget request briefing may assume more technical knowledge than a legislative committee possesses. A safer course is audience analysis, which usually involves *audience mapping* to identify intended and potential (although the latter may be unintended) audiences. It usually also means recognizing what functions each audience serves—immediate, primary, or secondary—and their respective priorities. Analysis may also involve constructing an *audience profile* for particularly important and recurring audiences, to learn their organizational positions and roles, educational and professional backgrounds, key affiliations, and communication preferences (for example, whether an audience prefers memoranda, briefings, or both, and whether it likes or dislikes jargon). To profile all potential audiences is impossible and counterproductive, but benefits result from profiling frequent audiences and those who can make or break a message. Profiles can be recorded on index cards, forms, or computer files and can be referred to as appropriate. Public administrators and staff professionals can avoid much wasted effort by constructing audience profiles and sharing them with colleagues or others who often speak or write to (or for) those audiences. Avoiding faulty assumptions will in itself make a public administrator a more effective communicator.

Organizational Position Affects Message Reception. Research shows that people interpret messages and react to them in different ways, according to their positions in an organization (Dearborn and Simon, 1958; Tompkins, 1984). Tailoring a message to a specific audience makes sense, because different groups speak their own occupational and social jargon and see things in different ways. What each person perceives as the issues or facts of a case depends largely on his or her position in the organization. Miles's Law, attributed to Rufus Miles, Jr., has great relevance to government communication. According to Miles's Law, where you stand depends on where you sit. Organizational role forces agency directors, for example, to take a broader perspective than program directors do who are concerned primarily with single programs or projects. Cost-conscious Office of Management and Budget analysts are predictably perceiving plans for a new AIDS research laboratory differently than are research administrators from the Federal Drug Administration and the Department of Health and Human Services. When receiving or sending messages, a public manager should be aware of his or her own organizational role, in order to avoid letting that role unduly affect the interpretation of messages.

Audience Segmentation Strategies Can Improve Communicating Effectiveness by Targeting Messages to Specific Audiences. Audience segmentation involves disaggregating a mass audience into different, smaller, homogeneous audiences. Segmentation avoids the "shotgun approach" of sending the same message to everyone via the same medium, a tactic often inefficient, ineffective, or both. For example, papering a town in leaflets was found to be an effective way to reach most citizens, but it was ineffective in reaching the elderly, the homebound, and other priority audiences (Rogers and Storey, 1987). Careful segmenting of these audiences would have indicated the use of different media, such as the telephone, television, radio, or door-to-door interpersonal contacts.

Segmenting can also help avoid information gaps. For instance, audiences better informed about and more favorably inclined to AIDS prevention are more likely to be reached by public health education campaigns than are those less informed, less favorable, and less likely to seek out, receive, or retain AIDS information. Public health education campaigns may therefore widen the information gap, unless the uninformed are segmented and specific media, messages, and content are designed for them.

Audiences Will More Likely Respond to Direct Appeals. Research generally shows that public information campaigns trying to change people's behavior by remote appeals—to "conserve our nation's energy" or "improve our public schools," for example—will probably fail (Rogers and Storey, 1987). Most audiences are more likely to change their behavior if a problem or a change is shown to affect them directly. For example, effective law enforcement campaigns to involve U.S. citizens in crime prevention must tell groups and individuals that they are vulnerable to crime but can do something to prevent it (Mendelsohn and O'Keefe, 1981).

Knowledge About the Message

Knowledge about the audience and the objectives for communicating helps in tailoring a message, whether that message is official or unofficial, aimed at an internal or an external audience. The following general points about messages add to our understanding.

Message Ambiguity Increases Interpretation. Generally, the more ambiguous a message, the greater the audience's need to interpret it, and the more difficult interpretation becomes (Berelson and Steiner, 1969; Kribbendorf, 1975). Ambiguity can provide needed flexibility in some management situations, such as in contract or diplomatic negotiations. When precision, rather than flexibility, is desired, however, ambiguous messages are often ineffective, because audience interpretations may differ drastically from the one intended. For example, studies of the Internal Revenue Service's performance in February 1988 found that the ambiguity and complexity of the new federal income tax forms and instructions were resulting in an error rate of 40 percent when taxpayers called the agency for tax advice. To minimize misinterpretation, effective communicators segment audiences, avoid ambiguous terms or phrases, and try to anticipate the various ways their messages can be interpreted or misinterpreted. They can then state how their messages should not be interpreted, as well as how they intend them to be interpreted. Trying a message on a test audience, one representative of the actual audience, usually helps in identifying sources of misinterpretation. Novices and knowledgeable reactors alike are useful in a test audience; novices, for example, often spot unclear assumptions or terms that experts bridge over with their knowledge.

The Structure of a Message Affects Impact and Retention. Research generally shows that material placed at intermediate points in a message is more difficult to remember than material placed at the beginning or the end. Structural devices—previews, reviews, summaries, digests, and the like—also generally increase retention (Frandsen and Clement, 1984).

Facts Are Often Insufficient to Change Attitude or Behavior. Relying on factual information—for example, about government service delivery, in order to change citizens' attitudes about government—will probably fail. Research has generally found that facts alone are usually insufficient to change a person's attitude (Abelson and Karlins, 1970). Confronted with facts that make them uncomfortable, people tend to ignore or distort the facts to reduce cognitive dissonance (see Miller, Burgoon, and Burgoon, 1984; Miller, 1987). Careful audience analysis is required to detect feelings, personal experience, prejudices, and other factors that influence human behavior. One way to address this problem is to recognize that, instead of attitude influencing behavior, behavior often precedes and influences attitude (Miller, 1987). If citizens, for example, can be motivated via inducement or threat of penalty to adopt a different behavior, attitude change may well follow. For many citizens, obeying civil rights laws and court decisions has led eventually to attitudinal change.

Extreme, Sensational Claims Are Likely to Hinder Persuasion. Research typically shows that when a claim far exceeds what an audience is conditioned or willing to believe, that audience is unlikely to be persuaded (Weiss, 1969). Audiences are often better persuaded by claims that differ from their positions but are sufficiently close to seem plausible. Even when one is not engaged in argument, omitting *always, never, impossible,* and other extreme words from writing or speaking makes the message more reasonable and realistic.

Direction of Message Affects Content and Perception. The direction of communication, whether downward, upward, or horizontal, affects the kinds of information conveyed and how that information is perceived. *Downward communication* usually includes one or more of the following: specific task directives, information related to task, information on organizational procedures and practices, feedback on job performance, and information to foster a sense of mission and team (Katz and Kahn, 1966). Gortner, Mahler, and Nicholson (1987) note a tendency for task directives and job instruction to dominate the downward channel, leaving the other kinds of messages (particularly feedback on performance) underused. If administrative superiors send only task directives and instructions, subordinates can become saturated with this kind of information and starved for other necessary information. Overemphasis on directives promotes a control orientation, possibly stifling subordinates' initiative and triggering behavior that rebels against the control mentality. Performance feedback and information that fosters a sense of mission probably have the greatest effects on employees' motivation but are too seldom communicated. Public administrators must diversify their downward communication for it to be more effective.

Upward communication carries information about program results, perceived organizational needs and problems, and other messages that subordinates deem important to convey to superiors. An organization's reporting system is handled primarily via upward communication flows (Kaufman and Couzens, 1973). Since much upward communication is crucial to the recognition of problems and to necessary decisions, the tendency of public administrators to selectively screen or interpret messages inhibits essential organizational intelligence. Public administrators must often overcome the limitations of formal communication systems by actively seeking additional and independent sources of information and by breaking through the conventional wisdom (Wilensky, 1967). The selective use of multiple media is one method for increasing upward communication. The supplementing of normal channels with modern technology (such as the Bureau of Land Management's use of a network of computer-monitored magnetic sensors to detect lightning fires) is another.

Research about government communication shows that *horizontal communication* is often most accurate and responsive (Gortner, Mahler, and Nicholson, 1987), but pressures to report important information up the chain of command can discourage lateral communication (Walton, 1962). Reinforcing (rather than discouraging) horizontal and even informal communication and providing meetings, locations, lunches, and other forums for specialists and others to exchange information have been linked with improved organizational performance (Peters and Waterman, 1982).

Knowledge About the Medium

A medium or a channel conveys messages. The range of media available to government communicators has been expanded by modern technologies. Standard communications media (the report, memo, letter, press release, magazine, newsletter, meeting, briefing, speech, hearing, rumor, personal visit, radio, and network television) have been supplemented to include cable and satellite television, computer networking, electronic mail, automatic message systems, and the like. Some media are used primarily for internal government communication (a memo, a bill). Other media are used more in communications to external audiences (a press release, radio, television). Almost all media can be used appropriately, internally and externally, depending on the message, the audience, and the goals for communicating.

Different Media Are More Effective with Different Audience Segments. Research summarized by Tompkins (1984, p. 688) shows that oral communication, allowing feedback from subordinates, is the "preferred single medium of downward communication" in organizations; writing is more effective when combined with oral messages to allow feedback, and "management is ill advised to depend on the written medium alone, particularly in one-message campaigns."

Some audiences prefer certain media. Mintzberg (1973) has documented the preference of busy chief executives for oral communication (even rumors) over formal, written messages. The preference of video-age young people for short, visually oriented messages has prompted some governments to emulate political campaigners in making their messages short and visual. The choice of an appropriate medium depends on content as well as on audience. Financial information, for instance, is difficult to convey solely by briefing, even when an audience prefers oral to written messages. Financial and other technical data are often conveyed more precisely by written documents, often with oral explanation available.

The creative use of modern technologies enables governments to reach audience segments better than ever before. Word processing and computer data banks can produce letters of instruction to voters, for example, which not only appear to be personalized, individually typed letters but also can reflect information about residence, past voting regularity, education level, and the like. Cable television provides a means of segmenting communication to groups with different interests, languages, and geographical locations. Some cable networks have two-way capability. Monrovia (California)

High School routinely calls parents to inform them about their children's attendance and academic progress or about upcoming school events. The "caller" is an automated calling system, a computer that delivers preprogrammed messages. The Federal Aviation Administration uses voice-recognition technology to provide a weather advisory system. It has a vocabulary of more than two thousand words, available to eight hundred thousand licensed pilots.

Modern technologies like these can help one segment audiences more effectively, but they also require accurate knowledge of audiences, to avoid the "garbage in, garbage out" problem. Furthermore, the logistical advantages of high-tech channels may be offset by the anxiety many groups and individuals experience in the presence of technology that they cannot understand. For these people, and for others who prefer social contact, the coffee klatch may be appropriate.

Goals for communicating also affect the choice of a medium. For example, Rogers and Storey (1987, p. 837) note that "while the mass media may be effective in disseminating information, interpersonal channels are more influential in motivating people to act on that information." People are more likely to act on information when there is social and environmental support. The use of people as role models or opinion leaders helps provide such support, as do on-site interpersonal channels for reinforcing appropriate behavior. For these reasons, neighborhood meetings and householder interactions are important to the success of the Neighborhood Watch crime prevention program (Rogers and Storey, 1987). In summary, different media have different strengths and weaknesses with different audiences and goals for communicating. There is no substitute for knowing which medium works best for a particular audience or goal.

Using Multiple Media Increases Communication. Some research indicates that conveying a message via multiple channels or media interferes with message retention, but the bulk of research supports the value of redundancy, especially when a message is within the audience's ability to process it (see Frandsen and Clement, 1984; Tompkins, 1984). A typical finding reported that within three days, people forget about 80 percent of what they read (Maude, 1974). If they both read and hear the message, however, they forget only about 35 percent. The importance of backing up oral messages with briefing papers, memos, or other documents is also supported by administrative experience, as is supplementing written messages with oral explanations. Using different media can especially help certain audiences. Many senior citizens, for example, need written and spoken information to piece together messages that diminished sight or hearing alone might miss.

Multiple media or channels are just as important when public administrators receive messages. Providing multiple media for citizens to communicate with government enables people who are inarticulate in one medium to voice their opinions or needs via another. In many localities, for example, citizens who are reluctant to write or to appear at public hearings can use radio call-in programs to communicate with public officials. The City of Tucson is just one government sponsoring television call-in programs with city officials and telephone access twenty-four hours a day.

Multiple media also help in gaining feedback from government subordinates and field offices. Kaufman and Couzens (1973) found extensive use in government of routine reporting, site visits, studies, and meetings to gather information about the activity and progress of subordinates. He noted the importance of other media to supplement and complement routine reporting, because of the natural tendency for subordinates to exaggerate their achievements and minimize their deficiencies.

Active Involvement in Communicating Generally Aids Retention and Behavior Change. Active participation in communicating aids retention and persuasion more than mere passive retention does (Berelson and Steiner, 1969; Rogers and Storey, 1987). For example, getting a public official to make a speech about a specific policy is a tactic that policy analysts use for getting an official's commitment to that policy (Meltsner, 1976). Asking subordinates to transmit messages to employees at lower hierarchical levels also has value, particularly if subordinates are responsible for supporting or implementing the policies or decisions that they are transmitting.

Implications for Practice

To be better communicators, public administrators must first recognize that effective communication is as complex as other managerial skills. A public administrator would rarely consider doing a capital budget, for example, without significant forethought about strategy, content, persuasiveness, and the like, but he or she may not be aware of giving less attention to planning and executing communication strategies. Communication is such a common process that it appears to be less technical and to have less mystique than many other management tools. Skillful communicating, however, requires as much analysis, planning, and careful use as other management tools do. Moreover, the public administrator has to utilize communication skills more than other management skills, because they typically are used in conjunction with other skills. In addition, communication skills often tend to be more crucial than other management skills, because they can ensure or doom outcomes of these other skills. For example, a skillfully budgeted allocation of resources that is sketchily written and sloppily presented risks undermining a sound budget.

Communication is no mechanical process. To base communication on guidelines (even those with broad support, like the ones presented here) is risky, if one does not carefully consider such factors as the personal strengths and weaknesses of the communicator, the audiences, the appropriate media, the management situation (crisis or routine, for example), and the goals for communicating. In other words, the knowledge presented in this chapter is not to be followed mechanically, but it must be applied intelligently if it is to have value.

Government communication should not be mechanical, but it should be ethical. For public administrators to earn and retain the trust of citizens and colleagues alike, communication must be based on ethical, as well as strategic or technical, considerations. Persuading public and private officials to support illegal arms shipments and deliberately burying the critical flaws of a proposal where few will see them are both examples of communication proficiency used for unethical ends. To be effective in the long run, government communication must be strategically, technically, *and* ethically sound.

Public administrators bear responsibility for the kinds and quality of communication that occur. If superiors reward vertical rather than horizontal communication, they should hardly wonder why lateral communication in their agencies is impoverished. If policymakers insist on stuffy "bureaucratese," when writing in a more personal style is more likely to be understood and retained (Frandsen and Clement, 1984), then policy analysts and other government writers will continue to produce turgid, pompous prose. For government communication to improve appreciably, public administrators, especially those at the top, must set a constructive example and expect others to match their standards.

Summary

This chapter has emphasized a contingency approach to communicating, recognizing that a message and a medium are generally contingent on goals for communicating, the audience, and the management situation. Knowledge about the key elements of communicating—the audience, the message, and the medium—is presented here in the form of research- and experienced-based guidelines for communicating, inside or outside government. These guidelines should not be followed mechanically but should be used within an overall contingency framework. Effective communication requires mastery of knowledge and techniques, some of the most fundamental of which are described in this chapter.

References

Abelson, H. I., and Karlins, M. *Persuasion: How Opinions and Attitudes Are Changed.* (2nd ed.) New York: Springer, 1970.

Arnold, C. C., and Bowers, J. W. (eds.). *Handbook of Rhetorical and Communication Theory.* Boston: Allyn & Bacon, 1984.

Barnard, C. *The Functions of the Executive.* Cambridge, Mass.: Harvard University Press, 1968. (Originally published 1938.)

Berelson, B., and Steiner, G. A. *Human Behavior: An Inventory of Scientific Findings.* San Diego, Calif.: Harcourt Brace Jovanovich, 1969.

Berger, C. R., and Chafee, S. H. (eds.). *Handbook of Communication Science.* Newbury Park, Calif.: Sage, 1987.

Corson, J. J., and Paul, R. S. *Men Near the Top: Filling Key Posts in the Federal Service.* New York: Committee for Economic Development, 1966.

Dearborn, D. C., and Simon, H. A. "Selective Perception: A Note on the Departmental Identifications of Executives." *Sociometry,* 1958, *21,* 140–144.

Frandsen, K. D., and Clement, D. A. "The Functions of Human Communication in Informing: Communicating and Processing Information." In C. C. Arnold and J. W. Bowers (eds.), *Handbook of Rhetorical and Communication Theory.* Boston: Allyn & Bacon, 1984.

Gortner, H. F., Mahler, J., and Nicholson, J. B. *Organization Theory: A Public Perspective.* Chicago: Dorsey Press, 1987.

Hood, C. *The Tools of Government.* Chatham, N.J.: Chatham House, 1983.

Katz, D., and Kahn, R. *The Social Psychology of Organizations.* New York: Wiley, 1966.

Kaufman, H., and Couzens, M. *Administrative Feedback: Monitoring Subordinates' Behavior.* Washington, D.C.: Brookings Institution, 1973.

Kilpatrick, J. "Tips for Reagan on Press Sessions." *Stars and Stripes,* Jan. 10, 1981, p. 12.

Kribbendorf, K. "Information Theory." In G. J. Hanneman and W. J. McEwan (eds.), *Communication and Behavior.* Reading, Mass.: Addison-Wesley, 1975.

Mathes, J. C., and Stevenson, D. W. *Designing Technical Reports: Writing for Audiences in Organizations.* Indianapolis, Ind.: Bobbs-Merrill, 1976.

Maude, B. *Practical Communication for Managers.* New York: Longman, 1974.

Meltsner, A. *Policy Analysts in the Bureaucracy.* Berkeley: University of California Press, 1976.

Mendelsohn, H., and O'Keefe, G. "Social Psychological Grounding for Effective Communication on Behalf of Crime Prevention." Paper presented to the American Psychological Association, Los Angeles, 1981.

Miller, G. R. "Persuasion." In C. R. Berger and S. H. Chafee (eds.), *Handbook of Communication Science.* Newbury Park, Calif.: Sage, 1987.

Miller, G. R., Burgoon, M., and Burgoon, J. "The Functions of Human Communication in Changing Attitudes and Gaining Compliance." In C. C. Arnold and J. W. Bowers (eds.), *Handbook of Rhetorical and Communication Theory.* Boston: Allyn & Bacon, 1984.

Mintzberg, H. *The Nature of Managerial Work.* New York: Harper & Row, 1973.

Murray, M. A. "Education for Public Administrators." *Public Personnel Management,* 1976, *5,* 239–245, 248–249.

"Official Suspended for 'Sickies' Letter." *Charleston (West Virginia) Gazette,* July 2, 1978, p. 8.

Peters, T. J., and Waterman, R. H., Jr. *In Search of Excellence: Lessons from America's Best-Run Companies.* New York: Harper & Row, 1982.

Rogers, E. M., and Storey, J. D. "Communication Campaigns." In C. R. Berger and S. H. Chafee (eds.), *Handbook of Communication Science.* Newbury Park, Calif.: Sage, 1987.

Tompkins, P. K. "The Functions of Human Communication in Organization." In C. C. Arnold and J. W. Bowers (eds.), *Handbook of Rhetorical and Communication Theory.* Boston: Allyn & Bacon, 1984.

Walton, E. *A Magnetic Theory of Organizational Communication.* China Lake, Calif.: U.S. Naval Ordnance Test Station, 1962.

Weiss, W. "Effect on Social Judgement of Prior Nonjudgement Responses to Related Stimuli." *Psychology Report,* 1969, *24,* 19.

Wilensky, H. L. *Organizational Intelligence: Knowledge and Policy in Government and Industry.* New York: Basic Books, 1967.

39

Irene S. Rubin

Managing Cycles of Growth and Decline

Individual agencies experience periods of growth, stagnation, recovery, or decline. Growth, decline, and recovery all pose different but sometimes related problems for managers. When young and encouraged by their own excitement and by political support, agencies may grow rapidly, but eventually their growth must bring them into conflict with other agencies competing for missions or money. When growth slows down, it is harder to attract creative and ambitious staff, which may further slow growth (Downs, 1967).

As an agency is growing, it may become less efficient, because communications and coordination become more of a problem. The organization may overexpand with respect to its resource base, or it may grow rigid (Merton, 1957; Kaufman, 1971; Weick, 1979; Schein, 1985). Ritual procedures may take the place of problem solution. The agency may grow by adding new support constituencies, becoming inflexible as it tries to respond to its diverse constituencies. Finally, an organization may grow too quickly, without adequate planning or proper balance, and it may stagnate. All these problems may bring about decline and a new set of managerial problems.

Managing Growth

Administrators cannot control many of the changes in the environment that influence the growth and decline of their agencies; they simply have to adapt to them. The skillful management of growth can help prevent decline and keep an agency functioning at its most efficient level.

Achieving Compatible Growth. Sometimes an agency gets a new mission because it has performed the old one well or efficiently, rather than because there is a consensus that the new function belongs there. For example, a building inspections and community development department may get the new function of economic development. Some may see the marriage as appropriate, since both missions deal with growth, but others may see the functions as fundamentally antagonistic, since one regulates business, while the other alleviates pressures and costs on businesses. One function may corrupt the other. If the bureau chief does not manage to define the new functions as compatible, the new unit may never be viewed as legitimate, and the economic development mission may be moved somewhere else when the opportunity arises. Agency heads should generally look for additional missions that are compatible with existing missions and should refuse those that are too patently contradictory. Another possible strategy would be to show how the apparent contradictions have been resolved.

Managing Problems of Coordination. As an agency grows, problems may arise concerning how labor should be divided and how coordination should be achieved (Mintzberg, 1979). As soon as the organization grows too large for informal coordination to work, or for the coordination to be accomplished by one person who controls the whole operation, problems may arise.

One way of improving coordination in a growing organization is to pay attention to the informal lines of communication that have grown up, and to pattern the formal units to include the major informal, work-related channels of information flow. Informal networks may be employees' way of overcoming deficiencies in the formal structure. Such networks often function well, but they are easily disrupted, and they depend on personalities and happenstance: Who meets whom and who gets along with whom may determine the ability of a unit to get its work done. When a nurse in an intensive care unit has to call someone he or she knows in the laboratory to get test results quickly on a new admission, there is too much dependence on the informal organization; the formal structure should be changed to improve links between units.

Coordination is sometimes achieved by standardizing the product. If people throughout the organization always deal with the same problem by using the same form, work can be coordinated without the necessity for new communication each time. Standardization can be used inappropriately, however. Consider the case of an elementary school, where teachers want to know what is taught in other grades, so that they can build on what students already know. Coordination can be achieved by standardization, forcing each teacher to teach only a specific curriculum and coordinating the curricula of teachers in different grades. Alternatively, it can be achieved in a more time-consuming manner by the holding of annual meetings in which teachers from separate grades talk about their plans for the year, their goals, and their students. The latter solution allows for more flexibility and professional autonomy and, hence, possibly for better education. Standardization can take the "juice" out of otherwise interesting work. Nevertheless, standard outputs may be particularly important in an agency, in which case the sacrifice of autonomy is appropriate. Agencies giving out welfare checks, or otherwise processing relatively routine matters in which equal treatment of equal cases is important, should emphasize standardization as their key coordination technique.

Preventing Rigidity. As an organization grows, and especially as its successes increase, it may gradually become more rigid. Managing growth involves learning how to remain flexible and adaptable.

An organization can grow rigid because of interest-group demands, especially if interest groups have become so powerful that they really control the agency. To prevent such dominance, or to moderate it if it has already happened, an agency can reorganize to make the relationship of the interest groups' agenda and the agency's structure more diffuse (Seidman and Gilmour, 1986; Salamon, 1981). If, for example, a department of energy is organized by industry, with oil research and coal research as separate units, it is clear where each industry needs to put its pressure and how it can dominate the policy agenda of each unit. If the department is organized in terms of basic research and applied research, however, the link between the interest groups and the agency units is less clear and, at the least, the interest groups have to go to two units in the organization, doubling their efforts, and may well have to wade through much material that does not involve them. Cities are often organized in such a way that it is difficult for interest groups to put pressure on one unit to get the results they want. If cities were organized to provide services to specific groups, however, they would be more vulnerable to interest-group pressure.

Sometimes an agency grows by adding programs or developing regulations that appeal to greater and greater numbers of interest groups, some of which may have competing demands. Powerful conflicting demands can render an agency immobile or, at best, slow down decisions to the point of massive irritation among legislators and constituents. For example, the Urban Mass Transportation Administration has been plagued by quarreling constituent groups, including the handicapped, manufacturers of equipment, and transit operators (Rubin, 1985).

In maximizing interest-group support, it is important to give thought to the compatibility and permanence of the alliance an agency puts together. If it is necessary to put together quarreling interest groups, the coalition should be temporary. For example, a temporary coalition was formed among business, city officials, and representatives of the poor to support the Urban Development Action Grant program (Rubin, 1985). A short-lived and uncomfortable coalition between mass transit and highway supporters was terminated when mass transit got its own funding source. Agencies can help spin off the parts of programs that attract particular hard-to-deal-with interest groups. When cities spin off services to other levels of government (usually for reasons of economy), they also spin off interest groups. Thus, it is possible to reconfigure the interest-group cluster around a particular program if that combination has been detrimental to good management. The techniques can be radical, however, and it is usually better to grow more carefully, selecting more compatible allies and keeping less compatible ones on a temporary basis.

To remain flexible as it ages, an organization must continue to monitor the environment. It is often tempting to assume that past successes mean that an organization is still in tune with public demands, and to stop seeking feedback from citizens. This can create a situation in which the organization is doing something not preferred by the public, and it can result in tax revolts, expenditure limits, and other reductions in autonomy. Public organizations can monitor their environments in a variety of ways—by providing easy-to-use complaint facilities, carrying out public opinion surveys, and monitoring the use of various facilities and services.

Some organizations handle complaints with skill, while others either ignore them or delegate the complaint function to the most junior person on the staff and destroy complaint messages after they have been handled. Citizens' complaints, while often demoralizing, are an important source of information and should be solicited and analyzed for patterns over time. If there are many complaints in one part of a city, or many complaints about one service (such as about breaks in water mains), there is likely to be an underlying problem that goes beyond the individual complainers. Such complaints should be supplemented by the organization's own monitoring system, such as sampling of roads after snowplowing and continual monitoring of water for cleanliness, odor, and color. Work done on streets and driveways should routinely be followed by letters requesting citizens' evaluation of their satisfaction with the work and the employees. Blocking driveways with heavy equipment, destroying lawns, and other work habits can infuriate citizens, but these are problems that can be handled, if city officials are aware of them. Since the vast majority of citizens are very satisfied with the public services they receive, such feedback (as opposed to complaint data) is likely to have a positive effect on workers' morale and simultaneously point out early the development of trouble spots. Solicitation of feedback also signals the public that the government is responsive and open.

Another way of remaining flexible is to review rules at intervals. Periodically, old rules need to be reviewed and thrown out, or replaced if they are no longer applicable. Such simplification not only makes the organization sensitive to changes in the environment over time but also reduces the image of red tape by reducing the number of regulations and increasing the clarity of what clients need to do. It also enhances the uniformity of decisions, since all employees are working from the same rules, rather than some from the old rules and some from the new. During slow times, it may be a good use of planners to have them weed out old ordinances or old regulations.

The possible use of some employees for other tasks brings us to another way of remaining flexible: the hiring of people who are multiskilled and the training of staff to be able to take over one another's jobs. While total cross-training is very expensive and time-consuming, some cross-training is often desirable. It not only increases flexibility but also improves the ability of units to communicate with one another and understand one another's missions. Consider the example of a probation office dealing with new drunk-driving laws that are bringing many more adults under court supervision. If some staff can be shifted from working with juveniles (where work may be slack) to working with adults, the organization can adapt to the changing environment, without overtime and with much less stress.

Hiring for flexibility requires sensitivity to position descriptions and to labor contracts, so that work that generally requires the same or similar skills is not classified into two or more rigid categories. In some cities, for example, water department workers and street department workers are in separate classifications. Street department workers, who are relatively idle in the winter, cannot be drawn on to help the water department repair crews, who are hard pressed in the winter. It is helpful to classify both sets of workers in the same way, so that they can substitute for each other as the need arises.

Organizations sometimes grow rigid in yet another sense. They tend to recruit like-minded people who reinforce each other, without bringing in real criticism or allowing ideas to be tested. Everyone pats everyone else on the back. In an emergency, if everyone thinks alike and does not test ideas, serious mistakes can be made (Janis, 1982).

To maintain flexibility in decision making, especially in crucial decisions, it is useful to recruit people from markedly different backgrounds who think differently. An engineer and a historian approach problems differently and are likely to offer different kinds of solutions. The chairman, president, or head of an agency should maintain a style of leadership that encourages criticism and examination of ideas. Employees should not fear the loss of their positions or status if their ideas do not work or if they criticize the ideas of others. Such an open atmosphere may have costs, in terms of hurt feelings, but it should help to maintain the organization's readiness to respond to crises.

Sometimes an organization creates its own problems by growing too quickly and without a plan. When there is plenty of money, it may not seem important whether one unit grows before another. The rate of growth itself can be a problem, because recruiting many people at one time can be problematic. There may be several excellent candidates for one type of job available at one time, but there may not be ten. To go out and hire ten, knowing that half or more of them are not strong candidates, often results in "deadwood"—employees who produce below standard rates or below standard quality levels, who are "careered in." An accumulation of "deadwood" reduces the agency's productivity. Some employees may have to pick up the slack for others, a situation that creates resentment. It is better to grow more slowly and get exactly the staff one needs. A general rule is to keep growth to 10 percent or less per year, if possible.

Overall, during the growth period, more attention should be placed on evaluating the costs and benefits of growth. Public administrators often assume that growth is wonderful because it creates internal mobility, motivates employees, and helps attract the best employees. Rapid and unplanned growth, however, can create numerous liabilities. Rapid growth may pit old-timers against newcomers in a bitter contest for influence and disrupt normally good morale. Too-rapid growth may disrupt the informal organization and its communication channels, which are often an important part of the functioning of the organization. Public organizations often grow fastest during brief "windows" of political support. The limited time available may make it difficult to acquire the best staff or equipment at the best price. Sometimes organizations overextend themselves during growth, acquiring staff or capital equipment that later remains underused. Slow growth is often the most comfortable option, but sometimes a no-growth policy can actually be more cost-effective. In any case, the costs of growth need to be looked at realistically.

Managing Decline

Because of a change in the environment or mismanaged growth or both, some public organizations are faced with the need to cut back and manage with fewer resources. Managing cutback is more difficult than managing growth: There are more continuing crises to deal with, and issues that are routine during growth become problematic during decline. Moreover, any mistake becomes more glaring during cutback, because it cannot be covered up with more resources.

Matching Cutback Strategies to Specific Problems. One strategy for cutback is to match the cutback tactics to the nature of the problem. For example, temporary solutions should be paired with temporary problems. A general rule is not to make irreversible decisions if it appears that revenues may rebound soon. A temporary downturn in the economy does not warrant irreversible decisions. The proper responses are those that delay cuts, such as hiring freezes and delays in equipment purchases and in the start of new capital projects. These tactics would do enormous damage over the long term, but they are perfectly appropriate during a short-term reversal. They prevent the loss of experienced staff and help maintain morale. Across-the-board cuts and attrition reductions may be appropriate for short-term declines (Greenhalgh and McKersie, 1980); targeted deeper cuts may be more appropriate for longer-term declines. Across-the-board cuts, made year after year, will reduce cost-effectiveness. In the short term, however, they may do no irreversible damage.

If decline results from too-rapid growth that has resulted in excessive "deadwood," targeted personnel cuts are required. Some reduction-in-force regulations make this kind of selectivity difficult, but at the federal level it is increasingly possible to save the best workers from cuts. In agencies where layoffs are carried out strictly according to seniority, some thought should go into renegotiating contracts or classifying positions in such a way that key employees with important skills can be retained. A system of seniority that lays off the most recent hires first, regardless of their jobs, can be devastating to productivity; but a system that requires layoffs according to seniority within job categories may allow a junior computer programmer to stay, while a more senior clerical employee is let go. The principle of seniority is maintained while the capacity of the organization to function is protected somewhat. Advance thought to how a reduction-in-force clause will work is helpful. It is very difficult to redesign a reduction-in-force mechanism while the organization is coping with reductions (Rubin, 1985).

If an organization's problem stems from growth that now exceeds the support base, the goal is to cut back expenditures, but the means is not so important, provided that the cuts are reasonably balanced—that is, to make a permanent reduction in size in order to accommodate a lower but stable resource base, one ought not reduce one budget line permanently. One can cut transportation to almost nothing on a temporary basis; for the long term, however, terminating travel may render the organization blind and ineffective. Unless the size of the staff or the complexity of the mission is also reduced, travel should not be cut for the long term. The size reduction, however, can be accomplished by reducing overhead (for example, by cutting the number of administrators), shedding some mission, cutting every unit across the board, or reducing staff according to seniority.

Managing Morale. During periods of cutback, morale drops precipitately, and the normal motivators either are not present or no longer work (Levine, 1978). Just getting people to work in the morning can be difficult if the agency is facing personnel cuts or program termination. Explicit thought has to be given to motivating employees and managers during a period of cutback. One reward that is often available in a shrinking organization is choice of tasks. Employees can rotate through a number of jobs to cover the work of employees who have left, getting much broader experience and many more job titles more quickly than they would otherwise be able to do. This experience may be invaluable in getting other jobs outside the agency, as well as in improving prospects for promotion when the agency is stabilized once more. The possibility of promotion, as well as the prospect of learning new marketable skills, is likely to keep a number of employees intensely interested in their work, despite the shrinking of the organization.

One way of helping crucial employees to stay motivated is to take control of the "rumor mill." Some managers think that if they announce forthcoming cuts, the result will be long periods of poor morale and low productivity, and so they keep the news a secret as long as possible. Actually, this kind of news is so important that it is impossible to keep quiet; there are too many potential sources of leaks. Moreover, when left to rumor, this information is likely to be distorted. Many versions, often incorrect, may circulate daily. The level of speculation will be high, and much of employees' energy will be spent on their catching up with the most recent version of a story, as each grain of information spins off interpretations. In this process, much time is spent unproductively, and everyone in the organization is likely to feel threatened. This situation encourages helter-skelter job hunts, during which the most skilled and most necessary employees are likely to leave first.

It is far better, as well as more humane, to make early and accurate announcements of anticipated layoffs, telling employees which groups are at highest risk. Those employees are then indeed likely to look for new jobs, but others may relax and begin to pay more attention to their own futures in the agency. For those not affected, the normal incentives and discipline can be reasserted. For those likely to be affected, the agency has given them the maximum amount of time to look for new jobs.

Recreating Flexibility. When an organization is shrinking, lack of flexibility can be a major managerial problem. At precisely the time when innovation may be most important, there are no resources for innovation. At precisely the time when flexibility is required to motivate employees, there may be no resources available with which to motivate them. At precisely the time when administrators need the most flexibility to shift money around and minimize damage from cuts, there may be almost no flexibility in the budget. If administrators can recreate some flexibility, the agency can minimize the damage brought about by cutbacks.

A number of techniques are commonly used to recreate flexibility in shrinking organizations. The first is to leave vacant positions unfilled for all or part of a year, or to replace a retiring, highly paid senior employee with a less experienced, lower-paid employee. A second technique is to disburse or commit capital expenditures slowly. Money still unspent for capital projects may create a short-term pool of funds to spend for emergencies. Money set aside for capital cannot always be spent for operating, but expenditures for office equipment, telecommunications, and automobiles and vans can function in this way. A budget can also be formally or informally restructured to allow more flexibility between lines. For example, in one state university, administrators developed a system of internal swaps, so that one department could trade surplus money in one line for another department's surplus money in another line. The university budget officer served as the monitor for trades. Flexibility was increased, but the totals in each line remained constant.

One of the key techniques for recreating flexibility is to create a pool of uncommitted funds. One way of creating such pools is to carefully estimate spending a little high and estimate revenue a little low (Rubin, 1980, 1987). If successfully created, not only can the pools of money help repair the damage done by cuts and provide incentives for innovation, they can also help in purchases of capital equipment, when such equipment will save money over several years.

Reducing Demand. If administrators have to plan for stability at a smaller size, or even for their agencies' termination, they may also have to reduce the demand for services. Cutting back the hours of the public library, or reducing the staff of any demand-driven agency, is likely to produce client protests, staff overload, and general frustration. If demand can be reduced as the agency shrinks, however, the process of shrinking may be much smoother.

How can one reduce the demand for services? One way is to charge fees. Much care needs to be given to when this strategy will be used, since there are times when one will not want to restrict services to those who can afford to pay for them. If public swimming pools are built to keep teenagers off the streets in summer, then charging fees for the use of pools is not a sensible strategy, since fees will discourage use. Charging fees for public ambulances may reduce unnecessary calls, but it may also reduce the number of necessary calls. To provide a public service, and then make it unavailable to those who really need it, does not make sense. Nevertheless, some services are overdemanded because they are underpriced. Free police services (unlocking cars when drivers lock their car doors with the keys inside) or free fire services (fetching cats down from trees) are probably not justifiable, and fees may reduce calls of this sort. What is less visible is that much police work in accident investigations is for the insurance companies. There is slight rationale for keeping a large police force to provide free services to insurance companies. The department can charge a fee or drop the service. In either case, demand-based work that results from car accidents can be reduced.

Another way of reducing demand is to shift emphasis toward prevention. This idea has prevailed in public health for some time, but it has not fully worked its way into the rest of the public sector. The emphasis in fire departments has long been on the more exciting and dangerous work of fire suppression, although prevention is a more cost-effective approach to saving lives and property. Emphasis on prevention reduces demand and allows an agency to shrink in proportion to the reduced demand.

Another way of handling demand is to shift a service to another governmental unit or to the private sector. The net demand may not be reduced, but the pressure on a particular agency to provide the service may all but disappear. For example, a city that was experiencing financial difficulties shifted animal control to the county, and animal lovers had to shift their focus to the county.

Adapting to Smaller Space Needs. Reducing size for the long term brings other problems besides those of reducing demand. In a very practical sense, the agency will probably take up less space, which may mean reducing the number of offices rented or even selling a building. Less equipment may also be required. If equipment and space are rented, there may be contracts that have to be renegotiated or even cancelled, to reduce operating costs. Agency managers will also have to think about how best to deploy remaining staff in the new, smaller configuration. Empty offices, with the stubs of telephone and computer hookups in the floors, are daily reminders of trauma and loss; the sooner the space fits the staff, the sooner the agency looks and feels stable. Reducing the number of telephone lines and issuing new telephone directories must be done quickly, because work is seriously interrupted if clients, politicians, and employees cannot find each other by phone.

Outplacement. As an agency shrinks, staff gradually find new jobs for themselves. This is traumatic for those who remain and can be a bitter experience for those who are leaving. They may feel utterly unappreciated and depressed, especially if they have been working for the agency for many years and have little idea of how to find a new job. Morale will improve if it is clear that the agency did not let people go for cause—that is, because of anything they did or did not do. It will be helpful for the agency to provide every possible assistance to those looking for new jobs. This task makes those who remain, including administrators, feel less guilty, especially as they succeed in helping staff find new jobs, and it reduces the bitterness of those leaving. An extensive outplacement effort is the humane way of handling the problem, and it need not be expensive.

There are several elements of a successful outplacement program. One is to provide photocopying, typing, and telephone services to those looking for new jobs. A second is the formation of a support group, to discuss job-hunting experiences, share advice on drawing up résumés, and discuss possible job options. People from this group are likely to feel loyalty to each other, and when one or more get employment, they may try to find jobs in the new locations for their former colleagues. A third is to assign work to job-hunting employees that will maximize their attractiveness to outside employers, help them improve their technical and supervisory skills, and make them eligible for better-paying jobs. Thus, rotating a secretary into a management training slot for a few months may greatly improve that employee's possibility of getting a managerial job.

There may be training opportunities inside the organization that can be used at low cost to help improve employment possibilities. For example, increasing exposure to the computer and data-analysis sections may improve the marketability of staff whose jobs are threatened.

Another way that an organization can aid outplacement is to assign work so that those looking for new jobs will have good contacts outside the organization. Some tasks of the agency may require more telephone or personal contacts with outside businesses or legislators who can provide jobs. These tasks should be reserved as much as possible, in the short run, for those who need to find new jobs.

If possible, negotiate a period of health insurance coverage for employees after they are laid off. If the agency absolutely cannot afford such a transition, then see that group coverage rates are extended to individuals. It is a good idea to inform employees about their options for early retirement, as well as about possibilities and procedures for appeal. It helps to make this information widely and accurately available. It also helps to have a manager available to answer questions and field complaints. This is not a time to close the door because of the discomfort of dealing with people in trouble. Managing outplacement well is not just humane, it is also good management. It maintains loyalty to the organization, reduces the "us versus them" sentiment that is likely to arise, and helps maintain motivation until new jobs are found.

If the agency is not just cutting back but is actually terminating itself, then it may wish to designate an agency historian and record keeper. Someone will have to receive mail after the agency has closed and see that accounts are closed out. Relevant material can be contributed to a library, a university, or another agency. Furniture and equipment need to be disposed of in accordance with law. This task is not technically difficult, but it requires some forethought.

Managing Turnaround

Turnaround management means taking an agency that is declining and has low budgets, low political and public support, and low morale and restoring it to moderate growth, support, and optimism. Turnaround management is not always possible or even desirable in the public sector. If an agency is reducing its scope of services because it has outgrown its resource base and the public does not want to fund it at prior levels, then it may have to stay at the new, smaller level for some years. If the problem the agency was designed to handle has diminished in size or salience, it may not be sensible to try to rebuild the agency. Sometimes a reduction in resources results from competition with other agencies or from the public's unfamiliarity with the program's goals and accomplishments, or there may have been some particularly damaging charges against the agency, which make further funding embarrassing to sponsors. There may have been mistakes in management during growth, or a loss of political support. Under these circumstances, it may be both possible and desirable to try to turn the agency around.

One crucial step in turnaround management is contacting and motivating constituencies to press for higher levels of support. Often, interest groups watch for opportunities to help an agency, but sometimes they need to be alerted to "windows of opportunity." An agency can also help create coalitions of supporters.

Another step in turnaround management is to document the agency's successes and publicize them. Sometimes this step is as simple as calling a meeting with field representatives to draw up a list of successes. At other times, it requires some evaluation research, in which the agency's goals are listed and careful studies are made of the program's public impact. It may be useful to emphasize money saved because of the program. Thus, the director of a day-care center can talk about the number of mothers who were able to take full-time jobs because of the availability of day care. These mothers paid taxes and did not draw welfare, and the dollar savings are relatively easy to calculate. Sometimes, while it may not be true or provable that a program saved money or generally accomplished its intended goal, it may be possible to show that the program did work in some cases. The agency may then want to describe those cases, showing why they were especially important, and how such successes can be expanded in the future. Sometimes an agency may be lucky enough to handle a crisis situation well just when refunding is being considered and come into budget hearings as a hero. The agency should not create crises in order to exploit them, but it may well want to take advantage of existing crises, putting extra resources toward their solution and publicizing its own role.

If a program is being threatened with phaseout in favor of private sector competitors, the agency head can point out the costs of the proposed alternatives, their impacts on the poor, and their relative lack of accountability to the public. A few vivid examples of situations in which contracting did not work out well may be helpful.

If an agency has been charged with inefficiency, lack of direction, or some other shortcoming, the charges should be responded to dramatically. For example, the agency can produce a five-year plan and demonstrate that it has a direction and is moving solidly in that direction. It might change agency heads, getting some good new publicity and symbolizing a change of direction. If the agency has been reasonably well run, it can open its books and publish the information. If there has been some problem, it can discover the source, fire the people involved, and set up new procedures to safeguard against recurrence. It is important to make a clean breast of the story at a single time, so that pieces do not continue to come out slowly. Symbolize the problem in one event or office, and clean out the office.

One way to try to turn an agency around is to propose new programs to meet the same needs the agency was originally designed to handle, or new programs to meet emerging needs. The new proposals should respond directly to criticisms of the old program. Thus, if the old program was attacked for being too regulatory, then the new program should be less regulatory but should still address the same kinds of problems in which the agency has experience and expertise. For example, when the Employment and Training Administration was suffering from the demise of the Comprehensive Employment Training Act program, which was being criticized for being too oriented to city government, a new program was proposed, which was more oriented to local businesses. This proposal resulted in the Job Training Partnership Act. The new program, with many of the same goals as the old one, gave the agency a new lease on life.

Internally, management has to stimulate innovation in order to bring about rejuvenation. When an agency is suffering from contraction and morale is low, employees are unlikely to want to risk more creativity and spend more energy on the organization. If turnaround is to take place, if new programs are to be designed and successfully sold, and if management is to be streamlined, then the agency has to be able to encourage innovation. If it has been able to keep a core of dedicated employees, the possibility of turnaround may itself be a motivation to innovate. It is much more comfortable to think of possible future successes than to wallow in apparent failure and disapprobation. The new, smaller agency may want to dispense temporarily with some of its formal hierarchy, in an attempt to solicit opinions and stimulate creative solutions, using influence on decision making as an incentive to employees' participation.

Whoever is in charge of the attempt to rejuvenate an agency must make sure that employees understand the severity of the problem and the need for potentially drastic changes. It must be clear that there are no risk-free, effortless, magic solutions. It is a good idea to involve as many employees as possible in the plan to rejuvenate the agency, so that the credit can be widely shared if there are some successes. The positive impact on morale is likely to be stunning when successes occur, and the employees who were simply left after the reductions in staffing are likely to be welded into a close and loyal group, willing to work incredibly hard to implement whatever they have wrought.

Summary

Most organizations experience cycles of growth and decline. Growth needs to be managed in such a way as to avoid or prevent many of the problems that lead to or exacerbate decline. It is important to control the rate of growth, to avoid excessive rigidity as the organization grows, and to plan for a division of labor and coordination as the organization outgrows its original, informal design. Managing decline well requires attention to the sources of decline, whether they are internal or external, over the long or the short term. Managers need to take control of rumors and announce personnel cutbacks as far in advance as possible, taking care to indicate who is most likely to be affected and stabilizing the remaining employees as early as possible. Extra thought has to be given to how to motivate employees during a period of cutback. The successful handling of decline can lead to stabilization at lower levels of operation or, in some cases, to turnaround and recovery. There are some things that good management cannot correct, however, such as long-term changes in the economy or long-term shifts in public opinion about appropriate levels of taxation or appropriate public sector functions. Some agencies or programs may have to be terminated, so that others more in keeping with the times can grow.

References

Downs, A. *Inside Bureaucracy*. Boston: Little, Brown, 1967.

Greenhalgh, L., and McKersie, R. "Reduction in Force: Cost Effectiveness of Alternative Strategies." In C. H. Levine (ed.), *Managing Fiscal Stress: The Crisis in the Public Sector*. Chatham, N.J.: Chatham House, 1980.

Janis, I. *Groupthink: Psychological Studies of Policy Decisions and Fiascoes*. (2nd ed.) Boston: Houghton Mifflin, 1982.

Kaufman, H. *The Limits of Organizational Change*. University: University of Alabama Press, 1971.

Levine, C. "Organizational Decline and Cutback Management." *Public Administration Review*, 1978, *38*, 316–325.

Merton, R. K. *Social Theory and Social Structure*. (Rev. ed.) New York: Free Press, 1957.

Mintzberg, H. *The Structuring of Organizations*. Englewood Cliffs, N.J.: Prentice-Hall, 1979.

Rubin, I. "Retrenchment and Flexibility in Public Organizations." In C. Levine and I. Rubin (eds.), *Fiscal Stress and Public Policy*. Newbury Park, Calif.: Sage, 1980.

Rubin, I. *Shrinking the Federal Government: The Effect of Cutbacks on Five Federal Agencies*. New York: Longman, 1985.

Rubin, I. "Estimated and Actual Urban Revenues: Exploring the Gap." *Public Budgeting and Finance*, 1987, *7* (4), 83–94.

Salamon, L. M. "The Question of Goals." In P. Szanton (ed.), *Federal Reorganization: What Have We Learned?* Chatham, N.J.: Chatham House, 1981.

Schein, E. H. *Organizational Culture and Leadership: A Dynamic View*. San Francisco: Jossey Bass, 1985.

Seidman, H., and Gilmour, R. *Politics, Position, and Power: From the Positive to the Regulatory State*. (4th ed.) New York: Oxford University Press, 1986.

Weick, K. *The Social Psychology of Organizing*. Reading, Mass.: Addison-Wesley, 1979.

Part Eight

The Professional Practice of Public Administration

Public administration is not a profession, in the classic sense of the term. It does not enjoy the status of law or medicine. Public administration lacks the attributes that have commonly been associated with the meaning of the term *profession,* because it neither monopolizes esoteric knowledge vital to society nor controls entry into professional practice. In many other respects, however, public administrators are professionals. Many public administrators require extensive training, apply their knowledge to practical problems, provide an important service to society, subscribe to ethical codes, and belong to organizations intended to advance the services they provide. Part Eight explores the implications and quandaries of the professional practice of public administration.

Like the traditional professions, public administration seeks to promote particular social values. Unfortunately, these values are not so clearly delineated as others—the health of patients or the salvation of sinners, the social values pursued by doctors and the clergy, respectively. Instead, public administrators must struggle to balance several values. The ultimate test of how well different values are balanced is whether instrumental techniques and professional means are constructively situated within a broader system of democratic values and processes.

In pursuing the core values of the modern state, public administrators must often choose from a variety of competing ethical orientations. Law serves as the basis of one ethical orientation. Unlike many other ethical precepts, the obligation to abide by the law may be enforceable by citizens through the courts. Public administrators may be liable for damages for a range of illegalities, from violations of due process to unlawful appropriation of private property to malicious prosecution. In addition to a legal ethical orientation, public administrators may choose from a variety of other competing and sometimes contradictory ethical precepts.

The ultimate goal of the practitioner of public administration is effectiveness: success at achieving results consistent with the values of modern government. What are the characteristics of the effective public administrator? One set of characteristics includes technical, human, and conceptual skills, but these alone are not sufficient for effectiveness. The public administrator must also be responsive to democratic control and concerned with results. The characteristics of an effective public administrator define the real meaning of professionalism in public administration.

Although professionalism in public service is highly valued, professionalism, in the traditional sense, is not compatible with democratic governance. If public administration sets itself apart, it risks alienating itself from the public and its representatives. Public administrators must use their discretion and judgment to facilitate the workings of the complex machinery of government on behalf of the rights and interests of all citizens. Part Eight offers guidance for public administrators who seek to integrate democratic and professional ideals.

40   *Charles T. Goodsell*

Balancing Competing Values

As public administrators, we are more than technical experts. We are also dealers in values. In the work we do, we continuously make value choices: Shall we fire or help a disturbed employee? Should our annual report merely brag or also reveal problems? Ought we simply announce public hearings or actively invite all affected parties? In making these kinds of day-to-day administrative decisions, we invoke or deny a number of important values. This makes our work far more important than it would be otherwise. Moreover, since we are public administrators, our value choices carry a special importance: They affect the lives of citizens and represent to citizens what their government really stands for.

The theme of this chapter is that American public administrators face distinctive difficulties in the realm of conscious value choice. In some countries, a system of administrative law or even administrative corruption is sufficiently rigid that the discretion of the administrator is minimal. In others, external political control is so strong that the administrator is given ample guidance. In contrast to these situations, the American public administrator operates with wide discretion, within the constitutional context of separation of powers. Except for rare instances (for example, the case of city managers), U.S. public administrators are not instruments of either chief executives or legislatures, but of both. In addition, they are responsible to the courts.

Another factor creating value discretion in America is the open and fluid character of our liberal society. No well-articulated ideology or public philosophy exists to provide a fixed value framework. On the contrary, the American value system is loosely structured and contains several competing strains of ethical thought. While the American culture and constitutional tradition embody a number of basic normative principles, these seldom give much help in day-to-day practical decisions. In fact, our normative principles sometimes diverge substantially and even contradict one another. In practical situations, administrators often face the dilemma of honoring one legitimate value orientation over another. This chapter seeks to illuminate such problems. The advice given in this chapter is that administrators should attempt to balance competing value orientations, instead of vehemently pursuing one at the expense of another.

Picking one's way through these value dilemmas is not easy. By deemphasizing any appropriate and accepted value, the administrator faces the likelihood of external criticism and possibly even internal guilt. To cope with these no-win situations, it is helpful to be fully aware of the value conflicts that exist, thereby assuring ourselves that there is often no one best solution. Value conflict can be particularly hard on American public administrators, who are not high-prestige civil servants, in the European sense, but mere bureaucrats. This status means that they do not automatically enjoy a protective envelope of political support or assumed competence when their actions anger or disappoint citizens and private groups. On the contrary, U.S. administrators, despite their being among the best in the world, are vilified and accused of misdeeds that are characterized as only confirming their lowly bureaucratic station; hence, attempting to pursue balanced values will never be easy, politically or personally. It will mean taking the heat for controversial decisions, perhaps the highest duty of the public servant in a liberal, democratic society like our own.

Diverse Value Orientations

The Five M's. Five value orientations may be said to prevail in contemporary American public administration. Each is correct in that it rests on a sound normative basis and can be defended successfully in the context of our society's traditions, but each differs substantially from the next, even to the extent of possessing opposite conceptual roots. I shall refer to them collectively as the Five M's.

One of these value approaches is the *means* orientation. This perspective depicts the public administrator as the passive tool of higher authority. The duty of the administrator is to implement statutes passed by legislative bodies, and lawful orders issued by elected executives or courts. Efficient, effective, timely, and faithful execution of these statutes and orders is the normative charge borne by the administrator. From a conceptual standpoint, his or her work is a means whose task is to achieve higher ends. The means-end dichotomy is parallel to the famous distinction made between administration and politics in traditionalist public administration literature. While the politics-administration dichotomy can be ridiculed as simplistic, it does point to the essential truth that, in a democratic society, public bureaucracies are supposed to be responsive to the people via elected officials. If this kind of popular responsibility ended, democracy as we know it would end as well (Goodnow, 1900; Appleby, 1949; Stene, 1975).

Another value orientation is *morality*. One can argue persuasively that government must be based not only on democratic responsiveness but also on the moral foundations provided by natural law, the Judeo-Christian ethic, or the founding fathers. Values such as equality, justice, honesty, fairness, and the protection of individual rights must prevail, despite election returns, the wording of statutes, or the orders of elected officials. Many present-day public administrators display codes of ethics on their office walls, a symbol of this higher normative orientation. Basic constitutional principles are what the courts interpret in reviewing the actions of administrators. In addition, the judiciary imposes on government agencies a large body of procedural law derived from the Constitution and court decisions made under it (Waldo, 1974; Wakefield, 1976; Rohr, 1978).

A third normative perspective can be termed the *multitude* orientation. In this instance, the administrator responds neither to elected officials nor to a higher morality, but to the citizens themselves, directly and immediately. It is an orientation that became popular in the 1960s under the rubric of citizen participation and was part of the "new public administration" of that time. The concept originally assumed inadequate public policies for the poor and the underprivileged, and it prescribed that the administrator should empower these groups by mobilizing and consulting with them. While in its more extreme forms this orientation calls for the administrator to become a radical activist, a more moderate position is that the public administrator should uncover hidden problems suffered by the disadvantaged and create mechanisms of popular participation that can actually work. These would include not merely traditional public hearing and advisory committees but also such mechanisms as client councils, coproduction of services, and negotiated decisions, as well as a "polis" of joint official-citizen dialogue (Marini, 1971; Cunningham, 1972; Rosenbaum, 1976; Stivers, 1988).

The *market* orientation is a fourth value approach. Just as the multitude orientation appeared in the 1960s under the sponsorship of radicals, the market orientation emerged in the 1970s under the egis of conservatives. Like the "new public administration," it calls for abandoning official elitism, but it substitutes market economics, rather than populist politics. According to this view, the dictates of the marketplace should determine, to the maximum possible extent, the organization and activities of the public sector. Based on the "public choice" school of political economy, this position argues that taxation and expenditure programs should be derived from marketlike signals that reflect the public's utility preferences. Examples of reforms advocated by this utilitarian approach are user fees, deregulation, contracting, service contracts, voucher programs, and other forms of privatization. By means of these devices, the market orientation values direct instructions from the public, in the form of statements of individual self-interest, something akin to what would occur via prices in a market system (Ostrom and Ostrom, 1971; Niskanen, 1973; Ostrom, 1974).

The last value orientation to be discussed here is *mission*. This perspective may be seen as a product of the 1980s, although its roots go back much farther. Here, neither officialdom nor the public is the sole source of guidance to the administrator. In addition to these influences, administrators should obey their own emergent conceptions of the proper missions of their agencies. These missions are initially stated in authorizing organic legislation, but over time they become developed with operational experience. Professional experts accumulate a body of institutional knowledge that enables them to interpret an appropriate adaptation of the mission to the ever changing current situation. This evolving mission is externally legitimized by an ongoing process of legislative reauthorization and appropriation, statutory amendment, legislative oversight, court litigation, press scrutiny, and dialogue within the administrative profession itself. Administrative agencies are seen as legitimate actors in the governance process in their own right, along with elected officers and the courts. Hence, their institutional strength and health are inherently of value, as is satisfactory service to their clients and other publics. These agencies pursue the public interest, which in this context is defined as fulfilling the adapted mission in the long-term interests of all affected parties, proceeding on the basis of an agency's past experience, and judiciously weighing competing claims and arguments in policymaking and implementation (Wamsley and others, 1987).

Selecting the Right Orientation. Each of the Five M's rests on its own justifiable normative foundation. These foundations are, respectively, representative government for means, higher law for morality, populist equality for multitude, economic efficiency for market, and the public interest for mission.

We should recognize immediately that, intellectually, these separate value orientations are not always compatible. At the abstract plane of the ultimate source of values, one cannot simultaneously look to the morality of natural law, on the one hand, and the popular wishes or utilitarian satisfactions of the people, on the other. At the practical plane of everyday public administration, however, such issues of ultimate compatibility are not the point. The task of the administrator is not to debate philosophy but to make practical decisions on what to do here and now. At this level, the administrator needs easily understandable normative bearings that can be applied to the immediate situation and thereby give some basis of proceeding with assurance. A practical normative map is needed, so to speak. It is the purpose of this chapter to furnish such a map.

The position taken here is that five reference points on this normative map—that is, all Five M's—are useful decision anchors in the everyday work of the administrator. None should be ignored, and all should be accepted for use at the appropriate times and in the appropriate circumstances. Indeed, in a given workday, it is possible and perhaps even likely that the administrator will encounter a succession of situations in which each of the Five M's should be called into play. An appropriate use of each orientation, rather than an overriding commitment to any one of them, is the order of the day. I shall illustrate the need for such eclecticism by describing what might occur during a single workday of a public administrator.

Consider an administrator in law enforcement (who we shall assume is male, for ease of use of pronouns). He comes to work on a given morning in a federal, state, or local governmental agency. At nine o'clock, he is called to the office of his boss, a political appointee. At this time, he is told that daytime police patrols will henceforth include one officer instead of two, in order to save funds. Then, at eleven o'clock, an unexpected visitor appears in the administrator's office. This person, known to be a member of an underworld family, has been seeking lighter enforcement of the vice laws for some time. The visitor casually mentions that some profitable real-estate investments have come to his attention, which he would be willing to share. Then, at a noontime luncheon, the administrator addresses a meeting of the Hispanic Improvement Association. In the question period, a spokesman of the association demands that only Hispanic police officers be allowed to patrol in Hispanic neighborhoods. After lunch, the administrator returns to his office to meet with his staff and formulate a policy proposal regarding police assistance to drivers who have locked their ignition keys in their cars. It is determined that, except when people or animals are locked in cars, police assistance will require reimbursement of a fifty-dollar locksmith fee. At the end of the day, the administrator attends a budget conference. The unfortunate news is that the central budget office seeks to terminate the department's Explorer Scout program next year, on the grounds that it is a "frill."

Which value orientations might be appropriate to these successive situations during one workday? The order to reduce patrols from two officers to one comes directly from a superior official and is probably best addressed by the means orientation. Hence, the policy change is reluctantly accepted. By contrast, the thinly veiled bribe offered by the underworld visitor should be handled by the morality orientation; the proffered investment tip is thus flatly rejected. The demand for Hispanic police patrols is best responded to in light of the multitude orientation. While this does not mean that the demand is automatically granted, it occasions a stepping up of dialogue with Hispanic community leaders. The locked-cars issue, which concerns the allocation of resources in a time of scarcity, brings the market orientation into play. The locksmith fee, a way of assigning service costs to service beneficiaries, is reluctantly adopted. Finally, the demand to terminate the Explorer Scout program is best addressed by the mission orientation. From this perspective, the program is not a "frill" but an important means of agency recruitment and socialization; hence, the administration fights for retention of funding for the program.

Such versatility may seem like common sense, yet our hypothetical administrator could have been much more rigid, from a normative standpoint. He could have insisted on following one of the Five M's all day. Let us imagine what extremists for each of the orientations might have done in selected situations.

An unbalanced adherent to the means orientation, a person we might label a *technocrat,* would have gone along without a fight in the scuttling of the Explorer Scout program, out of deference to the superior authority of the budgeteers. The morality extremist, whom we will call a *saint,* would have opposed the locked-car policy on the grounds that all locked-out drivers should be treated equally, regardless of circumstances. The promultitude administrator, a *populist,* may have been tempted to accept the real-estate tips of his visitor out of sympathy with his visitor's ethnic group. The market enthusiast, the *salesman,* would have proposed that neighborhoods have the option of purchasing two-officer police patrols if they pay a supplemental tax within their patrol districts. Finally, the mission extremist, the *zealot,* would have told the luncheon audience that he could not agree to discuss Hispanic patrols because this would infringe on professional staffing judgments, which can be made only by top managers, who "see the big picture."

In truth, most administrators are not technocrats, saints, populists, salesmen, or zealots, for which we can be thankful. Most public administrators are balanced enough in their normative grounding to make appropriate shifts from one value orientation to another, without engaging in the kind of bizarre conduct just depicted. Still, on some workdays, most public administrators do face genuine value dilemmas, for which appropriate orientations are not obvious, and wherein one is torn convincingly in more than one direction. Let us now shift the focus of our discussion to some illustrative decision areas, where these more difficult choices are encountered.

Value Dilemmas

When Things Go Awry. Difficult choices present themselves when we face conflicts between orders and our own conscience. For example, an administrator discovers possible misdeeds or illegalities going on inside his own organization. Should the administrator keep quiet and be strictly loyal to his superiors? This would be the posture of the technocrat, whose value orientation is means. Should the administrator blow the whistle on the discovered wrongdoing? This would be the response of the saint, anchored in the morality orientation. Both positions have a firm basis in the values of public administration; therefore, each can be defended indignantly as the only right posture.

The point is that the public administrator should be prepared to recognize the legitimacy of both orientations in this kind of situation and proceed accordingly. He should avoid being either a knee-jerk loyalist or a knee-jerk moralist; instead, he should creatively seek to work out a practical blend of the two relevant value orientations. Possible options include (in order of emphasizing means to emphasizing morality) discussing the problem with staff peers, confronting the offending superiors privately but firmly, threatening to take the matter higher, and searching for another influential higher official who may be predisposed to intervene. These intermediate options do not constitute a muddled value compromise that is inherently tainted by virtue of its being unpure; rather, they represent conscious attempts to recognize competing value claims.

When Constituents Grumble. Another common value dilemma is conflict between hierarchical and constituency demands. In a sense, this is the classic dilemma of the program manager, who must simultaneously satisfy policies being handed down from above by superiors and lawgivers, on the one hand, and demands being made from below by citizens and groups, on the other. The administrator is caught betwixt and between, at the cost of discretionary latitude. At times, he faces a complete no-win situation, in which forces above and below are so opposed that their positions do not overlap at all and even contradict each other.

The technician, following the means orientation, will opt in favor of hierarchical demands. The populist, obeying the multitude orientation, will be responsive to citizens' groups. Again, neither extremist position is solely right; the administrator has a duty to look for a balance between possibilities. The legitimacy of both sets of claims should be recognized; consequently, the administrator should seek ways to recognize each one, to some degree. Options might include convincing policymakers up the hierarchy that the only way their ideas can be implemented in the long run is by their giving the administrator some negotiating room; dividing the decision terrain into two parts, one subject to imposed control from above and the other subject to delegation to authorized constituencies; and promising citizens' groups that if they can hammer out a common position on specific disagreements, the administrator will attempt to sell this solution to superiors as the most viable one.

When the Work Force Is Dangerous. A third difficult area, coming increasingly to the fore, involves how to react when members of an agency's work force are perceived as dangerous because they are under the influence of drugs when on duty or because they have AIDS. Again, two value orientations compete. The zealot, who is concerned with mission, insists that everything possible must be done to curb drug use and infectious disease because of the damage these can do to the agency's performance, public reputation, and political support. The saint, concerned with constitutional rights, will approach the issue from the standpoint of protecting the work force against undue harassment. In particular, the saint will object to any signs of unlawful search and seizure, required self-incrimination, invasion of privacy, violation of personal dignity, and discrimination on the grounds of sexual orientation. The zealot will respond to these objections by arguing that these matters are less important than the safeguarding of the public interest and safety. Alcoholics and drug users should never drive locomotives or control air traffic, the zealot will say; moreover, such public needs as safe streets, national security, and the public health should never be jeopardized by our coddling drug users or tolerating the presence of employees who have AIDS.

How can these competing value claims be bridged? One way is to make judicious distinctions among types of government employees and to treat them differently. Workers whose daily judgment affects the lives of others can be monitored comprehensively, periodically or randomly, while those with less critical duties can undergo scrutiny only when evidence of unfitness arises. Another step might be to ensure that methods of testing for drug use, or for the presence of HIV antibodies, are reasonably efficacious, while also being respectful of individuals. Laboratory testing of urine and blood samples may be called for, yet the urine-sampling process can be kept private, and the names of people who have tested positive for HIV antibodies can be kept confidential. Finally, balance can be reflected in follow-up procedures. Automatic dismissal can be rejected, for example, in favor of mandatory treatment programs and job transfers.

When the Government Is for Sale. The final area of value dilemma concerns privatization. The salesman, reflecting the market orientation, will be enthusiastic about the sale of government assets, the contracting out of government services, and the institution of user fees and voucher programs. These, he argues, will reduce government spending and increase economic efficiency. The zealot, showing loyalty to the organization and its programs, will strongly resist these steps as violations of the public trust. To the zealot, the issues are not budget savings or economic efficiency; to him, asset sales mean loss of taxpayers' past investments, contracting out means deterioration of services, and user taxing and spending options mean the undermining of a public fisc dedicated to the common good.

A balanced approach in this area requires the assumption that privatization is neither a panacea nor a threat to the republic; its success depends on whether individual proposals are appropriate. Asset sales may be desirable for strictly commercial properties (hotels, factories, and surplus land), but not for items closely associated with nationhood or the historical heritage (capitols, monuments, and historic buildings). Strictly utilitarian services could be contracted out (garbage collection, building maintenance, printing), but not services that symbolize the protective power of the state (the police, the army, tax collection). A user fee may be acceptable for gaining access to a public beach, but not for being rescued from swimming or boating accidents. A voucher system may be appropriate for taxi transportation or health services for the elderly, but not for regulatory services to business.

Summary

The American public administrator probably makes more value choices than administrators commonly do in most other countries, because of our constitutional separation of powers and our liberal society. The exercise of this value discretion is not made easier by the generally low esteem in which American bureaucrats are held in political circles and in the public eye.

Five distinct value orientations are seen as legitimate in American public administration: means, morality, multitude, market, and mission. These five orientations can all be defended. Consequently, it is possible to become a logical extremist in favor of each. The extreme advocate of means is here called a technocrat; the advocate of morality, a saint; of multitude, a populist; of market, a salesman; and of mission, a zealot. As these pejorative names suggest, the thesis of this chapter is that balance rather than extremism should prevail. The administrator should recognize the particular circumstances in which each orientation is appropriate and not insist on always employing the same one, regardless of circumstances.

Occasions arise when it is not clear which orientation is appropriate. Two or more value orientations may compete as logical normative anchors, creating authentic value dilemmas for the administrator. In these situations, the administrator should be fully aware of the value conflict and attempt to find creative ways of partially satisfying the relevant conflicting orientations. This recommendation will not satisfy value purists or resolve underlying philosophical contradictions, but this is not what concerns the practicing administrator. He or she must make quick decisions based on value systems that are defined at the operational level. The Five M's offer a normative map that may give the practitioner some help in sorting through these value dilemmas. Balance, rather than extremism, is needed in a plural normative universe. Accepting this truism will permit administrators to cope better with the anguish of making difficult choices. Also, perhaps, it will produce better choices, and thereby a better society.

References

Appleby, P. H. *Policy and Administration.* University: University of Alabama Press, 1949.

Cunningham, J. V. "Citizen Participation in Public Affairs." *Public Administration Review,* 1972, *32,* 598–602.

Goodnow, F. J. *Politics and Administration: A Study in Government.* New York: Russell and Russell, 1900.

Marini, F. (ed.). *Toward a New Public Administration: The Minnowbrook Perspective.* Scranton, Pa.: Chandler Press, 1971.

Niskanen, W. A., Jr. *Bureaucracy: Servant or Master?* London: Institute of Economic Affairs, 1973.

Ostrom, V. *The Intellectual Crisis in American Public Administration.* (2nd ed.) University: University of Alabama Press, 1974.

Ostrom, V., and Ostrom, E. "Public Choice: A Different Approach to the Study of Public Administration." *Public Administration Review,* 1971, *33,* 203–212.

Rohr, J. A. *Ethics for Bureaucrats: An Essay on Law and Values.* New York: Marcel Dekker, 1978.

Rosenbaum, W. A. "The Paradoxes of Public Participation." *Administration and Society,* 1976, *8,* 355–383.

Stene, E. O. "The Politics-Administration Dichotomy." *Midwest Review of Public Administration,* 1975, *9,* 83–89.

Stivers, C. M. "Active Citizenship in the Administrative State." Unpublished doctoral dissertation, Center for Public Administration and Policy, Virginia Polytechnic Institute and State University, 1988.

Wakefield, S. "Ethics and the Public Service: A Case for Individual Responsibility." *Public Administration Review,* 1976, *36,* 661–666.

Waldo, D. "Reflections on Public Morality." *Administration and Society,* 1974, *6,* 267–282.

Wamsley, G. L., and others. "The Public Administration and the Governance Process: Refocusing the American Dialogue." In R. C. Chandler (ed.), *A Centennial History of the American Administrative State.* New York: Free Press, 1987.

41 *Charles R. Wise*

The Liability
of Public Administrators

There was a time when public employees and government organizations were immune to suits for damages for wrongs they were alleged to have committed that involved other citizens. Under the doctrine of sovereign immunity, the principle widely applied by American courts was that "the king could do no wrong"—that is, the government as sovereign could not be sued for legal wrongs. Borrowed originally from English law, in the American legal context the underlying principle was that a democratic government was the embodiment of the people, and a person as a part of the body politic may not sue himself or herself. Those days are clearly over.

Actions by Congress and the state legislatures, but primarily by the courts, have defined and broadened the scope of liability to the point that virtually all public employees are involved, to some extent, as are all levels of government. Activity by the courts has been particularly expansive in the last decade, leading one observer to state that it verges on an explosion (Eikenberry, 1985). In any event, the nature and extent of legal liability for public employees—and, to some extent, for public agencies—have become a factor in the management of all public undertakings.

The liability arrangements that have been developed, however, are not consistent across levels of government, types of officials, or kinds of governmental activities. This has resulted in part because the legislative and the judicial branches, at both the national and the state levels, have sometimes been involved in the same aspects of defining liability arrangements and sometimes in different aspects. Thus, for any given state-level administrator to develop a complete map of the potential liability exposure applicable to himself or herself or to an agency would require a review of several federal and state statutes and court decisions at both the federal and the state levels.

Concomitantly, a map for all state and federal administrators would entail an encyclopedic effort. This is clearly beyond the scope of this chapter. The purpose here, then, is to focus on liability for violation of constitutional torts, which has primarily been defined by the federal courts. This focus has been chosen not only for reasons of parsimony and general applicability but also because in the past fifteen years the growth of suits in this area has been significant. Public administrators would do well, however, to acquaint themselves with the other sources of liability that are applicable to them.

The Framework of Constitutional Liability

The first issue that may come to mind is why and how public administrators came to be exposed as individuals to suits for violations of citizens' constitutional rights. While the Bill of Rights was established shortly after the adoption of the Constitution, nothing in the constitutional convention or in early congressional actions declared that federal or state public servants or the governments themselves would be open to suit from individual citizens.

The doctrine of *respondeat superior,* which firmly established the liability of employers for the legal wrongs of employees in private tort law, did not extend to any actions by public employees. Not only was there no doctrine under which the federal government could be sued for violations that had counterparts in private law, there was also no doctrine for violations that were purely public in nature. In fact, when the early courts allowed suits against states to be filed in federal courts, the Eleventh Amendment to the Constitution was passed to preclude such actions—an occurrence that still affects the system of liability today. These circumstances, together with the doctrine of sovereign immunity, effectively accorded governments and public employees absolute immunity to suit. Only in a few small areas did the federal government and the states grant permission for claims to be filed. The courts held that the remedy for individual citizens lay with Congress, and private bills were the vehicle for redress (Schuck, 1983).

It may be said that the impetus for change in fashioning liability rules stemmed from the larger involvement of government in various aspects of citizens' lives, from the larger scale of government itself, and from citizens' growing experience with the injuries they could sustain as a result of governmental action. The Federal Tort Claims Act, which originally allowed suits in just a few areas, was passed after the expansion of government following World War II, but this act covered conduct among counterparts in the private sector. Wrongs that had their origins in the nature of the relationship between government and citizens' rights came to be defined largely by the courts.

What led to the courts' activism in this area? In no small part, the reason was the expansion of government, but the federal courts have asserted a leadership role in defining how expanded government activity can impinge unfairly on citizens' rights. The courts have enunciated policy reasons for their activity, including vindication of rights, deterrence of abuse, and accountability of officials (*Butz* v. *Economou*, 1978). In the course of defining this protective scheme, the courts have enunciated a structure of liability for public administrators within which governments and officials must operate. It is a constantly evolving structure characterized by uncertainty in a number of areas.

Thus, it is not possible to lay out definitive rules for even a significant portion of the public work force. It is possible, however, to delineate some of the principles that appear to guide judicial policymaking, and to discuss how they have been applied to some sectors of public service, in order to provide a basis from which public servants can consider areas of exposure and risk. Several questions will guide this analysis: What are the legal bases of the liability of public administrators? How do immunity rules define exposure and protection for public servants? What are the responsibilities of public employers and public employees?

Legal Bases of Constitutional Liability

The United States has no coherent system of official liability within which officials in particular types of agencies at one level of government would find themselves in the same risk position as officials at counterpart agencies at other levels of government. This circumstance stems from the different statutes and particularly from the different legal doctrines on which the courts have drawn to define constitutional liability.

There are numerous ways to secure actions from governmental officials through the courts, some of which are statutory and some of which are constitutional. For example, injunctions against state and local officials have been common since *Brown* v. *Board of Education of Topeka, Kansas* (1954). That type of relief is not the main target of analysis here. The primary (but not exclusive) focus is on the bases of suits wherein the relief sought is monetary damages to be paid to the plaintiff.

In order to delineate the legal bases, it is necessary to distinguish between the origins and applications of extant policy according to different levels of government. Three primary points of departure are two federal statutes and one Supreme Court decision.

State and Local Liability. The central statute, as far as state and local governments and their officials are concerned, is 42 U.S.C. Section 1983. Originally known as the Ku Klux Klan Act, Congress passed it in 1871 to counter acts of intimidation against newly emancipated black citizens. For most of its history, the Supreme Court invoked it to strike down unconstitutional voting restrictions. In 1961, however, the court sharply broke with that tradition and transformed the act into the potent remedial scheme of much more general purpose that it is today.

In *Monroe* v. *Pape* (1961), the court stated for the first time that a citizen could sue an individual city employee (in this case, a policeman) for violation of rights. A key interpretive point established in that case was that the "under color of law" language of Section 1983 was held to apply to the employee's conduct, whether or not that conduct was authorized by state law. It did not refer only to violations of rights sanctioned specifically by some state statute but included those committed under pretense of law. This meant that citizens suing under the act did not have to show that the actions of officials were somehow affirmatively sanctioned by laws governing their jurisdictions. The court has recently held that a physician who is under contract with a state prison to provide medical services to inmates at a state prison hospital on a part-time basis acts "under color of state law" within the meaning of Section 1983 (*West* v. *Atkins,* 1988). The court also held that the availability of a state statutory remedy did not bar citizens from seeking federal relief. Section 1983 is supplementary to the state remedy; and the state statutory remedy, as a general matter of policy, does not have to be exhausted before one can bring a federal action. Similarly, state administrative remedies do not have to be exhausted before one can bring a suit under this act (*Patsy* v. *Board of Regents,* 1982).

In terms of grounds for suit, it has been noted that Section 1983 has been found capable of supporting almost any type of claim related to the violation of constitutional rights (Spurrier, 1986). For violations involving state and local government officials, however, the Supreme Court opened the way for a major expansion in the case of *Maine* v. *Thiboutot* (1980). In that case, the court considered whether an official could be sued on the basis of a federal statute or only when a constitutional right had been violated. The court decided that claims for statutory violations could also be granted under Section 1983. This interpretive move has greatly expanded the options for plaintiffs in bringing suits. State and local officials need to be advised of the federal statutes that potentially confer rights on the citizens with whom they deal in their professional areas of responsibility.

Nevertheless, state and local administrators have to be concerned with more than federal law and federal courts when it comes to Section 1983 suits. As Schuck (1983, p. 50) observes, "Prodded by the civil rights movement and the 'due process revolution' the Court has transformed Sec. 1983 into a powerful engine of social control, supplementing and often supplanting state tort law." One way in which the states have been brought into it is through state courts. In *Martinez* v. *California* (1980), the court held that Section 1983 claims could be brought in state courts, although it did not require state courts to hear such cases. In addition, the court has also found that state statutes and even state regulations can create a liberty or property interest that implicates the constitutional right to due process. This means that the federal courts will impose constitutional due process requirements on state administrative and regulatory schemes that the states themselves have devised to govern interests that they have created (*Hewitt* v. *Helms,*

1983; *Cleveland Board of Education* v. *Loudermill,* 1983). Thus, state policymakers are well advised to consider that when they take actions that can be considered by the courts to create property or liberty interests, they are also implicating federal due process rights that can be the subject of suits under Section 1983.

The types of relief available differ somewhat, depending on the identity of the defendant. For example, Section 1983 authorizes injunctive or declaratory relief from state or local officials or from local governments. Such types of relief are not available from state governments themselves, because of the Eleventh Amendment (*Edelman* v. *Jordan,* 1974). Compensatory money damages may be obtained from state or local officials in their individual capacities. In addition, local governments themselves may be sued for compensatory damages, but only if a violation by a local government official is pursuant to an "official policy" or "governmental custom" (*Monell* v. *Department of Social Services,* 1978).

In terms of determining appropriate damages, the Supreme Court has stated that each type of constitutional rights violation calls for an independent judgment on compensation (*Carey* v. *Piphus,* 1978). The Supreme Court has also held that it is the responsibility of the plaintiff to demonstrate injury (for example, evidence of mental and emotional distress) and that, in the absence of such proof of injury, nominal damages for the violation per se could be awarded. Thus, for example, students who were denied their due process rights but who did not demonstrate actual injury were awarded one dollar in nominal compensatory damages for the per se rights violation.

Punitive damages—payments to the victim beyond those necessary for compensation—are also possible under certain circumstances. Punitive damages may be assessed against individual state or local government officials, but not against such government entities as municipalities (*City of Newport* v. *Fact Concerts,* 1981; *Smith* v. *Wade,* 1983). A jury may award punitive damages "when the defendant's conduct is shown to be motivated by evil motive or intent, or when it involves reckless or callous indifference to the federally protected rights of others" (*Smith* v. *Wade,* 1983).

Another key statute affecting state and local administrators is the Civil Rights Attorney's Fee Awards Act of 1976 (42 U.S.C. Sec. 1988), commonly referred to as Section 1988. It states that in any action or proceeding to enforce Section 1983 and other specified civil rights statutes, the court may award a reasonable attorney's fee to the prevailing party (other than the United States). This constitutes a striking exception to the American rule, whereby each side normally pays its own attorney's fees. It means that a state or local administrator found responsible for a rights violation under Section 1983 can expect to pay the plaintiff's attorney's fees in addition to any money damages assessed. In certain situations, the purpose of fee-shifting statutes such as this one is to make access to the courts possible and to vindicate the plaintiff's rights.

The significance of this statute, and of the court's interpretations of it, should not be underestimated. It is not unusual for attorney's fee awards to considerably exceed the assessed damages. In addition, the scope of Section 1988's coverage is much wider than that of Section 1983. For example, the Supreme Court has held that the Eleventh Amendment does not provide a bar to the award of an attorney's fee against a state itself (*Hensley* v. *Eckerhart,* 1983; *Maher* v. *Gagne,* 1980).

Because of Section 1988, there are clear incentives to initiate litigation early in a potential dispute. This is because the prevailing parties in such litigation are the only ones who may be reimbursed for their attorney's fees. Plaintiffs' attorneys have an incentive to file these cases, so that the meter starts running.

The interpretations of Section 1988 have also spawned a whole new area of litigation, which explicitly concerns the amount of attorney's fees to be awarded. There is no clear standard for determination of attorney's fees, and the public decision maker should realize that if he or she unsuccessfully contests what is believed to be an unreasonable fee award, the court will add the attorney's fees incurred in defense of the award to the fees already incurred in the case. The Supreme Court has decreed that the amount of the fee must be determined according to the facts of each case (*Hensley* v. *Eckerhart,* 1983). Thus, the amount claimed is subject to litigation.

Since attorney's fee awards can be much larger than damage awards, administrators need to carefully consider actions that may contribute to a plaintiff's prevailing. For example, a consent decree, in which the plaintiff receives some of the relief sought, does not weaken the plaintiff's claim to fees (*Maher* v. *Gagne,* 1980). The Supreme Court has stated, "A lawsuit sometimes produces voluntary action by the defendant that affords the plaintiff all or some of the relief he sought through a judgment" (*Hewitt* v. *Helms,* 1983). That is sufficient to have fees awarded (*Ashley* v. *Atlantic Richfield Co.,* 1986). In fact, the court has left open the question of whether the "catalyst" theory can be advanced by a plaintiff, in the absence of even a consent decree. If so, the plaintiff will be allowed to attempt to demonstrate that some administrative action that a public official took voluntarily was actually taken under pressure of the plaintiff's lawsuit; thus, if the suit is the catalyst for change, the plaintiff is the prevailing party for purposes of awarding the attorney's fees (*Hewitt* v. *Helms,* 1983). If the "catalyst" theory becomes law, administrators will need to be doubly vigilant to avoid such unforeseen consequences of their actions.

What can state and local administrators expect? If the other party prevails, he or she will almost certainly be awarded attorney's fees by the court. If the state or local official wins the case, that official, or his or her jurisdiction, will almost certainly not have attorney's fees awarded, unless the court finds that the plaintiff's claim was frivolous, unreasonable, or groundless, or that the plaintiff continued to litigate after it clearly became so (*Hughes* v. *Rowe,* 1980). With regard to the amount in fees that will be awarded, there is less certainty. It should be noted that this is still a developing area of law.

Citizens can look to more than federal statutes (such as Section 1983) in their desire to obtain money damages for constitutional violations from state and local governments. They can appeal directly on the basis of the Constitution itself. In what could potentially constitute the most significant expansion of governmental damages liability since *Owen* v. *City of Independence* (1980), the Supreme Court has decided most recently that citizens may sue state and local governments for compensation for unconstitutional land-use regulations directly on the basis of the Fifth Amendment's prohibition on the taking of property without just compensation (*First English Evangelical Lutheran Church of Glendale* v. *County of Los Angeles,* 1987; *James Nollan et al.* v. *California Coastal Commission,* 1987). In doing so, the court explicitly rejected the argument that the Fifth Amendment is a remedial provision furnishing the basis of a court's award of money damages against the government. Given the extensive involvement of state and local governments in land-use regulations, it is reasonable to expect significant litigation to decide, among other things, which specific governmental regulations constitute a "temporary taking" that requires compensation. The dissenters in *First Evangelical* (1987) predict a litigation explosion under conditions where the court itself has repeatedly recognized that it cannot establish any objective rules to assess when a regulation becomes a taking. It remains to be seen if the courts will narrowly or expansively apply Section 1983 and Section 1988 to land use regulation.

Federal Liability. In 1946, Congress passed the Federal Tort Claims Act (FTCA), which for the first time waived the sovereign immunity of the United States for most common law torts committed by federal employees within the scope of their employment. An individual federal official is absolutely immune to suit for common law torts. The only condition for immunity is that the official must have been acting within the outer perimeter of his or her official duties (*Barr* v. *Mateo,* 1959). Complainants may maintain an action for money damages directly against the United States under the FTCA for common law torts. The FTCA has been interpreted over time to provide a remedy against acts or omissions that are tortious under the laws of the states in which they have occurred. Congress passed the law so that the federal government itself would no longer be exempt when its agents committed wrongful or negligent acts that commonly constituted torts. In 1974, the FTCA was amended to cover assault, battery, false imprisonment, false arrest, abuse of process, and malicious prosecution by officials empowered to make searches, seizures, or arrests.

Congress has not passed a statute such as Section 1983 that applies to federal officials. Nevertheless, the Supreme Court created a similar remedial scheme "in the absence of affirmative action by Congress" (*Bivens* v. *Six Unknown Federal Narcotics Agents,* 1971). Through the *Bivens* or constitutional tort line of cases, the court has defined a system of litigation for adjudicating alleged violations of citizens' constitutional rights. While the

Bivens case itself was directed specifically at Fourth Amendment violations precipitated by illegal searches, in the sixteen years since *Bivens,* the constitutional tort doctrine has been expanded to include other violations of constitutional rights as well. The federal courts have expanded the realm of constitutional torts to violations of the First, Fifth, Sixth, Eighth, Ninth, Thirteenth, and Fourteenth Amendments (Wise, 1985; Lehmann, 1977).

The Supreme Court, in creating the constitutional tort doctrine, held that the United States did not become vicariously liable for the constitutional violations of its officials. Thus, the court has reaffirmed the doctrine that the United States has not waived its sovereign immunity in such litigation (*Brown* v. *United States,* 1970; *Francisco* v. *Schmidt,* 1982). In addition, the court has also stated that not every tort by a federal official may be redressed in damages (*Davis* v. *Passman,* 1979; *Beard* v. *Mitchell,* 1979). A suit in federal court for money damages must be based on the unconstitutional conduct of federal officials (*Rodriguez* v. *Richey,* 1977), and the plaintiff must first establish a violation of a valid constitutional claim (*Garcia* v. *United States,* 1982).

There is no fee-shifting statute comparable to Section 1988 for cases against federal employees. The Equal Access to Justice Act of 1980 has not been interpreted by the Supreme Court as a general counterpart to Section 1988. Nevertheless, in some circumstances, the circuit courts have related the two statutes and awarded attorney's fees against the United States. The circuit courts are split on this issue. The majority of courts read the Equal Access to Justice Act to hold that the United States is liable for attorney's fees only when federal officials act under color of state law. A minority has found the United States liable when federal officials engage in the same activities for which state officials would be liable (Ragozin, 1986). The Supreme Court has not ruled on the matter.

Immunity Comparisons of Federal, State, and Local Scenes

As already discussed, the legal bases of constitutional torts are somewhat different for the three levels of government. These legal bases and subsequent court interpretations have produced liability systems with both similar and dissimilar features, according to the level of government. One of these features is how attorney's fees are treated. Another of the key features is the framework of immunity defined by the courts.

The courts have defined two types of immunity that apply to constitutional tort suits for money damages: absolute and qualified.

Absolute immunity means that the public official is not liable for money damages. Officials who enjoy absolute immunity, however, may still be subject to suit for injunctive relief and, in the case of state and local officials, attorney's fees (*Pulliam* v. *Allen,* 1984). The availability of absolute immunity is determined at the start of litigation by virtue of a motion to dismiss. For those officials to whom it applies, absolute immunity extends to all acts performed within the outer perimeter of their official duties, no matter how malicious their motivations (*Barr* v. *Mateo,* 1959; *Wallen* v. *Domm,* 1983).

Absolute immunity has been carefully limited by the court to a few officials whose functions the justices have defined as requiring full exemption from liability. This functional approach has led the court to extend absolute immunity to those engaged in acts of a judicial, prosecutorial, or legislative nature. Thus, judges (*Pierson* v. *Ray,* 1967), prosecutors (*Imbler* v. *Pachtman,* 1976), and police officer witnesses (*Briscoe* v. *LaHue,* 1983) are accorded absolute immunity when engaged in their respective functions.

In a few limited circumstances, executive-branch officials have been accorded absolute immunity. The president is absolutely immune (*Nixon* v. *Fitzgerald,* 1982), but state governors are not. Federal officials subject to Administrative Procedure Act restraints, and who are performing adjudicatory functions within federal agencies, are entitled to absolute immunity for their judicial acts, as are agency officials performing functions analogous to those of a prosecutor. The court uses a comparison-of-roles test. If the official's role is functionally comparable to that of a judge, for example, the official is accorded absolute immunity (*Butz* v. *Economou,* 1978; *Francisco* v. *Schmidt,* 1982). In addition, the Supreme Court has stated that executive officials may be accorded absolute immunity in "exceptional situations" if they are "essential for the conduct of public business," but the court finds exceptional situations exceedingly rare. A governor's efforts to deal with "mob rule" (*Scheur* v. *Rhodes,* 1974), a cabinet secretary's law enforcement activities (*Butz* v. *Economou,* 1978), and the attorney general's national security activities (*Mitchell* v. *Forsyth,* 1985) have all failed to meet the criterion.

The Supreme Court has increasingly emphasized that, for almost all administrative officials engaged in discretionary actions, only qualified (also known as "good faith") immunity may be accorded (*Malley* v. *Briggs,* 1986). Whether the court will accord it in a particular situation depends on the "objective legal reasonableness" of the action, assessed in light of the legal rules that were clearly established at the time the action was taken. Qualified immunity is really a defense that must be pleaded by the public administrator in response to a suit; the defendant must demonstrate his or her good faith by objectively proving that there has been no violation of clearly established law (*Harlow* v. *Fitzgerald,* 1982, p. 819). Thus, whereas absolute immunity provides officials protection from both suit and liability, qualified immunity protects only from liability.

The justices have continually defined qualified immunity in a continuing attempt to accommodate conflicting concerns. On the one hand, the court has relied on a damages remedy to vindicate the rights of citizens. On the other, "permitting damage suits against government officials can entail substantial social costs, including the risk that fear of personal monetary liability and harassing litigation will unduly inhibit officials in the discharge of their duties" (*Anderson* v. *Creighton,* 1987). The sought-for "balance" has not come easily and has been the subject of continuing litigation.

One key issue has been what the court means by "objective legal reasonableness," on which the qualified immunity defense rests. In an attempt to further define this concept, the Supreme Court has recently ruled on two cases in which illegal searches by police officers were alleged—*Malley* v. *Briggs* (1986) and *Anderson* v. *Creighton* (1987). In *Malley,* the police officer had obtained a search warrant from a magistrate and had argued that obtaining the warrant per se met the criteria of objective legal reasonableness. The majority of justices rejected this argument and stated that the criterion was whether a reasonably well-trained officer in Malley's position would have known that the affidavit he presented to establish probable cause failed to do so, and that he should not have applied for the warrant. The majority excused magistrates, stating, "It is possible that a magistrate working under docket pressures will fail to perform as a magistrate should" (*Malley* v. *Briggs,* 1986, pp. 1098–1099). Thus, judges working under docket pressures are not expected to make correct constitutional determinations; police officers working in the law enforcement environment must.

In *Anderson,* an FBI agent participated in a warrantless search of a house, claiming that probable cause existed and that his failure to obtain a warrant was based on exigent circumstances. The owners of the house sued, but their suit was dismissed on summary judgment (before trial) on grounds of qualified immunity: The officer successfully claimed that he could establish, as a matter of law, that a reasonable officer could have believed that the search comported with the Fourth Amendment, even though it actually did not. The court ruled for the FBI agent.

The justices are trying to preserve the brake they introduced in *Harlow* v. *Fitzgerald* (1982)—against sending every constitutional tort suit to a full-blown trial—by continuing to direct the lower courts to consider qualified immunity at the summary judgment stage. They want the judges to make the determination on the basis of "clearly established law." They evidently believe that they have gone a long way in establishing clear law, at least in cases of search and seizure, and they have stated, "If officers of reasonable competence could disagree on this issue, immunity should be recognized" (*Malley* v. *Briggs,* 1986, p. 1096). Nevertheless, the individual court is left to decide whether an official of reasonable competence should have known that the law governing his actions was clearly established. Plaintiffs will have to do more than allege rights violations in a general sense (for example, that due process has been violated) in order to get to trial. They will have to be more specific. "The *contours* [emphasis added] of the right must be sufficiently clear that a reasonable official would understand that what he is doing violates the right" (*Anderson* v. *Creighton,* 1987, p. 5093). It should be expected, therefore, that public officials who are defendants in future cases will argue that statements of rights violation provided by plaintiffs are too vague to meet the test of clearly established law. Plaintiffs, of course, will argue the opposite.

One key area of difference among levels of government is in how the jurisdictions themselves are treated by the courts, in terms of holding governments liable. The United States and its constituent organizations are held absolutely immune to the constitutional torts of their employees, under the doctrine of sovereign immunity. For certain specified violations (false imprisonment, malicious prosecution, and abuse of process), the United States has consented to be sued pursuant to the Federal Tort Claims Act. In short, however, the FTCA is not as favorable to plaintiffs as the *Bivens* doctrine is.

The states' treatment by the Supreme Court is complex and cannot be fully explored here (see Brown, 1985). The general principles can be delineated, however. The court has held that the Eleventh Amendment does not prohibit prospective relief, such as injunctions or declaratory orders, but it does prohibit retroactive relief, such as money damages (*Edelman* v. *Jordan,* 1974). Prospective relief may require payment from a state treasury (such as court-ordered welfare payments) as a necessary consequence of compliance in the future, but compensation for past violations is not allowed. Citizens can sue state governments for money damages, however, if Congress specifically authorizes such suits. Such authorizations are complicated and have been subjected to continuing litigation. With respect to money damages based on Section 1983 specifically, however, the court has rejected the contention that Section 1983's reference to ''persons'' includes states (*Quern* v. *Jordan,* 1979).

This is small solace for state administrators, however, when they consider payments for judgments pursuant to federal injunctions (Melnick, 1985), attorney's fees under Section 1988, and damages awarded under other statutes (specifically authorized by Congress) that make states proper party defendants. (The court allows this last liability exposure under the Fourteenth Amendment, which overcomes the Eleventh.) The risk to state treasuries from these sources is much greater than the potential exposure from Section 1983 itself. The states are exposed because the Supreme Court has developed the concept of ''official capacity'' (which, the court itself acknowledges, ''continues to confuse laywers and confound lower courts''—see *Kentucky* v. *Graham,* 1985) in order to obviate the application of the Eleventh Amendment to several specific statutes, except for Section 1983. This doctrine creates the fiction that it is not the state itself that is being sued, but rather the administrator who is implementing the offending state's statute. A judicial declaratory order thus directs the administrator to pay for prospective relief (for example, welfare payments previously denied). This fiction has been recognized by the court itself as representing ''only another way of pleading an action against an entity of which an officer is an agent'' (*Kentucky* v. *Graham,* 1985, p. 3105). Of course, if the official-capacity suit is successful—achieving injunctive relief, for example—the state can expect to pay the plaintiff's attorney's fee. The slim remaining significance of the Eleventh Amendment is that of a type of process protection that requires Congress to specifically abrogate the states' immunity statutorily (Brown, 1985).

Local governments do not have the Eleventh Amendment. Citizens who wish to sue local governments no longer need to sue local administrators in their official capacities (*Kentucky* v. *Graham,* 1985). They can sue local governments directly. Further, in contrast to the court's ruling for states, local governments are treated as persons under Section 1983 and can be sued directly for money damages, as well as for injunctive and declaratory relief.

Local governments may not plead the qualified, "good faith" immunity of their officials. This means that even if local officials successfully escape Section 1983 liability by being accorded qualified immunity for acting in good faith, the local government will still be held liable if the court decides that a constitutional violation has been committed. Therefore, local governments are liable when actions are judged after the fact to have violated the law, even when the law has not been so clearly established as to ensure that, at the time of an action, a local official could have reasonably understood that he or she was violating it. As Justice Powell put it in his dissent in *Owen* v. *City of Independence* (1980), "As a result, local governments and their officials will face the unnerving prospect of crushing damages judgements whenever a policy valid under current law is later found to be unconstitutional" (p. 683). In effect, even the local government administrator who is most informed about current constitutional interpretations cannot be sure of limiting his or her jurisdiction's liability exposure before the fact; later decisions can expose the jurisdiction to liability for damages. The court does stipulate that the harm suffered by the citizen must result from some official "policy or custom" of the local government; the local government must be the "moving force" behind the deprivation. Beyond this, however, the meaning of the policy-or-custom standard is subject to considerable confusion and litigation. The justices themselves have recently opined in *City of Oklahoma City* v. *Tuttle* (1985, p. 2434) that "the development of municipal liability under section 1983 is in a somewhat sketchy state." In that case, the justices decided that it takes more than a single isolated incident to constitute a policy or custom, but the standard was able to command only a plurality of the justices. Recently, in another opinion, the court decided that a local government unit cannot be held liable unless the plaintiff proves the existence of an unconstitutional policy promulgated by officials who have relevant authority. The identification of officials who have "final policymaking authority" is a question of state (including local) law, rather than a question of fact for a jury (*City of St. Louis* v. *Praprotnik,* 1988). This last standard was agreed to only by a plurality of the justices, however, and may not hold in the future.

Alternative Avenues for Pursuing Grievances

Can the legislative and executive branches provide alternatives to litigation in the federal courts to protect constitutional rights? Is the award of money damages pursuant to the doctrines described here the only constitutionally permissible avenue recognized by the court? The answers to these questions are "Sometimes" and "Not exactly." Nevertheless, the Supreme

Court has reserved the prerogative of deciding when constitutional tort doctrines will be either controlling or supplemental, with respect to other remedial schemes. The court recently reiterated its holding that constitutional tort action "might not be appropriate" when there are "special factors counseling hesitation" or an "explicit congressional declaration" that another remedy is exclusive (*United States et al.* v. *Stanley,* 1987). The court has also declared that "such 'special factors' include existence of statutory mechanisms giving meaningful remedies against the United States even though those remedies do not provide 'complete relief' to the claimant" (*Schweiker et al.* v. *Chilicky et al.,* 1988, p. 4767).

There have been several decisions concerning which other statutory schemes for pursuing grievances will be accepted by the courts as precluding constitutional tort suits. Nevertheless, if a systematic framework is preferred, it has yet to emerge. One critic has charged, "These decisions have created apparent inconsistencies in the domain of federal remedies, seemingly attributable only to shifting Supreme Court majorities and disparate ideologies in the lower federal courts" (Rumeld, 1983).

On the one hand, the Supreme Court has refused to acknowledge the Federal Tort Claims Act as the exclusive remedy, even after Congress explicitly amended it in 1974 to cover assault, battery, false imprisonment, false arrest, abuse of process, and malicious prosecution (*Carlson* v. *Green,* 1980). Therefore, citizens can elect to sue the United States under the FTCA for such violations, as well as to sue individual federal employees (although they cannot prevail against both). Similarly, at the state and local levels, the court has ruled that the remedial provisions of the Railway Labor Act (*Hodges* v. *Tomberlin,* 1980) and the Aid to Families with Dependent Children program do not preclude bringing a Section 1983 action.

On the other hand, the justices have ruled that some other statutory remedial schemes are "sufficiently comprehensive" that they signal congressional intent to preclude resort to the constitutional tort cause of action. In *Bush* v. *Lucas* (1983), for example, the court found that Congress, through the Civil Service Reform Act of 1978, had erected a system of administrative appeal that provides meaningful remedies for employees who may have been unfairly disciplined for making critical comments about their agencies. In *Schweiker* v. *Chilicky,* the court upheld that Congress, in amending Title II of the Social Security Act, had provided for meaningful remedies in an administrative review process for denial of disability benefits. Previously (in *Brown* v. *GSA,* 1976), the court determined that Section 717 of Title VII of the Civil Rights Act was the exclusive remedy for plaintiff employees alleging discrimination by federal officials.

At the federal level, perhaps the clearest judicial statement applies to the military. In applying the *Feres* doctrine (*Feres* v. *United States,* 1950) to both *Chappell* v. *Wallace* (1983) and *United States et al.* v. *Stanley* (1987), the Supreme Court held, on the basis of the military's unique disciplinary structure and of Congress's activity, that the court must abstain from applying constitutional tort doctrine to injuries arising out of activity "incident to service." Thus, members of a military service must rely on the military justice system, instead of on constitutional tort doctrine. This ruling does not apply to civilian defense employees, however (Euler, 1986).

At the state and local levels, the court has stated, "When the remedial devices provided in a particular Act are sufficiently comprehensive, they may suffice to demonstrate congressional intent to preclude the remedy of suits under Section 1983" (*Middlesex County Sewerage Authority* v. *National Sea Clammers Association,* 1981). Thus, with regard to any particular statute, the court seems to focus on the remedial scheme in the statute and then seeks to infer whether Congress intended that scheme to provide the exclusive remedy, or whether Section 1983 may be used as a supplement.

Administrators must be careful, however, to follow the procedures provided in the qualifying administrative remedies. Courts have decided, for instance, when defendants who were public officials were alleged to have conspired or acted to deprive plaintiffs of procedures otherwise available, that plaintiffs could proceed with constitutional tort actions (*McIntosh* v. *Weinberger,* 1984; *Sonntag* v. *Dooley,* 1981).

Summary

Administrators can expect to work within an environment of liability in the future. Recent history in this area has shown an expansion of the possibilities for litigation, as well as some modest drawing of boundaries. This is likely to continue. Public administrators cannot expect to make decisions with certainty regarding court action. The system is still evolving. Thus, no absolute rules of practice are possible. Nevertheless, the following guidelines are offered as a basis for operating.

1. Become familiar with liability statutes (federal, state, and local) that show the potential of being implicated in your own organization's activities.
2. Consider the nature of the "rights" that may be affected by changes in regulations or practices that confer "liberty" or "property" interests.
3. Review agency operations for due process procedures (such as providing notice, opportunity to be heard, and a statement of reasons for decisions).
4. Analyze the extent to which proposed actions treat different groups or people differently, and determine whether any differences are justifiable under current legal standards.
5. Coordinate with legal staffs to avoid unnecessary litigation that could result in the payment of large fees to plaintiffs' attorneys.
6. If litigation has started, consider whether any administrative actions can be characterized as having been motivated by a suit (these could result in determinations for plaintiffs), and consider the fee implications of consent agreements.

7. Become familiar with constitutional standards affecting your functions, in order to be cognizant of practices that a well-trained practitioner "should have known," so that you can act in "good faith."
8. Follow scrupulously the procedures afforded persons within administrative remedies.
9. Investigate the availability and coverage of indemnity, representation, and/or insurance provided by your agency, and investigate the availability and particularly the coverages of private insurers.

List of Cases Cited

Anderson v. *Creighton,* 107 S. Ct. 3034 (1987).

Ashley v. *Atlantic Richfield Co.,* 794 F.2d 128 (3rd Cir. 1986).

Barr v. *Mateo,* 360 U.S. 564 (1959).

Beard v. Mitchell, 604 F.2d 485 (7th Cir. 1979).

Bivens v. *Six Unknown Federal Narcotics Agents,* 403 U.S. 396 (1971).

Briscoe v. *LaHue,* 408 U.S. 325 (1983).

Brown v. *Board of Education of Topeka, Kansas,* 347 U.S. 483 (1954).

Brown v. *GSA,* 425 U.S. 820 (1976).

Brown v. *United States,* 653 F.2d 196 (5th Cir. 1981), cert. den. 102 S. Ct. (1970).

Bush v. *Lucas,* 103 S. Ct. 3081 (1983).

Butz v. *Economou,* 438 U.S. 478 (1978).

Carey v. *Piphus,* 435 U.S. 247 (1978).

Carlson v. *Green,* 446 U.S. 14 (1980).

Chappell v. *Wallace,* 462 U.S. 296 (1983).

City of Newport v. *Fact Concerts,* 453 U.S. 247 (1981).

City of Oklahoma City v. *Tuttle,* 105 S. Ct. 2427 (1985).

City of St. Louis v. *Prapotnik,* 108 S. Ct. 915 (1988).

Cleveland Board of Education v. *Loudermill,* 461 U.S. 238 (1983).

Davis v. *Passman,* 442 U.S. 228 (1979).

Edelman v. *Jordan,* 415 U.S. 651 (1974).

Feres v. *United States,* 340 U.S. 146 (1950).

First English Evangelical Lutheran Church of Glendale v. *County of Los Angeles,* 107 S. Ct. 2378 (1987).

Francisco v. *Schmidt,* 532 F. Supp. 850 (E.D. Wi. 1982).

Garcia v. *United States,* 666 F.2d 960 (5th Cir. Unit B 1982).

Harlow v. *Fitzgerald,* 457 U.S. 800 (1982).

Hensley v. *Eckerhart,* 103 S. Ct. 1933 (1983).

Hewitt v. *Helms,* 459 U.S. 460 (1983).

Hodges v. *Tomberlin,* 510 F. Supp. 1280 (S.D. Ga. 1980).

Hughes v. *Rowe,* 449 U.S. 5 (1980).

Imbler v. *Pachtman,* 424 U.S. 409 (1976).

James Nollan et al. v. *California Coastal Commission,* 107 S. Ct. 3141 (1987).

Kentucky v. *Graham,* 105 S. Ct. 3099 (1985).

McIntosh v. *Weinberger,* C.A. No. 82-491c (5) (E.D. Mo. 1984).

Maher v. *Gagne,* 448 U.S. 122 (1980).

Maine v. *Thiboutot,* 448 U.S. 1 (1980).

Malley v. *Briggs,* 106 S. Ct. 1092 (1986).

Martinez v. *California,* 444 U.S. 277 (1980).

Middlesex County Sewerage Authority v. *National Sea Clammers Association,* 101 S. Ct. 2615 (1981).

Mitchell v. *Forsyth,* 105 S. Ct. 2806 (1985).

Monell v. *Department of Social Services,* 436 U.S. 690 (1978).

Monroe v. *Pape,* 365 U.S. 167 (1961).

Nixon v. *Fitzgerald,* 102 S. Ct. 1690 (1982).

Owen v. *City of Independence,* 445 U.S. 622 (1980).

Patsy v. *Board of Regents,* 102 S. Ct. 2557 (1982).

Pierson v. *Ray,* 386 U.S. 547 (1967).

Pulliam v. *Allen,* 104 S. Ct. 1970 (1984).

Quern v. *Jordan,* 440 U.S. 332 (1979).

Rodriguez v. *Richey,* 556 F.2d (5th Cir. 1977), cert. den. 434 U.S. 1047 (1977).

Scheur v. *Rhodes,* 416 U.S. 232 (1974).

Schweiker et al. v. *Chilicky et al.,* 56 LW 4767 (1988).

Smith v. *Wade,* 103 S. Ct. 1625 (1983).

Sonntag v. *Dooley,* 650 F.2d 904 (7th Cir. 1981).

United States et al. v. *Stanley,* 107 S. Ct. 3054 (1987).

Wallen v. *Domm,* 700 F.2d 124 (4th Cir. 1983).

West v. *Atkins,* 56 LW 4664 (1988).

References

Brown, G. D. "State Sovereignty Under the Burger Court—How the Eleventh Amendment Survived the Death of the Tenth." *Georgetown Law Journal,* 1985, *74,* 363–394.

Eikenberry, K. O. "Governmental Tort Litigation and the Balance of Power." *Public Administration Review,* 1985, *45,* 742–745.

Euler, J. "Personal Liability of Military Personnel for Actions Taken in the Course of Duty." *Military Law Review,* 1986, *113,* 137–161.

Lehmann, M. P. "Bivens and Its Progeny: The Scope of a Constitutional Cause of Action for Torts Committed by Government Officials." *Hastings Constitutional Law Quarterly,* 1977, *4,* 531.

Melnick, R. S. "The Politics of Partnership." *Public Administration Review,* 1985, *45,* 656–658.

Ragozin, A. S. "The Waiver of Immunity in the Equal Access to Justice Act: Clarifying Opaque Language." *Washington Law Review,* 1986, *61,* 217–244.

Rumeld, M. D. "Preclusion of Section 1983 Causes of Action by Comprehensive Statutory Remedial Schemes." *Columbia Law Review,* 1983, *82,* 1183–1205.

Schuck, P. *Suing Government.* New Haven, Conn.: Yale University Press, 1983.

Spurrier, R. L. *Rights, Wrongs, and Remedies.* Milwood, N.Y.: Associated Faculty Press, 1986.

Wise, C. R. "Suits Against Federal Employees for Constitutional Violations: A Search for Reasonableness." *Public Administration Review,* 1985, *45,* 845–856.

42

Ralph Clark Chandler

A Guide to Ethics
for Public Servants

Those who maintain that prostitution is the world's oldest profession have not studied their Late Pleistocene anthropology. A religious practitioner called the *shaman* was the first specialist, and most of the time he worked for the chief or ruler, who delegated certain administrative responsibilities to him. Even among the most primitive hunting peoples, such an operative existed primarily to execute the will of the leader. A strong case can be made that the public official was the first professional.

By the time history began to be recorded in the fourth millennium B.C., the role of the public official had assumed special importance in organized society. In ancient Egypt, the public service was so prestigious, and the training for it so thorough, that the vizier and his ministers partook of the same dignity as the pharaoh himself. In ancient China, the professional servants of the priest-kings were not only the supervisors of public works and public services, they were also the leading philosophers and poets of the day. As early as the Han dynasty (206 B.C.–220 A.D.), the merit principle was institutionalized in China, but merit was assigned more for literary prowess than for technical competence.

Given the enormous influence of public officials over the centuries and the extent to which they make public policy by their interpretations of ambiguous directives from above, the standards by which they define ethical behavior are a crucial factor in human history. What are the professional criteria to be applied to this or that case of discretionary choice? Of what set of postulates does morality consist? Is there a public good that supersedes private goods? Does the civil servant have independent constitutional status as a professional? Such questions as these have been answered differently throughout administrative history, but it is helpful to remember that few

602

of them are new questions. In the late twentieth century, American public administrators are struggling with such ponderous professional concepts as technocracy, trusteeship, and coproduction. The only thing we know for sure about these models of thought is that how we answer the questions they raise determines the quality of life for millions of people.

The last time a set of fundamental questions about the ethical behavior of public officials was raised and answered definitively was in Nazi Germany during the 1930s and early 1940s. It was widely affirmed then that the morality of public officials consisted in their doing the will of the leader as efficiently as possible. Whatever one's personal preferences might be, the legal order of civilized society required German civil servants to be obedient to duly constituted authority. Thus, otherwise moral men and women participated efficiently in the excesses of German National Socialism in its efforts to accomplish a final solution to the "Jewish problem." The fundamental mistake they made was an erroneous judgment about what constitutes ethical behavior. The guards at Auschwitz had to spend much of their time intoxicated in order to engage in ethical behavior as defined by their administrative system, but they managed to do it. When obedience was offered as the legal defense of the public administrators who were tried for war crimes at Nuremberg in 1945 and 1946, it was an unsuccessful defense, because the tribunal said that we are individually responsible for what we do. That simple determination left a generation of scientific managers in search of better moorings for ethical behavior than obedience.

American definitions of the professional, the moral, and the ethical are colored by the unique circumstances of American history. In our generation, we have celebrated the bicentennial of both the Declaration of Independence and the Constitution of the United States. In doing so, we have forgotten that there was almost as much American history before these founding events as after them. The colonial experience profoundly influenced the precepts that have guided the ethical behavior of American public administrators, but the normative influences go even farther back, to Greece and Rome.

The founders were students of classical civilization. In 1787, they envisioned the administrative class of the new nation doing many of the same things and adopting many of the same attitudes as public officials did in the ancient democracies. They would be virtuous, for example. Selfless service, for its own sake, would fuel both their sense of professional pride and their personal well-being. Aristotle's statement that virtue was hammered out on the anvil of hard moral choice was taken as descriptive of how good character would shape the American experiment in balanced government.

The Athenian polity is frequently celebrated for its democratic principles. The *archons,* or magistrates, who were responsible for all departments of government, were democratically elected. All citizens of Athens, minus the many people living there who were not citizens, were eligible to sit in the *ecclesia,* or general assembly, and do the electing. The Council of Five Hundred, which managed the daily business of the *ecclesia,* consisted of ordinary citizens chosen by lot. They could not serve more than one year. Thus, nobody would become expert in public administration and develop a vested interest in it. Citizen responsiveness was more important than efficiency.

Council members who filled administrative posts in Athens were under constant scrutiny for their fairness and integrity. Each year, outgoing council members screened their replacements before the *dokimasia,* or court, to inquire about the performance of military service, payment of taxes, fulfillment of religious obligations, and family heritage. George Washington took such practices so seriously that when he set out in 1789 to find men of superior reputation to serve in his administration, he consciously replicated the selection processes of the first democracy. The fact that Alexander Hamilton centralized the work of these men, and formed the first administrative state by the expert orchestration of their considerable abilities, was less important to Washington than the purity of their motives for serving.

A similar tradition came down from Rome. In republican Rome, the magistrates were called *praetors,* and, as in Athens, their duties were partly political and partly administrative. Similarly, they served for only one year, and they were amateurs with no particular skills in administration. As Rome expanded and the administration of the Roman government became more complex, however, the republic was replaced by the empire, and the magistracies became permanent positions. Specialization and professionalization ensued, and with this development came detailed rules for the recruitment, training, promotion, remuneration, and judicial privileges of the Roman civil service.

Today, the idealized American civil service is a blend of the Athenian and Roman models of professionalism. It is composed of men and women of good character who are under the constant scrutiny of others, to make sure they stay as virtuous as possible. Simultaneously, they are specialists who are circumscribed by detailed rules of recruitment, performance, and evaluation. Our administrative procedures are more Roman than Greek, but our insistence on democratic accountability is more Greek than Roman. We have also mixed some Puritanism into the classical pot, believing that the wicked shall not bear rule and that public service is as much a calling as it is a profession.

Meanwhile, the twentieth century has seen the rise of an independent profession of public administration, which has elements decidedly unlike any of the classical models. Like medicine and law and like corporate management and journalism, American public administration is in the process of sealing a social bargain between itself and the society in which it seeks legitimation. In return for social status, the profession is in the process of refining a code of ethics, complete with implementation guidelines and supporting committee structures. Much of the current activity in this regard is focused in the Professional Ethics Committee of the American Society for Public Administration.

Guild-forming processes run counter to the predisposition of American public administrators to deal with instrumental techniques and legal means. An ethics of character may have been good for the federalists and antifederalists, but, since the emergence of Jacksonian democracy, we have taken off the powdered wigs of dignified decorum. Practitioners—many of whom are young computer whizzes—tend to understand administrative behavior not in terms of who one is to be but in reference to political pressures and bureaucratic constraints, properly issued directives and aggregate data analysis, and hierarchical authority and practical problem solving. The means are the ends of government, and the efforts of ethicists to focus on moral abstractions are frequently denigrated as "egghead" exercises at best and as Sunday sermonizing at worst. Waldo (1980) has said that ethics is not a neglected interest in American public administration, but a rejected interest.

Nevertheless, certain ethical precepts have guided American public administrators from the earliest days of the republic. Some are implicit, some are explicit, several are contradictory to each other, and all are subject to differing interpretations. Let us now turn to a description of ten of these precepts, not claiming them to be the new decalogue, and let us consider them in the rough chronological order of their ascendancy. Each has held up over time, and each has been devoutly maintained by professional groups of varying and unknown size.

Ten Ethical Precepts

Demonstrate Fiscal Integrity. The principles that guided the administration of the Massachusetts Bay Colony in the seventeenth century, the establishment of the U.S. General Accounting Office in 1921, and the passage of the Ethics in Government Act of 1978 are very nearly the same. The common denominator is fiscal integrity. An important benchmark of ethical behavior is how one handles money.

The great Puritan migration of 1630 overwhelmed the separatist Pilgrim settlements in New England by sheer numbers and moral fervor. Puritanism established a legacy of values that endures today as the Puritan Ethic. It says that hard work begets prosperity and that the proper stewardship of prosperity is the chief end of the state. The related doctrine of "calling" means that everyone is called to take some part in building God's righteous empire. Some are tradesmen, some are fishermen, some are farmers, some are educators, and some are keepers of the hearth, but the highest calling of all is to bear rule.

The magistrates whom the Puritans elected, and the public officials whom the magistrates appointed to manage public property, were called *visible saints* by the people of Massachusetts Bay. The constitutional responsibility of the saints was to enforce the canons of sobriety, piety, and a balanced economy, so that capital could be accumulated. Their professionalism consisted of their ability to add to the common good by avoiding the foul disorders of the commonwealth associated with public assistance to rogues, beggars, and vagabonds. By being thrifty and frugal with tax monies, public officials could use them to increase the wealth of the state and thereby assure all its citizens that they were indeed the elect of God.

The Congress of the United States had the same fiscal integrity precept in mind when it created, in the Budget and Accounting Act of 1921, a comptroller general to investigate all matters related to the receipt, disbursement, and application of public funds. It reiterated this common understanding of ethical behavior both in the Budget and Accounting Procedures Act of 1950 and in the Legislative Reorganization Act of 1970.

Similarly, when Congress could no longer avoid the necessity of explicit ethics legislation for federal officials in the late 1970s, it asked witness after witness what were the essential characteristics of ethical behavior in government. The answers it frequently got and eventually acted on would have warmed the heart of John Winthrop and all those who equate high ethical performance with sound fiscal management. The Ethics in Government Act of 1978 deals extensively and almost exclusively with financial disclosure, as well as with the reporting of potential conflicts of interest among officers and employees of the federal government at the GS-16 level and above. The Puritan Ethic's preoccupation with the material signs of God's grace, later translated into the principles of the Yankee trader, is now and has always been a leading ethical precept in American public administration. When one handles the accounts right, he or she is a moral public servant by definition.

Avoid Moral Abstractions. By the time of the American Revolution, the Puritan Ethic had lost its primary references to the Holy Commonwealth and the City of God. It had gone secular and been translated into a practical utopianism that wished to avoid moral abstractions. Even in Puritan New England, English law had been a sobering influence on the theocrats. The colonists did what they had to do to retain their charters and their land titles, which meant that they kept finding new examples of how the laws of England and the laws of God coincided.

The deists of the Revolutionary period fully subscribed to the injunctions of the Puritan Ethic. No man more methodically industrious than Thomas Jefferson ever lived, but he was hardly a Puritan. Experience had taught the founders that public administrators were not saints after all, and that precautions had to be taken for keeping them virtuous. These precautions could not be based on such moral abstractions as duty or the public good, however. If they were, moral reductionism and indoctrination would carry the nation into the kind of moral tyranny that may have worked in Geneva and other Calvinist strongholds but surely would not work in a land as culturally diverse as the United States. The founders counseled moderation on moral matters. The real danger, they said, was that a self-consciously moral public service would relegate individual rights and private tastes to a subordinate place in a regimented civil society. The new consensus was that individual rights and all things private were more important than prosperity, although not by much.

Public servants and everyone else would henceforth be coerced by law, not by the sermons of Cotton Mather or any of his progeny, including Jerry Falwell. Moral purists do not understand the ways in which political liberty and economic energy inevitably produce some immorality. The institutions of government will control whatever evil is necessary, without the social consequences of religious sectarianism. The members of the new administrative class will live with immorality moderately, remembering that men and women are not angels. If they were, no government would be necessary. This was the sage advice of that former theology student James Madison.

This serviceable wisdom has been translated by subsequent generations of American civil servants into a legalist position, which equates ethical behavior with obedience to law. The paramount ethical responsibility of public administrators is to follow the legally constituted directives of hierarchical superiors and elected representatives of the people. The strength of this precept lies in its fit with fundamental democratic political values and principles. Its weakness is that it reinforces a technocratic and instrumentalist conception of professional practice, which glosses over the inescapable moral content of real administrative life.

Embrace Moral Abstractions. Standing alongside the founders' advice to be moderate on moral matters was their paradoxical impulse to be passionate about certain moral abstractions. The most common of these was the idea of virtue. By *virtue,* the founders meant good character, civic concern, a willingness to sacrifice comfort and personal wealth for the public good, and a commitment to the development of the soul of the state. In its Aristotelian context, virtue is related directly to action, and not just to thinking or feeling in a certain way. It involves cognitive activity that is not innate but cultivated. One acts virtuously because his or her will has been conditioned to do so.

If virtue is a character trait that can be taught, it follows that ethical behavior may be influenced by a code of ethics that encourages the public administrator to make prescribed choices and judgments and pursue approved actions. In the Athenian oath, for example, virtue included a promise to fight for the ideals and the sacred things of the city. In the Code of Ethics of the American Society for Public Administration (ASPA), virtue includes a commitment to demonstrate the highest standards of personal integrity, truthfulness, honesty, and fortitude.

Long before 1984, when the ASPA Code of Ethics was adopted, such administrative Platonists as Paul H. Appleby and Stephen K. Bailey, both former deans of the Maxwell School of Citizenship and Public Affairs at Syracuse University, described ethical behavior in terms of moral abstractions such as optimism, courage, fairness, and charity. Neither Appleby nor Bailey was very sentimental. Appleby (1952) offered a practical description of the moral administrator that included a sense of responsibility; skills in communication and personnel administration, with special emphasis on recruiting competent assistants, advisers, and specialists; the ability to cultivate and use institutional resources; a willingness to engage in problem solving and to work with others as a team; and enough personal confidence to initiate new ideas. Bailey was equally practical. He argued (1965) for a personal code of ethics for the public administrator because he or she must relate what is specific and private to what is general, public, and moral; because, when ethical codes are absent, the public loses confidence in public processes; and because controversial policy decisions focus inordinate political pressure on administrators. Adherents of Bailey's third precept believe that translating moral abstractions into the marketplace of professional practice makes ethical behavior the predicate of administrative being and thus the appropriate expression of civic virtue.

Affirm Pluralist Theory. The founders devised a political system of countervailing power in which public policy is the product of compromises among competing interests. The American political system is a balance of power among economic, professional, religious, ethnic, and geographical groups whose memberships overlap. Each of these groups seeks to impose its will on public policy, but each is limited in its ability to do so because it must accommodate the demands of the other groups. Pluralism is the expression of this bargaining process. It is the political reality that has displaced the ideals of civic virtue in the American republic. Madison was correct in his prediction that interest would play the role of virtue in American government.

The norms of pluralism define the agencies of government as arenas for the expression of self-interest. Since bureaucracies are representative institutions, they provide access to government for everyone in society. They ensure stability because multiple group pressures on government virtually guarantee that the most important policy questions will eventually be processed and resolved by the public administrators who preside over the bureaucracies. These officials behave ethically to the extent that they fairly moderate the interests brought to them. Theoretically, they serve all interests, but they can serve none exclusively. Therein lies moral public service.

The definition of administrative agencies as representative institutions was the result of the Jacksonian revolution of 1829. From the rise of the spoils system until about 1869, representativeness in administration meant that bureaucracies should reflect the dispersion of citizens demographically, and that administrative personnel should be mirror images of the majority party. There should be an integration of politics and administration.

A complete administrative ethic meant that society's plebeian interests were consciously being served.

In the place of majority rule, pluralism recognizes rule by minorities. This fact of American life is given theoretical justification in the works of John C. Calhoun and Alexis de Tocqueville, both of whom argued that majority opinion holds no claim on abstract standards of justice merely because it is the opinion of the majority. The doctrine of rule by minorities is reflected in the checks-and-balances provisions of the Constitution. The ethical quandary associated with pluralism comes at the point of democratic theory. Civil servants are expected, especially by presidents, to be responsive to the leadership of whatever administration has the trust and authority of the American people, as demonstrated at the ballot box. Civil servants are also expected to be efficient. Neither majoritarianism nor efficiency is a value honored by pluralism, however. Representation, service, and accommodation are much more important to the pluralist, which means that traditional techniques of motivating or evaluating employees are not applicable to many public sector operations. When goal ambiguity is the norm, market-based performance measures do not work. If civil servants respond to their environment as pluralist theory asks them to, the results are often at odds with the goals of classical majoritarianism.

According to pluralist ethics, public administrators act responsibly by representing important interests and attitudes that are excluded from Congress and other representative bodies. The principle of representation—or the lack of it for millions of Americans—is one of the most serious defects of the Constitution. The huge career public service helps remedy that defect by interpreting professionalism to include the role of the public administrator as representative citizen.

Believe the Dichotomy. The political efficacy and administrative egalitarianism envisioned by Andrew Jackson had degenerated into crass political opportunism by the 1870s. Public administration came to be viewed as a managerial extension of the political machine. A reform movement arose to redress the incompetence and corruption of the Jacksonian and radical republican eras by proposing administrative models based on professionalism and neutrality. In 1887, Woodrow Wilson posited a major distinction between politics and administration: Politics is the proper activity of legislative bodies and other policymaking groups, he said, and administration is the proper activity of a professional class of public managers who carry out the directives of the policymakers as efficiently as possible (Wilson, 1887). Reformers such as United States Senator George H. Pendleton had said four years earlier that the appointment of these public managers should be based on fitness and merit, rather than on partisanship; hence, the Pendleton Act of 1883.

It was left to Weber (1946), however, to offer the classic justification of the dichotomy. Weber said that the unique attributes of the politician are exactly the opposite of those of the civil servant. The essence of politics, he maintained, is to take a stand, be passionate, exercise conscience, take personal responsibility for policies, and admit the transitory nature of the political role. The public administrator, however, is to execute the orders of the political authority conscientiously, regardless of their compatibility with the administrator's convictions and values. Thus, the morality of the civil servant consists in obedience to higher authority.

It was said that ethical behavior results from administrative neutrality, because public officials are free to apply to government what Frederick Winslow Taylor called the principles of scientific management. Bureaucracy is a rational and legal system designed to attain precision and reliability in serving the needs of mass democracy. The best thing that can be said about government is that it is businesslike in its procedures. Two months before Wilson's (1887) essay appeared, *The Nation* ran an editorial lauding the secretary of the treasury, Charles S. Fairchild, for establishing "a great business institution." President Grover Cleveland had done the right thing by ensuring "a most notable extension of the system of conducting the affairs of the Government on business principles" ("Government on Business Principles," 1887, p. 288).

When the dichotomy discourages the public administrator from making value judgments, it leaves him or her in a relativist position, which assumes that ethical norms are matters of arbitrary preference and that no objectively valid moral statements can be made. Is this the way administrative life is actually lived? Is moral responsibility possible without administrative discretion? Proponents of the dichotomy precept say that the answer to this question does not matter, because rules are ends in themselves, and the facilitating devices of administration are invested with self-evident moral legitimacy.

Disbelieve the Dichotomy. Lasswell (1930) identified what he considered the real significance of the dichotomy: The internal bureaucrat would be able to exercise power that was informal, unseen, and greatly underestimated by doctrinaire proponents of the dichtomy. The defects of the dichotomy were clearly visible during the presidencies of Franklin D. Roosevelt and Harry S Truman, when the administrative energies required to overcome the turbulence of global depression and global war fashioned a public administration that combined political effectiveness (the Jacksonian ideal) and administrative efficiency (the Wilsonian ideal) in ingenious ways. The standing of civil servants in American public esteem has never been higher.

The dichotomy must be disbelieved, according to the proponents of this precept, because the sanctions of science claimed for the principles of administration could not be sustained, nor could American government be modeled after the cameralist traditions of Europe or the self-aggrandizing business practices of American capitalism. A constitutional system of divided powers and federal divisions of delegated functions simply cannot absorb the artificial distinction between politics and administration. The rulemaking and case-deciding activities of administrative agencies cannot be carried out by legislatures and courts, nor can they be abandoned.

Public administrators have independent standing before the law. There is no doubt that a dichotomy of a particular sort exists, but it is not a dichotomy between decision and execution. Waldo (1987) identifies the real dichotomy as creative tension between the civic culture and imperial traditions of American government. In the civic culture tradition of classical Greece, thinking about government and deciding what it should do are the most important responsibilities of political man. In the imperial tradition of the ancient Middle Eastern and Mediterranean empires, organizing and executing the functions of government are the most important responsibilities of political man. The United States is a blend of these distinct traditions. For Waldo, our politics are Greek, but our administration is Roman. Americans live with an anomaly: Expanded democracy has called forth imperial mechanisms of government.

Not wanting public administrators to assume the dignity of the Roman imperium, political leaders of both parties have tried in recent years to reassert the discredited dichotomy. Public administrators themselves have responded in three distinct ways to these efforts to bring them to heel. One strategy is to reestablish the old claims to technical competence, efficiency, and administrative rationality. Another is to retreat into the techniques of organizational "guerrilla warfare." A third is to search for a theoretical basis of trusteeship—the idea that civil servants are sworn to uphold the Constitution, just as other officers of government are, and that they are competent to define the public good on their own authority. The contest between the proponents of the first and the third positions describes much of the professional discussion in modern public administration. The proponents of the second position mostly keep quiet, because they still believe in the professional ethic described in Simon, Smithberg, and Thompson (1950, pp. 554–555): "The administrator is always to some extent an initiator of values, partly as a representative of some interest group or groups, but also independently, in his own right. He can never be completely governed by others, and, as a matter of fact, he has considerable latitude of choice before the consequences of his decisions will bring reactions that threaten his survival."

Advocate Social Equity. The public service fell on hard times in the mid 1950s, and in some sense it has not yet recovered. Gawthrop (1987, p. 198) identified the reasons for what he called "a steady deterioration of administrative competency" as the insidious psychological destructiveness of McCarthyism, which intermittently revived questions of disloyalty, distrust, and disdain; the decline of the bureau-chief component of the iron triangle of policymaking, occasioned by television's opening up of congressional committee oligarchies; the establishment of the supergrade positions of GS-16, 17, and 18, which drew a distinction between policy careerists and proceduralists and fragmented political and administrative power; the venture of the Eisenhower administration into the implementation of a global containment policy, which extended the competency of the American administrative system beyond its capacity; and the fragmentation of the bureaucracy into a multiplicity of sovereign fiefs, buffeted by the centrifugal forces of single-issue politics, the new politics of litigation, and a system of intergovernmental relations that defied administrative control.

While the Balkanization of federal, state, and local bureaucracies was taking place, civil servants were also being asked to meet the needs of greater and greater numbers of citizens. To do so effectively, they had to define people in the aggregate: as clients, cases, and categories, rather than as individual persons in discrete social circumstances. It was said that impersonal transactions actually facilitated expert solutions to social problems, and that compassion is an individual virtue, not an organizational one. The rule of law, it was believed, required that everyone in the same problem category be treated in the same way. Institutional stability was thought to be incompatible with deviations from universal norms.

The result of this subtle reconceptualization of the essence of democracy into terms of the greatest good for the greatest number led a generation of civil servants into a trained incapacity to discern the difference between means and ends, facts and values, and the processes and purposes of government. The career service had neither the time nor the inclination to consider the qualitative consequences of its actions. The qualitative aspects of democracy came to be understood primarily in terms of quantitative measurements.

A counterattack on this understanding of public morality was launched in 1968 at the Minnowbrook conference site of Syracuse University. A gathering of "young Turks" produced the Minnowbrook perspective, which tried to refocus public administration away from the technical and toward the normative, away from administrative science toward social equity. Social equity makes the actual delivery of public services the criterion for judging the value of administrative policy and the ethical behavior of the transfer agent. Is there a fair distribution of services? Are disadvantaged people adequately represented in the policymaking process? Are public administrators working to replace the politics of having and doing with the politics of being?

In the end, say the advocates of the social equity precept, the bureaucracy cannot be neutral. It must be involved with clients as human beings, and it must bend the rules for them and take risks for them, if necessary. Civil servants must actively advance the causes of social justice. At the same time, they must seek increased citizen participation in government and encourage the personal development of individual members of administrative organizations. The "young Turks" of Minnowbrook are now older, and they still face the problem of bringing programmatic fruition to their noble ideas.

Pursue Professional Discourse. One of the most striking characteristics of American public administration in the last decade has been the extent to which practitioners and academics alike have committed themselves to talking about who they are. The conversation began in the late 1970s, when a code of ethics was proposed in the original Professional Standards and Ethics Committee of the American Society for Public Administration. Initially, there was a good deal of resistance to a code for many different reasons. The most compelling one was that the lack of stated public purpose in American society was one of the nation's fundamental strengths. Throughout our history, continuing redefinitions of purpose and compromises of principle have allowed us to make the incremental changes necessary for political stability. Proceduralism must be a terminal value, because in a pluralist system truth, unity, and especially morality can never be forged from a single ideal form. Only from the clash of opposites, contraries, extremes, and poles can come the accommodations that are themselves American public service ethics. In this view, the process of discovery must never be sacrificed to the approved "word"; the "word" is always being spoken.

After years of debate, even proceduralists have come to see the fundamental moral problem of building consensus around an agreement to agree on nothing substantive. Assent was being given not to value but to value default. As the need for shared values in a professional context grew, adversaries who could no longer find in their disagreements a basis for common norms were transformed from adversaries into enemies. Thus, a code of ethics was approved by the National Council of ASPA on April 8, 1984. Next came a set of guidelines to interpret each of the twelve canons of the code. At this time, subcommittees of the Professional Ethics Committee are working on finding appropriate ways to impose sanctions on those who violate the code, as well as to aid members who get into trouble because they follow it.

It is certain that debate about the tenets and tone of the code will continue. There is already a movement to revise certain parts of it. The code of ethics of the International City Management Association (ICMA) has been revised six times since it was first adopted in 1924, and ASPA is no less adaptive an organization than ICMA. The self-correcting system that is now in place keeps the membership of ASPA involved in ethical reflection and committed to the results of ongoing negotiations about ethical norms. Professional discourse reduces the moral confusion that a lack of authority brings, and eventually it turns words into reflective human activity.

Maintain Constitutional Order. The Constitution of the United States implicitly and explicitly assigns a demanding role to public administrators. Historic practice has made administrative institutions the balance wheel of the constitutional order. Capitalism allows individual projects of personal aggrandizement to proceed virtually unchecked, until they are checked by government. Only government compares the designs of private interests to collective needs and social concerns. Thus, public officials are called on to employ the processes of moral reasoning, judgment, and, finally, lawful coercion to affirm the safeguards of constitutional democracy. In applying state power to humane ends, public officials regulate, distribute, and redistribute national resources to promote the general welfare.

Capitalism does not like the regulatory role, of course, and the result is a continuing battle between public and private interests. The size and power of the federal government lead many to believe the struggle is unequal; but when we consider that ten of the twenty-five largest organizations in the world, ranked by revenues, are American corporations, it may surprise us that public administration can hold its own. When General Motors has economic power significantly greater than that of Canada, and when Exxon doubles the receipts of Sweden, we cannot underestimate the power of American economic institutions.

The public sphere has been diminished and denigrated by the preachment that society exists apart from government and is prior to and greater than government. In the ethos of capitalism, life finds its essential meaning in the consumption of goods and services. The balanced interests of constitutionalism become an obstacle to the pursuit of happiness. (When someone asked John D. Rockefeller, Jr., how much money it would take to make him happy, he reportedly answered, ''Just a little more.'')

In the face of the values of economization, the civil servant is called on to assert the values of the polity. His or her basis for doing so, according to this precept, is the moral imperative of covenant. The public administrator has entered into solemn agreement with the citizens whom he or she serves to honor the promissory note of equal opportunity that the founders signed for all future generations. Public administration is a professed obligation, informed and constrained by constitutional principle, to maintain the public interest against all competing private interests.

Serve the Community. The Preamble to the Constitution is not exactly an ethics text, but it comes as close to that as any piece of writing in American history: ''We the people of the United States, in order to form a more perfect union, establish justice, insure domestic tranquillity, provide for the common defense, promote the general welfare, and secure the blessings of liberty to ourselves and our posterity, do ordain and establish this Constitution for the United States of America.'' Gouverneur Morris, he of the suave manners and wooden leg who actually wrote the Constitution as the amanuensis of the Committee of Style and Arrangement, believed that verbs should count for something, so he let them roll out: *form, establish, insure, provide, promote, secure,* and *ordain.*

That is what the profession of public administration does in American life: It forms, establishes, insures, provides, promotes, secures, and ordains. It does so in the interest of the community. Moral behavior in public administration is not just a matter of private preference and personal integrity. Judgments about right and wrong are community decisions, because the community is the final arbiter of what is ethical. The community looks at the nature of an act to decide whether it is moral. Moral vices can be made into relative goods by their context; moral virtue can have patently evil results in particular circumstances. Law is therefore an uncertain guide to ethical behavior. It is possible to obey every law and regulation in the books and still be highly unethical. The profession of public administration operates to mediate the particularistic interests of the civil society while it tries to increase the ability of citizens to comprehend society's total purposes and participate unselfishly in the making of policies to implement them.

The cutting edge of ethical theory and practice today, say devotees of communalism, is that public policy is coproduced by public administrators and affected citizens' groups. Public administrators are social partners, rather than autonomous state agents or pluralist-oriented brokers of competitive interests. Ethical behavior fosters a culture of reciprocity, obligation, and responsibility. Citizen coproducers are treated as colleagues, rather than as clients and supplicants. The model of the future is Habermas's (1981) vision of a communicative ethics, which breaks down the barriers between professionals and laity and reconnects political authority to the vibrant content of civic virtue.

Summary

This chapter has discussed ten ethical precepts that have guided American public administration at one time or another in its history. Obviously, some of these precepts are mutually exclusive and exist tenuously in relationship to one another, but each one does describe a legitimate point of view in the profession, and each one is represented in the profession's codes of ethics. Two of the best known of these codes are those adopted by the American Society for Public Administration, in 1984, and by the International City Management Association, first in 1924, with six revisions through 1987. The American Planning Association has also been a leader in developing ethical standards and guidelines for local government. The ASPA and ICMA codes are representative (see Exhibits 1 and 2).

**Exhibit 1. The Code of Ethics of the
American Society for Public Administration.**

The American Society for Public Administration (ASPA) exists to advance the science, processes, and art of public administration. ASPA encourages professionalism and improved quality of service at all levels of government, education, and for the not-for-profit private sector. ASPA contributes to the analysis, understanding, and resolution of public issues by providing programs, services, policy studies, conferences, and publications.

ASPA members share with their neighbors all of the responsibilities and rights of citizenship in a democratic society. However, the mission and goals of ASPA call every member to additional dedication and commitment. Certain principles and moral standards must guide the conduct of ASPA members, not merely in preventing wrong, [but] in pursuing right through timely and energetic execution of responsibilities.

To this end, we, the members of the Society, recognizing the critical role of conscience in choosing among courses of action and taking into account the moral ambiguities of life, commit ourselves to:

1. demonstrate the highest standards of personal integrity, truthfulness, honesty, and fortitude in all our public activities in order to inspire public confidence and trust in public institutions;

2. serve the public with respect, concern, courtesy, and responsiveness, recognizing that service to the public is beyond service to oneself;

3. strive for personal professional excellence and encourage the professional development of our associates and those seeking to enter the field of public administration;

4. approach our organizational and operational duties with a positive attitude and constructively support open communication, creativity, dedication, and compassion;

5. serve in such a way that we do not realize undue personal gain from the performance of our official duties;

6. avoid any interest or activity which is in conflict with the conduct of our official duties;

7. respect and protect the privileged information to which we have access in the course of official duties;

8. exercise whatever discretionary authority we have under law to promote the public interest;

9. accept as a personal duty the responsibility to keep up to date on emerging issues and to administer the public's business with professional competence, fairness, impartiality, efficiency, and effectiveness;

10. support, implement, and promote merit employment and programs of affirmative action to assure equal opportunity by our recruitment, selection, and advancement of qualified persons from all elements of society;

11. eliminate all forms of illegal discrimination, fraud, and mismanagement of public funds, and support colleagues if they are in difficulty because of responsible efforts to correct such discrimination, fraud, mismanagement, or abuse;

12. respect, support, study, and, when necessary, work to improve federal and state constitutions, and other laws which define the relationships among public agencies, employees, clients and all citizens.

**Exhibit 2. The Code of Ethics of the
International City Management Association.**

The purpose of the International City Management Association is to increase the proficiency of city managers, county managers, and other municipal administrators and to strengthen the quality of urban government through professional management. To further these objectives, certain ethical principles shall govern the conduct of every member of the International City Management Association, who shall:

1. Be dedicated to the concepts of effective and democratic local government by responsible elected officials and believe that professional general management is essential to the achievement of this objective.

2. Affirm the dignity and worth of the services rendered by government and maintain a constructive, creative, and practical attitude toward urban affairs and a deep sense of social responsibility as a trusted public servant.

3. Be dedicated to the highest ideals of honor and integrity in all public and personal relationships in order that the member may merit the respect and confidence of the elected officials, of other officials and employees, and of the public.

4. Recognize that the chief function of local government at all times is to serve the best interests of all people.

**Exhibit 2. The Code of Ethics of the
International City Management Association, Cont'd.**

5. Submit policy proposals to elected officials, provide them with facts and advice on matters of policy as a basis for making decisions and setting community goals, and uphold and implement municipal policies adopted by elected officials.

6. Recognize that elected representatives of the people are entitled to the credit for the establishment of municipal policies; responsibility for policy execution rests with the members.

7. Refrain from participation in the election of the members of the employing legislative body, and from all partisan political activities which would impair performance as a professional administrator.

8. Make it a duty continually to improve the member's professional ability and to develop the competence of associates in the use of management techniques.

9. Keep the community informed on municipal affairs; encourage communication between the citizens and all municipal officers; emphasize friendly and courteous service to the public; and seek to improve the quality and image of public service.

10. Resist any encroachment on professional responsibilities, believing the member should be free to carry out official policies without interference, and handle each problem without discrimination on the basis of principle and justice.

11. Handle all matters of personnel on the basis of merit so that fairness and impartiality govern a member's decisions pertaining to appointments, pay adjustments, promotions, and discipline.

12. Seek no favor; believe that personal aggrandizement or profit secured by confidential information or by misuse of public time is dishonest.

Is there a unifying thread that weaves the precepts and codes together? Obviously, one can pick and choose which of the precepts and which of the tenets of the codes form a coherent personal and professional value system. The thread is not in the combinations one can discern in this variegated quilt. It is in the symbolic power of words. They inspire, they set a tone, and they create expectations. They are rallying points for conceptual clarity. With them, we tell others who we are. Both the precepts and the codes, which try to translate words into habits of action, are images of what professional public administrators think we should live up to. Thus, ethical discourse brings order, direction, and idealism to public service.

References

Appleby, P. H. *Morality and Administration in Democratic Government*. Baton Rouge: Louisiana State University Press, 1952.

Bailey, S. K. "The Relationship Between Ethics and Public Service." In R. C. Martin (ed.), *Public Administration and Democracy: Essays in Honor of Paul Appleby*. Syracuse, N.Y.: Syracuse University Press, 1965.

Gawthrop, L. "Toward an Ethical Convergence of Democratic Theory and Administrative Politics." In R. C. Chandler (ed.), *A Centennial History of the American Administrative State*. New York: Free Press, 1987.

"Government on Business Principles." *The Nation*, Apr. 7, 1887, p. 288.

Habermas, J. *The Theory of Communicative Action.* Vol. 1: *Reason and the Rationalization of Society.* Boston: Beacon Press, 1981.

Lasswell, H. *Psychopathology and Politics.* Chicago: University of Chicago Press, 1930.

Simon, H. A., Smithberg, D., and Thompson, V. *Public Administration.* New York: Knopf, 1950.

Waldo, D. *The Enterprise of Public Administration.* Novato, Calif.: Chandler and Sharp, 1980.

Waldo, D. "Politics and Administration: On Thinking About a Complex Relationship." In R. C. Chandler (ed.), *A Centennial History of the American Administrative State.* New York: Free Press, 1987.

Weber, M. "Politics as a Vocation." In H. H. Gerth and C. W. Mills (eds.), *From Max Weber: Essays in Sociology.* New York: Oxford University Press, 1946.

Wilson, W. "The Study of Administration." *Political Science Quarterly,* 1887, *2* (2), 197–222.

43

James L. Perry

The Effective
Public Administrator

This concluding chapter seeks to summarize what we know about effective public administrators. How shall we describe the effective public administrator? What are his or her qualities and attributes? What behaviors are characteristic of effective public administrators? In answering these questions, I will attempt to synthesize the insights shared throughout this handbook.

Defining Effectiveness

Effectiveness is an elusive concept. It is one of those things we talk about but never seem able to define or achieve to our satisfaction. I do not pretend here to have solved either of these problems, but it will be helpful to start out with a general idea of what is meant by *effectiveness*.

One of the first to write extensively about the effective administrator was Drucker (1967, p. 1), who equates effectiveness with the executive's job: "To be effective is the job of the executive. 'To effect' and 'to execute' are, after all, near-synonyms. Whether he [she] works in a business or in a hospital, in a government agency or in a labor union, in a university or in the army, the executive is, first of all, expected to *get the right things done.*"

Boyatzis (1982, p. 12) associates the concept of administrators' effectiveness with job performance. He defines effective job performance as attaining results through actions that satisfy certain constraints: "Effective performance of the job is the attainment of specific results (i.e., outcomes) required by the job through specific actions while maintaining or being consistent with policies, procedures, and conditions of the organizational environment." One of the nuances of Boyatzis's definition is that results are a function of the job incumbent's actions, not of chance occurrences. His definition also takes note of the context in which an administrator's job is performed—that is, the organization and its environment.

Anderson, Newland, and Stillman (1983, p. 9) echo elements from the definitions of both Boyatzis and Drucker. Effectiveness "involves doing the right things well—whatever the contingencies."

These definitions imply some of the ideas commonly associated with public administrators' effectiveness. Effectiveness is doing the right job, doing the job well, overcoming impediments, and living within certain constraints. I am interested here in summarizing the determinants that contribute to these results—that is, to public administrators' effectiveness. By *determinants,* I mean any of a number of different kinds of causal factors—skills, traits, self-image, and motives—that result in effective performance.

What Makes an Effective Administrator?

This handbook has touched on many factors that influence a public administrator's effectiveness. Seven stand out: technical skills, human skills, conceptual skills, responsiveness to democratic institutions, focus on results (including the moral consequences of one's actions), networking ability, and balance.

Technical Skills. An effective public administrator has command over the specialized activities that are assigned as part of an organizational role. One of the hallmarks of modern organizations and, by extension, of modern public administration is the expansion of specialized activity. Administrators' effectiveness necessitates some capacity to perform specialized tasks. Technical skills imply proficiency in specific kinds of activity, particularly those involving methods, procedures, or techniques (Katz, 1974).

Some contributors to this handbook have explicitly addressed the importance of technical skills to administrators' effectiveness; others have recognized their importance implicitly. For example, technical skills are essential to the effective policy analyst, who must be able to critically assess sophisticated quantitative analyses and, on occasion, conduct such analyses personally. As House and Shull note in Chapter Seventeen, the technical demands for policy analysis have expanded since the advent of personal computers, which require proficiency in manipulating preprogrammed analytical packages and in testing a wide array of models and assumptions.

A government accountant must be proficient in different, but no less important, techniques and methods. According to Berne's discussion in Chapter Twenty-two, the accountant must possess, among other proficiencies, the ability to read and interpret financial statements, report financial information so that nonexperts can understand it, become familiar and comply with legal mandates for accounting information, and design and evaluate accounting systems that satisfy the multiple objectives of financial decision makers.

Technical skill is also an effectiveness prerequisite for public administrators who serve as legislative liaisons, financial and budget analysts, trainers and management developers, compensation and equal employment specialists, labor negotiators, and systems analysts. Because technical skills are the most concrete aspect of administrators' effectiveness and have held such a central role in public administration thought over the years (Kaufman, 1969), it is important to put them into perspective. Although technical skills are an effectiveness prerequisite in virtually every administrative position (see, for example, Lau, Newman, and Broedling's 1980 study on U.S. Navy senior executives), their relative importance usually declines as a public administrator ascends an organization's hierarchy. By the same token, technical skills are never likely to be the only characteristic that discriminates between effective and ineffective performers at any level of an organization. The effective public administrator needs to possess other skills and attributes as well.

Human Skills. Waldo (1955) has characterized the essence of administration as cooperative human action. Cooperative activity involves human interaction. The effective public administrator must possess the human skills to integrate people into all types of cooperative activity.

Human skills are complex and difficult to summarize. At a minimum, they involve an awareness of oneself and of how one's actions affect others, an orientation toward and sensitivity to others, perceptiveness regarding the motives and sensitivities of others, recognition of one's own responsibility to the group, and genuineness in relations with others (Katz, 1974).

As the contents of this handbook illustrate, the situations in which a public administrator must employ these human skills are extensive. The situation probably most identified with human skills involves the problem of motivating subordinates to achieve high performance. Using their human skills, public administrators seek to develop subordinates' identification with and commitment to organizational goals and to ensure organization members' satisfaction with available rewards and incentives.

In some cases, human skills must be applied to motivational issues involving clients—that is, to the facilitation of coproductive processes. Although citizens may realize cost and quality benefits from taking an active role in the production process, the public administrator is pivotal in energizing and channeling clients' support. For instance, volunteers can be excellent resources for particular types of public services, but if their enthusiasm and energy are not harnessed and directed toward organizational objectives, volunteers' commitment may be more harmful than productive.

The importance of human skills for the public administrator reaches into the political environment as well. Relationships with legislators, elected and appointed executives, and citizens are potential sources of confrontation, unless the public administrator brings the appropriate orientation and skills to the situation. Perceptiveness and empathy—that is, the ability to identify with other parties and understand their positions—are necessary starting points for constructive, nonconfrontational relationships.

To reflect on the situations in which human skills are important will demonstrate the tenuousness of the public administrator's position. Although government is the chief coercive institution in our society, it is obvious that much of what happens in government depends on cooperation, rather than on coercion. Public administrators, as agents, are therefore relatively helpless, unless they wield informal influence. Thus, public administrators need to develop their human skills to provide the "glue" that will bond people together in cooperative action.

Conceptual Skills. These skills involve the public administrator's ability to see the big picture—to conceive how decisions, events, and people are linked in time and space. Katz (1974) suggests that conceptual skill involves both recognizing how the functions of an organization are interdependent and visualizing the relationship of the organization to its broader context. In government, this means being able to visualize the relationship between one's own organizational activities and broader agency and governmental goals, to recognize the implications of action for many attentive groups and for the general public, and to anticipate the consequences of action or inaction over time.

As with human and technical skills, the situations that require well-developed conceptual skills are numerous. For example, the challenges discussed in Part One demand the application of considerable conceptual skill, if their ramifications for administration and governance are to be understood. Appropriate responses to growing global interdependence, to the evolution of science and technology, and to shifting social realities cannot be fashioned without a broad view of how decisions, events, and people are linked in time and space.

Similarly, effective public policymaking requires participants to visualize programs holistically over time. Conceptual skill is essential to the number and quality of policy options that can be defined for any public problem. Implementation of public programs requires public administrators to conceptualize the factors that ultimately will contribute to the success of a program, as well as to be aware of contingencies that will diminish its success. The ability to conceptualize a program in operational terms at an early stage must be complemented by the ability to conceptualize it in physical and human terms as well.

Each of these arenas illustrates the importance of conceptual skills to effective public administration. In a real sense, conceptual skills are to the administrator what strategic capability is to the larger organization. Such skills help to unify and coordinate the administrative process in a chaotic environment.

Responsiveness to Democratic Institutions. The effective public administrator not only complies with the letter of the law but also strives to facilitate all aspects of democratic process by promoting an informed citizenry, contributing to open debate of issues, and respecting the ultimate choices of citizens and their representatives. Carrying out the law is the first test of democratic responsiveness. As Cooper argues in Chapter Eight, failure to carry out the law cannot be justified on the basis of the ends of administrative action, because the administrator's authority is derived from law. For a public administrator to violate the law is illegitimate and undermines the foundations of constitutional democracy.

As Part Two illustrates, legal systems are but one mechanism for encouraging democratic responsiveness by structuring the public administrator's environment. Governance structures, organizational design, and strategic plans reinforce the importance of democratic values. The effective public administrator recognizes these structural imperatives and strives to use these mechanisms to further the goals of a democratic society. Even in relatively unusual contexts, such as the types of public enterprises discussed by Rainey and Wechsler in Chapter Thirty-five, the effective public administrator is aware of and attempts to be responsive to democratic control.

While formal control systems create an environment for accountability, they do not ensure that public administrators will respond to the needs and interests of citizens and their representatives. The public administrator who perceives and properly interprets environmental cues about popular control has probably also successfully internalized the values and ethical precepts of democratic governance. Among the normative perspectives that administrators internalize is what Goodsell, in Chapter Forty, calls the *multitude orientation,* which directs the administrator's attention to citizens and their interests. This is not the only guiding orientation, of course, but it is crucial to considerations of responsiveness to democratic control. Among the related ethical precepts identified by Chandler in Chapter Forty-two are affirmation of pluralist theory, advocation of social equity, maintenance of constitutional order, and service to the community.

Accountability is generally discussed in terms of process, but responsiveness to democratic control is not solely procedural. Citizens expect high-quality services at reasonable costs as part of their social contract with government. A democratic government's ability to satisfy the more mundane and daily demands of its citizens is essential to its continued legitimacy. The effective public administrator recognizes the link between routine operating responsibilities and the long-term viability of democratic governance.

Focus on Results. Despite the ambiguities often inherent in their positions, effective public administrators have a keen interest in the results of their actions. As stewards of scarce communal resources, public administrators are obligated to achieve the best possible results.

The results orientation is rooted in the very beginnings of American public administration. Among the results that have attracted the most attention from public administrators over time are efficiency, effectiveness, and equity. The effective public administrator's concern about results does not end with these three, however. He or she is interested in the moral dimension of action as well. Thus, the effective public administrator is cognizant of the ethical use of office. He or she is also aware of the consequences of institutional decisions and is actively engaged in mitigating their undesirable consequences.

Effective public administrators are interested not only in the obvious moral consequences of their actions but also in the more subtle and less perceptible consequences. In deliberations about tax policy, for example, the effective public administrator recognizes that decisions about taxes are not neutral; rather, they have important distributive, economic, and social consequences. It is the public administrator's role to help focus public debate on these consequences of taxes, as well as on taxes' revenue capacity and collectability.

Networking Ability. Chapter One discusses the challenge of managing complexity, uncertainty, and change. One by-product of this challenge is that effective public administrators must develop the capacity to operate within diffuse and complex networks. These networks have several facets. One is their human component. Public administrators must develop cooperative links with peers, subordinates, politicians, competitors, and constituents to be able to gather the information that is vital to effective operation within networks. Another component of these networks is their structure, and public administrators must know how to make sense of them conceptually.

A public administrator's capacity to work within diffuse, complex networks is a function of several skills and behavioral orientations. One of the most essential skills is the ability to bridge competing cultures (Ring and Perry, 1985). This skill involves the ability to integrate competing viewpoints in decisions. It also entails a self-other orientation, open-mindedness, and low levels of dogmatism. These attributes permit an administrator to adapt to situations that require the administrator to be versatile, look to new constituencies, and explain the facts in new circumstances.

Another networking skill is the ability to communicate, particularly within large organizations and across social cleavages. As Garnett notes in Chapter Thirty-eight, communication in the public sector is different, because government is often situated in the middle of information networks. Within such networks, communication skills become essential tools for effective operation.

Balance. Criticisms that public administrators are either risk-averse or overzealous originate from people's judgments about imbalances in administrative decisions or actions. The effective public administrator has the capacity to identify trade-offs and, ultimately, to recognize the need for balance in most public decisions and actions.

The contributors to this handbook have provided many illustrations of how balance is important to effective public administration. For instance, in Chapter Eighteen, Williams reminds us of the ''Goldilocks'' problem encountered in the implementation of public programs. Any good thing can be taken too far. Such advice as ''Plan'' needs to be moderated by an awareness that too much planning can bog down efforts at timely implementation.

The relationships that public administrators develop with others in their environment can precipitate serious problems if there is no recognition of the need to balance the interests of superiors, legislators, citizens, and clients. Balancing the interests of all environmental actors does not mean that the public administrator should cater to everyone's interests or should compromise on matters of principle. At the same time, the effective public administrator recognizes that bureaucratic rules and the directives of superiors should not automatically negate the entreaties of citizens, to whom the administrator is also obliged to be responsive.

Balance is also a consideration with respect to standards for professional conduct. The value and ethical frameworks for public administrators are multidimensional. Actions taken by public administrators should reflect the consideration of multidimensional frameworks.

Another respect in which balance is important to effective public administration is the fine line between broad purpose and daily routine. In Chapter Twelve, Eadie illustrates the value of thinking and planning strategically. Nevertheless, attention to strategy must be balanced against the importance of the types of day-to-day operations discussed in Part Seven. The building of strategic capability should enhance operational responsibilities, but the effective public administrator recognizes the need for balance between these competing responsibilities.

Public Administration as a Profession

Public administration has long been synonymous with public service: sacrifice on behalf of others in pursuit of the common good. Throughout much of American history, the call to public service has been a powerful motivator, a noble activity worthy of the best of our society. For example, President Kennedy's call to ask what one could do for one's country led a generation of America's best and brightest to seek careers in public service. Commitment to public service is part of our civic heritage.

As we have come to learn, however, effective public institutions in modern society cannot be built on commitment alone. Successful public institutions must be built on a combination of competence and commitment. Public administration scholars and practitioners have progressively developed the foundations for administrative competence. This handbook is the culmination of this evolutionary process. Although public administration will continue to evolve, it has arrived at professional status through a merger of commitment and competence.

Joining competence to commitment is a necessary formula for meeting the challenges that confront today's public administrator. As Chapter One notes, the public administrator faces five challenges, which stem from the American system of public administration and the technological, social, and international developments that currently surround it. From the perspective of our governance system, the most basic of these challenges is to maintain order according to the letter and spirit of the Constitution. Within their assigned roles, public administrators are challenged by the need to achieve technical competence. They must also learn to cope with the expectations of a pluralist, democratic polity. Given the technological and organizational imperatives of modern life, the public administrator is challenged by the realities of managing complexity, uncertainty, and change. The public administrator must also rise to the challenge of behaving ethically.

We have now reached the juncture, symbolized by this handbook, at which the public administrator can step forward with confidence to meet these challenges. The effective public administrator possesses a range of skills and attributes, each important to the successful performance of assigned and implicit responsibilities. These skills range from a grasp of the technical components of a job to the ability to work with others to a vision of the big picture. The effective public administrator is also attuned to the letter and spirit of democratic governance, and he or she works to facilitate processes and substantive outcomes that are supportive of democratic institutions. At the same time, the public administrator is attentive to results but is aware that they need to be defined more broadly than in terms of the economical and efficient operation of government. The configuration of public sector systems means that most public administrators must be capable of working within diffuse and complex networks. Finally, effective public administrators must become artful at balancing a variety of competing considerations, including values and ethical precepts.

Attaining the skills and attributes to be an effective public administrator is in itself a formidable challenge. To become effective, the public administrator must aspire to two potentially conflicting personal attributes: specialized knowledge, on the one hand; and an awareness of and sensitivity to common, shared values, on the other. Effective public administrators succeed in integrating these attributes because of their commitment to public service. Public administrators can take and anticipate great pride in past and future accomplishments of the public sector; it has been with their competence and commitment that these accomplishments have been crafted.

References

Anderson, W. F., Newland, C. A., and Stillman, R. J. (eds.). *The Effective Local Government Manager*. Washington, D.C.: International City Management Association, 1983.

Boyatzis, R. E. *The Competent Manager: A Model for Effective Performance*. New York: Wiley, 1982.

Drucker, P. F. *The Effective Executive*. New York: Harper & Row, 1967.

Katz, R. L. "Skills of an Effective Administrator." *Harvard Business Review,* 1974, *52,* 90–102.

Kaufman, H. "Administrative Decentralization and Political Power." *Public Administration Review,* 1969, *29* (1), 3–15.

Lau, A. W., Newman, A. R., and Broedling, L. A. "The Nature of Managerial Work in the Public Sector." *Public Administration Review,* 1980, *40,* 513–520.

Ring, P. S., and Perry, J. L. "Strategic Management in Public and Private Organizations: Implications of Distinctive Contexts and Constraints." *Academy of Management Review,* 1985, *10,* 276–286.

Waldo, D. *The Study of Public Administration.* New York: Random House, 1955.

Name Index

A

Aaron, H. J., 327, 334
Abelson, H. I., 551, 556
Aberbach, J. D., 197–198, 205
Abney, G., 196, 202, 205
Abraham, K. G., 404, 411
Adams, W., 344, 345, 352
Adler, T. A., 489, 497
Agranoff, R., 131, 133, 134, 139, 140, 144, 145
Aharoni, Y., 500, 501, 502, 503, 505, 507, 510, 511
Ahlbrandt, R. S., 521, 524
Albrecht, T., 420, 422
Albritton, R. B., 299
Aldrich, H., 134, 145
Allen, L., 391, 399
Allison, G., Jr., 430, 434
Altheide, D. L., 233, 235
Amidei, N., 75, 81
Ammons, D. N., 191, 192, 398, 399
Anderson, W. F., 136, 145, 620, 626
Anthony, R. N., 310, 311, 318
Appleby, P. H., 194, 195, 205, 576, 583, 607–608, 617
Aredal, A., 421, 422
Argyris, C., 151, 159
Aristotle, 98, 603, 607
Arnold, C. C., 547, 556
Arnold, D., 472, 482
Aronson, J. R., 345, 353
Astley, W. G., 151, 159
Auerbach, A. J., 327, 334

Auletta, K., 73, 81
Avolio, B. J., 394, 400

B

Bablitch, N. B, 211, 220
Backoff, R. W., 164, 175, 457, 464, 509, 512
Bahl, R., 316, 318
Bailey, J. J., 292, 299
Bailey, S. K., 607–608, 617
Bailyn, L., 463, 464
Ball, N. E., 413, 423
Ballard, C., 327, 334
Ban, C., 205, 206, 359n 412, 422
Banovetz, J. M., 44, 51
Barber, B., 216, 220
Bardach, E., 133, 138, 140, 145, 251, 253, 255, 257
Barnard, C., 149, 159, 404, 410, 546, 556
Barnekov, T., 46, 51
Bayton, J. A., 431, 434
Beck, M., 36, 38
Becker, F. W., 44, 51
Befort, S. F., 445, 449
Begley, S., 60, 65
Behn, J., 28, 38
Behn, R., 13, 14, 21, 28, 38, 296, 299
Bellow, N. J., 167, 175
Benda, P. M., 21–22
Benson, E. D., 340, 342, 350, 353
Bentham, J., 63
Benton, B., 80, 82
Benton, W., 471, 482
Berelson, B., 547, 551, 555, 556

Subject Index

Debt: acquiring and repaying, 337–355; administering repayment of, 350–352; background on, 337–338; bond issue design and sale for, 343–350; and bond registration, 351–352; bond trustee for, 350–351; costs of, 337–338, 342, 348–350; creative approaches to, 347–348; and credit enhancement, 346–347; and disclosure practices, 345–346; issue size for, 340; outside advisers for, 342–343; planning sale of, 338–343; rating municipal, 343–345; and repayment pledges, 339–340; sale methods for, 340–342; summary on, 352; types of, 338–339

Decline cycle: attributes of, 564–569; flexibility in, 566–567; morale in, 565–566, 568; and outplacement, 568–569; and reducing demand, 567; and space needs, 567–568; strategies for, 564–565

Defeatism, in civil service, 370–371

Delaware, executive branch in, 32

Delivery system. *See* Service delivery

Demands, competing, and strategic issue management, 171

Democracy: adversary, 216; pluralist, 209, 214–215; strong, 216–218

Democratic theory, and public administration, 194–195

Demographic and social patterns: and aging population, 72; aspects of changes in, 68–82; background on, 68–69; and birth dearth, 70–72; and global population, 69–70; and health care costs, 74–75; implications of, 75–77; and poverty and underclass, 73–74, 75–77; and role definition, 77–79; shifting, 69–75; summary on, 80–81

Demographic control survey, of salaries, 381

Demonstration Cities and Metropolitan Development Act of 1966, and coproduction, 513

DENDRAL, 59

Department of Employment Security (Missouri), and welfare reform, 77

Department of Environmental Management (Indiana), Water Quality Program of, 132

Department of Mental Health (Missouri), and interagency effort, 79

Department of Social Services (Missouri): and interagency effort, 79; and welfare reform, 77

Depository Trust Company, 352, 353

Design: development of, 169–170; purpose of, 168–169

Detroit, Michigan, performance measurement for, 478

Development. *See* Management development

Digital Equipment Corporation, expert system of, 59

Disabled workers, equal employment opportunity for, 453, 457, 463

Disaster policy, implementation of, 249

Discipline, for poor performers, 421

Disparate treatment and impact, and performance appraisal, 394

Donovan v. *Dewey,* and constitutional authority, 101, 112

Dow Chemical v. *United States,* and constitutional authority, 101, 112

Dow Jones/Retrieval Service, 58

DRILLING ADVISOR, 59

Due process: adjudicating, 107–108; and liability, 588–589

E

Economic development strategies, of local administrators, 46–47

Economic Opportunity Act of 1964, and coproduction, 513

Economy, and global interdependence, 85, 87

Ecosystems, and global interdependence, 85

Edelman v. *Jordan:* and immunity, 595; and liability, 589, 599

Education, for management development, 426

Effectiveness: and accounting, 311–312, 314–315; aspects of, 619–627; and citizen participation, 211–212, 215–219; concept of, 619–620; factors in, 620–625; policy, and federal government, 12, 18–19

Effectiveness evaluation, for program evaluation, 268, 270, 271

Efficiency: and accounting, 311–312, 314–315; cost, from coproduction, 517–518; internal, and organizational effectiveness, 149–150; operations, and federal government, 13–16; and organizational design, 154

Egypt, public service in ancient, 602

Employees: collective bargaining by, 437–450; compensation programs for, 375–387; controlling behavior of, 156–157; and coproduction resistance, 519, 522; cross-training of, 563; in cycles of growth and decline, 559–572; dangerous, and values, 581–582; as deadwood, 563, 564; development of, 389; equal opportunity for, 451–465; morale of, 565–566, 568; outplacement of, 568–569; performance appraisals of, 388–400; as poor performers, 412–423; reward systems for, 401–411; rights and well-being of, as value, 364–365; shared mindset of, 153–156; and turnaround, 571

Employment and Training Administration, and turnaround, 570

Empowerment: and citizen participation, 208–221; in public enterprises, 509

Please remember that this is a library book,
and that it belongs only temporarily to each
person who uses it. Be considerate. Do
not write in this, or any, library book.